AN ILLUSTRATED HISTORY OF RAF WADDINGTON 1916-1945

First edition, published in 2003 by

WOODFIELD PUBLISHING
Bognor Regis, West Sussex PO21 5EL
United Kingdom
www.woodfieldpublishing.com

ISBN 1-903953-44-8

An Illustrated History of
RAF Waddington

PART I : FROM LONGHORN TO LANCASTER 1916-1945

Raymond Leach

Woodfield

ABOUT THE AUTHOR

Squadron Leader Raymond Leach MBE served as a member of aircrew in the Royal Air Force and, in a career spanning 30 years, he logged over 5000 flying hours in more than 60 different types of aircraft.

During his time in the service he was instrumental in the restoration of the RAF's sole remaining Lancaster to flying condition. This gave rise to his first book '*A Lancaster at Peace*'. He subsequently flew with the Battle of Britain Memorial Flight for four seasons. Later in his career he flew five seasons with the Vulcan Display Flight.

He served at RAF Waddington on three separate tours of duty in flying and staff appointments. It was during his last tour at Waddington that he compiled the history of the Station, which included a ten volume series of photograph albums.

On retiring from the RAF he flew Jet Ranger helicopters on pipeline safety inspection patrols with British Gas and, subsequently, Transco. During his thirteen years with the company he logged some 10,000 flying hours. Now retired he works as a freelance consultant, specialising in aviation and military history. He is currently working on a novel set in the First World War.

CONTENTS

This book is dedicated to all who served in the Royal Air Force in two World wars, both in the air and on the ground.

INTRODUCTION

I commenced my first flying tour at RAF Waddington in February 1964 when I was posted to No 44 (Rhodesia) Squadron, flying the Vulcan Mk I. During my four years with No 44 Squadron, I compiled a precis history of the squadron. This precis eventually became the basis of a comprehensive history of the squadron by my friend and comrade, the late Flight Lieutenant Al White.

About half way through my tour, command of the squadron passed to Wing Commander Mike D'Arcy. On reading my precis history he commented that he noted with interest that No 44 squadron was the first squadron in Bomber Command to operate the Lancaster, and that Squadron Leader John Nettleton was awarded the Victoria Cross for his leadership of the No 44 Squadron component on the daylight attack on the U boat engine works at Augsburg near Munich. He went on to add that he felt that Waddington, as the first operational Lancaster station, should have its own Lancaster, to match that guarding the gate at nearby RAF Scampton. Accordingly, four of us junior officers were tasked with examining the possibilities.

Months later this culminated in the arrival at Waddington of Avro Lancaster PA474 on 18 August 1965. As the project officer I was privileged to fly on the ferry trip as the navigator from its storage home at RAF Henlow to Waddington. Our brief from the owners, the then embryo RAF Museum was to hangar the aircraft and to restore it to 'static' display standard. As is now a matter of history, we at Waddington, particularly the engineers, put the widest interpretation on this requirement!

I left Waddington in January 1968 when I was posted as an instructor to the Officer Cadet Training Unit. This was followed by a flying tour in Cyprus. Then, in August 1974 I was posted to Waddington as Officer Commanding Operations Squadron. It was during this tour that I flew four air display seasons in the Lancaster with the Battle of Britain Memorial Flight. While flying with the BBMF, I was fortunate enought to meet and talk with so many ex members of Bomber Command and RAF Waddington.

Other tours followed before I again found myself at at Waddington in October 1983, this time as officer Commanding Operations. It was during this period that I became aware that the history of the Station was contained in one A4 page of duplicating paper. On mentioning this to the then Station Commander, Group Captain Bettell, his response was: "*Well do something about it then*". This book and the ten albums of photographs held by the Station are the result of my '*doing something about it*'.

During my researches I was lucky enough to meet with many who served at Waddington during both World Wars, as well as those who were there between the wars and in the post World War II (Cold War) period. Sadly, many have since died, but my memories remain bright.

As will become apparent, much of this history of RAF Waddington concerns its wartime years as one of the main stations of Bomber Command. It was from the station during this period in its history that so many young men flew to their death in the assault on the enemy. Since that time, as is ever the case, numerous iconoclasts of varying hues and persuasions have denigrated both Bomber Command and its most successful commander. These same iconoclasts conveniently forget two major facts. Firstly, for many years, Bomber Command was the only weapon available to the British people capable of taking the war to the enemy's homeland. Secondly, as a democracy, led by a government of national unity, our political masters held primacy. As the Commander in Chief of Bomber Command, Air Marshal Harris carried out the policies passed down to him from the war cabinet. So, if criticism there be, which i deny, it should be restricted to that of his efficiency in carrying out the orders of his political masters. Hopefully, this book may go some small way towards setting the record straight; it is the least that they deserve.

Ray Leach
Cambridge 2003

1. The Early Days

To stand almost anywhere on the western part of RAF Waddington, is to stand amidst history. The old Roman road that linked London (Londinium) to York (Eboracum) runs right through this part of the station. It is better known as Ermine Street. In the year 61AD, the Ninth Roman Legion under Petillius Cerialis marched south along the road from their temporary camp at Lincoln, to do battle with the Iceni army under Queen Boudicca (Boadicea). Following their defeat by the rebellious British near Cambridge, the survivors of the Ninth Legion withdrew north back to Lincoln, once again travelling via the Roman road. Just over one thousand years later, King Harold Godwinsson marched his army south from his victory at the battle of Stamford Bridge, to his defeat at the hands of William of Normandy. Harold too used the old Roman road. Almost another thousand years were to pass before any further major military activity was to take place in the area known as Waddington Heath.

The Great War

Contrary to the belief held by General Sir Douglas Haig at the beginning of World War I, that aircraft *'had no worthwhile role to play on the battlefield'*, the Royal Flying Corps (RFC) had soon proved its worth, and by 1916 it had undergone considerable expansion. The allied air forces had suffered severe losses during the battles of the Somme offensive, with some 800 RFC aircraft being destroyed, involving the loss of 252 pilots and observers. These losses had to be made good and the result was a massive increase in the number of training units. To the War Office, Lincolnshire, with its flat, wide open spaces and sparse population was an obvious area to choose for the location of the proposed expansion. So, in 1916 a considerable number of training aerodromes sprang up in the Lincoln area; among these was Waddington. The airfield stands on the Lincolnshire Heights (such as they are!), five miles to the south of the city of Lincoln and astride the ancient Roman road Ermine Street. Apart from the absence of industrial haze in the Lincoln area, an added bonus was the benefit derived from the prevailing south westerly wind and the assistance it gave to take-off as it breasted the Lincoln Heights.

RAF Waddington takes its name from the nearby village and parish; a settlement whose recorded origins go back to the first 'English' or 'Angles', who established a settlement in the area after the departure of the Romans. The name Waddington is derived from the words 'tun', meaning township, and 'wadings', meaning the followers of Wada; ergo, the township of Wada's followers. A study of the area will ascertain the reasons for their choice of location. The village was sited close to established tracks and on the edge of a limestone cliff, which had rough pasture on the hilltop, fertile soil on its slopes and verdant water meadows in the lower reaches, which stretched to the banks of the river Witham.

On 16 November 1916 Sir Douglas Haig wrote to the Air Board requesting the formation of 20 additional fighting squadrons. This was in addition to the 56 that he had previously requested. This request was but further evidence of the desperate need for pilots and observers on the Western Front and the importance the Army now placed on the role of the Royal Flying Corps. Five days later, on 21 November, the Air Board wrote to the General Officer Commanding (GOC) of the British Expeditionary Force (BEF) RFC, informing him that they intended dividing the existing RFC training brigades into three Groups. At this time, Waddington was the home of No 27 Training Wing, which formed part of the Northern Training Group under the command of Lt Col P L W Herbert, with its headquarters in York. Five training stations had been opened in Lincolnshire in late 1916, namely: Harlaxton, Spitalgate, South Carlton, Brattleby (later to become Scampton) and Waddington. Initially all were under the control of the Training Brigade, but the decentralisation previously referred to had resulted in each station becoming the home of a Wing, with No 23 Wing at South Carlton, No 24 Wing at Spitalgate and No 27 Wing at Waddington.

A Training Station Is Built

The aerodrome at Waddington was typical of many built at this stage of World War I. It was approximately 3000 feet square and took up about one third of Waddington Heath, including the site of the old Waddington village race course. This connection with horse racing is commemorated in the village by the names of two out of three of its public houses: The Horse and Jockey and The Three Horseshoes. However, the race course had already fallen into disuse well before the outbreak of the war as a result of the enclosure of the village and the planting of hedges on the Heath. The creation of the aerodrome resulted in the loss of some twelve fields and a degree of discontent on the part of the local farmers, who had to find alternative grazing for their sheep. Another result of the aviation activities at the new aerodrome was the removal of the sails from the village windmill and a reduction in its overall height, it having been deemed a hazard to aerial navigation!

In his reply to the question "What were the criteria used by the RFC when selecting a site for use as an aerodrome"? The late Marshal of the Royal Air Force Sir Arthur T Harris replied that, as the then Captain A T Harris, Officer Commanding No 38 Squadron, he "...looked for aerodrome sites partly from the air, partly from maps and partly by car. The simple criteria in those days were to find a field flat enough, big enough and with a reasonable grass surface to be used either as a squadron or flight aerodrome... in those days, the War Office seemed to show a marked reluctance to undergo the expense of removing a few trees, or flattening a few hedges and ditches for such purposes, so one's choice was somewhat restricted. As examples, I could quote such aerodromes as Leadenham and Waddington etc..."

Large numbers of soldiers were drafted in to Waddington to construct the aerodrome and its hangars and buildings. Among the troops was Private Gonville Marshall of the Durham Light Infantry. He recalled that he and a party of assorted tradesmen were assigned to a place called Waddington to help build a new aerodrome. When they arrived there was only one hut on site, so they lived initially in tents. Their task was to build accommodation for the personnel and hangars for the aircraft. Marshall further recalled that not long after some of the hangars were completed, an aircraft crashed on to the roof of one of them, the pilot suffering two broken legs. Gonville Marshall remained at Waddington until the end of the war; an extremely fortunate posting for him in the light of what happened to his regiment in France.

Much of the building material for the aerodrome came via the Great Northern Railway, being unloaded at the village station at the foot of Waddington Heights. The route from the station, up the hill to the aerodrome, was a simple cart track which quickly proved quite incapable of supporting the vast increase in traffic flow and rapidly deteriorated into a deeply rutted ruin. Apart from the military lorries making numerous return trips, some of the heavier loads were hauled up the hill by a steam engine glorying in the name of *Lord Kitchener*. It was driven by an English boxing champion Joe Beckett, who in more peaceful times had used a steam roller to crush granite road stone into the ruts in the tracks caused by the relatively sparse local traffic. Even before the aerodrome was completed, it received its first aerial visitor. In September 1916 a student pilot from the Royal Naval Air Station at nearby Cranwell, landed at Waddington; certainly the first military aircraft so to do. Probationary Sub Lieutenant Leonard (Tich) Rochford had taken off in a Bristol Scout, but after climbing to 10,000 feet and carrying out a series of manoeuvres and spiral descents, he became totally lost. Seeing a large town which he thought he recognised as Lincoln, he made his way towards it - just to make sure! En route the budding aviator saw an aerodrome under construction just beneath him, so he decided to land and ascertain his precise whereabouts. On the aerodrome he found a small detachment of Royal Engineers who were rather surprised at his unannounced arrival among them. Having been advised of his position and located it on his map, Rochford spent an enjoyable few minutes discussing the merits and otherwise of the new aerodrome.

Deciding that he had tarried long enough, he asked the officer in charge for the assistance of his men to start the engine. In the event, this proved easier said than done as none of the soldiers proved capable of properly swinging the propeller. After numerous abortive attempts to get the engine to start, the engineer officer suggested that his visitor should go to the RFC Air Park on Lincoln race course and obtain the services of an air mechanic or some other suitably qualified assistance. Eventually Rochford got the engine of the Scout started and, after briefly buzzing the field, he set course for Cranwell. The young Rochford was subsequently to enjoy a long and successful combat career in France with No 3 (Naval) Squadron and later with No 203 Squadron of the newly created Royal Air Force. He was credited with over 30 confirmed victories and many others probably destroyed or damaged. He ended the war with the Distinguished Service Cross (DSC) and bar, plus a Distinguished Flying Cross (DFC). By coincidence, it was while flying with No 3 (Naval) Squadron that 'Tich' Rochford met Flight Sub Lieutenant H E P Wigglesworth. Many years later, Wigglesworth was to become a feature of the Waddington story.

As soon as it was considered that sufficient buildings had been completed, the assigned training units moved in. Number 27 Training Wing was declared to be active on 13 November 1916 when two squadrons arrived; Number 47 Reserve Squadron arrived from Cramlington near Newcastle, while Number 48 Reserve Squadron moved over from Narborough near Swaffham in Norfolk; better known now as RAF Marham. As with all training or reserve units, as they were then called, the two squadrons that formed No 27 Wing were equipped with a motley collection of aircraft types, which must have made servicing a nightmare for the groundcrews. Number 47 Reserve Squadron brought with it a selection of Maurice Farman Longhorns and Shorthorns plus some very tired RE8 aircraft. At the same time, No 48 Reserve Squadron came with its Graham White XVs, Shorthorns and RE8s. The situation was to get even worse when additional units moved in, bringing with them other diverse types of aircraft.

To house its aircraft, Waddington had been provided with a total of ten 'Belfast Type' hangars. These were of standard War Office pattern, built of wood and clad in timber and corrugated iron sheeting. The internal dimensions were anything from 170 to 200 feet in length by 80 to 90 feet in width; the rectanular space being divided into seventeen bays. Seven of these hangars were grouped together in a complex along the southern boundary of the aerodrome and formed the main technical and flying complex of No 27 Wing. In the same area and in addition to the hangars, there was a collection of wooden huts for use as stores and administrative offices. The administration complex was linked to the domestic and the other smaller, technical/flying site by an old road that linked the village of Waddington to the hamlet of Mere. The other technical/flying site consisted of three hangars, adjacent to, and following the line of, the old Ermine Street.

Obviously, the aircraft of this era, being constructed of wood and fabric, did not take kindly to inclement weather, so any aerodrome required a considerable amount of hangarage to protect them from the elements. Of the main group of seven hangars at Waddington, two were allocated to each of the Reserve (Training) Squadrons; one to the wing repair section and the remaining two for use by a planned additional training squadron. The three hangars along Ermine Street (now known as High Dyke), were originally intended for housing aircraft used for practical demonstrations, such as 'the effect of controls' and other flying related matters. In the event, it appears that two of them were eventually used as paint/dope shop and a wing repair shop respectively. An air-to-ground gunnery target was provided at a later stage, located on the airfield (!) to the east of the main landing strip. In due course this was to give rise to an unexpected problem. The young boys from the nearby villages used to raid the aerodrome at night in order to dig up the bullets from the area in and around the target circle, much to the consternation of the aerodrome guards.

By the time the War Office gave the go-ahead for the construction of an aerodrome at Waddington, the training organisation of the RFC had undergone many changes and considerable development. At the outbreak of war on 4 August 1914, the Royal Flying Corps possessed seven squadrons and a training facility commensurate with a force of this size. It soon became apparent that there would be a need for a rapid expansion in the size of both British air arms, the Royal Flying Corps and the Royal Naval Air Service. It was further appreciated that such an expansion would necessitate a concomitant increase in the size of the training organisation. The new training organisation would have to be capable of producing the large number of pilots and observers required and in addition, provide replacements for those killed or injured in action. In the early stages of the war, some qualified civilian pilots volunteered to undertake instructional duties, and to these were added some pilots withdrawn from front-line squadrons. Two months after the outbreak of war, a Reserve Aeroplane Squadron had been established at Farnborough equipped with five types of aircraft that were considered suitable for training purposes. These were, Maurice Farman Longhorns and Shorthorns, Moranes, Bleriot XIs and BE2a aircraft. This was to be the starting point, with other Reserve Aeroplane Squadrons (RAS) being formed as soon as instructors became available and aerodromes constructed. Initially, the problem was minimised by the departure of the original seven established squadrons to France, leaving three aerodromes in England vacant and available for use as training bases. In addition, the War Office took over such civilian aerodromes as were considered suitable and embarked on a plan of aerodrome construction throughout the British Isles.

The Training Organisation

Just over one month after its formation, the first RAS was accorded the formal title of No 1 RAS, while at the same time, No 2 RAS was activated at the famous civilian aerodrome at Brooklands in Surrey. Later that same month on 29 November, the RFC within the British Isles, was divided into three Wings, each commanded by a Lieutenant Colonel who was designated the Wing Commander. One of these Wings was called the Administrative Wing and was based at Farnborough. It comprised the RFC Depot, the Records Office, the Aircraft Park, and the two RASs. Initially, the Reserve Aeroplane Squadrons were required to give their pupil pilots their preliminary training only; the pupils being then sent on to the Central Flying School at Upavon, where they completed their training before proceeding either to their assigned squadrons or to the Pilot Pool in France. Later, as the numbers required increased, some service squadrons also had to produce their quota of trained pilots for duties with the British Expeditionary Force (BEF). At an even later stage, the Reserve Squadrons would be required to give advanced training in addition to the preliminary training.

This policy of forming new training squadrons on new aerodromes in Great Britain instead of simply enlarging the existing aerodromes had several advantages. Firstly, it had been found impractical to train more than approximately sixty student pilots on any one aerodrome. Secondly, in view of the fact that weather conditions vary enormously in different parts of the British Isles, it was most unlikely that flying would be inhibited at all aerodromes at any one time. Furthermore, with suitable sites being designated for use as aerodromes throughout the country, this would bring the RFC and its work to the attention of the many Army units throughout the land. This would, it was hoped, result in a better understanding of the role of the new Corps and to possibly boost recruiting for the RFC from within the Army. However, this dispersal system also had its disadvantages. It meant that the small pool of flying instructors was widely scattered, resulting in the need for more instructors for the increasing number of student pilots, who in turn were scattered throughout the land in their training units.

On 21 January 1915, No 3 RAS was formed at Netheravon and moved immediately to Shoreham, bringing the number of RASs to three. These three training establishments provided the nuclei of three new squadrons; namely, Numbers 15, 10 and 14 Squadrons respectively. At about the same time, No 4 Wing was formed at Netheravon, comprising Numbers 7 and 11 RASs, which between them trained the nuclei of Numbers 11 and 12 Squadrons. Meanwhile, Gosport became the base for No 5 Wing which comprised No 8 RAS whose task was to train the nuclei of Number 13 Squadron. So, throughout 1915 there was a steady expansion in the number of Reserve Aeroplane squadrons, resulting in a total of seventeen by the end of the year.

Among the new aerodromes were some whose names were to become synonymous with the RFC/RAF: Beaulieu, Castle Bromwich, Catterick, Dover, Joyce Green, Montrose, Norwich and Thetford. Most of these aerodromes housed two RASs, a practice that was to develop as the expansion of the RFC training organisation continued. The aircraft employed in training were many and varied, consisting in the main of types found unsuited to, or outdated for, operational duties. Among the aircraft assigned to training duties were Maurice Farman Longhorn and Shorthorns, Bleriots, Caudron G3s, Avro 500 and 504s, BE2s, Morane Parasols, monoplanes and biplanes, RE5s, Vickers FB5s, Bristol Scouts, Martinsyde S1s, Armstrong Whitworth FK3s and Voisins. Such a miscellany of types must have been something of a nightmare for the servicing and supply organisations.

On 13 January 1916 there were 13 Service Squadrons and 18 Reserve Squadrons on the Home Establishment, the latter's titles having been changed from the earlier Reserve Aeroplane Squadrons. The new plan coincided with an improvement in the types of aircraft used for training purposes. Among the newer types were BE2Es, BE12s, DH1, 2 and 5s, FK8s, FE2B and Ds, Sopwith 11/2 Strutters and Pups and RE7s. Despite this new equipment it became apparent that the old system of flying training was in need of considerable change and improvement.

A start had been made the previous December when, on the 15th, a School of Instruction (later to be called No 1 School of Military Aeronautics) was formed at Reading. Its purpose was to provide ground instruction to intakes of some 100 officers, prior to their proceeding on to flying training. Originally, the school at Reading was intended for the training of officers transferring from within the Army for duty with the RFC as pilots. But it later trained recruits straight from civilian life and school! Four months later, two additional ground instruction schools were opened; one at Denham, the other at Oxford. Their specified tasks were the training of Other Ranks and those joining the RFC from civilian life.

In the early part of 1916, a list of complaints was received by the War Office from the GOC of the RFC in the field (France), concerning the poor quality of pilots arriving on front-line squadrons as reinforcements. The result of these complaints was a revised set of instructions regarding the qualifying tests for pilots. The new tests of achievement were as follows:

A. *Qualification Tests in Flying*

- i The pilot must have spent at least 15 hours flying solo.
- ii The pilot must have flown a service aeroplane satisfactorily.
- iii The pilot must have carried out a successful cross-country flight of at least 60 miles. During this flight he must land at two other landing places under the supervision of an Officer of the RFC.
- iv The pilot must climb to 6000 feet and remain at that height for at least 15 minutes after which he is to land with his engine stopped, the aeroplane first touching the ground within a circular mark of 50 yards diameter. (NOTE: This test can be combined with (iii) if proper supervision can be arranged.
- v The pilot must make two landings in the dark assisted by flares.

B. *Further Training*

Newly qualified flying officers should be given every opportunity to gain additional air experience. They should be made to fly in bad weather on all possible occasions. In addition they should:

- i Practice landing over tape 10 feet from the ground.
- ii Carry out bomb dropping and the use of cameras and wireless.
- iii Practice fighting in the air.
- iv Practice night flying.
- v Fly in formation

By the end of the year the required minimum number of solo hours required was increased to 20 hours and the height of the climb raised to 8000 feet. Furthermore, fighting pilots were to fly five or eight additional solo hours according to the service type of aeroplane on which they were trained. In addition, they were to fly another two hours on the aircraft type which they were destined to fly on joining their front-line unit. Despite the increased standards required of tyro pilots, the quality of instruction was not always all that it should have been, as was made clear by Arthur Gould-Lee, an experienced fighter pilot who had been recalled from the Western Front for instructional duties. In his book 'Open Cockpit', he states "... *most crashes were the direct consequence of inadequate instruction...*" Later in the book he goes on to say: "...*As an instructor I was all too aware of my ignorance, for I had been given no opportunity to learn how to instruct, but with memories of how unhelpful some of my own mentors had been, I tried to be different.*"

Waddington as a Training Station

On 20 July 1916 the 6th Brigade, which had been formed on 15 January that year, became The Training Brigade, under the command of Brigadier General J M Salmon. Under this arrangement, the Reserve Squadrons were sub-divided into elementary training squadrons and higher training squadrons; a distinction that was not reflected in their titles. By this time there were 43 Reserve Squadrons and the number was increasing almost monthly. It was during this phase of the expansion of the RFC training organisation that No 27 (Training) Wing was formed at Waddington on 13 November 1916. Less than two months later, in January 1917, approval was given for an expansion of the RFC to 106 front-line squadrons and 97 Reserve Squadrons. This was a further increase in the already approved target of 37 Reserve Squadrons.

Such was the pace demanded by the pressing need for replacements on the front-line squadrons, that the two new training squadrons at Waddington wasted no time in getting their students into the air. Flying training in those days was a dangerous business; indeed, at times it must have seemed as dangerous to learn to fly as it was to fly against the enemy. An indication of the size of the problem can be gained by reference to a comment made by Major Louis Strange, a well known RFC pilot who commanded No 23 Wing at South Carlton, itself only a few miles from Lincoln. In reviewing the problems associated with training replacements for the active squadrons, Strange reported that *there were insufficient instructors and students to make worthwhile use of his available machines, albeit too many of the machines would be undergoing repairs at any one time.* At the same time,

he observed that the accident rate was far too high, averaging out, as it did, at one aircraft for every 140 hours flying, which in effect meant the loss of some 30 to 40 aircraft every month. These figures did not include the 70 or 80 aircraft damaged to some extent in minor crashes and other incidents.

Number 27 Wing at Waddington was commanded by Lt Col I E A Edwards. It was a typical training wing, possessing an average of something between 150 to 200 pupil pilots under instruction. With an establishment of 20 instructors, this meant that each instructor was responsible for the training of between seven and ten students; a far greater number than could be effectively handled. With approximately 70 machines serviceable at any one time, allied with an eight hour flying day, a total of 560 aircraft hours per day was feasible. Within this there was a practical target of 225 dual flying hours. At the time, the ratio of dual to solo flying hours was one to three, which resulted in a theoretical target of 75 hours dual and 150 hours solo per day. To the 20 or so instructors, their assigned task meant that each would be required to fly four hours dual and to oversee eight hours solo flying each day. In other words, a twelve hour working day compressed into an eight hour flying day! What this sort of thing meant to the students can be judged from the comment by Alan Cobham (later to be better known as Sir Alan Cobham of Flight Refuelling fame) when he wrote that he started the solo phase of his flying training by flying two or three times each day. He went on to record that it was the practice in those days to give student pilots experience on a variety of different aircraft; this presenting no real problem bearing in mind the wide range of types held by the training squadrons, but what it did for the students pilots is anybody's guess!

One of the students at Waddington in 1917 was 2/Lt C L Turnbull, who underwent his flying training there before being posted to fly Armstrong Whitworth FK8s with No 10 Squadron at Chocques in France. The first entry in his flying log book (Army Book 425) is dated 21 May 1917, in which he recorded a training trip with a Captain Blatherwick in a Maurice Farman Shorthorn (Serial No A6874). Further study of his log book shows that 2/Lt Turnbull went solo in two weeks after a total flying time of 8 hours and 25 minutes dual. During his stay at Waddington, he flew Avro 504s, FK3s and FK8s, completing a grand total of 22 hours and 45 minutes flying time before being posted to France. Of passing interest is the fact that Turnbull's flying boots and heavy duty coat are now in the possession of the Shuttleworth Trust collection at Old Warden. His instructor, Captain Blatherwick, was the Officer Commanding 'A' Flight of No 47 Reserve Squadron under the command of a Major Rodwell.

As with their contemporaries, the student pilots allocated to No 27 Wing at Waddington came from one or other of the Schools of Military Aeronautics, most probably either No 1 at Reading or No 2 at Oxford. At these establishments the embryo pilots studied such subjects as theory of flight, meteorology, magnetism, electricity, aero engines, map reading, morse code and compasses. In addition they were introduced to the intricacies of aircraft rigging, the use of the clock code for reference purposes, and the two standard aircraft weapons, the Vickers and Lewis machine guns. After one month they would be examined in these subjects and, if successful, passed on to one of the growing number of Reserve Squadrons. Unless the student pilot had previously served in the RFC as an Observer or as a member of the ground staff, the chances are that he would never have flown before in his life; nor would he have any idea of just what flying was like. His knowledge, such as it was, would be purely theoretical, so his arrival at the Reserve Squadron was the first step in putting theory into practice.

Student pilots were introduced to flying by way of the RFC's elementary training machines the Maurice Farman Longhorn and Shorthorn. Legend has it that these peculiar names came about as a result of a chance remark made by the then Major J F A Higgins (later Air Marshal Sir John Higgins). It was he who, on seeing a collection of Maurice Farman aircraft lined up on an aerodrome, was reputed to have remarked *"Voila; les vaches mecaniques"!* Thus, by virtue of their differing shapes the 'mechanical cows' were sub divided into the Longhorn and Shorthorn.

The Longhorn was one of the RFC's main primary training aircraft. As a trainer, it was a safe and forgiving aircraft, albeit of a rather ungainly shape. The forward elevator was carried on upswept forward extensions of the undercarriage skids. The tail-booms were straight and parallel in plan view, ending in a rectangular box shaped tail plane. The feature most appreciated by the student pilots was the forward elevator, as it provided them with a visual head-up display of aircraft balance. Those who did not commence their flying training on the Longhorn, would instead have received their first taste of flying in a Shorthorn or, in a few instances, a Graham White XV, an aircraft not all that dissimlar from the Longhorn. The main differences between the Longhorn and Shorthorn were the absence on the Shorthorn of the extended undercarriage skids and the forward elevator, the reduction of the box-like tail plane to a monoplane unit, and the sharp convergence of the tail boom of the Shorthorn when viewed in side elevation. The Graham White XV on the other hand seemed to combine some of the features of both the Longhorn and the Shorthorn. It possessed twin boxed rudders at the end of parallel (in plan view) tail booms, no forward boom extensions, and a biplane wing of unequal span, the upper wing being longer than the lower.

It should be remembered that at this time, flying was still looked upon as something quite extraordinary by the general public; solely the province of gallant young adventurers. Many of the fledglings who so eagerly volunteered for flying duty with the RFC had no flying experience whatsoever and in all probability, very little idea of just what it was like to fly. What today appears to resemble a collection of Roland Emmett constructions, were in those days, things of wonder - even something as ungainly as the Longhorn. Of the three initial flying training aircraft used at Waddington, the most common was the Shorthorn. This aircraft has been likened to a bird cage, a not inappropriate simile. Indeed, it was a popular joke among the mechanics of the RFC that the true test of a correctly rigged Shorthorn was to release a canary beside the cockpit. If the rigging was correct the bird would be unable to escape! The rather fragile structure was braced by a complex network of wires, frequently referred to as 'the birdcage' by many of its pilots. The wings were similar in design to those of the earlier Wright biplane, with the leading edges acting as the front spars carrying the front vertical struts. The whole structure presented a rather ungainly appearance, but was relatively safe and easy to fly. However, even the simple Shorthorn had its faults; the first being a basic weakness in the wing design. The centre section carried four pairs of struts, the innermost of which straddled the body, or what passed for a fuselage. This carried most of the load, consisting of the engine, propellor, fuel tank and, of course, the crew. Because the weight was concentrated in this area, the nacelle spars were bowed or arched across the nacelle to give added strength. Unfortunately, this vertical curvature proved to be weak point whenever these spars were subjected to a side load. This defect could well have been the cause of some of the Shorthorn in-flight wing failures.

The other design fault lay in the cambered, lifting tailplane. This part of the structure carried some of the aircraft weight when in flight. Unfortunately, it failed to provide sufficient fore and aft stability, with the result that the lift it generated could result in an increased angle of descent together with a delayed recovery to straight and level flight. At the time, such shortcomings were not properly understood and doubtless resulted in the death of many trainee pilots.

The embryo pilots had to be shown how to negotiate 'the birdcage' in order to reach the side of the nacelle (cockpit). Having got there, they (the pilots) had to be extremely careful where they put their feet. One carelessly placed boot would easily break through the thin, fragile fabric cover with embarrassing results, usually much to the amusement of one's comrades. With all these hazards safely negotitated and safely seated in the nacelle, the side door had to be lifted into place and secured with an ordinary door bolt. The student pilot would be seated in the front cockpit, well ahead of the wings, while the instructor sat in the reat cockpit.

The Maurice Farman Shorthorn, or to use its more popular name - *The Rumpety*, was equipped with dual controls and served to give many a fledgling pilot his first taste of flying. The aircraft cruised at approximately 50 - 60 miles per hour, but possessed very few instruments. Perhaps the most important was the airspeed indicator, which indicated the speed by means of a glass tube containing a red liquid. In the early days these training machines had no Gosport or speaking tube; if the instructor wished to pass a message to his student, he had to throttle back the engine and then shout. The problem with this system was the fact that the difference between cruising speed and stalling was a mere 20mph, so any throttling back had to be accompanied by a lowering of the nose. Indeed, most instructors used to push the nose down before closing the throttle, such was their dislike of stalling. In fact, according to Wing Commander Norman Macmillan, a nine victory ace and aviation writer, the only way that a student pilot would experience a stall would be through either incompetence or ill-advised bravado as it was seldom if ever demonstrated. Macmillan's book *Into the Blue* is considered to be an aviation classic.

The *'Rumpety'* was equipped with a control column surmounted by a pair of spectacle-type handles. The student, sitting in the front cockpit would be given directions by means of hand signals. A right hand placed firmly on the right shoulder meant 'turn right'; a left hand on the left shoulder meant 'turn left'. A push on the back of his leather helmet meant 'go down', while a tug would mean 'pull up'. This seemingly haphazard method of instruction frequently led to less able students dreading the day that their 'instructor' would send them off solo, especially if he was one of the nervous fraternity who never actually released their hold on the control column in the rear cockpit!

Another Waddington student, who commenced his advanced training on 16 August 1917, having previously served at Doncaster, Spitalgate and South Carlton, was 2/Lt Reginald Pohlmann. Although he flew mainly DH4s, he also logged some time in the BE2e, the FK8 and the Martinsyde Elephant. His log book (Army Book 425) also records that he spent quite a number of sorties practicing formation flying as he neared the end of his training.

On successfully completing his training, 2/Lt Reggie Pohlmann was posted on 14 September 1917 to a holding unit, or pilot pool, at St Omer in France. Eleven days later he joined No 25 Squadron at Auchel, flying DH4s. The squadron was engaged in bombing and reconnaissance missions well behind the front line. He must have been an above average pilot as he appeared in the RFC Communique No 121 dated 9 January 1918. Under the heading 'Enemy Aircraft' for 4 January, is the entry:

'Two enemy machines were driven down out of control - one by 2/Lts R Pohlmann and O Hinson of No 25 Squadron, who were attacked by seven enemy Aircraft (EA) scouts while doing a photographic recommaissance, and the other by…'

Sadly, Reggie Pohlmann was not destined to survive the war; he and his observer were shot down and killed on 5 February 1918 by Lt H. Bongartz; a combat career of just over four months.

Simple though the training machines were, there were the inevitable crop of fatal and minor accidents. On 3 March 1917, the local paper, the Lincoln Echo, reported the first of many minor tragedies; the report stating:

'We regret to announce that while Lt C R Nelds and Sgt Liddle of the RFC were flying a military aeroplane last Wednesday afternoon, the machine was seen to burst into flames and make a nose dive to earth. Assistance was promptly at hand, but both occupants were found to be dead'.

This was the first reference in the local press to an aircraft accident, but regrettably it was not to be the last. Two weeks later, the same paper reported under a banner headline: *Flying Fatality Near Lincoln – Young Flight Officer's Sad Death.*

"At the 4th Northern General Hospital in Lincoln, the city Coroner conducted an inquiry into the circumstances surrounding the death of a young flight officer, namely 2/Lt Colin Smith (age 18), who was killed through an accident to the machine in which he was making a test flight in the vicinity of an aerodrome near Lincoln on Sunday afternoon. Lieutenant W H Campbell gave evidence of identification. He also deposed to the nature of the accident. He said that on … he saw the deceased make one circle of the aerodrome; he reached a height of about 1000 feet and then switched off the engine to make a landing. He started to descend but apparently forgot to adopt the correct rudder [!] which was necessary when landing. The machine, as a consequence, spun to the left, but the deceased managed to right it. Then the machine immediately went into another spin and it seemed to be out of control. When at about 400 feet, the machine suddenly nose dived… Lieutenant R L S Maurice… added that the deceased seemed to get control of the machine once again and to then lose it… The Squadron Commander stated that the deceased was a learner. He had mastered two types of aeroplane, and the one he was in when the accident occured was his third type. He had been for flights alone on several previous occasions and was acquainted with this type of machine, which was in perfect order. So far as the deceased had gone with his training he had shown himself to be a capable and efficient aviator and would have made a good pilot…"

On 30 March 1917, No 82 Squadron had moved into Waddington from Beverley in Yorkshire. It brought with it an assortment of aircraft types including the Avro 504, BE2c, BE2e, RE7, RE8, FK3 and FK8. This squadron, which immediately commenced working up to operational status prior to proceeding to France, occupied one of the three hangars which flanked the old Ermine Street (High Dyke); however, it was not destined to remain at Waddington for very long. On 20 November 1917, No 82 Squadron moved to St Omer in France, equipped with the Armstrong Whitworth FK8; its role being that of Corps reconnaissance. Initially, the squadron pilots had trained in their motley collection of aircraft, but emphasis gradually centered on the FK3 and FK8. In appearance, the FK3 resembled the BE2c, though the undercarriage had a unique feature; it was one of the first aircraft to have oleo shock absorbers attached to the fuselage. This was at a time when nearly all other types employed rubber bungees as shock absorbers for the undercarriage. Despite this somewhat innovative feature, the FK3 was also provided with a central skid between the wheels.

As a training aeroplane the FK3 was reputed to be virtually viceless; some pilots comparing it to the popular DH6, with the reservation that the FK3 was much lighter on the controls. It was fully aerobatic, popular with its pilots and affectionately known as *'Little Ack'* to distinguish it from the later FK8, which was known as *'Big Ack'*. Once the pilots of No 82 Squadron had mastered the FK3, they progressed to the bigger and more powerful FK8. Throughout its use by the RFC and the RAF, the FK8 gave excellent service and was much respected by German fighter pilots. Structurally the 'Big Ack' was an unremarkable, typical wire-braced aeroplane of the period, with only one really unique feature. Unlike other contemporary World War I aircraft, it did not have a clear centre-section between the two wings. Instead, it had an inverted vee strut connecting the upper wings to the fuselage. Despite this restriction to forward vision, the FK8 was popular with its crews who considered it to be a safe, strong aeroplane that was easy to fly.

Alan Arnett McLeod VC

Among the young pilots of No 82 Squadron who underwent training at Waddington was a tall, big-boned young Canadian named Alan Arnett McLeod. This young warrior enlisted just three days after he had attained the minimum age for military service. Accepted for pilot training in the RFC, he commenced his flying training at Long Branch near Toronto, going solo on 4 June 1917. Just over one month later, on 31 July, he was awarded his wings and in August sailed for England. Following further training at Winchester, McLeod was posted to No 82 Squadron at Waddington. Here he flew a variety of aircraft including the squadron's operational aircraft, the FK8. His disappointment that he had not been assigned to a fighter squadron was mitigated to some extent by the knowledge that soon he would be on active service. On arriving in France, McLeod was eventually posted to No 2 Squadron at Hesdigneul in late November 1917. The squadron was equipped with the FK8 and was engaged in bombing, photographic and general reconnaissance duties.

The young McLeod quickly established a reputation for himself as being a most aggressive pilot. Regularly he would return from a sortie at low level in order to ground-straff enemy troops wherever he could find them. Such was his determination to engage the enemy on every occasion that he was described by his commanding officer as *'a young fire-eater'*; quite a compliment from a senior officer who himself wore the ribbons of the DSO and the MC. Despite the FK8's reputation as a cumbersome, stable aeroplane, the young McLeod threw it about like a fighter (or scout as they were called then). On 19 December, in company with his observer Lieutenant Comber, they attacked a formation of eight German Albatross scouts. Unaccustomed to being attacked by a lumbering bomber, the enemy formation scattered in surprise, but not before Lieutenant Comber had sent one spinning down out of control. One month later, on 14 January 1918, 2/Lt 'Babe' McLeod with Lieutenant Reginald Key as his observer were sent out to destroy an enemy observation balloon. This so-called 'balloon busting' was considered to be highly dangerous, even for a fast scout; for a bomber to attempt to negotiate the defending anti-aircraft guns sited all round the balloon, together with any enemy scouts providing air cover, was virtual suicide.

The pair approached the balloon from well above and then dived on their target. In the descent, McLeod spotted three Albatross scouts converging on him intent on his destruction. Ignoring the threat he continued his dive through the bursting anti-aircraft shells, closing to within a few yards of the balloon. He opened fire as soon as he was in range and continued firing until at point blank range, whereupon the balloon suddenly burst into flames, causing him to turn sharply to avoid the blazing wreck. Fighting their way back to the Allied lines, Lt Key got in a telling burst on one of the enemy scouts, which fell apart in mid-air. For their gallantry and determination, the two were mentioned in despatches.

In March 1918 the German Ludenforf offensive commenced and considerable gains were achieved in the early stages. Along with other RFC squadrons, No 2 Squadron was moved south to the Amiens area; being opposed in this sector of the Front by the German Air Force's Jagdgeschwader No 1; better known as 'The Richthofen Circus'. On 27 March No 2 Squadron despatched seven FK8s to attack enemy troop concentrations near the town of Albert. Because of the poor weather the crews were briefed to proceed independently. McLeod was flying with Lt A W Hammond MC, an experienced observer and gunner, but unfortunately they were unable to locate their assigned target. After flying around for two hours, McLeod elected to land and refuel.

Following lunch with the Sopwith Camel pilots of No 43 Squadron at Avesnes-le-Comte, McLeod and Hammond took off to resume their search for the target. The weather remained poor, and after a further fruitless two hours, McLeod was about to give up and return to base. Then, through a gap in the clouds, he spotted a German observation balloon and immediately dived to the attack. No sooner had McLeod got the balloon steady in his sights when Hammond tapped him on the shoulder and pointed to a Fokker Triplane above them. Abandoning his plan to attack the balloon, McLeod hauled the nose of the 'Big Ack' up and towards the Triplane.

The experienced Hammond held his fire until they were almost at point-blank range. With the first burst from his Lewis gun he damaged the Fokker and possibly hit the pilot. It fell away in an apparent uncontrolled spin and crashed just outside Albert.

The destruction of the Fokker had been witnessed by the pilots of a formation of eight other Triplanes, one of whom was the German ace to be, Hans Kirschstein. In the ensuing fight, McLeod and Hammond sent two of the enemy scouts down in flames, but by this time Hammond had been hit three times and McLeod once, in the leg. On his second attack, Kirschstein set the 'Big Ack's' fuel tank alight. The intense heat rapidly consumed the bomber and the crew's flying clothing. With his leather coat and boots burning, McLeod climbed out of the cockpit on to the lower left wing root, holding the burning control column in his right hand while still managing to control the aircraft in a sideslip to keep the flames away from himself and the badly wounded Hammond.

The observer had by this time climbed out of his cockpit and was astride the fuselage, still clinging somewhat precariously to his gun mounting. Seeing their victim going down in flames, seven of the scouts withdrew, but the eighth decided to follow the FK8 down to witness its final destruction.. Closing in to get a closer view he came in sight of Hammond who, despite the flames and his severe injuries, swung his Lewis gun round and fired a final defiant burst at the Triplane. He must have killed the pilot as the Fokker flicked over and crashed into the German trenches. Meanwhile, the blazing bomber crashed in a crater in 'no mans land'. Despite suffering from five wounds, McLeod managed to drag the unconscious Hammond from the burning wreck and carried and dragged him to the nearest British trenches, being hit on the way by shrapnel splinters.

The award of the Victoria Cross to McLeod was announced in the London Gazette on 1 May 1918. Sent home to Canada to convalesce, McLeod was doing well until he contracted a particularly virulent strain of influenza and died on 6 November, four days before the Armistice came into effect. Alan McLeod was 19 years old when he earned the VC, the youngest recipient in the RFC during the First World War. His gallant companion, Lieutenant Arthur Hammond received a bar to his MC - surely scant recognition for such an heroic performance? Their vanquisher, Lt Kirschstein went on to achieve a tally of 27 victories and to earn the German equivalent of the VC, the Pour le Merite, but he did not survive the war, being killed in an air crash.

Waddington and the Local Community

From the earliest days of an RFC unit on Waddington Heath, the soldiers had established close contact with the nearby village. Two months after the aerodrome opened, the local paper recorded that:

'A most excellent entertainment was given by members of the RFC in the schoolroom on Wednesday evening. The room was packed to the uttermost; the concert being given in aid of the old people's tea!' One month later, a similar event was recorded, this time reporting: '...a very interesting entertainment was given in the Waddington village hall by members of the RFC in aid of the Red Cross and the 4th Northern General (Military) Hospital. The programme was arranged by Corporal Watson, and songs sung by 2nd Class Air Mechanics (2 AMs) Travis and Davis. A cornet duet was performed by 2AMs Leach and Halliday.' In the same edition of the Lincoln Echo was a report of a quite different nature. Entitled 'Alarming Shooting of Officer Near Lincoln' it gave details of the shooting of an RFC Officer. The article went on to add

'Quite a sensation was caused in the Lincoln district on Thursday when it became known that in the early hours of Wednesday a serious and alarming shooting offence occured in the aerodrome camp in the vicinity of the city. The authorities were reticent regarding the affair, but it appears that the victim of the outrage was a young officer, aged about 22, who prior to the war was with the Connaught Rangers. He had only recently been attached to the RFC at the aerodrome after having seen service at the Front. In the dead of night, a pane of glass of the officer's window was suddenly broken and a shot fired through the opening.

The bullet, which upon investigation was found not to be a rifle bullet, penetrated the fleshy part of the victim's thigh. An alarm was raised, but every effort to trace the culprit was unsuccessful and the identity of the assailant seems to be a complete mystery. A curious feature of the affair is that the sound of the shot did not waken any of the men sleeping nearby. At the time the offence was commited, the officer was lying in his bunk. He was taken to the 4th Northern General Hospital where he received attention, and it is hoped that he will recover'. A mysterious occurence which appears to have remained unsolved, and one far different from that concerning one Albert Mason Keefe of the RFC who was fined £2 and ordered to pay 7/6d (37p) witnesses' fees, having been found guilty of driving a motor cycle and sidecar in a manner dangerous to the public in the High Street, and not stopping after knocking down two men!

That the newcomers to the district were popular with the villagers is further evidenced by an entry in the Lincolnshire Chronicle dated 3 February 1917. In the page under 'News From the Villages', is the following report:

'The members of the Wesleyan Church have started a Soldiers'Institute which is open every evening. Various games and papers are provided as are refreshments. There is a small charge for weekday evenings, but Saturday evenings are free'.

A popular haunt in the village for the soldiers and airmen of the aerodrome was Peatman's in the village

High Street. This was an old established general dealer and bakery. The shop sold cigarettes, sugar, flour, sweets, assorted medicaments, soap, general dry goods and some hardware. The bakery provided the bread for the aerodrome among other military establishments in addition to the local villages. During the Great War one of the rooms of the shop was emptied and turned into a cafe cum restaurant, whose clientele were mainly from 'the camp'. The menu was simple and unchanging; mainly eggs on bread and tea, though those who could not spare the time to use the cafe, would buy cakes, buns and bread straight from the oven.

The RFC Training Organisation Develops

On 31 May 1917 the Reserve Squadrons lost their totally inappropriate title and were renamed Training Squadrons. Two weeks before this change came about, a third training or reserve squadron joined Nos 47 and 48; this was No 51 Training Squadron, which came to Waddington from Wye near Ashford in Kent. It was equipped with the usual assortment of aeroplane types, including Avro 504s, RE8s, FK3s and the Martinsyde Elephants. This latter type was used to give advanced training to those who were destined for reconnaissance squadrons. It was a relatively large, single seat fighter type, but it lacked the manoeuvrability required of a fighter; hence it became a bomber and reconnaissance machine. Its correct designation was the Martinsyde G100, but the RFC only ever referred to it as 'the elephant'.

By the time No 51 Training Squadron arrived at Waddington, the two resident training units, Nos 47 and 48, had increased the range of aircraft types in their inventories, which now included the Avro 504, BE2, FK3, RE7, DH4, and RE8. This occurred as part of the continuous expansion and development of the RFC and was mirrored throughout the training organisation, not the least among those in Lincolnshire.

With such a collection of high spirited young men in and around the city of Lincoln, a state of friendly rivallry was bound to occur, and of course did. One pair of local rivals were No 27 Wing at Waddington and No 23 Wing at South Carlton, who frequently engaged in competitive events both on and off the sports field. Occasionally, on days when the weather was considered too bad for instructional flying, some of Waddington's instructors and advanced pupils would organise a bombing raid on South Carlton, using a variety of more or less harmless missiles. In return, the pilots of South Carlton would respond in kind. But on one notable occasion, an FE2b from South Carlton landed quietly one evening at Waddington, and the occupants planted a few healthy young saplings in the middle of the landing ground, the implication being that as Waddington did so little flying, trees had the time and opportunity to grow on the aerodrome. This did not amuse the new Commanding Officer, Lt Col H le N Brock and retribution was swift to follow. The Waddington pilots waited until South Carlton was indulging itself in a tennis match. Then, out of the blue, a group of 27 Wing aeroplanes swooped on the tennis courts dispensing home-made soot-ball bombs, makinga dreadful mess of players, spectators and the courts alike.

Rumours of Sabotage

It was at about this time that ugly rumours began to circulate that there was a saboteur at Waddington. So seriously was this allegation taken, that in October 1917 an official investigation was instigated, but nothing was ever proved, the evidence pointing to the accidents being the result of a variety of causes. The first of the incidents which gave rise to the suspicion of sabotage was recorded in the *Lincoln Echo* of 5 May 1917. Starting with the headine: '*Lincs Air Fatality*', the report went on to say:

'A flying fatality occurred in the Lincoln district on Thursday, the victim being 2/Lt C Royston Marks RFC, and an inquest surrounding his death was held at the 4th Northern General Hospital. One of the witnesses, Captain R Blatherwick RFC, said that Lieutenant Marks was 23 years of age. He (Marks) was a pupil of his (Blatherwick) and had received some 3½ hours of instruction. That morning the witness sent Marks up on his first flight alone. He got off very well and made a complete circuit when he reached a height of 500 feet. As he turned to come down, the machine (Shorthorn) dived into the ground, killing the pilot. The witness had flown with Marks in the same machine and it was in good order'.

Elsewhere in the same paper was a smaller caption: 'Funeral Service at Waddington Church on Saturday 5 May'. A brief note in one column stated that:

'The funeral of 2Lt C Royston Marks, who met his death on 2 May, took place here. The RFC, who were in attendance, fired the usual three volleys over the grave, and two of the buglers sounded the Last Post. Lieutenant Johnson represented the parents of the deceased. There were some very beautiful wreaths, including one from his mother and another from his comrades which was in the form of an RFC wing'.

Lt Marks grave is the only one in Waddington with a headstone from the Great War Others were lost when the church and graveyard were virtually destroyed in World War 2.

The day following the death of Lt Marks, another Waddington Shorthorn crashed. In this instance, the wings collapsed in mid-air, the resulting crash killing the pilot. The RFC Court of Inquiry found that the probable cause was that the pilot had dived the machine 'at an excessive speed' by mistake. It was much later, when rumours of a saboteur abounded, that it was recalled that the port wing only had collapsed and that this could have been due to sabotage of the wing spa. Thus began a series of accidents that were to bedevil Waddington throughout the war, though its accident rate was no greater than any other training station. On 16 June, a BE2c belonging to No 51 Training Squadron spun into the ground. At the time it was considered that the cause was the student applying excessive rudder in the turn. Only later was it to be suggested that a possible alternative cause could have been a jammed rudder; though how and why this could be a result of sabotage is not recorded. Less than one week later, a Shorthorn of No 47 Training Squadron stalled; its starboard wing collapsed and it crashed to the ground. Once again, the official findings blamed the pilot for over-stressing the aeroplane. Then, on 15 July, another Shorthorn, this one belonging to No 48 Training squadron, dived almost vertically into the ground. The crash was witnessed by several local people, but none of them had any knowledge of aviation and were unable to suggest any cause.

This spate of crashes by Waddington aircraft was not confined to the three training squadrons. No 82 Squadron, which was working up for its deployment to France, lost three of its aeroplanes in quick succession. The first occurred on 6 August when one of its Avro 504s appeared to stall, enter a spin and crash almost vertically into the ground, killing the pilot. Just under one month later, on 4 September, one of the squadron's RE8s was observed to enter a flat spin before nosing over and diving vertically into the ground, again with fatal results. That same month, on 28 September, a BE2e crashed while in a starboard turn.

These fatal crashes were accompanied by the usual run of minor accidents, so common among training units. However, the cumulative result was a marked lowering of morale. This growing problem had not been eased earlier when, in mid August, an inexperienced student pilot of No 48 Training Squadron crashed on landing. He had failed to notice that his intended landing run conflicted with the path of another training machine that was taxying. Too late, he saw the danger and hauled back on the control column. His Shorthorn, climbing steeply but with insufficient power and speed, fell out of the inadvertantly initiated loop and crashed to the ground, killing the pilot.

Just as September was drawing to a close, No 47 Training Squadron lost a pilot when his Shorthorn was seen to descend in a flat spin and crash. In retrospect it is easy to see that most if not all of the incidents could be attributed to the now so-called 'pilot error', but in the tense atmosphere of the time, sabotage was only too easily considered to be a likely cause.

The crash that resulted in the initiation of an official review of the accidents at Waddington occurred on 22 October 1917. The type of aeroplane involved is not known, nor its unit, but the accident report was, to say the least, succinct: *'The engine fell out whilst being flown'*. It was not unknown for engine bearer bolts to work loose, but what if a saboteur had deliberately loosened them? Again, in retrospect most unlikely, but by then the idea of a saboteur had taken firm hold of many imaginations. This catalogue of accidents was to continue, though the rate was no worse than at any other training unit.

Some idea of how accidents could occur that had nothing to do with aircraft structural failure can be gained from the recollections of 2/Lt Stevens:

'...there were some wild students whose antics were not confined to their off-duty hours. One day I was flying around in a Shorthorn; on coming in to land at about 56 mph, I happened to glance to my left and to my horror I saw another aircraft coming in to land straight across my flight path. To prevent a collision, I drew back on my control column, but not having sufficient speed to climb, my aircraft stalled and crashed on to its nose.

It should be remembered that in those days we had no runways, just a large green field and we made our landings and take-offs according to the wind direction. After the crash, both of us had to report to the Commanding Officer, where the Russian (!) student of the other aircraft apologised to me, stating that he was in the wrong.

On another occasion, I was flying with my instructor, Captain Gowdie of the Seaforth Highlanders. Having climbed up to 6,000 feet he told me to take the main road to Lincoln. After a short run he tapped me on the back and shouted to me over the sound of the engine, to keep my eyes on the spirit level as I was side-slipping. Some time later I wanted to speak to him so I turned my head to the rear; at this point I got the shock of my life - he was having '40 winks'! We students all knew that he was fond of a drop from the bottle, but sleeping in the air...? Luckily all went well and we landed back safely at Waddington'.

The Independent Force

The attacks on Great Britain by the German Zeppelin airships and giant bombers resulted in the RFC developing a strategic bomber force of its own; its task being to bomb targets in Germany, which hitherto had remained free from attack. Coincident with the formation of the special bomber squadrons, which were eventually to become the Independent Force under Major General Hugh Trenchard, were selected training squadrons which were required to specialise in training pilots for this new role. One of the training units selected to specialise in this training was no 27 Wing at Waddington. To enable this new training requirement to be undertaken, yet more types of aeroplane were added to the Waddington inventory. A selection of DH4, DH6 and DH9 aircraft arrived, causing even more headaches for the engineering staff and the recently formed Aeroplane Repair Section (ARS). To assist with the new training commitment, two additional training squadrons moved in to Waddington. No 44 Training Squadron came from Harlaxton near Grantham and replaced No 82 Squadron, which had moved to St Omer in France as an operational squadron. Then, on 14 November, No 75 Training Squadron formed at Waddington. Both the new units were equipped with a selection of DH4, 6 and 9s, though No 44 Training squadron possessed in addition a few BE2Es. However, Waddington was not really large enough for five training squadrons, so on 22 December 1917, No 75 Training Squadron moved out to Cramlington in Northumberland.

The breathing space was extremely shortlived, as one month later No 97 Squadron arrived. Like No 82 Squadron before it, this squadron was working up to become operational. It formed at Waddington, equipped with Shorthorns and DH4s and was intended to become part of the Independent Force.

Just over one month after its formation at Waddington, No 97 Squadron, under the command of Major V.A. Albrecht, moved south to Stonehenge where it converted to a brand new aircraft – the giant Handley Page 0/400 night bomber.

Lieutenant Colonel Loraine and Friends

Since early 1917 the Commanding Officer of No 27 Wing had been Lt Col Robert Loraine, who in more peaceful times had been a well-known actor. Lt Col Loraine was well-respected by all at Waddington, the general opinion being that he was a just, brave and patriotic man as well as a strict but fair disciplinarian. At this time No 47 Training Squadron was commanded by a Major Douglas, well known in civilian life in the control and organisation of the betting business. No 48 Training Squadron's Commanding Officer was a Major Impy. Among the ground staff officers, Lieutenant Albert Wyndham Payne RFC joined the staff of No 27 Wing in May1917. He was posted in from the Northern Aircraft Depot at Bradford, to assume control and responsibility for the equipment and supply department. During his stay at Waddington he got married and lived with his wife in a gamekeeper's cottage at nearby Coleby. His young wife was the first lady to be invited to a guest night in the Officers' Mess, which at the time was presided over by Lt Col I.A.E. Edwards, who lived away from camp at Mere Hall.

Lt Col Loraine came to Waddington from France, having commanded No 40 Squadron, which flew FE8 scouts from Treizennes. He flew regularly; indeed, he had his own aeroplane allocated to him (unofficially). On moving from France, he had brought with him his technical Warrant Officer (WO) L.O. Day. That these two had a very close personal relationship is evidenced by an event concerning the Colonel's aircraft. Apparently, on one occasion Colonel Loraine wanted to fly but found that his aeroplane (either a Shorthorn or a DH6) lacked a propeller. Persisting in his wish to fly, he raised the matter with WO Day who, experienced great difficulty in obtaining a replacement propeller through official channels. Determined to satisfy his colonel's requirements, Day broke into one of the hangars belonging to No 47 Training Squadron and removed a propeller from one of their aircraft, which he duly fitted to the colonel's aeroplane. Early the next morning the technical Warrant Officer of No 47 Training Squadron, Sgt/Maj Hart, reported the theft of a propeller. A Court of Enquiry was convened, presided over by the senior officer, Lt Col Loraine. Eventually, WO Day was called as a witness, but before he could speak, the president of the court said:

"Ah, Warrant Officer Day... Well, you won't know anything about this matter. Next witness please!"

Improvements to the Training System of the RFC

During the last quarter of 1917, the training system of the RFC underwent a change and marked improvement. Based on the teachings of Major R. Smith-Barry and his experiences at the School of Special Flying at Gosport, the RFC's approach to flying training was revised. Smith-Barry had developed a training system founded on the knowledge that it was possible to recover from almost any situation in which it was possible to put an aeroplane. This approach was based on the discovery that a spin, hitherto considered irrecoverable and fatal, could be recovered from simply by centralising the controls and pushing the aeroplane's nose down. Following Smith-Barry's proposals, all pupil pilots were taught how to recover from a range of unusual positions and were then required to practice these manoeuvres. An additional aid to flying instruction was the introduction of a speaking tube linking the instructor to the student. The overall result of these changes in the system of training pilots, resulted in the production of a far more competent pilot on completion of his training. However, despite this, Waddington was still experiencing a series of worrying accidents. On 10 November, a DH5 of No 51 Training Squadron flicked into a flat spin as it came into land and struck the ground killing the pilot.

Training Continues & New Machines Arrive

The requirement to train bomber pilots resulted in the arrival at Waddington of three DeHavilland types of aeroplanes: the DH4, DH6 and the DH9. It was said of the DH4 that with it, Captain deHavilland produced one of the truly great aeroplanes of its day, one which had no peer among aeroplanes of its class in any of the combatant air forces, allied or enemy. There was nothing unique about its design; it was typical of the period. The Central Flying School's report was most enthusiastic, stating that it was very stable, laterally, longitudinally and directionally. The report went on to add that the aircraft was exceptionally comfortable to fly, very easy to land and exceptionally light on the controls. The RFC was so impressed with the DH4, that in order to reinforce the Independent Force, a batch of 50 destined for Russia was held back on the understanding that 75 would be made available in their place in the spring of 1918. At this time, there were over 100 Russian student pilots undergoing flying training in England; a fair proportion of these being trained at Waddington. These Russian students had a fearsome reputation for brawls and knife fights. They were accommodated in wooden huts set apart from the other students, an area that the local airmen, soldiers and airwomen avoided, preferring to take a three-quarter mile detour to the village rather than pass by the Russians' billets. It has to be said also, that their record in the air left much to be desired.

Among the British students was a 2/Lt Branthwaite, who arrived on No 51 Training Squadron in September 1917. While in training at Waddington, he flew an assortment of BE2Es, Martinsyde Elephants and DH4s. His flying training period lasted for approximately two months, after which he was posted to No 25 Squadron at Boisdinghem in France. His log book shows that following several combat sorties he was posted back to Waddington in December 1917 to join No 51 Training Squadron, where he remained until February 1918, when he moved to No 44 Training Squadron for one month before being posted to No 1 School of Navigation and Bombing at Stonehenge.

A contemporary of Branthwaite's at Waddington was Lieutenant C.P. Thursley. He arrived on 20 December 1917 and flew his first training sortie on 7 January 1918. His instructor was Captain E.H. Pullinger, who commanded 'A' Flight of No 44 Training Squadron. This trip must have been an interesting introduction to the world of aviation, as they experienced engine failure soon after take-off! Two weeks later he moved over to No 51 Training Squadron, where he passed his bombing test successfully on 25 February. That same day, he flew a second trip during which he practiced air to air combat against Major Patterson, both of them flying DH6s. On completion of his training, Thursley was posted to No 110 Squadron on 17 March 1918.

The second of the new training machines at Waddington was the Airco DH6, one of the four Great War aeroplanes designed as a trainer from the outset. Towards the end of 1916, the RFC recognised that it could no longer use a mixture of operational aeroplanes for training. For one thing, they could barely be spared away from the Front. For another, with the growing size of the RFC, there were just not enough of them. What was needed were large numbers of aeroplanes that could be quickly and easily manufactured (and repaired) and which would possess safe flying characteristics. The result was the Airco DH6, of which it was said:

"Its wings were made by the mile and cut off by the yard".

In service, the DH6 gained several nicknames; for instance, as its wings possessed a marked concave aerofoil camber, they earned it the soubriquet 'The Clutching Hand'. Then again, its tall twin exhaust pipes that turned up vertically from the engine, gave rise to the name 'The Sky Hook'. The DH6's long undivided cockpit containing both instructor and student gave rise to two nicknames: 'The Flying Coffin' and the 'Dung Hunter'. The latter came from the Australian students who considered that it resembled a vehicle used for that purpose back home. Among the students, when in 'polite company', it was further known as either 'The Sixty', 'The Crab' or the 'Clockwork Mouse'.

The last of the three new RFC training machines was the Airco DH9. During a meeting at the War Office in June 1917, it was decided to increase the number operational squadrons in the RFC to two hundred, with most of the new squadrons destined to be bomber squadrons. An order was placed almost immediately for a further seven hundred DH4s, while plans were drawn up for a new type with greater speed, ceiling and bomb load. The prototype of the new machine was a modified DH4; the new machine being designated the DH9. Throughout its development and service, the DH9 was plagued with a poor, under-powered engine. This resulted in the DH9 barely matching the performance of the already obsolete DH4. In essence, the DH9 was almost identical to the DH4; the main differences being the engine installation and the disposition of the cockpits.

The DH9 had a unique feature in that instead of building the radiator around the propeller shaft, as was standard practice, it employed a retractable radiator located under the fuselage. If the DH9 had a really good feature at all, it was the fact that the two cockpits were much closer together than in most contemporary types. However, in this configuration the pilot was no longer situated between the engine and the fuel tank, as in the DH4, but further aft, resulting in reduced forward and downward visibility - not a desirable feature in any aeroplane, particularly not in a trainer. Those student pilots at Waddington who were trained on the DH9 were destined for operations with the Independent Force in its bombing of German targets, an ominous portent of 'things to come'!

Among the students at about this time was 2/Lt C G Stevens. This officer began his military career by running away from home and joining the Black Watch as a Drummer Boy in October 1908. Shortly after enlisting, his battalion was posted to India where it remained until the outbreak of war. Almost immediately after the commencement of hostilities, the Black

Watch moved to the port of Karachi to join a convoy carrying the Indian Expeditionary Force to France. The convoy, numbering 76 ships in all, was escorted by the Royal Navy all the way to Marseilles, where they disembarked. The troops were packed into cattle trucks and travelled north to the town of Bethune where, on the west side of the town, they clashed with German forces for the first time.

Having taken part in numerous battles on the Western Front, Stevens came home and, after professing an interest in flying machines, he was posted to the RFC cadet camp at Denham. This was the basic training camp for RFC officers and it was here that he met Captain Bowes-Lyon, (Queen Elizabeth the Queen Mother's brother). Bowes-Lyon had been the young Stevens Company Commander in India and informed him (Stevens) that Denham was intended for recruits, not serving regular soldiers. Accordingly, he posted Stevens to Farnborough. Following successfully completing the course at Oxford he was promoted to Second Lieutenant and posted to Waddington. On his arrival he reported to the Adjutant who, in turn, passed him over to the Orderly Officer who showed him to his sleeping quarters. The student pilots were accommodated in bell tents, which housed numerous young officers and cadets from Britain, Australia and Canada. Stevens recalled:

"The camp consisted of a few hangars, a wood and canvas headquarters building, some other sundry flimsy constructions and a large green field with no runway and, when it rained, a lot of mud. For the purpose of our flight training there was a motley collection of aeroplanes. Our dual control instruction was something like an hour every other day. I had flown about fourteen hours when my instructor said that we would go up for 'a height trip'. We had climbed to 7000 feet when my instructor indicated that I should take it down and land. I completed the descent and made a successful landing, whereupon my instructor climbed out, lifted his goggles and said "Now take off; its all yours". That was the end of my dual control phase. After completing the course I was posted to an RE8 squadron, later transferring to a Handley Page 0/400 squadron as part of the Independent Force."

As could be expected, the spate of accidents continued throughout the bad weather in December 1917, ensuring that the rumours of a saboteur remained as strong as ever. The New Year started badly with two unexplained accidents. Firstly, a BE2c of No 51 Training Squadron dived into the ground under full power. A similar accident occurred the very next day to a DH6 of No 48 Training Squadron. Almost immediately a rumour began to circulate suggesting that the control column, or 'joystick' as it was called in those days, had been tampered with. However, a study of the accident reports on three fatal crashes in January 1918 gives no indication of anything untoward. The BE2c was being flown by a Lieutenant Harrison and, just prior to the crash, he was performing aerobatic manoeuvres when the wing tip extensions broke away, the aircraft subsequently crashing. This particular aircraft (Serial No A1350) had a 'chequerboard' design painted on the fuselage. The second aircraft to crash, which occurred on 5 January, was being flown by Lieutenants Forster and Denham. This was Lt Forster's first ever flight and took place only a few hours after his arrival at Waddington. A third fatality which occurred that January involved an Officer Cadet Sharpe of the American Army, who was killed when his DH6 of No 48 Training Squadron crashed.

It was not only the students who suffered in accidents. One of the instructors, Sergeant Herbert Hallatt, was admitted to the military hospital in Lincoln suffering from injuries received when his pupil pilot panicked on the approach to land and crashed the machine. Another unlucky instructor was a 2/Lt Barker. He was posted to Waddington in the summer of 1918 where he instructed on the Avro 504K and the DH9. He too spent some time in the 4th Northern General Hospital in Lincoln, following a crash in one of the Avros.

An interesting insight into the life of an instructor at Waddington can be gained from the log book of one 2/Lt J.F. Duff, who served there briefly as a flying instructor. One entry in his log book states: '23 *January 1917 - Aircraft Type Graham White XV, Serial Number A1699.*' Then on 31 January of the same year is the rather laconic entry: *'Landings and Circuits. Engine failed at low altitude; landed across wind, machine overturned and crashed – passenger (student) unhurt'.*

The Women's Auxiliary Army Corps (WAAC)

As the war dragged on, it became apparent that the huge losses were becoming harder to replace. Earlier mistakes, such as recruiting skilled workers and miners for service in the combatant arms had been rectified, but the sobering fact was that the manpower shortage was becoming acute. Early in the war, in July 1915, the Marchioness of Londonderry had suggested to the War Office that they should form a 'Women's Legion', whose role would be to undertake certain administrative and domestic duties, thereby releasing numbers of able-bodied men for front-line duty. Following the success of the trial period, the plan was extended and included the employment of women as drivers, motor cycle riders, clerks, cooks, storekeepers and other trades. Many women volunteers were subsequently employed by the RFC in all these capacities and, on 7 July 1917, the War Office announced the formation of the Women's Auxiliary Army Corps (WAAC). In February 1918 the WAAC changed its name to that of the Queen Mary's Auxiliary Army Corps (QMAAC) and, following the formation of the Women's Royal Naval Service (WRNS) on 4 February 1918, the newly emergent Royal Air Force was joined by the Women's Royal Air Force (WRAF) on 1 April 1918.

The early days of the women's services was, as with the RFC, more than a little confused. For quite some time after its formation, the early members did not have uniforms. When they were eventually issued, the first uniforms were khaki in colour, remaining so until November 1918, when blue uniforms were issued. The WAAC, the QMAAC and subsequently the WRAF, were divided into two branches, 'Mobiles' and 'Immobiles'. Basically, the Mobiles could be required to serve wherever required, whereas the Immobiles could be only employed in the area of their home neighbourhood, thereby allowing them to live at home, from where they travelled in to their duty station each day. As one ex-Waddington Immobile recalled:

"...as an Immobile, I worked for most of the time in plain clothes...uniforms came much later...We were not on the ration strength, but brought our food in with us or bought it locally..."

The first Mobile members of the women's service to be employed at Waddington could not be accommodated on the station as there were no suitable buildings available. Instead, they lived in a large old house known to the people of Lincoln at the time as 'The Red House'. It was situated in an area known as 'Steep Hill' and is still there to this day. As another ex-Waddington Mobile who lived at 'Red House' recalled:

"We used to be collected each day in a big, noisy lorry that drove us the four miles to Waddington every morning and brought us back each evening. During the day we worked alongside the men, in my case it was in the Dope Shop".

This particular lady served in the QMAAC and the WRAF as a 'Member', in other words as a 'Private'. Ivy Whitby on the other hand, rose to the rank of 'Chief Section Leader (Sergeant) and was employed as a statistical clerk in the aeroplane engineering records department of No 27 Wing Headquarters. Of her duties in those days she remembered:

"My main problem was that of keeping track of engines and aeroplanes. It was simple when they first arrived as the documentation recorded just which engine was installed in the aeroplane. But, following the numerous accidents and minor crashes, it was difficult to keep a record of what happened to the engines. For instance, if an aeroplane was badly damaged, but the engine was all right, the mechanics would put the engine into whichever aeroplane needed one! Sometimes they would remember to note it down or to tell us, but more often they forgot or just didn't bother. So, at regular intervals, I had to go round the hangars and endeavour to match the engine numbers with aeroplane serial numbers and then to check these against our records. This was a never ending task and one that continued to be performed right up to our disbandment in December 1919.

On the disbandment of the WRAF, a grateful government gave the Immobiles seven days leave with pay, whereas the Mobiles qualified for 28 days leave with full pay. Both branches were generously accorded the privilege of wearing their uniform during their terminal leave! Ivy Whitby served as a Mobile despite coming from Lincoln, and lived there all her life.

Accommodation at Waddington

The accommodation problem at Waddington, was not peculiar to the women's service. The officers of the permanent staff lived in some degree of comfort in a complex of twelve wooden huts located beside Ermine Street, near the three maintenance hangars. At one end of this complex, a few huts were reserved for commissioned officer student pilots, though they were not made over welcome in the Mess ante-room by the aforementioned officers of the permanent staff.. Those pupil pilots who were not commissioned; namely the Officer Cadets and Senior NCOs, lived for the most part in a collection of tents near the junction of Ermine Street and Mere Road.

Most of the resident airmen and soldiers lived in rows of huts adjacent to Mere Road and close to the guardroom, but a few were billeted out either in the local villages or in the city of Lincoln. With the living accommodation rather cramped and spartan, the young high spirited students found various ways to let off steam, both in the air and on the ground. On 16 February 1918, the local paper reported that Lieutenant A.R. Oxley of the RFC was charged, together with another officer, with brawling in the Lincoln Theatre during the interval. The magistrates set aside any conviction provided they paid the cost of the damage.

Aerial Activity and Improvements to the Training System

Not all the high spirits gained expression on the ground. One of the Waddington pilots felt that the growing practice of flying aeroplanes through hangars was becoming commonplace, so he elected to try something different. Early one morning some of the citizens of Lincoln were more than a little surprised to see an aeroplane flying down the High Street, below roof-top height, before swooping under the railway bridge, better known (before it was demolished) as 'Bainbridge's Bridge'. Other 'young bloods' developed a competitive sport of their own. It started with them spinning the wheels of their aircraft on the roofs of moving railway carriages, much to the consternation of the passengers, and developed from there. The final scheme was to fly at the roofs of the Belfast hangars, ideally early in the morning when the dew was still on the roof, and to then attempt to fly up one slope and down the other. The proof of success was the sight of wheel tracks in the dew!

With the improvement in training techniques and standards, had come a more rational allocation of aircraft for training purposes. Although worn out front line types could still be found on training stations, in the main this role was increasingly being taken over by Avro 504s and DH4 and 6s. However, despite these improvements, a depressing number of accidents continued to plague the training squadrons at Waddington. On 19 February 1918, Lieutenant Gross, one of the first Americans to arrive for training, was killed when his RE8 stalled while undertaking a gliding turn and crashed. For once, even the most suspicious could not really suspect sabotage in this instance. The RE8, the workhorse of Corps reconnaissance and artillery spotting duties, did not have a particularly good reputation. From the start of its introduction into service, it had a nasty tendency to spin; this unpleasant characteristic being compounded by its design. Another poor feature was the fact that the petrol tank was located directly behind the engine, with the result that in the event of a crash, the hot engine was forced back into the fuel tank, inevitably causing a fire. A week after the death of the American, a British cadet pilot died in similar circumstances when he stalled his aircraft at low altitude. In the case of another unfortunate student pilot; while flying an RE8 (Serial No 4508) he made such a bad landing that the engine (140hp RAF) was torn from its mountings and thrown clear of the aircraft.

As part of the attempt to improve the quality of flying instruction, the RFC issued two pamphlets, both written by a service pilot who, more than any other, completely changed the whole practice of flying training. His name was Robert Raymond Smith-Barry. He had become totally disillusioned with the standards of, and approach to, instruction and made it his business to implement major improvements. One his first pamphlets to be issued was entitled 'Notes on Teaching Flying for Instructors', copies of which were distributed among others, to the instructors at Waddington. Earlier, Smith-Barry had written:

'The present day pupil is often discouraged on entering the RFC by being regarded (by his instructor) as an 'odious Hun'...he is taught to fly by people who are altogether without enthusiasm and whose indifference is, as always, contagious... It is suggested that the mental attitude towards flying of an instructor is reflected in all the pilots he turns out...'

The second Smith-Barry pamphlet, which was circulated throughout the RFC was entitled 'General Methods of Teaching Scout Pilots'.

Notwithstanding the overall improvement in the standards of instruction, the catalogue of accidents continued unabated at Waddington. Even the arrival of a new commanding officer, Lt Col J.R.W. Smyth-Pigott did little to improve matters. Indeed, at one stage in early 1918 the situation became so tense that some student pilots refused to fly! In the general interest, the authorities kept the matter very quiet. But, in a letter to the magazine 'Popular Flying', one of No 44 Training Squadron's students wrote that he was convinced that there was a saboteur at Waddington. T H Newsome went on to add that he felt that he had been lucky to manage to land his DH4 following the jamming of his controls. He claimed that an investigation revealed that someone had almost sawn through his controls. Two weeks after Lt Gross was killed in his RE8, another No 44 Training Squadron aircraft crashed. This time it was a DH4 flying on a dual control sortie, only one of the occupants surviving the crash. But, not all crashes were fatal; on 14 February Lieutenant Small, flying an FK3, crashed into a BE2e while landing, suffering only minor cuts and bruises. The following month an FE2b of No 51 Training Squadron crashed on the aerodrome, killing the pilot.

In keeping with the practice of forming new squadrons based on a cadre of experienced personnel, No 123 Squadron formed as a nucleus at Waddington on 1 March 1918, moving the same day to Duxford near Cambridge. The cadre in all probability came from among the staff of No 44 Training Squadron. The plan was for the squadron to train as a day bomber squadron equipped with DH9s, but in the event it did not reach operational status and was disbanded on 14 October 1918. There is brief reference to No 117 Squadron forming at Waddington, having possibly come as a cadre from Beaulieu. Be that as it may, it moved on 3 April 1918 to Hucknall. It had several subsequent moves, but failed to reach operational status and accordingly, it was disbanded and absorbed by No 141 Squadron on 6 October 1918.

The Zeppelin Attack on Waddington

Following the crashes in February and March, the commanding officer attempted to put the pupil pilots' minds at rest by ordering that a guard be mounted on the station's hangars at night. However, this increased level of security was no protection against one group of ill-disposed visitors. On the night of 12/13 April 1918, five Zeppelin airships of the German Naval Air Service carried out a series of attacks on the Midlands and East Anglia. The craft taking part were as follows:

- (i) L60 - Kptlt H K Flemming
- (ii) L61 - Kptlt H Ehrlich
- (iii) L62 - Hptmn K Manger
- (iv) L63 - Kptlt M von Freudenreich
- (v) L64 - Kptlt Arnold Schutze

The attack was carried out by these five Zeppelins, the latest type to enter service, equipped with the improved Maybach engines. These airships were sometimes referred to as *'Heightfinders'* because of their ability to achieve far greater heights than the earlier classes of Zeppelins. However, this ability to cruise at greater altitudes, thereby remaining much safer from attack by defending fighters, gave rise to a new set of problems. Firstly, flying at greater heights increased the navigation problems, particularly because of the frequency that these high flying airships found themselves above cloud. Secondly, in those days, the level of knowledge of upper winds and meteorology in general, was an even more inexact science than it remains today! These two factors, combined to make life very difficult for the crews of these night raiders. Each Zeppelin carried a bomb load of approximately 3,000kg and bombed from a height of about 18,000 feet whenever possible.

The raiders were led by Germany's most experienced Zeppelin commander, Fregattenkapitan Peter Strasser. Zeppelin L64, commanded by Korvettenkapitan Schutze, crossed the Lincolnshire coast just south of Donna Nook at approximately 2150 hours. It passed over Louth at 2200 hrs, dropping some bombs near Donnington-on-Bain about five minutes later. Continuing to steer south-westerly, the great airship reached Sudbrooke where its crew spotted the lights of South Carlton aerodrome! Carrying out a right hand orbit in order to position overhead, it dropped a stick of bombs in the vicinity of the aerodrome. The Zeppelin, still seeking its primary target of Lincoln, passed to the north of the city, but the blackout must have been effective as no bombs were dropped. Instead, the lights at Skellingthorpe and Doddington attracted fourteen bombs, some of which damaged the railway track and an engine shed at Skellingthorpe. Those dropped at Doddington resulted in breaking only a few windows.

Over Doddington L64 turned back to the east, still trying to locate Lincoln. Crossing the A46 road near North Hykeham, the crew of the raider observed a cluster of lights just ahead of them; accordingly, they dropped a stick of four bombs. These missiles fell on Waddington aerodrome and at nearby Mere at 2240hrs. The stick of four bombs seems to have been a mixture of high explosive and incendiaries.

Having bombed Waddington, albeit unknowingly, Schutze turned his craft south, following the line of the A15 road. In the vicinity of Ashby de la Launde the airship commenced a wide left hand turn back to the north, bombing Metheringham at 2315hrs. Over Nocton Hall it turned on to an easterly course, passing over Woodhall Spa and Stickford before turning south east towards Friskney. Here the Zeppelin turned back to the north, proceeding as far as Burgh le Marsh, where it again turned to the east and crossed the coast over Ingoldmells Point at 0025hrs. Then, instead of crossing the North Sea to its base in Belgium, for some reason Schutze turned his craft back to the west, crossing the coast just south of Sandilands; flying inland for barely four or five miles, L64 turned onto a north-easterly course, coasting out on its way home at 0400hrs, just south of Mablethorpe. Subsequent investigations revealed that the reason why the aerodromes at South Carlton and Waddington were 'lit up' during an air raid, was that the Lincoln 'buzzer alarm' had either not been operated, was not heard or had failed to work, this 'buzzer alarm' being part of the national air raid warning system. The following morning the aerodrome at Waddington was alive with souvenir hunters, all looking for pieces of the bombs, many of which were found and hoarded or sent to relatives and friends, together with graphic descriptions of the night's events.

On a lighter note... a popular story that circulated the Lincoln area after the night's excitement concerned the engine driver of the local train. Legend had it that on seeing that an air raid was in progress as he approached Lincoln, the driver stopped his train in the Greetwell Cutting, so as not to give away the location of the Lincoln railway station. Rumour had it that the poor driver was sacked by the railway company for making an unofficial stop!

Subsequent regional reports on the raid revealed that two of the bombs fell opposite the engine shed just to the east of the Pyewipe railway junction, apparently just missing the signal box. These two bombs created craters some six to eight feet deep and twelve feet wide. A bomb that fell near Moor Farm, which is just south east of the road junction of the Doddington to Lincoln and Skellingthorpe roads, must have been of a larger capacity, as the crater was reported as being seven feet deep and 24 feet in diameter. Of the bombs dropped in the immediate vicinity of Waddington, the report stated that the craters were four feet deep and eighteen feet in diameter. The weapons were identified as being a mix of 660lb and 220lb bombs and some incendiaries. One unexploded bomb was located just to the east of the Sleaford road beside the aerodrome. This bomb was successfully defused and recovered, having been identified as a 300kg high explosive weapon.

Further Changes in the RFC Training System

One week before the Zeppelin attack, the local paper The Lincoln Echo again reported a fatal crash at Waddington. This report indicates that American and Russian pilots were involved. Under the heading 'Flying Fatality', the paper went on to report:

'*...on Wednesday, a machine crashed into another aeroplane that was stationary on the ground and Lieutenant S Huguenin of the American flying contingent was killed, together with Corporal B J Seifend and Private N Krantow; a fourth man was badly injured...*'

The same paper, one week later reported that questions were being asked in the House of Commons about the completion of aerodrome works. At issue was the report that 'exorbitant and unnecessary wages' were being paid to labourers engaged in aerodrome work. Apparently these aerodrome workers were paid £3 a week, whereas farm labourers were paid only half this amount. Steps were being taken to prevent farm labourers changing their jobs!

With the coming of the better weather in the Spring and Summer, the accident rate dropped markedly, though some suggested that the hangar guard was also partially responsible. Whatever the reason, the number of unexplained fatalities decreased and morale improved, with many courses completing their training in shorter than the allotted time, thereby speeding up the flow of young pilots to the Western Front. At this time, one of the instructors was Sergeant Herbert William Hallatt who, though a very experienced pilot and instructor, was badly injured when his pupil panicked in a turn and crashed the machine. Sergeant Hallatt was taken to the 4th Northern General Hospital with both legs badly broken.

The Army surgeons told Hallatt that gangrene had set in and that all they could do was to amputate both legs. Regardless of the difference in their ranks, the good Sergeant told the senior surgeon, a Colonel, just what he could do and that he would have to amputate his (the Sergeant's) head first! As a result, Sergeant Hallatt kept his legs; indeed, his recovery was so remarkable that the Colonel presented him with a silver-topped cane when he was discharged from the hospital.

On a lighter note, one of the student pilots who was later to reach high rank, made a name for himself when he crashed his DH6 through the roof of the WRAF billet. Luckily it was empty at the time as the residents were away at tea. The pilot escaped with minor cuts and bruises, but his reputation did not so easily recover. Thereafter he was always accused by his 'friends' of being a sex maniac!

Yet another squadron formed up based on a nucleus of Waddington pilots. This was No 163 Squadron which formed at Waddington on 1 June 1918. However, it disbanded just over a month later having never proceeded beyond the nucleus phase. Just why such a course of action was decided upon is not recorded. Following another change in the overall structure of the RFC/RAF training system, No 48 Training Depot Station was created at Waddington.

The purpose behind the formation of the so-called Training Depot Stations (TDS) was one of economy. It had been decided in 1917 at the highest level that the creation of seven Training Depot Stations, each equal to three Training Squadrons, would result in economies in personnel and transport. Furthermore, it was felt that it would reduce the need to convert yet more badly needed agricultural land to aerodromes. As a result of this reorganisation, on 4 July, Waddington became No 48 Training Depot Station (TDS) which comprised Nos 44, 47 and 48 Training Squadrons, the Station being commanded by Lt Col J.R. Herring. Despite this change, No 51 Training Squadron remained at Waddington, though apparently not as part of No 48 TDS. In addition to the structural changes in the RFC/RAF training organisation, the introduction of TDSs brought with it a change in training methods. The new system was to take the novice pilots and teach them to fly the basic training machines such as the Avro 504, and to then convert them on to whichever operational type they were destined to fly. Once trained, the newly qualified pilots, together with their instructors would move, with their aircraft, to a front-line squadron and into the fray. The resultantly denuded TDS would then receive a new batch of instructors and students, when the cycle would begin again.

Among the ground staff was a young soldier, William Shepherd who, many years later, was to retire from the RAF as Warrant Officer William Shepherd MBE. He remembered working on a variety of deHavilland and other aircraft. Among his recollections are those of illness and humour:

'We suffered a severe outbreak of Asian Flu and I was the first person on the camp to go down with it. I was isolated in a large, empty wooden hut; just me and I was very lonely. My section came under the command of an old regular army sergeant who used to frequent the pubs of Lincoln most evenings. One night, while he was in town, we found some sheep wandering around the camp, so we rounded them up and put them in his bunk, which reeked for days after. Luckily for us, he never found out who the culprits were. There was a permanent firing party in our hut who were on standby for any military funerals; their services being called upon all too often. When we heard that the Armistice had been signed, members of the firing party celebrated by shooting holes in the chimneys of the American detachment's hut, whose occupants did not seem to find very amusing'.

Towards the end of 1917 Field Marshal Sir Douglas Haig was calling for a programme to provide sufficient aeroplanes and squadrons to meet the projected needs of 1919. His requirement was for 113 squadrons for employment in France and Italy, though this figure did not include the 66 squadrons planned for the long-range bomber force - The Independent Force - for use against targets in Germany. The War Office did not agree; they suggested that there would be a requirement for 240 squadrons, this figure representing an increase of 40 over the previously planned target of 200 squadrons. Such an increase would result in an increased manning requirement of some 2,360 officers, 1,400 men and 4,500 women (!). However, with the never-ending demands of the fighting units on the Western Front, there was no way that this target would ever be met, despite the most searching trawl through the Army. Somewhat reluctantly, the War Office approached the Americans for assistance. With the agreement of the American Commander-in-Chief, General J.J. Pershing, the Americans undertook to provide 155 mechanics. These men would be sent direct to England from the United States and would be allocated for service with the RFC/RAF in England. This arrangement worked to the advantage of both the British and the Americans. It enabled the RFC/RAF to release men from the home-based units for service with either front-line squadrons or those forming up for such service. On the other hand, it eventually provided the Americans with a pool of well trained mechanics who had completed their training on aircraft types that were actually in service with front-line squadrons. In addition, the Americans undertook to maintain the number of mechanics on loan while still passing the fully trained men on to their own squadrons in France.

The long-term plans for the development and expansion of the American air services was for the formation of a flying corps of some 4500 aeroplanes, together with 5000 pilots and 50,000 mechanics. As part of the agreement, the British offered every assistance based on lessons learned from the expansion of the RFC. As far as Waddington was concerned, the growth of American participation in the air war in Europe was evidenced by the arrival of increasing numbers of American student pilots and mechanics. During the later stage of the war, these newcomers could be easily identified in the local area by their strange way of talking and the rather dated boy-scout style campaign hats they wore. The first reference to the employment of American personnel at Waddington is contained in a letter from the 'General Officer Commanding the Training Division of the RFC', dated 5 January 1918. In this letter, a Major Pidgeon on the staff of the Director of Air Organisation tasked the addressees with making arrangements for nominated Flights of selected squadrons to be accommodated at certain RFC stations. Assigned to Waddington were 41 members of 'A' Flight of No 135 Squadron of the United States Army Air Service, among whom was a 1st Lieutenant F.O. Fearn. Unfortunately, no further records exist to detail just what became of this unit. As early as 12 January 1918, the American General Pershing had written to the War Office stating that:

'...all American cadets and flying officers under training in England will be (henceforth) treated as a common pool for ***American*** *squadrons overseas'.*

On 24 June 1918, the 11th Aero Services Squadron of the United States Army Air Service arrived at Waddington from No.1 Training Depot Station at Stamford. The squadron had been there since 1 May, having come from the American Rest Camp at Winchester. This was the first and only American unit to be stationed at Waddington during World War I. It had formed at Kelly Field in Texas on 26 June 1917 and, following several moves in America, the squadron eventually sailed for England on 17 December 1917 on board the SS *Orduna*. Arriving at Glasgow on 31 December, the squadron disembarked and moved by train from Glasgow to Winchester.

At the time of its arrival at Waddington, the squadron was under the command of 1st Lieutenant Joseph G.B. Molton. While at Stamford, all pilots and mechanics continued the training which had begun at Winchester, on BE2Es, DH6s and FK8s. Such was the quality of the personnel that they quickly completed their British led training and commenced work as a training squadron in their own right. During this period, the squadron was actually training both British and American personnel. The Squadron Commander's policy with regard to the training of all ground tradesmen was different from that of most of his British counterparts. He required that all men who were thoroughly trained in one aspect of aeroplane maintenance should then be trained in another. The result of this policy was that when eventually the 11th Aero Service Squadron arrived in France, most of the men were thoroughly trained in two or more trades, making for greater flexibility when the squadron became operational.

In mid August 1918 the squadron moved to Flowerdown, a non-flying unit close to Worthy Down near Winchester, prior to moving to France, whence it arrived on 13 August. Here the squadron flew its DH4 aircraft on bombing raids against German positions for the remainder of the war. Its aircraft were easily identifiable as they carried a logo of 'Mr Jiggs' on the side of their engine cowlings (Mr Jiggs was a popular American cartoon character).

During their stay at Waddington, the Americans took the opportunity to fly the Avro 504Ks of the resident British training units and were most impressed with the machine. This aircraft type had by then become the most widely used trainer in the RFC/RAF. Indeed, by the end of 1918, the Avro 504 had been issued in one form or another to every training unit in Great Britain. The reason for the success of the type as a training machine lay in the fact that its controls were light but powerful, thereby ensuring that the aircraft's response was immediate, lively and positive. This sensitivity of the controls served to highlight any pupil pilot's faults immediately, thereby enabling the instructor to take early corrective action. Such was the high regard of the Avro 504 that it was still in service with the RAF as late as 1940.

But even this type had its little problems. Although the tractor-type 504 was an improvement on the pusher-type Shorthorn, the student pilots who invariably occupied the front cockpit, found the location of the carburettor difficult to come to terms with. It was situated between the knees of the occupant of the front cockpit. While in itself not a major problem, the Gnome engine had an unfortunate tendency to backfire into the carburettor. To the discomfort of the said occupant of the front cockpit, this resulted in a flutter of flame between his legs - this in an aeroplane made of wood and doped canvas! Then again, on the positive side was the 504's control column. This was a universally mounted control column as opposed to the handlebar-with-spectacles type employed in the Shorthorn. Another interesting problem associated with the 504 was its engine. The Gnome was a rotary engine, which meant that the cylinders spun round with the propeller. As with all rotary engines, the fuel was fed to the cylinders through the crankcase; such a system requiring the lubricating oil to be immiscible with the fuel. The lubricating oil used for this purpose was castor oil. Yet another characteristic of rotary engines was that, with such a relatively large mass of metal rotating at high speed, a considerable amount of vaporised castor oil was released through the exhaust valves. This vapour, having been exhausted into the slipstream was blown back all over the wings, fuselage and pilot. Hence the unfortunate pilots became covered in a film of castor oil every time they flew. In time, the oil impregnated their flying clothing and became a permanent feature. The physiological effects of always flying in a cloud of castor oil leaves little to the imagination!

Having had a relatively accident-free four months, Waddington suffered a fatal crash on 1 July 1918, when an RE8 of No 47 Training Squadron crashed. Four weeks later, there occurred a quite horrendous fatal crash. Flight Cadet Filsher was flying in a DH9 carrying out air-to-ground firing practice against a target on the ground near Saxilby, which is just outside Lincoln. As he descended through 100 feet on another pass against the target, the tail of his machine (C1256) was seen to break away, causing the aircraft to flick into a tight spin. Almost immediately the wings folded back and broke away; the wingless and tail-less fuselage plunging to the ground.

Fortunately, in this case the authorities were able to stifle any upsurge of the saboteur rumours. A study of the records revealed that a batch of DH9 aircraft that had been built by G & J Weir of Glasgow, were experiencing more than the average incidence of crashes. The batch in question extending from Serial Number C1151 to C1450. Government inspectors carried out a detailed investigation of the firm's production methods and quality control, but could find no obvious reason for the spate of crashes among aircraft from this batch. After another relatively crash-free period, Waddington lost one of its remaining RE8s. The aircraft was being flown by Flight Cadet Ralph Mossop when it was observed at approximately 500 feet in a steep glide with its engine just idling. Those who witnessed it all agreed that there was no apparent attempt to take any corrective action, with the RE8 just continuing its downward path until it struck the ground. The subsequent inquiry could find no evidence to explain the cause of the crash.

On 14 October the long awaited move of No 51 Training Squadron took place when it moved to Baldonnel in Ireland, taking its DH4s and 6s plus its Avro 504ks to join No 23 TDS. Meanwhile the accidents continued, some serious and some not so serious. On 30 October an American pilot was killed in a crash involving an RE8 (D1567), followed the next day by Waddington's last crash of the war. In this instance, an Avro 504K suffered engine failure while flying in the vicinity of the aerodrome. The student pilot immediately attempted to make a forced landing, but in doing so lost control of his machine which crashed into a tree. Fortunately, the two occupants of the aircraft survived, though both were quite badly injured. Notwithstanding the legends and rumours of a saboteur at Waddington, the fact is that its crash rate was no more than average for similar RFC training stations.

Other Units Formed or Disbanded at Waddington

A study of the scant records of the day indicates that several squadrons either formed at Waddington, or at least established a cadre there before moving elsewhere. Those that have been identified as having been at Waddington for one reason or another are as follows:

No 97 Squadron

This squadron was based on a cadre from No 51 Training Squadron and was to be equipped with the Handley Page 0/400 bomber. It was scheduled to form at Waddington on 1 December 1917 and to be at full strength by the end of the month. During its stay at Waddington it flew the DH4s of No 51 Training Squadron until its eventual move to Stonehenge on 21 January 1918. Two months later it moved to Netheravon and equipped with the 0/400 bomber.

No 123 Squadron

This squadron formed at Waddington on 1 March 1918 as a nucleus flight and moved to Duxford the same day. It was scheduled to operate the DH9.

No 126 Squadron

This squadron was apparently scheduled to form at Waddington on 1 February 1918 and to be based on a cadre from No 51 Training Squadron. However, no record exists of it ever having done so; the squadron's own history stating that it formed at Old Sarum on 1 March 1918. It may be that it followed the same route as No 123 Squadron and was at Waddington for but one day.

No 117 Squadron

This squadron's history is confusing. Its own records show that it formed at Beaulieu on 1 January 1918, but there is documentary evidence to suggest that it may well have formed as a nucleus flight at Waddington before moving to Hucknall on 1 April 1918. it was scheduled to be parented by No 51 Training Squadron and to be equipped with either the DH4 or DH9.

No 129 Squadron

This squadron was apparently formed at Waddington on 3 September 1918, its personnel coming from Nos 35, 39, 43 and 48 TDSs. It was scheduled to move to

Stoneham on 4 September before moving to France on 8 November. Other records suggest that the squadron formed at Duxford on 1 March 1918 and remained there until it was disbanded on 4 July that year.

No 162 Squadron

The records of this squadron are also somewhat confusing. Directives from the Training Bridgade Headquarters state that No 162 Squadron was to form on 4 October 1918; its personell coming from Nos 21, 35, 48 and 55 TDSs. It was to then move immediately to Chingford, where it would receive its assigned aircraft type the DH9A. Following conversion to this type, the squadron was to move to France on 4 December 1918.

With the Armistice, life at Waddington quickly became far more pedestrian, with flying training virtually ceasing. The Americans wasted no time in getting their men back home; indeed, by the beginning of December they had all departed. Meanwhile, squadrons from France began flying in to Waddington to either disband or to await reallocation. As an indication of its reduced status, the rank of the station commander was reduced to that of Major; the new commanding officer being Major J R Herring.

On 7 February 1919, No 204 Squadron arrived at Waddington from Heulle in Belgium. They were equipped with Sopwith Camel scouts and remained at Waddington until December 1919 when it was disbanded. The next squadron to arrive was No 23 Squadron, which came from Clermont in Belgium on 15 March. This unit was equipped with the Sopwith Dolphin, a relatively late arrival on the Western Front. The Dolphin was heavily armed, with two Vickers 0.303" machine guns mounted on top of the engine and synchronised to fire between the propeller blades. In addition there was a pair of Lewis guns of similar calibre which were installed to fire upwards at an oblique angle - shades of the German night fighter 'Shrage Musik' of World War 2. A unique feature of the Dolphin was its 'back-stagger' wing configuration, with the upper wing behind the lower. This resulted in giving the pilot excellent visibility as his head projected above the centre section of the upper wing; albeit with the risk of serious injury if the machine turned over on landing! Many experienced RFC pilots rated the Dolphin as the best fighter of its day. With the four-gun fire power, No 23 Squadron had proved very successful in the ground attack role.

Next to return from the peaceful Western Front was No 203 Squadron, which arrived at Waddington from Boisdinghem in France in March 1919, together with its few remaining Sopwith Camels. The unit remained at Waddington until December 1919 when it moved to what was then known as Scopwick aerodrome; later to become better known as Digby. At the time, Scopwick was the home of No 59 Training Squadron. Unlike most of the Lincolnshire training aerodromes, Scopwick was not closed down as soon as was possible, instead it remained active until 1922. However, No 203 Squadron's stay at Scopwick was not destined to be a lengthy one, as it was disbanded on 21 January 1920.

Almost nothing is known about the immediate post-war activities at Waddington, other than the fact that little flying was carried out; just enough to keep the few pilots' hands in. This apart, the unfortunate units were progressively reduced to the status of cadres, lingering on with diminishing complements until their eventual disbandment.

As to the aerodrome itself, unlike most wartime aerodromes, the land was not returned to its original owners. Instead, it remained the property of the Air Ministry. In view of the alacrity with which aircraft were scrapped and aerodromes returned to more peaceful uses, it is hard to believe that the retention of RAF Waddington was a result of a policy decision at government level. Instead, it would seem more likely that it was a simply a case of oversight!

Regardless of how it came about, when the small expansion of the Royal Air Force took place in the mid twenties, RAF Waddington was still on the books.

❖ ❖ ❖

2. What Price Defence?

The Territorial Army has been a feature of the British Army for many years, its units having a magnificent record of service in two world wars. Speaking in 1919, when referring to the provisions of the Air Force Constitution Act of 1917, Sir Hugh Trenchard expressed the opinion that Air Force reserves should be organised on a regional basis similar to that of the Territorial Army. He went on to add that they should be located close to the larger industrial towns in order to draw on these pools of considerable manpower, both to fly and service the aircraft and to administer the personnel etc. Each unit should be entirely self-contained and not just an appendage to any nearby regular Royal Air Force unit. To this end, each squadron should have its own aircraft, headquarters and messes, and a distinctive life of its own.

Great Britain had greeted the outbreak of peace in 1918 with great relief. The 'war to end all wars' was over and the embryo League of Nations would see to it that war was relegated to the history books.(sic) Never again would civilised nations resort to war as a means of settling disputes. Unfortunately, such a euphoric state of mind was not destined to last for long. Notwithstanding the 'Entente Cordiale' and the alliance with France in the war against Germany and its allies, when the *Times* newspaper reported in March 1922 that the French Air Force possessed 300 bombers and a similar number of fighter aircraft, the British public became more than a little concerned.

In many minds France was our traditional enemy in Europe and therefore required careful watching. In any case, Germany had been effectively disarmed following the Armistice. The revelation by the Times that in answer to the threat posed to Britain by these large numbers of French aircraft, Britain could muster barely 40, as a result of the virtual dismemberment of the Royal Air Force, was received with dismay. What was not mentioned was the fact that the Air Ministry had been well aware of this imbalance, but had been unable to do anything about it. Furthermore, the fact that Anglo-French relations had reached a new low did little to placate the feeling of unease.

In 1923, the year following the disturbing revelations in the Times, Parliament decided to create a Home Defence Air Force of 52 squadrons. The stated requirement that they should be formed with as little delay as possible, was negated almost immediately by the so-called 'Geddes Axe', together with the equally so-called 'Ten Year Rule'. This latter piece of parliamentary policy stated that the government could not conceive of any war that might threaten Great Britain within ten years, and that such a review would be carried out each year; this with a view to continuing the ten year time frame indefinitely. The infamous Geddes Axe, which was the name given to a savage reduction in government spending, had reduced the number of RAF stations in Great Britain from four hundred in 1918 to less than fifty by 1925.

The Auxiliary Air Force and Air Force Reserve Act came into being in 1924 when Sir Samual Hoare was the Secretary of State for Air. Hoare, or Viscount Templewood, as he later became, was a convinced advocate of the need for reserve forces to supplement the regular air force. Indeed, he subsequently became Honorary Air Commodore of two Auxiliary Air Force squadrons; numbers 601 and 604 Squadrons. The Act in question envisaged the formation of six Auxiliary Air Force fighter squadrons and seven Special Reserve squadrons; the latter consisting of four single-engined and three twin-engined bomber squadrons.

There were notable differences between Auxiliary and Special Reserve squadrons. The Auxiliaries were to be raised and maintained by the already well established County Territorial Associations, and were to be manned by locally recruited part-timers. They would possess only a small cadre of regular personnel and would, in addition, be commanded by a non-regular commanding officer. For administrative convenience, all Auxiliary Air Force squadrons were to be allocated a squadron number in the six hundreds.

The Conditions of Service or Statement of Unit Policy for the Special Reserve squadrons were contained in Air Ministry Pamphlet No 2 dated June 1925. This document gave such details as: the programme of expansion, organisation, period of enrolment, promotion, liabilities, training, pay and allowances, uniform requirements, gratuities (if mobilised), medical benefits, and compensation in the event of disability or death on duty. Under the section covering the programme of expansion it listed the assigned unit numbers, their planned location and the type of aircraft that they were to fly. Among the units listed, were the following:

- No 500 Sqn - A single engined bomber unit (no assigned location).

- No 501 Sqn - A single engined bomber unit located at Filton near Bristol.
- No 502 Sqn - A twin engined bomber unit located at Aldergrove.
- No 503 Sqn - A twin engined bomber squadron located at Waddington.
- No 504 Sqn - A single engined bomber squadron (no assigned location).
- No 505 Sqn - A twin engined bomber squadron (no assigned location).
- No 506 Sqn - A single engined bomber squadron (no assigned location).
- In the event, the last two numbered squadrons were never formed.

Under the heading of 'Organisation', the pamphlet went on to state that 'Special Reserve squadrons will be raised and maintained in certain selected localities as part of the Air Defence of Great Britain. In peacetime each of these squadrons will be located at an aerodrome in the vicinity of the town from which the Special Reserve personnel of the squadron are recruited. Each squadron is associated for purposes of Home Defence with a regular air force aerodrome, which will form its war station and to which it will proceed when called out to take its place in the air defence of the country. Each squadron will, normally, be commanded by a regular officer of the Royal Air Force and will have a strong nucleus of regular officers and airmen. Approximately two-thirds of the squadron will be composed of Special Reserve personnel, living in the neighbourhood of the aerodrome and keeping themselves efficient by attendance at the aerodrome, and by compliance with their conditions of service.' These conditions were made as flexible as possible in order to minimise interference with the civil life of officers and airmen.

Under the heading 'Appointment', the following requirements were spelled out for those considering applying for a commission in the Special Reserve. Normally between the ages of 18 and 25, unless the candidate had previously served as an officer of the Royal Air Force, in which case the upper age limit would be raised to 31 years of age. Each candidate would be required to produce a certificate as to his 'good moral character' and produce written evidence that he had attained a 'fair' standard of education. Furthermore, any aspiring candidate had to "...be of pure European descent, a British subject..." Officers would be entered in the rank of Pilot Officer unless they had served in the regular air force and reached at least the rank of Flying Officer, in which case they would join as a Flying Officer. The initial period of service was to be for five years which, on completion, could be extended for further periods of five years by the Air Council.

Under the heading 'Training', AM Pamphlet No 2 went on to define the minimum training requirements and how they were to be implemented. The training would consist of initial training, instructional parades, periodical flying, periodical unit training, courses and voluntary training. On first appointment on probation, an officer would be required to undergo a period of initial training which would consist mainly of initial flying training. It was expected that this initial training might take a period of up to six months, either continuously or in aggregate if performed intermittently. During this phase the probationary officer would be required to qualify as a pilot and to pass certain prescribed tests. After the period of initial training had been completed, the officers of the Special Reserve would be liable to complete 20 instructional parades, plus fourteen days service at the periodic training (annual camp) of his unit each year. In addition, all Special Reserve officers would be required to carry out an annual minimum of twelve hours flying and to attend any special course or courses as laid down by higher authority.

Normally, and as long as they remained 'efficient', it was not anticipated that officers would be called upon to attend compulsory training in excess of the twelve hours periodic flying, supplemented by attendance at instructional parades. However, should an officer be considered inefficient in the performance of his duties, he could be called upon, in addition to all or any part of the training as specified, to carry out a period of training not exceeding 21 days in any one year.

Voluntary classes and courses of instruction in armament, air pilotage, wireless telegraphy, photography and bombing, were arranged at the headquarters of the squadron, as and when necessary. Furthermore, a Special Reserve officer could, with Air Ministry approval, attend on a voluntary basis any of the regular air force courses relevant to his duties. These part-time officers received the same rates of pay and allowances as laid down for officers of the same rank in the regular air force. For instance, a Pilot Officer (P/O) received a standard rate of sixteen shillings a day, while a Squadron Leader (S/Ldr) would receive 34 shillings (£1.70) per day. To guard against those who might have attempted to join the Special Reserve in order to qualify as a pilot at no cost to themselves, one of the clauses in AM Pamphlet No 2 read as follows:

'...Officers taught to fly at the public expense...and who do not complete five years satisfactory service...will be liable to pay liquidated damages of £20 for each year by which their period of satisfactory service falls short of five years...'

Each officer candidate received a grant of £40 to enable him to purchase the minimum obligatory items of uniform, namely: a service dress cap and jacket, breeches, trousers, boots, puttees, white shirts and collars, brown leather gloves, black ties, a haversack and water bottle, a greatcoat, and a walking stick (RAF pattern).

On 14 September 1926, Air Order 1647 was promulgated which gave authority for the creation of a Special Reserve squadron as part of the policy of strengthening the Home Defence Force. The squadron was to form at Waddington, coming under the control of the Special Reserve and Auxiliary Air Force Command, which itself formed part of the Air Defence of Great Britain. The new squadron was to be called No 503 (Special Reserve) (Bomber) Squadron, and its first Commanding Officer was S/Ldr R D Oxland, who assumed command on 5 October 1926. Years later, he was to become AOC No 1 Group and, subsequently, Senior Air Staff Officer (SASO) at Headquarters Bomber Command under Air Marshal 'Butch' Harris.

The official formation date of No 503 Squadron was 5 October 1926, and in addition to the Commanding Officer, the other regular air force officers on strength were Flight Lieutenant W R Cox MC AFC, Flight Lieutenant (F/Lt) H E Walker MC DFC, and Flying Officers E F Haylock, C P Wingfield and C E Aston. Cox was the Squadron Adjutant and a flying instructor, Walker was another instructor, while Haylock, Wingfield and Aston were, between them, in charge of stores and accounts. In common with all other Auxiliary and Special Reserve squadrons, No 503 Sqn came under the overall command of Air Commodore J G Hearson CB CBE DSO who, in turn came under the command of the AOC Air Defence of Great Britain, Air Marshal Sir John Salmond.

Initially, the new squadron possessed a reduced establishment of three Avro 504K basic training aircraft, two dual control Fairey Fawns and five two-seat Fawn day bombers. The first six Fawns arrived three weeks after the formation of the squadron. The Fairey Fawn was the first new type of light day bomber to enter service with the RAF in the nineteen twenties, when most of the regular squadrons were still flying types left over from the Great War. Designed in 1921 and first flown as an Army reconnaissance aircraft in March 1923, the Fawn could carry a bomb load of 450lb and was armed with one forward firing Vickers machine gun, together with a rearward firing Lewis gun. The aircraft had a top speed of 114mph, and in all, the RAF took delivery of 70 Fairey Fawns.

Having taken over the real estate of the re-opened aerodrome at Waddington and established an initial squadron organisation, No 503 Squadron opened a recruiting office in Saltergate in Lincoln in 1927. Prior to opening the office for business, posters had been displayed in various locations in Lincoln and the surrounding district some weeks previous. But the posters were not the first indication to local people that the Royal Air Force would be returning to the Lincoln area. Firstly, the hangars at Waddington had been cleared of all the accumulated agricultural machinery and other farming stores that had gathered there over the years. There had then been the report in the local paper on 7 September 1925 which stated that a team from the Air Ministry were in Lincoln in connection with the proposed formation of a *"Reserve Air Squadron"* at the former aerodrome at Waddington. Next, on 7 November came the headline that there was a need for an emergency water supply for the new aerodrome at Waddington.

The first successful applicant for details of a flying appointment in the Special Reserve was a 22 year-old bank clerk, Douglas Allison, who recalled;

"I remember meeting a chap dressed in a tweed jacket and smoking a large pipe. He did not identify himself, but I assumed that he had to be the Commanding Officer. I was later to discover that the gentleman I had met was in fact the Adjutant, Flight Lieutenant Cox. Following a discussion about the qualifications required and the sort of training I would be required to undergo, Cox gave me a copy of the Air Ministry Pamphlet 2 and told me to go away and read it If I was still interested, I was to return the following Monday when I would be interviewed by the Squadron Leader. Having read the pamphlet from cover to cover, I knew that the RAF Special Reserve was just what I had been looking for, so, on the following Monday I duly arrived at the recruiting office, where I was interviewed at some length by a Squadron Leader Oxland. At the end of our meeting Oxland told me that I was a promising candidate and that if accepted by the recently arrived Commanding Officer, I would in all probability be the first Special Reserve Officer in No 503 Squadron. I was delighted to have been successful in my application and looked forward to meeting the 'CO' for lunch the following Wednesday".

Although Douglas Allison did not know it, the new Commanding Officer was a member of an old established Lincolnshire family and a man with an impressive war record. Wing Commander the Hon L J E Twistleton-Wykeham-Fiennes assumed command of No 503 Squadron on 21 February 1927. The family connection with Lincoln was continue into the 1980s, as the then Dean of Lincoln Cathedral was Oliver Twistleton-Wykeham-Fiennes, he having held the post for a considerable number of years.

Douglas Allison's first meeting with his Commanding Officer took place in Boot's cafe in Lincoln. The introductions were performed by Squadron Leader Oxland who then sat back and left the young Allison to the tender mercies of the CO! Lunch turned out to be coffee and sandwiches; not quite what the young aspiring aviator had expected. Although the lunch did not quite come up to his expectations, the meeting with the Wing Commander exceeded them. As Allison recalled

"...he [the W/Cdr] had the sort of steel blue eyes that looked right through you, apparently missing nothing. Despite this, he combined it with the knack of putting you at your ease. His questions were direct, blunt and searching and he seemed determined to find out just what I knew, if anything, about the Royal Air Force and flying. Luckily, I had done my homework and I managed to satisfy him."

Once the interview was over, Douglas was introduced to Flight Lieutenant Cox, whom he had met on first entering the recruiting office. This time, Cox was in uniform and looked most impressive with his decorations and campaign ribbons. Over lunch, arrangements were made for Douglas Allison to commence training as soon as he had been 'gazetted', an event which occurred on 23 April 1927, making him the first Special Reserve officer of No 503 Squadron. Two days later, Allison was in the air on his first flight, a trip in a Fairey Fawn with Squadron Leader Oxland at the controls. This flight was not a training sortie as such, simply a familiarisation trip.

Douglas Allison's instruction began in earnest the next day when he was given his first lesson by Flight Lieutenant (F/Lt) Cox in a dual control Avro 504K trainer. This particular aircraft (Serial No 7211) was the same basic type as had been used by the RFC and RAF in World War One. However, the old Avro was in process of being replaced by an improved version, the Avro 504N, better known as the 'Lynx Avro', though sometimes irreverently referred to as 'The Crab'. This type was delivered to No 503 Squadron at the end of April, just in time for Allison and other early members of the Squadron to undertake their training on the latest model. The famous Avro trainer needs no description, but the Lynx version was a radical change in that it was powered by a radial engine as opposed to the old-fashioned rotary. It was the first new trainer to be accepted by the RAF since the end of the war. It was fully aerobatic and could fly quite happily inverted. In competent hands the Lynx Avro could be trimmed to fly in a glide with the engine just above idling power. In this configuration it was possible to leave the aircraft to land itself, albeit in a rather untidy fashion!

Even the Lynx Avro had its faults however, and one member of the squadron, Arthur Young, remembered being taken to task by one of the instructors for taxiing in with his flying goggles up on his forehead. On asking why, he was firmly told that the valves on the Lynx engine possessed an additional hairpin spring on the rockers and it was not unknown for these pins to flick out of their sockets and fly back into the pilot's face. Apparently, there was at least one recorded incident where the unfortunate pilot lost an eye as a result.

Although Douglas Allison was the first Special Reserve officer to join No 503 Squadron, he was soon joined by other aspiring young aviators. On or about the same day that Douglas first flew in the Avro, three new recruits signed on the dotted line; they were Pilot Officers R H Maw, T H Worth and R Wardrop. Roger Maw subsequently left No 503 Squadron on joining the regular air force in the early thirties. In the Spring of 1942 he assumed command of No 108 Squadron, flying Wellingtons in the Western Desert. He was shot down and badly injured in August of the same year, during an attack on Tobruk and spent the rest of the war as a prisoner of war (PoW), most of it in Stalag Luft III. It was while there that he designed and built the wooden horse that was to feature in the successful escape of that name. T.H. Worth was a farmer who farmed on a large scale near Boston. He was joined on the squadron a few months later by his brother G A Worth, another farmer. The two brothers remained with the squadron for many years, eventually becoming the longest serving reservists of all at Waddington. Among the other volunteer aviators were such locals as Messrs Barrow, Brooke, Canning, deMoleyns, Groves, Horsefall, Morris, Thompson, Eric Grieve, Alban Carey and Nathaniel Lindley.

Of these stalwarts, Eric Grieve served throughout the war, retiring as a Group Captain. Nathaniel Lindley, twice mentioned in despatches, became an Operations Officer in Coastal Command. Alban Carey also served throughout the war, retiring with the rank of Group Captain. Leonard Barrow eventually became a fighter controller and was one of a team tasked with establishing an Operations Room at Stratton Strawless Hall. He retired as a Squadron Leader. Geoffrey Horsefall also retired as a Squadron Leader. Lastly, Francis deMoleyns, or to give him his full title - The Hon. Francis E deMoleyns, was the second son of the Sixth Baron Ventry. On 6 June 1944, he carried an RAF Standard on to the beach at Normandy and planted on the shore. This was entirely in keeping with family tradition, as they were descended from William the Conquerer's Standard Bearer. At the end of the war he left the RAF and returned to the family estates in Scotland.

On 11 July 1927 the 'Special Reserve and Auxiliary Air Force Command' was renamed 'The Air Defence Group', coming under the command of Air Commodore E L Gerrard CMG DSO. On the tenth anniversary of the formation of the Royal Air Force, on 1 April 1928, the Waddington squadron was accorded the title *No 503 (County of Lincoln (Bomber)) Squadron.* Following the granting of this honour, the squadron adopted the coat of arms of the City of Lincoln, and painted it on all their aircraft - a tradition that continues to this day. On the aerodrome, the new Officers' Mess and Sergeants' Mess were built. The former, named Newell House, remained in use until the present Mess was built in 1935. Since then it has served in a variety of capacities: WRAF accommodation, married quarters and, as at present, a social and amenities centre. The new Sergeants' Mess too was superseded by a larger building in 1935. Following the sudden influx of sergeant aircrew soon after the start of the Second World War, it became the Non-Aircrew Sergeants' Mess. It is currently the home of the Corporals' Club.

The badge adopted by No 503 Squadron incorporated the coat of arms of the city surmounted by an eagle with its wings extended; the whole set inside a scroll containing the words *'County of Lincoln Bomber Squadron'* mounted on the numerals 503. Unfortunately, the badge was never formally approved by the Chester Herald. The result of this omission was that No 503 Squadron was to be the only Special Reserve squadron to never have an official badge. As a way of introducing the new squadron and its home to the local people, the commanding officer decided to hold an Open Day. Apart from the goodwill that it was expected to generate, it was hoped that it might lead to an increase in the number of local volunteers coming forward to join. By all accounts it was a successful venture, with over two thousand people attending, though just how many, if any, subsequently joined the squadron is not a matter of record. This apart, the major event of the year was the squadron's first Annual Camp, which was held at RAF Tangmere. By this time the squadron had two new Flight Commanders: Squadron Leaders Hugh Walmsley and C B Cooke.

Early in 1929 the squadron re-equipped with a new type of aircraft, which resulted in it changing its role from that of a day bomber squadron to a night bomber squadron. The first of the new aircraft, the Handley Page Hyderabad, arrived on 8 February, the last one being delivered on 31 May, with the last Fawn leaving Waddington the next day. The Hyderabad was the last heavy bomber of wooden construction to enter RAF service. By the end of the year the strength of the squadron was nine regular officers and thirteen reservists. This was to prove to be the highest number of volunteer officers that No 503 Squadron was to achieve.

Although the other Special Reserve squadrons, all of which were situated close to centres of much larger populations, achieved considerably higher recruiting figures, the Lincoln squadron possessed a unique esprit de corps. The squadron had been formed at Waddington in the expectation that it would attract officers and airmen reservists from the city of Lincoln and, in particular, from amongst the farming community in Lincolnshire. As events were to prove over the years, this was an optimistic expectation as there was a relatively limited pool of manpower in the district upon which to call. Consequently, the other Special Reserve squadrons, by becoming larger, became better known, which in turn led to more recruits wishing to join them.

On 15 February 1930, Wing Commander the Hon Twistleton-Wykeham Fiennes handed over command of the squadron to Wing Commander H P Lale DSO DFC, who became known affectionately as 'Daddy' to one and all. During his service on the Western Front, Captain Horace Percy Lale became one of the most successful Bristol Fighter pilots, being credited with the destruction of 23 enemy aircraft and earning the Distinguished Flying Cross (DFC). Post war, he served in Wurziristan and was awarded the Distinguished Service Order (DSO). By this time, the squadron had a well established structure and routine; the Commanding Officer, the Adjutant, plus two or three specialists were always regular officers. 'A' Flight was the operational flight and was manned in the main by regular officers and airmen, with a leavening of trained reservists in both the flying role and the ground trades. On the other hand, 'B' Flight was the training flight; manned by a regular officer as the Flight Commander, together with other regulars filling the flying instructional posts.

On the ground there was a nucleus of regular fitters and riggers who, apart from looking after the aircraft, were responsible for training the reservist airmen. Training took place over the weekends for all personnel, while Wednesday and Thursday replaced the weekend 'days off' for the regular staff, just as in today's auxiliary squadrons. Among the members of the regular air force cadre was Flight Lieutenant O.E. Worsley who, in 1927, had been a member of the successful British team that won the Schneider Trophy in the Venice competition. He was posted from No 503 Squadron in early 1930, having served for almost two years at Waddington. Sadly, he was to die in a car crash in October that same year. Keeping an eye on one and all, both regular and reservists, was the Station Sergeant Major, Sergeant Major Butcher, a daunting figure who would brook no argument or excuse. Among his many duties was responsibility for the night-time security of the aerodrome and the aircraft. To assist him in this he possessed two civilian night watchmen, both of whom were partially disabled!

With the arrival of the new commanding officer and a new aircraft, both elements of the squadron were kept very busy. During the conversion on to the Hyderabad, the new 'A' Flight Commander was a tower of strength. Squadron Leader H.E.P. Wigglesworth DSC, a well-known Royal Naval Air Service pilot, had transferred to the Royal Air Force on its formation and was a well liked and highly respected member of the squadron. Many years later in 1943, Air Chief Marshal Sir Arthur Tedder was to appoint Air Marshal Sir Phillip Wigglesworth to the post of Deputy Air Commander-in-Chief of Allied Forces in the Mediterranean area. As a result of his work in this theatre, he earned the nickname 'Tedder's Carpet Maker', for it was under Wigglesworth's direction that the Allied air forces laid a carpet of bombs through German tank defences from El Alamein to Tunis and wherever else General Montgomery required them. Prior to that appointment, Wigglesworth was to spend some time as Deputy Director of Intelligence at the Air Ministry in 1936.

However, all this was far off in the future when he served at Waddington. At about this time, No 1 Air Defence Group, of which No 503 Squadron was a part, came under the command of a new air officer, Air Commodore W.F. MacNeece Foster CBE DSO DFC.

The strength of the squadron stood at ten regular and nine Special Reserve officers, most of whom had completed their training on the Handley Page Hyderabad. This aircraft was a large twin-engined biplane of wood and canvas construction, powered by two 454hp Napier Lion engines. It was an extremely noisy aircraft and heavy on the controls. With an all-up weight of 13,535lb, the performance of the Hyderabad failed to match the noise of its engines! It had a range of 693 miles at a true air speed of 96mph at 10,000 feet and a top speed of 109mph.

The squadron was located in the south-east corner of the aerodrome, beside what had been Mere Road, and occupied the old RFC hangars. In true air force fashion, the squadron's domestic accommodation was, of course, on the other side of the aerodrome; the airmen living in huts near the junction of Mere Road and High Dyke (Ermine Street). The Officers' Mess was located in a collection of wooden huts running along the side of High Dyke, opposite what is now the married quarters complex. These huts had been the Officers' Mess during World War I and were showing distinct signs of severe dilapidation, so in 1927 a new Officers' Mess was built across the road from the huts. When opened, it was named Newell House, and is still in use today, though no longer as an Officers' Mess.

When talking of the original hutted Mess, Arthur Young recalled:

"...the walk across the aerodrome from the Mess each morning was an excellent 'prairie oyster', particularly in the winter!"

It was around this time that a report appeared in the local paper concerning three aeroplanes getting lost in fog and being 'rescued' by personnel from Waddington. Apparently, three DH9A aircraft belonging to No 603 'City of Edinburgh' Squadron took off from Hendon bound for Edinburgh. They had planned to land at Cranwell to refuel, but when they got to Lincolnshire they found the ground obscured by one of the well-known county fogs. The three aeroplanes flew very low over the city of Lincoln in early afternoon, but all they could see were the towers of the cathedral. Continuing on to the north, they eventually caught sight of two villages. Though unknown to the pilots, the villages were Cammeringham and Ingham. So, with their fuel running low, the pilots elected to land. Two of them put down in a seed field quite safely, but the third ended up in a wheat field, where it became bogged down in the soft soil. On reaching a telephone, the wanderers contacted Waddington and shortly afterwards an Avro Lynx landed beside the two DH9As. After a brief delay, the Lynx was followed by a fast car, containing three reservist pilots, who had been tasked with assisting the Scotsmen. The newspaper report went on to say: "*...the combined efforts of the rescue party; S/Ldr Wigglesworth, F/Lt Allison and Flying Officers M A Cowan and N A Lindley, resulted in two of the planes and the relief machine (Lynx) taking to the air...*" The remaining DH9A was eventually recovered from the wheat field and left the next day.

Another new addition to the regular component of the squadron was F/O D M T MacDonald. He arrived in early November 1931 and remained until April 1932. Although Dennis MacDonald was not with No 503 Squadron for very long, he has quite detailed memories of the squadron and the station.

"...at the time of my arrival there was just one unit on the station - No 503 (County of Lincoln) Squadron. Its establishment was roughly 60% regulars and 40% special reservists, comprising both officers and airmen. There was no Station Headquarters; the Squadron Commander, Wing Commander Hanmer was also the Station Commander. Flying supervision was the responsibility of the single Squadron Leader, Percy Barnett. At the time of my arrival the Squadron possessed one operational Flight only; hence there was a need for only one Squadron Leader."

Among the regular groundcrew at this time was AC2 Laing, who lives in Waddington village to this day, and he too has many memories of his time with the 'White Fridays', the regulars' name for the reservists. He remembered that the Waddington regular airmen were popular with the village girls, despite their poor pay and the fact that they were not allowed to wear civilian clothes; this privilege was not accorded to anyone below the rank of senior NCO. The local girls were very well informed, and it was of little use to claim to be on duty in order to avoid a date. It was rumoured that the girls knew details of the duty roster well before it was published. On the flying side, Laing remembered the Hyderabads with little affection. There was no form of Flying Control in those days and Laing recalled an incident involving one of these machines.

"As there was no Flying Control, the pilots just used to climb in, start up, check that all was clear and then taxi out and take off. One this particular occasion one pilot took off over Mere Road, which was used by all and sundry en-route from the domestic site to the flight line. Unfortunately, the pilot had forgotten to check the rear cockpit of the Hyderabad; if he had he would have seen that the control column was still strapped up. The result was inevitable: the aircraft failed to leave the ground and ended up on its nose at the far end of the aerodrome. Another problem related to flying was the frequent presence of cows on the aerodrome! The only RAF Policeman, Corporal Bob Connor, would regularly be called upon to clear the Waterloo Farm cows away. Normally, this presented no great problem as the ani-

mals were quite placid, but occasionally the farmer would leave a bull out with them. The results when this occurred were always a source of great amusement to the groundcrew, as the poor policeman raced for the hedge, hotly pursued by the bull. Away from duty, the Station possessed a very good football team and the village team were not above borrowing the odd star player whenever they had a particularly hard or important match to play."

Again, as F/O MacDonald recalled:

"There were two instructors on strength. One was F/Lt Gandy, who was superseded by F/Lt Power soon after my arrival, the other being Sergeant (Pilot) Simons. Apart from converting newly arrived regular pilots to type, the instructors' main function was the initial flight training of the Special Reserve pilots. I believe that there were about six regular pilots in addition to the instructors. These were, F/O Leborgne, who was later killed while commercial flying after leaving the service, and F/O Price, who transferred to the Fleet Air Arm after it was handed back to the Admiralty in 1937. The other four were Davies, Piper, Harris and Alderson (?).

Of the reservist pilots, I recall the two brothers Worth, who were local farmers. The elder brother, Tom, who owned his own DeHavilland Moth aeroplane, became a night fighter pilot during the war. His younger brother Dick, who married Air Marshal Longmore's daughter, subsequently became Armament Officer of No 5 Group around 1940/41. Then there were Brookes, Peel, Allison and Roger Maw, the latter leaving the squadron to take a short service commission in the regular air force.

Apart from two Lynx Avro 504s, the squadron was equipped with eight Hyderabads. Each aircraft had a crew of four: two pilots, one of which acted as navigator and bomb aimer, plus two part-time air gunners, who were volunteer ground tradesmen. The Hyderabad was very difficult to taxi in a strong wind because it possessed no brakes, had a large side silhouette and a tail skid shaped like a soup plate, with little or no grip. It was also the first aircraft that I had flown that was equipped with an Elsan chemical toilet!

At that time the aerodrome was a grass airfield about 1000 yards square. We had a sports field in the south-west corner, and a bombing target in the middle of the aerodrome! We used to drop 8.5lb practice bombs on the target, which was a white circle about 25 feet in diameter. The various administrative, domestic and technical sites were widely dispersed, which could pose problems for the Orderly Officer during his rounds, particularly when one of the thick Lincolnshire fogs descended on the aerodrome.

We got quite a lot of flying, carrying out such sorties as navigation exercises, bombing and, surprisingly, quite a lot of formation flying. We also carried out 'front seat flying', necessitated by the Hyderabad's two pilots being seated in separate cockpits in tandem. One amusing incident involving a Hyderabad concerned F/O Leborgne, who landed in error at the old World War I aerodrome at nearby Bracebridge Heath, which at the time was a bus depot. There was not much left of the old airfield buildings, so Leborgne had no difficulty in extricating his machine, but to the amusement of the interested squadron spectators".

Being a small unit, our sports activities were entirely domestic because we could not compete with the local large stations. In winter, two of us, Nicholson the Accounts Officer and myself, played rugby for Lincoln. Despite our lack of numbers, we held a dining in night once a week, and on one occasion, the Blankney Hunt met outside the Mess, where we entertained them. The Commanding Officer, W/Cdr Hanmer, was an enthusiastic member of the hunt and rode with them about once a week."

Dennis MacDonald eventually retired from the RAF with the rank of Air Vice Marshal.

On 11 May 1931, Wing Commander Lale had handed over command to Wing Commander H.I. Hanmer DFC. By this time 'A' Flight was commanded by S/Ldr B.J. Barnett but had lost its first Special Reserve officer, Douglas Allison. Douglas had served No 503 Squadron well, reaching the rank of Flight Lieutenant before leaving on taking up a civilian appointment in Malaya. There can seldom have been a more enthusiastic member of the Lincoln squadron than Douglas Allison. He had undertaken many courses of instruction, taken part in several formal parades and flown as a member of the No 503 Squadron team that so nearly won the Sassoon Cup at the Hendon air pageant in 1930. They were beaten into second place by the famous No 601 (County of London) Squadron, sometimes referred to as 'The Millionaires Mob', as rumour had it that to join this august outfit it was necessary to possess one's own aircraft.

Soon after the change of command of No 503 Squadron, one of the most popular members of the squadron, Jack Peel, lost his life in the first fatal crash suffered by the Waddington based squadron. In personnel terms, the year 1931 was not a good one for the squadron. Several stalwarts had to leave due to business commitments, while yet others took the opportunity to take up Short Service commissions in the regular air force. Of interest is the fact that there were two distinguished officers on the staff of No 1 Air Defence Group at this time. W/Cdr A.H. Orlebar AFC, who had been a member of the winning British Schneider trophy team of 1929, was a staff officer at Group Headquarters, as was Flight Lieutenant J.I.T. (Taffy) Jones DSO MC DFC MM.

'Taffy' Jones had been a distinguished fighter pilot on the Western Front in World War I and was a great friend of the legendary 'Mick' Mannock VC DSO** MC*. Indeed, at this time he (Jones) was writing his book 'King of Air Fighters', which was the life story of Mannock, the RFC's top-scoring fighter pilot.

By April 1932 there were ten regular officers and six reservists on the squadron. Among the regulars were two newcomers; Flying Officers H.E. Power and H.J. Piper. The latter was an enthusiastic snooker player and became something of an exponent of the game, seldom pocketing a ball without it vibrating between the shoulder cushions of the pocket. This shot eventually became known throughout the peacetime RAF as 'The Piper Shot'.

The other newcomer, Henry Power, was to make his mark on the squadron in a far different manner. He was to remain with No 503 Squadron at Waddington for almost five years, and in that time he was to have a strong influence in the training and the *esprit de corps* of the squadron. He was the grandson of a well-known ophthalmic surgeon of the same name and he joined the squadron on 7 March 1932. During his war service on the Western Front, he had been shot down over Holland on 1 September 1918, while serving on an RAF squadron as an observer. But, after the war he trained as a pilot at No 4 Flying Training School (FTS) at Abu Sueir in Egypt. He came to Waddington from No 2FTS at nearby RAF Digby, where he had been badly burned about the face as a result of a crash following a badly executed practice forced landing by a pupil pilot. He was a strong character with a mischievous sense of humour; a modest man who shunned publicity. Power was an exceptional pilot and instructor, though often unorthodox in his approach to teaching. He suffered from a marked stammer when on the ground, but it disappeared as soon as he got airborne. Although he could be a strict disciplinarian, he took full advantage of the minimum of 'red tape', which he detested. Apparently, there was far less of this material on No 503 Squadron than on most other Special Reserve squadrons.

Command of the squadron passed to W/Cdr A.P.V. Daly AFC on 9 August 1933. He too was a distinguished aviator, who had served with No 60 Squadron and flown the reputedly dangerous French-built Morane Scout, better known as 'the Bullet'. According to Arthur Young, Daly and Power were kindred spirits, and between them raised the morale of No 503 Squadron to something akin to that of a wartime RFC squadron. Indeed, Young was to recall that in fact he found that such a spirit was not always evident on some of the regular air force squadrons, which he subsequently joined.

By the time W/Cdr Daly assumed command, there were only four or five reservist officers on strength. However, one recruit, who joined the squadron in October 1933, was Pilot Officer J.H. Smith, and he was to remain with the squadron until its disbandment, when he joined its replacement No 616 Squadron, based at Doncaster. In due course Arthur Young was gazetted in December 1933, followed in January 1934 by Pilot Officers Michael Smith and Paul Ruston. They were followed the next month by P/O C.W. Rees.

One of the changes in the regular staff was the arrival of a new commander for 'A' Flight. This was S/Ldr J.L.M. de C. Hughes-Chamberlain, who arrived in April 1934. By this time the squadron had come under the overall command of the new Western Area, which was responsible for all bomber units and was commanded by Air Vice Marshal P.H.L. (Pip) Playfair CB MC, who was subsequently to become the AOC of the Advanced Air Striking Force (AASF) in France following the outbreak of World War II.

The regular element of the ground staff received a reinforcement in October 1933 in the shape of LAC Alan Towers, newly qualified from the RAF Apprentice School at Ruislip. On his arrival at the Waddington railway station he telephoned the Guard Room for transport, only to be told that walking was good for him! He was employed as one of the three Orderly Room clerks, working initially under the Adjutant, F/Lt McGuiness, who was subsequently succeeded by F/Lt J.H.C. Wake. Among the regular pilots that Alan Tower remembered were Henry Power, Moon, Geoghegan, Hardy and Critchley. The Unit Engineering Officer was Warrant Officer Shaw, while the Stores Section was commanded by F/Lt Jacobs. Among the LACs were three who were to eventually become NCO pilots; these were Messrs Beck, Lodge and Wilkinson. Tower's other recollections concern life in general at Waddington:

"Each summer the squadron spent two weeks at camp, quite often at RAF Hawkinge near Folkestone and, as I recall, we regulars let the Special Reservists get on with it while we spent our time consuming quantities of ale and seafood and generally letting our hair down. At Waddington we lived in the very old, single brick, single storey barrack huts beside the road opposite the Airmen's Married Quarters and local council houses. Life there was rather spartan; the only hot water was in the bath house and we had only two pot-bellied stoves per hut for heating in the winter. We paraded each morning at 0800hr and marched to work in Flights. Similarly, we were marched back for lunch etc. The food was plain, but I seem to remember that it was plentiful. In fact, we were very fortunate with our catering section, who were Corporal Hartridge and AC1 Leibrick, plus their two kitchen hands ACs Pirie and Smith. In general, discipline was fairly easy going until one stepped out of line; then 'Bang'.

Off duty activities were confined to a bit of football or hockey; remember, we could not play on Saturdays as these were working days for us. The other activities were girls, pubs and motor cycling; several of us having our own motor bikes. None of us airmen could really afford cars, though I did have a half share in a £5 'banger'. It was an Austin Tourer of uncertain vintage, about 1923 I should think. My co-owner was a service MT driver named Walford, who had been in an armoured car unit in Iraq between 1930 and 1934. We picked the car up in a scrap yard at Bracebridge Heath and we rebuilt the engine in our spare time. We had a lot of fun both in building it and driving it around the local pubs, and I recall that it regularly carried at least five bods.

Relationships between Officers and Other Ranks were far more distant than from 1939 onwards. Some of the regular officers were virtually unapproachable, but the part-timers were ebullient, slap-happy and generally good fun. On their parade days they would arrive in a variety of cars of all ages and value, although not many of them turned up every week. Our regular Senior NCOs were strict disciplinarians; making sure that we were out of bed spot on 6.30am and they would inspect our huts for cleanliness and tidiness at least once a week. Our relations with the locals, particularly those in Waddington village, were very good. I feel that we kept the Wheatsheaf and the Horse and Jockey in business. Beer (mild) was 4d or 5d (2p) a pint, while for 2/6d (12.5p) we could get several pints of beer plus cheese, pickles and bread."

In 1933 the squadron began exchanging its Hyderabads for an 'improved' version called the Hinaidi. Initially, three very second- hand Hinaidis were delivered from the Stores Depot at Cardington in Bedfordshire; one of them with only 30 hours left to fly before completing its scheduled life of 700 flying hours. The Hinaidi was a development of the earlier Hyderabad, which it superseded in some RAF night bomber squadrons. The main difference between the two aircraft were the engines and the fact that the Hinaidi possessed a metal fuselage frame as opposed to the wooden frame of the Hyderabad.

The new aircraft had two 440hp Bristol Jupiter radial engines. The Hinaidi was supposed to have a superior performance to its predecessor, but the pilots of No 503 Squadron had grave doubts about this and tended to fly their Hyderabads as much as possible in preference. This practice ceased when one of the Flight Sergeant groundcrew stuck his penknife through the wooden longeron of one of the remaining Hyderabads and demonstrated the presence of *fungae lachrymosis* (wet rot)!

In terms of performance, the Hinaidi was reputedly superior to the Hyderabad. The published figures gave it a cruising speed of 75mph with a maximum speed of 122mph at sea level. With a bomb load of 1448lb it had a range of 850 miles. However, these figures were received with some scepticism by the aircrews of the squadron, so, out of either professional interest or sheer cussedness, the squadron carried out its own performance tests.

On the 7th and 8th December 1934, full war load tests were carried out with what were reputed to be the best and the worst Hinaidis on strength. From the squadron diary the following figures make interesting reading:

Test	*Aircraft* K1070	*Aircraft* K1063
Climb to 500ft	63 secs	79 secs
Climb to 10,000ft	44m 47s	38m 50s[1]
Service Ceiling	10,200ft	7000ft
Absolute Ceiling	-	7000ft
Cruising Speed (ASI)	86mph	78mph
Maximum Speed (ASI)	97mph	85mph
Stalling Speed (ASI)	62mph	52mph

One of the Hinaidis that was passed to the squadron came from No 99 Squadron at Upper Heyford, and it was considered by many at Waddington, to have had a most appropriate serial number - K1066! In a height test, it took this particular aircraft 20 minutes to reach 5000ft. The same day, 22 October, further height tests were carried out on two unloaded aircraft. The recently qualified P/O Ruston reached 18,500ft, while P/O Rees could manage only 18,400ft. At the same time, one of the squadron's Avro 504N training aircraft was also climbed to its maximum altitude, reaching 12,750ft. Following these height tests, there was considerable debate concerning the 500 foot difference in the readings of the front and rear cockpit altimeters; this despite the fact that they had both read zero when on the ground before the commencement of the tests.

Some months before the comparative tests, the part-timers took part in an Empire Air Day flying display at Waddington on 24 May 1934. The public were thrilled by the formation flying of the Hinaidis and the aerobatic display flown by the Avro 504. Then in July, the squadron had flown to Manston in Kent for their annual camp. While there, they met up with other Special Reserve squadrons such as Nos 500, 501 and 502 Squadrons. While at camp all the squadrons took part in simulated bombing raids using 'Sachalite' flash bulbs, attacking a variety of targets, among them being the Ford works at Dagenham; the results of their attacks were assessed by teams of umpires.

With regard to the training of the part-time flyers, Arthur Young recalled that 'ab initio' training followed the standard RAF system, beginning on the Avro 504N, the engine of which was started manually by a member of the groundcrew swinging the propeller. But, if it proved difficult to start, they could call upon a Hucks Starter, though some old hands would carry a length of strong rope to assist them in swinging the propeller when and if a Hucks was not available. Young went on to add:

"During the period 1934 and 1935 we had very few incidents, with only a small number of undercarriages being 'bent'. However, on one occasion one of the less intelligent airmen leaned into the rear cockpit of a Lynx Avro between flights. The engine had been left running with the propeller was just ticking over, but unfortu-

[1] It made only 7,000 feet!

nately there were no chocks under the wheels. While working in the cockpit, the airman's hand slipped and he inadvertently knocked the throttle wide open. The result was that the machine shot across the aerodrome, pirouetted around an isolated petrol notice board and came to rest only slightly damaged, after the terrified mechanic, who had hung on like grim death, managed to knock off the ignition switches.

The advanced phase of our training on the Avro covered a wide range of activities, sometimes exceeding those of the regular air force. All the part timers were enthusiastic flyers and flew, at their instructors' discretion, in all but the very worst weather conditions. According to one of the pilots "...generally speaking, if we could see the trees on the Sleaford road, half a mile away to the east of the hangars, flying took place..." In very strong winds it was considered great fun to fly over the regular air force stations at Cranwell and Digby and to perform circuits when they (the regulars) were not flying. We even used to practice forced landings in poor visibility, having been taught the theory of forced landings in fog. Among our other aerial activities were formation flying and aerobatics, together with low level formation flying, which we all found most exhilarating. However, one of the less popular requirements was to fly cross countyr exercises 'under the hood', possibly because some of the 'under the hood' landings produced hilarious results".

Training on the Hinaidi commenced within a few hours of going solo on the Lynx Avro. The tyro pilots had to achieve 40 hours before qualifying as a first pilot by day, and a further ten hours by night to qualify as a first pilot by night. To again quote Arthur Young:

"Normally as heavy as a cow on the controls, the Hinaidi was quite light in a strong wind; but in such conditions taxiing on the aerodrome was a highly developed art. Unlike the Vickers Virginia bomber, later Marks of which possessed wheel brakes, neither the Hyderabad nor the Hinaidi had any at all. With their very large keel surfaces, together with the big single fin and soup-plate shaped tail skid, the two Handley Page aircraft would weather-cock into wind at the slightest provocation. The only sure way of taxiing across wind, generally along the fence leading to the 'B' Flight hangar, was to use all available rudder together with aileron drag, combined with judicious use of the up-wind engine. After landing, many a pupil was seen to be in mid-airfield cavorting round in high speed figures of eight, usually being callously laughed at by casual onlookers while he was left to sort it out, thereby learning the art of taxiing an Hyderabad/Hinaidi the hard way. Inevitably, there were those who eventually had to give up the struggle and admit defeat. These unfortunates would be rescued either by an instructor or by a twin-tracked motorised trolley. Using this device, the aircraft tail skid, which was equipped with an eye-bolt, was attached to a hook on the trolley, thereby lifting the whole tail unit clear of the ground. The aircraft would then be towed backwards to the hangars, much to the embarrassment of the unfortunate pilot."

Another way of avoiding the problems of taxiing the big bombers in a strong wind was to attempt a 'Tarmac Landing'. However, this practice too had its hazards, though by all accounts only one pilot used the nearby wire fence as an arrester-cable, when he caught his tail skid in it! To once again quote Arthur Young:

"The term 'Tarmac Landing' is purely descriptive. In actual fact the tarmac, such as it was, ended between the northern sides of the hangars; beyond it was just grass. This enabled the sharper pilots to land very close to the hangars, thereby obviating the need to taxi at all. My most vivid memory, even after more than 20 years, relates to one such landing. I had of course done some dual and solo bad weather flying, and indeed had performed one hair-raising 'Tarmac Landing' with Henry Power at the controls. On the occasion in question, a particularly strong wind was blowing and Henry Power was airborne, giving some dual instruction in a Hinaidi, while I was working in his small Flight Office.

Suddenly, I heard an increasingly loud wailing sound. Dashing out of the office into the hangar on my way to the aerodrome, I was just in time to see a Hinaidi sweep past the windows of the opposite wall; it was waiting like a banshee. Just as I reached the outside of the hangar, the Hinaidi plopped over the fence and landed, coming to a halt some 100 yards from the fence. Henry and his pupil, the latter somewhat shaken, left the engines running and proceeded to the office with myself in tow.

After a few minutes Henry remarked quite casually that it was time for me to increase my total of bad weather flying hours. He went on to add that he had left the engines running to save me time.

"Very well sir," I said and in my innocence I started to get ready.

Just as I was leaving the office in full flying kit, Henry added, seemingly as an afterthought "Do about 30 minutes and leave the kite on the tarmac when you have finished with it, as I want to take Paul up for a bit more dual".

I flicked a quick glance at him, but his expression was completely dead-pan as he casually shuffled some papers.

"OK sir," I said, with what I hoped was an equally, if insincere attitude, while at the same time trying to ignore the furious butterflies in my stomach.

The take off was no problem; I just gave a terrific burst of power on the port engine and the Hinaidi swung out towards the aerodrome. Of course, as soon as I moved away from the shelter of the hangar, the aircraft weather-cocked into wind. Luckily, in this instance it was of no consequence, as in the prevailing strong wind I was airborne in about 20 yards. I flew around for some time wondering just what game Henry was playing, but coming to no firm conclusion, I commenced to carry out a few 'circuits and bumps' as we called them in those days. I should add that the Hinaidi possessed a complete wheel on top of the 'joystick' (control column) for aileron control, and in the turbulent conditions I got plenty of exercise trying to maintain some form of control over the direction of my aircraft. I finally decided that Henry had in fact 'thrown down the gauntlet' - in my case a flying gauntlet - and it was up to me to pick it up! Having made up my mind that I was not going to be beaten, I flew one more circuit and turned the big, clumsy bomber into wind over the Sleaford road. Gliding slowly down the approach, using the minimum amount of engine power, I aimed the Hinaidi at the tarmac beside the 'B' Flight hangar. Just before I reached the fence I slammed the throttles closed and the aircraft just plopped down on to the ground and stopped in about 60 yards or so.

As I entered the Flight office I said, in my best dead-pan voice, "The kite is on the tarmac for you". Henry just grunted and left immediately, taking Paul with him. When he had completed the training sortie Henry once again performed a 'Tarmac Landing' and pulled up about 100 yards beyond the fence, as I watched from the hangar. As soon as he had rolled to a stop, I retreated to the office, sat in a chair in a corner and pretended to read a training manual. Eventually Henry came in and sat at his desk without a word.

Suddenly, without any warning, all hell broke loose; he started by throwing his waste paper basket at me, followed by his copies of King's Regulations, Air Council Instructions and sundry other publications. These were followed by his helmet, gauntlets and other items as I finally dived for cover. Such a reaction was typical of Henry Power's sense of humour. However, there are two morals to the story: Firstly, by flying in faster, Henry had far more control over the aircraft than I had in a glide, an approach which could have had serious consequences if I had been caught by a sudden gust of wind. Secondly, never out-fly your instructor and/or Flight Commander; it is extremely tactless!"

Night flying in the Hinaidi generally had moments of excitement when novice pilots practiced circuits and landings (bumps), particularly for the unfortunate officer in charge of the flare path. Paraffin flares, larger than the goose-neck variety, were laid out in the form of a 'T'; the tail consisting of four flares spread over a distance of some 250 yards, whilst the arms of the 'T' were terminated by flares positioned 100 yards from the head of the 'T'. Number one flare was at the end of the tail and it was here that the officer in charge of the flare path was stationed; this individual being usually known as 'Paraffin Pete'. It was a chilly duty in winter, and the duty Paraffin Pete would always dress in the warmest clothes he could; usually they consisted of flying boots, gauntlets and either a Sidcott suit or a greatcoat with the collar turned up as high as possible. Invariably, the final approach to land by a novice pilot usually increased 'Pete's' circulation with worried anticipation, whilst on occasion he was kept even warmer by having to run for his life! One of the No 503 Squadron reservist pilots, who never seemed able to succeed in night flying, once landed straight up the line of flares instead of to the right of them. This caused the duty 'Pete' to run for it before dropping to the ground as the huge lower wing of the Hinaidi swept over him. In the event he suffered only minor damage to his nerves and his confidence. The same reservist later bent the undercarriage of an Hinaidi as the result of a 'kangaroo landing'.

Paraffin Pete was usually accompanied by an airman equipped with an Aldis Lamp, the sole means, apart from Verey Lights, of controlling flying. A pilot wishing to take off had to flash his aircraft individual letter on his recognition light. Depending on whether he got a red or green response from the Aldis operator, he would either take off or wait. Similarly, a pilot wishing to land would also use his recognition light to flash the aircraft letter. It was not unknown however, for a pilot who had been kept circling for what he considered too long, especially on a bitter winter night, to get his revenge by landing so close to the 'T' that his left wing would pass extremely close to No 1 flare, thereby making the unfortunate 'Pete' and his airman beat a hasty retreat. This flare path duty was one of the least popular with the long-suffering groundcrew. They loathed the filthy, smelly paraffin lamps and spent their whole period on duty longing for it to end.

Practice bombing was carried out by day using 8.5lb practice bombs. The target was a white chalk circle marked out in the middle of the aerodrome. On one occasion one of the armourers, a dyed-in-the-wool Cockney, acting against standing orders and regulations, walked out to a waiting Hinaidi carrying two bombs with their safety pins out. He compounded his crime by carrying them in his fingers by the tail fin. As was to be expected, the thin edge of the metal fin cut into his fingers which he shifted uncomfortably. Inevitably, one of the bombs slipped from his grasp and the unfortunate armourer got the shock of his life when he disappeared in a cloud os stannic-chloride! Luckily he suffered nothing more than needing a new pair of uniform trousers to be purchased at his own expense; though being one of the squadron regular airmen, he got into more trouble than that!

Thursday 24 May 1934 was Empire Day and Waddington was one of the RAF stations to open its gates to the public. The Special Reservists in particular dominated the flying display, which was very similar in format to that of the present day Battle of Britain displays. There were displays of formation flying by Hinaidis and Avro 504s, though the latter's immaculate performance was slightly marred when, just as the formation landed, one Avro suffered a burst tyre. Luckily it swung away from the other aircraft without damage. Possibly the highlight of the day, as far as the reservists were concerned, was an aerobatic display given by one of their number.

Two months after the air display, on 22 July, No 503 Squadron flew down to RAF Manston in Kent for Special Reserve and Auxiliary Air Force exercises. They took with them two Flights of three Hinaidis and one of three Avros. This was the annual fortnight camp and all the Special Reserve squadrons took part, spread among various regular air force stations, RAF Manston hosting Nos 500, 501, 502 and 503 Squadrons. The area covered by the exercise was a Sector of the Air Defence of Great Britain system, extending from Orfordness in Suffolk to Brighton, and included the fighter stations of Biggin Hill, Hornchurch and North Weald. The two weeks spent at 'camp' were eventful to say the least; as Arthur Young, who flew as second pilot and bomb aimer to Henry Power recalled:

"My personal recollections and memories of these exercises are few, but two events stand out quite clearly. Of the three night raids carried out as second pilot/bomb aimer to Henry Power, we reached the target, which was a factory at Dagenham, only twice. This was duly bombed using Sachalite flash bulbs. On 25 July we had taken off for a raid at 0050hr, flying from Manston to Dover and thence on to Folkestone. Unfortunately we failed to find one of the navigation check points due to extensive low cloud. We decided to return to Manston, and had just turned back when we received a message over our radio ordering us to do just that. Over Dover once more, we set course for Manston, but as we flew on, the weather got worse, with low cloud cover thickening up all the time.

At one stage, we could see neither the stars above nor the ground beneath us. Just as we reached our ETA, without warning we suddenly saw the lights of another aircraft coming straight at us from the general direction of London, and it was travelling very fast! Henry Power put the Hinaidi into a very steep turn to starboard to avoid a collision, continuing the turn to roll out behind the other aircraft. As we flew flat out behind the stranger, we gradually caught up with it, or at least got close enough to identify it as a German Lufthansa Junkers Ju52 mail plane, outbound from Croydon. We let the Junkers go when we estimated that we were near the coast and cruised around looking for a gap in the clouds. Eventually we found a gap at 3000 feet and plunged through it. On breaking clear we saw the lights of Dover and homed in on them with a sense of relief. Following the coast at low level, we came upon the emergency flare path at RAF Hawkinge; a small fighter airfield shaped like a saucer and which was officially declared unfit for night flying. Henry handled the Hinaidi like a fighter, finally turning on to the flare path following a sweeping side-slip. We touched down beside the third or fourth flare, taxied up to the far side of the saucer and came to rest with considerable expressions of relief.

We returned to Manston the next morning and were told that we would be on again that night, so we had better go and get some rest. We took of at 0105hr for another raid, in the course of which our passengers, among them an air correspondent, were fortunate to experience one of the most amazing displays of Hinaidi flying I have ever seen. Our air correspondent passenger, Mr F D Bradbrooke, was the editor of 'The Aeropilot' magazine and he later wrote an article describing his experiences with us :

Off Southwold the Hinaidi took to waltzing over the North Sea in broken moonlight...killing time before crossing the coast...I lounged on my promenade deck, gazing aft over the restless tail as it heaved and swung across the moon, until I knew its sixteen bracing wires by heart. F/Lt Power has a happy hand on the wheel of his great kite, and its antics were almost graceful...I was leaning idly over the gunwale (!) braced casually against the knife-like hurricane when the light materialised. The airscrew discs and every strut and wire glowed like molten metal. I have never really considered a situation in which I might be falling from two miles high over sleeping London and wanting to fall faster. However, for a second or so now I quite wished I could drop rapidly enough to keep up with the bomber, to which I was attached officially, but insecurely, as F/Lt Power dived to escape the searchlight. I had heard of power dives, but this was the first time that I had ever experienced one at first hand. In what seemed a few seconds, Power had evaded the searchlights successfully and we were droning peacefully towards Dagenham, while the bereaved beams combed the night sky far to the rear.

Next time I was ready. Our pilot had developed a dislike of the limelight, a rather unusual characteristic in distinguished aviators! One inquisitive beam caught us and was quickly joined by a second, so I braced myself in the gun ring (Scarfe Ring). The Jupiter engines bellowed in wrath and the Hinaidi reared, shook herself, stood on her head and dived like a giddy comet until she howled in all her wires; the wind nearly planing me off neatly at the waist...we with a thousand thunderous horsepower, cut planetary capers in the thin, sharp midnight air, and a few million candle-power groped after us in vain. If the fighters had come my hands were so full that I could only have spat at them, but I was still ready for a squadron or two. All in the night's work and a dull technical exercise - for some maybe, but not for me by Jove!"

With the exercises over, the squadron flew to Hawkinge near Folkestone on 27 July for the remaining week of their camp. From there they carried out daylight bombing practices at Andover and Porton, sometimes in the most appallingly turbulent weather, when it was a struggle to simply hold the heavy old Hinaidis straight and level. Nothing else of note occurred and the squadron returned to Waddington on 4 August at the end of a successful camp.

During September 1934 a new Air Ministry Order (AMO) was issued requiring all 'ab initio' training aircraft to be painted yellow; this to include the fuselage, mainplanes and tail unit. Prior to this order, all training aircraft had been painted with a silver dope finish. Accordingly, on 2 October, No 503 Squadron's first Lynx was rolled out of the hangar in its new livery. The general opinion was that the effect was 'hideous' and it was promptly dubbed 'The flying Banana"!

Another of the requirements of Special Reservist Officers was that they should undergo a ten day armament course at a later stage in their training. This necessitated their attendance at the Armament School on the Isle of Sheppey. As Arthur Young recalled:

"...my own course, which was held at the beginning of November 1934, developed into a competition between myself and a Flying Officer McGrath of No 502 Squadron and the only other Reservist on the course, whose name and squadron I cannot recall. It was bitterly cold and a painful and lasting memory is of my landing after an air to sea Lewis gun firing sortie, firing from the rear cockpit of a Westland Wapiti. As we taxied in, all and sundry dissolved into helpless laughter at the sight of a student (me) with an icicle hanging from his nose"

Just before the end of the year, on 13 December, the annual inspection by the Air Officer Commanding (AOC) Air Vice Marshal P H L 'Pip' Playfair CB MC took place. The march past and ceremonial parade in the morning was undertaken in thick fog, which had a depressing effect on most of those taking part. Luckily, the weather cleared in time for the flypast, which was led by three Hinaidis of 'A' Flight, followed by three Avro Lynx trainers of 'B' Flight. All went well until suddenly the leading Hinaidi peeled off and turned into wind, executing a quick landing. The problem had been one that was to plague the squadron's Hinaidis throughout the time that they were at Waddington. The minimum permissible oil temperature of the Jupiter engines of the Hinaidis was, by specification, fifteen degrees centigrade. But in these ancient machines the crews regularly accepted a minimum of ten degrees, quite frequently flying at this temperature. On this particular occasion, just as the Lynxes had tucked themselves in to tight formation behind the bombers, a red flare suddenly shot from the leading Hinaidi and the aircraft landed with an oil temperature of seven degrees.

As the year drew to a close, rumours started to circulate concerning the future plans for the aerodrome. A party of soldiers of the Royal Engineers arrived and carried out a survey of the airfield. It was said that there were plans to extend it eastwards over towards the Sleaford road. Among the other rumours popular at the time was one that said that the squadron was to move out of the Mere road hangar complex and move into the three smaller hangars that lined High Dyke, just opposite the Officers' Mess. Another rumour was that two day-bomber squadrons were to move in, while yet another said that No 503 Squadron was to re-equip with two-seat day bombers. Very few of these rumours had much basis in fact. However, the arrival of hoards of contractors' men together with their plant and materilals indicated that something was indeed going to happen at Waddington. The airfield quickly began to resemble a building site; the over-long delayed expansion programme for the RAF was gathering momentum and considerable work was in hand across the country. Five of the new large hangars were under construction, as were the new Officers' and Sergeants' Messes, together with the new 'fort-type' control or watch tower. The new hangars were what was known 'C' Type Hipped; this name being derived from the fact that the roof gables were slanted. These large hangars, which dwarfed the aircraft then in service, had big sliding doors which opened to completely expose the sides of the hangars. This type of hangar was built in varying lengths, dependant upon the intended use; for example, a fighter station would have a seven bay version, while a bomber station would be provided with a ten bay model.

The new year opened with an interesting flight for two of the crews of No 503 Squadron. On 6 January the two crews in question flew from Waddington to Filton in a pair of Hinaidis.

One of the aircraft was piloted by F/O Geoghegan, one of the squadron's regular officers, together with the ubiquitous Arthur Young. The second aircraft was crewed by Pilot Officers Ruston and Smith. The trip to Filton near Bristol was uneventful and the crews enjoyed their lunch, albeit having taken it rather quickly. Both crews climbed into their aircraft and commenced the litany of checks prior to starting engines. Geoghegan's engines started quite normally, but Ruston experienced a problem with one of his engines that refused to start for some time. Eventually, after a lot of coaxing, Ruston finally managed to get the errant engine running, by which time the two crews decided to discontinue the rest of the navigation exercise and to return to Waddington together. On the way home the weather steadily deteriorated as they headed north into a strong headwind. It soon became apparent that the combination of bad weather and the onset of dusk would prevent the two aircraft from reaching Waddington. Accordingly, they elected to divert (an unknown term in those days) to the aerodrome at Castle Bromwich near Birmingham, the home of No 605 (County of Warwick) Squadron, Royal Auxiliary Air Force.

This squadron had been formed about the same time as No 503, being equipped at the time of the Hinaidis' visit with the Hawker Hind day bomber. When the visitors arrived at the Officers' Mess they found a party in full swing. Members of the squadron were saying farewell to one of their regular officers, Squadron Leader J.I.T. Jones DSO MC DFC* MM. As the party progressed, 'Taffy' Jones had to endure considerable teasing about his becoming a successful author; he had just had a book published - 'King of Air Fighters', the biography of the RFC's top-scoring ace, Major Mick Mannock VC DSO** MC*, who had been a close friend of his (Jones). The four pilots from the Lincoln squadron soon got into the party spirit and all thoughts of attempting to return to Waddington were forgotten. As a matter of record, 'Taffy' Jones had been no slouch in action over the Western Front, having ended the war with a score of 37 aerial victories. Recalled during the Second World War as a Group Captain, he flew several unofficial fighter sweeps over France, flying Spitfires. Not bad for a senior officer commanding an Operational Training Unit.

By mid January the Waddington squadron was in a desperate state, having lost virtually all its experienced regular fitters, most of whom had been posted overseas. In fact, at this time 'A' Flight had been reduced to two fitters, 'B' Flight possessed one, while even the workshop had only four. As a result of this and other problems, most of the squadron's aircraft were unserviceable. Regardless of this parlous state, the Squadron Commander decided upon an interesting exercise. All pilots were required to fly one daylight and one night circuits and bumps sortie, in four inches of snow! All the pilots commented on the strange effect that the snow had, the ground appearing to be much closer than it really was, thereby causing nearly all of the pilots to overshoot on attempting to land.

As the new year developed, definite signs of progress could be seen in the construction work on the aerodrome. The Royal Engineer surveyors had done their work well and their plans were being put into effect. The new giant hangars were reaching ever higher and the sound of riveting, welding and other activities became as much a part of the scene as the sound of aero engines. Then on 21 March 1935 three newly painted, gleaming Hinaidis took off for RAF Mildenhall in Suffolk, one of the largest and most modern RAF stations in the country. The aircraft were to take part in the first rehearsal for the Jubilee Inspection of the Royal Air Force by the reigning monarch, King George V. The actual inspection was scheduled for 6 July, but in true military fashion, this was to be preceded by numerous practices and rehearsals. The Hinaidis were painted in the standard dark green colour scheme of all RAF night bombers, the drabness being relieved only by the colourful individual letters and the Lincoln City coat of arms, carried on the nose of each aircraft.

On the great day, 6 July, the aerodrome at Mildenhall was covered in rows of silver fighter biplanes and day bombers, together with the dark green Heyfords and Hinaidis of the night bomber squadrons. (Five weeks previously, the prototype Messerschmitt Bf109 had flown in Germany). It was a most impressive display, possibly seen at its best at night when the whole array of aircraft was floodlit. Among those present representing No 503 Squadron was a young air gunner, Les Priestley, who had been given several days off by his employer to enable him to take part. Priestley had flown from Waddington to Mildenhall in Hinaidi 'D' (K1066), flown by F/O Jerry Bradford. Les Priestley was to retain his association with Waddington throughout his life. It was during his tenure of office as Mayor of the City of Lincoln, that RAF Waddington was granted the freedom of the city and the right to carry the city's coat of arms on all its aircraft. The highlight of the review at Mildenhall was the mass take-off by all aircraft. This was initiated by the firing of a Verey cartridge, the firing of which was the signal for the all the aircraft to roar off in turn, taking an hour in all to get off the ground and form up before departing for RAF Duxford for the Jubilee fly-past. This Royal review was the greatest gathering of aircraft of the RAF that had ever been seen, with all squadrons participating, including those of the Auxiliary and Special Reserve. Legend has it that in the course of his inspection, the King so disliked the RAF officers' uniform trousers, with their turn-ups, that they were dispensed with soon after in favour of the turn-upless style which has been retained ever since.

Alan Towers recalled an amusing incident that occurred at Mildenhall during the review. Apart from the aircraft lined up for inspection there was a wide range of motor transport. Among the vehicles on show was a six-wheel Morris Commercial fire tender from RAF Waddington. This vehicle was the pride and joy of one AC1 Walford, who spent hours polishing the brightwork and painting and re-painting the red bodywork. Having been selected to go to Mildenhall, he emptied the main water tank of its contents before departing, in order to make the long road journey easier. Came the big day, Walford was stationed with his beloved tender on one of the road approaches to Mildenhall. His fire tender gleamed so much that it caught the eye of the king. Noticing the monarch's interest, one of the escorting air officers asked if his majesty had ever seen one in action. The King is reputed to have replied that he had not and that it would seem an ideal opportunity so to do. Walford was duly tasked with demonstrating the capability of his charge. He started the engine, turned on the pump and operated the control, but to his horror, nothing happened; he had forgotten to refill the tank after his arrival! His Majesty's reaction is not on record!

During 1935 the squadron gained four new recruits to the flying strength: Pilot Officers J S Bell, J S F Hood, M P Forte and R H Smith; their addition being somewhat offset by the loss of Arthur Young, who left for No 2 Flying Training School (FTS) for training on the Avro Tutor, having been granted a six year Short Service commission. Of the new arrivals, P/O Forte was to die tragically in an air crash at Waddington in 1937. Another of the new arrivals, P/O John Swift Bell, subsequently joined No 616 Squadron of the Royal Auxiliary Air Force on the disbandment of No 503 Squadron. Sadly, he was shot down and killed in a head-on attack on a group of Bf109s over West Malling, while flying Spitfire X4248 on Friday 30 August 1940. His aircraft crashed near Percival Farm, Wrotham in

Kent at midday and he is buried with his mother and father in the Eastgate cemetery in Lincoln.

In January 1936 S/Ldr Hughes-Chamberlain was posted and S/Ldr A F James arrived to take command of the squadron on the departure of W/Cdr Daly, who in February was posted to Headquarters Coastal Command as the Senior Personnel Staff Officer. On 1 May the squadron was transferred to the Auxiliary Air Force as part of No 6 (Auxiliary) Group of Bomber Command. At the time, No 6 Group controlled the entire Auxiliary Air Force, plus the sole remaining Special Reserve squadron, No 502 (Ulster) Squadron, which had been re-equipped with Westland Wallace aircraft at its base at Aldergrove. Among the Auxiliary squadrons within the Group were the following:

500 (County of Kent) Sqn	Harts
501 (County of Gloucester Sqn	Harts
503 (County of Lincoln)	Hinaidis
504 (County of Nottingham)	Wallaces
602 (City of Glasgow)	Hinds
603 (City of Edinburgh)	Harts
605 (County of Warwick)	Hinds
608 (North Riding)	Wapitis
609 (West Riding)	Harts
610 (County of Chester)	Harts
611 (West Lancashire)	Harts

Towards the end of 1935, the members of No 503 Squadron had been looking forward to re-equipping with Hawker Harts or Hinds. Instead, the squadron was allocated the Westland Wallace Mk I, a two-seat day bomber. The new type's arrival was presaged by the arrival of a Westland Wapiti Mk VI, which was to be used to convert the pilots to the new type, pending the arrival of the Wallaces. The Wapiti was something of a hybrid, having been designed and built to incorporate as many DH9a components as possible. This was an attempt by the Air Ministry to reduce the strain on a slender budget, while at the same time going some way towards meeting the requirement for a replacement for the ageing Bristol F2b and DH9a aircraft. Most Wapitis went to the RAF squadrons in the Middle East and India, but a few were retained at home for training purposes. Several Auxiliary and Special Reserve squadrons were equipped with the Wapiti as a bomber, but No 503 Squadron possessed only two at the most, purely for training purposes. As an instructional aircraft, the Wapiti was a large, strong aircraft which was responsive to the controls and stable in flight. If required, it could be used for aerobatics without undue problems. If it possessed any vice at all, it was a tendency to swing quite sharply on take-off and landing.

Eventually, the Wallaces arrived in October 1935; the first batch being Mark I aircraft with an open cockpit and a 570hp Pegasus IIM3 engine. Later deliveries were to include the improved Mk II version, which possessed the more powerful Pegasus IV engine and, even more noteworthy, enclosed canopies for the pilot and observer/gunner. In the latter's case, his canopy folded back like a lobster shell, providing protection from the elements and the slipstream. In general, the Wallace was simply a Wapiti with a lengthened fuselage, spatted wheels, wheel brakes, and possessing a more powerful engine. The only units to operate the Wallace were Auxiliary and Special Reserve squadrons, namely: Nos 501, 502, 503 and 504 Squadrons. It was not a popular aircraft with the groundcrew, who were required to assist with the start- up procedures. As ex LAC George Gray recalled:

"Most of us were dead scared to start these aircraft. First you had to turn the propeller by hand to suck in the petrol; we would warn the pilot by calling 'Petrol On, Switches Off, Suck In'. We had then to remove the starting handle from its stowage in the engine bay, insert it into the inertia starter attached to the engine, then two unfortunate airmen would begin to turn the starting handle which was in the vertical position. This starter, being inertia, was initially difficult to turn, but became easier and faster as the happy pair of airmen turned it. Once it was felt that the starter was revolving at sufficient speed, one of us would call to the pilot 'Contact', while at the same time pulling on the starter wire, whereupon the pilot - if he knew what he was doing - cut the switches in. Then, if you were lucky, the engine would fire and the propeller would start to revolve.

Next came the really frightening part; one of the airmen had to remove the starter handle and replace it in the engine bay, the housing being very close to the nose. To achieve this, one had to stand in the slipstream as you replaced the handle, with a twelve foot propeller whizzing around just behind you, picking up the tunic tails in the draught and making them flap furiously. Having spent some time working on Wapitis and Wallaces, I never had to be told to straighten my back when on parade; my back was permanently straight"! With the arrival of the Wallaces, all but three of the Hinaidis were flown out to RAF Hawkinge, the last leaving on 19 November. For some reason, probably unserviceability, the remaining three were disposed of locally.

At about this time the squadron at Waddington possessed a Hawker Tomtit, but unlike the Wapiti/Wallace this was popular with the groundcrew. To hangar this lovely little aircraft, all that was needed was to pick up the tail, place it on one shoulder and tow it in by hand. The Tomtit was used by the Chief Flying Instructor (CFI) and pilots for general circuit training, though it was not much used. The type had been ordered by the Air Ministry as one of two types to be evaluated in service prior to the selection of one or other as a replacement for the Avro Lynx trainers. In the event, this competition was won by the Avro Tutor, which had first appeared at the annual RAF Display in 1931. The year 1936 also witnessed a major reorganisation of the structure of the RAF. The Air Defence of Great Britain organisation was scrapped, being replaced by a range of specialised Commands, namely: Bomber, Fighter, Coastal and Training, each of which was commanded by either an Air Marshal or an Air Chief Marshal.

A new arrival at Waddington in early 1936 was AC2 Jack Bury. He came to Waddington straight from training at the Electrical and Wireless School at Cranwell. Bury had joined the RAF in 1934 as a Boy Entrant, and on completion of his training he graduated as an AC2 Wireless Operator. As a product of the peacetime RAF training machine, Jack Bury was a welcome addition to the squadron and, as he himself recalled:

"A brand new graduate from Cranwell was more than welcome. It was an economical air force in those days, radio tradesmen being considered to be more than normally versatile; we could be in the air one moment, carrying out watch keeping duties the next, with aircraft servicing being thrown in for good measure".

Among the other regular air force personnel on the squadron at the beginning of 1936 were the following: F/O I R L Rumsey, the Adjutant; F/Lt W W Oliver, Flying Officers Gauntlett and 'Goofy' Govett, and F/Sgt Riley, the Disciplinary NCO, whose romantic reputation was much envied by the younger airmen! On his arrival at Waddington, Jack Bury was briefed on the difference between Auxiliary and Special Reserve squadrons, which included an explanation of the differences between being a member of the regular element of a part-time unit and being on a normal regular squadron. It was explained to Bury that he was to act as an instructor to the reservists, and that until further notice, his weekends would be in the middle of the week, leaving him free for his instructional duties on Saturdays and Sundays.

Jack Bury has many fond memories of his time with No 503 Squadron. As he recalled:

"When I joined the County of Lincoln Squadron, they were equipped with Westland Wallace Marks I and II. There was also a dual control Wapiti for training new pilots. The radio equipment in the Wallaces was extremely primitive. A low powered transmitter, the T21C and a TRF receiver (TF) were the equipments on which I had to instruct the reservists. The aircraft armament comprised a forward firing Vickers .303" machine gun plus, when fitted, a drum fed (96 rounds) free-mounted Lewis gun on a Scarff Ring mounting (1916 pattern) in the rear cockpit. The bomb-racks were of the 'light series' type and were fitted under each lower mainplane. The only bombs that I can recall being dropped during my time on the squadron, were the 10.15lb Stannic practice bombs. There was no Air traffic Control in 1936; a primitive hut on the grass aerodrome housed the 'airman of the watch'. It seemed to us that these characters were nearly all recruited from Ireland, and the standing joke was that they were recruited for two reasons: their inability to speak coherent English over the radio and their total lack of mental agility. Their main function was to ensure that the aerodrome was not unduly cluttered in the event of an aircraft wishing to land or take off. Notification of the wish to land was normally undertaken by wireless telegraphy (W/T) during working hours and by GPO telegram if it was to be after 1700hr! Any diversion by a Waddington aircraft was a rare occurrence and, in the event that it was unavoidable, it was the aircraft's wireless operator's (the observer) job to notify the Waddington W/T station, while hoping all the time that it was manned.

Not long after arriving at Waddington I volunteered for Air Gunner duties, though the title was something of a misnomer. The air gunner was expected to act as navigator, bomb-aimer, wireless operator and aerial photographer. Luckily for me, the regular establishment at Waddington was geared up for full instructional duties, which assumed that the unit would be at full strength. But, as the squadron was nowhere near full strength, there were at least two highly qualified SNCOs of the armament trade just waiting for a pupil.

No sooner had I volunteered than I found myself in the 'Bombing Teacher', a device that, with the aid of slides, acted as a primitive form of simulator. In the 'Teacher', one could undertake corrections of drift by the 90 degree method, the three course method and/or the timing bead method. After a considerable amount of time spent in this simulator, I eventually graduated to flying in aircraft. While under training I had no regular pilot and therefore flew with a variety of pilots, both regular and reservists. I metaphorically bombed the Lincoln gasometer on numerous occasions, though just how accurately I never knew.

Another little diversion, just to ease the monotony, would be the forced landing procedure. We would land in a suitable field, switch off the engine and wait. Sometimes the pilot would wander off and indulge himself in a spot of rough shooting. Eventually, when it was considered time, it would be my task to start the engine. Having negotiated this rather frightening task, I would climb up the side of the Wallace fuselage and strap in. We would then taxi to the downwind end of the field, turn into wind and take off.

Our navigation technique consisted mainly of map reading, which presented no problems to me at all. I obtained the 'seal of approval' when I successfully navigated the Commanding Officer to RAF Thornaby near Middlesborough, the home of No 608 Squadron, and returned to Waddington without incident. Being a radio tradesman, the signals element of the training was considered irrelevant, so I progressed to photography. I must admit that I found this, using the cumbersome hand-held camera a bit difficult, but the examiners seemed satisfied. Lastly came the gunnery training which, in the interests of economy, was mostly conducted using a camera gun, the results of which were marked most severely. As for firing 'real' bullets, this was a very rare occurrence, with every round having to be accounted for. Eventually, with my training completed, the neces-

sary entry appeared in Unit Orders and I was thereafter the richer by 1/6d (7.5p) per day. The money apart, I was then allowed to wear the coveted air gunner's badge - the 'winged bullet'. This had been introduced in 1923 and consisted of a winged bullet made of brass, worn on the left sleeve. This badge continued in use until December 1939 when the 'AG' brevet was introduced.

Legend has it that when the prototype of the new AG brevet was shown to Marshal of the Royal Air Force Sir Cyril Newell, he studied the proposed design at some length before commenting that the wing element of the badge consisted of thirteen feathers. It is not known if Sir Cyril was a superstitious man, but he is reputed to have decreed "Either add another feather or take one off". So, in true Air Ministry fashion, and in the interests of economy, the wing was reduced to twelve feathers."

With his background in the radio trade group, Bury was obviously far more adept at sending and receiving messages by W/T than most. However, at least one of the reservists must have had some ability in this direction. At the time, there were only two RAF D/F stations in Great Britain, and these operated only during normal working hours. On one occasion, a Wallace aircraft of No 503 Squadron was being flown by Squadron Leader Power, with an AC Blackburn in the rear cockpit. During the trip they ran into bad weather, including rapidly deteriorating visibility and a lowering cloud base. It was solely due to his ability with the wireless that Blackburn was able to make the most of the rather meagre radio aids available to them, and this, together with his navigational ability enabled them to return safely to Waddington. This was no mean feat when the only radio navigational aids available at the time were the Tangmere/Orfordness beacon service and the Adcock D/F system, controlled by Bircham Newton in Norfolk.

On the social side, the squadron would from time to time organise a 'Recruiting Dance' in the Lincoln Drill Hall. Just how this was funded remained a mystery to the regular airmen, but they were quite happy to go along with it. It must be assumed that the local territorial Association had something to do with it. Whatever the financial facts, the dances were popular with the airmen and also with the local girls, many of whom could be relied upon to provide most enthusiastic support. There were other forms of entertainment available to those serving on the aerodrome. Among the many Waddington airmen to savour the delights of the local hostelries, was Jack Bury. He, in company with his friend AC Ward of the medical section, were taken to the Horse and Jockey public house in Waddington village, not long after their arrival on the station. Their mentor was Corporal Bowditch, a 29 year old veteran NCO, who ran the medical section administration. Though not particularly convenient sited for access to the old aerodrome site, the domestic area was ideally placed for rapid access to the village. The airmen's billets were those left over from the First World War, though the popular rumour was that they had been first condemned in 1918, and every year since! The billets themselves were adjacent to the dining hall and close to the NAAFI and the games room.

Just outside the barrier on the Mere Road entrance, was George's Cafe. This establishment was owned and run by George Hewitt, who sold sweets, cakes, tea and cheap cigarettes (Walters at 30 for a shilling (5p)). George's was a popular rendezvous, acting as a meeting place for the RAF men and the nearby civilian residents, though relations between George and his RAF customers became strained for a time when his wife left him for an airman! Here was the source of all local news and scandal, and it was to remain so until long after the Second World War. One of the most popular subjects was that of 'ghost bombers'. The old sweats would happily regale any gullible new arrival with hair-raising tales of spectral bombers that could be seen and heard taking off from the old Great War site.

Another young airman serving at Waddington at about the same time as Jack Bury, was one George 'Dolly' Gray. He recalled that:

"During its Auxiliary days, Waddington was very much integrated into local life. It was part of the village; the vicar was our padre and the Wheatsheaf and the Three Bells were our locals where we played the 'old gaffers' at Shove Ha-Penny or old fashioned skittles. We went to the hops in the village hall where we danced to the music of a piano and a violin, and where we had rare old times with the local belles. We had close associations with the nearby mental institutions at Bracebridge, Navenby and Harmston, where we played the more peaceable inmates at football and attended various social events organised by their staffs."

In the mid to late thirties, parades were not quite such a feature of everyday life on a Special Reserve squadron as they would be on a regular unit. However, when King George V died in 1936, the station was required to hold a special parade which included the firing of a maroon to mark a specific moment in time. All participants were to wear their best (No 1) uniform. In itself this should have posed no real problem to the regular element, but unfortunately the rather relaxed approach to such mundane matters at Waddington had resulted in a much reduced standard of available No 1 uniforms! So it was that one of the newer arrivals, Jack Bury, straight from the home of drill and ceremonial in the peacetime Royal Air Force, RAF Cranwell, found himself fulfilling the role of 'Flight NCO' despite his rank of AC2. It should be remembered that at this period, promotion in the RAF was slow to say the least. It could take fifteen years to progress from Leading Aircraftman to Corporal; whereas the move from Corporal to Sergeant was very dependant on trade plus success in the requisite trade test. Even then, substantive promotion could be preceded by a lengthy period of 'Acting' rank.

The RAF Begins a Gradual Build-Up

With the completion of the first of the new hangars, No 1 Aircraft Storage Unit had moved in from Peterborough in December 1935. They occupied No 1 hangar together with its annexes. No 1 ASU was a civilian establishment administered by the Air Ministry. The Commanding Officer was S/Ldr C H Pownell; the Engineering Officer was F/Lt F J Knowler, while the staff consisted of fitters, riggers, carpenters, fabric workers and clerks. The ASU's task was the receipt, storage and maintenance of airframes, mostly new ex-works machines that had been flight tested and subsequently had their engines removed. The engines were not replaced until the aircraft was required for ferrying to a designated unit. According to Leslie Eede, one of the clerks, the types held were a varied collection, mostly biplanes such as Furies, Bulldogs, Harts, Hinds and possibly the occasional Audax. Some of the airframes arrived needing repairs or modifications. The ASU remained in No 1 hangar until the arrival of the first regular air force squadrons, when it then moved across the aerodrome to the old RFC site on the far side of the station. It subsequently left Waddington for Kemble in February 1939, where it became part of No 5 Maintenance Unit MU).

The Wallaces did not remain with No 503 Squadron for very long, but they were on strength long enough to be given the distinctive squadron colour scheme. Each Flight had its own colour; 'A' Flight was red, while 'B' Flight was blue. The design, the result of an in-house competition, was thought up by the Chief Flying Instructor's (CFI) clerk, Aircraftman R C 'Cyril' Browne. It consisted of a five inch stripe, red or blue, depending upon the Flight, running along the fuselage from the tail to the engine cowling where it broadened out as a concave curve to meet the top and bottom of the fuselage sides. In addition, the top third of the fuselage was also painted in Flight colours, as were parts of the main wheel spats.

Among the new part-time members to join the squadron in 1936 were Pilot Officer R O Hellyer and Harold Willers. As Hellyer recalled:

"I was accepted into the squadron in August 1936 as an Acting Pilot Officer. At that time the acting Commanding Officer was F/Lt Henry Power and I flew my first flight with him in an Avro 504N (Lynx), going solo after approximately two hours dual instruction!"

On the other hand, Harold Willers joined as an armourer under training, but subsequently qualified as a Corporal Air Gunner. Harold remained with the squadron until its disbandment in 1938. As he was unable to make the journey to the new squadron's headquarters at Doncaster and there were no other squadrons any nearer, he elected to leave the RAuxAF and transfer to the Class 'E' Reserve. He was recalled on 24 August 1939 and posted toNo 46 Squadron, going with it when it took part in the ill-fated Norwegian expedition in May 1940. It was No 46 Squadron that flew its Hurricanes on to the deck of the aircraft carrier HMS Glorious following the withdrawal from Norway. Harold remained with No 46 Squadron, serving in the Middle East for over three years, being demobbed in September 1945 with the rank of Flight Sergeant.

At about the same time that Harold Willers joined the squadron, Henry Power received a well-deserved promotion to Squadron Leader and assumed command of the squadron; this in addition to his already acting as adjutant and CFI. Fortunately, another regular officer was soon to arrive to ease the load on the Commanding Officer. This was F/Lt E J Palmer, who proved to be a welcome addition to No 503 Squadron. Eventually, F/Lt Rumsey was posted in to replace F/Lt J 'Jackie' Wake. A popular officer with all at Waddington, Jackie Wake had a problem. A local merry widow pursued him unmercifully, frequently enticing him into her pony and trap. This was the subject of much raucous comment among the 'erks', especially on meeting them in the trap in the many country lanes around the camp. Among the other 'characters' on the station in the mid thirties were two entirely different personalities. S/Ldr Chamberlain was well known for his habit of walking back to the Mess across the aerodrome. He would invariably be seen in conversation with some other officer, his hands and arms being waved about as he simulated the necessary flying positions as he talked, totally oblivious to any aircraft attempting to land or take off.

He was indeed a picturesque figure who almost always wore knee-length black riding boots and riding breeches. The other notable was Flight Sergeant Tim Riley, the Discipline SNCO. He was considered by the airmen to be a real 'sand-happy' character; a reference to his years overseas. He once raised a flock of geese in readiness for Christmas and used to march them around the airmen's billets shouting "Left-Right, Left-Right etc. On arriving to feed his pets one morning, Riley was not amused to find that they had been painted with black stripes during the night, though how this was achieved without them raising the whole camp was never explained, though it did indicate the most likely culprits. Riley threatened all and sundry with sudden death if the guilty party or parties did not own up. They never did, but all the NCOs and airmen enjoyed the eventual Christmas dinner

An Auxiliary or Special Reserve squadron had a life style all its own. In the case of the Waddington squadron, the fact that the living accommodation was quite a distance from the main working area, at least until the new barrack blocks and hangars were completed, meant that the airmen had a bracing walk to work twice a day. As 'Dolly' Gray recalled:

"With the morning parade over, about a dozen of us would straggle up the road. In winter, we must have made quite a picture. In the usual Stores issue fashion, long greatcoats were issued to the short men and short ones to the tall men. This, combined with 'squadron hats' (those having had the wire stiffeners removed) would have given any regular Station Warrant Officer (SWO) apoplexy. As we proceeded along the road, we had to pass within five hundred yards of a small copse. Among the trees a man named Gilliat, but called Yank by one and all, used to render down animal carcasses. He created the most awful smells, the memory of which still makes those who experienced them shudder. Eventually it was closed down, following the death from tetanus of one of the squadron's airmen".

Just one month after the squadron had been re-designated an Auxiliary Air Force Squadron, it took delivery of its first Hawker Hart training aircraft. This was in June 1936. These machines preceded the new operational type that the 'County of Lincoln Squadron' was scheduled to receive; namely the Hawker Hind, the first of which arrived two years (!) later in June 1938 (with Munich but two months away!). At about the same time, the first of the new basic training aircraft arrived. The Lynx Avro was being replaced by the Avro Tutor, a type that had beaten the Hawker Tomtit in the Air Ministry competition for the RAF's new ab-initio training aircraft. When they eventually arrived, most of the Hinds came from No 57 Squadron, a regular squadron based at Upper Heyford, which was in process of re-equipping with the Bristol Blenheim Mk I. As is to be expected, the change to the new type was not to be without its problems, as 'Dolly' Gray recalled:

"The first Hart that arrived at Waddington was in a terrible condition. It was covered in thick dust and bird droppings; we reckoned that it had stood in a corner of a hangar for some time before coming to us. Naturally, when it arrived everyone on camp came to look at it as it was reckoned to be a great improvement on our 1922 vintage machines. As soon as he saw the state of the Hart, the Flight Sergeant tasked the groundcrew to get the machine fit to see before the Chief Flying Instructor (CFI) arrived to check it out. The unfortunate rigger moved immediately to the cockpit. Now, to get into a Hart, one had to put the left foot on to the wing near the fuselage, place the right foot into the bottom foothold set into the fuselage, and then follow this by placing the left foot into the top foothold. The next step was to swing the right leg into the cockpit, not unlike mounting a horse. Of course, if you got it wrong you could end up facing the tail, much to the amusement of any onlookers. In this particular instance the rigger, quite correctly, placed his feet in all the right places until his left foot was safely in the top foothold. Unfortunately, as soon as he put his full weight on it while swinging his right foot towards the cockpit, it cracked with a loud retort and ripped its way down to the bottom of the fuselage, splitting the canvas, ribs and stringers all the way to the bottom. The appalled silence was eventually broken by the 'Chiefie' screaming at the top of his voice "What the hell am I going to say to the CFI "? Silence was the only reply as all present drifted quietly away, leaving the poor man bemoaning his fate, as the CFI was known to be a very mean man if anything interfered with flying. Luckily, on closer investigation, it transpired that the aircraft was totally unfit to fly."

On 13 February the local press reported a fatal air crash at Waddington which had occurred the previous week. The paper went on to say that two Auxiliary airmen crashed to their death while engaged in a service flight. The pilot was Pilot Officer M P Forte, a young company director from Cleethorpes; the observer/gunner was LAC F.W. East of Lincoln. The aircraft was Hawker Hart K3025 and it crashed in a field adjoining the aerodrome. According to the press report, the probable cause of the crash was lack of fuel, as the aircraft had been airborne for approximately 80 minutes and it was suspected that the only fuel available would have been in the gravity tank. This was normally used only for take-off.

As an adjunct to the report of the crash, the paper carried a brief article which hinted at the supernatural. Apparently, on the day that Michael Forte died, a clock in his office stopped at the precise time that he crashed. Some hours earlier he had reputedly been winding the clock when he knocked a framed photograph of himself off the wall; the picture in question hanging below that of an aircraft The crash had been witnessed by the landlord of the Horse and Jockey public house in Waddington village. According to his story, the Hart had circled the aerodrome three or four times before it nose dived, crashing to earth like a stone. Only a few months before, during the previous April, Michael Forte had a narrow escape when he made a forced landing at Kingsbury in Middlesex in the middle of a snow storm. He crashed into a tree and just missed running into a group of children that were playing in a nearby road.

Michael Forte was buried at Golders Green near London. The same day, the funeral of LAC Frederick William East took place in Lincoln. East was the step-son of Police Constable J Rudd of the Lincoln City Police Force and the cortege commenced its journey to the cemetery at Newport from the local police station. Henry Power represented the squadron commander and there was a ten-man firing party, complete with two NCOs.

The Station is Named

In April 1937, one month after the new Station Headquarters building was opened, the aerodrome was formally titled Royal Air Force Waddington, and the new Commanding Officer, W/Cdr P H Cummins DFC, assumed command; the Station forming part of No 3 (Bomber) Group. This created something of an anomaly as the only unit flying at RAF Waddington at the time, was No 503 Squadron R Aux AF which was still part of No 6 (Auxiliary) Group.

At the time W/Cdr Cummins assumed command, the station was heavily engaged in preparations for the forthcoming Empire Air Day, which was scheduled to take place on 30 May. In an advance report of the forthcoming 'At Home Day', the local paper announced : 'No 503 Squadron will give a display, while visitors have their first and perhaps only opportunity to inspect the new hangars and buildings which will accommodate two new squadrons; namely, Nos 50 and 110 Squadrons of the regular RAF. A set piece will be the main item in the show, in which Lincoln Territorials will participate. The theme of the piece is that troops are encamped nearby and a village girl seeks their help for her father, who is held captive by the natives of another village. The air force is invited to join in the offensive against the village. The village will be built in the middle of the aerodrome and will be attacked by both the Air Force and the Army'.

By all accounts, the weather was glorious and the Open Day was well attended. Sadly, the day was to be a tragic one for No 503 Squadron. During the show, Henry Power was killed in an air crash. He was flying a Hawker Fury having recently been posted to command No 2 FTS at RAF Digby. His display was reported as having been the finest and most daring aerobatic display that anyone had ever seen. Tragically, while attempting a slow roll at high speed, across wind and at very low altitude, he found himself drifting across the aerodrome, towards the new, large hangars. He checked the roll, performed an inverted turn away from the hangars (and the crowd) but had insufficient speed to recover and crashed in front of the crowd, which included his wife and two young daughters. At the subsequent inquest, the theory was put forward that during the manoeuvre, Henry Power had been blinded by the sun. This suggestion found few supporters among the many RAF personnel who knew Power, most of whom could not understand why he was performing aerobatics at low level, as it was completely out of character. With his death, the RAF lost an exceptional instructor and a first class leader of men, something it was soon to need. At the time of the crash, a formation of Blenheims was holding on the far side of the aerodrome with their engines running. They took off almost immediately in order to distract the attention of the crowd away from the rescue activities taking place around the wreck of Power's aircraft.

❖❖❖

3. The Regular Air Force Arrives

The first regular RAF squadrons had arrived at Waddington in May, just in time to take part in the Air Day. No 50 Squadron, under the command of S/Ldr R B Sutherland DFC, reformed at Waddington on 3 May 1937, equipped with the Hawker Hind. Two weeks later, on 18 May, No 110 Squadron reformed at Waddington. It too was equipped with the Hind, though this was intended as a purely temporary measure, as the squadron was scheduled to re-equip with the Bristol Blenheim Mk I, which it did the following January. Soon after its formation, the squadron's new commanding officer arrived, S/Ldr I McL Cameron. The new arrivals were part of the recently formed and rapidly expanding Bomber Command. The Hind was classified as a general purpose day bomber, having been developed from the beautiful and popular Hawker Hart. Essentially, the Hind was an interim replacement, issued to newly forming squadrons pending the arrival of the more modern monoplanes, the Blenheim and the Fairey Battle. The Hind was to be the last biplane light bomber to enter service with the RAF.

One month after the arrival of Nos 50 and 110 Squadrons, two further units of the regular air force took up residence at Waddington. Number 44 Squadron, under the command of S/Ldr J A Tindall, brought its Hinds with it from Andover, while the other new unit, No 88 Squadron, was formed from a Flight of No 110 Squadron and left for Boscombe Down on 17 July after only one month. All these changes culminated in the transfer of RAF Waddington and its squadrons to No 5 Group on 1 September 1937. The Hind, though obsolete, was popular with the Waddington fliers. Pilot Officer Peter Bagley, who was subsequently to transfer to the Fleet Air Arm, retiring as a Commander RN, joined No 50 Squadron at Waddington in September 1937. Bagley had been recommended to the Squadron Commander, S/Ldr R B Sutherland DFC, by a friend, P/O Cyril Vernieux. As Peter Bagley recalled :

"When I joined No 50 Squadron, they were neither fully manned nor equipped with all their aircraft. As far as I can recall, we had an establishment of 12 aircraft which were divided into two Flights of six each. These were further divided into two sections of three aircraft. I was a member of Section 1 of 'A' Flight along with two Australians, Pilot Officers R J Cosgrove and D F Good. Our Commanding Officer, Bruce Sutherland, was an ex-RFC pilot and always wore an old style flying helmet, with a fur flap at the front. Whenever he led the squadron in the air, we were all petrified as he flew as if he were still in a World War I aircraft, flying at a dangerously low speed, far too close to stalling speed for our comfort. When Bruce led a Balbo, as happened on a number of occasions, it was no joke trying to keep squadron formation One of our execises was for twelve Hinds, flying in sections of three in arrowhead formation, to simulate crossing the English Channel in order to bomb a 'continental target'. At least that is what Headquarters No 5 Group said we were practicing. A Hind carrying 2 x 250lb bombs was barely airworthy at a speed of 78 knots! " Peter Bagley went on to add " Our Hinds were collected direct from the factory at Brooklands, and I well remember flying down in the rear cockpit of one Hind to collect my own aircraft K6743".

Another Waddington resident who well remembered the pre-war regular air force was Jimmy Bennett. He too was a Pilot Officer on No 50 Squadron at the time, going on to eventually command No 144 Squadron flying Hampdens, followed by No 550 Squadron flying Lancasters. He recalled:

"When I arrived at Waddington the Station Commander was W/Cdr P H Cummins. Among the officers on his staff were: F/Lt Page (ex RFC) the Station Adjutant; F/O Petchel-Burt the Accounts Officer and F/O Fisher, the 'F' Maintenance Unit Equipment Officer. He later transferred to the flying branch and, following the award of his pilot's wings, was posted to fly Stirlings. On 17 September 1944, Fisher was among those Stirling pilots towing Horsa gliders to Arnhem - some change from 'the stores'! I last heard of him farming in Yorkshire. The Station Disciplinary Officer, was Warrant Officer Oakley, and there were two other Warrant Officers on strength, Robinson (Armament Officer) and Barnard (Engineering Officer), of whom more later.

The new hangars were complete, as was the water tower that remains in use to this day, complete with the identification beacon. In fact, the beacon was ready and flashing in time for the first ever regular squadron's night flying sortie. This particular event took place at 2240hr on 7 June 1937, when Hawker Hind K6742 of No 50 Squadron took off from the grass runway. The Station Commander when I arrived was the supervising officer, as the CO of our squadron, S/Ldr R B Sutherland, had yet to arrive. Other completed buildings were the guardroom, barrack blocks, NAAFI canteen, wireless station, equipment section, workshops, parachute section, the medical centre and the Sergeants' Mess. The Officers' Mess was still under construction, so we still used the 1927 building, Newell House. Similarly, the Station Commander's house and other Officers' married quarters were not completed until the Spring of 1938.

At this time, married officers, if accompanied by their wives, lived out under their own arrangements. All single Officers lived in the Mess which was solely single Officers' accommodation and which was governed by strict rules. No cash changed hands for any of the services provided; drinks were served by waiters in the ante room, each Officer being provided with a bar book, which was held by the Mess staff. Each drink ordered was signed for on the spot and the total value checked by the President of the Mess Committee (PMC) and entered on the monthly mess bill. Bills were paid monthly by cheque and included a deduction of 4/6d (22.5p) at source, for the RAF Benevolent Fund.

With the arrival of the new squadrons, the available accommodation in Newell House proved insufficient for the number of Officers on strength. An interim solution was the erection of eight tents behind Newell House. There was no shortage of volunteers to live in the tents as it was early Spring and the weather was particularly mild. Furthermore, the volunteers were granted 4/6d 'hard lying' allowance per night. Such a munificent sum could ensure an enjoyable night out, with cigarettes at 1.5d for twenty and a pint of mild beer at only 3d.

The usual haunts in pre-war Waddington days were 'The Horse and Jockey' in the village and the 'Saracen's Head' in Lincoln (now the site of Woolworths). The village pub was nicknamed 'The Whore and Jockstrap' and was in the benign hands of Mr Brian Alford, whose fillet steaks were extremely popular at 3/- (15p) a time. On the other hand, the Saracen's Head was run by Mr Dick Levene, whose wife held the licence of the White Hart hotel in the Bail in old Lincoln. Levene had a particularly soft spot for the RAF and, when 'Babe' Learoyd was awarded the Victoria Cross (VC) for his attack on the Dortmund-Ems Canal in 1940, he threw the Saracens' Head open to commemorate the occasion."

Prior to the arrival of No 44 Squadron from Andover, one of the World War I hangars was used by a Maintenance Unit (MU) for the assembly of Hawker Hinds. This small unit came under the command of Maintenance Command, though none of its Hinds were allocated to the squadrons of No 5 Group. Instead, the Waddington squadrons and other units were required to collect their aircraft from the Hawker assembly organisation at Brooklands near Weybridge. Like Peter Bagley, another of the Waddington pilots, Sergeant 'Lofty' Stenner of No 50 Squadron, was flown as a passenger in a Hind to Brooklands on 28 May 1937. He took passage in Hind K6747 and returned piloting K6812. 'Lofty' was to serve with distinction in Bomber Command throughout the war, leaving as a much decorated Wing Commander.

By mid 1937 the three regular air force squadrons at Waddington, Nos 44, 50 and 110 were sharing the recently built hangars. At the time, the allocation of hangars was as follows: using the current hangar numbers, No 1 was used by the ASU; No 2 by No 110 Squadron, though the office annex housed the Link Trainer belonging to No 50 Squadron. No 3 hangar was No 50 Squadron's home; No 4 belonged to No 44 Squadron, while No 5 was the property of the engineers. As is always the case, with the new large hangars available, units quickly expanded their empires to fill them. For instance, in addition to the squadron aircraft in No 110 Squadron's hangar, the next door ASU added a selection of nine Bristol Bulldogs plus an old Gloster Grebe. These hangars had not replaced the old World War I hangars, instead, they complemented them. In fact, the old hangars remained the property of No 503 Squadron. As to the three old hangars along the side of Ermine Street, one was used by the MU, another being employed as a garage for the private cars of those Officers who could afford to run one.

Not far from the third hangar was the previously mentioned notorious 'Yank'. The problems raised by this peculiar establishment came to a head following an aircraft landing accident. F/O R.J. Cosgrove was flying a Hind, when on coming in to land, he misjudged his approach and finished up much further up the landing strip than was usual. As he was rapidly running out of room to stop, he applied full brakes. Unfortunately, he applied them too firmly, with the result that he stood the Hind on its nose, some 20 yards from the hedge nearest 'Yank's' establishment. To recover the aircraft it proved necessary to sling a rope over the tail of the Hind in order to pull the machine down on to its tail wheel. By mischance, one of the No 50 squadron fitters who was pulling on the rope, was struck by the tail-wheel assembly, causing him to suffer a deep gash on his forearm. He was taken to the medical centre for treatment and a local doctor was summoned. He advised that following treatment the airman should remain in the medical centre ward overnight.

The following morning the unfortunate airman was found dead in his bed. The subsequent post mortem revealed that he had died of tetanus. Urgent action was taken with all station personnel being given anti-tetanus injections. Meanwhile, a detailed investigation of the ground near the scene of the incident revealed that the whole area was contaminated by tetanus bacteria. Yank's glue factory was closed down immediately and all remaining carcasses removed or burnt. The unfortunate innocent initiator of the incident, F/O Cosgrove, who was the son of the Prime Minister of Tasmania, was to be reported missing in action in June 1940.

Among the other personalities on the station at this time were two civilian employees of the Officers' Mess. The Chief Steward was Mr Bolton, who was ably supported by the bar steward, Mr Sendall. In addition, the doyen of the batmen was Mr Dennis Coote, whose preparations of 'blues' and Mess kit was beyond reproach.

The era of the biplane was fast coming to an end, but those who flew the Harts and Hinds at Waddington all seem to have nothing but the fondest memories of them. To again quote Peter Bagley:

"Lincolnshire so lent itself to low flying and hedge hopping. Among those who flew with me in my Hart/Hind days was my fitter AC Robinson. He would always try to fly with me whenever possible; obviously a glutton for punishment. In particular, he liked to hear the 'blue note',[2] as did an old friend, Captain Tod who was the peacetime Adjutant at RAF Grantham. Tod was an ex-RFC man and he would cycle from Grantham to Waddington at weekends just to fly with us. He loved aerobatics and steep dive-bombing. We did not have RT in the Hinds and the only way for the front and rear occupants to communicate with each other was by the well tried Gosport Tube. Whenever we flew members of the recently formed Royal Observer Corps (ROC) we could always tell whether or not our passenger was being ill; the Gosport Tube mouthpiece being gripped in their hands. They apparently got some comfort from grasping it when they were frightened, so they would hang on to it through thick and thin! I well remember asking one chap what he wished to see, and he asked if we could do some aerobatics. I did not think that this was a particularly good idea as the occupant of the rear cockpit was held in by only a thin wire, fitted with a quick release hook which was clipped into the 'D' ring at the bottom of the parachute harness. In other words, he would be suspended by that single wire whenever the aircraft was inverted.

Rather stupidly, I allowed him to persuade me that it would be alright, so I decided to commence with a loop which was a safe manoeuvre, or so I thought. I dived from about 3600 feet to build up speed to the required 180mph. On reaching it I began a very gentle pull back on the control column, intending to keep his feet firmly on the cockpit floor. Somewhere near the top of the loop, but just before going over on to our backs, I realised that my speed was too low and that at any moment my passenger would be hanging on the end of his 'G' string. Accordingly, I immediately kicked the aircraft into an almighty stall turn, which instantly dumped my passenger back into his seat. After landing I asked if he was all right, and he replied that he was but that it seemed to be a funny loop. He added that he never saw the horizon come round and as everything went black, he supposed that he must have fainted. I never again performed aerobatics in a Hind when flying ROC personnel".

Another Hind pilot was F/O Alan McFarlane of No 44 Squadron. He too enjoyed flying the Hind, though perhaps he did not always fly wisely. One evening, while night flying, he was intrigued by the neon 'HOVIS' sign mounted atop a building beside the Brayford Pool in Lincoln. To the young McFarlane it was too tempting to resist, so he carried out an impressive beat-up of the building, followed by a second for good measure. Unluckily for him, the beat-up was witnessed by Sergeant Pickworth of the Lincoln City Police. He telephoned the station and reported the incident, adding that the aircraft involved bore large number 44s on each side of the fuselage. When the unfortunate McFarlane landed, he was met by the Station Commander, W/Cdr Cummins. He interviewed the errant pilot in the Watch Office and decided that open arrest was appropriate. Though nothing was ever said, most of the pilots felt that the Station Commander discussed the offence with Sergeant Pickworth before seeing McFarlane the next morning. Be that as it may, the result was that he delivered a Reprimand, thereby avoiding the need for a Courts Martial. Notwithstanding this incident, Sergeant Pickworth was well known at Waddington as a man who knew the meaning of interpretation of the spirit of the law as well as the letter.

It is not only ex-pilots who have memories of their flying days. Phil Pinder eventually retired from the RAF as a Flight Lieutenant, but in January 1938 he was a new graduate from three years as an RAF Apprentice at the Electronics and Wireless School at RAF Cranwell. He joined No 50 Squadron as an AC2 Wireless Mechanic, coming under the watchful eye of Sergeant 'Brummie' Wells. Soon after his arrival, Pinder volunteered for training as an Air Gunner, subsequently being crewed with a Sergeant Windsor. Phil Pinder recalled that he enjoyed the flying and the practices with camera and Lewis guns. He too remembered the Gosport Tube and the fact that on altitude/oxygen tests he would hold on to a length of string, one end of which was attached to the top of Sergeant Windsor's helmet; this as an added safety precaution!

The groundcrew too have their memories of the inter-war years at Waddington. Edward Deeks was an LAC Flight Rigger on No 50 Squadron. He recalled that when he joined the squadron in May 1937, it was commanded by S/Ldr R B Sutherland, who was reputed to have been an ace in World War I. His particular aircraft was a rare bird - a dual control Hind (K6744). Deeks was personally responsible for this machine, together with a Flight Mechanic AC1 Ron Lumsden. During his time at Waddington, Edward Deeks remembered being most impressed by the formation flying of the Blenheims of Nos 44 and 110 Squadrons. He also recalled when F/O Cosgrove (sic) was involved in a mid-air collision over Woodhall Spa while flying Hind K6746. In the ensuing confusion (!) his passenger, AC1 'Jock' Crawford bailed out, thereby becoming the first man to make a successful parachute jump by someone flying from Waddington. All others

[2] The 'blue note' that they both liked so much was caused by the direct drive propeller reaching near sonic speed at the tips).

involved in the collision survived with minor injuries. Edward Deeks went on to describe the basic structure of a squadron at that time. No 50 Squadron possessed twelve aircraft, divided equally between two Flights. Each Flight had a Flight Sergeant Fitter in charge of maintenance, while each aircraft had a First Fitter (Engines) and a Rigger, who were personally responsible for the serviceability of their aircraft. Each pair would also be the Second Crew on another aircraft; this in order to provide cover for leave, sickness etc. Apart from being First Crew for the CO's aircraft (K6744) Deeks and his rigger were Second Crew for Hind (K6741), the mount of a Sergeant Smith. Edward Deeks also recalled some of the notable characters at Waddington during his stay.

Among the aircrew that he remembered were Cosgrove, Vernieux, Abbott, Smith, Bennett and Smissen, who apparently was Scandinavian and particularly remembered for surviving crashing his Hind (K6744) at Ollerton near Nottingham. From among the many groundcrew, Deeks recalled Flight Sergeant Lapidge, who was the SNCO of 'A' Flight of No 50 Squadron, together with his counterpart on 'B' Flight, Flight Sergeant Symonds, who was also a qualified pilot. But perhaps the best-known character was Bill Duffy, who was an LAC working in Station Workshops. Legend had it that Bill had been a Major in a Highland regiment during World War I and had been awarded the DSO. Like T E Lawrence (Ross), Bill Duffy had joined the RAF as an airman, but would say very little about his wartime service. It appears that from time to time he would be invited to dinner at the Officers' Mess of the Lincolnshire Regiment in Sobraon Barracks in Lincoln. This was the cause of some embarrassment on one occasion when a young junior officer from Waddington pointed out to his hosts that there was an airman among the guests. The look of astonishment on his face was a picture when his Army hosts explained just who Duffy was and his earlier history.

Farewell to the Biplane and No 503 Squadron - Enter the Blenheim

Despite its grace and beauty, the biplane had ceased to be a credible weapon of war. The initial RAF squadron to receive the first of the monoplane bombers was No 114 Squadron at RAF Wyton. This squadron had re-equipped with the Bristol Blenheim Mk 1 in March 1937. In December of that same year, No 44 Squadron converted to the Blenheim, followed in January 1938 by No 110 Squadron. In the meantime, No 50 Squadron was left to soldier on with its ageing Hinds. This phase of the reorganisation of the RAF coincided with increasing manning problems on No 503 Squadron. By January 1938 the squadron was left with a strength of one regular officer, F/Lt Harman and six auxiliaries; F/Os J S Bell, J S F Hood, C W Rees, J H Smith and R H Smith, plus P/O G Hellyer. Wing Commander Cummins was still the Station Commander, which remained under the command of HQ No 5 Group. Despite its lack of numbers, the County of Lincoln Squadron attended its annual summer camp at RAF Hawkinge near Folkestone. However, things could obviously not continue in this way. With the rapid expansion of the RAF getting under way, the service could not afford the luxury of padding out part-time squadrons with regulars. At the same time, there was a growing need for aerodromes and accommodation. Faced with these problems and the fact that No 503 Squadron had never reached its manning targets, the outcome was inevitable; the most likely cause being the lack of a large enough centre of population on which to draw.

So it was that on 1 November 1938, No 503 County of Lincoln (Bomber) Squadron was disbanded, its aircraft and regular personnel going to a newly forming unit, No 616 (South Yorkshire) Squadron of the Royal Auxiliary Air Force, based at Doncaster. Those part-timers who wished, were offered the choice of either transferring to the new squadron, joining another unit, or leaving. A few stalwarts opted to make the much longer journey to Doncaster, and in so doing, helped No 616 Squadron to become one of the fighter squadrons that played a full part in the Battle of Britain. Despite the move to Yorkshire, the new squadron did not completely sever the links with Lincolnshire; the first Commanding Officer was Squadron Leader the Earl of Lincoln.

The prototype Blenheim had made its first flight on 12 April 1935 at Filton, the home of No 501 Squadron, and by the following June the aircraft had aroused considerable interest in the Air Ministry, mainly on account of its performance. Its top speed of 307mph was considerably faster than that of contemporary fighters in squadron service with the RAF. The Air Ministry ordered the Blenheim 'straight off the drawing board' as part of the Expansion Programme. By the time of the Munich Agreement, the RAF possessed sixteen squadrons equipped with the Blenheim Mk I, among them being Nos 44 and 110 Squadrons.

The crews of No 44 Squadron were proud of their new charges and of being the first of the Waddington squadrons to exchange their biplanes for this fast modern monoplane. Unfortunately the initial arrival of the first Blenheims, flown by crews from No 44 Squadron direct from the factory, was inauspicious to say the least. Having beaten up the aerodrome in fine style, the aircraft landed one behind the other, led by one of the senior pilots. As the Blenheims reached their squadron hangar, they were turned to face their new home, lining up to the right of their leader. With a final burst of power, the first Blenheim's engines were shut down; this done, the pilot selected flaps up, or so he thought, but to the delight of the watching crews of Nos 50 and 110 Squadrons, the bomber sank gracefully on to its belly! Initially, the squadron's Blenheims carried large numbers '44' aft of the fuselage roundels, but around the time of Munich, this was changed to the assigned code letters **JW**. The conversion to the Blenheim, with its more modern features, was not without its problems, and by May 1938 Nos 44 and 110 Squadrons were experiencing a few teething troubles. Many of the ground accidents were apparently caused by the spade grips for operating the hydraulic undercarriage and flap selectors being identical.. The pilots would reach down alongside their seat as they approached the end of their landing run and, on occasion, pull the undercarriage spade instead of the flap selector. This would invariably result in breaking the back of the aircraft as there was a 25lb practice bomb carrier under the main fuselage. This would be driven up into the belly of the machine and break the main fuselage member. This design defect could have been overcome quite easily by a modification suggested by some of the Waddington officers, but for some unknown reason, it was rejected by the Air Ministry. The Waddington officers' suggestion involved the use of a Bowden cable controlled pin, which could not be withdrawn when the weight of the aircraft was resting on the undercarriage. The Bristol Aircraft Company took up the idea and subsequently introduced it as a company modification!

The Blenheim Mk I was the first aircraft for which the Central Flying School (CFS) introduced its 'Twin Technique', together with a mnemonic to aid cockpit drill. In due course this technique became standard practice throughout the RAF, the mnemonic for the Blenheim being 'HTMPFG' for the pre-take-off checks. Using this, the pilot's litany would be as follows: H – Hydraulics, T – Trim, M – Mixture, P – Pitch, F – Flaps, G – Gills.

Though pleasant and not difficult to fly, the cockpit layout of the Blenheim I left much to be desired; that is unless the pilot was a practicing contortionist. Some of the secondary controls were located behind the pilot's left elbow, while the previously referred to hydraulic controls were grouped close together below and to the right of the seat. In what could possibly be described as appropriate, these handles or spades were very similar to the Victorian era lavatory handles. One of the test pilots of the time felt that the Blenheim Mk I was the most pleasant of the many variants because of its relatively low all-up weight and the extremely good forward and downward visibility. To quote an article in Flight magazine, written in 1945:

'Getting into the Blenheim was always something of an affair and one soon learned not to attempt it while weighed down with a parachute. An assistant put this in the seat while the 'driver', hatted, gloved and intercomm'd, clambered on to the port wing - slippery if wet - and down through the roof hatch, letting himself down gently so that, if the direction was poor, he did not damage his nether regions on the various pointed items surrounding the seat. It was peculiar at first too, to find that the wings and ailerons were more or less invisible behind the engine cowlings; a disadvantage which was handsomely outweighed in the opinion of the crews, by the most unusual way in which the landscape could be seen through the transparent floor of the nose, apparently passing rearwards.'

Among the Waddington pilots who received their first taste of monoplane flying on the Blenheim was the then P/O D J Penman. He joined No 44 Squadron in October 1938 when the squadron possessed its full complement of eighteen Blenheims, albeit few being available to fly due to an acute shortage of spares. He was thrilled to have been posted to a squadron that flew the modern high speed Blenheim, though he was somewhat concerned that up to that time, he had never flown an aircraft equipped with a retractable undercarriage, flaps or variable pitch propellers, let alone two engines! Furthermore, the Blenheim also introduced the young Penman to the blind flying panel, complete with an artificial horizon. On recalling his early days on his first squadron, he remembered:

"The Squadron Commander was S/Ldr Tindall, an extremely experienced pilot with over 1500 hours to his credit. The second in command was F/Lt Withy, who with the two Flight Commanders, F/Os Morrison and Weir completed the squadron heirarchy. There were no facilities for dual control in the Blenheim; all you got were a few circuits with the Flight Commander, who would demonstrate how to fly on one engine, and then you were on your own! Because of the spares situation we were strictly limited in the amount of flying that we were allowed to do.

After I had accumulated approximately ten hours flying on the Blenheim, I was allocated what I was told was the squadron's last serviceable aircraft. I was briefed to carry out a short cross-country navigation exercise and jokingly told to break the aircraft while I was about it. As we progressed round our chosen route the weather got worse; in particular the increasing amount of low cloud gave me cause for concern. I had done very little instrument flying and had practically no experience of flying in cloud. Indeed, there was a general tendency for inexperienced Blenheim pilots to avoid clouds because of the number of occasions that Blenheims had been seen diving into the ground on breaking out of low cloud. Luckily, all went well and we arrived back at Waddington quite safely and I began to relax.

On the final approach I needed a burst of power to correct my rate of descent, but on pushing the throttles forward, the port engine stopped. The problems that caused me were compounded by the fact that the starboard engine had responded to the demand, whereupon the aircraft port wing dropped and it started to turn sharply to the left. To my horror I saw the port wing tip dig into the ground causing the aircraft to cartwheel round. Luckily it came to rest the right way up with both engines torn from their mountings and the fuselage split in two at the mid upper gun turret, which spilt the unfortunate gunner on to the grass. My observer and I climbed from the wreckage, picked up the gunner and started to make our way across the aerodrome to the hangar. On our way we were intercepted by the CO who asked me what I was laughing at. I was not aware that I had been laughing, so I assume that must have been a reaction, combined with the knowledge that I had done as instructed - I had broken it!"

David Penman's accident did not give rise to much comment; as the Blenheim's Bristol Mercury engines were prone to sudden stoppages, usually with fatal results. Some months later, in February 1939, Penman's Flight Commander, F/Lt Withy was killed with his observer AC1 Richardson when he lost an engine on taking off from North Coates. Possibly the reason why Penman's accident received so little attention could be explained by three earlier accidents. In January 1938 the local paper had carried the headline 'Waddington Pilot's Death Mystery'. The report went on to state that P/O A N McFarlane of RAF Waddington died in mysterious circumstances while flying solo near Horncastle. The only witness was a farmer who was working in one of his fields near Tattershall Castle when he heard an aircraft make 'a strange noise'. From his description it is likely that for some reason McFarlane had pulled the boost override as he pulled out of a dive preceding a loop, which he had commenced at about three thousand feet. It appears that as the Blenheim passed over the top of the loop, the complete empenage (cockpit canopy) became detached. McFarlane bailed out immediately, but tragically he was struck on the head by the aircraft tail as it spun to earth. The blow fractured his skull, but according to the farmer, he walked a short distance after landing before he collapsed and died in his (the farmer's) arms.

On 23 April the same paper carried the headline 'Fatal Crash at Waddington'. On this occasion the paper went on to report that 'The observer was killed and the pilot and passenger were injured when a Blenheim bomber on a training sortie crashed on take-off.' During the take-off run, one propeller was seen to be revolving rapidly as per normal, while the other was scarcely turning (engine failure on take-off). The aircraft swung into wind and one wing touched the ground turning the bomber over and tearing both engines from the wings.

The third crash involved P/O McDonald who, together with his gunner survived the crash. Sadly the observer was not so fortunate. On 22 April 1938, nine Blenheims flying in three vics of three and led by F/Lt Walter Lamb, were scheduled to carry out a flypast at the RAF College Cranwell. P/O 'Scotty' McDonald was flying as Lamb's No 2, but shortly after take off and while flying at about 20 feet, with his wheels and flaps still down, his starboard engine stopped dead. The Blenheim (K7127) commenced a slow roll to starboard, which was checked only when the wingtip hit the ground causing the machine to cartwheel. All this occured well before the formation had cleared the aerodrome boundary. McDonald's observer, Cpl Tidey, was thrown out and killed, but the gunner AC Marklew, received only minor injuries. The Blenheim's fuselage broke open just forward of the upper gun turret and, according to eye witnesses; the gunner was out of his turret and round to the front of the aircraft in something under ten seconds, helping to extricate his pilot. P/O McDonald survived the accident but, following his transfer to the Fleet Air Arm, lost his life when the aircraft carrier Courageous was sunk by U29 on 17 September 1939.

During the afternoon of the day of McDonald's accident, members of No 44 Squadron tried to reconstruct exactly what had happened and just how AC Marklew had managed to evacuate the aircraft so quickly. At the time of the accident the gunner had left the aircraft still wearing his parachute harness. However, in the re-creation organised by Walter Lamb, there was no way that Marklew could re-enter the shattered fuselage, even without his harness. All agreed that it was amazing what can be achieved in an emergency.

Corporal Tidey's replacement on No 44 Squadron was Gilbert Haworth; later S/Ldr Haworth DFC DFM. Gilbert came to Waddington from RAF Abingdon, from where he had been detached to RAF North Coates to undertake observer training. All in all he has happy memories of Waddington, but his first few hours were far from welcoming. After a long and tedious journey, he arrived at Waddington village railway station, some two miles from the aerodrome. A brand new observer, he was pleasantly surprised to find a service vehicle awaiting his arrival. Assisted by the driver, Gilbert loaded his kit which included his bicycle, and they set off up the hill for RAF Waddington. Having been dropped off outside a hangar, Gilbert leaned his bicycle against the wall and reported to the squadron office to complete the necessary arrival procedure. Twenty minutes later, formalities completed, he left the hangar to collect his bicycle, where he found two grinning RAF policemen standing beside it. In answer to their questions, he admitted that the bicycle was his, whereupon he was informed that he was on a charge for 'Negligently leaning a bicycle against the wall of a hangar'. His pleas of being a newcomer fell on deaf ears and he was duly paraded in front of his new Squadron Commander. This minor unpleasantness over, Gilbert Haworth was fitted up with the chevrons of Corporal together with the brass winged bullet badge to wear on his right arm. This badge was worn by air gunners and air observers on probation. After six months, and if considered to merit it, the tyro air observer would then qualify for the highly prized 'O', the air observers' brevet, the origins of which dated back to the RFC in World War I.

In August 1938, 'A' Flight of No 50 Squadron were detached for duties with elements of the Army garrison at Catterick. The Hind crews were told little or nothing about the purpose of the move, only that they would be engaged in a joint service trial with 'certain Army units'. Before departing from Waddington, the Hinds were fitted with 50 gallon fuel containers, located under the lower mainplane. These containers were further modified to accommodate bakelite discs in the front and rear. Both discs were electrically operated by the pilot; the front disc opened to allow air flow to pressurise the tank, while the rear disc opened to permit dispersion of the contents.

Early on the morning of 24 August, Hawker Hind K6820 took off with Jimmy Bennett at the controls and with AC1 Hughes as his air gunner. They flew direct to an Army unit deployed in the Catterick training area and, at a height of 2500ft, Jimmy Bennett operated the controls and released the liquid contents over the soldiers in the form of a fine mist. Three days later a further trial took place, this time being flown at a height of 100ft against troops deployed in open country and in woodlands. The soldiers had been issued with chemically treated cards, subsequent study of which by Army and RAF experts confirmed the success of the experiment. Less than one week later, the meeting between Chamberlain and Hitler took place. The gas trial over, the crews of No 50 Squadron returned to their Lincolnshire base in a rather sombre frame of mind. Indeed, the steadily deteriorating political situation had begun to affect all the crews at Waddington.

A few weeks before the detachment left for Catterick, the Station Commander had informed the new OC No 50 Squadron, W/Cdr Leonard Young that Bomber Command had decided that in the event of war with Germany, the crews of his squadron would be used as reserves for No 44 Squadron's Blenheim crews. This little gem was passed on to the No 50 Squadron crews by their CO at a briefing in their squadron crewroom. Their response was hardly surprising; one or two officers muttered something to the effect that 'some bounce higher than others', while a seasoned non-commissioned pilot was heard to remark that he knew a song about 'how Lord Trenchard loves us'. Eventually the briefing session came to a close and the squadron members dispersed to discuss the news among themselves. In the event, common sense prevailed upon high and the plan was quietly dropped.

Meanwhile, at the Bristol factory, the company were working on a solution to the engine failure problem; as indeed was one of the Waddington engineers, Warrant Officer Barnard. The cause of the problem was sticking exhaust valves, caused by over heating. As an interim solution, some new flight drills were introduced. The first concerned the start-up procedures, which entailed carrying out a quick run up to full power shortly after starting. This was followed by cutting out each magneto in turn. As soon as this drill was complete the pilot was required to taxi straight out to the runway. At the take-off point, another quick check of the magnetos was carried out, followed immediately by the take-off.

Another change concerned the actual take-off itself. In future, the aircraft was to be flown off the ground to achieve maximum speed as soon as possible. In this way, it was hoped to keep the cylinder head temperatures down. However, Warrant Officer Barnard tackled the problem in a different way in his determination to affect a more positive cure. He experimented in the station workshops by drilling down into the top of the valves stems and filling the resulting cavity with Sodium. This proved to be an effective cure, but the in-service life of the troublesome Mercury VIII engine was to be shortened by the advent of the Pegasus, which would also be used to power the yet to arrive Handley Page Hampden.

Warrant Officer Barnard was a highly respected engineering officer who was known for his, by the standards of those days, unorthodox solutions to problems, whatever their nature. In 1937 the station did not possess a boxing ring of its own and there were insufficient funds available to purchase the ring advertised in the NAAFI catalogue at £300. As S/Ldr Sutherland put it at the time, that was the value of his local bungalow. WO Barnard however had other views. He raised the matter with the Station Commander, who agreed to the use of the station workshops. A small committee was formed and between them, managed to raise £90 for materials. In a very short space of time, the carpenter riggers had produced a boxing ring which accorded exactly to that in the NAAFI catalogue. Doubtless such minutiae as patents etc, played no part in the proceedings. The following year, the time and effort spent on building the ring were fully justified when Waddington won several top honours. F/O Sam Lloyd of No 50 Sqn won the Bomber Command and RAF heavyweight titles; F/O Mulloy also of No 50 Sqn, won the middleweight title, while P/O Esson of No 50 Sqn, gained the lightweight championship.

On reflecting on the accident of 22 April 1938, Walter Lamb went on to say:

"When one thinks back, it is quite amazing how naive and unprofessional we really were and how little we knew about what we were doing. We puzzled for some time as to why the prang had happened, and I notice that in my log book I attempted to simulate the Scotty conditions three days later! One must remember that in those days it was considered the correct thing to get 'unstuck' as soon as possible. In formations, take-offs were unsticking at 90mph and getting the wheels and flaps up almost immediately. When I simulated this at a safe altitude, I found that on cutting one engine in the

take-off configuration, there was no way that I could stop the aircraft gyrating round the dead engine at any speed under 95mph. After my tests we markedly increased our unstick speed! Recalling this accident brought to mind our other shortcomings. One almost gets an attack of the shivers when one considers just how unaware we really were. Our conversion from Hinds to Blenheims was a case in point. Some of us did about five hours solo in Ansons at Manston and Martlesham Heath; we then flew our Hinds to the Maintenance Unit (MU) at Filton. We then proceeded to Bristol's where a chap called Washer (I think) gave us a quick circuit and landing in our assigned Blenheims. The aircraft were then refuelled and we were despatched back to Waddington.

Following our return we were then tasked with instructing the other pilots. At that time there was no such thing as a dual control Blenheim, so the best that we could do was to go through all the actions in an aircraft that had been jacked up in a hangar. Ground power was supplied to simulate the real condition - all very 'makey learney'.

Gilbert Haworth too remembered his introduction to the Blenheim, though in his case it was as an observer. He recalled:

"Within two or three days I was given my first exciting flight. The sensation of sitting in a cabin aircraft free from the merciless blast of a cold air slipstream was delightfully novel. So too was the very firm push that I could feel on my back as we rapidly accelerated along the ground for take-off under the influence of two powerful engines.

The forward field of vision from the Air Observer's seat in the front of the Blenheim was unobstructed by any structural parts, and this facility made a welcome change from the old biplanes. It all helped to contribute to an exhilarating impression of colossal speed. However, I had something of a shock awaiting me when the time for landing came. The pilot closed the throttles and the noise of the engines died away. To maintain safety speed for this high speed monoplane, the pilot was obliged to point the nose well down so that we appeared to be almost diving at the ground.

To me, this was a most unusual performance, having flown only far more sedate biplanes up to this time. It was at this point that the excellent forward view gave the alarming impression of very hard ground rapidly looming up in front of my nose. At what seemed the very last moment, my pilot pulled back steadily on the control column, though to me it appeared to be an almighty heave, and the Blenheim made a beautifully smooth landing."

On a lighter note was the headline in the Lincolnshire Echo: **'Landed at the Wrong Aerodrome. SOS Broadcast for Waddington Plane'** On this occasion the pilot, who was on land-away sorties for the weekend, landed at RAF Biggin Hill at half past one, parked his aircraft and left the aerodrome without bothering to check in with the Flight Office before leaving for London. To his horror, he heard a BBC broadcast at 10pm that evening regarding an SOS for an overdue aircraft (his) that had failed to arrive at its destination - RAF Kenley!

Another humerous incident involved the recently arrived Gilbert Haworth. He recalled:

"Our Blenheims had cockpit glazing made out of thick celluloid material, which had many limitations. It soon discoloured, developed cracks, and various panels were prone to cave in during high speed manoeuvres. Much thought had been given to the danger of crews being trapped in the event of a crash on take-off. So our instructions were to leave the sliding roof canopy in the open position until nearly airborne. The observer was then required to reach behind him and, using his left hand, slam the canopy shut; something which could not be achieved once the aircraft was fully airborne.

On one particular occasion, when I was dutifully attempting to carry out this duty, I was surprised to find that the canopy would not move. Obviously more effort was called for which, when applied, had startling results. The bulky metal handle and front framework of the canopy came away in my hand, the remainder of the canopy vanishing towards the tail. My arm, suddenly relieved of its burden, shot forward at some speed, fetching my unfortunate pilot a mighty blow on the back of his head; all this while we were tearing across the aerodrome at some 80mph. Our doughty Blenheim performed some remarkable evolutions as the dazed pilot abandoned the take-off, and we eventually came to rest only a few inches from the boundary hedge.

Within a short space of time I was following the pilot into the Flight Commander's office. The pilot began complaining that he could not be expected to fly aeroplanes if people were going to hit him over the head, or words to that effect! The verbal assault upon me which followed was of almost unbelievable intensity, especially from the formidable technical Flight Sergeant. As was the fashion in those days, no one asked me for an explanation. In fact the thought passed through my mind that there was little point in escaping death in a plane crash, only to meet it in the Flight Commander's office. I am not one of those people who can normally retain perfect composure, being able to silence my critics with a few well chosen words, while at the same time producing irrefutable evidence of complete innocence. However, on this occasion I managed to do just that.

Behind my back the offending piece of canopy frame, together with the remains of the celluloid embedded in it, was grasped in my left hand. Eventually, I produced the evidence, and one glance at the aged yellow crack which extended for three quarters of its width was plain to see; a fault that should have been picked up by any one of a dozen routine inspections by the much vaunted technical staff, working under the aforementioned technical Flight Sergeant. Accordingly, I left the office in one piece with my honour intact, but no apology was forthdoming, that would have been too much to expect."

Another new boy, Sergeant V.A. Coveyduck, had arrived in February 1938, fresh from No 9 FTS at RAF Hullavington. At the time, the squadron was in process of its re-equipment with the Blenheim. Accordingly, the Squadron Commander had little time or use for an embryo pilot, so Andrew Coveyduck was sent on leave until April. On returning, it was his turn to tackle the Blenheim, an aircraft that was a far cry from either the Hawker Audax or Hart, with which he was familiar. After several hours solo, he was blessed with a crew, which was then followed by several months of routine squadron flying training. As a break, he managed to get a trip in an Avro 504K that still belonged to the station. As he put it; for him in his first weeks, any flight had become something of an event.

That summer the squadron went to Warmwell for the annual Practice Camp, during which, on 26 July 1938, Andrew and crew made a forced landing at Studland Heath near Bournemouth. The inevitable Court of Inquiry followed and he was charged with endangering both His Majesty's property and the lives of His Majesty's personnel; accordingly, he was placed under Open Arrest pending further action. On their return from camp, the Squadron personnel, with the notable exception of the new boy, went on leave. Andrew Coveyduck was left holding the fort, aided by a few junior NCOs and airmen. In general there was little for him to do apart from answering the telephone on the occasion when Group Headquarters called to enquire as to the serviceability of the aeroplanes and weapons etc. Coveyduck tried to explain to the caller that he was the only officer around, commissioned or otherwise, and that he did not really know the answer. Eventually, he gave them the answer: *"Two aeroplanes and two machine guns"*. This was of course the time of the Munich Crisis, September 1938. In retrospect and with 50/50 hindsight, it was perhaps just as well that Mr Chamberlain, for whatever reason, returned with his 'worthless piece of paper'.

A last comment on the Blenheim period of No 44 Squadron comes from Gilbert Haworth:

"In the peaceful summer of 1938, it was my good fortune to be serving on No 44 Squadron. On 23 July I was programmed to fly on a practice bombing sortie. My pilot was F/O Moore, a barrel-chested Canadian known to one and all as 'Pony'. He was very bald and was held in some esteem for his ability to get his flying helmet strapped on before we more hirsute mortals had managed to tuck our hair inside ours. I clambered into the cramped position on the pilot's right hand side and plugged into the aircraft intercom system. Thereafter things proceeded as follows:

"Ya got the bomb safety pins out"? he drawled.

"Sure enough" I replied.

We raced across the grass aerodrome and took off. The exercise height was to be 10,000ft so we commenced a steep climb towards the bombing range. I noted with displeasure that there was enough cloud about to cause us some difficulties with acquiring the target. We were required to drop eight bombs from different compass headings, and there is nothing more annoying than to be cheated out of a successful exercise because the target is obscured. On reaching 10,000ft, Pony levelled off to enable me to carry out a wind-finding exercise as a preliminary to adjusting the bombsight. This task took just a few minutes and when I gave the word, we attacked the target, a large white triangle with 45 foot long sides.

The clouds were now definitely threatening to obscure the target, but although I had serious doubts of success, I applied myself to the task and persevered. The Blenheim settled on course, straight and level, almost exactly where I wanted it. 'Left left' I shouted over the poor, crackling intercom and Pony immediately altered a few degrees to the left. The target entered the drift wires of the bomb sight and began to slide satisfactorily down them. 'Steady... steady' I droned to the pilot; a quick glance confirming that the bomb sight compass was aligned, and another glance showed me that the spirit levels were as near correct as they were ever likely to be. The target rapidly approached the release point, and when it sat neatly in the sights, I pressed the bomb release button, calling 'Bombs Away'. Those two words were the standard call and signified to the pilot that he was free to relax his concentration a little. However, he had still to maintain his heading until the tell-tale smoke puff of the bomb bursting on impact, which would result in our drop being scored. The bomb took about 30 seconds to fall, I then saw the burst, roughly 70 yards short of the target, but absolutely in line with our line of approach. This gave me a vital clue.

From the bomb score and sight of the burst, I could assess the probable cause of the miss. Our bombing run had been straightforward and faultless; moreover, it so happened that we had attacked directly into wind. So, without doubt the actual windspeed was higher than that which I had set on the bomb sight. It was well known that the most common cause of bombing errors was incorrect windspeed settings on the sight. Therefore, while Pony was turning away from the target for the next attack, I made a swift mental estimate and boldly added 30mph to the windspeed setting on the sight.

The next attack was made through a convenient break in the cloud and we were rewarded with a bomb burst close to the corner of the target. Within a relatively short space of time, we completed most of our attacks; each time achieving a hit or a very near miss. We were delighted and began to fervently pray that the clouds would continue to be merciful and stay away from the range area. Alas it was not to be. On our next attack I was forced to call 'Dummy Run' when the target slid out of view at the vital moment. Considerable patience was required before we could complete our exercise, and I failed to achieve any further direct hits. Winds are notoriously capricious and the delay imposed by the clouds had given our particular bombing wind time to change. Nevertheless, we were by no means displeased with what we had scored in the closing stages of our detail.

We did not carry our radio operator/gunner or our lower gunner on practice bombing sorties as they would have been bored to death with nothing to do. In any case, the radio equipment of those days was of woefully inadequate standard and we had become used to flying without making radio contact of any useful kind. Once our bombing exercise had been completed we were free to do as we liked. As free as the birds and, rather like schoolboys newly released from the classroom, we made the most of it. Those irritating clouds now became our playthings and we cavorted in and around the many towering summits, tasting the excitement of really low flying among and about the cloud tops, enjoying a splendid impression of really high speed with no risk of collision with anything hard and dangerous. When we eventually tired of this sort of fun, we brought it to an end by diving steeply through a chasm in the clouds before setting course for our temporary home at RAF Warmwell, the base for our armament practice camp. At the time, Warmwell was simply a grass aerodrome which was completely hemmed in by trees. It was customary to motor the Blenheim in at a height which narrowly cleared the treetops and to then throttle back and drop as gently as possible on to the grass. We all used the excuse that as there was no Air Traffic Control (ATC) we needed to carry out low level circuits; the only control being situated in a small watch tower from which occasionally a signal cartridge would be fired whenever a particularly 'hairy' approach was being made. In general, each pilot selected and made his own approach, and it was in this fashion that we came into land after our successful bombing exercise.

*We skimmed the treetops in fine style until we were about 500yds from the ground when, to my dismay, the starboard engine stopped. In the slang of the day, I thought that we had 'bought it' - that was, that we were as good as dead. Thoroughly alarmed, I looked across at Pony, whose instant reaction had been to apply full rudder to correct the swing into the dead engine, his face betraying the strenuous effort required of him. He could not afford to use full throttle on the remaining engine because the result could have been disastrous. Instead, he opened it up just enough to keep our airspeed at the minimum safety level. We both felt and heard the bottom of the fuselage scraping the top branches of the last few trees before we dropped heavily to the ground. After we had come safely to a halt, I could not refrain from muttering '***** Dangerous' into my microphone. 'Ya can say that again' was the reply. Eventually we made our way to the Bomb Plotting Office to where the results of our efforts had been passed by the range party. We were elated to learn that we had averaged a 52-yard error for the eight bombs that we had dropped and that this was the best score that had so far been recorded for the high performance Blenheim Mk I."*

September 29th 1938 is noted in history as the date of the signing of the Munich Agreement ('Peace in our Time'). While Prime Minister Neville Chamberlain was engaged in talks with the German Chancellor, Adolf Hitler, No 44 Squadron was on detachment to RAF Evanton in Scotland on an Armament Practice Camp. For some reason, long since lost in the mists of time, the squadron received an urgent message recalling them to Waddington immediately. In no time at all, Blenheims were getting airborne and heading south. As they were about to taxy out for take-off, the W/Op Air Gunner (W/Op AG) in the Blenheim crewed by Gilbert Haworth, reported that he could see an hydraulic leak under his gun turret. A brief inspection revealed that there was a leak from a section of one of the hydraulic pipes. Reacting to the general air of urgency, Gilbert suggested to his pilot that if he were to hammer part of the pipe flat, this would prevent hydraulic loss to the undercarriage and flaps, though it would render the gun turret temporarily unserviceable. His proposal was accepted and duly carried out, thereby enabling the Blenheim to follow the rest of the squadron with the minimum of delay.

On arriving at Waddington, Gilbert reported his unauthorised modification to the squadron Technical Flight Sergeant. This worthy gave vent to a tirade of abuse, the gist of which was that he considered that the crew should have remained at Evanton until such time as the squadron could get a servicing team up to them by road, regardless of the delay. Having made his feelings abundantly clear to the crew, he then felt it his responsibility to report the matter to the Flight Commander. Unfortunately for the Flight Sergeant, the Flight Commander too was imbued with the general air of urgency and gave him very short shrift, adding that among other reasons, that was why aircrew were selected from ground specialists; to come up with practical solutions to minor technical problems.

Hampdens For No 50 Squadron

Following the Munich Agreement, the national re-armament programme continued, one of the results of which was that No 50 Squadron flew its Hinds for the last time on 17 November 1938, when Hind K6820 was flown by Jimmy Bennett, by now the Squadron Adjutant, on a 30 minute local sortie. Five days later, the instructor pilots of No 44 Squadron began to initiate the No 50 Squadron pilots into the intricacies of twin-engined monoplane flying. The programme was intensive and, by 16 January 1939, the conversion was complete; just in time for the arrival of No 50 Squadron's new mount, the Handley Page Hampden.

Some time previously, in 1937, the Admiralty had finally succeeded in wresting control of the Fleet Air Arm from the Air Ministry. To overcome the resulting manpower shortage, the Royal Navy offered any suitable RAF officer who was willing to transfer to the Air Branch of the Navy a step up in rank. Thus in 1938, some six officers left Waddington to join the Royal Navy; these were P/Os T W Lamb and McDonald of No 44 Squadron, P/Os Bagley and Pollard of No 50 Squadron and P/Os H I A Swayne and Wellham of No 110 Squadron. Of the six, three were to be particularly successful; both Swayne and Wellham being awarded the DSC for their part in the attack on the Italian fleet at Taranto. Wellham further distinguished himself in other attacks, once sinking both a submarine and a coaster that were tied together in Derna harbour, during the Western Desert campaign. Walter Lamb retired from the Royal Navy as a Captain after a full and distinguished career.

In 1938, at about the time that the volunteers left to join the Navy, command of Waddington had passed to Wing Commander W J Dado-Langlois, though he was to remain for only six months, leaving the station in January 1939. In the meantime the station had held another Empire Air Day. The show began at 2.30pm with a display of towed banner target practice, involving a Hawker Hind carrying out dummy attacks on a banner towed by a Westland Wallace. Then came a display of solo aerobatics by a Hart of No 503 (County of Lincoln) Squadron. The next event was a demonstration of anti-aircraft cooperation. This event was a combined operation between No 385 (Lincoln) Anti-Aircraft Searchlight Company, Royal Engineers (TA) and a Blenheim. The purpose of the demonstration was to show how the anti-aircraft (AA) units detected and located raiding aircraft. Their display over, the Army left the area just before the air above Waddington was torn apart by a formation of Gloster Gladiators from RAF Church Fenton. The last item before the tea interval was a demonstration of dive bombing by a Hind of No 50 Squadron. Immediately after the tea interval, a formation of Blenheims from nearby RAF Hemswell gave an impressive display of close formation flying. The penultimate event was a 'flypast of types' which included Hinds, Harts, Blenheims, plus a Miles Magister, a Lynx and a Tutor. The final event in the programme was a set piece display based on the pacifying of a rebel chief by a combined force of RAF aircraft and the Army. Of interest was an advertisement in the programme for the day which announced that there were 1400 vacancies for Short Service Commissions in the RAF!

In January 1939 the Air Ministry decided to promote all Air Officers Commanding (AOCs) Groups to the rank of Air Vice Marshal. At the time, the AOC No 5 Group was Air Commodore W B Galloway AFC, whose headquarters were at St. Vincents, a large house on the outskirts of Grantham, owned by the Lord Lieutenant of the County, Lord Peregrine Brownlow. That same month, command of RAF Waddington passed to Group Captain (Gp Capt) L H Cockey, who would be in command on the outbreak of war. Gp Capt Cockey proved to be a popular commanding officer, particularly among the colonial members of the flying squadrons. They were particularly impressed with his skill with his 12 bore shotgun and the fact that he kept his married quarter lawn like a billiard table - using a scythe! It was under his aegis that the 'colonists' managed to get showers built in the Officers' Mess, an unheard of luxury in most messes at that time. Some indication of the colonial input to the squadrons of Bomber Command at the time, is the fact that, of 23 pilots on No 50 Squadron, eight of them were Australian.

With No 50 Squadron busy converting to the Hampden, No 44 soon followed suit, exchanging its Blenheims for Hampdens, begining in February 1939. It had been decided upon high, that apart from converting to the Hampden itself, No 44 Squadron would become a training unit for other No 5 Group squadrons scheduled to receive the type. To assist it in this task, the squadron was allocated some Avro Anson Mk I trainers. In due course, the Ansons were passed to No 76 squadron at RAF Finningley in June 1939, when the Waddington squadron's training role came to an end. The Hampden, though of a rather peculiar shape, was regarded as a very impressive machine, particularly by its crews. It compared favourably with the other bombers in service with Bomber Command. It could match the larger Whitley and Wellington bombers for range, while it could carry a heavier bomb load twice as far, at about the same speed as the Blenheim Mk IV. Altogether, the Hampden was a promising prospect that sadly, was not to be realised in the crucible of war.

Air Officers were not the only ones to obtain promotion in early 1939. In January, the Air Ministry decreed that with immediate effect, all Air Observers were to be appointed to the rank of Sergeant. The newly promoted young Corporals and Airmen were delighted, but the same could not be said of the long serving senior non-commissioned officers and Warrant Officers, particularly the RAF Waddington Station Warrant Officer, Mr Turk. All these long serving worthies had taken many years to reach their exalted ranks and now they were faced with 'babies in uniform', full members of their Mess! However, before long it was decided that the young air observers were far too rowdy and they were moved out of the Mess building into a nearby barrack block. This particular solution was to be of short duration, as the expanding strength of the station put a premium on barrack blocks; a situation that was to get worse as the war went on. With the arrival of the big and more complex four engine bombers, there came the introduction of 'two tier' bunks by the middle of 1944. In the meantime, the next move of the less than popular young sergeants, was into the old World War I huts beside Mere Road, situated conveniently close to 'George's Cafe', more popularly known now as 'Smokey Joe's'. This was too good to last; on the outbreak of war the observers were moved again, this time back behind the barrier posts into the recently vacated Warrant Officers' and Sergeants' married quarters. This was a particularly popular, if short lived, move with one group of observers. They shared the semi-detached residence with a group of NAAFI girls, who lived in the other half of the building. This also was too good to last and, on the grounds of security, the young sergeants were all moved back to the main camp site. Eventually, the new, larger Sergeants' Mess was opened in the Spring of 1941 and all aircrew WOs and SNCOs were to be accommodated there. This building remains in use for the same purpose to this day. The original Sergeants' Mess is a single story building opposite Station Headquarters across the road from the main guardroom. Soon after their elevation to the exalted rank of Sergeant, the Air Ministry issued an order to the effect that all Air Observers were forthwith relieved from any technical duties associated with their previous ground trade. Hitherto they were to concentrate solely on flying duties. This change was universally welcomed by the Air Observers, though not so well received by some of the ground trade SNCOs, who had made a point of unloading the less popular tasks on the 'part-time' aircrew, whenever they were not flying.

Among those at Waddington when the first Hampdens arrived was Gilbert Haworth. He remembered the aircraft well; indeed so he should, for he was destined to fly the Hampden on many operational sorties. His recollections were as follows:

"The arrival of the Hampdens excited us all and our hearts went out to the Handley Page newcomers; perhaps it was just as well that they did, for we were destined to have our lives linked with the Hampden for a long time. To us they were sleek and fast with an ability to fly well on one engine, a virtue not possessed by some of their rivals. From our Hampdens we were to witness many unforgettable scenes within Hitler's Fortress Europe."

For all the members of the 'navigators' union', the new machine was a marked improvement, with a comfortable position in the transparent nose which gave a wide field of view in most directions. A large chart table facilitated the work of navigation and it could be easily folded away to gain access to the bomb sight and a single Vickers K-type 0.303" machine gun. There could be no intrusion from other crew members; the pilot sitting above and behind, hidden from view except for his feet, which could be seen over the navigator's shoulder, resting on the rudder bars. It was very convenient to be able to pass a message slip to the pilot, having tapped gently on his foot to attract his attention. The main problem for the navigator was the tiresome business of just getting to his station. The troublesome journey inside the fuselage could well have served as a training course for Commando units. For a grown man encumbered by bulky flying kit, plus parachute pack and other items of flying and navigation equipment, the narrow fuselage (only three feet at its widest point) bristled with difficulties. Numerous projections lay in ambush to catch clothing or harness, and to generally impede progress. It could all be very vexatious, but the navigators (observers) soon learned that it was quite useless to hurry, whatever the degree of urgency; the pace just had to be slow and deliberate. Although bad language was known not to help a great deal, it was frequently used, especially in the dark.

The navigator had to enter from the underside of the fuselage at the lower rear gunner's position, then squirm through a small door in order to negotiate the gigantic main wing spar, which had to be climbed over in the manner of a miner at the coalface, until reaching a small rectangular aperture. This was the final lap of the obstacle course and it called for just one more session of squeezing and wriggling before being rewarded by reaching the 'office', which had room for everything. But, this compartment was ruled as being too dangerous as a take-off station, so after stowing everything in its correct position, a laborious backtrack was obligatory, to reach a safer if more uncomfortable position behind the pilot. Once the aircraft was off the ground there followed yet another wriggling operation before the navigator could congratulate himself on being ready for duty.

The cabin heating system was in no way a strong selling point in the Hampden. The crews frequently endured intense cold, with instances being reported of frost forming on the pilot's boots. On more than one occasion, crews would find that on unpacking their flying rations, the juicy oranges so considerately issued to them, had frozen solid. The nose compartment had the rare virtue of not being particularly noisy, being located well ahead of the engines, which were heard as a muted roar, which could be quite soothing - until the engines stopped, which was not at all comforting.

One month after the arrival of the first No 44 Squadron Hampdens, a Waddington machine was lost in a crash near Lincoln. The local paper of 25 March 1939 carried the banner headline **'Four Killed in Bomber Crash'**. It reported that a Hampden bomber from Waddington fell in flames (!) near Boultham Baths on the outskirts of Lincoln. The Hampden was in a formation of four when it vanished into cloud. A large explosion was heard and the aircraft emerged from the cloud and dived steeply into the ground, killing all four crew members.

Writing for the local paper, a Lincolnshire aviation enthusiast, Mr Bill Baker, reported the Empire Air Day which was held at Waddington on 20 May1939. The show opened with a display by three Fairey Battles of No 98 Squadron, based at Hucknall. This was followed by a brilliant aerobatic display by a Hawker Fury from

Ternhill, the aircraft looking rather strange in its camouflage colour scheme. Towed target practice was demonstrated next by a Westland Wallace tow being attacked by a Hind, both aircraft coming from No 5 Flying Training School (FTS). Three Hampdens from No 50 Squadron then gave a demonstration of supply dropping by parachute. Apparently one of the parachutes failed to open, thereby giving rise to the joke that the airmen would be eating scrambled 'bully' for supper that evening. Next came a combined attack on a dummy village set up in the middle of the aerodrome. The attack was carried out by a combined force of No 50 Squadron Hampdens together with Blenheims of No 110 Squadron. Soon after this event, a DH86B (Dominie) arrived carrying Sir Kingsley Wood, Secretary of State for Air, together with the Chief of the Air Staff, Air Chief Marshal Sir Cyril Newell. The VIPs did not remain too long, leaving after a short stop to move on to Hucknall.

Once the smoke from the simulated bombing attack had cleared, three Ansons of No 44 Squadron' s training flight gave an impressive display of formation flying. After the tea break, a party of recruits gave a display of drill and physical training, which was followed by nine Hampdens of No 50 Squadron demonstrating formation flying in three vics of three. Solo aerobatics by a Fury II (K8299) was next on the programme; this being followed by a flypast of the fourteen aircraft which had been on show in the static park. Among those taking part in this were the following: Hampden (L4074) and Anson (N5000) of No 44 Squadron; a Waddington Station Flight Miles Magister (L5947); a Harvard (N7017) from No 10 FTS, a Fairey Battle (K9386) of No 98 Squadron; Hurricane (L1827), Oxford (L4626); Audax (K7467); Tutor (K3263); Hart (K8268), the last four all coming from Cranwell. These were followed by a Wallace (K6020), a Fury and a Blenheim of No 110 Squadron. The last in the stream was a Westland Lysander (L6867), which gave an extremely impressive demonstration of its short take-off capability. Admission to the show was free, with cars costing 6d (2.5p) for parking! So ended the last pre-war air display at Waddington and the last of the Empire Air Days.

At about the time of the last air display, No 110 Squadron left Waddington for RAF Wattisham. This was as a result of an Air Ministry policy to rationalise its equipment policy and to locate similarly equipped units together. Accordingly, No 110 Squadron, which was destined to retain its Blenheims, no longer belonged at Waddington, which was declared to be a Hampden base. As with the crews of No 44 Squadron, No 110 Squadron had experienced some teething troubles during its conversion to the Blenheim. It lost its first aircraft on 22 April 1938 when Blenheim K7146 crashed at Crowland near Peterborough, when its pilot became disorientated in cloud. Less than two months later, Blenheim L1157 overshot the runway at Ronaldsway on the Isle of Man and was written off. Apart from their own training task, the squadron was further required to undertake the training of crews for Nos 49 and 83 Squadrons, both based at the time at nearby Scampton. This task was purely to introduce the crews of the other two squadrons to twin-engined monoplane flying, as both were destined to re-equip with the Hampden. That No 110 Squadron attained an extremely high standard was recognised when the squadron was selected to provide six aircraft for a detachment to Carlisle for special bombing trials at Gretna Green for one week in April 1939. One month later, the squadron left Waddington.

Decoy Airfields

With war clouds gathering, in June 1939 the Air Ministry formulated its policy regarding dummy airfields. This policy directed that night dummy airfields should be established for all aerodromes east of a line joining Southampton, Birmingham and Perth. Furthermore, daylight dummy airfields were to be established for all satellite stations. These decoys were to rely on imitation huts, tents and vehicles, and for effect, were to be manned by service personnel. However, it was stressed that such decoys were not to be located near any populated districts. The C-in-C Bomber Command,, Air Chief Marshal Sir Edgar Ludlow-Hewitt was not convinced of their value. He pointed out that the presence of hangars was going to be a major give-away. Better, he argued, to rely on effective 'blackout' at night.

Notwithstanding the the reservations of the commander of Bomber Command, construction work began in September 1939. At first, the night sites employed 'goose-neck' lamps to simulate runway lighting, which must have been convincing as quite often, returning Bomber Command aircraft would endeavour to land on them. These sites became known as 'Q' Sites and were progressively developed. Once completed, they possessed electric runway and flare path lighting, obstruction lights and other facilities. Movement was simulated by using cars moving around the airfield and along the runway. The resident personnel were equipped with a special signal to warn off RAF aircraft attempting to land, but it was of limited effectiveness. The operating rules for a 'Q' Site were as follows:

When the main base seemed likely to be the target for an attack, the 'Q' Site lights were to be switched on as the raiders were reported approaching. Cars with headlights switched on were to move about the airfield to simulate aircraft. Landing aircraft were simulated by means of a carriage fitted with a headlamp running along a wire the length of a fictional runway. When the enemy aircraft were sighted, the carriage was propelled along the wire by means of a cordite cartridge, which drove the carriage at about the same speed as a landing aircraft. Initially, the 'Q' Sites had a high success rate. By the end of 1941 there were over 100 recorded attacks on them. Between June and October 1940, they were attacked twice as often as their parent stations.

The construction of the daylight dummy airfields, known as 'K' Sites, began during the period of the so-called 'Phoney War'. Obviously, these were harder to make realistic. However, by mid 1940, there had been thirteen attacks on 'K' Sites; half the number of attacks on parent stations. The dummy aircraft used were manufactured by the film industry.

One other form of decoy system employed to distract the enemy's attention was that of 'Fake Fires'. These were known as 'QF Sites' and were first installed in August 1940, and by the following November there were 30 in operation. They were originally called 'Crashdecks', but were re-named 'Special Fires' or 'Starfish'. Their purpose was to simulate burning towns or ports. The usual arrangement was two groups of 120 metal baskets containing combustible materials; the second group was for use on a second night if required. The groups of baskets were linked in smaller groups. A standard 'Starfish' Site was divided into three sections, each of which could burn for one hour. In all, a total of 235 'Starfish' Sites were created.

RAF Waddington possessed three combined 'K'and 'Q' Sites, located at Potter Hanworth, Branston Fen and Gautby. The city of Lincoln was protected by two 'Starfish' Sites, one at Branston Fen, the other at Canwick. All five sites had closed by September 1943, once the threat of enemy air attack had been considerably reduced.

The Last Days of Peace

The unfortunate Sergeant Coveyduck, who had been placed under Open Arrest following his forced landing, recalled the last halcyon days of peace at Waddington:

"When I first reported for duty with No 44 Squadron, it still possessed three Blenheim Mk I aircraft, but these were eventually ferried to the Middle East. During the Summer of 1939 we took part in a number of exercises over France. These sorties were designed to provide experience of long distance navigation over unfamiliar countryside, as well as showing the flag. We also gained valuable data on the fuel consumption of the Hampden, albeit without war loads. According to my log book, I note that we flew to Bordeaux via Le Havre on 11 July, while on the 25th we flew a 'Round Robin' to Paris-Lyons-Avignon."

Having converted to the Hampden, Andrew Coveyduck was detached to the School of Air Navigation at RAF Manston in Kent, returning in May having successfully completed the course. He recalled that at about this time:

"...the new Squadron Commander, Wing Commander Boothman, of Schneider Trophy fame, took command of the squadron. He was a terrific man who firmly believed that aircrew should be in the air. At the Horse and Jockey, he introduced us to the 'Flaming Oyster'. This consisted of a tumbler 2/3 full of boiling water, to which was added brandy, which was then lit. Castor sugar was sprinkled through the flames, turning to caramel in the process. Provided that the mixture was correct, and therein lay the art, the result was delicious and very effective, particularly when the pub ;ights were turned off and some half a dozen 'Flamers' were alight. Personally, I felt that 'Burning Depth Charge' would have been a more appropriate name for it".

Despite all the activity involved in building up experience on the Hampden, some of the pilots retained an affection for their old biplanes. 'Lofty' Stenner and Wally Gardner decided that the six heaps of Hind wreckage in their hangar could be put to good use. Between them these two young Hampden pilots constructed a complete Hind (K6679). According to 'Lofty', they must have flown thousands of miles in their search for missing parts. In due course, on 26 September 1939, Lofty air tested the Hind, but the two enthusiasts were not to enjoy the fruits of their labours for long. The Air Ministry soon got to hear of a serviceable Hind at Waddington and allocated it to Hullavington. Although their efforts had been successful, the project had not been without its problems. During the rebuild, they omitted to tighten up the bolts of the access plate on the bottom of the oil tank. A Hind engine oil tank held some 4.5 gallons of oil, and all of it ended up on the hangar floor!

In those days, hangar floors were scrubbed regularly, with each aircraft parking slot being defined with brightly painted lines. To drop anything on a hangar floor was considered to be a crime, but to spill nearly five gallons of oil on it...!!! Very much aware of the heinousness of their crime, the two erstwhile plane builders spent many hours working with caustic soda to put things right. With the hybrid Hind virtually complete, the lack of available incidence boards when the rigging was being carried out soon became apparent. After several weeks of painstaking attempts, the two pilots swallowed their pride and called in a rigger, Sergeant Walters, to assist them. On his arrival, he appeared to give the aircraft a quick look, adjusted two turn buckles, and all was correct. Being ex-fitters themselves, Messrs Stenner and Gardner never heard the last of it.

It was at about this time that the crews heard that a lucky few might be able to get away on a 'swan'. Apparently, there was a plan to ferry some elderly Bristol Bombay aircraft out to Singapore; the Air Ministry having earmarked Waddington crews for the task. Unluckily for those who felt that they stood a fair chance of the job, somebody started a war in Europe and the plan was dropped.

Dave Penman, by now an established member of No 44 Squadron, really liked the Hampden. His recollection of the aircraft which was variously nicknamed 'The Flying Tadpole', 'The Flying Suitcase' or the 'Flying Frying Pan', to name but a few of the more printable sobriquets, is as follows:

"The Hampden was a single pilot aeroplane and nobody had seen fit to produce a dual control version. Our conversion to the aircraft comprised a briefing with one's Flight Commander, followed by a few circuits sitting behind him on the wing spar. Having demonstrated one landing to me, F/Lt Weir climbed out and handed the machine over to me. I found it a very responsive aircraft with excellent view all round and a delight to fly. The controls were light to the touch and the large flaps and leading edge slots gave it good slow speed handling characteristics. Perhaps most appreciated by the ex-Blenheim crews though, was the relaibility of its Bristol Pegasus engines."

No 50 Squadron had been the first of the Waddington squadrons to equip with the Hampden, their first aircraft arriving on 27 January 1939, when Hampden L4077 arrived with S/Ldr John Flemming at the controls. As OC 'B' Flight, he had collected the aircraft from the Handley Page factory at Radlett and wasted no time in commencing a training programme for the squadron pilots. As with all Hampden instructors, S/Ldr Fleming talked his way through the litany of checks and procedures, so that the 'tyro', who was plugged into the aircraft intercom system could get the gist of just what was going on.

Squadron Leader John Fleming was a very experienced pilot who had been the chief instructor at the Royal Australian Air Force (RAAF) base at Point Cook. He was 40 years of age and instilled a feeling of confidence in all his young charges. One of his first was Jimmy Bennett, to whom he not only demonstrated take-off, circuits and landings, but went on to show how to fly the Hampden on one engine, emphasising the use of the lateral trimmer. At this time, No 50 Squadron possessed five Hampdens: L4065, L4077, L4081, L4083 and L4097.

No 44 Squadron received their first Hampdens approximately one month after No 50 Squadron. In addition to converting themselves to the new type, the squadron had a secondary task; that of converting selected pilots from other squadrons to the Blenheim in readiness for their re-equipping with the Hampden. S/Ldr Ken Cook of No 83 Squadron at Scampton recalled:

"...we were to be re-equipped with Hampdens. At the time, we were flying Hinds and I for one had little or no experience with twin-engined aircraft. We had been warned that there were no dual control Hampdens, so we were to be allocated a few Blenheim Mk Is. I was given three hours dual and instrument flying, followed by a 20 minute test for solo by S/Ldr Cameron at Waddington. I was then sent on my way back to Scampton with the annotation in my log book 'Qualified to fly a twin-engined aircraft...'

It was a No 50 Squadron Hampden that had crashed near the Boultham Baths on 25 March 1939. F/O McAllister of 'A' Flight, was flying his aircraft in the Lincoln area on a routine training sortie. He came up on the R/T, requesting permission to land and was advised by Flying Control that the cloud base was 500ft and that visibility was good. At this point he gave his altitude as 3000ft, whereupon Flying Control passed him the barometric pressure setting. Having set this, McAllister corrected his height readout to 2550ft. Carrying out a left hand circuit, the Hampden was seen approaching Waddington on a heading of 160 degrees. It was seen to enter cloud as it passed over Skellingthorpe on the outskirts of Lincoln; its height being estimated to be at about 1800ft. Then, without warning, the Hampden broke clear of cloud in a steep descent, hit the ground and exploded. The cause was to remain a mystery.

In July/August 1939, a special group of Territorial Army Light Anti-Aircraft (LAA) Regiments were raised for the express purpose of defending RAF airfields. By and large, they were recruited from older men, and their area of deployment was adjacent to the area in which they lived, or as near as possible. These LAA regiments of the Royal Artillery were rotated around the regional airfields, using aerodromes which saw little action as 'rest and recuperation' stations following a spell at an airfield of high defence activity. Their primary equipment was the 40mm 140/60 Bofors gun, supplemented by Lewis guns on pole mountings. RAF Waddington was defended by batteries of No 27 LAA Regiment RA.

One of No 50 Squadron's young pilots was F/O Derek French, who was a prolific letter writer, particularly to friends and family at home in Australia. One of his letters gives an interesting insight into the rather cynical aircrew view of British war preparations.

'...every week or so, we 'flap' in our squadron. That is to say that there is some silly war scare and we go scampering around painting things camouflage, putting war code letters on our aircraft and other such activities...we recently witnessed the painting of false hedges on the aerodrome, using a black mixture of soot and linseed oil. If nothing else, the mixture produced a good crop of mushrooms...these flaps usually last for only a few days and then die out...'.

Among the No 44 Squadron aircrew was Sgt Jim Taylor, who had joined the squadron in June 1939 from the RAF Cranwell Wireless School as a Wireless Operator Air (W/Op(Air). His air gunnery training was undertaken on the squadron and included detachments to Manby, Leuchars and West Freugh. Of his time undergoing operational training, he recalled three incidents which occurred during various gunnery sorties The first involved a cow, which was accidentally hit while browsing in a field at Theddlethorpe village near the range. The second concerned a Hampden that was damaged as a result of an emergency landing on the beach at Southport (Andrew Coveyduck) - luckily the tide was out! The third incident involved a Hampden's wireless aerial being shot off, for which the offending gunner was fined five shillings (25p). It was as a result of this that the W/Op AG's gun position was equipped with a gun guide to prevent a recurrence of the incident. On recalling the months leading to the outbreak of war, Jim Taylor went on to state:

"Training was intensive both night and day. Our CO was W/Cdr Boothman and he drove the squadron hard to prepare it for what was to come. I recall flying one night as the sole 'look-out' in a Hampden with no wireless. The pilot was P/O MacIntosh and the sortie was a circuits and bumps detail. During the course of our circuits, the pilot lost sight of the aerodrome. He searched for it for half an hour without success and we were both getting very cold, as we had not bothered to wear our flying suits or boots. Totally unsure of our position, MacIntosh became very nervous about our flying near the high ground of the Pennines, so he climbed to what he felt was a safe altitude. This of course added to our discomfort, as with increasing height we experienced decreasing temperatures.

Luckily, we finally spotted the lights of another aircraft and followed it in to land we knew not where! On climbing out of our aircraft we discovered that we had put down at RAF Sutton Bridge near Boston. That night, I slept on the floor of the Wireless/Telegraphy (W/T) section. After a hearty breakfast we took off for Waddington, trying to arrive as unobtrusively as possible. We both had a vested interest in exciting the least possible attention; MacIntosh for getting lost in the first place, and me for not carrying an Aldis Lamp for emergency use. At this time, we WO/AGs, and indeed the u/t Observers (navigators), flew with the rank either AC2, AC1, LAC or Acting Corporal etc and would normally gain promotion only through our respective ground trades, but this was soon to change".

On 11 July 1939 the Station's navigators were given the chance to sharpen up their skills when W/Cdr Boothman led a formation of 36 Hampdens on a 'show the flag' trip over France. The formation was led by twelve Hampdens from No 44 Squadron; the whole formation taking off early in the morning and landing first at Tangmere to refuel. From Tangmere the route was Le Havre - Tours - Bordeaux - Angers - Caen - Beachy Head - Waddington. In all, the formation flew 1,000 miles in 6½ hours, at an average speed of 160mph. A similar, but slightly longer trip was flown two weeks later. The crews of No 44 Squadron were always happy to follow their CO. He was respected and liked, his image being somewhat enhanced when it was rumoured that he had flown with the French Air Force (L'Armee de l'Air) in World War I at the age of sixteen, and that furthermore, he had been awarded the Croix de Guerre.

Among the navigators taking part in these and other training flights, was a young man who had been among the first to join the RAF direct from civilian life to train as an observer. Alan Nichol arrived at Waddington on his posting to No 44 Squadron on 26 June 1939. He was one of ten so-called Direct Entry Observers, a new type of non-commissioned engagement which had been introduced to fill the many aircrew vacancies occasioned by a rapidly expanding air force. Following basic training, these young men attended a civilian navigation school, followed by a service bombing and gunnery course. They arrived on their first operational squadron as sergeants, though they were not awarded the coveted brevet, the flying 'O', until they had satisfied their commanding officer who would, hopefully, recommend confirming them in rank and the award of the observer brevet. Among the other Direct Entry stalwarts at Waddington were Bernard Bardega, Jack Bulcraig, Cecil Harding and Harry Moyle. Sadly, of these only the late Harry Moyle was to survive the war.

As the year progressed the political situation deteriorated rapidly. The training schedules of the squadrons of Bomber Command took on a new urgency and significance, with the young aircrews beginning to take their flying more seriously. No 44 Squadron was detached north to Leuchars in Scotland for their annual practice camp in early August, but on the 27th they were hurriedly recalled to Waddington. Four days later, on 1 September, they were dispersed to Tollerton near Nottingham; this civilian aerodrome, together with RAF Swinderby, having been taken over as Waddington satellites. The next morning some of their girl-friends motored over and in due course a convivial gathering got under way; being eventually disrupted by the order to return to base. As the girls drove home along the Fosse Way, they were escorted by the Hampdens, mostly at very low level, much to the consternation of other road users.

Gilbert Haworth, who was by now an established observer on No 50 Squadron, having moved from No 44 Squadron with the arrival of the Hampdens, was to find that even though war had not broken out, things were no longer as predictable as they had been in earlier times. The young Haworth was looking forward to meeting an attractive young Lincoln lass whom he was due to take to a dance at the Assembly Rooms in Lincoln. That day, the squadron had been tasked with providing seven aircraft for a daylight sweep over the North Sea to search for and report on any suspicious shipping activities. Gilbert had not been detailed for the operation, so watched the crews' preparations with mild disinterest. Just as the aircrews were about to leave for their aircraft, one of the Flight Commanders began berating one of his gunners who had chosen that moment to decide that he was unfit to fly. Thinking that the trip could be an interesting one and that he would be back in plenty of time for his date, Gilbert volunteered to fill in. Besides, he reasoned, it would make sure that he was not detailed for evening duties later in the day. So, grabbing his flying gear and parachute, he snatched the sick gunner's bits and pieces and ran to the Hampden, just having time to strap in as the aircraft was taxied out by an impatient pilot. Not long after taking off, Gilbert's Hampden was part of an immaculate 'V' formation heading for the Lincolnshire coast. As his aircraft was on the extreme right, he had an excellent view of the formation from his position in 'The Tin', as the lower rear gun position was more commonly known. The day was clear and warm and the formation flew at 4000ft with no need to wear the uncomfortable oxygen mask.

About 30 minutes after take-off, the coastline had faded from view and the Hampden crews concentrated on looking out for any lurking U-boats or German battleships! All went well for the first hour of the patrol and Gilbert's crew had settled into a quiet routine when the navigator suddenly shouted over the intercom to the pilot that the starboard propeller was wobbling badly. From then on things started to happen quickly. The pilot confirmed that he was aware of the situation, which was followed by the sound of the engines being throttled back. This was followed soon after by a disconcerting thud as the offending propeller broke away from the engine and struck the Hampden, leaving a large gash in the nose compartment. Flying on only one engine, their aircraft quickly lost speed and the formation started to draw away, blissfully unaware of the problem. Not wishing to be left alone to sort out the problem, the crew made several unsuccessful attempts to contact the formation by radio, but as so often happened in those days, the radio failed, leaving them very much on their own.

Their problem presented the pilot with a situation for which he was totally unprepared to handle; through no fault of his own. P/O Luxmore was a young, relatively inexperienced pilot, who had never flown the Hampden on one engine. He inevitably made the classic blunder of selecting fine pitch on the remaining engine, in the circumstances, the most inefficient setting possible. Fortunately, as the sortie had been intended simply as a reconnaissance patrol, the aircraft had not been loaded with bombs, so they did not have the added problem of 4000lb of extra weight.

Not knowing why the propeller had failed, the crew contemplated the possibility of the other one following suit at any moment. Realising that they might soon be faced with having to ditch, Gilbert Haworth unplugged his helmet from the intercom socket and moved forward to the inflatable dinghy stowage, in order to have everything ready. As he was squeezing his way forward, he went through in his mind the recommended ditching drills: Wait until the aircraft has finally stopped before hurling the dinghy pack over the side, while at the same time pulling the inflation handle. Once fully inflated, the dinghy should be boarded by the crew without delay, as the Hampden could be expected to remain afloat for only two minutes at best!

To his horror, Gilbert discovered that the dinghy stowage was empty. His thoughts regarding a crew that took off for a flight over the North Sea without a dinghy are unprintable. In view of the problems being faced by the pilot and navigator, Gilbert decided not to inform them of the additional one, but feeling the need to share the bad news with someone, he confided in the Wireless Operator. This proved to be unwise as the young sergeant panicked and in seconds had his parachute clipped to his harness and was preparing to jump from the aircraft. Reasoning that there was nothing to be gained from jumping into the North Sea at their height of 500 feet, Gilbert grasped the W/Op's harness and dragged him back from the escape hatch. Having calmed him down, Gilbert left him crouching by the exit looking pale and dejected. Returning to his station in 'The Tin', Haworth plugged back into the intercom just in time to hear the navigator saying that the nearest airfield was at Martlesham Heath near Ipswich, and that their estimated time of arrival (ETA) was in approximately 30 minutes. To the crew, this was the longest half hour of their lives. The once friendly sea looked decidedly hostile, with the noise from the remaining engine sounding more and more ominous as time went by, a situation made worse by falling oil pressure and rising engine temperature.

Eventually they crossed the coast at a height of 200 feet, passing over crowds of holidaymakers who waved and cheered, totally unaware of being at risk had the other engine failed. On sighting the airfield at Martlesham Heath, Luxmore did not bother with the standard joining procedures or circuit; instead he aimed straight for the runway and landed. Once their nerves had returned to something like normal, the crew inspected the damaged engine with a party of fitters, who explained in graphic detail just what had happened. As the aircraft required a new engine, which was not available at Martlesham Heath, the crew were transported back to Waddington by road. The final outcome to what had been an eventful day for Gilbert Haworth was to be the loss of his date; the lady went to the dance with someone else!

At the end of August, all Army and RAF reservists were called up and the Royal Navy was mobilised. RAF Waddington received its share of reservists, some coming gladly, others not so gladly. This was followed on 1 September when General Mobilisation was ordered; war was not far off! Among the reservists that reported to Waddington were some of the pre-war volunteer members of the Women's Auxiliary Air Force (WAAF). The forerunner to the WAAF, the Auxiliary Territorial Service (ATS) had been formed in September 1938. The ATS was an army territorial force and as such its members wore Khaki, even those attached to RAF units. Khaki was not a popular colour with the Air Ministry, so in May 1939 the Air Council decided that it required its own women's service. Accordingly, on 28 June 1939, the WAAF was formed. Among the many messages broadcast by the BBC on 1 September 1939 was one to all members of the WAAF, ordering them to report to their assigned units. One of the first of these ladies to arrive at Waddington was a WAAF Motor Transport (MT) driver. She was the daughter of Lord Brownlow, the owner of St Vincent's in Grantham, which had been taken over by the Air Ministry as Headquarters of No 5 (Bomber) Group, to which Waddington belonged.

Within a few days of the outbreak of war, No 5 Group received a new AOC. Air Vice Marshal A T Harris was to lead his Group in the difficult transition from peace to war and he wasted no time in visiting the many components of his new command. RAF Waddington was the first station that he visited, possibly because it was the home of No 50 Squadron, which he had commanded for a time in the First World War. On the morning of his visit, all the officers of the Station were assembled in the peace-time Operations Room, located on the top floor of the Station Headquarters building. Seating himself on a raised dais overlooking the assembled company, he surveyed the room, looking over the top of his spectacles before commencing his address. He began by saying that from then on, short of Courts Martial or accident, no resignations would be accepted by the Air Ministry until further notice. He then added a personal rider; any future social or domestic problem that brought the Service into disrepute, would result in the immediate dismissal of the offender. He (Harris) would not wait for authority from above; the dismissal would be instant. It appears that there was at least one very red face in the audience!

The new AOC's command at the outbreak of war consisted of six operational and two reserve squadrons. The operational units were Numbers 44, 49, 50, 61, 83 and 144 Squadrons. All six were equipped with the Hampden and located at Hemswell, Scampton and Waddington. The two reserve squadrons were Numbers 106 and 185 Squadrons, both based at Cottesmore. These eight squadrons were the component elements of No 5 Group on the day war was declared. The Group, together with Numbers 2, 3, 4 and 6 Groups represented the total front line force of Bomber Command. In all, the Command had at its disposal a total of 33 squadrons comprising 480 aircraft. This was a far cry from the projected 990 front line bombers, backed by a further 200 in reserve. A dynamic man, Harris set about reviewing his command within days of taking over. He was not particularly impressed with the Hampden, with which No 5 Group was equipped. He wrote a detailed letter to the C in C Bomber Command, in which he listed the shortcomings of the Hampden. This was followed very soon after by a further letter in which Harris listed in detail the major weaknesses of the Hampden's defensive armament. In his letter, he pointed out that the mountings for the rearward firing guns were flimsy and impractical; that the gunners had no idea as to the contents of their magazines once they had commenced firing, and that the guns were magazine fed which required a correct tensioning of the spring, for which there was no indication. He went on to add that the discomfort experienced by the gunners from draughts and oil leaks around the gun positions seriously degraded their ability to shoot accurately. He concluded his second letter as he had his initial one, by stating just what he intended to do to rectify the situation.In the case of the weak rearward defences, Harris introduced a doubling of the guns in both the top and the bottom firing positions. To this end, he personally approached the firm of Alfred Rose & Sons of Gainsborough and arranged for them to manufacture twin mountings for the Vickers 'K' guns, which he intended should replace the existing Lewis guns. Thus equipped, RAF Waddington and the country went to war; as before, a war that 'would be over by Christmas'.

To quote the official (contentious) history of Bomber Command:

'...when war came in 1939, Bomber Command was not trained nor equipped either to penetrate into enemy territory by day, or to find its target areas, let alone its targets, by night...'

On the outbreak of war, the Command was led by Air Chief Marshal Sir Edgar Ludlow-Hewitt, he having taken over the Command on 12 September 1937. On paper his command was quite impressive in terms of numbers, if not in quality. A study of Bomber Command's Order of Battle, three weeks after war began, shows that it possessed six Groups, excluding the five Wings of the Advanced Air Striking Force (AASF) which, with their obsolete Fairey Battles, had been sent to France on 2 September 1939.

Each of the six Groups possessed from between four to six stations, each of which housed two squadrons. As to the Command's equipment, it was a mix of Whitleys, Wellingtons, Hampdens, Blenheims and Battles. No 1 Group was in process of reforming at Benson and possessed no operational aircraft of its own. No 2 Group was spread between Wattisham, Watton, West Raynham and Wyton, with all its squadrons equipped with Blenheims. No 3 Group's squadrons were based at Bassingbourn, Feltwell, Honington, Marham and Mildenhall, with all its squadrons, both operational and reserve being equipped with the Wellington. No 4 Group was located on three stations in Yorkshire, namely Dishforth, Driffield and Linton-on-Ouse, all of which were equipped with Whitleys. No 6 Group, with its headquarters at Abingdon, was a hybrid mixture of all the aircraft types in the Command. Its stations were Abingdon, Benson, Bicester, Cranfield, Harwell,

Hucknell and Upper Heyford. Between the six Groups the Command possessed seventeen operational squadrons, seven reserve squadrons and thirteen general purpose (?) squadrons. In theory, the seventeen operational squadrons each possessed sixteen aircraft, giving a theoretical total of 242 bombers available for war. Unfortunately, a more accurate figure of effective aircraft would have been twelve machines per squadron, making 204 bombers available. To all intents and purposes the Blenheim, with its pathetically small bomb-load of 1000lb, could be ignored when considering strategic targets, thereby giving a more realistic figure of approximately 130 bombers ready for operations; not much with which to take on the might of the Third Reich!

At Waddington meanwhile, preparations were under way that had been put in hand some time before. In August the station had been brought to wartime readiness; aircraft were dispersed around the airfield, gun emplacements were sandbagged and yellow gas detectors erected all around the camp. On 1 September, Headquarters No 5 Group issued Operation Order B1 which tasked No 44 Squadron with despatching nine Hampdens to carry out bombing attacks on elements of the German Fleet. These attacks were to be undertaken on whichever day war was declared. Accordingly, only a few hours after Neville Chamberlain's melancholy speech to the nation, the nine assigned Hampden crews took off to locate and attack German naval units, reported to be off Heligoland. Meanwhile, on the Station, the Peacetime Operations Book was closed and the war Operations Book (Form 540) opened.

The flying units whose activities would be recorded in the new book were No 44 Squadron under the command of W/Cdr J N Boothman, No 50 Squadron under the command of W/Cdr L Young and 'F' Maintenance Unit Ferry Flight, under the command of S/Ldr G J Spence. Two of the Station's War Posts were activated when S/Ldr J A Tindall took over as the Administration Officer, while S/Ldr H A Stokes took up one of the newly created Intelligence Officer appointments. The Ferry Flight had been formed on 31 May 1939, its purpose being to accept and deliver aircraft to re-equip units in the Middle East. Little is known of this unit, although two of its ex-members recalled their time at Waddington. John Fisher arrived on 14 December and left two years later to the day. He was the Equipment Officer and recalled that the unit was located in the old World War I hangars on Mere Road. Apart from the ferry tasks, 'F' MU was a storage unit for signals vehicles, tractors and parachutes for use on sea mines. The other ex-member, Arthur Upton, was a Fitter/Air Gunner, serving with No 21 Squadron at Watton. In May 1939 he was detailed to join a scratch crew to ferry a Mk I Blenheim to Heliopolis via Marseilles, Malta and Mersah Matruh. The pilot was Philip Joubert de la Ferte, who was later to become C in C Coastal Command. The crew joined their aircraft at Waddington where the machine, fresh from the factory, was inspected, air tested and flown on a long cross-country. The purpose of the cross-country was to check the fuel consumption and the reliability of the overload tanks before setting off on their ferry trip, which they completed successfully.

World War One - Round Two

One of those taking part in the Station's first war sortie was F/Lt T C Weir, who recalled:

"On Sunday morning (3 September) the Station Commander, Gp Capt Cockey, told us that we would soon be mounting our first operational sortie. Later that afternoon a list appeared detailing the nine aircraft and their crews, together with their respective positions in the proposed formation. The leader was identified as **A N Other**, *as our Squadron Commander, W/Cdr Boothman was on the sick list. The rest of the formation were to be myself, Pilot Officers Penman, Robson, Sansom and Stuart; F/Sgt Cook and Sergeants Farmer and Jeffrey. During the early afternoon the ladies room in the Officers' Mess gradually filled up with girl friends who had been invted over for afternoon tea. There was a feeling of elation mixed with an air of unreality. At about 4.30pm we got the word that the trip was definitely on, and the assigned crews moved down to the Operations Room, where we were briefed and introduced to a naval officer, who told us that a group of enemy warships were reported as heading out into the North Sea. If all went according to plan we were expected to make contact with them in the vicinity of the island of Heligoland. Our naval visitor was to navigate the formation from the leading aircraft and would be also responsible for identifying our targets once we found them.*

Accompanied by the ladies, we went to the Squadron crew room, changed into our flying kit, kissed the ladies farewell and left for the dispersals. Each Hampden had been loaded with four 500lb general purpose bombs; the first time for some of us that we had ever taken off with real bombs on board. While I was sitting in my aircraft with the engines running, waiting for them to warm up, my particular friend Frankie Eustace, climbed on to my wing and wished me good luck, adding 'Don't bring your bombs back'. The way I felt then, if I had found the enemy I would certainly not have returned with my bombs. We taxied across to the north east side of the airfield and lined up in formation. The A N Other formation leader turned out to be W/Cdr Johnny Boothman, as we all knew it would be. He gave the signal and all nine Hampdens took to the air in a neat formation. It must have looked impressive from the ground; I know that leading the right hand 'vic' I certainly felt good, though I must admit to having felt a few moments of concern as I took off for the first time with a full war load of bombs and ammunition.

The weather deteriorated the further East we went, eventually forcing us down to 500ft in rain. Our formation had by then changed to line astern, but soon began to break up. My No 2 was Dave Penman and I became very concerned when I lost visual contact with him . Pressing on, we eventually ran into a thunderstorm, not long after which, we turned for home having seen nothing of the enemy. Sergeant Smythe, my navigator, was not too happy about our course because, according to his calculations, our formation would make landfall near Newcastle. He jokingly suggested that our 'naval bloke' had included the tide in his calculations.

Regardless of his humour, Smythe was absolutely right, because as we approached the coastline, seen dimly in the distance, we suddenly made a large alteration to port; eventually making good our arrival at Waddington via Skegness. As we neared the overhead we switched on our navigation lights, which was eventually responded to by the ground crews lighting the Goose Neck flares. Aided by a brilliant Moon, seven of us landed safely one by one. I was still concerned about the absence of Penman, but luckily he turned up some time later. I taxied up to the squadron hangar and, once the chocks were in place, the armourer signalled for me to open the bomb doors. Up to this moment there had been quite a crowd milling around the aircraft, looking for bullet holes and or shrapnel damage, but they all disappeared rapidly when it became known that my four bombs were still nestling in the bomb bay. Apparently the other crews had jettisoned theirs in the sea on the way home."

The missing Penman had been through some worrying moments of his own. He was the right hand man in the right hand 'vic'. He coasted out over Skegness at 2000ft, below the cloud base, saw no sign of the enemy and eventually lost contact with the formation, due to lowering cloud, rain and the onset of darkness, by which time the Hampdens were in line astern. He pressed on for some time unaware that the others had turned back. Finally, deciding that there was nothing to be achieved by pressing on, he too turned back to the West. Having been briefed not to bring the bombs back, he opened the bomb doors and jettisoned his four bombs 'safe' into the North Sea. Relieved of its load the aircraft performance improved markedly and he climbed quickly up to 10,000ft. Fortunately they broke cloud before levelling off so there was no requirement for him to fly completely on instruments. Perhaps this was just as well, because up to this time, Dave Penman had a total of only three hours and forty-five minutes night flying to his credit. Of that, only two and a half had been flown in a Hampden!

Eventually, they saw ahead of them a beacon flashing **WD** - the Waddington code. Descending slowly to 2000ft Penman could make out the lights of the hospital at Cranwell and the glow from the steel works at Scunthorpe, but there was no sign of the Waddington flare path; even the hangar lights had been extinguished. Realising that the Station beacon must have been moved to a new location, remote from the airfield, Penman flew a course between Cranwell and Scunthorpe in an attempt to locate Waddington. Someone must have realised what the problem was for suddenly there they were, the hangar lights and the Station Chance Light. A considerably relieved Dave Penman landed in the beam of the Chance Light, the Goose Neck flares having long since been gathered up and put away when he had been given up for lost.

Another member of the Waddington formation to fly that first day of the war, was Sgt Jim Taylor. On reminiscing on the days leading up to the outbreal of war and those which followed, he recalled:

"Our August camp at Leuchars was cut short and we hurried back to Waddington to be put on alert. For several days we were all confined to camp; the aircrew dressed in flying kit and the aircraft bombed up. I remember hearing Chamberlain's tired voice at 11 o'clock on that Sunday. We of No 44 Squadron were lying on our beds in full flying kit and it was in some respects a relief to know the worst. Our take-off was delayed until after 6pm because we had to wait for the reconnaissance pilot to report the position of the German fleet in person, as his radio was not working properly. Once airborne, we flew in formation with small blue formation lights dimly lit, but they were not much help in the very poor visibility. The weather was squally and cloudy near Heligoland Bight and we returned home having seen nothing. At least one of our aircraft (Penman) strayed from the formation and coasted in north of the Skegness Corridor, causing the first Lincolnshire and South Yorkshire air raid warning of the war."

So ended Waddington's first of many operations of the Second World War.

If all at Waddington expected that the first day of the war was to set the pattern, they were in for a surprise. In the early days, both sides abided by President Roosevelt's plea not to bomb civilians (sic). Consequently, Bomber Command concentrated on searching for naval targets, provided they were not in harbour. It also initiated the dropping of leaflets over enemy territory. This was a boring but dangerous pastime and was carried out throughout the period of the so-called 'Phoney War'. It was more commonly known in the service as 'Nickelling', the leaflets being termed 'Nickels'. Certainly the new AOC of No 5 Group was not convinced of their efficiency. He is quoted as having said that in his opinion it was nonsense and that all it achieved was to provide the German population with sufficient toilet paper to last them through the war. That apart, it must be said that the 'Nickel' sorties did provide an element of operational and navigation training for the bomber crews, few of whom had much experience in night flying, let alone operational night flying.

Having expressed his feelings regarding leaflet raids, 'Bomber' Harris came up with an alternative way of blooding his crews at minimum risk. He strongly advocated the dropping of sea mines in enemy waters, a subject close to the Admiralty's heart and which earned its full support. By pure chance, it transpired that the Hampden was Bomber Command's most suitable aircraft for the mine-laying role; hence the squadrons of No 5 Group were soon to find themselves the major sowers of mines By the end of the war in Europe, aircraft of Bomber Command had laid over 47,000 sea mines, resulting in the sinking of over 700 vessels. The mines all had names of vegetables, according to type, while the mined areas were names after flowers. The task of mining was known throughout the Command as 'Gardening', and within No 5 Group, was carried out in accordance with Group Operation Order No B.57. A typical entry in a Waddington squadron's War Diary could therefore read 'Three aircraft carried out successful Gardening sorties, dropping one Onion each in the Daffodil area'! On the ground, the aircrews were given lectures on Escape and Evasion in enemy territory, with most of the speakers being veteran escapers of World War I, many of them being quite well known in other fields of endeavour.

As part of the defence against surprise attack, the Waddington aircraft were dispersed, some going back to their 'scatter base' at Tollerton. However, the lack of any enemy air activity over mainland Britain early in the war, led to the Hampdens eventually being recalled to their main base. By the time they returned, the Station defences had been strengthened (!) by the presence of members of the Local Defence Volunteers (LDV), the forerunners of the Home Guard. Jimmy Bennett recalled that most of the LDV men were ex-World War I soldiers and extremely keen. Their help was invaluable in patrolling the aerodrome and bomb dump during the small hours and definitely eased the load on the groundcrews.

During Christmas 1939, Sir Frederick Handley Page presented the three Lincolnshire Hampden stations with 30,000 Players cigarettes for the aircrews. However, the Station Commander had other ideas; he presented the Waddington share to the LDV men.

The 'scatter base' of Tollerton is fondly remembered by Jim Taylor, who recalled that whenever the squadron was stood down, a liberty wagon would run the aircrews into Nottingham, where they would savour the delights of their favourite pubs, such as The Trip to Jerusalem, The Black Boy and the Salutation, all of which were destined to become 'bomber territory' for the remainder of the war. Jim Taylor, together with three of his friends, Bob Bert (WOp/AG), Ken Houghton (Observer) and Jack Little (WOp/AG), bought a 1935 model Jaguar from a local farmer for about £5, which they ran until late 1940. A rigger friend of theirs sprayed it the colours of the year - black, green and brown (!) and they 'scrounged' petrol from various sources. One strole of luck was the discovery of a small biplane that had crashed in the woods near Tollerton. It had about 20 gallons of fuel remaining in the tank which they gratefully siphoned into cans before reporting their discovery. Another useful source of illicit petrol for the car was a grounded Fairey Battle. They discovered this machine parked in a quiet corner of the airfield. Apparently it had been flying in a formation when the Battle above it got too close and its propeller chewed through the rear fuselage and the unfortunate WOp/AG.

On the flying side, the period of the 'phoney war' was used to give the Waddington crews an opportunity to improve their operational effectiveness. Whenever the crews were not on standby, they would carry out reconnaissance patrols over the North Sea, fly cross-country exercises, or undertake fighter affiliation sorties with the Hurricanes of No 504 Squadron which was based at nearby RAF Digby. Despite all this activity, there was a general feeling of anti-climax; a situation well described by Jimmy Bennett:

"...so the month of September, with its hot dry weather was a bore, only partially enlivened by alarms and excursions. Enemy ships would be reported (inaccurately) and we would be soon taxying across the airfield in 'vic' formation, only to have a red Verey cartridge fired at us cancelling the whole thing. On No 50 Squadron two things helped to ease our sense of frustration; the first was the availability of the open air swimming pool at Boultham Park, and the second was 'The Wall'! S/Ldr John Fleming was a much older and wiser man than any of us and he had his own ideas concerning the easing of tension. Having first calculated his requirements, he ordered a quantity of Lincolnshire stone from the Works and Bricks Department and had it delivered to the front of the Officers' Mess. Thereafter, whenever a false alarm and the subsequent cancellation occurred, all No 50 Squadron aircrew were required to report to the Mess where, under the supervision of a local expert, they built a traditional dry-stone wall"

This wall took six weeks of hard work to complete, but it was a job well done and still stands to this day outside the front of the Mess, a tribute to Fleming and the builders. These same builders were those who pioneered the routes to all the main targets in the Ruhr and Berlin, truly the first Pathfinders! All this construction activity was viewed with some quiet amusement by soldiers of the 6th Battalion Leicester Regiment, who had recently taken over responsibility for airfield defence from the King's Own Yorkshire Light Infantry (KOYLI). The Station was awaiting the arrival of the first RAF Ground Gunners, the forerunners of the RAF Regiment. Had they arrived however, they would have had little with which to defend the Station. A few Lewis guns were held in the armoury for Station defence purposes, but there were no rifles, these having been withdrawn in 1937 in favour of a light automatic weapon, which the powers that be had been in no position to issue before calling in the rifles!

A Hampden Crash at Waddington

In November 1939 the Standard Blind Approach System was not widely available. At the time, Waddington was the only Hampden airfield to have it installed, the system being more commonly known as the 'ZZ' System. Other Hampden squadrons had to fly their aircraft to Waddington in order to carry out the required practice approaches. On 23 November a Hampden (L4034) belonging to No 49 Squadron at Scampton, and piloted by S/Ldr P McG Watt, was tasked with carrying out 'ZZ' practices at Waddington. On board were four airmen Wireless Operators and their instructor, Corporal Keating. Visibility was poor when the practice approaches were commenced and deteriorated quite rapidly until the cloud base was nearly at ground level, almost obscuring the tops of the hangars. At the time that the visitor was carrying out his approaches, Sgt Harry Moyle, an Observer on No 44 Squadron, was standing outside the squadron W/T office, which was located in the front of the hangar.

One of the squadron's W/Ops had tuned in the signals office radio to the control frequency and was giving a running commentary, as all approach instructions by Air Traffic Control were given by W/T using the 'Q' code. The Hampden made two successful approaches and was given clearance to land each time. On the third approach the pilot was given the "Go round again" signal and Harry Moyle heard the roar of engines as the pilot opened up and turned away. Later on he again heard the sound of engines gradually getting louder, when suddenly he saw the Hampden, which was almost at ground level. S/Ldr Watt must have caught a glimpse of the Watch Office (ATC) almost in front of him, as the aircraft banked hard to starboard, just missing it. Tragically, it struck the main hangar door girders at the corner of No 50 Squadron's hangar. The building was covered in camouflage netting, which caught fire when one of the engines broke off and crashed through the roof of the Armourers' Office, killing Corporal Henderson and injuring several others who were there at the time.

While Harry Moyle was standing in the W/T office, Jimmy Bennet was talking to the squadron armourer, Flight Sergeant Martin, in the Armoury Office. The noise of the overshooting Hampden kept disturbing their conversation, seemingly coming closer each time. To Bennett, it sounded as if one approach had brought the aircraft directly over the hangar roof with little room to spare. Knowing that the visibility outside was very poor, Bennett was not convinced that all was well and suggested that they continue their conversation across the other side of the hangar if the Hampden once again passed low over the roof. The noise got louder as the machine approached once again, so the two men left the office and started to walk across the hangar. As they reached the other side the engine note became deafening and there was a resounding 'bang' as the bomber struck the roof. One of the engines fell into the office that they had just vacated!

Another airman to have a lucky escape was Sgt 'Lofty' Stenner. He was in the Link Trainer room with another pilot while the visiting Hampden was carrying out its approaches. He had not paid a great deal of attention to the noise or to what the aircraft in question was doing; he was more concerned with the Link Trainer exercises. Suddenly, without any warning, there was an ear-splitting crash and the room was deluged with aviation fuel from one of the Hampden's ruptured fuel tanks. The two pilots, their uniforms soaked in fuel, fled to the safety of the aerodrome, pulling off their uniform jackets as they went.

As soon as the Hampden crashed everyone rushed to the scene, including the young Harry Moyle and one or two other Observers. As they ran across the tarmac between two of the hangars, they were stopped by a grizzled old Flight Sergeant who ordered them to go away and have their lunch, adding that there were more than enough people available to deal with the situation. On reflection Moyle thought that the SNCO was trying to spare them the sight of the mangled bodies. In the event it was a forlorn hope, for as the young Observers turned away to go to their Mess, Harry Moyle accidentally kicked against what turned out to be a flying helmet. As it rolled away, he saw to his horror that it contained pieces of flesh and blood. On looking around them with a new sense of awareness, Moyle and his friends realised that there was quite a lot of blood and human debris floating in the puddles on the tarmac. They hurried away, and by the time they reached the Sergeants' Mess, the Station personnel had the fires well under control, this despite exploding ammunition. After the chaos and confusion had died down, 'Lofty' Stenner was leaning against the wall of a small building near the damaged hangar, talking to one of the Wireless Operators, who had miraculously survived the crash, but as they talked the W/Op nearly collapsed, so he was rushed off to the Station Medical Centre, where he subsequently died of ruptured kidneys. The casualties in the Hampden were S/Ldr Watt, Cpl Keating, AC1s McGarvie and Taylor, and AC2s Kelly and Talbot.

With the mess cleared away and the damage under repair, things on the Station quickly reverted to what had soon become normal. Most of the operational tasks consisted of sweeps over the North Sea hunting for units of the German Navy (Kreigsmarine). On 24 November No 50 Squadron was detached to RAF Wick in Scotland in preparation for a planned attack on the German battleship Deutschland. After a frustrating week of fruitless waiting, the operation was cancelled and the detachment returned to Waddington on 2 December. During this early phase of the war,

Blenheims, Wellingtons and Whitleys occasionally found and attacked enemy vessels, but the Hampdens of No 5 Group were continually out of luck. Then, on 18 December, a force of 24 Wellingtons were detailed to attack enemy ships reported to be anchored off the port of Wilhelmshaven. Unknown to the crews of the Wellingtons, they had been detected by an experimental Freya radar station located on the island of Wangerooge as they approached the target area. In the ensuing encounter with German fighters of IV/JG2, twelve of the British bombers were shot down. This disaster, coming only four days after the loss of five other Wellingtons from a twelve strong force attacking shipping in the Schillig Roads north of Wilhelmshaven, led to a reappraisal of the Bomber Command policy on daylight attacks. Unfortunately, others were to die in further daylight attacks before the Command finally switched to a policy of night bombing; though this too was subsequently to prove costly.

Blue on Blue or Friendly Fire

The morning of 21 December dawned grey and cheerless, and the workers hurrying along the streets of Lincoln to their eight o'clock deadline, looked upwards to the sky above them as their ears were assailed by the sounds of another group of workers also making for a deadline. 96 young airmen, after hurried breakfasts and urgent briefings, had climbed aboard their cold and damp aircraft and taken off into the wintry sky from their aerodromes at Scampton and Waddington. As they circled the city of Lincoln, each aircraft with its navigation and recognition lights glowing, took up its allotted station in the formation. At a pre-determined time, twelve Hampdens of Nos 44 Squadron plus twelve from the two Scampton squadrons, set course for their planned coast-out point. As the sound of 48 Bristol Pegasus engines died away, the air above the cathedral city seemed strangely quiet, as though hushed by silent, unspoken prayers from the townsfolk below. Many of the people in the city had recognised the signs; there was 'something on' and some of the Air Force lads, who nightly livened up the pubs of Lincoln, were on their way to work.

The airmen's mission was to fly across the North Sea to the southern tip of the then neutral Norway, and to then turn north and search for 300 miles along the coast in a hunt for the German battleship Deutschland. This elusive leviathan had been reported as making a bid to break out into the North Atlantic. Their somewhat optimistic order was to the effect that if found, the enemy warship was to be 'destroyed'! Only four days earlier, another German capital ship, the Graf Spee, had been scuttled on the orders of Hitler, after she was damaged in a battle with three British cruisers off the coast of Uruguay. It would indeed have been a most acceptable Christmas present for the government and people of Britain if the RAF could dispose of another of the enemy's battleships.

The Hampden bombers that were going about their business across the North Sea, were variously nicknamed by their crews as either 'Flying Tadpole', 'Flying Suitcase' or the 'Flying Frying Pan'. These names were derived from the shape of the Hampden, with its narrow fuselage, in which the four crew members were housed, together with the slim rear fuselage which in reality was simply a boom to support the tail with its twin fin and rudders. Despite these sobriquets, the Hampden was considered by its crews to be a good flying machine, particularly with regard to its manoeuvrability at low level, even when carrying its maximum bomb load of 4000lb. However, its qualities as a fighting machine had yet to be determined, though there was already an ominous question mark over the fate of a formation of five Hampdens of No 144 Squadron, which disappeared without trace while attacking German naval units in the Heligoland Bight. Rumours concerning their fate abounded: they were shot down by anti-aircraft fire; blown up by their own bombs or, according to the German version, shot down by fighters. Unfortunately, nobody really knew what had happened apart from the crews involved and they were not available for comment.

The two hour flight across the cheerless North Sea had but two highlights as far as Observer Sergeant Harry Moyle was concerned, as he sat hunched up in the lower rear gunner's position in the rearmost aircraft of the whole formation. The first was when, after they had left the Lincolnshire coast far behind, the air gunners were ordered to test-fire their guns. He always found it fascinating to watch the coloured tracer bullets curving away downwards, to end in a line of splashes in the sea. On this occasion, by the time the Vickers K machine guns had all been fired, a smell of cordite pervaded the fuselage, which somehow seemed very reassuring. The second highlight concerned food. Harry had scrounged some bacon sandwiches to augment his flying rations and, feeling hungry and in a generous mood, decided to offer a share of his extra rations to AC1 'Two Tee' Lyttle, the Wireless Operator. He hoisted himself up on to the fuselage floor, to sit between the W/Op's feet and together they enjoyed their coffee break as they flew at 180mph, with the grey waters of the North Sea slipping away 1200ft beneath them. Meanwhile above, a layer of stratus cloud stretched monotonously to the horizon all round them.

Just before eleven o'clock, 'Ferdie' Farrands, a sergeant pilot who was acting as navigator in Moyle's Hampden, called up the pilot, P/O R J 'George' Sansom on the intercom to ask if he had spotted the two coasters ahead of them. Sansom confirmed that he had and added that he was going to carry out a beat-up of one of them. Suiting actions to words, Sansom put the bomber into a dive. When the coaster flashed into view a few feet below them, Moyle, from his position in the lower gun position, could see two startled seamen looking up at them. Then, from a mast on the vessel's stern, the crew of the bomber could see a red, white and black German flag stretched out in the wind, taut and taunting. The temptation to perforate the flag with a burst from his guns was overcome with the greatest difficulty, but their orders forbade then to attack anything in or near Norwegian waters unless it was their target the Deutschland. In the latter case, it would be a matter of attacking first and answering questions afterwards.

The bomber's progress along the Norwegian coast for the next two hours passed without incident. All they spotted were a few coasters and fishing boats, all of which were studiously ignored. As the formation progressed northwards, the weather began to deteriorate, but they did get brief glimpses of snow on the higher ground. To pass the time, Harry Moyle used the expensive issue Leica camera to take shots of the scenery, if only to prove that they had been to Norway. By one o'clock in the afternoon the Hampden crews had reached the end of their assigned search area and, with mixed feelings of relief and anti-climax, turned to head for home, which in this instance was to be RAF Lossiemouth in Scotland. Though they were not aware of it, their quarry the Deutschland was safely in harbour at Gdynia in the Baltic. As the returning bombers flew back across the North Sea, the weather gradually deteriorated. At times it seemed as if the cloud base was so low that there was hardly room enough to fly between it and the mountainous waves. To make matters worse, heavy rain squalls reduced visibility to such an extent that eventually the two squadrons became separated and had to proceed independently.

After about an hour of really bad weather, the cloudbase lifted slightly and the crews were able, for the first time that day, to climb to 3000 feet, much to everyone's relief. Their morale improved even further when at about three o'clock, Sansom and Farrands, having noticed a change in the course they were following, announced to the crew that they could see land a few miles off to port and that as the new heading was northerly, they were probably on course for Lossiemouth. To Harry Moyle, there seemed little point in his continuing his seven hour squat in the cramped lower rear gunner's position, so he asked for and obtained Sansom's permission to join the W/Op in the cabin. Crawling past the feet of 'Two Tee', Moyle passed through the doorway to the forward part of the fuselage where he was able to sit in relative comfort on the wing spar behind the pilot.

Once in place Moyle lowered the armour plate extension behind the pilot's seat so that he could see what was happening ahead of them. He also opened the downwards-folding doors of the astro-hatch above his head, so that he could enjoy the approaching scenery. Ahead of them, the rest of the squadron was spread out, having given up any attempt at maintaining close formation. By this time they had less than one hour's fuel remaining and an early landing was becoming imperative. It therefore came as a great relief to hear Sansom say that he recognised just where they were and that they would be landing at RAF Leuchars in about 20 minutes. This news was doubly welcome as most of the crews were familiar with Leuchars and its personnel, having carried out their annual practice camp there just before the outbreak of war.

On their way back across the North Sea, the Squadron Commander's W/Op had sent the required recognition signals, but these had not been received and consequently not acknowledged. Unfortunately, because of the weather and other factors, their landfall had been 100 miles further south than intended, while their revised track took them north towards the Firth of Forth. By coincidence, this was a favourite route of enemy bombers attacking targets in Scotland and as a result, defending fighters were scrambled to intercept. The Hampden crews were blissfully unaware of these facts and as such were not at all concerned when three Spitfires appeared and took up position some 20 yards behind the bombers. Harry Moyle gave the Spitfire pilot behind his Hampden a cheery wave, thinking to himself what jolly decent chaps they were to come up to welcome the crews back home. After a few minutes, the leading fighter broke off and dived away, leaving two others still trailing the Hampdens. Despite the friendly waving, the Spitfire pilots made no attempt to leave or to carry out a few practice attacks, such as would have been the case with Waddington's neighbours, No 504 Squadron at Digby. Gradually this inexplicable attention and the lack of any response became rather ominous and Moyle began to feel uneasy. This unease prompted him to ask Sansom to pass him the Verey pistol so that he (Harry) could fire off the appropriate colours of the day. Suddenly, just as Sansom was extracting the pistol from its stowage, all hell broke loose; the friendly fighters had opened fire on them!

Moyle could hear the sound of their guns firing, even over the noise of the Hampden's engines, while the even louder noise of the bullets striking the bomber sounded like *"somebody was emptying a can of nails on a corrugated tin roof"*. Harry Moyle's immediate reaction was to put as much aircraft as possible between himself and the bullets. He dropped down beneath the pilot's seat to huddle against the wing root, from where he could see vicious wisps of smoke as incendiary and tracer bullets whipped into the fuselage. They were attacked by both of the remaining Spitfires; the first attacker blasted away with his eight machine guns, using up all his 2400 rounds of ammunition in three long bursts before diving away to leave the way clear for his companion to have a go. As a defensive manoeuvre, Sanson had pulled back on the control column so that the Hampden climbed steeply, making it a more difficult target for the second attacker who, after firing a few short bursts, stalled and fell away. Almost immediately, the bomber followed suit, stalled, dropped a wing and flicked into a spin. Moyle immediately scrambled back on to the wing spar to see what was happening. His first impression was that his pilot had 'bought it'. He was slumped over the control column, not moving. Realising that unless something was done pretty quickly, they would dive straight into the sea. Harry leaned over the inert pilot and hauled back on the control column. The movement caused Sansom to stir and it was with a great sense of relief that he (Moyle) saw him move. Sansom gave a thumbs-up sign as he turned his blood-covered face towards the gunner. Fragments of his shattered windscreen had cut his face, but apart from this and shock, he was uninjured and soon had the Hampden under control.

Looking out of the astro hatch, Moyle could see blue smoke streaming from both engines; the Hampden had suffered a mortal blow and all that the pilot could do was to try to ditch the aircraft safely. Ferdie Farrands emerged unscathed from his station in the nose, so Harry decided to check on the W/Op 'Two Tee'. As he turned to do so, he saw the W/Op's face framed in the window of the door. Moyle made frantic signs that he and Farrands were taking up their crash positions and that he (W/Op) should do the same. 'Two Tee' acknowledged the message, indicated that he was OK and vanished from view as he too braced himself for the impact with the unforgiving sea.

As Farrands and Moyle sat back to back on the wing spar, hanging on to the fuselage sides, the latter's main concern was that they would hit one of the rocks that he had seen sticking up through the waves. Suddenly, without any warning there was a juddering thump as the bomber hit the sea. Foolishly, Harry Moyle released his hold thinking they were down - they were not, they had simply bounced off the sea back into the air. In a matter of seconds the Hampden hit the sea once again with another mighty splash, but this time it was down to stay. The second impact had caught the unfortunate gunner unawares and he was thrown about the narrow confines of the fuselage, ending up in a dazed heap on the floor by the wireless operator's door. Water was pouring in everywhere but luckily the aircraft dinghy pack was almost under Moyle's hand. Obviously it was going to be needed, but Harry was unable to push it out of the hatch as one of Farrand's legs was in the way; the navigator was standing with one foot outside the fuselage on the wing root, while the other was still inside the cabin on the wing spar. To attract his attention, Moyle thumped him on the flying boot, but before Farrands could respond, the problem was resolved by the Hampden sinking. As it sank and Farrands drifted away Moyle managed to push the dinghy pack out of the hatch and attempted to follow it. But the clips on the front of his observer-type parachute harness caught in the downward folding door. Still struggling to free himself, Harry Moyle sank with his aircraft some 80 feet to the sea bed. As the bomber sank, the force of the inrushing water effectively prevented him from getting out of the hatchway. Holding his breath and feeling pain in his eardrums, Harry felt the Hampden (L4089) crunch to its final resting place on the sea bed. He hastily freed himself and started swimming upwards to the surface, which at first was only visible as a dark green blur above him. He was barely conscious that he was alive when he finally broke the surface and would possibly not have made any effort to remain so, if he had not heard urgent voices shouting his name. Looking about him in a dazed fashion, he spotted Sansom, Farrands and Two Tee clinging together in a huddle. As his senses cleared he realised that they were calling to him to inflate his Mae West life-jacket. In those days this aid to survival did not possess a CO2 gas bottle; the only way to inflate them being to blow them up orally; not an easy task when gasping for breath in the North Sea in winter! Luckily for him, he managed to get some air into his life-jacket before he passed out.

The aircraft dinghy had failed to inflate and Harry's three companions were some way from him when he regained consciousness. Totally at the mercy of the waves, he quite enjoyed the sensation; each wave picking him up and giving him a short ride before lowering him, to be passed on to the next wave. He felt that as a lone figure his chances of rescue or survival were remote. It was the shortest day of the year and daylight, such as it was, was fading fast. He knew that in no time at all the cold sea would penetrate his flying clothing and when that happened he would be finished. From his wavetop vantage points he had seen no sign of life, his contact with the rest of the crew having long since ceased. He knew that he was going to die, but there was no feeling of fear, only a sadness that his mother would be getting the dreaded telegram about him, and that, just before Christmas; unless of course the authorities decided to leave it until the festival was over. His past life did not flash before him either, though what would it have shown to an eighteen year old who had not seen a lot of it?

Suddenly these melancholy meanderings were stilled; a distant throbbing, which gradually increased in volume was becoming insistent. Then, there it was, only a few hundred yards away - a fishing boat. The small vessel, manned by a father and three sons of the Pearson family from North Berwick, was heading in his direction when suddenly it stopped; was it picking up the other three crew members? The boat started moving again but Harry could not decide if it was coming his way or not. He felt surely, after all this he was not going to be left behind. Summoning up all his reserves of energy he began shouting as loud as he could and waved his arms about. To his delight he saw the boat turn towards him and, in no time at all, it was almost on top of him. One of the crew threw him a line which he grabbed and held on to while he was dragged through the water to the side of the boat. The crewman with the line grasped hold of him and without ceremony hauled him over the side and dumped him in a wet soggy heap on the deck. This was followed by one anxious moment when the fisherman advanced on him knife in hand. Sensing his concern, his rescuer assured him that he wished only to cut through his collar and tie, for if he did not do so they would strangle him as they shrank; as they most surely would.

In what seemed like no time at all, the Hampden's crew were landed at North Berwick, where their arrival caused quite a stir, particularly when it was realised that they were 'RAF Boys'. On reflection, Harry Moyle felt that even had they been members of the Luftwaffe, the kindly folks of North Berwick would not have been too hard on them. As it was, they were certainly the men of the moment, the stars of the show and the centre of attraction. Eventually, they were bundled into the back of what appeared to be laundry van and driven to a nearby nursing home. Here they were led to the kitchen where, stripped of their wet clothes and draped in bath towels, they were plied with brandy while sitting in front of a cheery coal fire which blazed in an old-fashioned kitchen range. In due course an RAF ambulance arrived to take them to RAF Drem, the home of their assailants from No 602 (City of Glasgow) Squadron. The unwitting villains of the piece being F/O D Urie and P/Os Archie McKellar and P C Webb. Of these three fighter pilots, Archie McKellar had already scored his first victory when he led the attack on the first enemy aircraft, an HE 111, to be shot down on British soil. McKellar was to become an ace during the Battle of Britain, his score standing at 22 when he was killed in November 1940.

Ten Hampdens of No 44 Squadron had landed at Drem without incident. Once in the station medical centre, the Sansom crew were met by their Flight Commander, S/Ldr Watts, who said that in his opinion the whole affair had been 'good experience' for them! They had to admit that apart from the loss of their aircraft, it had not done them any great harm. Only Sansom had any injuries, even these being limited to superficial cuts about the face. However, when they enquired about the other crews, they were told that a second Hampden (L4090) had been shot down, resulting in injury to the observer, Sgt W.K.Lodge and the death of the air gunner, LAC 'Tich' Gibbin, who had tried to bail out and was killed in the attempt. The injury to Ken Lodge was a 'bruised' eyebrow, he having been hit there by either a tracer or incendiary bullet. Unfortunately, it had caused more damage than at first thought and Lodge lost the sight of that eye. The pilot and observer, P/O P F Dingwall and Sgt J.A. Reid both escaped unhurt. A few weeks later, Sgt Reid, who had been a pre-war airline pilot, was moved to Sidney Cotton's hand-picked Photographic Development Unit (PDU) at Heston, having been specifically asked for by Cotton. Shortly after joining the PDU, Reid was again shot down by 'friendly' fighters - Hurricanes of No 32 Squadron. Again he survived, though this time he suffered severe burns.

The atmosphere at Drem following the arrival of the ten Hampden crews was tense to say the least. One of N0 602 Squadron's Flight Commanders, 'Sandy' Johnstone, remembered *"The uncanny silence and an atmosphere that could have been cut with a knife"*.

On leaving the medical centre the survivors were taken to the clothing store where they were kitted out with some badly fitting uniforms. These were taken straight off the racks and had no badges or rank or brevets on them. So attired they were escorted to the Sergeants' Mess for a meal. Their arrival through the blacked-out hallway into the Mess ante room was enough to send one Flight Sergeant (Discipline) into an almost apoplectic fit. He proceeded to harangue them for appearing in the Sergeants' Mess with unclean buttons etc etc, and took some persuading that the visitors were not some of his raw recruits, but genuine bomber squadron aircrew types whose visit to Drem was not entirely intended; indeed it had been almost compulsory!

This minor domestic matter solved, they were taken into the kitchens where eggs and fried bread were prepared for them. After eating their fill the 'heroes of the hour' were offered the armchairs in the ante room, while the residents vied with one another to buy them as much beer and whiskey as they could drink. It became apparent that these trade SNCOs were still not used to eighteen and nineteen year old aircrew sergeants being around their Mess, but it was gratifying to hear a Flight Sergeant with World War I medal ribbons on his chest remark: *"They seem a chirpy lot, considering..."* There was no room in the Mess, so the visitors were assigned beds in the medical centre. Once there the combined effects of shock, seawater, fried food and alcohol resulted in the inevitable reaction! If nothing else, it ensured that they all had clear heads for the journey home the next day.

The next morning the visitors were driven to the nearest main line railway station where they caught an express train. In view of their dress they were not considered fit to be seen by the general public, so they spent the journey in the guard's van. On arrival at Grantham the returnees were met by service transport and whisked back to Waddington. An unexpected spell of Christmas leave followed, so for the survivors of the two crews, it all had a relatively happy ending. All in all however, it had not been a very auspicious operation. Apart from the misadventures experienced by No 44 Squadron, one of the nine No 49 Squadron aircraft (L4072) from the Scampton component had crashed with the loss of all on board while attempting to land at RAF Acklington. So, of the 24 Hampdens which set out on this 'Phoney War' sortie, two were at the bottom of the sea in the Firth of Forth, while a third was a mangled wreck in Northumberland. Of the 96 crew members, five were dead, one had lost the sight of one eye, while at the same time, none of the participants had fired a single shot or dropped a bomb in anger. As one of the welcoming party at Waddington was heard to remark on their return: "*Well, things can only improve...*"

The cause of all the effort, the pocket battleship *Deutschland*, had been safely in harbour in the Baltic all the time. This warship was later re-named Lutzow on the orders of Hitler, as he feared the effect on national morale if a ship named after the Fatherland were to be lost.

The Hampden as an Engine of War

On Christmas Day 1939 most station personnel were on duty - "there was a war on" - and No 44 Squadron was tasked with carrying out a sweep of the North Sea (sic). W/Cdr John Boothman AFC had recently handed over command of the squadron to W/Cdr W J M Ackerman, but had not actually left the station. Boothman persuaded Ackerman to let him have 'one more go' and accordingly led the sweep, which was carried out in formation, unfortunately finding nothing. The squadron returned to Waddington just before nightfall, each Hampden landing singly; that is except for the formation leader. W/Cdr Boothman climbed his aircraft to 3000 feet and, while crossing the aerodrome, executed a slow roll, followed by a full power climb to 4000 feet where he performed an immaculate loop. Nobody at Waddington had seen a twin engined aircraft handled in such a fashion, and in the ensuing minutes the watchers were treated to a demonstration of the handling capabilities of the Hampden, its strength and its virility. All in all it was great morale booster, coming as it did so soon after the tragedy at Drem.

Throughout December and January, crews from the two Waddington squadrons flew their Hampdens to RAF St Athan. They were told that it was to have something called IFF fitted, but were not advised as to what IFF stood for, or what it did! Their operational briefing being restricted to "You switch it on when your told to and off when your told to". This apart, the crews thoroughly enjoyed the delights of South Wales during the two days it took to install. Cardiff was not as used to the presence of RAF aircrew as were Lincoln and Nottingham and the crews made the most of it.

Despite German activity on the Continent, most of the flying carried out at Waddington until February 1940 was confined to training. As Jim Taylor, the Wireless Operator/Air Gunner (WOp/AG) recalled:

"Training by now had taken on a sense of urgency. Whenever the weather permitted, we carried out high and low level bombing, plus air-to-ground gunnery. For the latter, we went either to Hornsea or Roman Hole. There, twin Vickers 'K' machine guns would be mounted on tripods and we would blaze away at the silhouettes of German aircraft or, occasionally, at any bird foolish enough to put in an appearance. As a change, the squadron was tasked to carry out a simulated attack on Tollerton aerodrome, in order to provide the Army gunners with some practice at engaging aircraft. At the briefing for the attack, the Army briefing officer foolishly voiced the opinion that he doubted the Hampden's ability to fly as low as the German Ju 87 Stuka. Taking this to be a challenge, S/Ldr Watts led the subsequent formation so low that their propeller tips must have been virtually in the long grass. Unfortunately, the jape turned sour when the tail wheel of the Hampden (L4077), flown by Sgt Wild, struck the barrel of an anti-aircraft gun, causing fatal injuries to Army Sergeant Fretwell and injuring Gunner Wardle, both of No 53 LAA Regiment, Royal Artillery". This tragedy did little to endear the RAF to its Army brothers in arms in the Nottingham area.

On Sundays it was quite common for cyclists, mainly young girls, to come up to the aerodrome to see the young fliers. Almost inevitably, whenever they took off using the south western runway, which began at the Sleaford Road (A15) boundary, the younger pilots would hold the aircraft on the brakes, until at the word from the W/Op, they would open up to full power. If judged correctly, the result would be skirts blown over the girls' heads, a performance enjoyed by both the air and groundcrews alike. Another antisocial custom was to make a low pass over the boats sailing on the Witham at Boston, in the hope of frightening the occupants into abandoning ship. There were no reports of any crew ever having succeeded, and all they achieved was needlessly to endanger life, including their own. During the winter of 1939/40, the crews were always looking around for ways to relieve the boredom of endless 'Standbys' and sundry sudden panics, neither of which seemed to result in a take-off.

To add to the problem the weather that winter was particularly severe. Low flying practice, often in formation, was carried out at every opportunity and the consequent foolhardy practices led to several incidents. One of the Hampdens hit a wave top and both propeller tips were neatly bent at right angles, six inches from the end. In a similar incident, another aircraft shed a propeller which, as it flew off, sliced off the front of the observer's compartment. Fortunately, in both incidents, the aircraft made it back safely to Waddington. On another occasion, P/O Smith was carrying out 'circuits and bumps' when he had the urge to show off to this parents who lived near Kettering. He and his crew le3ft the circuit and on arrival at the parental home, proceeded to beat up the village in some style. On their return they were met by a reception committee, consisting of S/Ldr Watts and other menacing figures. Apparently, the Smith's neighbour had telephoned the Station Commander to say that he had lost part of his shrubbery; adding that although he was quite happy to watch young Smith kill himself, he had no desire to join him. Leaves sticking out of the engines provided irrefutable evidence of 'the crime' and Smith was duly grounded. This lasted for only a few days as the squadron was very short of operational aircrew.

The Hampden's rather feeble defensive guns were normally loaded with ammunition in the sequence, incendiary, tracer, armour piercing and three ball. The armourers maintained the pilot's fixed machine gun and the bomb bay, while the air gunners cleaned and serviced their own guns and looked after the electronics. This they did as part of their routine 'Daily Inspection' (DI), as well as undertaking the necessary air tests. The crews frequently used the nearby range at Theddlethorpe in the Wash, where they fired at a drogue target towed by a Fairey Battle. Each gunner had to dip his bullets in a different coloured paint, thereby enabling several gunners to fire at the same target. The hits were counted from the smudges of red, blue, green etc which were found on the drogue. On one noteworthy occasion, one 'Fiji' Stanley was so busy changing the ammunition pans of his Vickers 'K' machine gun, which were stacked between his feet, that he missed the Battle pilot's 'wing-wag' signal which indicated that they were now out of the range safety area and all firing should cease. With new, full magazines clamped to his guns, Fiji promptly opened up when the target came into his sights. At the time the drogue was between his Hampden and a village, which was liberally sprayed by 0.303" bullets, killing a cow and badly frightening several range workers. Despite their age and sedentary occupation, these worthies displayed a fine turn of speed as they headed for the safety of the bunker, which also took a few hits.

It became the practice at Waddington to man the upper guns of any Hampden parked on a dispersal whenever there was an air raid alert. Jim Taylor's Hampden KM-P was parked adjacent to the bomb dump near the Coleby/Sleaford crossroads. In the event of an alert, Jim had to double across the aerodrome to his aircraft - there was never any transport to spare for such activities. His problem was that not only did he suffer interruptions to his sleep, followed by the physical discomfort of galloping across the aerodrome, but also that he did so at the risk to life and limb. One of the LDV picquet was a Lascar seaman, who was in the habit of challenging everyone. In itself this was no bad thing, apart from the fact that he was stone deaf and could not hear the password, even when it was correct. Accordingly, following his challenge, he would open fire! After a few very near misses, he was either pensioned off or issued with a hearing aid.

From the very earliest days of the war, the RAF bomber crews used German radio beacons to assist with their navigation. Those at Borkum, Sylt, Aachen and Kiel were great favourites and the crews would practice switching from one to the other, even during air tests. By judicious use of the loop aerial it was possible to obtain an accurate position if a quick switch could be made from one beacon to another. But, as the operation was manual, constant practice was required to remain proficient. Aircraft callsigns were changed daily and the crews were given a list of them together with the appropriate frequencies, all printed on edible rice paper. In the event of an emergency or being likely to end up in enemy hands, the crews were briefed that they were to ensure that the pages were eaten. In addition, the aircraft were equipped with Verey light cartridges corresponding to the German colours of the day; though these were for use in extremis. At low level over an enemy aerodrome or flak ship, the correct signal was always likely to make the gunners at least hesitate; or so it was said!

The WAAF

The Women's Auxiliary Air Force (WAAF) was activated on 28 June 1939, with the express purpose of "...releasing men for operational front line duty and to assume a wider and more active role within the Service itself..." The uniform and rank badges were to conform to those of the RAF, and the trades available initially to women were armourer, balloon operator, parachute packer, bomb plotter, electrician, plus flight, instrument and MT mechanic. In time, as the war dragged on, the range of trades and duties were to be considerably expanded. During the war, members of the WAAF were to be found in almost all sections of the Station. Among the early arrivals was ACW Nora Townsend, who arrived from Cranwell in October 1939 along with nineteen other girls. Their proper uniforms were not ready when they left Cranwell, so they arrived at Waddington wearing a WAAF shirt, a navy blue skirt, black shoes, black tie, navy blue beret complete with cap badge; the whole topped off by an air force raincoat.

It soon became obvious to this first batch of WAAFs that the Station did not know what to do with them. Their first WAAF officer was the daughter of Air Marshal Leigh Mallory, though they saw little of her. Nora was sent to work in the Sergeants' Mess as a stewardess, alongside the civilian staff, all of whom treated the WAAFs with great respect, calling them all 'Miss'. They were billeted in Newall House, the old Officers' Mess, which had been superseded by the new larger building in use to this day. The Station gradually got used to having women about the place and romance was continually in the air. The first Station Dance after the arrival of the WAAF was held in January 1940, Miss Leigh Mallory having given her permission for the girls to wear dresses because their proper uniforms had still not arrived. However, in true service fashion, the arrival of the WAAFs in the Service as a whole, resulted in a proliferation of orders detailing the regulations covering the conduct and behaviour of all personnel, ending in a range of implied threats about what would happen to any transgressor!

Another of the first WAAFs to arrive at Waddington was an ex Fire Service Sub Officer, Wyn Clark. She too recalled that on arrival the girls found no dedicated WAAF accommodation, no suitable shoes or great-coats, and a general atmosphere of unpreparedness for the arrival of a batch of young women. Wyn Clark was to serve in the telephone exchange at Waddington for most of the war, reaching the rank of sergeant.

❖❖❖

4. From Phoney War to Real War

By the end of 1939, mobilisation was well under way, though people had begun to call it 'The Phoney War', as little of any significance had occurred. However, the war was far from 'phoney' to the men of the Royal and Merchant Navies. To them, the real war began on 3 September 1939. Following their first war sorties flown, rather inconclusively, the Waddington crews settled into what was generally assumed to be the wartime routine. Most of their flying was still training of one sort or another, occasionally interspersed with North Sea sweeps, still hunting for the elusive German Navy (Kreigsmarine).

Most of the bomber pilots of the RAF were young, junior officers, the majority of which were, or had been, on peacetime short service commissions. These young inexperienced pilots were to some extent carried by the older regular officers and SNCO pilots, many of whom began their service careers as Halton Apprentices (Trenchard Brats). The observers, wireless operators and air gunners were, in the main, ex groundcrew tradesmen, though the first of the direct entry observers (navigators) were begining to arrive in some numbers. Scattered among all aircrew categories, particularly among the pilots, were volunteers from the old Empire or Commonwealth, who had joined an expanding Royal Air Force during the last months of peace.

Despite the high quality of the training in the peacetime RAF, the problem, all too soon to be tragically demonstrated in the crucible of war, was that it was just that - peacetime training! Little thought and even less practice had been given to appreciating just how different it would be in war, flying against something more lethal than a camera or an umpire. As Guy Gibson stated in his book 'Enemy Coast Ahead', no Hampden crew at RAF Scampton had ever taken off in a Hampden with a full bomb load before the outbreak of war; of which the same could be said of the Waddington crews - through no fault of their own. Similarly, none of the pilots had any experience of landing at night under operational conditions, with or without a full bomb load.

As to navigation, there were few if any answers to the problems posed by a requirement to fly over a blacked-out enemy country and find the target. The answers to these and many other questions would be found in time by the front-line crews of Bomber Command, and paid for in blood.

Among the stalwarts of No 44 Squadron was S/Ldr Watts, one of the Flight Commanders. Watts was a regular officer with experience gained in the undeclared war on (they were informed) the North West Frontier of India. A typical (sic) regular officer, Watts was always immaculately turned out, punctilious and very correct. However, he did slip up on at least one occasion, following an opening briefing by the Squadron Commander, W/Cdr Ackerman. Watts assumed the the Wing Commander had left the briefing room immediately after concluding his address. Accordingly, he (Watts) opened his own presentation of the detailed procedures by saying in effect: "Don't take the Wing Commander's comments too literally". Whereupon, the CO stood up from tying his shoelaces and quietly invited Watts to call upon him in his office after the briefing!

One of the first pre-war members of the Royal Air Force Volunteer Reserve (RAFVR) groundcrew to report for duty was F T Thurlby. He had been called up prior to the outbreak of war and was already on duty when war was declared. One of his first tasks at Waddington was to drive a tractor towing bombs out to the Hampdens, many of which had been dispersed in the fields on the far side of the Lincoln to Sleaford road (A15). During the weeks following the declaration of war, the frequently changing requirements meant that Thurlby became very familiar with the remote, widely dispersed sites, as he trundled back and forth with different loads. Occasionally, before the section of the A15 that adjoined the aerodrome was closed to the public, some of the trailer loads of bombs were towed along this active road at night! This practice caused more than a little consternation to passing motorists and cyclists, who would suddenly come upon this train of death, moving slowly along the road, illuminated only by the dim lights of their semi-blanked out headlights.

Another member of the ground personnel at Waddington during the early days of the war was AC1 Rowland, an armourer. He and his friend Cpl Stevenson were detached from Farnborough to Waddington on the day war was declared. Corporal Stevenson owned a car and the two airmen were given permission to use it to get to the Lincolnshire base. As they neared Waddington, they were stopped by a police constable who informed them that there was a suspect aircraft in the vicinity, and that their headlights were too bright;

this despite their having stuck brown paper across the lenses. In deference to the law, the two stuck a second layer of brown paper over the headlamps, leaving barely one half-inch diameter hole from which to illuminate the road. Having satisfied the guardian of the law, the two airmen proceeded on their way, made all the more hazardous by their virtual lack of light. Eventually they came within sight of Waddington, easily identified by its flashing beacon, which lit up the sky in the vicinity of the aerodrome! On reporting to the guardroom, they were informed that there was no accommodation available for them that night. Accordingly, they were directed to a hut, situated on the far side of the aerodrome (naturally!). Their overnight accommodation proved to be that used by the Local Defence Volunteers (LDV); later to be re-named Home Guard. The LDV detachment used the hut as their combined HQ and guard post. Most members of the LDV platoon were veterans of various Colonial wars or World War I and they made the two young men very welcome, passing the time by regaling them with stories of the Boer War, the Boxer Rebellion and the Great War. None of these reminisencies did much for the two airmen's peace of mind on this, the first day of their war.

The actual purpose of Cpl Stevenson and AC1 Rowland's detachment was to install an Air Ministry Laboratory Bombing Teacher. The task took them about one month to complete, but by the time they left the Station, they had one quite a few shillings in competitions with various pilots and observers, in practice bombing exercises in the Teacher.

On the outbreak of war, the two southernmost of the new hangars were occupied by No 44 Squadron, while No 50 Squadron occupied the two northern ones. The hangar to the rear was used by the partly civilian Aircraft Storage Unit (ASU). In the case of No 44 Squadron, their briefing room was to the right of the central fire doors of what is currently No 4 hangar. It was kept extremely warm throughout the year by a number of parafin heaters, as it housed the aircrew flying clothing. The Hampden's cockpit heating system was notoriously ineffective and the crews were always at risk from frostbite. Getting airborne in damp flying clothing would have been asking for trouble, hence the room temperature.

Following the unrewarding sorties during the first weeks of the war, the days passed alternating between training flights, ground training, standby duties and the occasional sweep over the North Sea. When on standby, the crews would spend much of their time in the briefing room or their crew room. Some would read the latest Air Ministry publications, while others would pass the time playing cards, reading Men Only, or writing letters. On the odd occasion that an 'Alert' came down from Group Headquarters, the squadron commander and the flight commanders, Squadron Leaders Norris and Watts, would arrive and give details of the proposed sortie. Their briefings would include such things as the name and type of the target, the bomb load, routing, the recommended attack direction, and the allocation of aircraft to crews. There would be particular emphasis on the tactics to employ should they be attacked by enemy fighters (sic). There would be also detailed coverage of the safe return lanes to Waddington, which crossed the east coast at either Cromer or Skegness. Further information would follow covering such factors as fuel management, WT procedures and the bearing and distance to selected diversion aerodromes. The latter to be used if for any reason a crews was unable to land at Waddington on their return.

Once the crews had been fully briefed, they would be confined to the briefing room and were allowed no contact with anyone who was not scheduled to take part in the operation. This condition would remain in force until take-off or until the Alert was cancelled, which happened more often than not. From time to time, the alarm would sound, sending the crews rushing out to the waiting transport; usually lorries at this stage of the war. Encumbered as they were with flying kit, navigation bags, pigeon carriers, helmets, rations, sextants etc, the scene would be little short of chaotic. On arrival at their aircraft, each crew would waste no time in boarding, particularly if it was raining. The engines would be started, warmed up, checked for 'mag drop', after which the aircraft would be taxied out to the marshalling point.

After all this, all too frequently, the operation would be cancelled and the crews either returned to the briefing room or be stood down - until the next time. During these early days of the war there was no such thing as mass attacks by large formations. Invariably, each crew made their own way to the target, quite often never seeing any other friendly aircraft, even in daylight. Later on, once heavy daylight losses had forced Bomber Command to switch to night attacks, the procedure became even more 'ad hoc'. To again quote Gibson, crews were often left to decide their own route and take-off time, within certain limits. In one instance, Gibson wrote of his crew electing to take off late in the evening so that they could take in the early evening show at a cinema in Lincoln! Another crew decided to go early in order to be able to make it back in time to get into Lincoln before closing time!

Despite their AOC's reservations, the two Waddington squadrons opened the New Year by carrying out two leaflet raids on 11/12 January. No 44 Squadron despatched two Hampdens to Hamburg, while No 50 Squadron sent two to Bremen. Each aircraft dropped 324,000 leaflets or 'Nickels' as they were more commonly called. Air Marshal Harris of course, felt that mine laying was a far better way of giving his crews operational experience, and in this he had the full support of the Admiralty. Eventually, the Air Council would come to agree with him and this soon supplemented, and in time almost replaced 'Nickelling' as a training vehicle for new crews, who also felt that this was a more worthwhile task than the dropping of leaflets. Indeed, such was the feeling of frustration at dropping only paper on enemy territory, that some crews resorted to dropping the weighty bundles unopened, in the hope that they might at least break a skull or a greenhouse!

On 1 February, elements of Nos 44 and 50 Squadrons were detached to RAF Lossiemouth in Scotland for two weeks, with the crews being rotated every two or three days. The purpose of the deployment was to enable the Hampdens to range further afield in their searches for the elusive German battleship the Deutschland. After two fruitless weeks, the detachment returned to Waddington as a thirteen aircraft formation. Three days later, on 17 February, No 44 Squadron crews were placed on Readiness 1 Hour, for operations against the German pocket battleship Graf Spee's auxiliary supply ship, the Altmark. As before, nothing came of it. Indeed, the only definite contact made with any real or possible enemy vessels during the early weeks of 1940, was by a No 50 Squadron aircraft flown by F/Lt Jimmy Bennett on 10 February. Flying in Hampden L4062 with Sgt Potts (a pilot) as his observer, Bennett was carrying out an anti-shipping sweep off the coast of Denmark. The other two members of the crew were Sgt Fawcett as the W/Op air gunner and Sgt Woud as the lower gunner. Observing a large vessel sailing parallel to the coast, some 20 miles off shore, Bennett descended to sea level and circled the ship, which was carrying no identification. The crew were well aware of the recently issued Air Ministry rules of engagement with regard to unidentified shipping - they were allowed to attack only if fired upon. Obtaining no response from the vessel, the crew of the Hampden turned reluctantly for home.

In March, command of the Station passed to Gp Capt C T Anderson DFC. Among the many personnel on the Station who were sorry to see Gp Capt Cockey leave, was 'Lofty' Stenner's W/Op air gunner, Sgt Bake. This worthy was forever getting into one sort of trouble or another, resulting in frequent appearances before his Station Commander. Apparently, Sgt Bake knew that the Group Captain was an ardent motoring enthusiast and used this knowledge to his advantage. On one memorable occasion, he was seen leaning on the Station Commander's desk debating some finer point of motor racing, while supposedly there on a 'charge'!

During February and March, three No 44 Squadron crews had been detailed to undertake practice mine-laying on a simulated stretch of canal at the nearby Coleby Meadows. The eventual intended target was to be the Kiel Canal, and the leading exponent of accurate mine dropping, proved to be P/O Smythe. Meanwhile, the two Waddington squadrons, together with others in the Command carried out more of the despised leaflet raids. Among the defects that were highlighted when flying the Hampden under operational conditions, was the previously mentioned heating system. On 20 February, Corporal W Crooks was flying as the W/Op AG on a leaflet raid on Bremen. On his return he reported that while carrying out a successful 'Nickel' drop, he experienced problems with the intense cold. It was so intense that his fingers became so stiff that he could neither hold a pencil nor operate his morse key. At one point, while attempting to adjust his radio receiver, a blast of cold air struck him in the face and, on blinking, he found that one eyelid remained firmly closed. He had to use air from the hot air pipe to free (thaw out) his eyelid. Some time later he either dozed off or passed out from the cold; whichever, on regaining consciousness he found that both his eyelids were firmly glued shut. Fumbling for the hot air pipe, he eventually located it and succeeded in freeing both eyelids.

Feeling that he could not tolerate much more, he called his pilot on the intercom and asked if they could descend to a lower and, hopefully, warmer altitude. Later, despite being at a lower height, Crook found that the controls of his radio too were frozen, requiring applications of hot air to free them. By this time he was experiencing severe pains below the right knee. Deciding to ask the lower gunner, another W/Op AG, LAC Simpson, to take over the radio, he tapped him on the shoulder with the toe of his boot. On his (Simpson) looking up, Crooks could see that he looked as miserable as he felt himself, so he did not have the heart to make his request. Eventually, after what seemed an eternity, they reached Waddington. After landing, his right hand was found to be badly frozen, so the Medical Officer took him to Sick Bay where they thawed out his hand using cold water and massage. Three months later, on 25/26 May, Cpl Crooks was killed in action flying with S/Ldr C E Johnson on an attack on Borkum in support of the British Expeditionary Force (BEF). Soon after this, the Air Ministry decreed that the minimum rank for a member of aircrew was forthwith to be Sergeant.

Although the Hampden crews were happy with their aircraft, they became only too well aware of its weeknesses. A heated pitot head did not become available until until late in 1940, hence, during the winter months of 1939/40 it was quite common for the pitot head to freeze up, rendering the airspeed indicator useless. Similarly, the Kilfrost anti-icing paste did not become available until the end of 1940. This paste was the only form of protection against icing up of the leading edges of the wings, unlike their opposite numbers, the Ju88s and He111s of the Luftwaffe. Their aircraft were equipped with heated wing leading edges before the outbreak of war. Consequently, the build up of ice on the leading edges of the wings of the Hampdens when in icing conditions, was an ever present danger and, probably, many crews were lost as a direct or indirect result of it. In severe cumulo-nimbus cloud icing conditions, a Hampden was reputedly capable of taking on its own weight of ice in little over ten minutes. Another weakness was the Hampden's fuel tanks. These were made of aluminium without any form of armour plating or rubber sealing. Hence even the smallest hit in a fuel tank could have grave consequences. Equipment weaknesses apart, one of the main problems for pilots flying the Hampden was the phenomenon known as 'stabilised yaw'. Basically this was not so much an aircraft problem as a pilot problem, particularly for new, relatively inexperienced pilots. The Hampden possessed very small keel surfaces aft and any coarse use of the rudder, coupled with insufficient bank, was likely to convert a flat turn into a potentially fatal sideways skid. This would render the ailerons useless, thereby preventing any increase in the angle of bank, while at the same time locking the rudders hard over, due to the strong sideways flow of air against them. One pilot who found himself in this situation was, at the time, over Berlin at night! He reported that even with both feet on one rudder pedal, he was unable to move it. His control column was slack, the ailerons ineffective and the aircraft was descending rapidly. In desperation, the pilot throttled one engine right back while at the same time opening up the other engine to full power. This 'brute force and ignorance' solution worked, but only just in time.

In February, aircraft of Bomber Command were increasingly engaged in 'Security Patrols'. The purpose of these sorties was to patrol off the German seaplane bases, most of which were either on the coast or located on some of the islands off the North German coast. Once the assigned seaplane base had been located, the patrolling bomber would drop the occasional bomb on the take-off lane; the aim being to keep the seaplanes confined to base. It was from these bases that the enemy seaplanes took of on their mine-laying sorties over the coastal waters of Britain. It was while returning from one of these sorties on 17 March, that Hampden L4063 crashed into Cocklaw Foot in the Cheviots killing the crew. That same day, while attacking Royal Navy ships in Scapa Flow, German bombers dropped bombs on land, killing one civilian working on an airfield and seven others in a nearby village. The War Cabinet immediately ordered Bomber Command to carry out a reprisal raid on one of the German seaplane bases *"Provided that there is no civilian property nearby"*. The target chosen was the seaplane base of Hornum on the southern tip of the island os Sylt, off the west coast of North Friesland. According to the Operation Order, the crews were to aim for the hangars, slipways, oil storage tanks and the Hindenburg Dam. The two Waddington squadrons each despatched five Hampdens, the total force comprising 30 Whitleys and 20 Hampdens. The attack was pressed home in the face of heavy anti-aircraft (flak) fire and numerous searchlights. One Whitley was lost, but all the Hampdens returned safely.

First to bomb were the Whitleys, which had been allocated a four hour bombing period. The Hampden force was allocated a two hour slot and fifteen of the 20 crews reported that they had bombed accurately. This raid was the first real bombing operation for either the Whitleys or the Hampdens of Bomber Command. The combined force dropped a total of 20 tons of high explosives and 1200 incendiaries. (Note: Post-war research indicates that some of the attackers bombed the neutral Danish island of Bornholm in the Baltic Sea by mistake!).

Among the crews taking part in the attack on Hornum was that of F/Lt Jimmy Bennett of No 50 Squadron. For his part in this attack, Bennett was awarded the DFC for: "*...the precise and efficient way he carried out his attack...*" This, the first attack on German soil, was given full coverage in the British press and on the radio. The famous American correspondent, Ed Murrow, and the lesser known F B Bates, both interviewed Jimmy Bennett following the attack, the result being broadcast to America by CBS and their rival NBC. During the recorded interview, Jimmy Bennett stated:

"On Tuesday (19 March) we got the orders for which we had been waiting for a long time. We had been carrying out training sorties and security patrols for some time and we all felt that it was about time that we were given the chance to make good use of the knowledge and experience we had gained. I am not saying that the security patrols were not exciting or well worthwhile, but they were rather monotonous. We simply used to go over to the German seaplane bases in order to make them keep their lights out, thereby preventing them from operating effectively. You see, as long as any of our aircraft were in the vicinity, they would consider it too dangerous for them to illuminate their take-off lanes. In this way, we prevented the seaplanes from taking off to lay mines in British waters. But even if the monotonous nature of the task was relieved by the odd burst of flak or a searchlight beam, we still felt that all we were doing was simply making things difficult for the German flyers. I feel that every one of us on those patrols would have welcomed the chance to take a crack at the foe. So, when we got our orders to proceed to the island of Sylt and carry out attacks on the seaplane base itself, everyone felt that at last we were going to get some of our own back. The weather was about the best we had experienced since commencing the security patrols.

We took off in moonlight and flew out over the North Sea. After about forty-five minutes we ran into low cloud and rain showers, which persisted for some 30 minutes before the cloud lifted and partially cleared. Thereafter we flew the rest of the way to the target area below cloud and in reasonable visibility. The Germans no doubt thought that it was the usual security patrol and that we had no intention of being any ruder than we had on previous visits. Whatever they thought, they took the usual precaution of activating their blackout plan. We identified the northern end of Sylt while approximately five miles out to sea and turned southwards. On arriving at the southern tip of the island we turned inland over it and flew north. As we flew across the coast of Sylt we could see the lights of Esbjerg, a town in neutral Denmark. At this time we were flying very low, soon turning eastwards towards Germany. As we neared the mainland we ran into anti-aircraft fire, but it was not very effective. We again turned towards our target and climbed to our assigned attack height. We were now ready to carry out our attack.

We approached the seaplane base and, as we got closer, we could see a slipway at the edge of the water. We dived towards this feature and released our four 250lb bombs. On hearing my observer call "Bombs Gone", I turned away from the target and continued my dive to sea level. I saw the flashes of our bombs as they exploded and my W/Op AG told me that he saw them hit the slipway. I immediately turned out to sea and set course for home feeling well satisfied. During our attack the flak guns had opened fire, but although the barrage was fairly intense it was neither accurate nor effective. We knew that some of the shell bursts were quite close because we could feel the concussion, even though we could not hear them.

The Germans must have had an extremely uncomfortable time of it while the attack was in progress and I should think that they began to wonder when it was going to end, as it went on for six hours in all. We crews are pretty used to these long flights by now and when we were all talking about the raid afterwards, I think that we felt that the German gunners and searchlight crews were probably a lot more tired than any of us. It was not until we had all landed safely that we realised just how tired we were, but we all went to bed with the satisfaction of having done the job required of us. It was not a big show as shows go, but it was a good show and a promising start".

While the raid on Hornum was taking place, the Secretary of State for Air, Sir Kingsley Wood, dramatically cut short his speech to the House of Commons to announce that: "*...at this very moment our aircraft are dropping bombs on Sylt...*" Among the Waddington crews taking part in addition to Jimmy Bennett, were S/Ldr Watts, F/O French, Pilot Officers Crossley and Eustace, and Sergeants Harbourne and Jeffrey. In order to ensure that his attack was accurate, French had made two runs over the target before releasing his bombs.

While the aircrews were taking the war to the enemy, other events were taking place on the ground at Waddington. Among the routine, mundane but nevertheless essential duties performed by the non-flying personnel, was that of administration and accounts. The Station Accounts Officer was P/O Petchell-Burt, a local lad from nearby Wellingore. For an accounts officer, he was somewhat unique in that he was quite popular with the aircrews, who used to fly him from time to time. Later in the war he remustered to aircrew and was subsequently killed in action during an attack on Berlin. On a less dramatic note; the WAAFs were finally issued with complete uniforms. Another among the ground crews was Arthur Jacklin, who had volunteered to join the RAF on the day that war was declared. He recalled one afternoon in March when a Hampden was carrying out an air test.

The test over, the bomber came into land, at which point the starboard undercarriage collapsed, leaving the aircraft stranded in the middle of the aerodrome. As operations were scheduled for that night, the obstructing Hampden had to be cleared away. The collapsed wing was raised using a Coles crane and lowered on to an empty oil drum positioned under the wing and padded with airmens overalls! When preparations were complete, the wing was lifted off the oil drum and repositioned on to the top of a fuel bowser, to which it was fastened by ropes. Then, with tractors attached to both aircraft and bowser, the combination began its journey to one of the hangars.

Unfortunately, the notorious Lincolnshire fog came down and none of the working party were quite sure which way to go. Eventually, one volunteer left on a bicycle in order to locate the hangar. Once there he climbed up to the roof and periodically fired off a Verey cartridge. This ad hoc method proved successful and the party successfully made it to the hangar. Another crash involving a Hampden was potentially far more dangerous. The aircraft, flown by Sgt Clayton, was being ferried back to Waddington from Finningley. On selecting undercarriage down, it failed to function and no amount of manoeuvring or emergency drills could free it, so Clayton elected to carry out a forced landing. The landing was almost copy-book, but before the Hampden came to a halt, it burst into flames. The crew abandoned their aircraft without delay, but the wireless operator's flying clothing caught fire. Seeing this, Sgt Clayton knocked his friend to the ground and rolled him in the grass to smother the flames, saving his crewman from serious injury. Not long after this incident, Sgt Clayton was promoted to Flight Sergeant.

Yet another crash caused more than a few smiles, when a Hampden flown by P/O Quicke overan the grass aerodrome and ended up embedded in the rear of George's Cafe. Among the resulting damage and minor injuries was that suffered by George himself, who lost what few teeth he had left. When Quicke visited George to apologise (!) his (George) comment was to the effect that at least he would not have to go to the b— — dentist again.

On a more serious note, Hampden L4102, flown by Sgt S A Williams and crew, failed to return from a security patrol in the area of the Elbe Estuary on the night of 25/26 March

Following the German invasion of Norway and Denmark in April, Bomber Command was ordered to do what it could to slow the rate of the enemy advance in Southern Norway, while a joint British and French expeditionary force landed at Narvik in the north of the country. This was a task for which the aircraft of the Command were singularly unsuited. Any attack from Britain involved a round trip of approximately 1000 miles, flown almost entirely over the sea, thereby making accurate navigation almost impossible. The other major weakness, one that was to prove fatal, was that the distances involved meant that there could be no posibility of fighter escort.

On 9 April, aircraft from Waddington formed part of a force of 24 Hampdens, tasked with attacking enemy ships in the Bergen area. The subsequent recall was heard by only twelve of the crews, all of which returned to base. The remainder pressed on, two of which later claimed to have bombed a cruiser. All the Hampdens returned safely, though the Waddington element landed all over eastern Scotland due to a combination of fuel shortage and bad weather. The following day, W/Cdr R T Taafe took over command of No 50 Squadron from W/Cdr Young. That same day all Station personnel were pleasantly surprised at the receipt of a signal from the C in C Bomber Command, in which Air Marshal Sir Charles Portal said:

"Please convey to all ranks in your squadrons my warm appreciation of their operation against Bergen yesterday. The resolution and skill of the crews in finding their objective and pressing home a successful attack in the face of heavy fire, is worthy of the highest praise, especially as they had been kept at instant readiness all day, prior to take-off. That all aircraft should return safely after a thousand miles over the sea is evidence of the high standard of maintenance in your unit. The whole operation reflects great credit upon you and all ranks under your command".

The First Heavy Losses

The blood-letting that Bomber Command was to experience for most of the war came early to Waddington. As part of their continuous patrols and attacks on airfields and shipping around the coast of Norway and into the Baltic, a composite force of twelve Station Hampdens was briefed to attack enemy shipping on 12 April. Led by S/Ldr Watts of No 44 Squadron, their prime target was the enemy battle cruiser the Hipper, together with its cruiser escort, all of which were reported to be steaming towards Kristiansand. The alternate target was specified as any ship, merchant or otherwise, under way or at anchor. The twelve bombers took off at 0820hr, intending to make a landfall at Lister Fjord. Among the crews detailed for this attack were those of S/Ldr Good, F/Lt Rogers, F/Os Donaldson, Robson and Taylor, P/Os Bull, Homer, Johnston, Pilcher and Thomas, and Sgt G M Wild. The weather over the North Sea en-route to the target area was 10/10 very low cloud and heavy rain. As the formation neared the Norwegian coast, the sky cleared and the crews found themselves flying in bright sunlight and unlimited visibility S/Ldr Watts decided that if the enemy warships were in the area of bad weather, there would be no chance of finding them, let alone carrying out an attack. Accordingly, he ordered the formation to climb to 9000 feet, divide into four sections of three aircraft each and to fly parallel to the coast searching for any shipping targets.

Each Hampden was carrying four 500lb semi-armour piercing bombs, and as such needed to be at least 9000 feet in oredr to maximise the bomb's effectiveness. When approximately 20 miles from Kristiansand, some shipping was observed in the bay. S/Ldr Watts elected to attack these ships, well aware that the vessels own anti-aircraft defences would certainly be supplemented by those on the nearby shore. Before attacking, Watts led his formation in a sweep of the bay in order to identify just what vessels were present and which should be designated as targets. In the centre of the bay two large cruisers lay at anchor, so Watts nominated these as the primary targets. Doubtless he hoped to emulate the successful attack on the enemy cruiser Konigsberg by Skua dive bombers of the Fleet Air Arm two days earlier.

The Hampdens bombed in sections of three in line astern, all four sections carrying out their attacks at the same height and on the same heading. This resulted in the combined anti-aircraft fire from the ships and the shore batteries becoming increasingly more accurate as successive sections ran in to bomb. At about the time that the first section was releasing its bombs, enemy fighters were sighted closing in on the formation. Calling a warning to the following crews, S/Ldr Watts put the nose of his aircraft down and dived to sea level, accompanied by the other two Hampdens of his section. As this first section descended and headed for the open sea, the second section was making its bombing run. By this time, the German gunners had accurately assessed the range and height and soon began to hit the attacking aircraft. F/O W G Taylor in L4099 was hit and badly damaged, but managed to complete his attack and dive for the sea. Unfortunately, the damage to his aircraft meant that he was unable to keep up with the other two aircraft of his section and he soon became isolated. In no time at all he fell victim to the Bf109s of II/JG77 and was seen to crash into the sea in flames. The W/Op AG in another Hampden later reported as having seen L4099's upper gunner, Cpl Harold Brown, still firing his guns as the blazing bomber hit the sea.

The next aircraft of the second section to be attacked by the fighters was that flown by P/O Homer. He was flying in KM-B (L4074) and his Hampden was badly damaged by cannon and machine gun fire from the Bf109s. One cannon shell passed through his cockpit without exploding, missing his head by less than six inches. Other cannon shell hits did far more damage; one blowing a large hole in the starboard wing, while another destroyed the port engine oil tank. In addition, there was a rash of machine gun bullet strikes on the wings, fuselage and nose section. During the attacks, the W/Op AG, Cpl Caldicott shot down one of the fighters, thereby making the others keep at a respectful distance. Taking violent evasive action, Homer opened up to full throttle and endeavoured to close up on his section leader, F/Lt Rogers. With mutual protection, Rogers and Homer then closed up on S/Ldr Watts section, their rear gunners reporting that the aircraft of the third section were attempting to join them.

Despite accurate heavy flak, the three Hampdens of the third section managed to complete their attack without suffering apparent damage. But, as they endeavoured to join up with the leading sections, they were attacked by fighters. F/O Robson's aircraft (P1173) was hard hit and set on fire. Other crews reported seeing the dreadful sight of flames streaming back from the fuselage out of the open upper and lower gun positions. Inevitably, the Hampden fell away and crashed into the sea. The next to be hit was L4064, flown by P/O Bull of No 50 Squadron. Though not badly damaged, the Hampden had been hit in the fuel tanks and was steadily losing fuel. Despite the damage, Bull managed to join up with his section leader, S/Ldr Good, whose gunner, Cpl Wallace, had also sent a fighter down in flames. Together, these two aircraft succeeded in joining up with the other two sections.

Not one of the three No 50 Squadron aircraft of the fourth section survived. First to go down was Sgt Wild; hit by flak. His bomber was seen to go down almost vertically and explode on hitting the sea. Next to fall was Hampden L4081, flown by P/O Thomas. His aircraft was shot down by fighters as he tried to catch up with the leaders. The W/Op AG in Thomas' aircraft was Cpl Barrass, who had been 'borrowed' for the mission from Derek French's crew. The third aircraft of this section, L4083, flown by F/O 'Weasel' Donaldson, was unable to catch up with the retreating leaders, this despite opening up the engines to Emergency Full Power. Alone, he stood no chance. Repeated attacks by the Bf109s reduced his Hampden to a blazing wreck. With his lower gunner dead and his W/Op AG badly burned, Canadian Donaldson crash landed his still burning Hampden on a small island off the Norwegian coast. Donaldson and his remaining crew members survived the landing and were rescued by Norwegian fishermen. Before their eventual capture, they made several spirited attempts to escape, including an attempted take-off in a Bf109 that had made a successful landing in a field having run out of fuel during the attack on the Hampdens. But that is another story!

Fortunately for the remaining seven Hampdens, the enemy fighters had to break off their attacks due to fuel and ammunition shortage. But for this, it is doubtful if any of the Hampdens would have survived. As one of the surviving pilots stated at the debriefing: *"It could only have been a matter of time before they shot the lot of us down"*. Heading back across the North Sea, the Hampden flown by P/O Homer began to suffer the after effects of flying at full power for too long using a damaged engine. The port engine, with desperately low oil pressure began to overheat. Realising that his chances of making it back to Waddington were slight, Homer elected to divert to the nearer RAF station at Acklington; landing there at 1535hr.

The remaining six aircraft pressed on, but when only 100 miles east of Newcastle, P/O Bull was forced to 'ditch', having run out of fuel from his damaged tanks. S/Ldr Good circled the crippled Hampden as Johnny Bull carried out a successful ditching. The battered Hampden remained afloat for some time and the crew were seen to abandon the aircraft and board their dinghy, carrying their injured gunner with them. Sgt Nevinson, the lower gunner, had been hit in the leg during one of the fighter attacks and had been in considerable pain for some time. Safely settled in their dinghy, the crew waved cheerfully to the circling Hampden, while S/Ldr Good transmitted an SOS. It was a mild, fine day and it seemed that a successful rescue would be mounted in no time, especially as the emergency service reported back to S/Ldr Good that they had got an accurate fix of his position. Though satisfied that the crew would be soon picked up, Good remained over them as long as he could before setting heading for base.

Back at Waddington, the Hampdens were expected to land at about 1400hr. So, some time before this, most of the aircrew who had not been detailed for the attack, made their way out to the flight line to await the returnees. There had been some surprise that no message had been received from the force since take-off. No sighting report report had come in, nor had any other communication, causing some of the waiting crews to suggest that all was not well. By 1430hr it was obvious that something was indeed amiss and the aircrews were joined by a crowd of groundcrews and other off duty personnel, all asking anxiously if there was any news. Then, there there they were, three Hampdens in loose formation.

One after another the three aircraft flew low over the aerodrome before breaking downwind to position for landing. The onlookers all moved to the first machine to taxy in, eager to hear what had happened and to enquire as to the whereabouts of the other aircraft. The W/Op AG of S/Ldr Watts aircraft was the first to speak as he slid back the canopy over his gun position. In a shaking voice he said that he thought that they had got one, but one what was not specified. The rather puzzled crowd did not know what to make of this; that was until the rest of the crew vacated their aircraft. Then, another crew member exclaimed: *"We ran into fighters! Jerry jumped us in the target area; the others didn't have a chance*". By the time the fourth crew climbed from their aircraft, it seemed apparent to all that there were no more to come, though in fact, S/Ldr Good had yet to leave the Bull crew and make his way home. The news that one had diverted to Acklington and another had made a successful ditching, was seized upon with some relief, but nothing could ease the shock of realising that five crews had been lost. That night there would be 20 vacant places in the messes. These were not strangers, they were friends, team mates on the rugby, football and cricket pitches; drinking partners on pub crawls in Lincoln and Nottingham and, worst of all, longstanding colleagues of the peacetime air force. As one or two of the older hands commented: "*At this rate the old regular air force will soon cease to exist.*"

Among those who took some comfort in thinking that it was just one of those things - an incredibly bad piece of luck, were a few who were to survive long enough to experience the scale and magnitude of the losses that were to be suffered by the crews of Bomber Command in the forthcoming five years of war.

After the initial shock over the losses, there was a rush of volunteers to provide overhead cover for Johnny Bull and his crew until such time as they were rescued. One of the first to take off was Sgt 'Lofty' Stenner of No 50 Squadron. He and his crew wasted no time in getting airborne in their Hampden (L4164), followed soon after by a No 44 Squadron Avro Anson trainer. This machine was flown by P/O Crossley, together with his observer, Sgt Harry Moyle. Neither of the searching aircraft managed to locate the dinghy and the hunt was called off reluctantly at last light. The next morning, Hampdens and Ansons from both squadrons were airborne at dawn, as was a Hudson of No 220 Squadron of Coastal Command. The Hudson crew found the missing fliers and remained circling them until midday. On their return the crew of the Hudson reported that the survivors were showing signs of distress. By this time, feelings at Waddington were running high regarding the apparent lack of any effort to effect a rescue.

The Station aircraft involved in the search deployed north to RAF Thornaby near Middlesborough, in order to be closer to the search area, but they failed to locate the dinghy and its occupants. One of Waddington aircraft taking part was an Anson (W5193). Flying from Waddington, Sgt 'Snub' Pollard, together with a volunteer crew, took off loaded with emergency supplies of food and survival equipment. It was Pollard's stated intention to ditch (!) alongside the dinghy and render whatever assistance they could until help arrived. Following a lengthy search, Pollard located the dinghy, but there was no sign of the crew. Descending to very low level, the crew of the Anson searched desperately for some sign of their friends. Finding nothing, they sank the dinghy by gunfire and set course for base. Soon after crossing the coast near Grimsby, the Anson's engines started to misfire. It is probable that Pollard had forgotten that the Anson did not possess the endurance of a Hampden. Realising that he was not going to make it back to Waddington, Pollard elected to make an emergency landing on a deserted road. Unfortunately, during the landing run, the Anson swung off the road and crashed, injuring all members of its crew, including Pollard, who lost an eye.

Not satisfied that all possible assistance had been forthcoming, the Station Commander, Gp Capt Anderson, made formal representations on behalf of his angry crews. In due course they were told that the sea at the time was too rough for an Air/Sea Rescue launch and that as the dinghy's reported position placed it in the middle of a minefield, the Royal Navy would not risk a larger vessel. Sadly, Johnny Bull and crew were not destined to be the last Waddington crew to find their final resting place under the cold grey waters of the North Sea.

It is believed that as a result of this tragedy, members of No 50 Squadron developed an air droppable set of survival equipment. By the time that it was formally accepted by the Service, the squadron was based at RAF Lindholme; hence its title 'Lindholme Gear'.

With five aircraft out of twelve having been shot down, plus one lost at sea and another forced to land away, Gp Capt Anderson decided that something more comprehensive than the standard intelligence debriefing of the crews was called for. All members of the surviving crews were called upon to give a full report and to add their own comments. Among the most telling reports was that of P/O Homer and crew. In his report, Homer stated:

"...anti-aircraft fire was intense and accurate, and during the bombing run my aircraft was rocked severely several times by near misses. Immediately after dropping my bombs, I took violent evasive action. At this time I saw nine Bf109s just inland of Kristiansand, all climbing rapidly. I immediately opened up to full throttle in order to catch up with my section leader, who was himself moving into box formation on the leading section. At that moment, I saw the aircraft of my No 2, F/O Taylor, losing height slowly, with the pilot slumped forward over the controls. Soon after this the fighters attacked him and he hit the sea in flames. I eventually got into formation with my leader and almost immediately, S/Ldr Watts led us down to sea level. At this time there were eight in our formation; S/Ldr Watts' Section, S/Ldr Good's Section, F/Lt Rogers and myself. When we reached sea level, Rogers moved out to the left of No 1 Section, while I remained outside him in the No 3 position, on the extreme left of the formation. I saw one aircraft of No 4 Section trying to catch up with us, but it was shot down in flames before he could reach us.

By this time, we were flying at 210mph and under constant fighter attack which continued for a further half hour. I estimate that there were twelve Bf109s, one of which in particular attacked me initially from dead astern, breaking away to the beam as soon as my upper gunner, Cpl Caldicott, returned fire. This same fighter then attacked from the port quarter, coming in very slowly in a gentle dive with his propeller just ticking over. He came in from an angle just outside the arc of fire of the rear guns, firing continuous bursts with his cannon and machine guns, sweeping my aircraft by lowering his nose. One cannon shell hit the right wing between the roundel and the outer fuel tanks.

The shell exploded inside the wing causing considerable damage to the internal structure. Also, it blew quite a large hole in the top of the wing and ten or more smaller ones in the bottom. Another cannon shell exploded inside the port engine oil tank, making a large hole in the top of the tank, thereby causing considerable loss of oil. Yet another shell came through the open astro hatch, passed over my armour plating and exited the fuselage, six inches behind my head, without exploding, leaving a hole about three inches in diameter. The cannon shells were observed (!) to not explode on impact, but to have a slight delay.

We experienced various hits by machine gun fire, one passing through the port aileron, one in the port engine cowling, two through the prespex in the navigator's station, which must have entered near the tail before exiting beside the bombsight. The fixed aerial was shot away. At some stage, the fighter broke away across our tail and Cpl Caldicott (W/Op AG) put a burst into it. Flames were seen to come from its engine and I am certain that it was destroyed.

After 30 minutes, the enemy broke off their attacks and left us. I had then to throttle back as my port engine was losing a lot of oil. The rest of the formation went on ahead, leaving us to continue alone at reduced speed. With the loss of oil, my port engine was running very hot and I did not want to overtax it. My observer obtained two good fixes and at 1512hr we made landfall at Holy Island. I decided to divert to Acklington, where we landed at 1535hr."

Having studied all the crew reports and inspected the damage to the Hampdens, Gp Capt Anderson arrived at several conclusions, which were duly passed on to the Air Ministry, and copied to the crews involved. In his report, Anderson concluded that it had been a mistake to bomb in line astern, at the same height and on the same heading. He went on to add that the formation leader should have collected all his aircraft and formed a defensive formation as quickly as possible. He (Anderson) felt that the wide 'vic' formation, flown at very low level on leaving the target area was ill-advised. All it achieved was to render the lower gun position inoperative, as the lower gunner was unable to bring his guns to bear. Similarly, the wide 'vic' formation meant that those aircraft on the flanks were subject to individual attacks without the benefit of mutual support from other Hampdens in the formation. Another point highlighted by the Station Commander in his report pointed out that by being at very low level, the formation was unable to carry out any steep turns. Had they flown higher, at around 200 - 300 feet, with the bombers in a box formation, they would have been more manoeuvrable. He added that a further advantage of flying higher would have been that the enemy fighter pilots would not have found it so easy to use 'bullet splash' on the sea as a guide to the accuracy of their deflection shooting.

Gp Capt Anderson's report went on to observe that some of the enemy fighters had attacked by flying parallel to the Hampdens until slightly ahead, at which point they turned in to carry out a beam attack, against which none of the Hampdens' guns could be brought to bear. This latter point came as no surprise to the crews, most of whom had long been aware of the Hampden's defensive fire deficiencies. Indeed, before the outbreak of war, articles had appeared in the aviation magazines *Aeroplane* and *Flight*, showing sectioned side elevation diagrams of the RAF's newest bomber. Doubtless the fighter pilots of the Luftwaffe had studied them and worked out that the Hampden was virtually defenceless against a beam attack. The contention by certain pundits in the Air Ministry that the Luftwaffe pilots were not competent enough to carry out accurate beam attacks, had been received with more than a little scepticism by the crews of Bomber Command. The performances of the German pilots of the Condor Legion in Spain, not to mention that of the Luftwaffe in Poland, did nothing to support such a crass claim. Post attack examination of, among other things, bullet and cannon shell holes in the Hampdens provided ample evidence that beam attacks had indeed taken place, and accurate ones at that. The 'experts' went back to their drawing boards and the installation of beam gun positions was proceeded with as a matter of urgency, though the quality left something to be desired.

Despite the heavy losses and the failure to hit any of the German warships, it had not been a completely one-sided battle. The War Diary of II/JG77 records the loss of four Bf109s and their pilots during the air battles of 12 April 1940. A fifth fighter made a forced landing and was written off ('Weasel' Donaldson doubtless had a hand in this). Two months later the Fleet Air Arm was to suffer equally heavy losses, when its Skua dive bombers attempted an unescorted attack on Trondheim in Norway. It seems that some lessons just have to be learned the hard way!

For their part in the action at Kristiansand, Acting Corporal Coldicott of P/O Homer's crew, and Corporal Wallace of S/Ldr Good's crew, were both awarded the Distinguished Flying Medal (DFM), the first to be awarded to any No 5 Group aircrew members. A further DFM was awarded to Sgt Pilot J Clayton, who had been flying as a navigator on this operation, in accordance with Bomber Command policy at the time. The purpose of this was to give pilots straight out of training, some operational experience before having a crew assigned to them. Sgt Clayton, flying in Hampden L4154, could see the German fighters coming in on the undefended beam, so taking his Vickers 'K' machine gun from its nose mounting, together with some drums of ammunition, he crawled to the hatch behind the pilot; no mean feat in itself under normal conditions, let alone while under attack. On opening the hatch, he stood up in the full force of the slipstream and fired the cumbersome gun from the shoulder, in order to discourage the fighters from making their beam attacks. Some years later, this gallant feat had a sad postscript. Later in the war, Clayton was shot down and became a prisoner of war (PoW). Following his repatriation at the end of the war, he was delighted to be posted back to RAF Waddington. After enjoying a good lunch in the Sergeants' Mess, he sat down in an armchair for a nap and was found later to have died from a heart attack.

The Station had barely come to terms with the losses over Kristiansand, when another sad loss occurred. On the night of 13 April, F/Lt R J Cosgrove, the son of the Premier of Tasmania, took off in Hampden L4065 on a mine laying sortie. His was one of fifteen Hampdens tasked with laying the recently modified naval Mk I magnetic sea mine. With his mission completed, Cosgrove set course for base. The Hampden was picked up on radar as it approached Mabelthorpe, but it then inexplicably disappeared from the screen. No trace of the aircraft or its crew was ever found.

The success of the German campaign in Norway and Denmark, had given added impetus to the development of a British sea mine that could be delivered by air. By coincidence, the German successes in Scandinavia coincided with the 1500lb air dropable magnetic mine becoming available. An ugly weapon, it was given the nickname 'vegetable'. It was a large device, carrying an explosive charge weighing 750lb (340kg). In 1940 the Hampden was the only Bomber Command aircraft capable of carrying this latest weapon in the air/sea war. The air-dropped mine had a parachute attached to prevent it from breaking up when entering the water, having been dropped from a height of between 400ft and 1000ft, at a speed not exceeding 200mph. The action of the seawater activated a release mechanism, which separated the parachute from the mine. The availability of the 'M' mine initiated a campaign of mining of the enemy coastal waters and harbours, which was to continue throughout the war.

On the night of 13/14 April 1940, a force of fifteen Hampdens, including that flown by F/Lt Cosgrove, each planted one magnetic mine off the coast of Denmark, thereby initiating Bomber Command's mining campaign. Six of the crews were from Waddington and, apart from Cosgrove, were flown by the crews of S/Ldr Weir (44 Sqn), F/Lt Bennett (50 Sqn), F/Lt Dutton (44 Sqn), F/O Corr (50 Sqn) and Sgt Smythe (44 Sqn). Of these, only Cosgrove failed to return, though F/Lt Dutton was shot down a few days later and became a PoW. Sgt Smythe was to go on to be a highly valued member of his squadron until being killed in a low level attack on Bremerhaven docks on the night of 11/12 September 1940, while flying in Hampden P1338. By the time of his death in action, he had been commissioned, promoted to the rank of Flight Lieutenant and awarded the DFC. F/O Corr survived his time on Hampdens, subsequently being killed in action piloting a Lancaster on the daylight attack on Le Creusot.

Mining Operations

As was stated earlier, mining operations were given the codename 'Gardening', with the mines being described as vegetables. Later, specific mines were alloted the names of specific vegetables. The mining areas too were given agricultural code names. In the main, the various areas were named after flowers, shrubs, fish or the more exotic vegetables. Among the earlier mining areas were the Baltic Sound (Daffodil), the Elbe Estuary (Eglantine), Kiel Bay (Quince) and North Heligoland (Yams), to name but a few. In general, Gardening was considered to be less hazardous than attacking enemy land targets. That is not to say that it was without dangers, as F/Lt Dutton and crew were to find out ten days after taking part in the first mining operation.

On the night of 21 April they took off in Hampden L4088 as part of a 36 strong force tasked to drop mines in the Kattegat. Having completed his timed run in to the drop point and released his mine, Dutton commenced a climb. As he did so, he saw what he took to be the lights of a fishing fleet dead ahead. Considering this to be 'a self-evident target of opportunity', Dutton dived to attack them using his two wing mounted 250lb bombs. Unfortunately, the fishing boats were in fact flak ships, which proceeded to fire everything they had at him. Badly damaged, the Hampden, with one engine out of action, could barely maintain height.

The crew could see the lights of neutral Sweden beckoning like a beacon off the starboard wing, but resisted the temptation to head for them. Rather than risk a forced landing in the dark in unknown territory, Dutton elected to make for neutral Holland, intending to put his aircraft down on a beach. As they struggled along over the sea, the crew jettisoned everything that could safely be removed from the aircraft. Despite their best efforts, the bomber was still unable to maintain height. Eventually, the battered aircraft just slid on to gently rising ground, not far from the German naval base at Kiel. As the Hampden skidded along, the upper gunner reported that he could see pieces breaking off and disappearing into the night. Once the bomber came to a stop, the crew tried to evacuate it, but the lower bulkheads had collapsed, jamming the escape hatches. By energetic use of the crash axe and some deft footwork, the crew extricated themselves from the wreck only to step into the arms of some jubilant German troops. For Dutton and his crew it was the start of five years as PoWs (Kriegies). Sadly, the W/Op AG, Cpl Watson, was to be killed in March 1945 while being marched in a PoW column from one camp to another. He was among 50 PoWs killed when the column was straffed by RAF Typhoons.

Another crew who were to experience the very real hazards of mining, was that of S/Ldr Good of No 50 Squadron. On the night of 4/5 May they took off to lay their mine in the approaches to Oslo harbour (Onions). On reaching their planned timing point, from which they would commence a timed run to the designated drop point, S/Ldr Good set course flying just above the waves. The Hampden was picked up almost immediately by the German defences which laid a curtain of medium and light flak across his approach path. In addition to the defensive fire, Good had also to contend with the blinding light coming from the numerous searchlights directed at his aircraft. An experienced pilot, the Australian Good had undergone his baptism of fire during the attack on Kristiansand, being one of the five to make it back to Waddington. Pressing on towards his drop point, Good kept his Hampden as low as he dared, but despite this he was unable to escape the defenders' fire. Just before reaching his release point his aircraft was hit repeatedly by a burst of either 20mm or 40mm flak shells. S/Ldr Good was struck several times by fragments from the exploding shells and by pieces of his aircraft. Hit in the face, with his right arm broken and his left wrist torn open, Good had great difficulty in controlling the damaged Hampden. He was unable to call for assistance as the aircraft intercomm system had been put out of action. With both arms badly injured and with blood pouring from the wound in his face, Good was rapidly losing control of the machine. In the nose compartment, his observer, P/O W G Gardner, himself a pilot, concentrated on releasing the mine in the designated spot, totally unaware of the grievous injuries suffered by his pilot.

Following the release of the mine, the change in trim caused the nose of the bomber to drop. Unable to use his arms to pull back on the control column, the by now barely conscious Good felt completely helpless. Through the fog of pain he realised that their only chance was the trimming wheel. With both arms useless, Good managed to hook one finger in the wheel and slowly work it back, initiating a gradual climb. He then commenced kicking the rudder pedals from side to side in an attempt to attract the attention of his crew. Initially, the crew thought that this was evasive manoeuvres and took little notice. It was not until the Hampden almost struck the mast of an anchored ship that Gardner wondered if all was well. Switching on his cockpit light, he was horrified to see a growing pool of blood in the tunnel under the pilot's seat. Scrambling up through the blood spattered tunnel, Gardner managed to get to the well behind the pilot's seat and to stand up. One glance was enough to tell him that Good was very badly injured. A quick glance at the airspeed indicator and altimeter spurred him into action. Reaching past the wounded Good, he grasped the control column and pulled back on it, while at the same time pushing the throttles fully forward. As soon as they had reached a safe height and had moved out of range of the flak, Gardner throttled back the engines and trimmed the bomber for straight and level flight. This accomplished, he then struggled to undo Good's blood soaked seat and parachute harnesses. Having achieved this, Gardner had to then lower the back of the pilot's seat. In the Hampden the released rear of the pilot's seat overlapped the well in which Gardner was standing, so it was with great difficulty that he managed to wriggle over it and to crawl over the recumbent Good. Having accomplished this he had then to sit on his badly injured companion while he flew the aircraft, while at the same time trying to attract the attention of the other two members of the crew. Eventually, newly promoted Sgt Wallace, another survivor of Kristiansand, realised that something was wrong and worked his way back to the well. As he stood up with difficulty in the confined space, he could see that the cockpit resembled a slaughterhouse, with blood everywhere.

With considerable difficulty, Wallace managed to drag the injured Good from under Gardner, but could not get him clear of the rear of the seat. Leaving Good with his head resting on the main spar, Wallace ducked down to the lower gun position and indicated to Sgt Smith that he needed assistance. Together, they managed to get Good into the well and to then raise the back of the pilot's seat. By the light of a torch Sgt Wallace inspected Good's injuries. One arm was bleeding profusely, so Wallace improvised a tourniquet and succeeded in stemming the flow of blood. To ease the pain while he tried to deal with the other injuries, Wallace gave the wounded pilot a morphine injection in his leg.

Covering Good with their Irvine jackets, Wallace and Smith made him as comfortable as possible before Wallace attended to his other wounds. The injuries were enough to daunt the most hardened doctor; there was a hole in one cheek, the tongue was torn, while part of the nose was almost severed. In addition, several teeth were broken and Good managed to indicate that he had swallowed a couple of others. Despite his injuries and the injection, S/Ldr Good remained conscious throughout the return trip. Rather than make the injured man suffer the long return trip to Waddington, Gardner elected to land at the much nearer station of RAF Kinloss near Inverness. Good survived despite his wounds, thanks to his crew and the dedication of the Scottish surgeons who attended him. Both he and

Gardner were awarded the Distinguished Flying Cross (DFC).

These were the early days of Bomber Command's mining campaign and the Hampdens were to continue to perform this role right up to their withdrawl from front-line service with Coastal Command in December 1943. In modern parlance, mining was to prove a most cost-effective activity. Though not headline material, and largely ignored by the press, it forced the Germans to allocate a considerable proportion of their war effort to countering the mine threat. In addition, they were forced to allot scarce resources into building replacements for the shipping lost to mines. By the end of the war in Europe, 40% of all German naval personnel were engaged in mine-sweeping and related activities.

The Station Commander

On the Station itself, the new Station Commander, Gp Capt C T Anderson DFC was making his presence felt. Toar Anderson was something of an enigma. A pilot in the First World War, he limped as a result of the injuries he had suffered to his left leg. The injuries prevented him from flying as a pilot, so he would often fly as an observer or air gunner with crews from the two squadrons on his Station. In the years before the outbreak of war, Anderson had been a Wing Commander on the staff at Air Ministry. It was while here that it is thought that he provided Winston Churchill with classified information regarding the true state of the nation's air defences. Churchill would then use these accurate figures to discomfort government ministers, who knew only too well that they were indeed correct, despite their protestations to the contrary. Not popular with all at Waddington, he was considered by the majority to be a first class leader, if sometimes inclined to be irascible and unpredictable.

Jim Taylor recalled Anderson flying in their crew as lower rear gunner on an attack on Hamburg on the night of 17 May 1940. On landing back at Waddington, the elderly Group Captain had to be lifted bodily from 'the tin', suffering acute cramp caused by the cold. Despite this, Toar Anderson continued to fly on operations on an 'as and when' basis. F/O Mike Lewis, a Canadian flying on No 44 Squadron, recalled that when he (Lewis) was declared tourex and posted on to the staff of Station Headquarters as Link Trainer Officer, he actually spent much of his time flying as unofficial staff pilot to the Station Commander. Whatever the truth or otherwise concerning Toar Anderson's pre-war activities, Lewis noticed that during a visit to the Station by Winston Churchill in early 1940, the two men spent a considerable time together - alone!

Indicative of Anderson's irascibility was his reaction to the actions of two Hampden pilots. In June 1940, a No 50 Squadron pilot, Derek French, was injured by pieces of shrapnel from a near miss while carrying out a low level attack on the railway junction at Eindhoven in Holland Despite his injuries, French flew his aircraft back to Waddington, passing out as he climbed out of the bomber. In a stormy interview, Anderson upbraided French for flying too low over occupied territory. A few days later, the Station Commander was to repeat his somewhat strange behaviour when S/Ldr Oxley of No 50 Squadron returned from an attack on Hamburg. On 19 June, Oxley was one of five Waddington crews detailed to attack Hamburg. Despite his feelings that it was immoral to carry out an act of war on the Sabbath, Oxley completed a successful attack on an oil installation. Ten days later he was detailed for another attack on Hamburg. As Oxley recalled:

"We were mostly very young men entrusted with lethal cargoes, so there was tight political and military control over us. Bomber Command was constrained at the time by the politically motivated target policies of SEMO (Self-Evident Military Objective) and that of MOPA (Military Objective Previously Attacked)".

These seemingly bizarre regulations were introduced in June 1940 following revised government instructions to the Air Ministry regarding the need to minimise civilian casualties. In essence they made some improvement to the lot of the bomber crews, many of whom died unecessarily in attempting to land a badly damaged aircraft, still with its bombs on board. Prior to the introduction of SEMO and MOPA, crews were required to return to their base with their bombs if they were unable to identify their assigned target. The introduction of these new regulations at least enabled crews to achieve something useful with their bomb load, in the event that the planned target could not be attacked. To continue S/Ldr Oxley's story:

"On the night of 29 June, I was briefed to bomb a particular warehouse in a particular street in Hamburg (sic), that particular warehouse and nothing else... ...on this occasion our take-off had been delayed until almost four hours after all the other aircraft had departed... ...we crossed the enemy coast just before dawn and proceeded inland to the target, much too late to have any real chance of surviving their defences. I therefore decided instead to attack the German aerodrome on the island of Sylt. As we approached the sea-plane base, we were fired upon by the aerodrome's flak batteries. The base had been attacked before, so it was clearly (to me at least) a MOPA. However, in view of the intensity and accuracy of the Sylt flak, I decided on another change of target, this time taking on the Hindenburg Dam, which carried the railway line across the mudflats to the island of Sylt. To me this was an obvious SEMA which, in any case, was miles away from any civilian property. On my return to Waddington I submitted my post-attack report and was promptly placed under arrest by the Station Commander, who considered that I should have brought my bombs back. Following communications with HQ No 5 Group, the official report stated that the bombs had been 'jettisoned in the sea'."

Operations Continue

Sergeant V A 'Ginger' Coveyduck had been posted from No 44 Squadron to a Crew Training Unit in March 1940 'for instructional duties'. This did not appeal to him, feeling that he was avoiding the war, so he applied to return to his old squadron. Doubtless as a result of mounting losses, his request was approved; so following a navigation course at RAF St Athan, he returned to Waddington at the end of April. On his return to the fold he was anxious to hear what had really happened at Kristiansand and the survivors were only too willing to tell him. Some time later, following the announcement of the award of a number of DFCs and DFMs for the action, one of the Orderly Room sergeants was overheard to express the opinion that they were being given away; he was very lucky to escape severe injury.

'Ginger' Coveyduck had noted that the air gunners were taking their job much more seriously than they had done before the war. He recalled that not long after his return, during a training session on the 400 yard range at Catfoss near Beverley, a large flock of seagulls flew across the butts, resulting in twelve Vickers 'K' machine guns blazing away at them; without one feather being disturbed! In May, Coveyduck made a number of trips to the Handley Page factory at Radlett. Here, their Hampdens were fitted retrospectively with self-sealing fuel tanks. On one of his visits, Coveyduck, flying as navigator, together with his crew witnessed the Handley Page test pilot, Major Cordes, looping a Hampden. This obviously impressed his young Canadian pilot, F/O Dave Romans, because on the return trip Coveyduck noticed that Romans was steadily gaining height. Tactfully, it was pointed out that if the navigator thought that the pilot was going to try a loop, he, the said navigator would bale out. The idea, if such it was, was forgotten.

On 1 May, a combined force of Hampdens from the two Waddington squadrons carried out two simultaneous separate attacks. One formation headed for the aerodrome of Fornebu near Oslo, while the other proceeded to Aalborg, an aerodrome in northern Denmark. Despite intense flak and numerous searchlights, the attack on Fornebu was pressed home with each Hampden dropping its load of six 250lb bombs, one of which was fused to explode on impact. The other five had been fitted with delayed action fuses. None of the attackers were hit and all returned safely to base. Meanwhile, the four Hampdens tasked to attack Aalborg, carried out another successful attack, led by Jimmy Bennett The crews had been briefed that Aalborg was being used by the Germans as a staging post for Ju52 transport aircraft, engaged in ferrying troops to Norway. The aim of the raid was to crater the runway and to destroy the fuel installations, thereby hopefully hindering the enemy reinforcement plans. Each crew had decided upon its own method of attack; most preferring to overfly the target at between ten and fifteen thousand feet, thereby remaining above the worst of the flak. Their leader, Bennett, decided to try a different approach. He flew past Aalborg, heading north and continuing on his way for several minutes. He then reversed his course and headed back towards the target. With the aerodrome identified, he closed the throttles at 15000ft and commenced a shallow glide down to 5000ft. On reaching his chosen height, he carried out a circuit of the airfield while he and his crew studied the layout. Satisfied that he knew where he wanted to drop his bombs, Bennett carried out his final approach at 700ft, from which height his navigator, Malcolm Potts, released a stick of six bombs. As soon as Potts called "Bombs Gone", Bennett opened the throttles wide and headed for the safety of the open sea. All four Hampdens returned safely, landing at Kinloss to refuel before continuing on to Waddington.

During the first week of May, the Waddington Hampdens, together with those from other stations, carried out an intensive minelaying programme. By this time, the Hampden crews were gaining in experience, as night after night they prowled along the hostile coastlines of northern Europe.

A typical mining sortie of the period was recalled by S/Ldr Watts:

"On the night of 3/4 May, three crews of No 44 Squadron were detailed for mining sorties. Our drop area was near Fornebu and as it had been mined only recently, we anticipated a warm reception. After studying the weather report, we decided to fly over the North Sea at high altitude, returning at medium level in order to take advantage of the winds, which we felt would result in a relatively quick trip. We planned to make our approach from West to East and, if possible, to be the first of the three aircraft in the target area, thereby achieving maximum surprise. However, by the time we took off in KM-B (P4290) at 2010hr, the other two crews had a ten minute start on us. One of the other aircraft KM-P (P1338) was flown by F/Lt Smythe and crew. Apart from 8/10 cloud, visibility was excellent and, climbing steadily, we set course from Skegness to Lister Fjord. At 12000ft we levelled off, and sometime later, calculated our groundspeed as being 150mph. I ensured that all my crew were on oxygen and carried out frequent checks.

We made our landfall at Lister Fjord within six minutes of our planned Estimated Time of Arrival (ETA) and we followed the by now familiar coastline. While we were still about 30 miles from the drop area, we saw the German reception committee welcoming the Smythe crew! Deciding that our planned run-in point would be a dangerously alert place, we elected to reverse our approach, intending to use the effect of the Northern Lights to silhouette the off-shore islands. As we were positioning ourselves out to sea, we saw the flak directed at the second Hampden lighting up the sky. With the throttles almost closed, we were making a glide approach as we studied the outlines of the various islands. Spotting our new planned run-in point, I steep turned towards it.

By this time, searchlights from the direction of Oslo began searching for us, accompanied by considerable light flak. The sound of exploding shells accompanied us throughout our final run-in to the drop point. Having released our vegetable in the exact spot, we dived down to sea level and escaped at full throttle down Oslo Fjord. I ordered my gunners to return fire, and at some point, Cpl Crook, my W/Op AG, reported that he had seen his tracer strike the centre of a group of three searchlights which appeared to be collocated with several guns on the promontory that we had intended originally to use as a run-in point. After a few moments the searchlights went out. None of the lights had succeeded in holding us for more than a few seconds, and only one heavy calibre gun was observed firing at us from somewhere near Fornebu aerodrome. On landing back at base, we found that our only damage was a severed aerial stay wire".

At about this time, government legislation was enacted closing the A15 road to the general public between Bracebridge Heath and the junction of the A15 with Mere Road. In due course, this stretch of the road was to be equipped with hinged roadsigns (!). This enabled repaired aircraft fuselages to be towed from the Avro repair facility on the site of the old aerodrome at Bracebridge Heath along the road and across the grass verge on to Waddington aerodrome. Once at Waddington, the wings would be fitted prior to engine runs and air tests. Much later in the war, when the likelihood of invasion had receeded, the road was re-opened to the public, but controlled by traffic lights.

The Blitzkreig

The German offensive on the Western Front commenced at dawn on 10 May. Once the situation became clear, the Waddington squadrons were put on standby, along with most other Bomber Command squadrons. Their intended role was to attack bridges, railways and other lines of communication. Later in the day the tasking was changed to one of attacks on industrial targets in the Ruhr. Following this change, three Hampdens of No 50 Squadron took off to attack an important road/rail junction (sic) near Munchen Gladbach, close to the German/Dutch border. The crews were unable to identify their target area in the dark, so two dropped their bombs on ETA, while the third crew returned to base with their bombs.

At debriefing, all three crews reported that they had encountered considerable flak and searchlight activity in Germany and Holland, but that they had seen no sign of enemy fighters. No other attacks were called for that night; the crews assuming that the embargo on bombing targets in mainland Germany was still in force. In fact, they were wrong; a force of nine Whitleys had bombed bridges and columns of road transport in northern Germany, again near the Dutch border. In truth, the British cabinet had still not completely lifted the embargo, this was not to take place until 15 May when Bomber Command was authorised to extend its operations beyond the immediate battle areas and their associated lines of communication.

Indecisiveness and an unwillingness to face facts had characterised British political policy throughout the second half of the nineteen thirties. Despite all the warning signs in resurgent German nationalism, the British government remained inordinately optimistic; that was until the return from Berlin in 1935 of the Foreign Secretary, Sir John Simon and the Lord Privy Seal, Anthony Eden. Making no progress at all during discussions on arms levels and armament in general with Adolph Hitler, Simon put the crucial question quite bluntly. He asked for the present strength of the German Air Force. Quite calmly, Hitler replied that Germany had already reached parity with Great Britain.

From then on, a series of Schemes and Air Plans poured forth from the government and the Air Ministry. It is unlikely that any details contained in these schemes and plans were received, let alone studied in detail at Station level. Indeed, it is highly unlikely that the crews were ever aware of whichever scheme or plan was in force at any one time. In all probability, at Waddington as at all other RAF stations, even after war broke out the only perceived manifestation would have been a change in emphasis from coastal targets to others in the Ruhr and the German oil industry; though here too, a far too optimistic assessment of the potential effectiveness of Bomber Command was assumed. In the event, these schemes and plans were subject to political controls during the early months of the war; later to be followed by tactical considerations which were forced upon the government and the Air Ministry by the German 'Blitzkreig'. As in the past, the cost of appeasement and indecisiveness was to paid for by the pre-war regulars and early volunteers of the armed forces of the Crown. To quote G W Hegel: "What experience and history teach is this - that people and governments never have learnt anything from history, or acted on principles deduced from it."

At Waddington, minelaying was becoming a way of life. The technique used was to fly at low level at night to an easily identifiable coastal feature in the assigned mining area. From this feature, known as the run-in point, a timed run was made on a pre-determined course, the mine being released at the calculated elapsed time. These sorties were most productive and provided the crews with valuable experience of war operations at night. They were also considered to be relatively safe. However, an ominous portent of the future was experienced by a crew from No 50 Squadron which, for some reason or other, had taken off from RAF Scampton. On their return, the crew reported that low cloud in the assigned area had prevented them from identifying their timing point, despite loitering in the area for some time. They went on to report that they had been intercepted by enemy fighter aircraft. These fighters (or fighter) were able to locate the Hampden at low level over the sea and had also been able to follow the bomber through cloud.

By mid May the Hampden crews were begining to refer to themselves as 'Gardners' or 'Horticulturalists'; an oblique reference to the perceived ban on bombing 'proper' targets in Germany. Then, on 15 May 1940, everything changed. The German armies smashed their way through the French defences at Sedan. That night 99 aircraft, including nine from No 44 Squadron and two from No 50 Squadron, attacked targets in the Ruhr. Of the total force, 36 were Hampdens, all but one of which returned safely. The strategic bombing campaign against Germany had begun and was to continue unabated for the next five years. Among the targets attacked that night were Cologne, Dortmund, Kamen, Sterkrade, Munster, Rotterdam and Breda. The missing Hampden (P4286), flown by F/O L J Ashfield of No 44 Squadron, was reported as having crashed near Oosterhout in Holland; there were no survivors.

Two nights later, Waddington aircraft formed part of a force of 48 Hampdens that attacked Hamburg, while Whitleys and Wellingtons attacked Bremen and Cologne. The Hamburg attack was a success, with 160 buildings reported as destroyed or damaged, including two chemical factories. In all, 130 British bombers were out over Germany that night and all returned safely, though the Waddington crews had to divert on return when the station became fogged in.

The Air Ministry plan was for the bombing to concentrate on attacking oil targets in the Ruhr, but as the German advance progressed remorslessly across Belgium, France and Holland, the aircraft of Bomber Command were called upon increasingly to support the hard pressed Blenheims and Battles of No 2 Group and the Advanced Air Striking Force (AASF). These units were suffering grievous losses in their attempts to help stem the German advance. The new AOC in C Bomber Command, Air Marshal Sir Charles Portal, had replaced Air Marshall Sir Ludlow Hewitt the previous April. He (Portal) immediately called a halt to the leaflet dropping sorties in order that his small force of bombers could concentrate on the night bombing offensive. By this time, aircraft of the Command had dropped approximately 65 million leaflets over Germany to no apparent effect, other than that predicted by Air Marshal Harris! However, this paper offensive was to continue throughout the war, but only as an adjunct to the dropping of more lethal cargoes.

The crews of Bomber Command were now being called upon to carry out their night attacks against oil installations within Germany, while at the same time undertaking tactical bombing operations in support of the sorely pressed British Expeditionary Force (BEF). At the many briefings, the crews were told that their task was to interfere with road and rail movements; create blockages and delays by destroying bridges over the river Oise; bomb trains and railway lines; destroy and derail trains etc etc... The crews were further informed that one way to block approach roads through towns and villages, was to bomb the houses on either side of the road (sic), thereby blocking the road with rubble and other debris. In retrospect, there was little chance of achieving this, bearing in mind the relatively small bombs carried by the Command's aircraft at the time. Furthermore, the bombers' primitive navigation and bombing equipment made it almost impossible to locate a particular blacked-out town or village, let alone carry out precision attacks.

Nothing daunted, though fully aware of their shortcomings, the Waddington crews, together with their counterparts on all the other bomber stations, took off night after night, either carrying out attacks in support of the BEF, attacking oil installations, or laying mines off the coasts of Norway, Denmark, Holland and Germany. These attacks became so frequent that they seldom rated a mention in the press, but they were no less dangerous. Losses mounted, with more and more of the old faces from pre-war days disappearing from the messes. Among those posted as missing during this period were three crews from No 44 Squadron. S/Ldr C E Johnson and crew were shot down by flak near Aachen during the night of 23/24 May, while carrying out an attack on the railway complex around the town of Borchum. In the early hours of 4 June, Hampden P1340 hit a barrage balloon cable and crashed in the river Orwell near Harwich while returning from an attack on an oil installation near Emmerich. The pilot, Sgt E J Spencer, managed to bail out, but the other three crew members perished. The remains of the aircraft and crew were finally recovered in August 1995 during work on extending the container port of Felixstowe. This was due in the main to the efforts of ex-Sgt Observer Harry Moyle of No 44 Squadron.

Two days after the loss of the Spencer crew, Sgt W Jeffrey and crew were shot down while attacking tactical targets in the La Frere and Laon area of France; there were no survivors. Meanwhile, No 50 Squadron was having a run of good luck, as they had not lost a crew for some time. On 10 April, W/Cdr Taafe had handed over command of the squadron to W/Cdr N D Crockhart, who had come to the squadron on promotion, from No 106 Aircrew Pool Squadron at RAF Finningley.

Among the aircrew of No 50 Squadron at this time was Sgt Alan James Coad. An ex Halton Apprentice (No 26 Entry), he had volunteered for aircrew duties and had been psoted to No 9 Flying Training School (FTS) at Hullavington in January 1939. He was awarded his Observer brevet in June of the same year and was posted to No 50 Squadron. He took part in numerous bombing and minelaying sorties, which included attacks on Dortmund, Hamburg, Salzbergen, Binche, Duren, Givet, Laon, Frankfurt, Beauvais, Tjerborg, Borkum, Lunen, Norderney, Soest, Oldenburg, Wismar, Harburg and Osnabruck. All these attacks were carried out between 7 April and 5 August 1940. In all, Coad flew 33 operational sorties during a total of 203 flying hours. His last six operations were flown as the aircraft captain; an extremely rare honour for an Observer at that time. He was awarded the DFM on 24 December 1940, the citation making reference to his courage, determination and his skill as a navigator/bomb aimer. Sadly, he did not live long enough to receive his award, which was presented to his widow. He was killed in a flying accident on 7 December 1940, while instructing at No 16 OTU at Upper Heyford.

Meanwhile at Waddington, something new was under way. As Jim Taylor recalled:

"Crews from Waddington and other stations were tasked with carrying out practice mining of the Kiel Canal. The training took place at the nearby Coleby Grange meadows. A line of sacks, simulating the canal banks was constructed and the crews were required to place their dummy bombs on target from 500 feet. On the actual attack, all aircraft were subjected to heavy flak and searchlights. Several attacks were carried out, with those taking part being given the German colours of the day, plus daily beacon codes (ULTRA?). Some crews reported that the dropping of flares during an attack appeared to confuse the German gunners."

Along with the other squadrons of the Command, the two Waddington squadrons continued to bomb oil, communications and tactical targets right up to the completion of Operation Dynamo - the evacuation of the BEF from Dunkirk. The night following the end of Dynamo, Bomber Command carried out its largest effort of the war, when 142 bombers, including 48 Hampdens, attacked numerous targets between Hamburg and Frankfurt. Throughout the rest of June Waddington aircraft conrinued their wide range of attacks, but by this time, minelaying was back on the agenda.

Survivors From France

On 15 June 1940, following the debacle in France, some of the remnants of No 142 Squadron arrived at Waddington. This Fairey Battle squadron had been part of the AASF, based in France. Understandably, the personnel of No 142 Squadron were not a particularly amenable bunch, having experienced the trauma of the Blitzkreig at first hand. After a stay of only three weeks, the permanent residents of Waddington were not sorry to see them depart for Binbrook. Among the visitors was a young airman, Ron Rainford. He recalled their brief stay at Waddington quite clearly:

"The rear party consisted of the crew of our last Fairey Battle that made it back to England, together with a few 'erks' (airmen) who were crammed aboard just before it took off from our last aerodrome in France, Villiers-Faux. They were joined quite soon by those of the squadron groundcrew who had the good fortune to have been on home leave when the Blitzkreig began. The remainder of us did not manage to leave France until the night of 16 June, landing at Plymouth in the early hours of the next morning. After a brief stay at RAF Locking, we were put on a train and told to report to RAF Waddington. On arrival, it was obvious that nobody knew what to do with us, so we were dumped in an old World War I hangar, located beside the camp road. We were told that we were to live there until some instructions were received regarding our future.

The Waddington aircraft were kept pretty busy and their flying hours did little for our chances of recovering from what had been for all of us, a shattering experience Throughout the Blitzkreig our life had seemed to us to have been one of complete chaos. We were short of fuel, spares, aircraft and replacement crews. Owing to the manpower shortage, I flew as an 'ad hoc' rear gunner on two operations. On the day that we of the rear party were told to evacuate, we possessed only two Battles that were fit to fly, though neither of these was in any great shape. We prepared them for flight and they both started up and taxied out to the far side of the muddy field which was our aerodrome! As they commenced their take-off run, we climbed aboard our trucks and started to depart when, without warning, one of the Battles' undercarriage collapsed. I was in the last truck and our driver tore across the field towards the wreck, totally regardless of his fragile load of airmen. By the time we arrived at the Battle, the crew were out on the grass, with the pilot busy draining some fuel out of the tanks so that he could set fire to it using his Verey pistol. As soon as the wrecked Battle was well alight, we and its crew climbed aboard the truck and set off for the coast.

Almost all our equipment had been lost in France and few of us had more than the clothes we were wearing. I recall that my total possessions were: one shirt, one pair of trousers, a pair of gym shoes, a 'tin hat' and a rifle. For the last few days in France we had lived in a stable and our turnout reflected this fact. Obviously we could not continue to walk about in this condition; at the very least it was setting the Waddington people a bad example, so we were paraded outside the stores section for a kit issue. The stores personnel could not seem to understand how we could have lost our equipment and were insisting on us filling in vast sheets of paperwork. This annoyed us intensely and the atmosphere got rather unpleasant until, sensing that it could get out of hand and sympathising with our problem, our squadron adjutant countersigned all the forms with the words 'LOST THROUGH ENEMY ACTION', much to the obvious disgust of the stores clerks. Having kitted us out, the authorities then made a grave error; they paid us all our accrued back pay! This was a mistake of considerable proportions, which was compounded by our then being left very much to our own devices. The Station was more concerned with fighting the war than with dealing with a bunch of recalcitrant airmen and we made the most of it. We spent most of the first few days following the pay parade in the hotels and pubs of Lincoln and the surrounding area, getting either very merry or maudlin as we drowned our sorrows. I do not know how the unfortunate Waddington people viewed us, but I know that we all felt rather remote, as though we had come from another World. We lacked the ability or maturity to convey a picture of what we had experienced in France; perhaps some of our problem was an unconscious sense of guilt at being part of a great defeat. Whatever the reason, we were irritated by the sight of people going about their duties, and to all intents and purposes, living a normal life. Our minds were still filled with images of refugee-filled roads, Stukas dive-bombing, bombs exploding and the constant fear that we might never reach home. As the national war effort got into its stride, this feeling gradually faded, but never before nor since have I ever felt so alone and so different as I did during those few weeks at Waddington.

Not long after we had been re-kitted, I recall some air ranking officer turning up to address us. We were all paraded for him, whereupon he proceeded to give our officers a savage dressing down. It was all about poor leadership, lack of morale and even cowardice. I cannot imagine what the powers that be thought this sort of approach would achieve, but it failed dismally. We, the airmen, most of whom were under 20, felt that our officers had done much to steady us, both by what they said and what they did. In those days, 20 year olds were not very mature and we looked upon up to our officers and never found them wanting. So, this tirade was, as far as we were concerned, unjust and typical of those who had no idea.

To keep us occupied, out of mischief and away from the pubs, the Station Commander decided that he could find useful work for idle hands. We were set to digging slit trenches all over the station, but mainly in front of the hangars. On asking what they were for, we were told that in the event of an invasion, we were to man them and defend the aerodrome. We used to stand to at dawn and dusk each day, all very martial if not very meaningful. In any case, the effect was diminished by the fact that we had only one rifle per ten men! From our expeiences in France, it did little for our peace of mind, though it did achieve what I imagine was its main purpose; it kept us out of mischief".

Ron Rainford eventually returned to France, in June 1944. This time he went as a member of the Grenadier Guards as his eyesight had precluded his being accepted for aircrew, so he transferred to the Army.

Among the aircrew of No 142 Squadron to arrive at Waddington were F/O Doug Gosman, Sgt Peter Baker and Sgt Les Frith. These three were among the thirteen crews who took off from Villiers-Faux on 15 June. The aircraft were flown by S/Ldr Wight, F/Lt Hewson, F/O Gosman, P/Os Franklin, Sutton, Ricalton, Edwards, Bilton and Childe, and Sergeants Heslop, Spear, Tweed and Ebert. Three other Battles had been destroyed on the ground by the groundcrew as they were unfit to fly. One of the Battles experienced problems in flight and had to make an emergency landing at Rennes. The remaining aircraft continued on their way, eventually landing at RAF Abingdon near Oxford. Doug Gosman had been a contemporary of F/O Donald Garland, who won a posthumous Victoria Cross (VC) for his attack on the bridges at Veldwezelt on 12 May.

On the day of their scheduled departure for England, the Battle assigned to Les Frith and his pilot, was unserviceable as a result of battle damage sustained during an attack on German tanks near the river Seine outside Paris. Accordingly, they were detailed to fly another aircraft, this despite it too being riddled with bullet holes. The Squadron Commander, W/Cdr Falconer, elected to remain behind with the rear ground party, but persuaded Les and his pilot to carry his dog back to England. The CO and his party eventually arrived in England having sailed from France on the SS Vienna. They were more fortunate than those of the main ground party, who were assigned to the Lancastria, which was sunk on the return journey.

Peter Baker, who was to retire many years later as S/Ldr B P Baker DFM, flew as Observer to P/O Ricalton. As Peter Baker recalled:

"On arrival at Waddington, all we had was what we stood up in. We were treated with much kindness by the Hampden crews, some of whom took me out to Lincoln on my first night. I remember coming round at some late hour at a dance in the Assembly Rooms. I found this rather surprising as I did not dance. I was still wearing my flying boots and sporting two days growth of beard. The two or three hours immediately preceeding my regaining awareness in the dance hall, remain a complete blank; presumably caused by an unaccustomed intake of English ale..."

Among the Waddington residents who came into contact with the Battle squadron was Bob Forster. He remembered going into No 50 Squadron's hangar first thing one morning and being surprised to find it full of Battles. He was even more surprised to note that all the wings and fuselages were covered in messages and addresses from the groundcrew left in France. Forster further recalled walking round the aircraft looking at the bullet holes and other signs of battle damage.

Enemy Shipping As A Priority Target

One month after the last British soldier had been evacuated from Dunkirk, Bomber Command issued a directive requiring that first priority should be given to attacks on docks and enemy shipping. There followed raids on Hamburg, the home port of the mighty battleship Bismark, and on the port of Keil wherein lurked the pocket battleship Lutzow (nee Deutschland) and the battle cruiser Scharnhorst. In addition, the ports of Bremerhaven, Rotterdam and others in Holland were also attacked. Meanwhile the mining campaign continued unabated, though German defences were becoming more active off their coastline. The minelaying Hampdens were reporting increasing contact with enemy fighters and flak. On the night of 5 June, six Hampdens nof No 50 Squadron were detailed to attack an oil refinery near Wedel. All crews reported heavy flak and searchlight defences. All six bombers returned safely, but one crew reported being chased by seven enemy fighters out to a point some 60 miles off the coast.

Derek French and his No 50 Squadron crew were detailed to attack a railway junction at Eindhoven. His navigator/bomb aimer was a newly-joined young pilot, P/O Smetten who, the evening before, had crashed a Hampden (P4289) while delivering it to the Waddington satellite aerodrome at Coleby Grange. He had been caught out by engine failure and was still shaken by the experience. In the target area, visibility was poor, so French gradually lost height and dropped flares at intervals in the hope of finding a landmark while continuing eastwards. Eventually, when down to 1000 feet one of the flares showed them to be over a densely built-up area. At first there was no sign of life or opposition, but this quickly changed and they became the target for searchlights and both medium and light flak, with tracer coming at them from all directions. One shell hit the Hampden on the starboard side of the fuselage, just to the rear of French's seat. The resulting explosion destroyed the hydraulic control box and part of the pilot's instrument panel.

Luckily for French, most of the shrapnel was stopped by the armour plate that had been fitted to the Hampden a few days earlier. However, a few pieces of shrapnel struck the pilot in the upper right arm which was not protected by the armour plate. With the hydraulic lines cut and the hydraulic fluid spurting about the cockpit, French began to think that he was bleeding to death, particularly as he could feel warm, sticky fluid in his flying boots. A quick taste check served to calm his fears. To escape the flak, French put the bomber into a steep dive, pulling out when almost at ground level. At one point, the crew could see that they were flying along a wide river, with multi-storey warehouses on either side of them! Once clear of the flak, the W/Op applied a tourniquet to French's arm, who in due course made a successful flapless landing back at base. On climbing out of his aircraft, Derek French passed out and was immediately rushed to the medical centre at nearby RAF Cranwell. Here, he was operated upon to remove the pieces of shell splinter and aircraft metal from his arm. In fact, some pieces of metal were to remain in his arm as a permanent reminder of his younger days. French had been accompanied to Cranwell by the Waddington Medical Officer, F/Lt Cullinan, a delightfully eccentric South African who turned the return journey to Waddington into a pub crawl. As was previously mentioned, it was this incident that resulted in French being upbraided by Gp Capt Anderson for flying too low over occupied territory.

While the crews of Bomber Command continued to take the war across the North Sea, the enemy decided upon reciprocal activity. The first air attacks on Lincolnshire took place on the night of 5 June 1940, during which incendiaries fell on RAF Hemswell. Two weeks later, while Derek French was recuperating from his injuries, the German intruders carried out widespread attacks, mostly in the North Kesteven, Spilsby and Louth districts. During one of the attacks, two high explosive bombs were dropped in a field near the vicarage beside Hykeham Road; luckily there were no casualties. On another occasion, two bombs fell at Mere, damaging a cottage. Obviously the Germans knew where Waddington was, so it could be only a matter of time before they found it.

Seven Hampdens of No 50 Squadron took off on the night of 25 June to attack the German bomber airfield at Langenhagen near Hannover; their alternative target being the marshalling yards at Osnabruck. The total bomber force out that night was 107, comprising Hampdens, Wellingtons and Whitleys. Three aircraft failed to return, all of which were Hampdens, two of them belonging to No 50 Squadron, whose run of luck had finally ended. P/O Luxmore and crew (L4078) were shot down by flak over Hannover, while the squadron commander, W/Cdr Crockhart and crew went down in the North Sea. A message was received from the Wing Commander's aircraft (P1329) - "Going down 15 miles off the Dutch coast" at 0359hr.

Nothing more was heard from either crew, but post war investigations revealed that the Luxmore crew were buried outside Hannover. Of the Crockhart crew, two bodies were later washed ashore and buried by the Germans. The day following the sad loss of two crews, W/Cdr G W Colledge assumed command of No 50 Squadron. By this time, his opposite number on No 44 Squadron, W/Cdr D W Reid, had been in post since 12 March. Just over one week after losing their commanding officer, No 50 Squadron were stood down from all operations in order to prepare for a move to their new base at Hatfield Woodhouse near Doncaster. The squadron moved to its new home on 10 July, though on 18 August the name of the aerodrome was changed to Lindholme in order to avoid confusion with the de Havilland aerodrome in Hertfordshire.

On 13 July a further Air ministry directive ordered that priority now be given to attacking enemy aerodromes and aircraft factories. The following evening, P/O Price of No 44 Squadron was about to carry out his attack on the aerodrome on the island of Borkum when he spotted two Bf110s in the circuit. Wasting no time, he turned in behind the nearer of the two and shot it down in flames, using the single fixed machine gun mounted on the upper port side of the nose of his Hampden, possibly the only recorded instance of a Hampden achieving such a success.

Among the other pilots on No 44 Squadron at this time was Sgt 'Dim' Wooldridge. He successfully completed a tour of operations with the squadron before being posted to other duties. Later in the war he reappeared at Waddington on a visit from the Air Ministry having been promoted to Wing Commander and awarded the DSO and DFC and bar, to go with his DFM. He became a noted intruder Mosquito pilot, later ferrying a Mosquito across the Atlantic in 1944. After the war, among his many musical and literary achievements, he wrote the screenplay and composed the music for the film about a bomber squadron entitled 'Appointment in London', starring Dirk Bogarde.

On the ground at Waddington, despite the fact that the war had been in progress for almost a year, life in the Officers' Mess retained a vestige of peacetime routine. At lunchtime on Sundays, there was invariably a social hour during which a string quartet would play to the assembled company, which included wives and girl friends. The Station Defence Officer, a retired Army Colonel, had some theatrical connections and he could be relied upon to provide some interesting entertainment. On one occasion, Douglas Byng and Alice Delysia of World War I 'Byng Boys' fame, appeared with the quartet. Inevitably, the increase in German intruder activity against aerodromes brought such peacetime pursuits to an end. It also resulted in some flying personnel being billeted off-base for a brief period. Some of the lucky ones lived in a large country house at Branston. This happy band joined in village life with enthusiasm, the two elderly ladies who ran the village store and post office, keeping 'their boys' well supplied with chocolates and cigarettes throughout their stay. Living out with local families in nearby villages was very popular, but eventually the authorities decided that the aircrew were more at risk from enemy infiltrators (sic) than air raids and the practice was discontinued.

Apart from the Hampdens, the other aircraft on the Station were the squadron Ansons and the Station's Fairey Battle Flight (!) The Ansons had arrived on the Station some time after the Blenheims and were well remembered by AC Alan Sadler, the Fitter Rigger assigned to look after the aircraft. As he recalled:

"...and I made several flights in the old crates (sic). I remember cranking up the undercarriage; over two hundred turns on one occasion. We once took the Station Commander to RAF Cottesmore and returned at 200 feet and below, via the Grantham railway line. We actually flew through the smoke from the engine's funnel, much to the apprehension of the train's passengers. On another occasion, on returning from a trip to RAF Horsham St Faith (now Norwich airport) the pilot was unable to find Waddington as it was in the middle of a snow storm at the time. He force landed in a field almost opposite the Dunstan Pillar and the 'Annie' was to remain snowed in there for two weeks. To keep an eye on the aircraft myself and another airman were billetted at Coleby Grange farm..."

The Fairey Battle Flight was commanded by F/Lt Bassett, and their task was to tow drogue targets over the East Coast ranges, where they were fired at by both ground and air gunners.

By this time 'Ginger' Coveyduck had become one of the more experienced Observers, and he recalled the early summer at Waddington:

"In June we flew numerous sorties in support of the BEF in France. On the 11th and 13th we were tasked with carrying out attacks on enemy troop concentrations and communications at La Frere and Laon. The fact that we were not given the targets until the very last minute summarised the confused state of the whole situation. We dropped our bombs as briefed and were aware of activity below us, but in reality they could have been anybody's troops, such was the muddle. Most of us felt that these tactical attacks at night were ineffective, but they were the best that we could do. I further recall that during June and July our crew made a couple of training trips to Coleby Grange. Selected crews were preparing for a special trip involving operations against a canal (the previously mentioned Kiel Canal operation). A sandbagged outline of the proposed target was laid out on the Coleby aerodrome and crews carried out low level attacks with practice bombs. In the event, the Waddington squadrons did not participate in the actual attack. This was undertaken by crews from Nos 49 and 83 Squadrons based at Scampton and for which F/Lt Learoyd was awarded the Victoria Cross for his part in the attack.

Towards the end of June we took part in an attack on Soest, during which, shortly after I had dropped our bombs, there was an almighty explosion, which to us at the time, seemed to light up the whole of Germany; we had obviously hit something expensive! On 5 July our target was the docks at Kiel. The flak was extremely heavy and as we approached our release point, several near misses threw us off and we were forced to go round again. In all, we made three unsuccessful runs before Macintyre (the pilot) decided that the only answer was a low level attack. He put our Hampden into a steep dive towards the target area where I released the bombs before we made off at high speed, staying low until well clear of the defences. Four days later we were tasked with laying a mine in the Schillig Roads. We had been briefed to plant our vegetable in the harbour complex from a height of less than 500 feet. Macintyre decided to approach our timing point in a steep diving glide from

6000 feet, so that we would arrive silently, at low level and at high speed. Then followed a short sharp dash to our designated release point, in the course of which we flew right over an anchored flak ship! We then planted our mine and departed, breathing sighs of relief. We were well aware that several crews had frightened themselves using this method of attack, with the fuel mixture set at the economy weak setting. In this condition, carburettor icing was likely to result in a distinct lack of power at the bottom of the descent.

The Hampden

By mid July the newspapers, radio and cinema newsreels were concentrating their attention on the fighter pilots of the RAF. They were the 'glamour boys' of the war in the air, or at least so the media seemed to have decided. There was not a lot of media mileage in pictures of bombers taking off in the dark and returning at dawn. Unseen, a bomber reaching its target, dropping its bombs and returning to its base had little public impact, or so it seems to have been considered by those in control of the media. Conversely, if the unfortunate crew did not return, there was no story to tell, at least not in the British press. Accordingly, the crews of Bomber Command went about their dangerous, deadly business with little public recognition for their work or their sacrifices. At Waddington, as on all bomber stations, the crews of the resident squadrons were a carefree bunch, preferring to live for the day rather than to dwell too long on what might happen tomorrow or the next day.

Although their AOC had misgivings about the suitability of the Hampden as an effective instrument with which to wage the air war, the crews were happy with their 'kite', though not uncritically so. While the Hampden's slim fuselage reduced drag and made it faster than either the Wellington or the Whitley, this very feature could prove a disadvantage under certain circumstances. Of the four crew members, the navigator's (observer) lot was a vast improvement on the types that had preceeded the Hampden. Gilbert Haworth had been most impressed on first climbing into this, the latest product of the Handley Page stable. He was delighted with his comfortable position in the nose, which gave him a wide field of view in most directions. The large plotting table facilitated chart work, while it could be easily folded away to gain access to the bombsight and the single, nose-mounted moveable Vickers 'K' machine gun. Following the heavy losses over Kristiansand this was augmented by two beam gun positions, which necessitated the observer moving his gun from one position to another as required (sic). The navigator was alone in the nose; the pilot sat above and behind him and was hidden from view, apart from his feet which could be seen resting on the rudder pedals. It was convenient to be able to pass a message slip to the pilot after tapping him on the foot to attract attention. The one real inconvenience for the navigator was the rather tiresome manner of access to his position in the nose. It was said that the journey from the access hatch to the navigator's station could well have served as an assault course for the Commandos. For a grown man in bulky flying kit, encumbered with a parachute pack, a bag of navigation equipment and documents, rations, the machine gun and ammunition pans, plus a chemical hot water bottle (!), the latter being activated by urine, the route posed an almost impossible task. The narrow fuselage positively bristled with difficulties. Numerous projections lay in ambush to snag on clothing, harness or other impedimenta, and generally impeded progress. The navigator of a Hampden soon learned that it was quite useless to hurry, whatever the degree of urgency; the pace just had to be slow and deliberate. Bad language was not known to help much, although it was frequently employed.

The navigator entered his domain from the underside of the fuselage at the lower rear gunner's position and had then to squirm through a small door in order to negotiate the huge main wing spar, over which he clambered in the manner of a miner at the coalface. Eventually he would then reach a small rectangular apperture, the last obstacle before reaching 'the office'. Having negotiated the obstacle course, the navigator could then stow his equipment, fit the machine gun and carry out his pre-flight checks. Then, because higher authority had decreed that the nose position was too risky to occupy during take-off, the unfortunate navigator had to then backtrack to a safer, if more uncomfortable position, in the well behind the pilot. Once the Hampden was safely airborne, the wriggle, writhing and swearing act had to be repeated in order to regain his crew station.

The pilot entered the narrow cockpit by either stepping off the wing or, if he had long legs, via the main spar and over the lowered back of his seat. Behind his seat, the well was approximately four feet deep and just big enough for one man. At the bottom of the well was a sloping chute leading to the navigator' station. Having lowered the seat back, the pilot had to then squeeze past before sliding over it to his seat. Once there he had to pull the seat-back into the upright position, thereby cutting himself off from the navigator once the latter was in the well or the nose. Behind the entrance into the navigator's station, in the centre section, was a small space containing the inflatable multi-seat dinghy and other equipment. Moving towards the rear, the next obstacle was a metal door which allowed access to the W/Op AG's position which, when closed, completely cut him off from the rest of the crew other than by intercom. The W/Op AG sat in a small space completely filled by a radio, machine guns, ammunition pans, parachute pack, documents, rations and the chemical hot water bottle. He might also have to make room for the messenger pigeon and its container. At times he would be further encumbered with a supply of leaflets (Nickels) and/or Razzles, of which more later.

After Kristiansand the two rear gunners were provided with twin mounted Vickers 'K' machine guns which added to the cramped conditions. When not actually manning his guns, the W/Op could pull down a spring-loaded perspex canopy to afford some protection from the elements. Below the W/Op AG and even further aft, the rear lower gunner lay stretched out on a padded floor, part of which acted as the access door. He too was squeezed into the minimum possible space, made even more cramped by the addition of the extra machine gun.

As can be seen, space was at a premium in a Hampden, each crew member being effectively cut off from the others, access to whom was achieved only with great difficulty. This was the situation faced by S/Ldr Good and Derek French's crews when their pilots were injured.

It was to present even more difficulties to another No 44 Squadron crew when they were faced with a totally incapacitated pilot.

On the Ground at Waddington

By mid 1940 the population had become almost paranoid regarding the possibility of 'fifth columnists' within their midst. The police were inundated with reports of suspicious lights, resulting in hundreds of investigations, none of which proved to have any substance. From 28 June to 8 July 1940, church spires, water towers, RAF buildings and other vantage points were manned throughout Lincolnshire during alerts. The purpose of this activity was to establish the location of suspicious lights by cross bearings. The only useful information gained from this exercise was that many of the lights which had been, or were, considered suspicious, turned out to be signals from aircraft, which when in the distance, appeared to be coming from the ground. Owing to the consequent drain on manpower, this practice was quickly dispensed with.

As part of the enhancement of the Waddington ground defences, a batch of 50 airmen was posted in for ground defence duties. The Officer Commanding the station defences forces was S/Ldr Streeter, who had been an Observer/Air Gunner in World War I and was nearly 50 years of age, if not over it. In addition to the OC, there were three equally elderly Pilot Officers, one Warrant Officer and a Flight Sergeant. Among the newcomers were three airmen wearing First World War campaign ribbons, all of whom were promoted to Sergeant within days of their arrival. Those younger members, who had been in their school cadet corps and who had actually handled rifles, were promoted to Acting Corporal!

The ground defence troops (airmen) were allocated to sectors around the station, though in the main they were employed in manning the two entrances to the station, much as is the situation today. The password was changed daily and those wishing unrestricted access to the station had perforce to memorise it. On one occasion the defence force Flight Sergeant either forgot the password or omitted to obtain it. So, it was with much delight that he was duly escorted to the main guardroom. Inevitably, he had the last laugh when, soon after this incident, he introduced night foot patrols of the aerodrome perimeter and the distant dispersals.

Among other personalities on the station at the time was the Flight Sergeant, later Warrant Officer, Catering Officer. WO Randall was a strict disciplinarian of the old school and took no nonsense from anyone, service or civilian. He demanded high standards in all aspects of catering and would accept no excuses. A tarter who was, perhaps surprisingly, quite well liked, albeit preferably from a distance.

On the maintenance side, the engineers were kept busy repairing and modifying the Hampdens, as operational experience dictated essential changes. Civilian working parties were brought in to handle some of the more complex tasks. The aircraft were fitted progressively with Marconi HF radios, auto-pilots, self-sealing fuel tanks, beam gun positions and long range fuel tanks. The reason given by the Air Ministry for the latter modification was to provide an enhanced safety margin for attacks on Berlin. Already flying long trips over an inhospitable North Sea and enemy occupied territory, the aircrews were not too enamoured of the prospect of being required to fly further and for longer. Their comments tended to be colourful, to say the least. These forebodings were soon to be realised when two crews were despatched to attack Danzig; the stated aim being to raise Polish morale (sic).

New Ideas

Among new weapons being tried out at this stage of the war were 'Deckers' and 'Razzles'. To quote one of the No 44 Squadron navigators:

"Deckers and Razzles were rather wierd objects. Both were incendiary devices and were very unpopular with both air and ground crews. A Razzle was a celluloid sandwich containing a phosphorus pellet. They came in a tin of alcohol and water, each containing up to 500 Razzle leaves and we were required to pour the contents down the flare chute when over an identified area of crops or forest. The idea was that when the phosphorus pellet dried out it would ignite itself and the celluloid and, hopefully, start a fire. The Decker was a development of the Razzle and incorporated a latex rubber insert which increased the surface area. A Razzle was about three inches by one inch, while a Decker was about four inches square. There were numerous instances of aircraft returning to base having been damaged by rogue Razzles or Deckers. On one occasion a W/OpAG, 'Bags' Bagley, was about to drop a loose Decker over-

board from his gun position when his aircraft was attacked by an enemy fighter. In the ensuing excitement he forgot about the Decker, which he had dropped in his haste to man his guns. Sometime later, he recalled that he had dropped the device and began a feverish search for it. Being unable to locate the Decker, he warned the crew to watch out for any sign of fire. Inevitably, in due course it ignited, but it was in an inaccessable area and Bagley was badly burned trying to retrieve it. It was still burning when they landed at Waddington. After this incident, crews were issued with a liquid-filled syringe with which to keep any rogue devices moistened. Despite their reputation, there were instances of members of the groundstaff pocketting one as a souvenir, sometimes with unfortunate results. These wretched devices achieved little if any success and their use was eventually discontinued, much to everyone's relief".

Another weapon appeared at about this time, but it had little to do with officialdom. Somewhere or other, a rumour spread to the effect that enemy sound locators could be upset by falling beer bottles! (sic). Accordingly, those who believed it would hurl empty beer bottles from their aircraft whenever fired upon by enemy flak. Prior to take-off, it became common practice for some air gunners to visit their Mess and 'acquire' a supply of empties. As one gunner reported: "*I once had the pleasure of dropping some beer bottles over a car that was travelling along an autobahn...*" In reality of course, the bottles had no effect on the enemy defences whatsoever, other than to provide an alarming, though harmless noise.

The Air War Develops

With the move of No 50 Squadron to its new home in early July, the only operational unit at Waddington was No 44 Squadron. On 19 July, Sgt 'Ferdie' Farrands, together with four other crews were despatched on minelaying sorties. Two of the Hampdens went to Samso Island while the other three flew to Frederikshaven. Just after midnight, RAF Aldergrove picked up a message from an unidentified No 44 Squadron aircraft, reporting that they had been hit by flak and were going down just off the Danish coast. With the return of the other four crews it was apparent that Sgt Farrands and crew, flying in L4087 were missing. Subsequent Red Cross reports advised that two of the crew, Sergeants Miller and Nixon had been buried at Skagen in Denmark. Farrands and his lower gunner, P/O Green, were reported to be PoWs. P/O Green, known to one and all at Waddington as 'Pop', was a veteran of World War I and a holder of the Military Cross.

At this stage of the air war, crews were still more or less free to decide on the route and timing to and from their designated target. The days, or more accurately, nights, of mass attacks adhering to rigid routing and timing, were still far off. So too was the introduction of technological aids to navigation and target finding. However, some useful improvements were coming along and were being retrospectively fitted to the Hampdens of Bomber Command.

On 28 July, S/Ldr J G Macintyre and crew were assigned Hampden P4375 for an attack on Hamburg. On arriving at their aircraft they were met by the Station Armament Officer, who pointed out to them the newly fitted cable-cutters on the leading edges of the wings. Their target that night was an oil refinery at Blankensee near Hamburg. The navigator, John Coveyduck, noted that this would be the third time that they had attacked targets in the Hamburg area. Between them, Macintyre and Coveyduck elected to cross the North Sea to make a landfall at the island of Wangerooge. The plan was to then fly past Hamburg, keeping well clear of its defences, before turning back to attack their target on a westerly heading. This was not the normal approach, most crews preferring to spend as little time as possible over enemy territory. However, the Macintyre crew hoped to achieve surprise by coming on the target from the East and to take advantage of the fact that they would be heading for home at the moment of bomb release.

On their run-up to the target they were subjected to very heavy anti-aircraft fire. Then, just after Coveyduck had called "bombs gone", their Hampden suddenly reared upwards, stalled and fell off into a spin. Ironically, it was later discovered that they had hit a high altitude balloon cable. On orders from their pilot, the three crew members bailed out. Coveyduck was the first out, leaving via the escape hatch in the floor of the nose compartment. On pulling the 'D' ring of his parachute, he realised that his chest-type parachute was fastened to his harness by only one hook. He attempted to fasten the other clip several times, but the load on the harness was too great and he had to give up the attempt and prepare for landing. He then became aware that he was descending over clouds that appeared to be illuminated from below by various fires. His discomfiture was further heightened by the realisation that he was dropping through a flak-filled sky.

On hitting the ground he injured his ankle, but managed to rid himself of his parachute before reviewing his situation. He was down in Germany, very near Hamburg, with a damaged ankle and little hope of escape. He then became aware that shrapnel from bursting flak shells was falling all around him, so he hobbled across some fields to a nearby cowshed which he had seen in the glow from the fires in Hamburg. As he neared the cowshed he came to a small stream which he attempted to jump across. Unfortunately for him, what appeared to be the far bank turned out to be a bed of bullrushes, which left him up to his waist in mud and water. 'Ginger' Coveyduck, together with Sergeants Cross and Edgar all eventually became PoWs. S/Ldr Macintyre's body was found by the Germans near the remains of his aircraft. His parachute had opened, but for whatever reason, had failed to function properly - too low perhaps. It was to be some time before the experts (!) accepted that the Germans had developed a high altitude barrage balloon. This had always been discounted when returning crews reported seeing them well above the accepted 3000 feet maximum.

Although the loss rate among the aircraft of Bomber Command was not yet at the levels that would be suffered later in the war, the gradual diminution of the pre-war aircrew was becoming quite noticeable. Aircraft of the Command were out bombing or mining virtually every night. Some crews were given a brief break from operations in order to practice for another unamed 'special operation'. The Hattersley crew was one of a small number selected for such training. This involved flying at night at approximately 50 feet along a river. The crews practiced with lights on the extremities of the wings, angled to converge when the aircraft was at a pre-determined height. In the event, nothing came of it, although No 617 Squadron was to employ a similar system to good effect during their attack on the Ruhr dams.

Pilot Officer H P Clarke was a new pilot, flying as a navigator in the Hattersley crew at the time of the special training, and he recalled their return to operations following the end of the practices:

"We were despatched to the river Elbe on a mining operation and decided to put what we had practiced into effect. As we flew up the river, a boat challenged us for the colours of the day. Intelligence had provided us with a list of German challenges and responses, but on this occasion we decided to reply by releasing our wing bombs as we passed over the boat. This was nearly our undoing, because we were so low that the explosions rocked us quite badly. We subsequently heard of another of the specially trained crews who tried this low level approach against a fishing boat, but to their surprise they found it to heavily armed with machine guns and they were lucky to survive the encounter.

The night of 31 July was not one of the better ones for Bomber Command. 42 aircraft, including Battles, Blenheims and Hampdens were despatched to a variety of targets in Germany, Holland and France; some to bomb, other to lay mines. Of these, only thirteen located and bombed their targets, though nine managed to lay their mines in the assigned area. One Battle was shot down by RAF fighters, crashing into the sea off Skegness on its way to its target. On their return flight, three Hampdens ditched in the sea. One of the latter was L4085, flown by Sgt E D Farmer and crew of No 44 Squadron. Their target had been Misburg, which they found and attacked before turning for home. Radio reception was very poor and the crew became completely unsure of their position (lost!). They let down through low cloud and fog on ETA, hoping to see the East coast somewhere near Skegness. Instead, they were presented with the lights of what could only be neutral Eire. Relieved to be at least aware of his position, Sgt Farmer turned the Hampden around and headed for the nearest RAF aerodrome. Unfortunately, they ran out of fuel before they could coast in and were forced to ditch just off the coast of Aberystwyth. With the fuel tanks empty and in a calm sea, the Hampden remained afloat for some time. While Farmer fired off Verey cartridges, the W/Op fired his guns in an attempt to attract attention. Despite all this there was no indication that they had been seen. In fact, the Coastguard had seen them and had initiated the launch of a rescue boat. Deciding that they were on their own, they elected to paddle ashore using the aircraft dinghy. The large, round multi-seat dinghy burst on inflation, rendering it useless, though the navigator Sgt Hobbs and the lower gunner Sgt Don Seager managed to hold on to it until their rescuers arrived. Sgt Farmer and his W/Op Sgt Wood decided to swim ashore and get help, but sadly neither of them made it, both being drowned.

Misfortune had not finished with the crew of L4085. While returning to Waddington from his convalescent leave, Don Seager was waiting for his train on a Kings Cross station platform while an air raid was in progress. An unexploded anti-aircraft shell landed near him and exploded, the resultant injuries causing Don Seager to lose a leg above the knee.

Dave Romans DFC

During their off-duty time in the summer of 1940, the Lincoln open air swimming pool was a popular spot with the Waddington aircrew. One afternoon there were quite a number of aircrew desporting themselves around the pool, including the Commanding Officer of No 44 Squadron, W/Cdr Reid. A keen, if not particularly proficient diver, Reid was standing on the high board when a Hampden buzzed the pool so low that he leaped off the board in fright. As soon as he had clambered out of the water, he was on the telephone to Waddington ordering the arrest of the pilot concerned. The guilty party was a young, high spirited Canadian, F/O Dave Romans, who had been left behind at Waddington when the swimming party departed, because his aircraft required an air test Brought before his Commanding Officer, Romans was restricted to navigator duties until further notice; an inauspicious start to the subsequent award of the DFC.

Some time after the swimming pool incident, Dave Romans was in the nose of a Hampden being flown by P/O Walker, en route to the German aerodrome of Eschwege. They reached their target, which was bathed in bright moonlight, and commenced their bombing run at 3000 feet. Almost immediately, searchlights probed the sky searching for them, while at the same time, the flak defences opened fire, gradually getting nearer. As he called the course corrections to his pilot on the bombing run, Romans noted that the shell bursts were getting dangerously close. The nearer the Hampden got to the release point, the more dense the flak became; so much so that Walker was forced to take evasive action. Suddenly, two nearby explosions rocked the Hampden, followed almost immediately by the bomber pitching up into a steep climb. With no change in power setting, the bomber stalled and fell off into a spiral dive which threatened to develop into a spin. In the nose, crouched over his bomb sight, Romans felt the two wxplosions and was aware of the violent manoauvres which followed. Feeling that his pilot might be in trouble, he called out to him to watch his increasing speed and the threat of a spin. Receiving no response, Romans pulled off his helmet and struggled back through the tunnel to the well space behind the pilot. All this time, the Hampden had continued its erratic descent.

On reaching the well, Romans stood up behind the pilot's seat, to find Walker slumped forward over the controls. Romans immediately clambered up on to the padded rest on the main spar and began tugging at the pilot's seat straps in order to lower the back of the seat. Without his helmet, Romans was unable to make contact with the other two members of the crew. All this time, the Hampden continued its downward plunge. As he struggled with the straps Romans was surprised to find no sign of blood or injury to the unfortunate Walker, but neither was there any response. Eventually, after what seemed an age, Romans managed to get the straps undone and the seat-back down. Grasping the shoulders of the unconscious Walker, he managed to drag him over the back of the seat. With height and time running out and unable to move the inert pilot into the well without assistance, the young Canadian had to overcome his reluctance and sit astride the still body of his pilot. Having done this, he was then able to lean forward and grasp the control column and the throttle levers. While he carried out recovery action to correct the near spin, he had to kick the unconscious Walker's feet free of the rudder pedals.

By this time the aircraft was well below 2000 feet and was still being fired upon by the flak defences. Despite the strange manoeuvres, the other two crew members remained blissfully unaware of the problem facing their navigator. Eventually, by rocking the wings violently, Romans managed to attract the attention of the W/Op, who wriggled forward into the well and started to drag the still form of Walker from under Romans, who had to stand on the rudder pedals in order to take his weight off the body. In the cramped space and in almost total darkness, the W/Op's task was almost impossible. However, by the time Romans had got the Hampden up to 6000 feet, he had succeeded in turning the body over and lowering it into the well, where he turned the unconscious pilot around and sat him on the well floor. Despite careful examination, the W/Op could find no sign of injury until he removed Walker's helmet. He then found a small puncture just behind one ear, from which there was little sign of bleeding. He bandaged the wound and gave the pilot a shot of morphine. The wound, though small, had proved fatal. A piece of shrapnel had penetrated the brain, killing Walker instantly.

Having, as he thought, made the pilot as comfortable as possible, the W/Op moved behind Romans to provide any further assistance. The young Canadian was indeed in need of assistance, but there was little that the W/Op could usefully do to help. The two near misses had peppered the bomber with shrapnel, most of it striking the starboard wing between the engine and the fuselage. The damage had wrought havoc with the instruments and destroyed the prime navigation instrument, the gyro compass. As soon as he had gained control of the aircraft, Romans had carried out a quick check of the instrument panel. He had been momentarily horrified to see that both RPM guages were reading zero; however a brief glance out of the side windows of the cockpit showed that both engines appeared to be functioning normally.

Although they were now clear of the flak and searchlights, Romans had other problems. Not only did he have to fly the aircraft, he was the only one on board who knew how to navigate it; though how he was to do this with his master gyro out of action was another matter. He despatched the W/Op down to the nose station to collect his maps, charts and navigation equipment, including the astro sextant. During the three hour trip back across the North Sea, Romans somehow managed to work out and take an astronautical fix of his position, using the stars. His calculations must have been reasonably accurate as they eventually recovered to Waddington via the approved approach route. Even then his troubles were not over. Realising that their damaged aircraft might pose a threat to other landing aircraft, Romans decided to orbit the aerodrome until the other returning aircraft were down. During the final stages of the approach, the W/Op nursed Walker's head in his hands to protect it. After touching down it became apparent that the brakes were inoperative. That, allied with a punctured tyre, caused the Hampden to swing off the line of the grass runway and head for the hangars! As it careered across the grass, it struck an obstruction which tipped it up on one wing and slewed it around. The bomber then collided with the Station Commander's car (luckily empty at the time), followed by that of the Station Adjutant, before skidding over a gunpit, finally coming to rest with its lower fuselage completely torn away.

For his gallantry that night, Dave Romans was awarded the DFC. In view of the problems that he had to overcome in the cramped confines of a Hampden, in the dark and under fire, had the navigator not been a man of the calibre of the young Canadian, the BBC announcer may well have reported "One of our aircraft is missing".

This was not to be the only remarkable performance by Romans during his time on No 44 Squadron. During the night of 31 August 1940, he was the pilot of Hampden P2123. They had taken off at 2005hr for an attack on Berlin, but on the return their aircraft ran out of fuel at 0620hr the next morning, as they approached Cromer. Romans' ditching was near perfect, enabling the crew to take to their dinghy and paddle ashore, reaching safety after unknowingly strolled across a heavily mined beach! Four days later Romans, flying with a different crew, took off at 2035hr for an attack on distant Stettin. Almost ten hours later he had to ditch his Hampden (P4290) off Lowestoft, from where a naval patrol vessel collected them, none the worse for the experience.

Dave Romans completed an eventful tour on No 44 Squadron at Waddington and was posted just across the way to the recently arrived No 207 Squadron, which was in process of equipping with the new Avro Manchester. He was not destined to remain with No 207 Squadron for long, leaving on posting at the end of June 1941 to another newly forming unit, No 90 Squadron. This squadron was in process of exchanging its Blenheim IVs for the American Boeing B17 Flying Fortress. Sadly, he did not survive for very long, being shot down by Bf109s over Norway on 8 September 1941 during a daylight attack on the German battleship the Admiral Scheer, moored in Oslo harbour. None of the crew survived and all are buried at Bygland near Oslo. Two weeks later, Bomber Command decided against using the Fortress in daylight as the type, few in number, had proved to be inadequate for daylight operations over Europe. The remaining No 90 Squadron aircraft were sent to the Middle East.

Two Crews Who Didn't Quite Make it

During the early stages of the air war, it could be said that at times, Bomber Command had a rather cavalier approach to the problems associated with carrying out attacks on long range targets. As Sgt G E Harris, who flew with P/O H P Clarke recalled:

"Six crews from our squadron (No 44) attended a briefing for an attack on a factory that was building Ju87 Stuka divebombers, near Dessau. We were informed that the estimated flight time for the trip was a little under nine hours. As the endurance of the standard Hampden was approximately eight hours, we were more than a little concerned; making our feelings known. In reply, we were told that...favourable winds at high level would facilitate the necessary fuel economies...

Furthermore, we were advised that Royal Navy Motor Torpedo Boats (MTBs) would be patrolling off the East Coast near our planned return route in order to pick up any ditched crews. During our attack we were hit in the starboard wing by a flak shell. Despite jettisoning all removeable equipment, our Hampden ran out of fuel while we were still over Holland. Our pilot belly-landed on the beach at the water's edge, where we destroyed all our maps and charts etc. We tried using pieces of parachute to act as wicks in order to set fire to what little fuel remained. After numerous unsuccessful attempts, we finally managed to set fire to our parachutes by firing Verey cartridges into them at close range. This in turn set our aircraft alight, which burned fiercely, the ammunition and remaining Verey cartridges making quite a display. Some exploding debris set fire to a nearby wheatfield, which attracted the attention of two Bf109s, which circled overhead. Despite our efforts at escape and evasion, we all ended up as PoWs".

P/O Hynes and crew, also of No 44 Squadron, were not quite so lucky. Tasked to attack the oil refinery at Gelsenkirchen, flying in Hampden P4372, they were hit just as the navigator, P/O Dunkels, called "Bombs Gone". At that instant their aircraft was rocked by a tremendous explosion and immediately burst into flames. Over the intercom came the anguished cry "Christ, I've lost my leg!" It was Dunkels, whose position had taken the brunt of the explosion. Hynes managed to keep control of the stricken bomber long enough for the crew to abandon it. Sgt Wicker, the W/Op, joined Sgt Wainwright, the lower gunner, at the lower escape hatch just in time to snatch his (Wainwright) intercom and oxygen connections from their sockets as the gunner dropped out. Sgt Wicker lost one of his flying boots in bailing out, but despite this, together with heavy rain and the fact that he landed inside a German Army camp, he remained free for some time. With the exception of P/O Dunkells, who died of his injuries, the three remaining crew members spent the remainder of the war as PoWs.

Since the outbreak of war, Bomber and Coastal Commands had carried out numerous attacks on a variety of targets in occupied Belgium, France, Holland, Denmark and Norway as well as those in Germany. In July1940, the two commands flew a total of 383 sorties against enemy airfields alone, while in August, the total rose to 714 sorties. These attacks were, in part, intended to assist the hard pressed pilots of Fighter Command in their epic struggle with the Luftwaffe. Then, in September, a new threat became apparent. Following the fall of France, the German High Command commenced preparing plans for a possible invasion of Britain. To counter the threat of attack by the Royal Navy and aircraft of the RAF, the Luftwaffe was alloted the task of gaining air supremacy over the Channel and South Coast areas; hence the Battle of Britain. Meanwhile, preparations were under way in many of the Channel ports for the assembly and subsequent launching of Operation Sealion - the invasion of the British Isles.

The Other Battle of Britain (The Battle of the Barges)

During July and August of 1940, the pilots of Fighter Command took on the might of the Luftwaffe in the

Battle of Britain. Meanwhile, the crews of Bomber and Coastal Commands went about their business largely unheralded.

Considerable activity had been observed on the rivers and canals of Germany and Holland as barges of all types made their way to the Channel ports. Many were sea-going barges, some of which had been modified to carry tanks, guns and lorries in addition to troops, ammunition and other essentials. Following on from their successes in France and the low countries, the Germans moved in hundreds of anti-aircraft guns, searchlights and balloons to defend the vulnerable masses of barges. In addition, thousands of assault troops were moved into the nearby assembly areas to await the order to sail. The barges were massed in the ports of north-west Germany, Holland, Belgium and northern France.

Within No 5 Group, the practice was to allocate a particular port to a particular squadron and a particular basin, which might contain several hundred barges, to a particular crew. In this way, all crews became familiar with their assigned target and it engendered a spirit of competition as to who could destroy the most barges in any one night.

As September wore on, the tempo of the 'Battle of the Barges' increased and continued by day and by night. The concentration of searchlights and flak guns, together with the fires from burning barges and dock installations caused the aircrews taking part to christen the Channel ports - 'The Blackpool Front'. Despite the defences, the bomber crews took delight in being able to attack targets that were easy to locate and large enough to hit. On 8 September, three crews of No 44 Squadron attacked barge concentrations at Ostend. All three crews completed their attacks successfully, although W/Cdr Reid's aircraft was hit three times in the tail section. The following day twelve crews attacked barges at Boulogne and Ostend, followed that night by a five aircraft attack on barges at Calais. The Hampden (P4371) flown by F/Lt Rogers and crew failed to return; there were no survivors.

Among the crew members taking part in the attacks on the barges was Sgt Jim Taylor,a W/OpAG on No 44 Squadron. He recalled: "I was enjoying a show in the Theatre Royal in Lincoln when they announced that all RAF aircrew were to return to their stations immediately. On arriving back at Waddington, we were told that the barges were reported as being loaded and moved to the outer harbours. I became part of a scratch crew flying with our CO, W/Cdr Reid. Our bombs were fitted with seven second delay fuses and we went in at low level to recce our target before attacking. Having identified his target, W/Cdr Reid climbed up to 1000 feet, the worst possible height for flak as virtually all calibres could get at you up there! Almost immediately we were coned by the searchlights and pounded by what seemed to be all the flak in the World - light, medium and heavy. Inevitably, we were hit and I was fascinated to see lumps flying off our tail, that is until lumps started flying off my radio set right next to me. I fired off a mixture of Verey lights in the hope of distracting the flak crews. Both the under gunner and myself fired off long bursts at the searchlights, but as it was almost as bright as day over the docks, I doubt that it made much difference, though it did make us both feel better to be actually doing something vaguely militaristic."

For his gallantry in this attack on the barge concentrations, W/Cdr Reid was awarded the DFC. The citation read 'One night in September 1940, this officer successfully carried out a dive bombing attack on an assembly of barges in Ostend harbour. On arrival over the target area, he made reconnaissance runs at an altitude of 1000 feet, during which he carefully selected the most vital parts to attack. He then climbed to 6000 feet and made a dive attack to 500 feet, obtaining direct hits on the target with a stick of eight 250lb bombs. During the preliminary runs and in the attack, intense anti-aircraft fire seriously damaged his aircraft, affecting its controls and shattering the pilot' compass and the rear gun hatches. Despite these difficulties, W/Cdr Reid pressed home his attack with great determination, courage and skill, showing complete disregard for his personal safety."

On the night of 11/12 September, Bomber Comand despatched 106 aircraft to bomb the Channel ports, Berlin and Bremerhaven. Most of the effort was directed against the barges, but F/Lt Smythe DFC, of No 44 Squadron, had volunteered, together with three other crews, to attack the liners Bremen and Europa in Bremerhaven docks. Sgt W H Jones took Jim Taylor's place and his flying kit, to fly with Smythe. The four Hampdens attacked the liners from 2000 feet and scored several hits. F/Lt Smythe and crew flying in Hampden P1338 and P/O Stewart and crews in Hampden X2913 did not return, both falling victim to the heavy defences. There were no survivors from either crew.

The loss of Smythe was a bitter blow to the squadron and Station, as he was one of the most experienced pilots on the squadron. In peacetime, he had been a pilot in one of the popular travelling circuses and in one year of war he had progressed from Sergeant Pilot to Flight Lieutenant DFC; he would be sorely missed.

The attacks on the Channel ports continued without respite, with the total of destroyed and damaged barges mounting. So too were the losses to Bomber Command which, while not particularly heavy in any one attack, there was a constant, steady draining away of the old and not so old hands. In order to demonstrate its flexibility and growing strength, the Command despatched a force of 129 aircraft to attack Berlin on the night of 23/24 September. Of the total force, 112 claimed to have identified and attacked their designated target. Then it was back to the Channel ports, including an attack on the battle cruiser Scharnhorst, berthed in Kiel harbour. Unbeknown to Bomber Command at the time, the German High Command had ordered the invasion shipping to be dispersed in order to reduce losses resulting from RAF attacks. At the height of the Battle of the Barges, the Germans had amassed 994 invasion craft at the ports of Boulogne, Calais, Dunkirk, Gravelines, LeHavre, Nieuport and Ostend. Furthermore, there were an additional 1497 vessels in transit to the Channel ports.

As the pilots of Fighter Command had won their battle, so too had the crews of Bomber and Coastal Commands. In a report to Hitler, the German Admiral Raeder advised him that: 'Interuptions by the enemy's air forces...have assumed major significance. The harbours at Ostend, Dunkirk, Calais and Boulogne cannot be used as night anchorages for shipping because of the danger from English bombing...further delays are expected in the assembly of the invasion fleet...' Each September the nation rightly recalls the heroism of the pilots of Fighter Command in their epic struggle against the odds in the Battle of Britain. But few if any seem to remember that the other half of the battle, the Battle of the Barges, was also won and was equally critical. To put it in its right perspective, three quotes might be appropriate: In A J P Taylor's 'The History of World War Two', he writes:

"...On 17 September, Hitler postponed his invasion plans indefinitely, having realised more clearly than Goering, that no longer could vast concentrations of barges, troops and military stores be maintained in the face of Bomber Command's devastating attacks...Bomber Command had destroyed a great part of the shipping and war material on which the invasion depended..."

Taylor goes on to say that the British people had for centuries become accustomed to the idea that battles always took place on distant high seas or in far away countries; now the battle was at home!

Another well-known historian, John Terraine, writing in his book 'Right of the Line', goes on to say:

"...I consider it a blemish in existing accounts that British air losses in the fight for national survival almost never include those of Bomber and Coastal Commands...the Roll of Honour in the Battle of Britain Memorial Chapel in Westminster Abbey contains the names of 718 aircrew of Bomber Command and 280 of Coastal Command, plus 537 of Fighter Command, making a total of 1535. In other words, Bomber Command suffered just under 50 per cent of the RAF casualties during the Battle of Britain in the loss of 246 aircraft on offensive operations. Furthermore, in all probability this figure for Bomber Command does not include those bombers which, having returned to the British Isles, failed to make a safe landing."

The last reference, surprisingly, is contained in the August 1976 edition of the British Army Review. In this, a writer states:

"Traditionally, the comparison has been made in terms of British fighters against German fighters and bombers combined. For some reason, Bomber Command has usually been left out of the calculations. Yet Bomber Command's strikes against the invasion fleet in the Channel ports were to play a major part in forcing a decision on the German High Command to disband their Sea Lion forces. No one would wish to detract for one moment from the magnificent achievements of 'The Few', but history must be served. It does no service to the RAF to preserve a myth which in fact conceals a very considerable achievement (by Bomber Command) in terms of organisation and logistic support, that contributed quite as much to the success of the Battle of Britain as the heroism of the Hurricane and Spitfire pilots in the air".

One comment that frequently occurs when talking to the handful of survivors from the early days of the war, is to the effect that civilians who lived and worked near the bomber airfields of Lincolnshire and Yorkshire, could not properly comprehend that the men in blue uniforms, that they saw in the local pubs and cinemas, were frequently engaged in fierce, deadly battles. An often heard remark was "But he can't be dead... He was sitting here only last night..."

So, from their remote bases, far removed from the major British cities and the representatives of the media, the crews of Bomber Command went about their deadly and dangerous business, unsung and virtually unoticed. As Gilbert Haworth, one of the Waddington participants recalled:

"When most members of the British public thought about barges, they mentally pictured an English canal with a horse plodding along a towpath, pulling a brightly painted long, narrow boat - not much of a target, surely? ...our briefings were sketchy and we took off in our own good time...it did not matter if you were 30 minutes late getting off. Crews could more or less pick their own route to and from their target, although there might be a recommended route. Most of us had to walk out to the dispersal points; it was quicker than waiting for the transport...the Germans were always more than ready for us with their countless and formidable flak batteries. There was never any element of surprise in our favour. We were briefed that our enemy hoped to deter us by skillful deployment of anti-aircraft weapons.

The inclusion of an abnormal proportion of tracer ammunition made their 20mm calibre barrage extremely conspicuous and doubly threatening. Their strategy was to cover target areas by an intense and continuous barrage of unaimed light flak. Shooting usually commenced well before any attackers were within range; the whole idea being to create a frightening display as a deterrent. Our orders were to ensure that their hope was a vain one. ...Calais for instance seemed to have an especially fiery ceiling, provided by endless streams of tracer. A most apt description was 'like a giant incandescent waterfall laid on its side'..."

The Second Year of the War

The Battle of the Barges over, the pace of operations eased slightly. This gave time to celebrate some of the awards gained by Waddington personnel. In addition to W/Cdr Reid, S/Ldrs Collier and Gardner, F/Lt 'Frankie' Eustace and P/Os K Jones, W J Lewis and P M deMestre were all awarded the DFC. Sgt Don Wintle gained a DFM, as did two members of two other crews. F/Sgt J F Clayton and his navigator Sgt J C Chesters and Sgt E E Collins and his navigator Sgt R S Ayton.

During August the Germans had dropped thousands of propaganda leaflets entitled 'Hitler's Appeal to Reason'. These contained extracts from his various speeches and the Lincolnshire based aircrew, among many others, found them mildly amusing. On 1 September the German bombers dropped more lethal cargoes, when Lincolnshire suffered its severest air attack to date, with some 144 high explosive bombs, plus 250 incendiaries being dropped. The nearest to Waddington were dropped at Harmston Hall; the enemy was getting nearer! From then on enemy bombers were frequent visitors to the area, though they did not actually attack Waddington until 28 September, when a lone intruder dropped a stick of incendiaries near the bomb dump without causing any damage Then, much later, on 9 November, a Bf110 coming from the direction of Harmston, attacked the aerodrome with cannon and machine gun fire, hitting one of the hangars. The ground defences engaged the intruder with enthusiasm, curbing any ideas the enemy pilot may have had for a second pass.

Towards the end of the year, Jim Taylor was coming to the end of his tour. He had flown over 200 hours on operations and was posted to the newly forming No 207 Squadron, which had taken up residence at Waddington. He recalled:

"Most of the pre-war aircrew could see little prospect of surviving the war, so we were inclined to live for the day, making the most of booze, women and leave. I noticed towards the end of 1940 that some of us at Waddington were showing definite signs of stress, but we were afforded scant sympathy and even less help."

Jim's last trip on No 44 Squadron nearly resulted in his going out with a bang. He was flying with S/Ldr Broad when they had to return early from a mining sortie and land at Upper Heyford. Something went wrong on the approach and their Hampden (P1324) crashed, still with its 1500lb mine on board! Jim Taylor's comment on returning to Waddington was a paraphrase of the words used by the Duke of Wellington - "I don't know what effect he has on the enemy, but by God he frightens me!" A few days later, the unfortunate S/Ldr Broad had an even more unsettling experience. On the night of 16 October, Waddington Hampdens formed part of a mixed force of 73 bombers attacking targets in northern Germany and France. The weather over the target was a problem, but of little consequence when compared with that which greeted the returning aircraft. After a long and tiring trip, the returning crews found that Waddington was fogged in. Sgt Neil, flying in Hampden P2142, made two attempts to land using the 'ZZ' procedure but, after nearly colliding with the Station water tower, he diverted to Bircham Newton near Hunstanton. By the time Neil got there, Bircham Newton too had fogged in, necessitating a second diversion, this time to Mildenhall in Suffolk. Unfortunately, after nine hours in the air, the aircraft ran out of fuel and Neil was forced to land in a beet field near Ramsey, close to RAF Upwood. The crew evacuated their aircraft having suffered only minor cuts and bruises; their aircraft being declared Category 'R' and flew again following repairs, some time later.

The remaining crews had no better luck, two of them crashing at Waddington while trying to land. F/Lt Ogilvie in P4414 struck the corner of one of the remaining World War I hangars sited near High Dyke, but luckily none of the crew were injured. Their aircraft being declared Category 'A' repairable. S/Ldr Broad meanwhile, was flying in Hampden X2997 with Sgts Hammond, Logan and Egar, having returned from their attack on Merseburg. In attempting to land, Broad too hit the roof of one of the World War I hangars, bounced off and fell to the ground close to one of the bulk fuel installations. Broad suffered a broken leg, while Sgt Hammond suffered injuries to both knees. Their aircraft was declared Category 'W' - a write off.

The autumn and winter weather forced a reduction in the tempo of operations, though whenever the weather was flyable, the crews of Bomber Command would be out either attacking targets in Germany and the occupied countries, or busy laying mines in the enemy's main shipping channels. At about this time, an additional campaign was conducted, this one in the city of Lincoln. The details are well documented in Gibson's excellent book 'Enemy Coast Ahead', but basically it appears to have started as a result of too much beer. The battlefield was a popular watering hole for aircrew in Lincoln, the Saracen's Head hotel, more often referred to as 'The Snakepit'. The main protagonists were No 44 Squadron, representing the 'Bomber Barons', with Nos 29 and 151 Fighter Squadrons representing the 'Glamour Boys'. Whatever initiated what came to be known locally as 'The Battle of the Snakepit' is lost in the mists of time, but the opening move was made by No 44 Squadron when three Hampdens took off fully loaded with toilet rolls and old leaflets. Arriving overhead RAF Digby at lunch time, the three bombers proceeded to beat up the place in some style. The roar of engines attracted the lunching fighter pilots, who ran out of their Mess to see what was going on. By the time they got to the Mess forecourt, the Hampdens had departed, leaving the sky full of paper. Such a challenge could not be allowed to go unanswered!

The following day began with low cloud and rain. With the routine flying programme cancelled, the crews of No 44 Squadron were either undertaking administrative chores or lounging around in their crewroom. Out of the grey murk, a black Blenheim night fighter, carrying no identification markings, landed and taxied up to the control tower. Over the radio, the visitor asked to see the No 44 Squadron Gunnery Officer at the aircraft. When this worthy appeared and climbed into the Blenheim, a bag was pulled over his head, his arms pinioned and he was unceremoniously flown to Digby. Once there, he was given a long stick with a spike in the end and invited to pick up all the paper that his crews had delivered the previous day. His task done, he was returned unharmed to Waddington.

Several days passed without further incident. Then, one lunch time, the Officers' Mess at Digby played host to a few visitors, among whom were a padre, an engineering officer and one or two others. They were not particularly talkative, had lunch and went on their way. Some time later it was discovered that the collection of unit crests was missing from the entrance hall of the Mess. Suspecting 'foul play', cars were despatched in hot pursuit of the so-called visitors, of which of course there was no sign. Meanwhile at Waddington, the 'visitors' were explaining to an admiring audience how well they had done. The crests were duly photographed adorned by various insulting appendages, before being returned to Digby as surreptitiously as they had been taken. To add insult to injury, there on the Mess notice board was a selection of the insulting photographs for all to see.

For some days nothing happened; indeed the fighter boys were conspicuous by their absence from The Snakepit. Then one afternoon, the air above Waddington was rent assunder as two squadrons of Beaufighters proceeded to beat up the aerodrome in no uncertain fashion. The show over, the Beaus left leaving the No 44 Squadron boys agreeing that it had been a good performance, but that there seemed to have been little real purpose in it. But purpose there was, which became all too apparent when it was time to leave the Mess for the Flights. The cloakroon had been denuded of that most prized possession of bomber pilots, their operational caps. Such a low, cunning, dastardly act ensured that there were few Waddington faces in the Saracen's Head that evening. Worse was to follow; the following day a Beaufighter appeared low over Waddington, beat up the Mess and jettisoned all the hats into the mud of the sportsfield. There was an immediate rush to retrieve the headgear, but the Digby team too had added insult to injury. They had carefully removed or obliterated all identification markings.

From then on the battle raged fast and furious, with some schemes verging on the homicidal. Indeed, one of these was a western style gunfight which began in the Snakepit and ended up through the arches of the Lincoln Stonebow. Luckily, neither the participants nor any innocent bystanders or passers-by were injured. Eventually, when it became known that the numerically superior 'Bomber Barons' threatened to debag any 'Glamour Boy' so unwise as to appear in the Snakepit, the two Station Commanders gave orders that the battle was to cease. Both sides were told to concentrate on the other war.

On 5 November, the newly promoted Gp Capt J L Kirby took over command of RAF Waddington from Gp Capt Anderson, who left to become Deputy Director of Training for Canadians serving in the RAF. Meanwhile, on the international political front, the Soviet Foreign Minister, Vyacheslav Molotov, was on a visit to Berlin. In the course of the discussions, during which the German Foreign Minister, von Ribbentrop was offering parts of a dismembered British Empire to Russia as part of the Nazi/Soviet understanding. He went on to assure a sceptical Molotov that Britain was as good as finished. Molotov was not convinced, and not being a patient or diplomatic man, snapped "If England is in fact defeated and powerless, why have we been conducting this business in your air raid shelter?" Seven months later, Hitler unleashed Operation Barbarossa, the German invasion of Russia.

At about the time of the meeting between Molotov and von Ribbentrop, P/O H R 'Socks' Stockings of No 44 Squadron took off from Waddington in Hampden P1332 for the long flight to Danzig in occupied Poland. His aircraft had been specially modified to carry extra fuel tanks under the wings in place of the standard bomb racks. The purpose of the trip was to let the Poles know that they had not been forgotten. Having identified the target and dropped his bombs, Stockings returned to Waddington, landing after a flight of over twelve hours, for which feat he was subsequently awarded the DFC.

With the Luftwaffe now concentrating on night bombing, the Hampdens of No 44 Squadron were given an additional task. As the recently arrived S/Ldr Ken Smales recalled:

"The idea was to scramble from Waddington and climb to 20,000 feet over whichever English city was under attack. We were then supposed to locate the enemy bombers and shoot them down (sic). For this purpose, we carried an extra air gunner, who manned a hand-held machine gun which was fired from amidships through slots in the fuselage. At night this position was worse than useless as all it achieved was to let a blast of freezing air into the fuselage, much to the disgust of all

concerned. Although we saw several Ju88s, Dorniers and Heinkels during the three or four nights of the trial, they were always either too high or too fast for us. The trial was considered a failure, if for no other reason than the fact that the Hampden carried only one 0.303" fixed forward firing machine gun. However, the flying was a welcome if brief relief from bombing operations". Ken Smales, who retired as Gp Capt Smales DSO DFC, went on to add: "It was often said that if you kicked a Hampden it would burst into flames, and to the crews it did at times seems like it. But on at least one occasion in a snow storm, a burning Hampden on the Waddington aerodrome enabled half a dozen other aircraft to get in by the light of the fire".

S/Ldr Smales was to go on to complete two tours of operations with No 44 Squadron at Waddington. His first tour running from October 1940 until June 1941 as OC 'B' Flight; his second was as the CO, from May 1942 to January 1943, by which time the squadron had been equipped with Lancasters.

The Introduction of Area Bombing

Following the heavy attacks by the Luftwaffe on Coventry and Southampton, the War Cabinet authorised the C in C Bomber Command, Air Marshal Sir Richard Pierse, to undertake a general attack on the centre of a German city in retaliation. Mannheim, south of Frankfurt, was selected and a force of 200 bombers assigned to the task. The attack was code-named Operation Abigail Rachel, and took place on the night of 16/17 December. The weather forecast indicated that conditions over the British bomber aerodromes would deteriorate throughout the night. Accordingly, the size of the force was reduced to 134 bombers, which included 29 Hampdens, three of them from Waddington. The weather over the target was almost cloudless and there was a full moon. The attack commenced with eight experienced Wellington crews endeavouring to mark the city centre with incendiaries. This was to be the first time that Bomber Command was deliberately aiming for a town rather than a specific factory, oil installation or marshalling yard. It was to be however, the forerunner of what the Germans would come to call 'Terror Bombing', but which the Allies would term 'Area Bombing'. Despite the reduction in the size of the attacking force this was still the largest attacking force directed against one target to date. The results were disappointing, mainly due to the inaccurate marking by the Wellington crews, but Mannheim was located and attacked, thereby pointing the way ahead.

The operation against Mannheim indicated the type of attack best suited to the true capabilities of Bomber Command at the time. Most of its crews were just not able to locate blacked out targets in most of Germany, certainly not with a view to carrying out precision attacks. It also indicated to the Luftwaffe the need for a better organised and equipped night defence organisation. Unfortunately for the crews of Bomber Command, the Germans took this lesson on board only too well. Meanwhile at Waddington there were strange 'goings on' in one of the hangars. A batch of American built Douglas DB7 twin engined bombers, known in the RAF as the Boston, had arrived. That they had originally been intended for the French Armee de l'Air was evident from their markings and the cockpit instrumentation. Six of these machines arrived at Waddington in December 1940 and were formed into 'The DB7 Flight'. This so-called Flight came under the command of OC 'A' Flight of No 44 Squadron, S/Ldr Stubbs.

Throughout its brief existence, the DB7 Flight was administered by No 44 Squadron. The purpose of the Flight was to investigate the possibility of converting the Boston bomber into a night fighter, which was subsequently known as the Havoc. In addition to S/Ldr Stubbs, 'Paddy' Ayton and several other Waddington pilots were checked out on the DB7. All agreed that it was a beautiful aircraft to fly. Among the navigators and W/Ops assigned to the DB7 Flight were Sergeants John 'Totem' Wells, Jim Bloor, Jock Bryce and Grindley, the latter becoming the resident expert in arming the eight nose-mounted 0.303" machine guns. Jock Bryce recalled:

"The plan was for us to operate from satellite aerodromes between London and Grantham, but how we were supposed to locate enemy aircraft was never explained. The Flight never became operational before it was disbanded, without us ever firing a shot in anger."

Another stalwart of the DB7 project was John Wells who recalled:

"The Bostons were to be painted matt black and it was to be called the Havoc. We were told that once the Flight was fully worked up, we were to become night fighters. I was really quite thrilled at the prospect of something different, having just completed my first tour while on No 50 Squadron, during which I took part in one of the first leaflet raids over Germany, dropping our 'Nickels' over Bremen. On the DB7 Flight, we flew cross country flights, practiced night flying and fired our guns over the Wash ranges. Later, we became the subject of a Fighter vs Bomber Command squabble. Fighter Command insisted that as the DB7 was to be a fighter, the unit should come under its control. On the other hand, Bomber Command's position was that as its pilots had more night flying experience than those of Fighter Command, the unit should remain under Bomber Command control. This was finally resolved on high towards the end of February 1941 when the DB7s were assigned to Fighter Command. However, Bomber Command would not release the crews, so the DB7 Flight was disbanded and the aircraft flown away. Only one Waddington aviator went with the DB7s, a chap called Martin.

I enjoyed flying in the DB7, though I remember being surprised to find an emergency control column in the rear gunner's position, apparently for use (!) if the pilot should be killed. I recall also being somewhat concerned to find that the observer/navigator, unlike in the Hampden, was unable to leave his station in the nose in flight."

A last word on the DB7 comes from Jock Bryce, who recalled:

"...during the months of January and February 1941 I was with the DB7 Flight, which was attached to No 44 Squadron at Waddington. The Flight Commander was S/Ldr Stubbs, but we never became operational. When we were disbanded, towards the end of February, John Wells and I asked for an interview with W/Cdr Hyde, the CO of the recently formed No 207 Squadron, which was bringing the new Manchester aircraft into service. The Wing Commander accepted us as volunteers, John Wells going to 'A' Flight, being subsequently shot down flying with W/Cdr Hyde in an attack on Kiel. I went to 'B' Flight, where I crewed up with my DB7 pilot, P/O 'Paddy' Ayton. 'B' Flight became the nucleus of the second Manchester unit, No 97 Squadron, and we moved with it to Coningsby under the command of W/Cdr Balsdon in March 1941. My stay with No 207 Squadron was so brief that I hardly had time to unpack my gear, though I did manage to make a one hour local flight with P/O Gardiner. Later, while on No 97 Squadron, we were returning from an attack on Berlin on 10 may when we were forced to ditch in the North Sea due to catastrophic engine failure This was our first operational sortie in a Manchester as a crew and ended after almost five days at sea in our dinghy, when we were picked up by some Dutch trawlers and landed at Ijmuiden and into captivity. That was the sum total of my Manchester experience; brief and not much to show for it."

Possibly the last Waddington aircraft and crew to be lost in 1940 was that of S/Ldr N H J Tindall. He and his crew were on a minelaying sortie off the mouth of the Gironde in Hampden X3049 when they were hit by flak which punctured their fuel tanks. At 0901hr on 11 December the RAF listening service picked up a message from them saying 'OK. Down in France'. Sgt Peter Tebbutt was flying as a second W/OpAG and had returned to the aircraft to send the message when it failed to burn, despite their best efforts. While he was transmitting the message, one of the crew managed to release some incendiaries which exploded, detonating one of the aircraft oxygen bottles, which shot skywards from its rack. Peter Tebbutt left the Hampden at speed voicing his displeasure!

Enter the Avro Manchester

With the departure of No 50 Squadron, Waddington had a decidedly empty appearance, but with an expanding Bomber Command, it was obvious that such a situation would not last for long. One of those experiencing such thoughts was the newly arrived Flight Commander on No 44 Squadron, S/Ldr Norman 'Hettie' Hyde. He had arrived on the squadron in July 1940, his first operational posting. As he recalled:

"After only one month on operations as a Flight Commander on No 44 Squadron, I was sent for by the AOC, Air Vice Marshal Harris. During an interview at his No 5 Group Headquarters, he told me that I was to reform No 207 Squadron at Waddington with the express purpose of introducing the new heavy bomber, the Avro Manchester, into squadron service. On returning to Waddington I carried out a rapid clearance and departed for the Aircraft and Armament Experimental Establishment (A&AEE) at RAF Boscombe Down. I arrived there towards the end of August 1940 and went solo on this monster aircraft in a few days, flying the second prototype L7247. During the next two months I gained considerable experience of the new aircraft, flying L7247 and the first production Manchester L7276. I remember that on 9 September, I flew from Boscombe Down to Grantham (RAF Spitalgate) to fly the AOC. For this trip we had the Director of Engineering at the A&AEE, Mr Rowarth, as our Flight Engineer.

While I was gaining experience on the Manchester, I was in frequent contact with Group personnel staffs in order to select capable, experienced captains for the new aircraft. I was fortunate in that a number of the pre-war air force pilots were about to complete, or had recently completed, their first tour of operations flying Hampdens. My first selection was an Australian, F/Lt Johnny Siebert, who had been on my Flight on No 44 Squadron. Shortly after this, I was delighted to be offered S/Ldr Charles 'Captain' Kydd, a great chap who had already earned a DSO and a DFC on Hampdens. Among the others assigned to me were Peter Burton-Gyles, Derek French, Frankie Eustace, Mike Lewis and Ronnie Stubbs. Others came after the squadron was officially formed and included Hugh Morgan, Dave Romans, John Nunn, 'Golly' Bird, Chris Frost, Harwood, Taylor, Gardiner, Paape, Stewart, Herring, Hall, Heartland, Robson, and Stevens. I was also fortunate to get Sgt Panton, a navigator who had flown with me before the war at the A &AEE when it was located at Martlesham Heath. Then, shortly before the new squadron was declared operational, 'B' Flight was detached to form the nucleus of the second Manchester squadron, No 97 Squadron, under the command of W/Cdr D F Balsdon. On 1 November 1940, No 207 Squadron was officially reformed and seven days later,S/Ldr Kydd and I flew Manchester L7279 up to Waddington from Boscombe Down. We were given just under four months in which to get all our aircraft and to train the crews up to operational standards."

In the meantime, the advance element of the ground staff flew into Waddington in a Harrow transport aircraft, followed almost immediately by a steady flow of Manchesters. By the end of the year the squadron possessed eight Manchesters on charge, which increased to a full compliment of eighteen by 24 February 1941. Among the captains was Derek French who had been on No 50 Squadron at Waddington before its move to Hatfield Woodhouse (Lindholme). He had joined the new squadron from his six month 'rest' at No 16 OTU. In referring to 'Hettie' Hyde, French recalled: *"Although our CO had been non-operational prior to joining No 44 Squadron, the aircrew of No 207 Squadron still admired him because of his record of test flying"*. The squadron personnel quickly developed a great affection for their CO and he in turn, fully acknowledged their operational experience. In Derek French's opinion, No 207 Squadron had the highest morale of any squadron that he ever encountered.

In addition to working up to operational status, the new squadron was given two other responsibilities. The first was to act as a test and development unit for the new aircraft; the second being that of a training unit for converting aircrew of No 5 Group that were assigned to the new bomber. No 207 Squadron, under its energetic CO set about these three tasks in determined fashion. One historian commented, on referring to this phase of the squadron's history: "...the level of experience on the squadron at this time was higher than that of No 617 Squadron when it was working up for the dams raid..."

Signs of coming problems with the Manchester had been evident from the very first. On landing after the first test flight of the prototype, the test pilot, Captain Brown, reported that the aircraft was directionally unstable and that the engines were not giving full power. Following further investigation, the specialists at the Royal Aeronautical Establishment (RAE) advised fitting a third fin for stability. Captain Brown also reported that the Manchester was difficult to land and that its single engine performance was not acceptable. Further research by RAE, AVRO and Boscombe Down resulted in an increase in both the span of the wings and the tailplane. Unfortunately, the major problem, that of the Rolls Royce Vulture engine was never to be overcome. The Manchester was powered by two Vulture engines, rated at 1760hp. In effect, the Vulture comprised two V12 Peregrine engines mounted in opposition on a common crankshaft, resulting in a 24 cylinder 'X' configuration. The purpose behind such a combination was to achieve high power output at a lower power/weight ratio than that of four engines. It was considered also that two powerful engines created less drag than four less powerful ones. As with so many proposed technological advances, the principle was fine, but there had been insufficient facilities and time available to develop the engine and to overcome its problems. The crews who flew the Manchester were to pay a heavy price for this omission. But perhaps the last word on the much-maligned Manchester should come from 'Hettie' Hyde. During a visit to Waddington in 1985, he expressed the opinion that "...the Manchester was a fine aircraft, plagued with unreliable engines..."

As part of his brief to bring No 207 Squadron up to an operational standard without delay, W/Cdr Hyde had been instructed to initiate a programme of intensive flying, in order to achieve 500 hours as quickly as possible. Acknowledging that there remained many unresolved problems with the new bomber, the Air Ministry arranged for a specialist AVRO team to move into Waddington to assist in resolving technical problems. In all, six Manchesters, fitted with the original smaller tailplane were the first to be supplied to the squadron, four of which were held in readiness for the first operation.

One of the early arrivals among the engineering personnel was P/O Eric McCabe. He was posted to the new squadron as the Squadron Engineering Officer on 8 November 1940. When No 207 Squadron was moved to Bottesford one year later, Eric McCabe remained at Waddington as the Station Technical Officer, specifically tasked with seeing in the soon to be received AVRO Lancaster.

By the end of December 1940, No 207 Squadron possessed eleven Manchesters and sixteen crews. Six of the crews were considered to be fully operational by day, but had yet to commence night flying. Between them, the 112 aircrew on the squadron possessed one DSO, six DFCs and seven DFMs. Training was delayed at the start of the new year owing to bad weather, though priority was given to the crews that had reached the night flying stage and to an attached officer S/Ldr D F Balsdon. This officer was attached to No 207 Squadron from HQ No 3 Group, prior to his forming and taking command of No 97 Squadron.

In December, 'Hettie' Hyde had performed a demonstration flight in front of the new AOC No 5 Group, Air Vice Marshal Bottomley. During his visit the Air marshal warned Hyde that in the near future there would be a Royal visit to the station and to his squadron in particular. Accordingly, on 27 January 1941 their majesties King George VI and Queen Elizabeth visited RAF Waddington, where the King conducted an investiture. Among those honoured on this occasion were seven members of No 207 Squadron. Acting Squadron Leader C J F Kydd was decorated with his DSO, while F/Os F E Eustace, W J Lewis, J A Siebert and H Y Matthews were presented with their DFCs, as was P/O G F Reid. In addition, Sgt K H L Houghton was presented with the relatively rare DFM.

The citation to F/O W J 'Mike' Lewis' DFC stated that "...this officer successfully pressed home, in the face of intense and accurate anti-aircraft fire and searchlight glare, a dive bombing attack on a concentration of barges in Antwerp docks. During the dive his aircraft was severely damaged by gun-fire from the ground defences and was rendered temporarily out of control. Since March 1940, P/O Lewis has taken part in 38 operational flights over enemy territory, and as a captain of aircraft has displayed outstanding coolness, determination and devotion to duty..."

Though unknown to anyone at Waddington at the time, just over two weeks before the Royal visit, a new four-engined version of the Manchester, known then as the Mk III, had flown its first flight from the AVRO factory at Woodford near Manchester.

The crews that had been hand-picked to join the new squadron, did so with mixed feelings. In the main they were experienced veterans who had gained their experience the hard way, flying Hampdens against the increasingly heavy defences of the targets in enemy occupied Europe and over Germany. They had seen their comrades in arms go missing, both in action and as a result of flying accidents. Many of them were pre-war regulars and were only too well aware of their dwindling number.

The peacetime RAF had been similar to an Army regiment, or club, with everyone knowing everyone else; or almost. To these men, it was readily apparent that in fourteen months of war, their losses had been grievous. So, in their opinion, to be required to commence another tour of operations, was to say the least hardly conducive to a long and happy life. However, allied with this realistic assessment of their chances was a feeling of pride in being selected to be among the first to fly the new heavy bomber against the enemy. It says much for the courage of the crews of No 207 Squadron that they persevered with the Manchester for over a year; much longer than any other of the units that were equipped with the aircraft. Sadly, few of those joining the squadron on that November day in 1940 were to live to see the Manchester's successor develop into the most successful heavy bomber of the war in Europe

Notwithstanding the many technical problems which plagued the Manchester, particularly in the early period of its front-line service, the youthful exhuberance of the crews resulted in numerous 'hairy' incidents. Among the more experienced crews on the squadron, was that captained by the recently promoted F/Lt Johnny Siebert of the Royal Australian Air Force. At one period during the squadron's work-up phase, Siebert and crew were detached to RAF Duxford for a few days in order to undertake fighter affiliation exercises with the resident fighter squadrons.

On arriving at their dispersal one morning, there was no sign of the groundcrew. Being impatient to take off, Siebert and the three experienced members of his crew, George Formison, Jim Taylor and Pete Gurnell, decided to start up and see themselves off. With both engines running, they removed the chocks and taxied out with a full dummy bomb load aboard. They were well into their take-off run when they realised that the airspeed indicator was not registering. A quick glance outside confirmed their worst fears, the pitot head cover was still in place! Accepting that they would have to land faster than usual in order to ensure that they did not stall on the approach, Siebert decided to divert to the aerodrome at Newmarket, rather than have to admit to their error when questioned by Waddington. En route to Newmarket they spotted a new. large aerodrome under construction. At this point they made their second bad decision of the day and chose to land at the new field. They reasoned that there would be no duty pilot or air traffic controller at an aerodrome under construction, and as such they would probably manage to hide their indiscretion. Unluckily for them, on touching down on the main runway, at what proved to be RAF Waterbeach, they found that the surface of the runway was coated with loose gravel. Consequently, Siebert was unable to bring the Manchester to a halt before it overshot the end of the runway and ploughed through an unoccupied gun position. On the way, their propellers had picked up strands of barbed wire, great lengths of which wrapped themselves around the spinners before the engines could be shut down. Eventually, the chastened crew were collected by a truck from Duxford and the Manchester duly recovered, having suffered a burst tyre and minor damage.

Johnny Siebert and crew were later involved in a second incident, which served to highlight the unreliability of the Manchester's engines. On this occasion they were airborne, having been detailed to check the single-engine performance of the new aircraft. On board was a flight crew of five plus a few soldiers from the airfield defence force, who were along just for the ride. Over Lincoln at 7000 feet, Siebert experienced no problem in maintaining height on one engine (almost unique!), so he decided to shut down the other engine, feather the propeller and initiate a glide. As the big bomber reached 3000 feet he commenced the engine re-start procedure. To his dismay, he found that the unfeathering solenoids were inoperative. So, with the engines roaring but providing little or no motive power, the Manchester continued its downward path. Siebert called for everyone to take up crash positions at the rear of the aircraft, which they did with the exception of Jim Taylor, the W/Op, as he was too busy trying to wind in the trailing aerial. Picking his spot, the Australian made his approach, lowered the flaps and undercarriage and touched down in a ploughed field.

With the speed barely reduced and with the bomber's tail still up, Siebert realised that he was fast approaching the raised bank of the river Witham. With no chance of stopping in time, Siebert hauled back on the control column and just hoped! The Manchester reared up, just crossed over the river and flopped down into another ploughed field on the other side, near the Bardney sugar-beet factory. Breathing a sigh of relief, the crew and passengers evacuated the aircraft and took stock of the damage. Surprisingly, this was confined to the loss of the trailing aerial which Jim Taylor had not managed to fully wind in before the first touch down.

The crew were soon joined by a representative of the local branch of the constabulary, in the form of one village bobby. Minutes later, he was joined by two shotgun armed farmers, all ready to capture 'the Germans'. Taylor made contact with Waddington on the R/T and the assembled party were collected by road transport. Later on, with most of the fuel having been drained and the propellers restored to normal, the Manchester was flown out of the, by now, frozen field, by W/Cdr Hyde flying alone.

The Siebert crew were involved in yet another escapade, though this time not of their own creation. As one of the most experienced crews, they were tasked, towards the end of December, to carry out an endurance test, with the equally experienced Derek French flying as co-pilot. Their duties required them to fly at approximately 17,000 feet between two nominated turning points at RAF Debden in Essex and RAF Dishforth in Yorkshire. As the trial took place on a Sunday, the crew were joined by two Army officers, who had obviously never met the earlier Army passengers! After almost eight hours of monotonous flying back and forth, they were passing over Dishforth for the umpteenth time when Siebert decided that enough was enough and chose to terminate the test. Rather than fly another leg above cloud, he decided to descend to below cloud and return home at low level. The crew and passengers took little interest in the proceedings; indeed Jim Taylor was playing noughts and crosses with one of the Army officers on a page from his Signals Log. As he broke clear of cloud, Siebert found that they had emerged directly overhead RAF Linton-on-Ouse, which had just been attacked by German intruders! They immediately came under fire from the airfield defences which were, by rare chance for once, accurate. One shell burst very close, tearing away part of the starboard wing tip and peppering the rest of the wing with shrapnel. Siebert commenced to take violent evasive action, while Jim Taylor searched feverishly for the colours of the day Verey cartridges which he repeatedly fired off. All this activity was accompanied by various unprintable comments regarding the lack of intelligence and legitimacy of the ground gunners and their aircraft recognition capabilities. This latter point was unfair as there had been very little information made generally available regarding the RAF's new bomber. At one point the crew considered landing at Dishforth and taking issue with the offending defenders in person. Perhaps just as well, good sense prevailed and they flew back to Waddington where the Manchester was repaired.

Another incident, this time not involving the Siebert crew, occured when F/O Frankie Eustace suffered an engine failure shortly after take-off; a feature that was to become all too prevalent in the months to come. Contrary to all the teachings, Eustace carried out a turn-back at very low level and executed a successful downwind landing. The squadron commander congratulated him on his luck and flying skill, while at the same time tearing him off a strip for bad airmanship. It was also about this time that the squadron located its missing silver. On taking command, W/Cdr Hyde was surprised to find that for a squadron whose existence went back to World War I, and which had continued throughout the years of peace, there was a remarkable lack of squadron silver. Purely by chance, one of the squadron's officers paid a visit to RAF Benson in Oxfordshire where, at lunch time, he was somewhat surprised to find himself drinking from a silver tankard engraved '207 Squadron'. Further investigation revealed that Benson were holding over £500 of No 207 Squadron silver. Following the completion of numerous forms, in triplicate at least, the silver was duly transferred to Waddington.

The Manchester was still giving considerable cause for concern, particularly with regard to the engines and hydraulic systems. On the last day of the year, a conference took place at Waddington, the attendees including a high ranking Air Ministry official, the chief designer of AVRO and various Group, Station and other engineering specialists. By this time No 207 Squadron possessed eleven Manchesters and this, together with No 44 Squadron's full compliment of Hampdens, meant that there was insufficient suitable parking space or dispersals on the aerodrome. It was decided to deploy some of the Manchesters to the nearby fighter aerodrome of Coleby Grange.

On 20 January, another officer assigned to the yet to form No 97 Squadron arrived, to join W/Cdr Balsdon. F/Lt J S Sherwood came on attachment to No 207 Squadron from No 144 Squadron, which was flying its Hampdens from Hemswell. John Seymour Sherwood, known to his contemporaries as 'Flap', was later to have a miraculous escape when he was blown out of his exploding Lancaster near Augsburg. At the time, he was leading the No 97 Squadron element of the daring, but ill-fated low level daylight attack on the U-boat engine works. Three days after Sherwood's arrival, the AOC No 5 Group, AVM Bottomley visited the Station to discuss the possibility of limited operations by the Manchesters. The outcome of these discussions was a general, but qualified agreement that the aircraft should begin to join in the war.

Despite the fact that the results of the 500 hour trials on the six specified aircraft had not been fully analysed, it was decided that by imposing selective restrictions, and ensuring the engines did not overheat while climbing after take-off (sic), the Manchester could be cleared to carry out attacks on relatively short range targets, albeit with a reduced bomb load of 6000lb. On 24 February six Manchesters of No 207 Squadron carried out the first operational attack of Bomber Command's newest aircraft. The target was the German cruiser Admiral Hipper, in dock in the French port of Brest. The crews taking part were: W/Cdr Hyde (L7300) flying with F/Lt French's crew;

S/Ldr Kydd (L7288); F/Lt Siebert (L7279); F/O Burton-Gyles (L7284); F/O Eustace (L7286) and F/O Lewis (L7294). In addition, some of the No 44 squadron Hampdens took part in the attack which was carried out by a total of 57 aircraft.

None of the Manchesters taking part in the attack were fitted with a mid-upper gun turret, while the retractable ventral turret, though fitted, was not manned. Each Manchester carried a crew of six, which included a second pilot, as Bomber Command had yet to cease this wasteful practice. The results of an analysis of each Manchester's engine performance dictated its flight profile. Some were cleared to climb to 15,000 feet carrying twelve 500lb bombs, while others were restricted to 9500 feet carrying eleven 500lb bombs. In addition, all had been specifically briefed to abort the raid if for any reason they were unable to climb above 8000 feet. That the bombs carried were of the 500lb semi-armour piercing type, that were quite incapable of penetrating the deck or turrets of the Hipper, may have been indicative of the degree of confidence that Command Headquarters had in its crews ability to hit a relatively small target like a warship from high altitude. Presumably, it was hoped that any 'overs', 'unders' or 'wides' would inflict collateral damage to the dockside installations, thereby achieving at least something worthwhile.

This, the first raid in which Manchesters participated, was considered to be a success, though subsequent photographic reconnaissance sorties could provide no evidence that the Hipper had been hit. On returning, four of the Manchesters landed without incident, despite a snow storm affecting the Station at the time. The fifth aircraft, flown by Burton-Gyles had to force land as he could lower only one main wheel. Whether this was due to flak damage or a simple hydraulic susyem failure, is unknown. The sixth aircraft, that flown by W/Cdr Hyde, diverted to Boscombe Down with leaking hydaulic oil covering the windscreen.

The day following the attack on Brest, No 97 Squadron was officially formed at Waddington under the command of Acting Wing Commander Balsdon. The two Flight Commanders were F/Lt Gerald Oscar Laidler Bird DFC and F/Lt John Seymour 'Flap' Sherwood DFC. Some of No 207 Squadron's aircraft were passed on to No 97 Squadron to enable it to undertake its own conversion training. By coincidence, No 97 Squadron had formed at Waddington once before. The first occasion being on 1 December 1917 when it formed as an RFC training squadron, later moving to Stonehenge on 21 January 1918. When at almost full strength, the Command's second Manchester squadron left Waddington for Coningsby on 15 March 1941.

The second Manchester operation took place during the night of 26/27 February. The target was Cologne and the five Manchesters taking part each carried the same weight of bombs, though on this occasion they were a mix of 1000lb and 500lb General Purpose (GP) bombs. A total of 126 bombers of various types took part in this attack without loss. However, the Manchester's problems continued to affect their operational effectiveness. Frankie Eustace, flying in L7286, suffered a loss of oil pressure en route to the target and bombed the docks at Flushing instead (A classic case of a MOPA). Meanwhile, F/O Mike Lewis (L7294) had to return to base with hydraulic failure, having jettisoned his bombs in the North Sea. Eustace and Lewis were in fact among the pilots assigned to No 97 Squadron, but continued to operate with No 207 Squadron.

The continuing problems with the Vulture engines limited the number of operational sorties that No 207 Squadron could mount, though they did put aircraft up for another attack on Brest and one on Hamburg. By this time another problem with the Manchester's engines had become apparent. This concerned the exhaust, which was reported by crews flying the aircraft at night as being similar to a fiery comet-like trail of sparks, even when the engines were functioning correctly. As one Manchester air gunner recalled:

"...these were visible for miles and all kinds of schemes were devised to overcome the problem, without success. No German night fighter needed radar when Manchesters were about. To my mind, this might have accounted for more than a few Manchesters being easily stalked and shot down..."

On the night of 13/14 March, No 207 Squadron put up five Manchesters for an attack on Hamburg, for the second night in succession. Four of the Manchesters took off on time and took part in the 139 aircraft attack, which proved to be the most effective against Hamburg to date. The Manchester EM-C (L7313), flown by F/O Hugh Matthews and crew, was late taking off because of a burst tail wheel. Having got airborne, Matthews set course for the rendezvous, but unknown to him, the Waddington flare path and his late take-off had been spotted by a low flying Ju88 intruder of I/NJG2, flown by Feldwebel Hans Hahn. Earlier in the night, Hahn and his crew had shot down a Blenheim near Lincoln.

Matthews had barely enough time to raise the undercarriage and flaps and to select climbing power, before his aircraft was struck by a storm of cannon and machine gun fire. Watched by many horrified Waddington personnel, the Manchester caught fire immediately and crashed near Whisby, some five miles from Waddington. Some of the bombs exploded in the crash and ensuing fire. F/O Matthews and Sergeants Hemmingway, Redgrave and Welch were killed outright, but Sergeants Cox and Marsden were thrown clear in the crash, both with multiple injuries. They were taken to Lincoln hospital, where Sgt Marsden died of his injuries. Sgt Bill Cox was the only survivor, though he lost a leg. F/O Matthews and Sergeants

Redgrave and Welch were buried in the graveyard of Waddington Parish Church on 18 March 1941.

Angered by this attack so close to home, 'Hetty' Hyde and Charles Kydd planned to carry out a semi-official sortie against the home airfield of the intruder, Gilze Rijen in Holland. The Station Intelligence Officer had identified the intruder's base and Gp Capt Kirby agreed to the plan. However, the proposal was firmly vetoed by HQ Bomber Command.

No 207 Squadron's Manchester operations continued at a low level, again because of serviceability problems, together with various modification programmes, one of which involved the installation of the mid-upper gun turret. Despite these problems, on the night of 20/21 March, three of the squadron's aircraft took off to join 21 Whitleys in an attack on the U-boat base at Lorient. Accompanying the Manchester crews were two American naval officers. Commander McDonnell flew with S/Ldr Kydd, while Lt Cdr Wannamaker flew with Derek French. The political implications of their participating, should either have ended up in captivity, appears to have been accepted!

Among the three Manchester crews was that captained by Sgt Harwood DFM, flying in EM-A (L7278). During the take-off run, the navigator, F/Sgt Holland had been tasked with keeping an eye on the oil pressure, which could be easily seen from his position. After about 20 minutes flight, Holland reported to his captain that there was a serious drop in oil pressure in the port engine. Almost immediately after his warning, the engine burst into flames. With little chance of maintaining height, Harwood ordered his crew to bail out. The rear gunner left his turret and jumped from the rear fuselage door, while the front gunner, the second W/Op Sgt Aitken, jumped from the nose escape hatch, closely followed by the navigator. F/Sgt Holland realised that they had been losing height and accordingly, pulled the ripcord of his parachute immediately he cleared the hatch. He felt his parachute open and retard his descent just before he hit the ground in the middle of a ploughed field. The last to leave the aircraft was the co-pilot, Sgt Birch, by which time the Manchester was extremely low. The only other crew member in the aircraft with the captain, was the W/Op, Sgt Hogg, who had remained with Harwood to try to assist him. Realising that they were by now too low to even consider bailing out, they endeavoured to carry out an assymetric landing straight ahead (in pitch dark!) They so very nearly made it, but sadly the Manchester struck a tree, slewed violently to port and exploded, killing the two crew on board. Of the four who bailed out, only two survived the low level drop. F/Sgt Holland and Sgt Hallam spent the night in the medical centre of RAF Cottesmore before being collected by road and returned to Waddington. As John Puyenbroek recalled: "*...whilst at No 14 OTU at Cottesmore, a Manchester crashed nearby and two members of the crew were brought into the Sergeants' Mess late at night. One of these was an ex-neighbour of mine from 'digs' days at Tooting. Among the things he said to me that evening was - 'Never get yourself posted to Manchesters...'' Two months later I joined No 207 Squadron at Waddington!* "

On 27 March, four of No 207 Squadron's crews were briefed for an attack on Dusseldorf as part of a 39 strong bomber force, which included Hampdens of No 44 Squadron. The four Manchester crews were S/Ldr Kydd, F/Lt Siebert and F/Os Paape and Romans. Johnny Siebert and crew were flying in EM-P (L7303). The crew members with Siebert were Sgt Robson as co-pilot; Sgt Formison as navigator; Sgt Jim Taylor as W/Op; Sgt Pete Gurnell as rear gunner and Sgt McDougal as mid upper gunner. This was one of the squadron's most experienced crews, most of whom had already completed a full tour of operations on Hampdens. The newly arrived Station Commander, Gp Capt John Boothman, saw the crews off at around 1930hr. His parting words to George Formison as he climbed into the back of the lorry which would take them out to their aircraft, were to be sure to look out for a nice fat maternity hospital in Dusseldorf as his aiming point. This was an oblique reference to 'Lord Haw Haw's' propaganda claims that the RAF only bombed hospitals and non-military targets.

F/O Paape DFC, flying in EM-K (L7318) had to return to base without reaching the target, due to a marked drop in oil pressure and overheating in the starboard engine. He landed with his load of four 1000lb GP bombs and 420 x 4lb incendiaries still on board. The other three crews carried out accurate attacks, having clearly identified the bridge over the bend in the river. In addition to the Manchesters of No 207 Squadron, there were six Hampdens of No 44 Squadron taking part in this attack. John Siebert and crew carried out two bombing runs, dropping half their load on each run, during which they encountered the usual heavy flak barrage that they had come to expect over any Ruhr target. One burst of flak in particular exploded just under the bomber, blasting the starboard wing high in the air. As they left the target area, the crew speculated as to what if any, damage their aircraft had suffered. As the Manchester approached the searchlight belt on the Dutch border, the flak died away; a sure sign that night fighters were around. At that moment, the starboard engine began to smoke, lost power and had to be shut down. The bomber began to lose height and almost immediately, the port engine started also to lose power.

Siebert called to the crew over the intercom that he could not maintain height, as the aircraft fell off into a descending sideslip to port, though still under some semblance of control. Jim Taylor, in his wireless operator's position, switched on his W/T set and began transmitting without waiting the customary fifteen seconds for it to warm up. As he transmitted a situation report to base, he noted tracer passing his window on the port side. They had been intercepted by a Bf110 night fighter of 3/NJG 1 from Eindhoven, flown by Oberfeldwebel Herzog and crew. This particular crew had already shot down a Whitley of No 78 Squadron, though at the time, they reported it as having been a Wellington. It later transpired that Herzog and crew accounted for both the aircraft shot down in this attack on Dusseldorf.

While he was busy transmitting to base, Jim Taylor missed his captain's order to bail out. By this time the starboard engine was well alight, while Siebert had also to contend with a total hydraulic failure into the bargain. As both these occurences had become all too common on Manchesters, it is by no means certain that Herzog actually hit the already crippled bomber. None of the surviving crew members could recall their aircraft being hit, though by this time, they were more concerned with leaving the doomed aircraft.

As the mid upper gunner, Sgt McDougal, made his way to the forward escape hatch, he slapped Jim Taylor firmly on the shoulder and indicated that he should follow him. Before leaving his seat, Taylor clamped his morse key to 'transmit', unplugged his oxygen hose, ripped out his intercom jack plug and, grabbing his parachute pack followed McDougal down into the nose. By this time the Manchester was in a steep dive and side slipping viciously to port.

One engine was racing and the hydraulic failure had caused the undercarriage to drop down. In the rear turret, Pete Gurnell found that without hydraulics he was unable to rotate his turret to the abeam position which was required for abandoning the aircraft. One attempt to rotate the turret by hand proved useless, so he scrambled backwards over the tail plane spar and made his way up the fuselage, arriving in time to follow Jim Taylor out through the hatch. As they fell from the side slipping bomber, both Taylor and Gurnell narrowly missed being struck by the starboard mainwheel. John Siebert was the last to leave the stricken Manchester, but in all probability he struck either the starboard undercarriage or one of the engines which had broken away from its mounting. In either case, his body was found by the Germans some way from the site of the crash. Siebert's body lay in a depression, indicating violent impact with the ground. His parachute, though out of its pack, was not fully deployed, indicating that he either bailed out too low for it to have time to fully function, or that he had been rendered unconscious on leaving the aircraft. So perished a very gallant young man, thousands of miles from his homeland.

The German pilot had attacked the Manchester from behind and below and, as he broke away, he observed five parachutes in the glow of the searchlights. Herzog dropped a flare beneath the descending parachutes, thereby enabling the survivors to see that they were heading for what appeared to be open water. On seeing this, both Taylor and Gurnell were feverishly attempting to inflate their life jackets when they splashed down into four inches of water covering two feet of mud! Jim Taylor sprained an ankle on landing, but dumped his parachute and life jacket and waded through the mud and water for about one hour before reaching firm ground. On coming upon what appeared to be an inn (The Golden Lion in Bakel) Taylor knocked on the door. Quickly ushered in, he was given first aid and food before being sent on his way with the name of a 'contact' in the Dutch underground.

Unfortunately fortune does not always favour the brave, and by next morning all five survivors were 'in the bag'. Taylor and Gurnell were taken by the Germans to identify the body of their captain, before being driven to the Luftwaffe aerodrome at Eindhoven. Here they were entertained by Herzog in his Mess. Later, they were moved to the Gestapo Headquarters in Amsterdam for lengthy interrogation. As the days passed and the technical examination report on the wreckage of their aircraft came to be studied, the Germans realised that what Herzog had reported as a Whitley, was in fact an entirely new type of aircraft to them. The survivors were threatened with a firing squad if they did not cooperate. In particular, the Gestapo wanted the names of any Dutch citizens who had aided them. Pressure was brought to bear on the crew by their interrogators, who asserted that their bomber had crashed on a Dutch farmhouse, killing the entire family. (Returning to Bakel after the war, Jim Taylor was relieved to meet the 'dead' Dutch family. In fact, the Manchester had fallen on a barn, killing only some cattle. Throughout their interrogation, the crew stuck to their story that they had not been lucky enough to meet any of the local people; adding that if they had they would never have been caught so quickly.

The evening following their failure to return, a carrier pigeon arrived at a loft in a house in Rookery Lane in Lincoln, which was only a few yards from the home of Jim Taylor's girl friend, who was later to become his wife. Just before leaving his turret, Pete Gurnell had released the bird rather than let it perish in the crash. It is little wonder that Pete returned to farming after the war.

During the attack on Dusseldorf, the Station and No 207 Squadron in particular, was visited by the AOCinC Bomber Command, Air Marshal Sir Richard Pierse. He remained until after all the crews had been debriefed.

Towards the end of March and in early April, No 207 Squadron despatched four or five Manchesters on each of three attacks on Brest. In most cases, the bombers carried three 2000lb armour piercing bombs. The primary targets, the battle cruisers Gneisenau and Scharnhorst, were not seriously damaged by these attacks, though F/O Graham Ross of No 44 Squadron claimed a hit on one of the warships. During the attack on the night of 4/5 April however, one bomb fell in the dry dock in which the Gneisenau was berthed. The next day the warship was moved out into Brest harbour to permit the unexploded bomb (UXB) to be defused. It was while moored in the harbour that a Beaufort, flown by F/O Campbell of No 22 Squadron, Coastal Command scored a direct hit with a torpedo, causing damage that kept the ship out of action for six months. The Beaufort crew all perished in the attack, for which Campbell was awarded a posthumous Victoria Cross. The only other serious damage suffered by the enemy was a direct hit on a nearby hotel containing several German naval officers, some of whom perished

On the night of 8/9 April, W/Cdr Hyde, who did not have a crew of his own, 'borrowed' F/Lt French's crew for an attack on Kiel. Their Manchester EM-R (L7302) carried four 1000lb GP bombs and four Small Bomb Containers (SBC), each containing a load of 90 4lb incendiaries. The crew members on this occasion were F/O Morgan and Sergeants Buck, Budden, Hedges and Wells. All went well until they reached the target area, where they were coned by searchlights and subjected to the concentrated efforts of the flak batteries. The aircraft suffered some obvious damage, but nothing that appeared to be serious. Just as 'Hettie' Hyde was turning away from the bomb run, his co-pilot, F/O Morgan, called that the starboard engine was on fire. Hyde closed the throttle, feathered the propeller and operated the fire extinguisher. It soon became apparent that this was a fire that was never going to be put out, so Hyde instructed the crew to bail out before the fire reached the wing fuel tanks. Having seen his crew safely away, Hyde remained at the controls hoping that the fire would subside, enabling him to attempt a return on one engine. Unluckily for him, the fire showed no signs of abatting so, reluctantly, Hyde followed his crew into the night, landing some way north of Hamburg. As Hyde recalled:

"After arriving with a bump in a frosty field, I spent a couple of days making my way to Flensburg, a small Baltic port, where I hoped to find a Swedish ship on which I could stow away. But no such luck; I was picked up by the civil police while trying to find the dockyard. They handed me over to personnel from the local Luftwaffe station, the start of my four years as a Kreigsgefangener (Kriegie or PoW)".

In due course W/Cdr Hyde arrived at the Dulag Luft, the Luftwaffe distribution centre for captured aircrew. Here he met up with Jim Taylor, and together they walked around the football pitch discussing their plight - the rooms were known to have been 'bugged'. Hyde told Taylor that he had written to his (Taylor) mother when he had failed to return, little realising that in a few days time, someone would be doing something similar for him!

During operational flights, the standard procedure was for a brief signal to be transmitted by the W/Op reporting that the target had been attacked. The method used was a simple four-letter code group. This air-to-ground code system had been used by the RAF world-wide between the wars, in such places as the Middle East. Similarly, strips of material could be laid on the ground to form the letters of the code group, thereby simplifying ground-to-air communications. 'Hettie' Hyde was studying the list of code groups on one occasion, many obviously for use in desert-type operations, when he came across one four letter group that decoded as 'The inhabitants appear hostile'. As he later recalled:

"I arranged with that excellent character S/Ldr Charles Kydd that we would attach this particular code group to our normal 'Mission Accomplished' code group. We felt that it would cheer up the return flight and make the signals and operations staff at Waddington scratch their heads. Charles Kydd duly sent his, but I did not - the inhabitants of Kiel being rather too hostile!"

The squadron mourned the loss of their popular commanding officer, though it is likely that the Station gardeners may have felt some sense of relief. It appears that 'Hettie' Hyde had a penchant for eating flowers, particularly daffodils! It is indicative of the calibre of the man that Hyde should maintain the spirit of the squadron, even in captivity. On the anniversary of the squadron's formation in 1916, he would hold a Squadron Dinner every 1st of November.

The Hampden Soldiers On

While No 207 Squadron had struggled to resolve the problems with the Manchester, the rest of Bomber Command had continued their nightly visits to Germany and the occupied countries. In late 1940, a number of changes took place among the higher echelons of the RAF. Sir Charles Portal had handed command of Bomber Command to Air Marshal Sir Richard Pierse on his (Portal) appointment as Chief of the Air Staff(CAS). Some weeks later, AVM Harris handed over command of No 5 Group to AVM Bottomley and joined Portal as Deputy Chief of the Air Staff (DCAS).

Soon after his appointment, Air Marshal Pierse received a directive from the Air Ministry, requiring him to make oil his continuing priority target. At the same time he was to continue attacking other targets as and when the opportunity arose, or when called upon so to do. So, throughout the closing months of 1940, Waddington aircraft had joined others of the Command in attacking a variety of targets. These attacks varied in their effectiveness but, as ever, continued to be paid for by a steady loss of crews, as the Germans improved and strengthened their night defences.

On 6 January 1941, No 6 Blind Approach Training (BAT) Flight formed at Waddington under the command of S/Ldr C W Bromley. The unit had an establishment of three instructors, one of which was the Officer Commanding, eight W/Ops, two air gunners and 44 ground staff. It was equipped initially with three Blenheims Mk I (L1304, L6646, L6738). The plan was for No 6 BAT Flight to commence training courses in March, with an intake of four student pilots and W/Ops. During the course the student crews were scheduled to fly just over ten hours. with a further four and a half hours in the Link Trainer (simulator). In the main, they concentrated on flying the Standard Beam Approach (SBA). During its stay at Waddington, No 6 BAT Flight was to eventually operate a mixture of Blenheims, Oxfords, Ansons and Hampdens.

Bad weather curtailed operations during the period January to March, and those crews that did fly, were well aware that the Hampden did not respond well to landing on frozen, snow covered grass.

It appears that not all those serving at Waddington at this time, were cast in the heroic mold. It came to the attention of the aircrew that one of the administrative officers had developed a personally profitable sideline in selling off the cars of those posted as missing. Nothing was ever said and no formal action taken, but during a Mess rough house one evening, the said officer mysteriously suffered two broken ribs; it appears that he got the message!

During the first twelve months of the war, Bomber Command had flown approximately 12,000 individual sorties and dropped 6,766 tons of bombs. On the debit side, the Command had suffered the loss of 1,381 aircrew killed in action, with a further 269 wounded plus 419 becoming prisoners of war. An additional 600 had been killed or injured in non-operational incidents. In total, this represented almost 2,700 aircrew permanently or temporarily out of action – a number greater than the total operational aircrew strength of the Command at the commencement of hostilities!

In addition to the hazards of operating over enemy territory presented by flak, searchlights and night fighters, were the activities of the German night intruder force. On the night of 14/15 February, the Waddington Hampdens were returning from a minelaying operation in the Gironde, when the intruders of I/NJG2 struck. As the then S/Ldr Ken Smales of No 44 Squadron recalled:

"*...several Hampdens were circling Waddington waiting to land, others having already touched down and taxied to their dispersals. The pilot of one of the latter, a very wide awake chap called Ross, was looking up at the circling Hampdens, all with their navigation lights on, when he spotted the silhouette of an unlighted aircraft closing on the tail of one of the Hampdens. He pushed the lever of his T/R 9 radio to 'transmit' and shouted to the World in general "Break! He's on your tail". By some chance, several of the Hampden pilots heard him and immediately initiated steep turns, myself among them. It was just in time, as I received a burst of fire through the port engine instead of through the fuselage and wings. An incident of this sort was the signal for an immediate blackout of the flarepath, leaving myself and the other pilots to make a landing of sorts by what little light there was, damaging the aircraft but not, mercifully, ourselves*".

The incident with the night intruder was not Ken Smales' only stroke of luck that night. Some time after Smales and crew had left their damaged aircraft (X3025), it was struck in its dispersal by a landing Wellington from No 301 (Polish) Squadron from nearby Swinderby. By coincidence, a similar accident was to happen to the same Hampden seven months later, though on that occasion the culprit was another Hampden.

In addition to the attack on aircraft in the Waddington circuit that night, a No 44 Squadron aircraft flown by F/O Dave Penman, was attacked and damaged over Lincoln by an enemy intruder. The most likely culprit in both attacks, was one of I/NJG2's aces, Oberleutnant Kurt Herrmann.

Oil was still the prime target for Bomber Command, despite the growing evidence that the Command's crews did not possess the ability to locate and hit small targets at night. Luckily for Bomber Command's rather battered reputation, the bad weather of the past few months had prevented any real concentration of effort. Then in March, British shipping loses rose to over half a million tons. The causes of this dramatic increase were the new U-boat wolf pack tactics, combined with the use of Focke Wulf Kondor long range patrol aircraft, plus the activities of surface raiders. Seriously worried, the Prime Minister directed that with the exception of oil targets, Bomber Command was to concentrate its attacks on German capital ships in harbour or dry dock, U-boat pens, German seaports and factories engaged in the production of long range aircraft.

On the night of 2/3 March, eight Hampdens of No 44 Squadron, together with two Manchesters of No 207 Squadron had set out for an attack on the German capital ships Scharnhorst and Gneisenau, but bad weather over the target meant that all crews had to bomb blind. Later reconnaissance proved that neither ship had suffered any damage. Over the next twelve months, Brest was to feature regularly among the Command's list of targets attacked - at considerable cost. Indeed, by the time of the successful 'Channel Dash' by the German Battle Cruisers Scharnhorst and Gneisenau, in company with the heavy cruiser Prinz Eugen on 11 February 1942, Bomber Command had despatched a total of 1700 aircraft to attack maritime targets in Brest harbour. These aircraft had dropped 3500 tons of bombs and lost 127 of their number.

In mid March, Hampdens from Waddington had taken part in two attacks against Hamburg on consecutive nights. On the night of 12/13 March No 44 Squadron's Hampdens, together with the four Manchesters of No 207 Squadron formed part of an 88 aircraft attack; all returning safely to base. The next night, another mixed force from Waddington joined in the attack by a force of 139 bombers. It was while taking off late for this attack, that F/O Matthews DFC was shot down by the intruder. All the Hampdens returned safely.

Six Hampdens set off from Waddington on the night of 20/21 March as part of a combined bombing and mining operation. Five of the aircraft dropped their mines in the alloted position, codenamed 'Beech'. Having planted their 'vegetables', each Hampden then searched for targets of opportunity, more formally known as a 'Self Evident Military Objective (SEMO). S/Ldr Smales dropped his two wing bombs (250lb) on the docks at Brest, while Sgt Lauderdale dropped his two on the pundit light at Vannes-Meucon aerodrome. Meanwhile, P/O Graham Ross and crew bombed the building complex on St Brieuc aerodrome and followed this up by machine-gunning the flarepath and runway.

At this time, the Spring of 1941, Bomber Command was still sending new pilots as the navigator/observer with an experienced crew, before turning them loose with a crew of their own. Such was the experience of Sergeant Pilot D B Nixon. He joined No 44 Squadron in March, having come from No 61 Squadron at Hemswell. He flew his first 'navigator' sortie with P/O Ross and crew, which was in effect his check trip. This was followed by a similar trip with the same crew the next night. This second trip was a 'Gardening' sortie to the approaches to the docks at St Nazaire. Having successfully planted their 'vegetable', they decided to drop their two wing bombs on a French aerodrome near the coast. During their attack, they spotted two enemy night fighters, but managed to evade them in the dark. Nine days later, once again with Ross, Sgt Nixon navigated Hampden (X2982) on another Gardening sortie; this time their area was the approaches to Brest.

On 4 April, still with Ross and crew, Nixon took part in an attack on the Scharnhorst. On 12 May, he flew with another very experienced crew, captained by F/O Clayton, on a night cross-country training exercise. It was then considered that his apprenticeship was over and he was sent to RAF Finningley to undergo his First Pilot's Course with No 25 OTU. Sgt Nixon rejoined No 44 Squadron as an aircraft captain on 19 June 1941. In July of that year he was posted to No 207 Squadron and flew his first operational trip with his new squadron in Hampden (!) AE219. This was a mining sortie to the Elbe. Following his conversion on to the Manchester, Nixon flew his first operational sortie on his new aircraft, as co-pilot to S/Ldr Murray in EM-C (L7317). On this occasion, the target was the distant port of Rostock.

The two German capital ships, Scharnhorst and Gneisenau, or to give them the nicknames assigned to them by the aircrew of Bomber Command, 'Salmon and Gluckstein', were high priority targets. Accordingly, towards the end of March it was decided to try a different tactic. If, as was evident, the Command's crews were unable to hit them from high level, then a new approach was required. A low level attack against the two ships would be little better than suicide, but if they could be bottled up in their harbour, this would be an effective way of neutralizing them.

On the night of 29 March, eight Waddington crews took part in a mining operation by 25 Hampdens against the approaches to Brest. In addition, S/Ldr Smales led seven crews on detachment to RAF St Eval in Cornwall to stand by for a bombing operation against Brest; this time in daylight! As can be imagined, the idea of a daylight operation against a heavily defended target like Brest, was not popular. Each one of the crews was well aware of the disastrous losses when the Command had carried out daylight attacks against targets within range of enemy fighters. The crews had practiced formation flying before they moved to St Eval carrying their load of 500lb Semi-Armour Piercing (SAP) bombs, but were less than sanguine about their chances of survival. Their brief was to bomb below cloud and to then retire immediately into the cloud. After a nerve wracking wait for suitable weather in the target area, a combined force of 16 Hampdens, eight from each of Nos 44 and 144 Squadrons, took off for Brest. On the climb the formation entered thick cloud and became separated. A number of individual crews pressed on until the cloud cleared, well before they reached Brest whereupon, in accordance with their brief, all but one crew turned back. It will never be known if the crew that pressed on did so despite the risk or because they were unaware that the others had turned back. Whatever the reason, the crew in question failed to return.

The Station's Hampdens also took part in the attack on Brest during the night of 4/5 March, together with the four Manchesters of No 207 Squadron. In all, 54 aircraft took part in the attack, from which one Hampden (not No 44 Squadron) failed to return. As part of the operation, P/O Graham Ross and crew of No 44 Squadron, had volunteered to carry out a low level attack using a 1900lb GP bomb. While the other aircraft drew the enemy's fire, bombing at medium level using 500lb SAP bombs, Ross and crew pressed on at very low level. By the time of this attack, Brest had become a daunting target at any altitude, let alone at low level. The harbour was set inside a ring of hills, all of which housed literally hundreds of anti-aircraft guns of all calibres. Between them, the flak defences at Brest could throw up a virtually impenetrable curtain of cross-fire. In addition, there were three flak-ships moored in the harbour, all of which could add their considerable fire power to that of the capital ships and ground batteries. In total, there was something in excess of one thousand guns defending the harbour at Brest, at least a quarter of which were heavy calibre.

With their sights and fuzes set to engage targets at short range, within the harbour area, the Brest defences were a virtual death trap for any attacker.

Among the awards promulgated in the London Gazette of 25 April 1941, were the following: 'The King has been graciously pleased to approve the following awards in recognition of gallantry displayed in flying operations against the enemy:

Distinguished Flying Cross: P/O G R Ross RAFVR

Distinguished Flying Medal:Sgt E T Street RNZAF

The citation read:

'In April 1941, P/O Ross and Sgt Street were captain and rear gunner respectively of an aircraft detailed to carry out an attack upon two enemy cruisers at Brest. Flying over the target at low altitude, P/O Ross finally located his objective and in the face of intensive and concentrated anti-aircraft fire and searchlights, descended to 1000 feet, scoring a direct hit on one of the ships with an extremely heavy bomb. During the attack, Sgt Street coolly directed his machine gun fire against searchlights and succeeded in extinguishing many of them, thus assisting his captain greatly during a hazardous part of the attack. P/O Ross and Sgt Street have completed numerous operational missions and both have, on all occasions, displayed great keeness, courage and determination in pressing home their attacks'.

Graham Ross and crew reported having seen their bomb hit what they thought was the Scharnhorst.

Graham Ross gave a graphic first-hand account of his attack, together with observations on life on a bomber squadron at that stage of the war:

"When a crew appeared on the Battle Order for a night attack, they would gather together in the morning to carry out an air test of the aircraft; known as a 'night flying test (NFT)'.On one such occasion I found that my assigned Hampden had a crack running across the navigator/bomb aimer's front perspex panel. I protested that it was not fit to fly and the Engineering Officer duly appeared. He pronounced it 'Quite OK' and so, despite my misgivings, off we set. During the course of the NFT I initiated a maximum speed check by entering a dive from 10,000 feet. On the way down at some 300mph, the suspect window imploded. The Hampden promptly went into a bunt and pitched over on to its back, a manoeuvre that I had not anticipated. We eventually recovered with about 2000 feet to spare, although exactly what I did to achieve this I do not know to this day!

The afternoon would then be free. Those who could, slept, while the rest of us wrote letters or chased the Mess copy of the Daily Mirror, with its 'Jane' cartoon. Briefing usually took place two hours before take-off, hence the timing of the briefing would inevitably provoke wild guesses as to the target. A very early briefing would usually denote Hamburg or even Berlin. The Station Master (Commander), Johnny Boothman, conducted the briefings. He loved his crews and made it a friendly and communal affair, even introducing some humour where circumstances permitted. We were still in the days of individual effort, consequently a latest take-off time would be 'suggested' to ensure that we were at least clear of enemy territory before daybreak. Each crew chose its own take-off time and route; variations being introduced in the light of the 'Skipper's' previous (bad) experiences, knowledge of hot spots, the W/Op's brief on serviceable DF stations and the expertise of the navigator. By the time all these factors had been discussed, matters would usually end in as direct a transit as possible, out and back, not only because such a procedure provided the greatest fuel reserves, but also because by this time the navigator had drawn the route on his map! After kitting up, a vehicle of some sort would be waiting to take us out to the aircraft, though we seldom got such treatment on our return! The order of take-off was a matter of preference; first in to the target was away before the flak and searchlights were on form. Later arrivals had the target already identified (hopefully) for them. First back, if he was lucky enough to be promptly collected from the dispersal, got a good measure of post-flight rum, and also made sure of his beer. The beer and post-op fried egg were more a traditional celebration of a safe return than a pleasure in themselves.

Take-off from the grass runway with two 'Peggy 18s' (Bristol Pegasus 18 engines) always seemed a little hit or miss. Well wishers were advised to stand well clear of the take-off area because the Hampden, with its diminutive rudder surfaces, was prone to swing to starboard during take-off. Prior to rolling, I had adopted the technique of raising the tail on the brakes, thereby giving me effective rudders early in the take-off run. Others on the squadron considered this somewhat 'dicey', but it worked for me. We would climb to our chosen altitude, normally around 8000 feet and settled down to a steady cruise at 140 mph. At this stage we would switch in 'George' (the autopilot), which in itself could be a hazardous undertaking. The crew were always pre-warned as 'George' invariably crept to port or starboard, climbed or dived. Frequently, the autopilot unit would develop a combination of these - quite disturbing really! Navigation was principally a matter of forecast winds which, all things considered, were surprisingly accurate, with the navigator laying them off in the appropriate direction. A check on the actual drift was provided by the lower gunner. He would point his guns at a flame float or a prominent feature directly below the aircraft and read off the drift on a scale. The direction finding (DF) loops were none too reliable at this stage of the war and we all experienced, at some time or another, a 'fix' that placed us somewhere in the middle of the Alps!

The target could well be identified by the strength of its defences, or the 'Well this is where it ought to be and anyway it looks something like it' approach. The bombs would be dropped and whenever possible, the results observed. I favoured a steep dive attack down to a comparatively low level, as the target could be better identified and the accrued speed was useful on the way out. It was a lovely feeling when the Hampden gave a little jump as the bombs fell away. Then it was a case of 'due West' while the navigator sorted things out. Operations, which we termed 'playing', were normally mounted at half squadron strength in order to preserve both crews and aeroplanes. This meant that we had the day and night following a raid, free. Depending on the state of individual finances, it enabled us to find a pub with some beer or to go to the pictures. Invariably, we ended up in 'The Snake Pit'. Here we could usually find out where the other half of the squadron were off to that night; usually from remarks dropped in the bar - the barmaid always seemed to know. In time, the intelligence and security people tightened things up and the barmaid was screened, but found to be completely innocent; at least in the security sense!"

During the winter and spring of early 1940/41, No 44 Squadron was called upon to take part in night defence trials. The idea was to scramble from Waddington and climb to 20,000 feet or higher over a British city under aerial attack. Their task was to locate enemy bombers by the 'cats' eyes' method (sic) and to then shoot them down! This proved to be a complete failure; the crews taking part all saw several enemy bombers on the three or four nights of the trial, but they (the enemy) were always too high and too fast. Armed with only one forward firing machine gun, the crews involved considered their chances of actually hitting an enemy aircraft remote to say the least. However, all agreed that it made a welcome change from bombing sorties over enemy territory.

It was at about this time, the spring of 1941, that a new aircraft type paid a visit to Waddington. One of the first 20 Boeing B17C Flying Fortresses flew in and the Waddington aircrews were allowed to view this, the latest product of the American arsenal to be ordered for the RAF. The B17's flight crew were loud in their praises of the new bomber, though it had yet to see operational service. It was made known that anyone interested and possessing sufficient experience, could volunteer to transfer to the first RAF Fortress unit, No 90 Squadron, based at West Raynham. The idea appealed to Dave Romans who, along with others of No 207 Squadron, was disenchanted with the Manchester and its inherrent serviceability problems. In due course, Romans left to join the new squadron. Sadly, he was shot down and killed on a daylight (!) attack on Oslo on 8 September 1941, when his Fortress WP-D (AN525) was attacked by Lt Alfred Jakobi, flying a Bf109 of 13/JG77.

Meanwhile, also at Waddington, other events were taking place. On the night of the attack on Brest by Graham Ross and crew when they hit the Scharnhorst, a Whitley (D4947) crashed in a nearby field while trying to land at Waddington. The bomber was destroyed by fire, there being no survivors. On a more historical note, a notable feature of the Lincolnshire landscape, the Dunstan Pillar, was reduced in height at the insistance of the Air Ministry, who considered that an edifice over one hundred feet high, only two miles from Waddington and the nearby fighter station of Coleby Grange, to be 'a hazard to navigation'. Accordingly, it was reduced to a mere 60 feet in height. The Pillar had been a feature of the Lincolnshire countryside since its erection in 1751. The then local squire, Sir Francis Dashwood of Nocton Hall, the notorious founder of the 'Hellfire Club', erected the pillar as part of a wager. It was originally surmounted by a fifteen foot lantern, but this was dislodged in a storm in the year 1808. Two years later, Lord Hobart, the Earl of Buckinghamshire, who was by then the owner of the Nocton Hall estate, had the remains of the lantern removed and replaced by a twice life-size statue of King George III, to commemorate the King's fiftieth year on the throne. The mason, one John Willson, while engaged in erecting the statue on its plinth, stepped back on the wooden platform erected around the top of the Pillar, to admire his handiwork, and plunged to his death. He was buried in the nearby churchyard at Harmston, where the inscription on his headstone reads: 'He who erected the noble King, is here now laid low by death's sharp sting'.

Apart from considering the Pillar to be a hazard to aircraft flying nearby at night or in bad weather, it was also considered that it could be used by the Luftwaffe as a landmark. (Assuming that they could not see the Cathedral!). Some years ago, the many legends and tales concerning the Dunstan Pillar, were put into words by a local poet, Winston Kime. In his poem entitled 'Dunstan Pillar', he told the tale:

Dunstan Pillar on Dunstan Heath
Capped by a lantern which shone beneath;
A beacon that gleamed o'er the darkened down
Twixt Lincoln city and Sleaford town.
A place where footpads lay in wait
To prey on travellers passing late.
The Postboy riding home one night,
Warned to keep the beacon on his right,
Did that, and round and round he went
'Till the dawnlight found him almost spent.
But still going round the lantern light,
As he'd been doing all that night.

Still on the ground at Waddington; what can only be assumed to have been an Air Ministry experiment took place. Fifty trainee pilots were sent to Waddington in early May 1941 to undertake their Initial Training Wing (ITW) course. In the event, only two such courses took place at Waddington, the second commencing in October that same year. As one of the students, Noel Davidson, recalled:

"This was, I believe, the first of an experiment to run such courses on operational stations. Our instructional staff comprised one Education Officer, one Wireless

Operator, who had been seconded from one of the resident squadrons, plus one Physical Training Instructor. Our classroom was at one end of the NAAFI/Dining Hall building and our domestic accommodation was a set of condemned buildings on the far side of the aerodrome (the old World War I hangar complex by Mere road). During our course, we shared guard duties with the Station personnel, dug trenches and took part in several parades in the local area. I had my first air experience flight in one of No 44 Squadron's Hampdens. The course proper, was scheduled to last six weeks, but someone must have lost our files as we remained at Waddington for some four months!"

Ex Master Pilot C M Ward was a member of the second ITW course run at Waddington and remembered arriving on the Station on 13 October 1941. As he later recalled: "There were only two ITW courses at Waddington and I attended the second of these between October 1941 and January 1942. There were approximately 30 of us, all AC2s, paid two shillings (10p) a day, which we received fortnightly. We wore the distinguishing white flash in our forage caps and the course was commanded by a F/Lt Hammerton. At the time he was an Education Officer, but occasionally flew the Station Tiger Moth, much to our admiration. He later trained as a navigator. At the time I was there, the Station was commanded by the Schneider Trophy winner Gp Capt John Boothman. No 44 Squadron was commanded by a VC winner, W/Cdr Learoyd, and was busy converting on to the Manchester while waiting for their first Lancasters. Most of us managed to get a trip in a Manchester, one of which crash landed with some of our course on board; luckily, no one was seriously injured. Among the students on the course ahead of us was Eric Rogers, who went on to be trained as a fighter pilot I believe. Much later, he became the Musical Director of the London Palladium. On my own course, we had Chris Curwin of a musical publishing family. He was considered quite wealthy by our standards, but insisted on existing on his RAF pay, even to the extent of hitch-hiking home at weekends, like the rest of us. He went on to be trained as a navigator."

By the end of 1940, the RAF had over 35,000 men serving as ground gunners which, in April 1941, were organised into squadrons. The Waddington unit then became No 729 Squadron. This organisation culminated in the formation of the RAF Regiment on 6 January 1942. Of the 150 ground defence squadrons which formed part of the newly created RAF Regiment, one was the Waddington squadron, which was renumbered No 2729 Squadron RAF Regiment.

Also in April 1941, the government formally recognised the valuable part being played by women in the defence of the nation. On 25 April, the Defence (Women's Forces) Regulations came into effect. This, among other things, declared that all members of the Womens Auxiliary Air Force (WAAF) were members of the armed forces of the Crown and as such, the Air Force Act now applied to the WAAF, which hitherto had not been the case. By this time, the initial few trades open to the WAAF had been increased to eighteen, including several technical trade groups.

With the expansion of Bomber Command and the introduction, early in the war, of the rank of at least Sergeant for aircrew personnel, it was inevitable that there would be the occasional clash between the 'young bloods' of aircrew and the 'old hands', all of whom had taken years to reach their much coveted membership of the Sergeants' Mess. One minor incident at Waddington serves to highlight the problem, as ex W/OpAG Norman Beattie recalled:

"...In the Sergeants' Mess we had a gramophone and quite a stack of records. The most popular record at one time was 'The Shrine of St Cecilia' by the Andrews Sisters. I imagine that the gramophone would be played only about half a dozen times during the course of an evening, but five out of the six times this would be the record played... There was something about that song which seemed to suit the feelings of the time. Although the 'old hands' were tired of hearing the same record time after time, night after night, the steady flow of aircrew newcomers kept the record at the top of the hit parade in the Mess. On one occasion, I was reading a newspaper when a newcomer went over to the gramophone and, despite having just heard the tune, put it on again. The singers were two lines into their song when the crusty Station Warrant Officer, who was reading in the corner of the ante room, carefully folded his newspaper, placed it on the chair beside him and walked over to the gramophone. He removed the record from the turntable and, without a word, broke it over the head of the newcomer. He then placed the two pieces of the record on top of the pile of records and resumed his seat, leaving a bewildered newcomer staring after him. It was a futile gesture, as two days later a new copy of the record was belting out the tune as before.

I recall also that it was at about this time, that British Intelligence got word that the Germans had decided that as they could not stop our bombers in the air, the next best thing would be to kill the aircrew on the ground. Apparently, this was to be carried out by teams of commandos, dropped by parachute at night. To counter this threat it was decided that aircrew would be billeted out for sleeping purposes. Each evening, at around ten or eleven o'clock, the Station transport would collect us at the Mess and drop us off at various houses in the surrounding villages. Early the following morning they would collect us and take us back to the Mess for breakfast. This was an extremely popular system with the NCO aircrew, but sadly it did not last very long."

The Manchester's engine and other problems continued to cause concern, resulting in them all being grounded for some days in April 1941. However, the crews of No 207 Squadron continued to operate, flying some of No 44 Squadron's Hampdens. In the meantime, Bomber Command despatched aircraft on operations virtually every night. Group Captain Boothman was officially forbidden to carry out operations, as indeed were most Station Commanders. But, as he was about the same size as S/Ldr Ken Smales, he would from time to time, join Smales in his office just before a night take-off, don Smales' flying kit and go off on the operation with the Smales crew.

On the night of 9/10 April, a mixed force of 80 aircraft attacked Berlin, while nine others went for the U-boat construction yards at Vegesack on the river Weser near Bremen. F/O Burton-Gyles and crew of No 44 Squadron took part in this attack, and were additionally tasked with dropping packets of tea (!) to Dutch residents of Leeuwarden and Groningen. The Waddington Hampdens that attacked Berlin that night all returned safely, having flown an average of eight hours and forty minutes each; very nearly running their fuel tanks dry. Apart from dropping their bombs, the crews were tasked with scattering the dreaded 'Nickels' over the German capital, thereby indicating to the residents of that unfortunate city that they could not expect total war to be one-sided.

Berlin was again the target on the night of 17/18 April, when a mixed force of 118 aircraft scattered their bombs all over the city. This lack of concentration was caused by dense haze obscuring the two designated aiming points. Flight Sergeant J E Sneeston and crew, flying in Hampden X2999, failed to return, all four being killed when they were forced to ditch in the North Sea.

With the loss of W/Cdr Hyde, S/Ldr Kydd had assumed temporary command of No 207 Squadron, but on 30 April, W/Cdr J N D Anderson OBE arrived to take over command once he had completed his conversion on to the Manchester. In the event, W/Cdr Anderson never really took command of the squadron, as he was posted to other duties on 6 May, his place being taken by W/Cdr K P Lewis on 21 May 1941.

In March, the new aircrew category of Flight Engineer (FE) had been introduced. An Air Ministry Order (AMO) decreed that fully qualified Fitter II (Engines) personnel were eligible to volunteer to become Flight Engineers on aircrew duties in the new four-engined heavy bombers. Appropriate aircrew rank and rates of pay would be authorised for successful applicants, but initially, it was to be clearly understood by all volunteers, that on completion of their operational flying duties, they would revert to their basic ground trade in their substantive rank! (One wonders how they could resist such a generous offer).

The month of May opened badly for Waddington. On the night of 2/3 may, the Station despatched two Hampdens and three Manchesters as part of a 95 strong force attacking Hamburg. This was to be the first time that Manchesters were to carry the 4000lb High Capacity (HC) blast bomb, better known as the 'Cookie'. Good bombing results were claimed, but P/O Tripp and crew of No 44 Squadron, flying in AD864, failed to return. Three of the crew are buried near Hamburg, but the fourth is still listed as missing in action. One of the Manchesters also failed to return. Flying in EM-T (L7379), F/O D F Pinchbeck and crew were hit by flak as they were in the middle of their bombing run. The port engine immediately burst into flames, but the quick reactions of the pilot minimised the damage. Unfortunately, it was to be the old story of the Manchester's problem of flying on one engine. In no time at all, the starboard engine too burst into flames, with the fire spreading along the leading edge of the wing towards the fuselage. Left with no choice, Pinchbeck ordered his crew to bail out. All five left the aircraft, though the rear gunner made it only just in time. Now alone, Pinchbeck decided that it was time he too abandoned ship. Looking around for his parachute, he was horrified to find that one of his crew members must have taken it by mistake. The only parachute remaining was visible in the nose compartment, but well out of reach. As soon as Pinchbeck tried to leave his seat to reach for the parachute, the bomber pitched over into a near-vertical dive, leaving him no alternative but to remain at the controls. The problem had been caused by the fact that he had been forced to use an observer-type parachute instead of his normal pilot-type, as his own parachute was being repacked and there were no spares available.

Pinchbeck was now faced with having to stay with the blazing Manchester, hoping all the time that the fire would not reach the wing tanks. His only chance was to force land the bomber dead ahead, as when he tried to manoeuvre the aircraft, it proved virtually impossible. Unknown to him he had lost all hydraulic, which had resulted in the flaps and undercarriage dropping fully down. It was this that was the cause of his high rate of descent and lack of control. So, left with no directional control and a high sink rate, he would have to put the blazing bomber down where it would. In the final stages of his descent, he readied himself for a belly landing, hoping all the time that there would be no obstructions in his path. As the Manchester passed through 20 feet, he was appalled to see a farmhouse looming up in front of him. Luckily, his high rate of descent resulted in the undercarriage bouncing his aircraft high over the farmhouse (!) On striking the ground for the second time, the undercarriage collapsed and the big bomber slid along the ground. As soon as his aircraft came to a stop, Pinchbeck jettisoned the escape hatch canopy and left the still burning bomber at the run. He had covered about 200 yards when the fuel tanks exploded. Pinchbeck and crew all survived to become PoWs.

The other two Manchesters, flown by S/Ldr Kydd and F/O Romans, both attacked their assigned targets and returned to Waddington, though not without incident. Dave Romans was lucky in that his aircraft was hit by heavy flak over the target, but fortunately it failed to damage anything vital. Charles Kydd had been specially briefed to attack the city some hours after the main force, in order to create the longest possible period of disruption. The Kydd crew did as they had been briefed, but it resulted in their becoming the sole object of the attention of a very alert flak defences. In the target area, the bomb aimer had great difficulty in locating their assigned aiming point due to the persistent ground haze. When he called out that they were overshooting, Kydd calmly replied that he would go round again! On their second pass, they dropped their bombs on target and left the area in a diving turn to the west. Realising that by now there was every chance that fighters had been alerted as to their presence, Kydd descended to ultra low level and hedge-hopped his way to the coast. On the way back, the two air gunners reported visual contact with German fighters which were obviously looking for them. Luckily, they remained undetected and made it to the coast without being seen, eventually making a safe return to Waddington.

The following night, Bomber Command despatched 101 aircraft to Cologne and an additional 33 to Brest. Waddington provided nine Hampdens and two Manchesters for the attack on Cologne, and one Manchester for the attack on Brest. Having dropped his 'Cookie' from 12000 feet, Mike Lewis descended to low level in order to give his gunners a chance to take on the searchlights and flak battery crews. They also straffed some of the main streets. This in itself says much for the crew, who must have been aware of their chances of getting back, if even only one of their engines was damaged. Luckily, they got away with it and lived to fight another day. Meanwhile, over Brest, Gardiner dropped his three 2000lb AP bombs, but was unable to observe any results. All the Waddington aircraft returned home safely.

On the night of 9/10 May, Manchesters attacked Berlin (The Big City) for the first time. No 207 Squadron put up three aircraft, flown by F/Lt Burton-Gyles, P/O W S Herring and F/Lt G R Taylor. At the same time, another Manchester, flown by F/O T C Murray carried his Cookie to Mannheim. Of the three Manchesters assigned to the attack on Berlin, Burton-Gyles and Herring attacked their target, but Taylor had to return early with a radio problem. En route to their target and while still over the North Sea, Herring and crew were intercepted by a Bf110 night fighter. Following an exciting few minutes, the rear gunner, Sgt 'Tiny' Hallam reported that he had shot the fighter down and the crew proceeded on their way to Berlin.

The following night, the target was again Berlin, and No 207 Squadron put up two Manchesters for this attack. They were flown by S/Ldr Kydd and Dave Romans, the latter apparently having an uneventful trip. Not so for Kydd and crew, who found themselves involved in a running battle with two Bf110s, not long after crossing the enemy coast. Luckily, this experienced crew, working together, managed to thwart most attacks and even succeeded in driving down one of the night fighters, though it was not actually seen to crash. The second fighter continued a series of attacks until the German pilot made a mistake, enabling the rear gunner, Sgt Oliver, to score numerous hits causing the second fighter to dive away towards the sea. This engagement had been witnessed by the crews of other British bombers who confirmed that the fighter crashed into the sea. Following their subsequent return to base, the ground crew recorded over 350 strikes on Kydd's Manchester EM-J (L7309). For his performance that night, Sgt Oliver was awarded the DFM, as was Sgt Linklater, the W/Op who had acted as a defence coordinator between the two gunners and the pilot.

Mannheim was the target on the night of 12 May, which was attacked by a force of 141 aircraft. Waddington provided four Manchesters and eleven Hampdens for this operation. With solid cloud cover all the way to the target, this was not a particularly accurate attack, causing minimal damage. On the other hand, the German defences were not successful either as all the bombers returned, albeit not all safely. When Mike Lewis recovered to Waddington, he found that there was an intruder in the area and consequently, the Flying Control Officer would not allow any landing lights to be illuminated. With low oil pressure and then temperature in the red on the starboard engine, Lewis was faced with landing to all intents and purposes from memory. As he turned on to finals over Waddington village, the airfield defence unit switched on one of their searchlights and illuminated the bomber, making it a sitting target for the intruder. In desperation Lewis's W/Op fired off the colours of the day which eventually resulted in the searchlight being switched off. However, Mike Lewis was only too well aware that they had just demonstrated the colours of the day to the intruder. Lewis did not switch on his landing lights until he was just about to flare for landing and, having done so, switched them off again as soon as he touched down. Mike Lewis was still braking towards the end of his landing run when the intruder dropped a stick of four bombs, parallel with the landing strip and about 400 yards from the Manchester. Fortunately neither the aircraft nor the crew suffered any damage, though it would a long time before the crew could bring themselves to be civil to the searchlight personnel.

Bomber Command was making the most of the improved weather, despatching forces of varying sizes out over enemy territory virtually every night. The night after the attack on Mannheim, a force of 115 aircraft attacked Hamburg. Only two Waddington aircraft were operating that night, both from No 207 Squadron. Meanwhile, No 44 Squadron's Hampdens had been involved in an 89 aircraft attack on Brest. On the return flight, the Hampden flown by Graham Ross diverted to Boscombe Down in order to get urgently needed medical treatment for his injured navigator, P/O Brunicardi. The latter was a newly arrived pilot, doing his stint as a navigator. No 44 Squadron had a particular success that night when F/Lt Broadhead and crew scored a direct hit on the Gneisenau with a 500lb SAP bomb, dropped from 12000 feet. Their claim was subsequently confirmed following intelligence reports.

German bombing raids and intruder activity had become commonplace by the time of the first Manchester attack on Berlin, with most of the local attacks being aimed at Lincoln. The Waddington aerodrome was attacked several times, but little damage was caused. One pair of intruders, doubtless on their way home, strafed the Station with cannon and machine gun fire. One had a go at the hangars and flight line, while the other shot up High Dyke from the Sergeants' Mess to Mere road. In neither case was there any report of casualties or serious damage. Then on the evening of 9 May, the Station and the village shared a common tragedy, when bombs fell on both of them. Two parachute mines were released over the aerodrome, but the wind carried them over the married quarters near Mere road and on into the village. The first struck the village church, destroying it completely. The second mine fell into the vicarage garden, making a huge crater and causing widespread blast damage. In all, nineteen houses were destroyed, 71 seriously damaged with a further 160 being slightly damaged. Miraculously, only one person was killed, though six were seriously injured and 43 slightly injured. The infants' school was destroyed and 400 village people were rendered temporarily homeless. Among those injured, were Mr and Mrs Peatman, who were hurt when their bakery was badly damaged by blast. Although work in the bakehouse had to cease while the buildings were made safe, the bakery re-opened the following December for the business of supplying the village and the Station with bread and cakes. That night, the villagers witnessed a less light-hearted side to the 'boys in blue' as both air and groundcrews, deeply affected by what they saw, gave all the assistance they could to the stricken village. The shattered church lay as a pile of stones in a cruciform shape, with the bells clearly visible atop the rubble. It is said that the lectern still stood by the altar steps, with the church bible open and undamaged! The Horse and Jockey inn, the favourite haunt of the Station's aircrews, was designated an emergency dormitory, while the Methodist chapel across the road was used as a casualty clearing station.

The next day the village presented a scene of utter devastation, but despite this, red, white and blue bunting was to be seen fluttering from the eaves of one of the damaged houses, while a rather tattered Union Flag flew from another. The village church dated back to the sixteenth century and had two clock faces, one facing North, the other to the West. Typical of the village reaction to their loss was that of Mr George Lilley who, like many villagers, regulated his life by the church clock. As he looked out from his house, he recalled: *"It was a moonlit night and I looked across towards the church - nothing!"*

Later in the month that saw the destruction of the church, a local lady, Elsie Scarborough, penned an ode to her church entitled 'The Death of Waddington Church'.

I now lie crushed and broken
No one will see me more
Though many people stand and look
The rich as well as poor
I know they all feel sorry
To see me rent and torn
But some day I will rise again
A new church will be born.
My spirit will be in that church
Whenever it is reared
And God will bless both old and new
Our foes need not be feared.
Some day the bells will ring out clear
The clock the time will tell
And peace will come to this sad world
God will do all things well.

A new church was built on the site of the old one in 1954 and the five original bells were re-hung, being joined in 1959 by a sixth, a treble. Many of the headstones in the churchyard were either destroyed or displaced, many of them being lost for ever. Among those lost were all but one of the RFC graves from the First World War.

About two hours after the mines struck the village, a lone intruder dropped a stick of six bombs on the Station. The first two exploded in a field behind the Sergeants' Mess, while the third fell in the road leading to the Mess. The fourth bomb struck an air raid shelter and the fifth hit the building containing the NAAFI. The sixth bomb exploded on the parade square. The bomb that hit the shelter killed eleven WAAFs and NAAFI girls, including the manageress, Mrs Constance (Nellie) Raven. One girl, Lily Green, was pulled out of the wrecked shelter alive. The sole RAF casualty was Sgt J Vigar, a navigator on No 44 Squadron. As a tribute to Mrs Raven, the rebuilt NAAFI was named after her - 'The Raven Club', a name it bears to this day.

Some nights later the Luftwaffe had another go at Waddington. This particular raid is well remembered by ex-Sgt Charles Ball (later F/Lt DFC):

"My room mate, Sgt Dave Walker and I were asleep in the Mess when we were awakened by a series of crumps, frighteningly close to the building. Dave immediately got up and dressed rapidly, urging me to do the same. I ridiculed him for his panic, saying that it was probably just a lone intruder, who had just missed us. Not much later, we experienced another series of explosions; these being obviously much closer. This time we both panicked and dashed down the stairs to the shelter at high speed. Once the 'all clear' sounded, we wandered

back to our room in the Mess. When we entered our room, our first action was to draw the blackout curtain as it was by now daylight. While so doing, we noticed a one inch diameter hole in the glass and a smaller diameter companion hole in the door behind the head of my bed. In the corridor outside, there was a lump of masonry missing from the wall and a piece of shrapnel lying on the floor. This caused me considerable retrospective fright, because if I had remained sitting up in bed arguing with Dave Walker, either my head or chest would have interupted the trajectory of the bomb fragment!"

Dave Walker survived the war, during which he served a second tour on No 44 Squadron and took part in the first one thousand bomber raid. He retains a fondness for Lincoln and its people, possibly occasioned by the fact that he met his wife-to-be, Barbara, in the Montana Ballroom, which was opposite the Theatre Royal in the city.

Among the minor legends concerning RAF Waddington, is that of the supposed mysterious arrival of a German Dornier on the night of 20 May 1941. In his book 'The Great Coup', the author Robert Hill, refers to a German pilot named Schmitt (!), who claimed to have landed at RAF Lincoln (sic) in a Dornier 217 and to have delivered a package to a waiting RAF Officer, before returning to Germany. It would appear that the contents may have had something to do with further peace overtures, which finally ended when Hitler ordered the attack on Russia. There is no reference in any of the official records to such an event (it is unlikely that there ever would be), but several local people are adamant that it did occur - one can but wonder!

In mid 1941 Waddington was still a grass aerodrome, with no concrete runways and few, if any, aids to recovery and landing apart from the 'ZZ System'. But on 14 May, the installation of the 'Drem' lighting system was completed. This was a system of aerodrome and approach lighting, designed to replace the rather crude, existing system of the 'Chance' runway floodlight and the gooseneck, or glim lamp runway lights. The Drem Mk I system comprised three main components: the actual runway lights, the approach lights and the outer circle lights. The procedure adopted required the returning pilot to first identify the 'pundit' light, which would be flashing (all being well) the Station code letters in morse. Having identified the pundit, the pilot then looked for the outer circle of lights which would be approximately 2000 yards from the centre of the aerodrome. This outer circle consisted of 23 lights mounted on poles. By flying around the circle of lights, the pilot would eventually locate the approach lights for a particular runway. These approach lights were also mounted on poles, located in six groups of six, three on each side of a 90 degree 'V', pointing towards the runway. The actual runway lights comprised four main components; the runway flarepath, the totem pole lights, the angle of approach indicators (AAIs) and the runway floodlights. The AAIs were located on the left-hand side at each end of the runway. Using coloured slides in an optical projector, the AAI would give a pilot approaching at too low an altitude, or at too flat an angle, a red beam. Alternatively, if he was too high or too steep, he would see a yellow beam. If the approach was at the correct height and angle, the pilot would see a green light.

At about the same time as the new aerodrome lighting system was ready for use at Waddington, the Ministry of Supply requisitioned most of the old World War I aerodrome site at nearby Bracebridge Heath. It was allocated to the AVRO organisation for use as a repair and salvage depot. From then on, throughout the remainder of the war, battle damaged AVRO aircraft were repaired there and returned to the front line squadrons. The site was no longer large enough to fly from, so repaired aircraft such as Manchesters and later Lancasters would be towed the short distance down the A15 road to Waddington aerodrome. They would have their outer wing sections removed because of the trees lining that part of the road. In addition, all road signs along this stretch of road, which had not been removed, were hinged so that they could be laid flat as the shortened wings passed over them. On arriving at Waddington, the aircraft would be re-assembled and flight tested before being collected and flown to their assigned units.

The Manchester was again under scrutiny as a result of its lack-lustre performance. An analysis of results of the aircraft's first three months revealed that the 65 Manchesters that had been delivered to the RAF, had managed to fly only 112 operations between them. Furthermore, these had been flown with a reduced bomb load. No 207 Squadron had flown 87 sorties, while No 97 Squadron had achieved only 25 sorties. Of the total, 23 had been aborted early for one reason or another. Between the two squadrons, five Manchesters had been lost due to assumed enemy action and six from mechanical failure. A further three had been lost in training flights. In human terms, this had resulted in 49 aircrew being posted as killed or missing on the two squadrons, with an additional eleven with training units.

As a consequence of the appalling statistics, on the 17th May both Manchester squadrons were ordered to cease operational flying and instead, institute a programme of intensive test flights and training sorties, all of which were to be carried out flying with a full bomb load. Aircraft performance and behaviour were to be noted and reported to Command Headquarters. The very next day a Manchester, EM-V (L7393), flown by S/Ldr Mackintosh and crew, left Waddington on the first of the intensive trial flights. While flying at 16000 feet between Land's End and the Welsh coast, the glycol temperature of the starboard engine suddenly reached danger level. In no time at all the Vulture engine caught fire. Having carried out all the remedial actions, it soon became apparent to Mackintosh that the bomber was losing height rapidly. He sent one of the crew into the nose to jettison the bombs, but though it helped, it was obvious that they had to land at the nearest serodrome without delay. Mackintosh accordingly set heading for the small Spitfire station at Perranporth. During the approach, he could see that at their rate of descent, they would be unable to clear the cliffs on which the aerodrome was located. Initiating a flat turn, the pilot ordered the crew to jettison guns, ammunition and anything else heavy and removeable, while he commenced to jettison fuel. Mackintosh put the Manchester down as near the cliff edge as he dared, but even so, they very quickly ran out of aerodrome. As the boundary approached, he raised the undercarriage; but even this failed to prevent the bomber crashing through the boundary hedge and crossing a road before coming to a stop after having hit a parked lorry. Not a promising start to the trials!

Two days after the Perranporth incident, W/Cdr K P Lewis formally assumed command of No 207 Squadron. He was the obvious choice for the troubled squadron as, in the peacetime air force, he had been a specialist engineer. That same day, all Manchesters were grounded in order that an inspection of engine oil filters and viscosity valves could be carried out. All the engine oil filters of No 207 Squadron's aircraft were found to be unserviceable, so S/Ldr Kydd flew to the AVRO factory in Manchester in a Hampden (!) and returned with a supply of serviceable filters.

Wing Commander S T Misselbrook had taken command of No 44 Squadron in mid March and the subsequent announcement of the award of the DSO was popularly received. Among other newcomers at this time was P/O R Kee, who joined the squadron as a replacement pilot, but as usual, he commenced his operational flying as a navigator. In later life, Robert Kee was to become a well-known TV commentator, broadcaster and author. Another new arrival was P/O H Maudesley, who also joined the ranks of No 44 Squadron. Henry Maudesley was well remembered by Sid Green, a member of the squadron instrument section. He recalled: "*...I remember him as a most charming man; an officer and a gentleman in the truest sense of the word. He was unassuming, considerate and extremely good looking; hence our nickname for him of Tyrone Power*". S/Ldr H E Maudesley DFC was later to die flying with No 617 Squadron on the dams raid some two years later. Another, most welcome visitor to the Station in June was Marshal of the Royal Air Force, Viscount (Boom) Trenchard, who gave an informal talk to the officers. Still an imposing personality, he held his audience's attention throughout.

On the night of 13/14 June, Gp Capt Boothman joined sixteen other crews from No 44 Squadron in yet another attack on Brest. All but one of the Hampdens returned safely, most having experienced varying degrees of flak damage; Brest was living up to its reputation. Sgt S P C Saunders and crew, flying in Hampden KM-C (AE129), called up on their radio to say that they were returning with a problem. All members of the crew perished when their aircraft crashed a few miles south of nearby Metheringham.

Operational losses had continued to mount, with No 44 Squadron losing three crews in the first two weeks of June alone, having operated on only three nights. It was therefore particularly tragic when two crews were lost on non-operational sorties. On 19 June, Hampden KM-H (AD747), flown by the recently commissioned P/O Lauderdale, was departing on a ferry trip from Ternhill to Waddington when it lost an engine on take-off, necessitating a forced landing. Things did not go well; Lauderdale fractured his spine and the three members of his crew all suffered severe burns. Meanwhile, another squadron Hampden (AD904), flown by Sgt C F Greig, circled the wreck radioing a report to Ternhill. In his endeavours to keep the wreck in sight, Greig stalled his bomber and crashed near the wreckage of AD747, killing all on board.

Towards the middle of June, No 207 Squadron started to receive replacement Manchesters, with modified engines and oil cooling systems. By 20 June, all modifications were complete and this, together with the replacement aircraft, meant that No 207 Squadron was declared available for operations.

P/O Leslie Syrett had been on No 207 Squadron for some time and had almost completed his squadron acceptance training. On 21 June, with the squadron tasked to provide the maximum number of aircraft for an attack on Boulogne, Syrett approached his Flight Commander, S/Ldr Kydd, and asked if his final check could be combined with the forthcoming night flying test (NFT). Unable to locate all the members of Syrett's crew, it was agreed that he would fly as first pilot with Kydd and his crew on their NFT in Manchester EM-H (L7310). In due course they taxied out for take-off, with Kydd standing in the second pilot's position. The grass runway in use was that which ran parallel with and close to the A15 road. Just after take-off, when the bomber was passing 150 feet, the port engine failed. Subsequent investigation revealed that a piston had broken through the crankcase. Over the radio, listeners heard the clipped voice of Kydd reporting that they had engine failure and were returning to base. In true Manchester style, the aircraft was unable to maintain height on one engine and the crew were faced with a forced landing as their aircraft crabbed to port. Syrett saw a field ahead of them that looked suitable, but it was preceeded by a line of trees, which they could neither avoid nor climb over. Just after Syrett called for the crew to brace themselves for a crash landing, the Manchester crashed through the trees and stalled. It fell heavily into the field, sliding along on its belly before striking a grassy bank and coming to a dead stop, just east of the Dunstan Pillar. The final deceleration forces had been extremely violent and far more than Kydd could resist standing, as he was, in the co-pilot's position. With no head protection other than his leather flying helmet, he suffered a severe blow to the head when he was forced up and forward, making violent contact with the canopy frame.

The occupants of a passing Army ambulance witnessed the crash and immediately turned in through a gate and tore across the field to the wrecked bomber. Though seriously injured, Les Syrett remained conscious and directed the soldiers to get the other two members of the crew out first. Charles Kydd remained unconscious throughout, but the W/Op, Sgt Arnott was in great pain and required morphine. Eventually, all three members of the crew reached the hospital at Bracebridge Heath where, sadly, both Kydd and Arnott died of their injuries. Les Syrett survived despite an horrendous catalogue of injuries, which included a fractured skull, broken back, neck, arms and leg, crushed left shoulder, elbow, wrist and fingers, plus internal injuries. By virtue of his many months at the Queen Victoria Hospital in East Grinstead, Syrett became a member of the Guinea Pig Club.

In his youth, S/Ldr Charles John French Kydd DSO DFC had been an enthusiastic member of the Boy Scout movement. When this had became known in America, he was awarded the Eagle's Feather by representatives of the North American Indians. This award was given by the Indians to the eleven best pilots of the RAF. Charles Kydd was buried at Upminster on 27 June 1941. The loss of such a young, courageous leader was yet another that Bomber Command could ill afford.

As if the loss of Charles Kydd in such futile circumstances was not enough, that night another crew was lost by No 207 Squadron in even more distressing circumstances. The squadron had put up seven aircraft for an attack on the docks at Boulogne. At the time that the Waddington aircraft took off, German intruders were active over Lincolnshire, one of which was following a similar course close to F/O Withers and crew in EM-Y (L7314). Beaufighter night fighters had been scrambled and one was homed on to what the controller thought was an enemy intruder. The fighter pilot closed to within sight of Withers' Manchester and reported to his controller that it was displaying RAF roundels. At the same time, the Manchester's crew sighted the Beaufighter and fired off the colours of the day. Despite all this, the controller insisted that the contact was hostile and ordered the Beaufighter to attack. Obeying his orders, the night fighter pilot opened fire with his four 20mm cannon and six 0.303" machine guns. Fatally hit, EM-Y crashed near Woolaston near Northampton. There were no survivors. Strangely, the Station Signals Log for that night contains a pencilled entry against the Withers crew - 'Probably F/L in France near target'.

One recent arrival on No 207 Squadron who had cause to thank his lucky stars that night was Sgt (later S/Ldr) John van Puyenbroek, a newly arrived W/Op. As he recalled:

"My first operational flight in a Manchester should have been on the night of 21/22 June 1941, but the pilot, F/O J D G Withers objected to my lack of operational experience, so at the last minute I was dropped from his crew. They were flying in EM-Y which was shot down by a Beaufighter... On My birthday, 27 June, I was in charge of the funeral party at Nottingham for the mid-upper gunner who had replaced me..."

With the continuing problem of engine trouble in the Manchester, despite the so-called corrections and modifications, they were again withdrawn from operations, but not grounded entirely. In the meantime, to keep the Manchester crews fully operational, they were assigned to No 44 Squadron to fly Hampdens on 'a voluntary basis'. Among the pilots of No 44 Squadron sharing their aircraft with the No 207 Squadron crews, was the recently arrived F/Lt J D Nettleton. John Nettleton had flown his first operational Hampden sortie on 29 June, when his squadron put up fifteen Hampdens as part of a mixed force of 106 bombers attacking Bremen. Another new pilot to fly that night was P/O John Sauvage from the Seychelles. He was to survive the war and go on to become a well-known figure in the post-war airline business.

There was no let up in the pace of operations; aircraft of Bomber Command were out operating over enemy territory virtually every night. The losses continued at a steady, acceptable (unless you happened to be one of them) rate, with new faces appearing to fill the gaps. However, some of the older ones seemed indestructable and able to go on for ever. For instance, Joe Dacey DFC DFM eventually completed three tours of operations, his last with No 617 Squadron. But for the Gods of Chance however, he might never have completed his first tour, which was on No 44 Squadron. As he recalled:

"...it was an attack on Hamm. My pilot was Sgt Ron Jessop DFM who had been recently married when I joined him...while approaching the target we were picked up by the dreaded master blue searchlight, which immediately resulted in our being coned by all the other searchlights. The standard procedure when coned in those days was to shove the nose down and hope to escape its clutches. Ron did this, but to no avail, so he just kept going down at an incredibly steep angle. I was the first W/Op, manning the upper gun turret of our Hampden KM-V (P4285). As usual, I had my turret cupola open as I searched for night fighters, and as Ron pushed over to dive even more steeply, my rations, flask and wireless operator's log floated out of my turret and away into the night. I called to Ron that I had just lost

my rations, to which he replied "... your rations; what about my wife!" He kept the Hampden's nose down, finally bombing from 900 feet and continuing on down to avoid the flak. He finally levelled off at what I reckoned was about 50 feet and I occupied myself by machine gunning the searchlights and their crews. When we got back, we walked round our aircraft inspecting all the holes in it. ...one of my particular friends on No 44 squadron at that time, was Frank Gregory who, as P/O G H F G Gregory, flew and died as the front gunner in F/Lt John Hopgood's Lancaster on the dams raid."

Notwithstanding continuing losses, Bomber Command maintained its relentless assault on enemy targets, despite the shorter summer nights. On the night of 8/9 July, eleven Waddington Hampdens took part on a 73 aircraft attack on the railway marshalling yards at Hamm.. Of the total of seven aircraft lost that night, two of them were from No 44 Squadron. Sgt A W Wilson and crew in KM-Z (AD840) were shot down and crashed near the target, while P/O E D Tyler and crew, flying in KM-N (AE153) were presumed to have ditched in the North Sea.

The recently arrived P/O Henry Maudesley had flown his first operational sorties as a pilot on a mine laying trip on 10 June. At around this time, the Royal Navy were still flying in RN armourers to fuse the sea mines. The navy specialist was usually flown in by Swordfish aircraft, but in time the RAF acquired sufficient qualified armourers to do the job itself. Maudesley was quickly identified as one of the 'press on types', destined for great things - if he lived! One of the No 44 Squadron W/Ops recalled:

"One night I was somewhat dismayed to find that I was to fly as a stand-in W/Op with Henry Maudesley. It was quite an experience, with Maudesley handling the old Hampden like a fighter. He exuded confidence, which quickly rubbed off on the crew. En-route to the target, I was busy logging the half-hourly broadcasts, in case of a target change, general recall, etc etc. Suddenly I realised that our aircraft was in a steep dive. Feverishly switching over to intercom, I expected to hear the 'Prepare to bail out' order. To my surprise, I found the intercom chat to be entirely normal. I heard Maudesley saying to the navigator that he would go down another couple of thousand feet; adding that if he opened up again the navigator was to plot his position and we would teach him a lesson on the way back., which would teach him to think twice before firing on a single Hampden!

Apparently, while I was tuned in to the radio, a lone gun position had fired on us. This deliberate picking a fight with a gun position was an entirely new experience to me. To date, I had always understood that our remit was to take off, bomb the target and return home. Obviously, the Maudesley crew had other ideas. Sure enough, when we reached the plotted position on our return, down we went, but there was no response. Not satisfied, Maudesley switched on the navigation lights in an effort to persuade the lone gunner to fire. However, either we were in the wrong place, or the gunner would have none of it, leaving us to set course for home."

Frankfurt was the target for a 70-strong force of Hampdens and Wellingtons on the night of 21/22 July. Waddington put up eighteen Hampdens, flown by crews from both Nos 44 and 207 Squadrons. Two of the aircraft were tasked with laying mines off the island of Borkum. On returning, one of the minelayers KM-N (AD983), flown by Sgt D M Bruce and crew, crashed into the Girls High School on Lindum Hill in Lincoln, very close to the cathedral. All four crew members perished in the crash, as did a Miss Fowler, one of the teachers, who died of shock.

❖❖❖

5. Things Can Only Get Better

Bomber Command had been planning a major daylight attack on the German warships in Brest harbour for some time. With bitter memories of heavy losses in the early daylight raids, this attack was planned to be different (sic). A mixed force of 100 bombers would take part, escorted by three squadrons of Spitfires equipped with long range fuel tanks. The operation was scheduled for 24 July and the plan of attack comprised three phases. The first phase consisted of three Boeing B17 Flying Fortresses of No 90 Squadron, bombing from 30,000 feet which would, it was hoped, draw the enemy fighters up to attack. The second phase consisted of 18 Hampdens escorted by the three Spitfire squadrons. It was hoped that the Spitfires would engage the German fighters thereby reducing their effectiveness against either the Fortresses or the Hampdens. Lastly, came the main bomber force of 79 Wellingtons, which would have to fly unescorted as there were no other fighters equipped with long range tanks available for the operation. The attack took place in clear skies and several hits were claimed on the Gneisenau and the Prinz Eugen. Unfortunately, but as was to be expected, the Luftwaffe reacted in strength and the cost to Bomber Command was ten Wellingtons and two Hampdens.

No 44 Squadron put up six Hampdens for this operation, which cost the squadron the loss of one of its most experienced pilots. F/O J F Clayton DFM and crew, flying in KM-A (AD962), were attacked by a Bf109 and seen to go down in flames, though crews reported seeing three parachutes leave the aircraft. Clayton and his two gunners survived, but their navigator, P/O J Grant RCAF, was killed in action. Of the five other Waddington crews, Collier, Gammon, Nettleton and Ridpath claimed one enemy fighter each, while P/O Tew and crew claimed a probable. Many years later, Allan Clark, who was the W/OpAG in the Clayton crew recalled: "*...my four month stay on No 44 Squadron came to an end over Brest in daylight, when we were shot down by an enemy fighter just after releasing our bombs...*" Three days after the attack on Brest, Nora Townsend, who worked in the Officers' Mess, heard Lord Haw Haw announce over the radio that F/O Clayton was alive and well and in a PoW camp.

The daylight attack on Brest was not the end of the day for the Hampden crews at Waddington. That night, fifteen Hampdens took off for an attack on the shipyards at Keil. They formed part of a mixed force of 64 Wellingtons and Hampdens. Four of the fifteen Station crews, F/Lt Lewis, P/Os Bayley and Green, and Sgt Armstrong, were provided by No 207 Squadron, their Manchesters having been taken off the Command Order of Battle. A fifth No 207 Squadron crew, that of S/Ldr MacIntosh, suffered engine failure on starting up and did not take part. In addition, a sixteenth aircraft set off alone on a mine laying sortie.

On the night of 5/6 August, the Command despatched nearly 300 bombers to a variety of targets. Mixed forces of 98 went to Mannheim, 97 to Karlsruhe, and 68 to Frankfurt. In addition, small forces attacked Aachen and Boulogne, with yet others undertaking minelaying operations off the Danish coast. The Waddington contribution consisted of fifteen Hampdens, flown by crews from No 44 Squadron, plus six more flown by No 207 Squadron crews. All the Station's aircraft returned, though one of the No 44 Squadron crews had to make a force landing at nearby Bassingham.

Two days after the multi-target attacks, the Station received a signal from Bomber Command releasing the Manchester for operations (again). Almost immediately, a tasking signal arrrived requiring a maximum effort that night for a three target attack on Essen, Dortmund and Hamm. In all, 179 bombers took part in the night's activities, which included numerous minelaying sorties. Waddington despatched thirteen Hampdens and three Manchesters to Essen, plus two Hampdens tasked with minelaying. As on previous occasions, crews from No 207 Squadron flew some of the Hampdens; seven on this particular occasion.

On 12 August, Command ordered another special daylight operation! The purpose of this attack was to initiate a partial withdrawl of fighters from the Russian Front to reinforce their defences in the West. A force of 54 Blenheims was to attack two power stations; one at Knapsack and the other at Quadrath near Cologne. As part of a diversion, two formations of six Hampdens each, eascorted by seven fighter squadrons, were tasked with attacking the airfields at St Omer and Gosnay. Six Hampdens of No 44 Squadron, led by W/Cdr Misselbrook, took off in formation and joined up with their Spitfire escort. Bad weather prevented the scheduled attack on the airfields; instead they bombed the railway some three miles south of St Omer. All six Hampdens sustained varying degrees of damage from flak in the target area and near Dunkirk, but all recovered to

Waddington. Later that day, a second operation was scheduled in support of the Blenheims' withdrawl, but just as the Hampdens were taking off, it was cancelled due to poor weather in the target area. F/Lt Ridpath did not receive the recall message and pressed on alone. The weather forced him to seek an alternative target and he eventually bombed Hannover before returning to base. This 'Circus' operation was considered to have been a success, with both power stations being damaged, but the tally at the end of the day made for sober reflection. Twelve Blenheims and six Spitfires lost as against ten German fighters claimed as destroyed or probables.

When No 207 Squadron recommenced operations on 7 August with an attack on Essen, the three crews flying on the first operation of their 'new season' were those of F/Lts Mike Lewis and T C Murray and F/O W M R Smith. Seven other squadron crews flew in 'borrowed' Hampdens and all returned safely, though Murray had been forced by marked 'tail flutter' to bomb a SEMO at Duisberg. Subsequent analysis of the attack on Essen concluded that it had not been a successful attack, with far too many crews unable to locate the target.

In another attempt to assist the Russians in their opposition to the German attack, codenamed Operation Barbarossa, Berlin was selected as the target for a mixed force of nearly 70 bombers. No 44 squadron put up six Hampdens, whose participation was cancelled just after the first of them had taken off. Meanwhile, the six Manchesters of No 207 Squadron pressed on to Berlin, while at the same time another mixed force, this of 65 aircraft was targetted against Hannover. En route to Berlin, F/O Gardiner and crew, flying in EM-W(L7380) experienced severe tail flutter and decided to bomb the nearby docks at Emden, rather than press on all the way to Berlin. This they did and recovered safely to Waddington.

Of the five remaining Waddington Manchesters pressing on to Berlin, the rearmost was that flown by F/Lt Mike Lewis. The experienced Canadian was well aware that on a clear, cloudless night, there was a distinct likelihood that night fighters would be active and warned his crew to be particularly alert. Some time later, dead ahead, Lewis saw an exchange of tracer fire, followed almost immediately by the distinctive spreading pink glow of an exploding 'Cookie', followed in turn by the vivid flare of exploding fuel tanks. So perished Mike Lewis' close friend, 21 year old F/O M R Smith together with his crew. They had fallen to the guns of a budding night fighter ace, Oberleutnant Ludwig Becker, who would be credited with 44 night victories before himself being killed in action against a daylight attack by bombers of the American Eighth Air Force in February 1943.

Of the four remaining Manchesters of No 207 Squadron, Lewis, Hill and Keartland dropped their bombs on or near the aiming point, despite intense heavy flak and searchlight defences. The last of the four, S/Ldr Taylor was somewhat later than the others, but made a good run up to the target despite the thoroughly aroused Berlin defences. Just after releasing their bombload of one 4000lb 'Cookie', Taylor's aircraft was coned and held by the searchlights. The German gunners set up a box barrage in front of the Manchester in addition to the fire from the radar predicted flak. The bomber was hit several times, one of which ignited the flares which were stowed just below the mid-upper gunner. This was a fire that was never going to be put out and very soon developed into a raging inferno. The crew were left with no alternative but to bail out. Seeing that his fellow crew members appeared to be having problems escaping from the nose escape hatch, the W/Op, Sgt Bill Wetherill, decided that if he was to escape before being either burnt to death or killed in the inevitable explosion, he would have to get out through the starboard cockpit window. He opened it and started to wriggle out, pushing his chest-type parachute out in front of him. Too late he realised that he was attempting to leave the aircraft right in front of the starboard engine!

As he tried to reverse back into the cockpit, he found that he was firmly wedged in the window, unable to move in any direction. Meanwhile, the cockpit had become a sea of flames which had reached his legs. At this point, probably because of the intense pain from his burning legs, he must have passed out, coming too as he fell through the cold night air. Later, he assumed that Manchester EM-G (L7377) had exploded, hurling him clear of the still spinning propellers. For reasons which his captors never satisfactorily explained to him, Bill Wetherill was the only survivor from his crew. The rear gunner, Sgt McPhaill, joined Wetherill in a French Pow hospital, but died soon after from his burns. His interrogators told Wetherill that the other members of his crew drowned in a lake. Because of his injuries, Bill Wetherill was repatriated through the Red Cross in October 1943.

Bill Wetherill's pilot, S/Ldr George Taylor DFC, was one of those tasked with solving the problems with the Manchester. He had joined the RAF in 1938, having previously been a Cadet in the Royal Australian Air Force. He flew with No 50 Squadron from July 1938 until August 1940, when he was posted to No 16 OTU as an instructor. He joined No 207 Squadron in February 1941 and operated with the squadron until being shot down and killed. His last and fatal operation was his 47th and was flown almost a year after he had taken part in the first night attack on Berlin on the night of 25/26 August 1940. Two weeks before his death, Taylor had given S/Ldr Petchell-Burtt some dual instruction in the Station Tiger Moth. Petchell-Burtt had been the Station Accounts Officer in 1938, later remustering to pilot. He was subsequently killed in action while flying a Lancaster of No 50 Squadron on his fourteenth operation.

Another three target combined attack took place on the night of 14/15 August, with Waddington despatching nine Hampdens and three Manchesters to Magdeburg, plus a further two Hampdens to lay mines off the Frisian Islands. All fourteen of the Station's aircraft returned safely, but such was not the case two nights later, when then targets were Dusseldorf, Ostend, Duisburg and Cologne. No 44 Squadron despatched eighteen Hampdens to Dusseldorf and one to Ostend, while No 207 Squadron sent two Manchesters to Dusseldorf and two to Ostend. The old hands of No 207 Squadron, Keartland and Gardiner, went to Dusseldorf, while the two new boys, Birch and Gilderthorpe, took on the easier target of Ostend.

P/O Keartland experienced a minor problem just after start-up. When he ran his engines up to full power prior to a 'mag drop' check, he found that despite having the brakes fully on, his aircraft slid across the grass. Nothing daunted, Keartland taxied Manchester EM-F (L7311) out of his dispersal and on to a part of the A15 road! Once there, he applied the brakes and ran his engines up to full power with no further problems, apart from delaying the passing Sleaford to Lincoln bus! Of the other Manchesters, Gardiner located and bombed his target, as did P/O Birch. P/O Gilderthorpe on the other hand failed to locate Ostend, but bombed another dock installation on the River Scheldt. Meanwhile, P/O Keartland was having trouble with his aircraft, as the engines would not produce full power. By careful management, always conscious of the unreliability of their Vulture engines, the crew managed to get their bomber up to 15000 feet.

Just after they crossed the Dutch/German border, they were illuminated by a master searchlight. Other searchlights quickly joined in until they were thoroughly 'coned'. Fully illuminated, they were attacked by a German night fighter, their assailant being Hauptman Werner Streib, flying a Bf110. Streib had struck with deadly precision which, though Keartland managed to avoid his second pass, proved critical. Their port engine burst into flames, they lost hydraulics and their flying controls were badly damaged. Realising that there was no chance of saving their aircraft, Keartland gave the order to bail out, which they did, at almost the last minute as their Manchester struck the ground soon after the last crew member left the bomber. Streib shot down a second Manchester that night, this from No 97 Squadron. At the end of the war, Major Streib was the fifth highest scoring German night fighter pilot, with 65 victories to his credit.

The Station's other loss that night was Hampden KM-F (AE239) flown by Sgt J G Armstrong and crew. They were reported as missing, presumed to have ditched in the North Sea having been hit by flak or fighters off the Dutch coast.

Although the Station's Hampdens were out on two nights following the attack on Dusseldorf, the Manchesters were not called upon until the night of 25/26 August. Two targets were attacked that night, Karlsruhe and Mannheim. The latter being the target for a 38 strong force of Hampdens plus seven Manchesters. Five of the Manchesters were from No 207 Squadron, none of which did anything to dispel the crews' poor opinion of their aircraft. Only 'Kipper' Herring actually bombed the assigned target, and this despite experiencing tail flutter, which had become more prevalent of late. Gardiner was unable to get his aircraft above 8000 feet and he too experienced tail flutter. Deciding that discretion was the better part of valour, he jettisoned his bombs in the North Sea and returned to base.

P/O Paskell experienced similar problems and elected to bomb Dunkirk and to then return to base, which he duly did. One of the new boys, P/O Birch, found that his engines were overheating so badly that he was forced to jettison one of his 1000 lb bombs before pressing on. Such dedication merited a better end to his sortie, but it was not to be. With little or no navigation aids, they had to rely on dead reckoning, but on the elapsed ETA, they were unable to identify any ground feature, so dropped their remaining bombs on a group of searchlights. Meanwhile, Mike Lewis also had problems. He too was unable to locate Mannheim in poor weather, so dropped his bombs on 'an unidentified urban concentration'.

On returning to Waddington, the crews understandably were quite vocal in their opinion of the aircraft in which they were asked to risk their lives. Two days later, Bomber Command set up a test team to ascertain whether or not things were as bad as the crews claimed. Mike Lewis and Gardiner joined Gp Capt Lewis Roberts and the AVRO test pilot, Bill Thorne as part of the team. Their trials, flying a war loaded Manchester served to prove that the production version of the aircraft had a pathetically poor performance. Part of the problem was found to be the position of a modification to the engine oil cooler system. These cooling lips, as they were called, had inadvertantly been sited so as to create turbulent airflow over the wing, which in turn affected the tail fin. Among the test team's other findings was the need to revise the recommended power settings on the climb.

Meanwhile, the Hampdens continued with the war. On the night of 27/28 August, the Station put up ten as part of a 91 aircraft attack on Mannheim, while five others carried out mine laying operations off the Frisian Islands. One of the Hampdens involved in mine laying was KM-P (AD917), flown by Sgt B W Johnson and crew. They returned desperately short of fuel, which virtually ran out as they neared Waddington. Realising that he could not make it to base, Johnson attempted to land at the nearby 'Q' Site at Potter Hanworth, but did not quite make it. In the ensuing crash landing, Johnson and his W/opAG survived, but his navigator and lower gunner received fatal injuries.

The recommendations of the Manchester test team were put into immediate effect, just in time for the six crews despatched to Cologne four days later to notice the improvement. Four of the crews located the target area and dropped their bombs where they thought the aiming point was located. Luckily for Cologne, the weather in the area was overcast and few bombs actually fell on the city. The other two crews, those of P/Os Birch and Gilderthorpe, did not have such an easy time of it. Birch and crew, flying in EM-V (L7422), were intercepted by a Bf110 which caused considerable damage to their aircraft, fortunately hitting nothing critical. The Manchester fell out of control into a steep dive from which Birch had the greatest difficulty in recovering. Such a traumatic experience seems to have unerved the second pilot, who was flying on his first operation. Switching on the aircraft lights, he left his seat and made his way to the entry door and bailed out! Birch had in fact only warned his crew to 'prepare' to abandon the machine. Jettisoning his bombs, Birch succeeded in getting the aircraft back to Waddington, despite great difficulty in keeping it under control, for which he was awarded the DFC.

The sixth Manchester, EM-U (L7316), flown by P/O Gilderthorpe and crew, had only managed to reach 8000 feet when they were illuminated by searchlights. Almost immediately, they were subjected to a heavy, accurate flak barrage, being hit by a heavy calibre shell which started a fire in a wing fuel tank. This was obviously a fire that was never going to be extinguished, so Gilderthorpe gave the order to bail out. He and his navigator, Sgt Parker, left via the nose escape hatch, but no other member of the crew got out before the bomber crashed at Oberkruechen.

The Manchesters were not the only Station aircraft operating that night. As usual, ten of No 44 Squadron's Hampdens made up part of the 103 aircraft attacking Cologne, one of which failed to return. Hampden KM-Y (AD726), flown by Sgt S A Harvey and crew, were forced to ditch 30 miles east of Harwich; there were no survivors. A further five Hampdens carried out mining operations off the Frisian Islands without loss. Sadly, the Station had lost one of its aircraft earlier in the day, when P/O P R Owen and crew were carrying out an air test in KM-N (AD939). They were involved in a collision with a Spitfire of No 412 Squadron RCAF, flown by the Hon P Hughes. The Hampden crashed near Waddington, killing all three occupants, one of which AC2 Prest, was only on board for the ride!

On 1 September, a conference took place at HQ No 5 Group, which was attended by the squadron commanders of the three operational Manchester units, Nos 61, 97 and 207 Squadrons. The outcome of the meeting was that while 'A' Flight of No 207 Squadron would remain on operations, 'B' Flight would be withdrawn to concentrate on the training of new crews. At the time, the squadron possessed eight operational aircraft captains and a further ten under training. At about this time, the final (improved!) version of the Manchester, the MkIA was coming into service. On this Mark, the central tail fin had been dispensed with, while the shape of the two remaining fins had been revised to that which would be found later on the Lancaster. The ventral turret had been dispensed with, the aircraft carrying instead the FN7A mid upper gun turret.

The cities of Berlin and Frankfurt were the targets on the night of 2/3 September. A total of 201 aircraft were operating that night. 126 going to Frankfurt while 49 others went to Berlin. Other bombers were engaged in mine laying operations off Ostend, the Frisian Islands and the Danish coast. Of the total, Waddington despatched nine Hampdens to Berlin and four to Frankfurt. This was to be a very bad night for No 44 Squadron, with three crews failing to return, and one crew bailing out near Dorking on their way back. The crews of Sgts D N DeBrath and L A Robertson failed to return; their fate unknown. The crew of P/O E A W Thompson, flying in KM-R (AE152), were believed to have ditched in the North Sea. Sgt Knight and crew were returning on one engine when it too failed and they were forced to bail out near Dorking. Knight and two of his crew landed safely by parachute, but the wireless operator, Sgt Stevens, was struck by the aircraft as he bailed out and was killed. Lastly, on this night of disasters, P/O Anekstein and crew, flying in KM-A (AE192), crashed on landing at Waddington, as did Sgt Musgrave and crew when they diverted to North Luffenham.

Those aircraft that did make it back to base, found most of England covered in fog. The Station's Hampdens and Manchesters landed all over the country, with only four managing to put down at Waddington; some getting damaged in the process. To make matters worse, the Hampdens of No 50 Squadron, now based at Swinderby, attempted to land at Waddington. Four made it safely, but three others crashed in the attempt. Of these crashes, one was a complete write-off when it collided with a parked Hampden of No 44 Squadron.

One member of the unfortunate Sgt Knight's crew that had to bail out near Dorking, was the under gunner, Sgt Churchill. He recalled that particular night only too well:

"Our target was Frankfurt; a fairly long haul for the Hampden. Adding to our discomfort was the fact that our aircraft had developed a habit of one engine cutting out in flight for no apparent reason. The problem could not be reproduced on the ground, nor so in the air whenever we carried an engine fitter on an air test. With nothing to go on, our aircraft was pronounced 'serviceable'… …The trip out was uneventful, but the target area was a sea of flak and searchlights. As we approached our aiming point on the bomb run, the flak seemed to redouble its efforts. We comforted ourselves with the thought that it would at least keep the fighters away. Our bombs gone, Terry the pilot stood the old Hampden on its side and we left the target in a diving

turn to escape the attention of the troublesome searchlights. Unfortunately, our steep turn took us back into the flak, which made the most of the opportunity. Suddenly, we were hit very hard, the shock almost pitching me out of the aircraft. Among the instant confusion, I heard the skipper say that the port engine was out of action and that he was trying to feather the propeller. As soon as we had flown clear of the flak, we reviewed our situation. We were flying at a much reduced speed, added to which, we were steadily losing height. We reckoned that provided the fuel cross-feed cock was still functioning, we should be able to make Holland where, if we bailed out and were lucky, we might make contact with the Resistance.

In our damaged condition we would be unable to retaliate or evade if we were intercepted by a fighter, or fired upon by flak. We were still losing height, so Ted Knight ordered us to jettison anything not essential. Accordingly, out went the guns and ammunition, plus sundry other items of non-essential equipment. Gradually, we noticed that our rate of descent was decreasing and that we were flying in a layer of cloud. For what seemed like hours we worked our way towards Holland, with the tension building up with every turn of the propeller. Eventually, we reached a break in the cloud, and from his position in the nose, Fred (Spanner) our navigator, called that we must have crossed the coast as all he could see was the sea. On hearing this, Ted ordered us to remove our parachutes and to be prepared to ditch. By this time we were more or less straight and level at eight thousand feet, with plenty of fuel remaining.

After another interminable wait, Fred identified a flashing beacon and called for a 90 degree change of course. Just as we rolled out of the turn on to the new heading, our remaining engine stopped and our battered Hampden commenced its last descent. We all groped feverishly for our discarded parachutes and harnesses as Ted called 'Bail Out; Everybody Out'. The door to 'the tin' flew off as I pulled the release handle. I lay on the floor with my back to the open hatch and pushed hard with both feet, making a clean exit. As soon as I was clear of the aircraft I pulled the ripcord and felt a wave of relief as I felt my parachute snap open. Looking down, I saw to my horror what I thought was the sea, but it turned out to be cloud, which enveloped me in its clammy folds. Suddenly, the top of a tree flashed past me, indicating that my rate of descent was much faster than I realised.

Before I had time to consider what I should do, I jerked to a halt; my canopy having snagged in the branches of another tree. While hanging there, swinging in the breeze, I thanked my lucky stars for my survival. I then heard a voice calling my name It was our navigator, impolitely telling me to stop hanging about and to hit the quick-release box. This I did without thinking and promptly fell on him! I had lost my flying boots in my descent, so Fred offered to carry me on his back. We had hardly covered a hundred yards when a squad of heavily armed Canadian soldiers burst upon us, ordering us to stop. Fred's colourful response soon convinced the soldiers that we were anything but German and, from then on, they couldn't do enough for us. It transpired that we had come down near Dorking in Surrey. Tragically, 'Big Steve', our W/OpAG had not made it; his body being found near the wreckage of our aircraft. In due course the Squadron sent a Hampden to a nearby aerodrome to collect us. On getting back to Waddington, one of the first things we did was to apply for our Caterpillar Club badges."

All three Manchesters despatched to Berlin from Waddington that night, bombed their aiming point and returned safely. The only other Manchester operating that night was that flown by the Squadron Commander of No 61 Squadron, W/Cdr G E Valentine. His aircraft was shot down over Berlin by flak; as a result, orders were issued by Bomber Command that Station and Squadron Commanders were not to fly on operations without specific permission. Another result of this loss, together with other factors, was that No 207 Squadron became the only operational Manchester squadron; a situation that was to continue until 20 October.

Berlin was again the target on the night of 7/8 September, when No 44 Squadron despatched five Hampdens to Berlin and another four on mining operations. Some of the minelaying aircraft were among the first to take off, the second of which, KM-Z (X2921), flown by Sgt A A Watt and crew, crashed on take-off, killing the crew. The next aircraft in line was another Hampden, followed by Mike Lewis in the first of the Manchesters. The Hampden pilot got a 'green' from the runway caravan, but appeared to be mesmerised by the inferno in the field beside the runway and made no move to take off. Behind him, Lewis was watching his engine temperatures rising and knew that he could not afford to hang around. So, in true blunt Canadian fashion, he pressed the transmit button on his microphone and called: *"Hampden on the runway; either p*** or get off the pot!"* The young Hampden pilot duly rolled down the runway and took off, despite the possibility of unexploded bombs being set off by the fire. Some weeks later, Mike Lewis and the reluctant Hampden pilot were to meet in a PoW camp. It was there that the young pilot admitted that if Lewis had not made his call, he would in all probability not have been able to make himself take off, such was the state of his nerves.

In retrospect, Mike Lewis could have felt that it was a pity that the Hampden pilot made way for him that night. He (Lewis) had just been declared 'tourex' and was destined to move to No 44 Squadron as their conversion pilot for the forthcoming new bomber, the Lancaster. But, with a high profile target like Berlin, his Squadron Commander had asked him if he was willing to make 'one more trip'. It would have been completely out of character for Lewis to refuse, so off he went. During the preparations for that night's activities, Lewis' aircraft was declared unfit to fly and he was allocated the reserve. It was this aircraft that Lewis and crew air tested. To use his own words: *"It was a clunker among clunkers"*. Even without a bomb load, it proved incapable of maintaining height on one engine; a comforting thought to take all the way to Berlin!

On their way to the target, Lewis managed to drag the reluctant bomber up to 13000 feet; but while still over the North Sea, they were intercepted by a German night fighter. Just as Sgt Miller, the rear gunner, called *"Night fighter astern"*, they were hit by a burst of cannon and machine gun fire in the port wing and engine. The fighter made two more passes at them but failed to inflict any further damage. Surprisingly, the port engine continued to run as if nothing was wrong, though it soon became apparent that they had suffered considerable loss of fuel from the punctured wing tanks. Berlin was no longer an option, so Lewis decided to head for the much nearer Wilhelmshaven (MOPA), where they dropped their 4000lb 'Cookie' plus the incendiaries.

Their bombs gone, they set heading direct for Waddington at their stabilised height of 8000 feet. After a few minutes, without warning, the port engine temperature started to rise rapidly. Looking out of his cockpit window, Lewis could see that parts of the cowling were already glowing red hot. In the brief space of time that it took to shut the engine down and feather the propeller, the cowling had become white hot. Just as it had during the night flying test earlier, EM-W (L7380) failed to maintain height on one engine and, despite the experienced Lewis' best efforts, it quickly became obvious that they would end up ditching in the North Sea. As they were only a few miles off the enemy coast, Lewis elected to turn back towards land and try to put the bomber down on one of the Frisian Islands' beaches. Eventually, he put the Manchester down on the beach on Ameland, in about six feet of water.

The crew abandoned the inside of their aircraft and gathered on the top of the fuselage, clear of the water. Realising that their arrival appeared to have gone unoticed, they went back inside the fuselage and proceeded to systematically destroy all the internal fixtures and fittings. Having made sure that the Germans would obtain little of any value from their aircraft, they waded ashore. Thinking that such a flat, inviting beach might be mined, Lewis walked alone up the sand before allowing his crew to follow in his footsteps. Finding a large lifeboat on a wheeled cradle, the crew considered the possibility of launching it and sailing it back to England. Unfortunately, it proved too heavy to move without either a tractor or a team of horses, so they had to abandon the idea. Rather than compromise the Dutch inhabitants by asking for assistance, they were eventually captured by German troops while still near the beach.

At about the time that Mike Lewis was putting his bomber down on the beach at Ameland, F/O Gardiner and P/O Paskell were dropping their bombs on or near the aiming point in Berlin. Having witnessed the explosions, both crews turned away and headed home. Meanwhile, P/O W S 'Kipper' Herring was running in to bomb when his Manchester was coned by searchlights and subjected to intense flak. His aircraft was struck numerous times, but he pressed on with his attack and his bomb aimer released their bomb load in the target area. Just as Herring was about to take evasive action, the Manchester was hit near the port engine, followed almost immediately by more close bursts of flak which peppered the aircraft. The port engine was seen to be losing coolant and at the same time the engine temperature began to rise ominously.

The crew were now faced with the unlikely prospect of a single engined return to England, all the way from Berlin. Knowing that the chances of success were remote to say the least, Herring offered his crew the opportunity of bailing out, or staying with the aircraft and attempt the virtually impossible. They were unanimous in electing to stick with their aircraft. As was to be expected, the Manchester was slowly losing height, so their only chance was to reduce the weight of the machine as much as possible. With the loss of the port engine, they had lost all hydraulics, thereby rendering the guns and their turrets virtually useless; so guns and ammunition were the first to go over the side. There followed all moveable items such as oxygen bottles, the rest bed, recce flares etc. Having passed all these items to the rear gunner to dispose of, they set about the fuselage with crash axes, removing as much of the actual airframe as they safely could. This included the armoured doors situated between the cockpit and the main fuselage.

Back at Waddington, the Station had received the standard 'Q' code message for mission successful, but it had been followed by the additional comment that EM-Z (L7432) had experienced heavy defensive fire. A coded damage state followed, which was received with gloom at Waddington; there was no way that they would make it back on one engine in a Manchester.

After an epic five hour return flight, Kipper Herring landed his empty shell of a Manchester at West Raynham, where the bomber swung violently off the runway due to a punctured port mainwheel tyre. On climbing out of their aircraft, the crew were somewhat disturbed to find that they had flown all the way across the North Sea without the crew dinghy. It had been blown out of its wing stowage by one of the flak bursts. So much for their comforting thought that if all else failed, they could take to the dinghy!

Pilot Officer Wilfred Stanley Herring DFM was awarded an immediate and well deserved DSO for his actions that night; a rare distinction for a junior officer.

As for the battered Manchester, it was repaired and returned to the squadron, where Herring made it his own, christening it 'LONDON PRIDE'. On the squadron it was considered to be a lucky aircraft and as such was much sought after if Herring was not flying it. Indeed, it lived up to its reputation by once again bringing a crew back from a target on one engine; surely unique among Manchesters? Avro of course, made quite a thing about it and invited Herring and crew to dine with the Managing Director and the Chief Test Pilot. After the meal, each member of the crew was presented with a silver cigarette case. Sadly, S/Ldr Herring did not survive the war. He was killed on 4 July 1943 when the Liberator in which he was flying as co-pilot crashed on take-off from Gibraltar. One of the passengers was the Polish leader, General Sikorski.

Four days after the loss of Mike Lewis and 'Kipper' Herring's near miraculous return from Berlin, the Station played host to a Russian military mission. Among the visitors was the Soviet Air Attache, Major Shvetsov and a Russian test pilot, Colonel Fedrovi. The two men were given a 45 minute demonstration flight in a Manchester flown by F/O Geoff Hall, who was on secondment from No 61 Squadron to No 207 Squadron. During the flight, Colonel Fedrovi took the controls, causing Hall no little concern as he carried out rather unconventional manoeuvres while engaged in fighter affiliation with a Boulton Paul Defiant. But after a while, it became apparent that the Colonel was a most accomplished pilot and Hall managed to relax - a little! After lunch in the Mess, the visitors departed, leaving Station personnel wondering about the purpose of the visit; were we really going to supply Manchesters to our Allies the Russians? If that was the plan, nothing came of it; perhaps just as well.

At about this time, letters of congratulations were received from on high, regarding the speed with which No 207 Squadron had completed yet more trials with the Manchester, in an attempt to improve its fitness for operations. The Station Commander, Gp Capt Boothman, relayed congratulatory messages from the VCAS, Air Chief Marshal Sir Wilfred Freeman, and the AOC No 5 Group, Air Vice Marshal Slessor.

As the war progressed and the many new training units got into their stride, more and more personnel arrived at Waddington and other stations. Some had been trained to maintain the more complex equipment coming into use, while others arrived to assist with the many non-technical tasks. Among the latter were three members of the WAAF. Assistant Section Officer Jean Barclay arrived on commissioning, posted in for intelligence duties. She had joined the WAAF in October 1939 and had served initially as a plotter at Fighter Command Headquarters. During her two year stay at Waddington, she kept a diary (now published) that gives a very human insight into life (and death) on an operational bomber station. Another member of the loyal band of Waddington WAAFs was ACW1 'Pip' Beck. She arrived at Waddington as one of the first WAAF R/T Operators and was employed in Flying Control for almost two years before moving to Bardney, when Waddington was temporarily closed in 1943 for runway construction. In 1989, 'Pip' published her memoirs in a moving book, 'A WAAF in Bomber Command'. Her book describes clearly the unique contrast of joy and sadness that characterised a small, close knit community; only part of which lived in the shadow of sudden and violent death, while flying on operations.

The third member of the WAAF to arrive at this time was ACW1 Doreen Byrne. She arrived as one of a batch of seven new WAAFs. Doreen was employed in the Intelligence Section during her time at Waddington, and was eventually to marry a No 44 Squadron W/Op when he completed his Lancaster tour. One of her abiding memories was her first sight of the WAAF accommodation. It was referred to as 'the old camp', which indeed it was, having been left over from the First World War. As she recalled:

"It really was a dreadful place, and my first thoughts when I saw it was that it looked as if it had been there since the last war; which of course it had..."

On 12 September 1941, No 44 Squadron became known officially as 'No 44 (Rhodesia) Squadron'. In the words of the official bulletin, it was 'in recognition of that country's generous donations to the war effort'. The title was particularly apposite, as at the time, about a quarter of the squadron personnel were either Rhodesian or South African.

On the night following the announcement of its title, the squadron despatched two Hampdens to Boulogne, seven to Rostock and four on minelaying sorties. In addition, No 207 Squadron despatched five Manchesters to Rostock. All but one of the Station's aircraft returned safely, with the exception of Sgt Dedman and crew, who ran out of fuel and were forced to ditch Hampden KM-A (AD981) off Cromer. Luckily, they were picked up by the destroyer HMS Garth after only 35 minutes in their dinghy; returning to the squadron little the worse for the experience.

Luftwaffe intruders carried out another attack on Waddington on the night of 13 September, preventing three out of eight Hampdens from taking off for an attack on Frankfurt. While apparently searching for the aerodrome, the intruders dropped incendiaries on Mere Hall farm and at Branston. Eventually finding their target, they dropped a mix of high explosive and incendiaries on the aerodrome, but caused no damage or casualties. It had been this sort of threat, among others, that had resulted in aircrews being billeted off camp at night. As Dick Ikin of No 207 Squadron recalled:

"...we were not allowed to sleep on the station at night in case of air raids. Instead, we were housed in 'civvy' billets in the surrounding villages. The host

families were paid nine pence (just under 4p) per day to provide sleeping accommodation only. I was extremely fortunate in that the couple that I was allocated to, made me very welcome, giving me a key to their cottage and allowing me to come and go at any time. At about ten o'clock in the evening, they would give me a hot supper and follow this with a cup of tea in bed in the morning, before I had to catch the service transport to Waddington and breakfast..."

Despite all the best efforts of both service and civilian engineers, No 207 Squadron's problems with the Manchester had not been resolved. The Avro company based a permanent team on the Station, who worked closely with the squadron engineering personnel. An example of the problems facing them was the inexplicable loss of Manchester EM-K (L7318), which dived into the ground near South Hykeham while in the circuit. The aircraft was carrying a total of ten aircrew and groundcrew; none of which survived. Despite this tragedy, five Manchesters and thirteen Hampdens took off that night, all but one returning safely. The Hampden flown by Sgt Musgrave and crew crashed close to nearby Harmston, killing two members of the crew.

During the autumn of 1941, not all the excitement was confined to the two operational squadrons. On the night of 8 October, two Oxfords of No 6 Beam Approach Training (BAT) Flight were airborne when the weather closed in, making safe landings impossible. Accordingly, S/Ldr Bromley ordered the crews to abandon their aircraft and bail out. This order was duly acknowledged and obeyed. Oxford V4033 crashed in a field at Welbourn, while V4034 crashed near Stubton. The occupants of both machines all landed safely by parachute. At the time of the incident, No 6 BAT Flight possessed six Oxfords, two Blenheims and had the use of the No 44 Squadron Anson (N9835). A little over one month after the loss of the two Oxfords, the Flight was renumbered on 16 November, becoming No 1506 BAT Flight. The change of title made no difference whatsoever to the training task, which continued unabated.

On the night of 10/11 October, Bomber Command despatched 78 aircraft to Essen; 69 to Cologne and 85 others on various duties. The Hampdens of No 44 Squadron divided their attentions between Essen and Dunkirk, while No 207 Squadron put up a total of ten Manchesters, its biggest effort to date, all of which went to Essen. All the Station aircraft returned, though P/O Birch and crew were lucky, putting down at Horsham St Faith (now Norwich Airport) with their fuel gauges all reading zero!

An indication of the growing strength of Bomber Command was given by the effort on the night of 12/13 October. A total of 373 sorties was mounted; this being the highest number achieved in any one night so far. A mixed force of 152 aircraft attacked Nuremburg, while a 99 strong force went for Bremen. Meanwhile, a third force, of 79 Hampdens and 11 Manchesters attacked the chemical works at Huls. In addition, a further 32 aircraft carried out minor supporting operations. Waddington's part in these combined attacks, was to send 10 Hampdens and 11 Manchesters to Huls, and two Hampdens to Bremen. All but one of the Station's aircraft returned safely; the missing aircraft being the Manchester EM-L (L7312), flown by P/O Bowes-Cavanagh and crew. While over Belgium, they were attacked by a Bf110 of II/NGJ1, flown by Oberfeldwebel Gildner. The attack was extremely accurate and left the Manchester damaged from nose to tail. Seriously damaged and on fire, Bowes-Cavanagh had no option but to order the crew to bail out. He ordered his navigator, Sgt Jack Cheesman to move into the nose and jettison the bombs. This Cheesman did, by which time he could see that his aircraft was doomed. Without wasting more time,Cheesman releasd the nose escape hatch and bailed out. Almost immediately, after he fell away, the blazing bomber nosed over and dived into the ground taking the rest of the crew with it.

Jack Cheesman's injuries rendered his efforts at escape and evasion unsuccessful and he was captured not far from the crash site. The next day he was taken to the wreckage where he was required to confirm that it was his aircraft. Following this traumatic experience, his captors deigned to then transport the injured Cheesman to hospital by motor-cycle side car! The memories of the burnt and shattered bodies of his friends lying in and around the wreck were to remain with him for many years.

The following night the targets were Dusseldorf and Cologne. Of the 39 aircraft attacking Cologne, Waddington provided twelve Hampdens and nine Manchesters. This was to be another bad night for the Station, with three of its aircraft failing to return. No 44 Squadron lost Sgt E Owen (a Rhodesian) and crew, flying in Hampden KM-J (AD975). They were shot down by a night fighter over Waasmunster in Belgium. A similar fate befell two of the Station's Manchester crews. The first to fall was that flown by F/O Joe Unsworth and crew in EM-D (L7321). They were illuminated by searchlights near Liege and were attacked by a Bf110. The attack was extremely accurate, with hits on the engine and fuel tanks in the starboard wing.

Despite instantly operating the engine fire extinguishers, the entire wing burst into flames. Realising that there was every chance that the fuel tanks would explode, Unsworth gave the order to bail out. In the nose gun turret, Sgt Tom Cox dropped into the nose compartment, donned his parachute, jettisoned the escape hatch and followed it out into the night, being quickly followed by the co-pilot, P/O Carroll. These two were to be the only survivors from their crew. Neither have ever understood why no other crew members left the aircraft, other than that they might have been hit by the fighter's cannon and machine gun fire. Both Carroll and Cox were picked up by the Belgian 'Comete' escape organisation and returned to England.

The second Manchester to fall that night was EM-T (L7373), flown by P/O 'Jock' Pascell and crew. They reached their target, dropped their bombs and were on their way home when they were caught in the searchlights surrounding Louvain. Almost immediately, the rear gunner, Sgt Arthur Smith, reported a night fighter closing in from the rear. Smith and the German pilot opened fire simultaneously, though the effect of the fighter's cannon and machine gun fire far outweighed Smith's four 0.303" machine guns. The rear gunner felt the enemy's fire hitting the Manchester and at almost the same time, heard a call over the intercom that they were on fire. This was soon followed by Paskell giving the order to bail out. Arthur Smith experienced great difficulty in getting out of his turret and into the fuselage to collect his parachute, and by the time he did so, the interior of the fuselage was an inferno. Despite the flames surrounding him, he managed to locate his parachute, snap it on and jump from the fuselage door, just missing the tail. Just before leaving the aircraft, he was horrified to see that the mid upper gunner was still strapped, unmoving in his turret and was ablaze. The only other crew member to escape was the navigator, Sgt Ken Houghton, who had bailed out from the nose escape hatch.

Ken Houghton made his own way across occupied Europe to Switzerland and eventually to Portugal, from where he was repatriated to England; the details of his journey reading like a novel.. Arthur Smith's burns precluded any attempt at escape, but in any case the Germans had followed his descent by the light of the searchlights. As he hit the ground. there was a reception committee waiting for him, but on seeing his injuries, the German troops did all they could for him before passing him on to a military hospital in Brussels.

The 20th October marked the end of No 207 Squadron being the only operational Manchester squadron. No 97 Squadron, based at Coningsby, was tasked with joining in a 153 aircraft strong attack on Bremen. Meanwhile, No 207 Squadron despatched four Manchesters on mining operations in the 'Willow' (the Baltic off Sassnitz) mining area. Three of the four planted their 'vegetables' in the assigned area; the fourth crew having jettisoned theirs when they were unable to locate an identifiable run-in point. All four aircraft were scheduled to land at Horsham St Faith, but the crew of EM-L (L7487) were forced to ditch some eighteen miles off Cromer on the Norfolk coast. Nothing further is known about the circumstances of the deaths of P/O Ruck-Keene and crew; they were never found, despite several of the squadron aircraft participating in the search.

Although the Manchester's engines were now somewhat more reliable, there remained a problem of uninitiated feathering of the propellers! By 26 October the problem appeared to have been resolved, and two of the Station's Manchesters were programmed for air tests. By chance on that day, a party of local Air Training Corps cadets was visiting the Station as part of their training programme. As a special treat, it was decided to give them all an air experience flight in a Manchester. For some of those chosen, it was to prove an unforgetable experience! The air tests were carried out by the two Flight Commanders, Squadron Leaders Beauchamp and Murray. Murray's trip passed off without incident, his cadets thoroughly enjoying the opportunity to fly in the RAF's latest bomber. At the same time, S/Ldr Beauchamp and crew took off with a newly arrived sergeant pilot and a complement of eleven cadets. It had been decided to combine the air test with a propeller feathering exercise for the sergeant pilot, which was duly commenced once Beauchamp had climbed the aircraft up to 1500 feet.

The pilot under instruction carried out the correct shut-down and feathering drills and was told to proceed with the re-start procedures. Having initiated the re-start drills, the propeller was unfeathered and the boost and rpm increased accordingly. It was immediately apparent that the engine was not responding, and that in coarse pitch the propeller was creating considerable drag. As ever, the Manchester was unable to maintain level flight on one engine and was steadily losing height. Left with no alternative, Beauchamp ordered all aboard to take up crash positions while he looked for a suitable place to force land. There was nowhere really suitable, so he was forced to pick a small field and go in with the wheels up. The big bomber skidded along the field, smashed through the boundary hedage and ended up, still in one piece, in the adjoining field. Immediately their aircraft came to a stop, the crew jettisoned all escape hatches and concentrated in getting the cadets out of the machine. Having ensured that all the cadets were out of the aircraft, the crew followed them to a safe distance, where Beauchamp carried out a roll call.

Beauchamp despatched one of the crew to find a telephone while he made a careful, long distance study of his aircraft. After some time it seemed unlikely that the bomber would burst into flames so, cautiously, Beauchamp approached the machine and climbed inside. Having made his way to the cockpit, he studied the controls and instrument panel in an attempt to discover what might have caused the problem. There, glaring at him, were the engine fuel taps, all in the OFF position. It was a very embarrased Flight Commander who had to fill out an accident report.

Losses continued throughout the autumn and winter among both the Hampden and Manchester squadrons at Waddington. While crews of No 207 Squadron were still endeavouring to overcome the problems still plaguing their aircraft, selected crews from No 44 Squadron were being detached to Boscome Down. Among those chosen was Sgt T D Moore, a Hampden under gunner. He recalled:

"That autumn we were detached to Boscombe Down to take part in performance trials with the new, yellow painted Lancaster. During one trip, when we were in the vicinity of Carlisle, I casually glanced out of one of the side windows. To my horror, I saw that the wing was opening up into huge cracks. On my shouting a warning, our pilot, F/O McLaglan, promptly jettisoned our dummy load of concrete and headed back to Boscombe Down. We also experimented with a mid-under gun turret, which had a 360 degree traverse. Unfortunately, I found it difficult when using the periscope aiming system, to judge the relative movement between ourselves and the target, quickly becoming disorientated. My adverse comments were not, understandably, particularly well received. However, the next air gunner experienced the same problem, to the extent that he peppered the target-towing Lysander aircraft instead of the drogue! In due course, a second Lancaster arrived at Boscombe and was parked on the opposite side of the aerodrome from our aircraft.

Access to our Lancaster had been limited to the detached squadron personnel only and I imagine that the appetite of the Boscombe test pilots had been thoroughly wetted. Sure enough, within a short space of time the new arrival was taxying out for its first trip from the A & AEE. As it lifted off, one of the huge main wheels fell away and careered in our direction at high speed. Being out of its immediate line of flight so to speak, I was able to stand and watch as a group of terrified ground gunners disappeared below ground like a bunch of rabbits. The wheel struck their weapon pit with a resounding crunch before finally coming to rest; luckily without injuring anybody.

All this had occured without the knowledge of the flight test crew. As their Lancaster carried no radio, the problem then was how to inform them of their predicament. Eventually, a Lysander was launched carrying a blackboard (sic) inscribed with a hastily scrawled message. Closing on the Lancaster, the board was waved in the rear cockpit until the message was acknowledged. Then followed a most professional example of flying. The test pilot landed across wind with the main undercarriage retracted. It was raining at the time and the pilot put the huge bomber down so gently that it just slid across the grass, coming to rest out of the way in a corner of the aerodrome. Subsequent flying at Boscombe that day was unaffected, and the damage to the Lancaster was confined to four bent propellers and a bomb aimer's compartment full of earth"

A combination of bad weather and poor bombing results obviously led to a feeling of frustration at Bomber Command Headquarters. In an (ill advised) effort to overcome criticism, the CinC, Air Marshal Sir Richard Pierse, ordered a major effort with Berlin as the main target. Despite a revised weather forecast which predicted storm clouds with icing and hail over the North Sea, through which the bombers would have to fly on their way to and from the target, the order was given to go. The AOC No 5 Group, Air Vice Marshal Slessor, objected to the plan, particularly in view of the distance to Berlin, and was allowed to despatch his crews to a nearer target, Cologne. All in all that night, the Command sent 392 aircraft to Berlin, Cologne and Mannheim. It proved to be a disaster, with a total of 37 aircraft failing to return (9.4%). This figure represented a 100% increase on the previous highest loss for one night. It is probable that many of those lost fell in the North Sea from fuel shortage, icing, or a combination of both. To make matters worse, not one of the attacks was particularly successful; the attack on Berlin being the last on the enemy capital until January 1943.

As part of No 5 Group, the Waddington crews were spared the trip to Berlin, going instead to Cologne. No 44 Squadron despatched fourteen Hampdens, while No 207 Squadron put up nine Manchesters for Cologne and one for Boulogne. All the Station aircraft returned safely, though several Manchesters suffered hydraulic problems.

Following the attack on Cologne, No 207 Squadron was warned that it was to move from Waddington to Bottesford in the near future. However, before the move, the squadron was called upon for one more operation from Waddington. For the crews of Bomber Command, it was back to Hamburg on the night of 9/10 November. A mixed force of 103 aircraft was despatched to Hamburg, which included six Hampdens and six Manchesters from Waddington. In addition, five Station Hampdens carried out mining operations off the mouth of the River Elbe, while one Manchester joined eight other aircraft in an attack on Ostend.

Three of the Station's Manchesters experienced a variety of problems which, allied to other matters, resulted in only three of them managing to locate and bomb Hamburg. Among those unable to attack Hamburg was a newcomer to the squadron, F/O John De Lacey (Dim) Wooldridge DFM. His navigator had misidentified the Jade Bay for the mouth of the Elbe, and by the time they had realised the error, the defences of Hamburg were fully activated. Rather than take on the flak, searchlights and night fighters defending the city by himself, Wooldridge elected instead to attack Wilhelmshaven. He was convinced that a power-off dive attack was the best method of attacking a heavily defended target; so having managed to drag his Manchester up to 12000 feet, he commenced a diving glide, releasing his bombs as his aircraft passed through 10,000 feet. In view of the heavy defensive fire, Wooldridge continued his descent, but this time with full power on, eventually coasting out at around 1000 feet.

On 17 November, No 207 Squadron left Waddington for the recently opened RAF Bottesford in

Leicestershire. Six days before the move, the squadron had been stood down in order to play host to a party of Air Ministry press officers. In due course, the interviews and photographs appeared in the 'Aeroplane' periodical. The articles laid great stress on the courage and determination of the crews, flying in the face of strong enemy defences, and went on to state that the new Vulture engine was reliable etc etc! While the crews agreed wholeheartedly with the first part, they expressed the opinion that the section on the Vulture engine must have been written by a promising novelist! Among those leaving Waddington with No 207 Squadron, was 'Dim' Wooldridge. He was to survive the war, eventually moving on to the Mosquito. Post war, he became a highly regarded composer and writer. He wrote the script and the music for the film 'Appointment in London', a story of a bomber squadron.

Although No 207 Squadron and its troublesome Manchesters had left Waddington, the Station had not heard the last of them. Some were assigned to No 44 Squadron for use as training aircraft, pending the arrival of the Lancaster. Five days after No 207 Squadron's departure, P/O Bill Hills DFM, was flying EM-F (L7300) to Waddington. On board, apart from the crew, were three passengers who had hitched a ride. Hills and crew had flown at low level from Bottesford to Boston, where they picked up the canal linking Boston to Lincoln. For part of the way, the canal ran beside the London to Lincoln mainline railway, and the crew enjoyed flying close to, and level with the trains as they overtook them. At times they were down to around 50 feet as they passed some of the trains. As they neared Lincoln and prior to making their approach into Waddington, the port engine failed. Hills wasted no time in shutting down the engine and feathering the propeller. Unfortunately, the feathering mechanism worked only partially, leaving them with a dead engine and a drag-inducing propeller. Advising Waddington that they would be coming in on one engine, Hills increased power on the starboard engine in order to climb high enough to get into Waddington which, being on the Lincoln edge, was higher than Hills' aircraft at the time of the incident!

Almost immediately, the starboard engine failed also. This left Hills and crew at low level with no engines, committed to crash landing dead ahead. Luckily, there was flat open ground in front of them, with a small tree-lined lake off to one side. As the Manchester struck the ground, the tail section broke away, leaving the remains to skid along the field at about 100mph. The bomber eventually came to a stop when it flopped over some banking and pitched into Fiskerton Lake. As the terrifying apparition careered towards the lake, the participants in a fishing competition decided that they would be better off somewhere else and ran for their lives! All the anglers got away safely apart from the sole occupant of a punt who was stranded in the middle of the lake. This unfortunate piscatorialist got thoroughly drenched by the Manchester-caused tidal wave, to say nothing of the effect on his nerves.

After something verging on a comedy of errors, the soaking wet, frozen crew reached the edge of the lake, some suffering from shock or concussion. Eventually, an ambulance and a private car arrived to take them off to Lincoln hospital. Those with more serious injuries were stripped of their soaking wet clothing and wrapped in blankets. On the way to the hospital, the ambulance had to stop at a road junction, at which point, the concussed co-pilot leaped from the vehicle and dashed naked down the road, much to the consternation of the passers-by! He was eventually caught and returned to the ambulance, which continued on its way to the hospital without further ado.

At about the same time as No 207 Squadron left Waddington, 'F' Maintenance Unit (MU), which had come to the Station from RAF Kenley in 1938, returned whence it came. This unit had been responsible for the care and custody of a reserve transport pool and the despatch of vehicles to units in the area. Meanwhile, in preparation for the scheduled arrival of the new Lancasters, the Station received an influx of highly experienced Warrant Officer pilots from RAF Scampton and other stations. Among these 'old hands' were such stalwarts as Hubert Crum, 'Lucky' Wright, 'Pi**y' Jones and Frankie Stott, a man with a prodigous capacity for beer.

On 13 December, No 44 Squadron carried out one of its last Hampden operations; a special 'daylight' minelaying task off Brest. The Squadron Commander, W/Cdr Misselbrook, protested in the strongest possible terms that such operations inevitably resulted in appalling casualties for little or no worthwhile result. He went on to add that the Command could not afford such losses in men and machines, particularly at a time when questions were being asked in high places as to the effectiveness of Bomber Command's operations. However, as a true professional and an honourable gentleman, once he realised that his objections had fallen on deaf ears, he determined to lead the mission himself. After a brief period of training with a new weapon, three Hampden crews took off for Brest. The crews involved were W/Cdr Misselbrook DSO, S/Ldr Burton-Gyles and Sgt Hackney.

It had been the Wing Commander's expressed intention that he would be the last to drop his mine, knowing only too well that the flak and fighters would be at their most deadly by then. Burton-Gyles was the first to attack, dropping his mine from 400 feet before turning to engage the enemy fighters. The second Hampden, that flown by Sgt Hackney and crew, lost the protective cover of low cloud on their run in to the assigned drop point, so elected to drop their mine in the estuary, some seven miles short of the briefed location. W/Cdr Misselbrook's forebodings had been well founded. He pressed home his attack in the face of intense fire; he and his crew, F/O Jeffcoat and Sergeants Gumbley and Leggett, perishing together in their aircraft KM-F (AE196). Meanwhile, Burton-Gyles was under attack from a Bf109, but by a skilfull combination of evasive manoeuvres, directed by his W/OpAG, Sgt Pool, combined with accurate return fire from both gunners, the Hampden survived the attacks and limped away badly damaged. Much later, following a forced landing at Boscombe Down, which was witnessed by some No 44 Squadron aircrew on detachment, the damage to the aircraft was assessed. The starboard wingtip and rudder had been shot away; the main plane and starboard aileron badly damaged; the starboard engine fairing torn away and the nacelle damaged.

The squadron felt keenly the loss of the Commanding Officer, particularly in view of the circumstances. He had been the driving force behind their gradual conversion to the Lancaster, and had died as he had lived, leading from the front. His loss was felt well beyond the squadron. Gp Capt 'Gus' Walker, commanding RAF North Luffenham, sent a message of sympathy, in which he expressed his sorrow at their loss. Saddened too was Jean Barclay, the Intelligence Officer. As she confided to her diary:

"...a loud hoot of laughter and a merry hail to see a comical vision stroll into the room, a ridiculous schoolboy's pepperpot of unruly fair hair, sticking inevitably aloft... ...studying the target (Brest) prior to take-off and commenting - Well I'm glad it isn't Wilhelmshaven; I'd be a bit windy about that..."

For his performance that day, S/Ldr Burton-Gyles was awarded the DSO.

Despite the tragic loss of their Commanding Officer, the squadron continued to operate on any night that the winter weather permitted. The new CO, W/Cdr R A B Learoyd VC arrived on 19 December and immediately commenced conversion flying, using one of the squadron's recently acquired Manchesters. That same day, the squadron lost another of its leaders, but this time in much happier circumstances. S/Ldr J D Collier DFC was promoted to Wing Commander and posted to the newly established No 420 (Snowy Owl) Squadron RCAF, which was forming at Waddington. In due course, this Canadian squadron would inherit seventeen Hampdens from No 44 Squadron and carry out operations alongside the Rhodesian squadron, which was by then flying its new Lancasters.

It appears that at some time later, the Air Ministry's plan to re-equip No 420 Squadron with Manchesters was rejected by the RCAF Overseas Headquarters (who could blame them). The squadron eventually moved to Skipton-on-Swale and re-equipped with Wellington Mk IIIs. On its formation, No 420 Squadron was Canadian in name only, as the personnel were mostly RAF, but an increasing number of RCAF air and ground crew were posted in, until the squadron became Canadian in fact as well as in name.

A Legend is Born

On 24 December 1941, RAF Waddington and No 44 (Rhodesia) Squadron in particular, received the best possible Christmas presents. That day, the squadron's first three Lancasters arrived (L7530, L7537 and L7538); four days later a further four arrived. Despite the pleasure and excitement at the arrival of the new four-engined bombers, it was not the first time that Lancasters had been seen on the Station. During the previous September, one had appeared in the circuit, but had been dismissed initially as 'just another b****y Manchester'; that was until it was seen to be powered by four engines, not two! This was the prototype Lancaster (BT308), which was being used by the No 44 Squadron crews on detachment to Boscombe Down. The purpose of the earlier visit had been to ensure that there would be no unforseen problems operating the RAF's new bomber from Waddington.

Having undergone some conversion training on both the Manchester and the Lancaster, the new Commanding Officer, W/Cdr Learoyd, was not to see the new bomber into operational service. Instead, he was posted to Headquarters Bomber Command; acting command of the squadron passing to OC 'A' Flight, S/Ldr J D Nettleton. His brief was to ensure that that at least eight crews were fully operational by the end of January.

Long before the arrival of the first Lancasters, Waddington had been the scene of considerable building work. The sergeants' Mess was extended in order to accommodate up to 140 SNCOs. In addition, the bomb storage facilities were expanded and extra fuel storage tanks were installed; all this in addition to the construction of numerous technical facilities. Many of the older buildings were replaced or extended, while others underwent a change of use. One building however remained undisturbed. This was the Station Pigeon Loft, which was housed in what appears to have been a building left over from World war I. This minor facility was the domain of an elderly Corporal, who was an avid pigeon breeder and racer. One of his charges was later to win the animal VC, the Dickin Medal.

So ended 1941; a year of mixed achievement by Bomber Command, with doubts being expressed in high circles as to the comparative value of its efforts, costs and losses. Inevitably, such doubts were enthusiastically endorsed by the Admiralty and the War Office, ever keen to increase their share of the defence budget (nothing changes!). It had to be admitted that up to the end of 1941, the German defences had kept the Command's effectiveness in check. German industry had not been seriously affected and civilian morale showed no sign of weakness. Among the many problems the the Command had still to overcome was the inability of its crews to accurately navigate by night over a blacked out continent. Denied navigation aids, while having to contend with inclement weather and unreliable weather forecasts, the gallant crews did their best, but they badly needed scientific assistance if their sacrificies were not to be in vain. Their lot was not an enviable one; being forced by flak and searchlights to fly at oxygen height with a rudimentary aircraft oxygen system, while carrying a volatile combination of high explosives and high octane fuel. Indeed, in some cases they were required to fly in aircraft that lacked any form of self-sealing fuel tanks or armour protection. Theirs was a courage that defies adequate description. Yet despite the odds stacked against them, they kept going back, always endeavouring to find and hit their assigned target. That they were so often unable to do so, was not for the want of trying. Years of peace at any price, together with a blind, parsimonious defence vote in succeeding years, were being paid for in blood; but as ever, not the blood of those responsible.

The one bright spot on the horizon was the knowledge that the country, Commonwealth and Empire were no longer alone; there was a new ally. Following the Japanese attack on the American Pacific Fleet at Pearl Harbour on 7 December 1941, the United States of America had declared war on the Axis powers. It remained to be seen how long it would take for the American intervention to become effective.

The New Year at Waddington commenced with a new squadron and a new aircraft. The crews of No 44 Squadron were converting enthusiastically to their new charge, while No 420 Squadron worked up under the energetic drive of its Commanding Officer, W/Cdr J D Collier DFC*. Joe Collier had been promoted from his position as a Flight Commander on No 44 Squadron, to what was eventually to become almost an entirely Canadian squadron. That he more than achieved the Command's requirements was a testimony to his sheer determination and hard work. To again quote Jean Barclay:

"...Joe Collier, a young and very keen Flight Commander of No 44 Squadron, had been promoted to lead the new Canadian squadron...he put heart and soul into the task and his keeness and determination to make a success of the job, seemed to galvanise us all into excitement and enthusiasm. The most junior Squadron Commander in No 5 Group, he was anxious to compete successfully with his old squadron, from which he had emerged with a DFC and bar. He had every known difficulty to contend with, but overcame them by sheer determination and hard work. Many of his ground crews were some of those who 'were not required' by No 44 Squadron; tools failed to arrive, and some of the Hampdens handed over to him from No 44 Squadron were, to say the least, war weary.

All this and other problems had to be dealt with, but through it all, Joe Collier remained undaunted and on 21 January 1942, No 420 Squadron operated for the first time, the target being Emden. It was not an auspicious start; the aircraft were late taking off due to a hitch in fuel loads. Even worse, their 'B' Flight Commander, S/Ldr Wood, failed to return flying in PT-S (AT130). They had been hit by flak and crashed near Harlingen; all four crew members becoming PoWs... 'Woody' was a tall, delicate looking South African who had been in Burton-Gyles Flight on No 44 Squadron. Originally a fighter boy, his was a thoroughly lackadaisical manner and appearance. He always looked as if he had been hauled through a hedge backwards and then through a rubbish heap. This, together with his slow quiet drawl, gave one the feeling that nothing would ever be finished or accomplished. Yet, when the squadron came to operate, there was 'Woody's' Flight, quietly ready and on top line...he was clever with a pencil and paper and many were the strange devices floating around his Flight. His Sidcott suit bore a most monstrous demon known as 'The Harbinger of Death', which also adorned his log book and even his aircraft."

W/Cdr Collier's efforts resulted in No 420 Squadron becoming accepted quickly as part of the Waddington scene. In this he was ably assisted by his other Flight Commander, S/Ldr Campbell, who commanded 'A' Flight. Campbell was a Canadian who had come from No 83 Squadron at Scampton, and who, like his Squadron Commander, believed in leading from the front; despite which, he succeeded in outlasting three 'B' Flight Commanders! The unfortunate S/Ldr Wood was succeeded by S/Ldr Harris, later killed in action during the German 'Channel Dash' in February. This was the name given to the break out from Brest of the battlecruisers Scharnhorst, Gneisenau and Prinz Eugen, during which they made their way up the English Channel to north German ports, further away from Bomber Command. In turn, S/Ldr Harris was to be succeeded by S/Ldr Tench, who was to ditch near Heligoland and be taken prisoner, following an attack on Lubeck on 29 March.

Although morale was high at Waddington, the New Year was not a particularly cheerful one for the British people. The German assault on Russia was going well for the Wehrmacht; the Japanese had struck a devastating blow to the American Pacific Fleet, while the Royal Navy had lost the Battleship Prince of Wales and the battlecruiser Repulse to Japanese air attack. In addition, the U-boats of the Kreigsmarine appeared to have the upper hand in the battle of the Atlantic. The only apparently successful British offensive action was that of Bomber Command. It was therefore just as well that the British public were not aware of the contents of the Butt Report, which had been completed in August 1941. Having analysed over four thousand individual aircraft target photographs, taken in the course of one hundred night raids in June and July 1941, Mr Butt, a civil servant in the War Cabinet Secretariat, concluded that only one crew in four which claimed to have bombed the assigned target in Germany, were found to have been within five miles of that target. This analysis was all the more disturbing in view of the fact that under normal circumstances, only the best crews carried cameras!

Closer to home; although the aircrews at Waddington and elsewhere were not aware of the findings of the Butt Report, they were only too well aware of their casualties, if not the overall loss rate. This latter point too made disturbing reading. In four months, from July to October, the Command had lost 414 bombers at night and 112 in daylight attacks. In comparative terms, this was approximately the equivalent of the Command's entire front-line strength being lost in only four months. In percentage terms, the losses were 3.5% at night and 7.1% during daylight. Following a meeting between the Prime Minister and the CinC Bomber Command, Sir Richard Pierse, the War Cabinet had ordered that the bomber offensive, in its current form, was to be curtailed during the winter months while a new policy was formulated. Accordingly, on 13 November, the Air Council directed that only limited operations were to be undertaken until the whole future of Bomber Command was determined. In other words, the Command was fighting for its life! Ever eager to press their case for more resources, the Admiralty wasted no time in pursuing their oft-repeated demand that Bomber Command's aircraft be assigned to convoy protection duties. The aim being to reduce the crippling losses being inflicted on our merchantmen by the U-boats.

At Waddington, as elsewhere, the reduction in the number of operations was put down to the severe winter weather. As one of the groundcrew recalled:

"No 44 Squadron was a Rhodesian squadron, and was made up in the main of volunteers from Rhodesia and South Africa, plus a few of us British lads to bring the squadron up to full strength. The Colonial lads had never seen snow until their first winter in England. The first snow in Lincolnshire fell overnight, and one of the Rhodesians, who had been drinking heavily the night before, left his billet at around four in the morning to pop outside and relieve himself.

On opening the door he was confronted with a carpet of virgin snow. He let out an almighty yell and in no time at all, he and his fellow countrymen were outside, playing in the snow while the rest of us tried to get back to sleep. it was not to be many days before the novelty of snow wore off and the newcomers were feeling the cold. On their return to their barrack blocks at midday, the baths in the ablutions were half-filled with hot water, when as many as possible would stand in it in their wellington boots in an attempt to get their feet warm. Later on, some sheep farmer in Rhodesia sent over a batch of sheep-skin coats to be issued to the Rhodesians. These coats helped keep out the cold, though the colonials never did find an effective way of keeping their feet warm."

In January 1942, further awards were promulgated in the London Gazette. S/Ldr Burton-Gyles DFC was awarded the DSO, while DFCs were awared to F/Lt Jean Sauvage from the Seychelles, F/Os H E Maudesley and D R Taylor and P/O C Salazar. In addition, F/Sgt A J T Moon was awarded the DFM. Later that month the Station aircrew were given a lecture on escape and evasion techniques by a F/Lt Shore. Normally, aircrew tended to treat this subject and its instructors with scant regard. However, Shore commanded attention by virtue of his having evaded and escaped after being shot down over Germany.

During the first weeks of 1942, No 44 Squadron was non-operational while the crews familiarised themselves with their new aircraft. Apart from the usual circuits and bumps, most of their flying training involved long coastal flights to the north of Scotland, carrying four inert sea mines. To the majority of the squadron aircrew, this indicated that they would first use their new bomber in the same old minelaying role as the Hampden, only this time they would carry four mines instead of just one. In the main, the crews were all experienced operators, who considered the mining role to be a waste of the Lancaster's potential, though post war analysis proved just how wrong they were. What they did not know was the concern at high level regarding the latest German battleship the Tirpitz. This leviathan, which was markedly superior to even the latest Royal Navy battleships, was nearing completion in the port of Kiel in the Baltic.

The Tirpitz and her sister ship the Bismark, were the largest and fastest battleships to have been built up to that time, and although the Royal Navy eventually managed to sink the Bismark, the Tirpitz was to all intents and purposes 'a fleet in being' throughout the war. The First Sea Lord wrote of the necessity of always having three modern battleships available to cope with the Tirpitz. Churchill was to write that he regarded the destruction of or crippling the Tirpitz to be the greatest event at sea at the time. He considered that no other target was comparable to it and regarded the matter to be of the highest urgency and importance. In its turn, the Admiralty laid great stress on the need to keep the Tirpitz bottled up in the Baltic and away from the Atlantic.

Despite Bomber Command's best efforts, in mid January Tirpitz broke out of the Baltic and sailed to Foettenfjord near Trondheim in Norway, reaching it on 16 January 1942. Almost immediately, Bomber Command was tasked with sealing the Tirpitz in by mining the exit through Aas Fjord. The plan was to mount a series of minelaying sorties using three of No 44 Squadron's Lancasters, each carrying four mines; hence the training flights. The three aircraft were to be detached to Wick in north east Scotland on 25 January and commence operations immediately on arrival. However, the prolonged severe weather rendered Wick unusable by the heavily laden Lancasters and the operation was cancelled. Meanwhile, back at Waddington, the Lancaster crews continued to work up on their new aircraft, though not without incident.

The new AOC No 5 Group, Air Vice Marshal J C Slessor visited the Station and flew in Lancaster KM-H (L7536) which was to be later lost on the Augsburg raid. The AOC found the squadron morale very high and all delighted with the new bomber.

As was to be expected with any new aircraft type, the odd problem arose from time to time. The acting Squadron Commander, S/Ldr Nettleton, lost a tail wheel when his aircraft struck a mound of snow. Later the same month, F/O Henry Maudesley and crew, flying in Lancaster L7535 on a routine test flight for the A & AEE at Boscombe Down, could not obtain permission to land at Stanton Harcourt in Oxfordshaire when they found themselves low on fuel. The nearest alternative aerodrome was Cheddington near Aylesbury, so Maudesley elected to divert there. Unfortunately, unknown to the Maudesley crew, the aerodrome at Cheddington was still under construction and their Lancaster struck a pile of concrete posts on landing. Their aircraft slewed off to one side of the runway and the undercarriage collapsed, resulting in the bomber sliding backwards (!) through the mud and builder's debris, suffering extensive damage. The Lancaster was subsequently recovered, but was found to be so badly damaged that it was relegated to ground instructional airframe status only. Luckily, none of the crew were injured and returned to Waddington, little the worse for the experience. Henry Maudesley went on to serve with distinction on Nos 44 and 50 Squadrons before joining Guy Gibson on No 617 Squadron. He and his crew perished near Emmerich, following their attack on the Eder Dam.

As soon as No 44 Squadron's mining operation against the Tirpitz was cancelled, some of the squadron's specialists were detached to Coningsby to assist in converting the crews of No 97 Squadron to the Lancaster. This was the second squadron to equip with the Lancaster, and to say that the crews were relieved to see the back of the Manchester, would be putting it mildly. As F/Lt David Penman DFC, then a member of No 97 Squadron, recalled:

"...and F/Lt 'Nicky' Sandford of No 44 Squadron flew in with a Lancaster to convert a few pilots. Our conversion consisted of one demonstration circuit flown by 'Nicky', followed by one circuit each by the pilots to be converted; about six of us in all. We then climbed into a Manchester and flew to the Avro factory at Woodford, where we collected six brand new Lancasters."

David Penman had previously served on 44 Squadron when it was equipped with the Blenheim Mk I.

Back at Waddington, the recently renumbered No 1506 BAT Flight had its establishment of aircraft increased, in order to double the intake of trainees. At about this time, Sgt Wilfred Bickley joined No 44 Squadron as one of the additional air gunners required by the new aircraft. Wilfred was a pre-war regular, having joined in 1936 as a Fitter Apprentice. On joining his first squadron, he became a part-time air gunner, sporting the brass winged bullet on his right sleeve. In March 1940, he joined No 613 Squadron, flying as a Corporal air gunner in Lysanders of Army Cooperation Command. He flew both Hampdens and Lancasters with No 44 Squadron before eventually joining No 617 Squadron in November 1943. In all, Wilf Bickley flew 71 operations and was awarded the rare Conspicuous Gallantry Medal (CGM). He flew regularly with W/Cdr Leonard Cheshire during the time that the latter commanded No 617 Squadron. Commissioned in July 1944, Wilfred Bickley retired from the service in 1946.

Among the Station groundcrew was John Thompson. He joined No 44 Squadron in early 1940 and served at Waddington for most of the war. For a time he was billeted out with a family named Farrier, who lived just opposite the Horse and Jockey public house in the village. He was one of John Nettleton's groundcrew at the time of the Augsburg raid, later moving to No 617 Squadron at Scampton before returning to Waddington on posting to No 463 Squadron RAAF. John recalled the visit of Roy Chadwick to Waddington during the early days of the Lancaster. Having met and spoken with the to him, unknown 'civvy', the young Thompson remarked to his Flight Sergeant that: *"That Avro bloke is very clued up on the Lancaster"* to be informed *"So he should be son, he designed it!"*

Another of the stalwarts on the ground was one 'Paddy' Keating, a young Gen/Armourer, who came over from Southern Ireland to join the RAF. A bit of a wild man, his method of lighting the barrack room stove was to acquire (!) a 4lb incendiary bomb, bang the nose cap on the floor until it ignited, pop it into the stove and top up with coke; a very effective if unorthodox system, which necessitated regular stove replacements.

On 1 February 1942, 44 groundcrew of the Royal Canadian Air Force arrived at Waddington on posting to No 420 Squadron. The Station's newest squadron was begining to reflect its title.

Six days after the Canadian influx, Sgt D F Nicholson misread the landing indicator at nearby RAF Skellingthorpe and made his final approach downwind. Realising his mistake at the last moment, he attempted to rudder his Lancaster (L7542) on to the cross-wind runway. In so doing, he lost control of his aircraft and collided with a frozen snow bank, writing off the bomber's undercarriage, rendering the aircraft 'beyond repair'. A similar accident was to befall Sgt Rowan-Parry, not many weeks later. In addition, the very experienced Warrant Officer Hubert Crum, discovered that the landing run of a large heavy aircraft on a wet and greasy grass runway, used up more countryside than he expected! On delivering a new Lancaster from the manufacturers, he ended up crashing through the airfield boundary hedge and straddling the Lincoln to Sleaford (A15) main road.

On 12 February, three major units of the Kriegsmarine broke out of their much-bombed harbour at Brest and sailed up the English Channel on their way to the north German ports - the so-called 'Channel Dash' was on! In all, Bomber Command committed 244 aircraft in an attempt to counter this move; some bombing while others laid mines. From Waddington, No 420 Squadron despatched six Hampdens on a bombing sortie. Of these, three failed to locate the warships, while one, that flown by F/O Smith and crew, carried out an attack but was unable to observe the results. The other two Hampdens; those flown by S/Ldr Harris (AT134) and P/O Topping (P4400), failed to return. As a result of the Command's efforts, the battle cruisers Scharnhorst and Gneisenau were damaged by mines; the Scharnorst seriously; while the heavy cruiser Prinz Eugen escaped undamaged. During the course of these operations, the RAF lost 42 aircraft, while the Fleet Air Arm lost six Swordfish in torpedo attacks on the three ships.

On the night of 18/19 February, No 420 Squadron despatched four Hampdens on minelaying sorties off the Dutch and German coasts. Among the pilots taking part was P/O Kee, flying Hampden PT-F (AD915). Robert Kee had joined No 44 Squadron in May 1941 and had served his apprenticeship flying as second pilot/navigator. He flew his last trip as a navigator with S/Ldr Nettleton and, having completed his captains' course, he returned to Waddington to join No 420 Squadron. Apart from a leaflet dropping sortie, this was to be his first operation as an aircraft captain; his 24th in all. The target area for his mine was off the Frisian Island of Terschelling. Their first attempt to commence a timed run to the drop point, was met by a barrage of flak, which drove them off and above a thin layer of cloud. Kee decided to try a glide approach to their timing point and to then set course for the drop point as quickly as possible. Unfortunately, the German flak crews had remained alert and, as Kee opened the throttles wide as they passed over their timing point, the searchlights and anti-aircraft guns found them. One of the first shells hit the port engine, causing the bomber to immediately fall off into a spin at the dangerously low height of 800 feet.

Acting by instinct, Kee somehow managed to bring the Hampden under a semblance of control, just before it mushed on to the ice and snow-covered mud flats in something like a landing attitude. As he later recalled, if they had been about 300 feet higher, they might have got away with it. As it was, there was a grinding, sliding sensation and 'more noise than he had ever heard in his life'. Eventually, the noise and the violent movement ceased and the expected pain did not materialise. On removing his arms from in front of his face, he found it difficult to believe that the wreckage he was sitting in had once been an aircraft. The wings had been torn away, the cockpit had disintegrated and he was sitting on the ice with the broken control column lying across his knees. Having struggled clear of what had been his aircraft, he began to search for his crew. The two gunners were patently beyond help, but the navigator was alive, though badly injured. Kee dragged the injured man to safety, fearing that the mine might explode at any moment. Having made his navigator as comfortable as possible, Kee decided to make a break for it before some approaching German troops reached them. The sound of bullets whistling past his head convinced him that for the time being at least, the war for him was over! This incident had an interesting postscript. At approximately 2pm on 22 February, a pigeon was picked up by an Army unit located at Spurn Point at the mouth of the Humber River. The bird carried a message:

"SOS AD915 - F. Time of despatch 10 o'clock 21.2.42. Position Oosterbierum, Friesland, Netherlands".

Added along the side of the message sheet were the letters '**OZO**'. As none of the crew had time to send a message, it can only be assumed that some Dutch people had found the bird in its container somewhere near Kee's aircraft and had released it with a message. The position given was incorrect, but the letters OZO were the Dutch initials for 'Holland Will Rise Again'.

The pigeon was named 'Billy' and carried the ring number NU41HQ4373. It had been bred and trained by Mr Joe Greenwood of North Hykeham near Waddington. When found by the Army, the bird was in a state of collapse, having flown 250 miles through a gale-force snowstorm to deliver its message. On 8 September 1945, the People's Dispensary for Sick Animals (PDSA) awarded Billy the Dickin Medal, the animal equivalent of the VC.

On 23 February 1942, Air Marshal Sir Arthur Harris was appointed AOCinC Bomber Command. It was not an auspicious time to take over, the Command being at the nadir of its fortunes. At the time, Bomber Command possessed only 58 squadrons, seven of which were temporarily non-operational, including No 44 Squadron, which was busy converting to the Lancaster. The 58 squadrons possessed just over six hundred aircraft available for operations, less than one hundred of which were the new four-engined bombers. Add to this the continuing calls from the Admiralty and the War Office to disband the bomber force and share out its assets among more needy (their) causes, and it becomes apparent that the new Commander's position was hardly an enviable one. Something had to be done to convince the doubters and critics alike, including those with less than honourable motives, that Bomber Command had a role to play and a major one at that. Despite the misgivings in high places, Bomber Command remained the only Allied component capable of carrying the war into Germany, even though the results were far from satisfactory. Luckily, a new radio navigation aid named Gee was coming into service, and it was reputedly capable of ensuring accurate track keeping at least as far as the Ruhr Valley.

In the same month that he was appointed, the new CinC received a directive from his political masters. This directive stated that the new strategic objective should be focussed upon the morale of the enemy civil population and, in particular, of the industrial workers. To say the least, this was an interesting policy directive, emanating from the War Cabinet, particularly when viewed in the light of the subsequent endeavours of some politicians in 1945 to distance themselves from the cataclysmic results achieved by the Commander and crews of Bomber Command. Harris was to join the unfortunate GOC Singapore, General Percival, in carrying the can for political shortcomings of one sort or another.

Bomber Command's main targets were now those that came within range of the Gee equipment. This included the towns and cities of the Ruhr Valley, together with the ports of Bremerhaven, Emden and Wilhelmshaven. The list of secondary targets included Berlin, Lubeck and Schweinfurt among many others.

On 3 March, four Lancasters of No 44 Squadron carried out minelaying operations off the northwest coast of Germany - the Lancaster had been blooded! Among the four crews taking part in what was the first Lancaster operation of the war, were three who were to take part in the costly attack on Augsburg the following month. The crews involved were those of S/Ldr Nettleton, F/Lt Sandford and Warrant Officers Crum and Lamb. All four aircraft returned safely to base, each aircraft having laid four mines in the area of Heligoland Bight. S/Ldr Nettleton and F/Lt 'Sandy' Sandford laid their eight mines in the southern approaches to Heligoland, while the two Warrant Officers mined the northern approaches. These particular mining areas were known as 'Yams' and 'Rosemary' respectively in the Bomber Command mining area code. Each crew had with them a Royal Navy officer, who had been sent by the Admiralty to see just how the crews of Bomber Command carried out the requirements of the new mining directive.

The first Lancaster to take off that auspicious night was KM-Q (L7549), flown by Warrant Officer Hubert Crum, watched by the AOC No 5 Group, AVM Slessor. The significance of the Lancaster as a minelayer was its ability to carry four mines as opposed to the Hampden's one, and to be able to lay them at much greater ranges. This latter feature meant that mines could now be laid in areas such as the Baltic, which hitherto had remained immune. Under its new dynamic CinC, Bomber Command undertook to lay one thousand mines per month. By the end of the war, air dropped mines had accounted for 152 enemy warships sunk, with a further 340 damaged in the coastal waters of northwest Europe. While the Lancasters were carrying out their first operation of the war, four crews of No 420 Squadron joined a mixed force of 235 bombers in an extremely successful attack on the Renault factory in the town of Boulogne-Billancourt, just west of Paris.

The weather in early 1942 remained extremely bad, with little flying taking place. Because of their relative inexperience on the new aircraft, the crews of No 44 Squadron were severely restricted as to when and in what conditions they could fly. Apparently, higher authority wanted no repeat of a pre-Christmas fiasco when, without warning, fog descended over the Lincoln area. Despite the hazardous conditions, most of the returning Hampden crews of No 420 Squadron elected to land back at base, rather than divert to other distant aerodromes. The next morning the fog having partially cleared, the early shift workers on their way to their duties throughout the Station, were greeted by the sight of Hampden tails protruding through the fog in all sorts of unlikely places. There was one particular Hampden up on its nose right in front of the Sergeants' Mess. Amazingly, there were few serious injuries among the crews involved.

On 8 March, one week after a visit to the Station by Marshal of the Royal Air Force, Viscount Trenchard, eight Lancasters took off for Lossiemouth in preparation for an attack on the German battleship Tirpitz. The aircraft left in two flights of four, but not in formation as they had not had the opportunity to practice this in the Lancaster. As a Canadian rear gunner, F/Sgt 'Bud' Gill recalled:

"I had crewed up with F/Sgt 'Lucky' Wright, an experienced operator who put all his crew members through a thorough test before accepting them fully as a member of his crew. Wright gave 100% and demanded 100% in return... ...at the briefing for our trip up to Lossiemouth, we were warned that British ground defences had not been issued with silhouettes of the new Lancaster and as such, we were to fly up the coast over the sea. We took off in KM-F (L7534) around midday and proceeded out to the coast near Skegness before turning north up the North Sea. There was 10/10 cloud at about 10,000 feet and we got bored flying over it, so 'Lucky' decided to drop down and fly just below it. We broke cloud around 6000 feet right over a British convoy, which opened up with everything they had. Being a new boy, I had never been fired on before and did not realise what all the pretty lights were! I had been told that when you could smell the cordite, it (the shell) was close, but on this particular occasion, I could actually taste it!

No sooner had we got clear of the Navy, when two Spitfires closed in on us from behind and started firing. I just did not know what to do; sit there and hope, or fire back. 'Lucky' told me to hold my fire and called to our wireless operator, Terry Byrne, to fire off the colours of the day, while he (Wright) took evasive action and climbed for the clouds. The Verey pistol was in its stowage, but nobody had felt it necessary to check it. Terry quickly loaded the colours of the day, put the safety catch to fire and pulled the trigger. Unfortunately, during the construction of this particular Lancaster, someone at the factory had omitted to cut the hole in the skin which allowed the pistol to fire into the airstream. The result of this oversight was, that when Terry fired, the fuselage filled with red, bue and green lights, which ricochetted around the cabin in all directions. Fortunately, we reached the clouds and escaped the not very accurate attentions of our two erstwhile assailants. It was a very chastened Lancaster crew that landed at Lossiemouth some time later..."

The detachment remained at Lossiemouth waiting for good weather which never materialised, so on 13 March they returned to Waddington. In the meantime, those crews that had been left behind had continued with their training programme until 10 March, when the squadron was tasked with taking part in a 126 strong attack on Essen. The distinction of being the first crews to fly the Lancaster on a bombing operation fell to F/Os Ball and Wilkins, flying in KM-H (L7536) and KM-A (L7566) respectively. In the attack, F/O Ball's aircraft suffered minor flak damage, but both aircraft returned safely.

On 24 March, Waddington despatched three Hampdens and two Lancasters as part of a 35 strong force minelaying off Lorient. All No 420 Squadron's Hampdens returned safely, landing at St Eval in Cornwall, but Lancaster KM-N (R5493), flown by a South African, F/Sgt Warren-Smith, failed to return. This was a particularly heavy blow to the squadron as the crew consisted of two pilots, two navigators and two wireless operators, together with a mid upper gunner and a rear gunner. It also represented the loss of five Englishmen, one Rhodesian, one South African and an Australian. A No 420 Squadron pilot reported seeing a four-engined bomber coned by searchlights and being heavily engaged by heavy flak over Lorient itself. So, R5493 was to be the first of hundreds of Lancasters to fall to earth (or sea) over occupied Europe.

Two days after the loss of the first Lancaster on operations, the Station's Lancasters were taken off operations following the loss of a No 97 Squadron Lancaster (L7531), flown by S/Ldr T H Boyland and crew on 24 March. The signal from HQ No 5 Group ordering restrictions on Lancaster flying, read as follows: 'Lancaster aircraft are to be inspected immediately for failure of flush rivets attaching the wing-tip skin to rib attachments to the mainplane, and for wrinkling of the skin on the top surface of the wing. Aircraft found to be defective are to be grounded until further instructions. Aircraft that are not defective, are to be flown for practice flights only, with light inboard tanks only; remaining tanks are to be empty'. As a result of this signal, eight Waddington Lancasters were found to be defective and in need of rectification, and were accordingly grounded.

A few days prior to the grounding of the Lancasters, their Majesties King George VI and Queen Elizabeth, visited the Avro works at Yeadon, where the King named Lancaster R5498 'George', while the Queen named R5548 'Elizabeth'. These two bombers were subsequently delivered to Nos 44 and 97 respectively, neither surviving the year. Lancaster 'George' was later moved from No 44 Squadron to No 207 Squadron, which had got rid of its Manchesters to become the third Lancaster squadron in the Command. The aircraft was destroyed when it crashed on the approach to Bottesford on 8 April 1942.

During the early months of 1942, new aids and equipment were being introduced into service along with Gee. This latter aid had soon proved to be of limited use over the continent, as the Germans quickly countered it by jamming. However, it remained invaluable for navigation in the early stages of a sortie and in recovery to base. One of the aids introduced at about this time was more concerned with saving aircrew lives than in attacking the enemy. The 'Darky' Scheme entailed the installation of an additional radio in RAF aircraft. The device itself was a small transmitter/receiver of limited range, operating on a fixed frequency of 6440Kcs. Similar sets were located in the control rooms of the many aerodromes that possessed a Flying Control Section (Air Traffic Control). These ground-based 'Darky' sets were invariably monitored by WAAF R/T Operators.

The principle behind the 'Darky' system was that any aircraft so equipped, could make a 'Darky' call, which should be heard by at least one 'Darky' station, which would then give navigation assistance. This assistence could be in the form of illuminating balloon barrages by searchlights, thereby revealing the hazard. Another, more commonly used form of assistance, was the use of searchlights to steer lost aircraft to an airfield; a system which was later developed into the 'Sandra Lights' aid. In addition, lighthouses could be contacted and requested to switch on their coded flashers. These 'flashers' were marked on aeronautical charts and aircraft near enough to see them could thereby establish their position.

Flying Control at Waddington was equipped with a 'Darky' set and, on 25 April 1942, ACW 'Pip' Beck was on watch when she picked up a 'Darky' call. Having identified herself as Waddington, she asked what assistance was required. Eventually, the reply came back "May we land; may we land. One engine u/s." As Pip passed permission to land, Flying Control switched on the aerodrome lighting and the Chance Light. It appeared to those in the control room, that from the sounds outside, the pilot overshot his first approach and was attempting to go round again. Tragically, the young, inexperienced pilot made the fatal mistake of turning into the dead engine. A few indecipherable words came over the radio, followed almost immediately by an explosion and a sheet of flame, just off the end of the runway. Vickers Wellington (R1661) of No 11 OTU at Steeple Morden, crashed killing all on board.

With the grounding of the Lancasters, the operational committment at Waddington was left to No 420 Squadron. The Hampden crews of the Canadian squadron continued their nightly offensive against enemy targets, suffering steady losses in the process. On the night of 28 March, eight of the squadron's aircraft took off for an attack on Lubeck. All but one returned safely; the missing aircraft being that of S/Ldr Tench and crew, who were flying in PT-V (AE246). They managed to transmit an SOS at 0245hr, in which they reported engine failure. In fact, they had been intercepted by Luftwaffe night fighters and were eventually forced to ditch off Heligoland. All four members of the crew were picked up from their dinghy by a German naval vessel and became PoWs. Meanwhile, the squadron had despatched a Hampden to search for them which, on the return flight, was attacked by Spitfires (!) and had to make a forced landing at Driffield.

An indication of the domestic and administrative problems posed by a burgeoning Bomber Command can be gathered by reference to the recollections of the late Ken East. He arrived at Waddington in March 1942 as a newly qualified Flight Mechanic and was posted to 'A' Flight of No 44 Squadron. As he recalled:

"I arrived at the Main Guardroom and was told to report to the building across the road (now called Anson Block). I entered the empty building and eventually found an empty bedspace in a large unpartioned room. I later learned that this building housed some 40 airmen, most of whom had arrived within the last 48 hours. The next morning, I reported to the No 44 Squadron offices, was duly booked in and sent over to the 'A' Flight dispersal. After three days I was told that I was being relocated; I was to pack my kit and join ten or more other individuals for transport to Ashfield House in the village of Branston. Ashfield House turned out to be an almost derelict farmhouse, with what accommodation there was already taken. So, we new arrivals were billeted in a wooden hut some distance from the house itself. The twelve of us not only filled the hut, we overflowed it somewhat.

Neither the house nor the hut possessed anything but the most basic facilities. There was one cold water tap over a large sink, and two soil toilets! The only lighting we had was provided by candles. In all, there were approximately 40 of us billeted at Ashfield House, most of whom were Rhodesians. They coped with this rather strange situation very well and soon had fires burning in the large fireplaces every night, there being plenty of wood around the house. They also used to catch fish in a nearby pond, though we never did find out who it belonged to.

We were transported to camp for breakfast and the working day, at the end of which, the same transport took us back to the house. Once there it was a case of 'out of sight, out of mind', and we used to explore the local countryside and the Branston pubs. However, we were not the only ones billeted off camp. Another large house, called 'Longhills', served as a billet for WAAF personnel. I believe that the WAAFs who lived at Longhills were operators at the Mere Lane radio station. In addition to these remote billets, a number of Station personnel were accommodated in the village of Navenby, along with some airmen from the RAF Stations at Digby and Coleby Grange.

The 'A' Flight dispersal was located to the east of the Lincoln to Sleaford road (A15). I recall that between our dispersal and a nearby one belonging to No 420 Squadron; later passing to No IX Squadron, was a large pyramid of camouflage netting. this pyramid was 30 to 40 feet high and covered a cache of gas bombs. We were told that they were there for use should there be an invasion. The Lancaster to which I was assigned was parked within 100 yards of this frightening pyramid, but I never saw anyone ever enter or leave it. The pyramid was still there when the squadron moved away to Dunholme Lodge at the end of May 1943."

The attack on Lubeck, carried out during the night of Palm Sunday 1942, was the first really successful attack by Bomber Command on a German target. For those crews whose aircraft was equipped with the new navigation aid Gee, it greatly assisted them in the initial stages of the route, though the target itself was beyond Gee range. The force of 234 aircraft carried out an area bombing, fire-raising attack, which destroyed 190 acres of the old town. This was to be the only large scale attack on Lubeck throughout the war. Following representations by the Swiss President of the International Red Cross, it was agreed to leave the port of Lubeck alone, as it was used by vessels carrying Red Cross supplies.

It was during this attack on Lubeck that No 420 Squadron lost S/Ldr Tench and crew, their place being taken by S/Ldr Forsythe and crew, who were subsequently posted to make way for a Canadian Flight Commander, the newly promoted S/Ldr 'Tiny' Ferris. As if the loss of another 'B' Flight Commander was not bad enough, the squadron had to say farewell to the popular Joe Collier, who left to assume command of No 97 Squadron. This was the second squadron in the Command to be equipped with the Lancaster and was based at Coningsby. Joe Collier was succeeded in command of No 420 Squadron on 30 March by a

Canadian, W/Cdr D A R 'Doug' Bradshaw, who wasted no time in making his mark on the squadron.

In Daylight to Augsburg

Despite the temporary withdrawl of the Lancasters from operations, the Waddington crews continued to fly training sorties during the first week of April. During this time, rumours of something special coming up were reinforced when eight crews were selected for an as yet unspecified task. Unbeknown to those at Waddington, a similar process was being enacted on No 97 Squadron at Coningsby. At Waddington, the acting Squadron Commander, S/Ldr Nettleton, began his initial briefing to the selected crews by telling them that unlike a normal briefing, there would be no questions asked at the end! They were to pay close attention and keep what they heard strictly to themselves. As they could see for themselves, they were among the most experienced crews on the squadron and were forwith withdrawn from operations. They were to undertake special training, in the course of which they would develop techniques for flying in daylight (sic) in close formation, at low level and high speed. The assembled crews felt that it sounded both exciting and fun, but Nettleton added a warning: 'Low flying at speed is dangerous'. He closed his briefing by reminding the crews to say absolutely nothing about the flying they would be doing; concluding by saying: 'Think what you will, but keep your mouths shut!'

With the briefing over, the crews naturally began speculating as to what it all meant. Some thought it presaged the formation of a special force, something akin to the later Pathfinder Force. Others felt that they were to be targetted against German defences in France, prior to an invasion. But in the main, the feeling was that it did not much matter what the long term future held for them; in the short term it meant a reprieve from operations and more opportunity to savour the delights on offer in Lincoln and the surrounding area.

The chosen crews began their training with loose formation flying over the sea which, as their skill improved, got progressively tighter and lower. This first phase of the training culminated in the crews flying with the wing tips of their Lancasters overlapping at almost sea level. Next came the mixture as before, but this time over land. The flights were long and far ranging, mostly over the sparsely populated regions of Scotland. Freed from the anonymity of night attacks, the crews exhilarated by flying down valleys and up and over ridges, scattering sheep and cattle in the process. Occasionally, they would surprise the passengers in railway carriages by flying alongside them or, whenever the track surmounted an embankment, below them!

Though screened from operations and the attendant hazards, these training sorties were not without hazards of their own. One Lancaster, that flown by F/O MacLagan and crew, lost three engines in quick succession, ending up force landing in a field near RAF Upper Heyford. As Sgt T D Moore recalled:

"I locked my rear gun turret fore and aft and hung on for dear life to my gun controls. On the first impact I was thrown forcefully back on to the turret doors; on the second I was hurled back into the fuselage, badly gashing my head in the process. When I eventually got around to taking an interest in my situation, I found our wireless operator struggling to open the rear fuselage door. Being stronger and possibly more motivated, I virtually tore it off its catches and we both 'made for the hills'! On reaching a safe distance, we stopped and looked back at our badly damaged aircraft. It then dawned on me that there was no sign of the rest of the crew, so I very gingerly made my way back to the wreck, very much aware that we could not have used much fuel and that consequently, there was still a lot of it on board, just waiting to explode. Fearing the worst, I looked inside the fuselage, expecting to find the rest of the crew dead, injured and/or trapped. Finding no sign of my fellow crew members, I walked round my turret to the other side of the fuselage. It was then that I saw the rest of the crew; in the distance and still running! I was still in hospital when the Augsburg raid took place."

A few days before the scheduled date for the attack, and while the No 44 Squadron crews were carrying out a delayed last training sortie, S/Ldr 'Flap' Sherwood and F/Lt David Penman (ex No 44 Squadron), both of No 97 Squadron, were called to Headquarters No 5 Group to be briefed on the forthcoming attack. When the details were revealed to them, their reaction was 'This is suicide'! Despite their misgivings, the two pilots were impressed by the thoroughness of their briefing and of the excellent, detailed model of the target. Great stress was laid on the need to fly at low level in order to avoid radar detection. The two pilots were also given basic details of the large number of diversionary raids that were to be mounted, in order to draw enemy fighters away from their planned route. With regard to the defences in the target rea, they were told to expect little or no flak of any sort.

The last training sorties for both squadrons took place on 15 April, two days before the raid was scheduled to take place. On 17 April, take-off was planned for 1515hr. Following an early lunch, the crews changed into their flying kit and headed for the briefing room. As one of the pilots recalled:

"When the briefing officer revealed the map with the route depicted by a length of red wool, there were audible gasps as the crews saw just how far they were expected to go." Similarly, as Sgt Charlie Churchill, Nettleton's wireless operator recalled: "We knew that this was going to be different, but just how different was soon apparent...the course shown on the wall map went across one section of the wall and well into that of the adjoining section. I thought that I was dreaming; I just

could not believe what I was seeing. I thought - it takes us right down to Bavaria..."

Apart from the usual group of briefing specialists and the Station Commander, there was a number of very high ranking officers which, what with everything else, made the briefing a very solemn affair. The briefing for **Operation Margin** was opened by one of the visiting high ranking officers. He stressed the threat to the British war effort posed by the success of the German U-boat wolfpacks in the Atlantic. Indeed, he went so far as to state that the situation was critical and that because of this, Bomber Command had undertaken to assist the gallant efforts of the Royal Navy convoy escorts by attacking, and hopefully destroying, the main source of U-boat diesel engines, the MAN factory at Augsburg. The crews were told that this single factory supplied more than half the German U-boat fleet with diesel engines. He went on to add that the Lancaster was the only aircraft in the Command that could attack a target some one thousand miles inside enemy territory in daylight and stand any chance of getting back (sic).

Following this exhortation, there followed the specialist briefings. The Station Navigation Officer gave details of the rendezvous with the six Lancasters of No 97 Squadron, and the route to the target, which was as follows: Waddington - Grantham (RV with No 97 Sqn) - Selsey Bill - Dives sur Mer - Sens - Ludwigshaven - Ammer See - Target. Next to speak was the Intelligence Officer who gave a resume' of the Luftwaffe fighter strength in northern France, followed by details of the planned diversionary raids laid on by No 2 Group and Fighter Command. The plan was for Bostons of No 2 Group, together with a strong escort of Spitfires, to bomb various targets in northern France. These attacks were scheduled to commence at the time the Lancasters would be crossing the French coast, thereby drawing the Luftwaffe fighters away from the planned route. It was intended that these diversionary attacks would keep the enemy fighters busy while the Margin force crossed occupied territory in daylight.

Once the briefing had been completed, the crews were carried out to the waiting bombers, just in time for a last cigarette and a chat with their groundcrew, before boarding their aircraft and commencing the litany of checks. Both squadrons had two reserve aircraft; one in case of failure prior to take-off, while the other was to take off and shadow the formation as far as Selsey Bill where, if all went well, it would turn back to base. In the event, neither were needed by No 44 Squadron, but No 97 Squadron had to use their 'on the ground' reserve. In the air, the planned rendezvous did not take place, neither formation spotting the other, but it was of no real consequence as both elements had planned their route to and from the target. In the light of subsequent events, it was perhaps just as well that the No 97 Squadron element did not follow John Nettleton's force.

Passing over Selsey Bill at around 4.15pm, the crews bad a silent farewell to the reserve crew and set heading for the French coast. The No 44 Squadron element, callsign 'Maypole', was led by John Nettleton in KM-B (R5508). The other two crews in his three-aircraft 'vic' were F/O John 'Daisy' Garwell DFM in KM-A (R5510) and Sgt 'Dusty' Rhodes in KM-H (L7536). The other 'vic' was led by F/Lt 'Sandy' Sandford in KM-P (R5506) and included Warrant Officer Hubert Crum DFM in KM-T (L7548) and Warrant Officer Joe Beckett DFM in KM-Y (L7565).

Spot on time, the six Waddington Lancasters crossed the French coast at 4.45pm; the time at which the Bostons of No 2 Group were scheduled to commence their diversionary attacks. For reasons still unexplained, the considerable effort by the Bostons and their Spitfire escort had in fact commenced early, at 4.01pm and had ended at 4.15pm, some 30 minutes before the first of the Lancasters crossed the French coast! Slightly behind and further south, 'Flap' Sherwood thought he saw the No 44 Squadron element as they climbed to clear the cliffs, well to the North and, in the opinion of his navigator, well off the planned track!

Soon after coasting in, the six Lancasters of No 44 Squadron, flying at very low level over the wooded countryside, were engaged by enemy flak. Black bursts stained the otherwise clear sky around the formation, two aircraft being hit. The damage to Lancaster 'V' Victor (Beckett) rendered the rear gun turret inoperable. The knowledge that they had been seen and would be reported, only served to heighten the awareness of the crews. To again quote Nettleton's wireless operator, Sgt Churchill:

"As we flew clear of the flak we felt that we had been lucky to have got away with so little damage to the formation. At one stage, we were flying alongside a train travelling along an embankment. We could see straight through the windows, but the passengers must have been lying on the floor as there was no sign of them. On other occasions we would see the upturned faces of farmworkers in the fields."

The actions of one elderly Frenchman in particular heartened those who saw him; as he swept off his hat and performed a courtly bow.

The inexplicable change in the timing of the diversionary attacks in northern France was now to have tragic consequences. Among the Luftwaffe fighter forces drawn away to counter the Boston attacks, was a mixed force of Bf109 and FW190 fighters of II Gruppe/Jagdgeschwader 2 'Richthofen'. This force, led by one of the Luftwaffe's leading aces, Major Walter Oesau, was in process of recovering to its base at Beaumont-le-Roger near Evreux, when they spotted an unidentified group of four-engined aircraft virtually flying along the aerodrome perimeter. Joe Beckett was the first to spot the threat and called a warning to the formation: *"One-O-Nines, eleven o'clock high!"* John Nettleton ordered his force to close up and took them down even lower. However, despite their combined firepower of 48 0.303" machine guns, they were no match for the cannon armament of the attacking fighters. Hubert Crum's aircraft was the first to be hit, with strikes on his cockpit canopy which sent perspex splinters flying in all directions. With blood running from numerous cuts to his head and face, Crum waved away the offer of help from his navigator, Alan Dedman, a Rhodesian.

The combined firepower from the Lancasters, such as it was, apparently came as something of a surprise to the enemy fighter pilots, but they soon realised that with their cannons, they could open fire at 700 yards, breaking off their attacks at 400, which was the maximum effective range of the Lancasters' machine guns. To add to the bombers' problems, almost all the Lancasters' gun turrets experienced gun stoppages. At his subsquent debriefing, John Nettleton's mid upper gunner, F/Sgt Frank Harrison, reported that by the time the engagement with the German fighters was over, only one of his twin Browning machine guns was functioning. Post war analysis has revealed that this was not an uncommon problem.

With his rear turret completely out of action, Warrant Officer Beckett's aircraft was the first to go down. In no time at all, his Lancaster was a mass of flames and fell back out of formation. Scattering burning fuel and fragments in its wake, the stricken bomber struck a clump of trees and exploded, hitting the ground just outside the village of Le Tilleul-Lambert near Ormes. Next to go was Hubert Crum's aircraft. Despite the efforts of his two gunners, both of whom were wounded in the engagement, the enemy fighters' fire soon set the port wing alight. With the bomber wallowing along at about 100 feet above the ground and rapidly falling behind the formation, Alan Dedman jettisoned the bombs 'safe'. Struggling to control his doomed aircraft, Hubert Crum called a warning to his crew before closing the throttles and flying the Lancaster into the ground. The big bomber sliced through the top of a hedge and settled gracefully on to its belly in a wheat field, near the hamlet of Folleville near Conches.

After having assisted Sgt Bert Dowty, his front gunner, to extricate himself from his damaged turret, in which he was trapped, Crum made sure that the rest of his crew were safe. He remained with his crew beside their aircraft until he was certain that the fire would destroy it completely. He then wished his crew the best of luck in their escape endeavours, before setting off back the way they had come, towards the funeral pyre of his best friend, Joe Beckett. The crew's bad luck continued, all ending up as PoWs, though Bert Dowty and Saunderson very nearly made it to Vichy France before being captured; but that is a story in itself.

The last of the rear 'vic' of three aircraft was that flown by F/Lt R R 'Sandy' Sandford. Without the supporting fire of the other two aircraft of his section, Sandford's bomber was soon riddled by cannon and machine gun fire. With all four engines ablaze, the great bomber ploughed into the ground and exploded. Sandford's 'lucky pyjamas', which he always wore on operations, had not worked their magic this time. His dog Nelson, which he had adopted when its original owner, a New Zealander, failed to return from an operation, waited in vain at Waddington for his return. In due course, Sandford's parents collected the dog and took it home with them to Twickenham.

With the rear section of three aircraft down, it was now the turn of the leading 'vic'. Realising that the volume of defensive fire from the bombers was now considerable reduced; gun stoppages having compounded the problem, the enemy fighter pilots began to press home their attacks much closer. One of the Bf109 pilots closed in on 'Dusty' Rhodes' Lancaster to almost point blank range before opening fire. All four of the bomber's engines were hit and set on fire. In all probability, Rhodes too was hit, as his aircraft suddenly reared up out of formation. For a moment, it appeared to the two remaining crews that it might collide with the pair of them.

With great sadness, the crews of Nettleton and Garwell's aircraft watched as Rhodes' bomber stalled, fell inverted and crashed to the ground, making it JG2's one thousandth victory of the war. It was John Garwell's turn next; but after one pass which left his starboard wingtip flapping like a wounded bird's, the fighters broke away as quickly as they had come. By this time, the fighters were out of ammunition and low on fuel. Ignoring orders to the contrary, the two remaining Lancaster crews pressed on despite being less than half way to their target. They were faced with flying for over two more hours before they would reach their target; this in the knowledge that as far as they could tell, 28 of their friends had died in a matter of minutes. It was not until much later that they were to learn that all seven of Crum's crew had survived, largely due to his skill and experience.

Although the two surviving aircraft of the No 44 Squadron element were to experience no further fighter attacks, the German defence controllers kept a careful check on their progress, eventually deciding that the likely target was Munich. However, to be on the safe side, they also sounded the warning sirens in Augsburg. As Nettleton and Garwell neared the town of Augsburg, Nettleton realised that a group of factory chimneys would obstruct their planned bombing run, forcing them to climb to clear them. Instead, he elected to use a different line of approach and indicated the change of plan to John Garwell. As the two Lancasters ran in, they were engaged by the medium and light flak defences of the town and its factories. Despite this, both crews dropped their bombs on the

MAN factory, but during the run-in to the target, Garwell's aircraft was hit and set alight. The wireless operator, Bob Flux DFM, standing behind his pilot in the capacity of 'fighter spotter', called out that they were on fire as they came up to the bomb release point. Glancing over his shoulder, Garwell could see that the inside of the fuselage was like a furnace; the flares that they had been refused permission to leave behind, had been ignited by the enemy fire. Ordering Flux to close the fire doors that shut the cabin off from the rest of the fuselage, Garwell concentrated on obeying his bomb aimer's instructions. Only after the call 'Bombs Gone' did he turn his attention to survival.

The terrain to the west of Augsburg was wooded, undulating and abounded in villages and tree-lined lanes; not a good area to force land a big aircraft! By this time, dense choking smoke had penetrated the cabin, making the pilot's task all but impossible, as he could not see ahead. Realising this, Bob Flux reached up and jettisoned the cabin roof escape hatch; the resulting draft immediately sucking the smoke from the cabin. This action was to cost Bob Flux his life; for as soon as the blazing Lancaster hit the ground, he was thrown up and through the open escape hatch. As it careered across a rough field, the big machine broke in half just aft of the wings, where the fire had been most severe. The moment their aircraft came to a stop, Garwell, Dando, Kirke and Watson scrambled out of the wreck, eventually finding the body of Bob Flux lying under one of the wings. Of the two gunners, F/Sgts Edwards and McAlpine, there was no sign.

John Nettleton and his crew in the sole surviving Lancaster of the No 44 Squadron element, set off on their long journey back to base as the light from the setting sun began to fade. It was still too light to climb and fly the planned route home, so Nettleton elected to return the way they had come. After dark, they climbed and continued homewards, somewhat concerned that the aircraft's master gyro-compass was behaving erratically. It was possibly this that had caused them to wander off track and fly so close to the the aerodrome at Evreux on their outbound leg. Not trusting his gyro, Nettleton decided to fly using the P4 magnetic compass. Above cloud, in the dark and with no navigation aids to assist them, they had to rely on the dead reckoning skills of their experienced navigator, the Australian P/O Des Sands.

Eventually, the bomb aimer, F/Lt Doug McClure, a Rhodesian, spotted a coastline through a break in the clouds and reported it, adding that it did not look much like the French coast to him. On hearing this, Nettleton ordered Charlie Churchill to break radio silence and call for a 'fix' (a 'Darkie' call?). Using the top priority SOS SOS... followed by their special call-sign, prefixed by the letter 'V', Churchill called for a fix and a homing. To his immense relief, through all the mush and static in his earphones, Churchill heard "*...the most beautiful resonant morse*" he had ever heard. They were directed to turn on to a northeasterly heading and to land at Squires Gate, just south of Blackpool. The coast that McClure had seen had been that of Lancashire. Des Sands' navigation must have been quite accurate as they must have passed close to Waddington, but he was possibly caught out by a wind that was different to that forecast.

John Nettleton and his crew landed with their fuel tanks almost empty, after flying for nine hours and forty-five minutes. The following morning Nettleton asked his crew if they wished to fly back to Waddington or to travel by train. To a man, they chose to go by train! That same morning, the WAAF Radio Operator, 'Pip' Beck, thought that the Station seemed unduly quiet and subdued as she walked to work in the Watch Office. On being told the reason, she later said:

"It was such a shock that five of the six aircraft that had set out yesterday, had not returned. That those five pilots and crews would never again appear on the Battle Order. So many empty places in the Officers' and Sergeants' Messes. We learned then what the target had been and the reason for the attack, but we grieved and wondered if it had been worth it."

The crews of the No 97 Squadron element reached Augsburg without being attacked, but as they ran in on the planned bombing run, they too were subjected to heavy fire. The tall chimneys that Nettleton had elected to avoid, caused them to climb and may have been the root cause of their losses in the target area.

There was a rather sad postscript to the Augsburg raid. P/O 'Buster' Peall, another Rhodesian, was flying as co-pilot with Sandford. Just before leaving his room in the Mess for the briefing, he started a letter to his mother, written on Officers' Mess headed notepaper. It was marked: 'To be posted if I die'. The letter, in its unfinished state was subsequently published, and is a most moving document. It began:

'My Darling Mother, I knew from the start that this was bound to happen in the end and I have always thought that my only regret would be not saying thank you and goodbye. It seems strange writing so, but I feel I must...'

At the time of his death, Peall was 21 years old and had already survived a ditching in the English Channel. He was to be but one of the many young men from the Commonwealth and Empire who were to die in the service of the mother country.

For his leadership, John Nettleton was awarded the Victoria Cross; with DFCs going to Pat Dorehill, Des Sands and Doug McClure. DFMs were awarded to Churchull, Harrison, Huntley and Mutter. Later, when it was confirmed that they were prisoners of war, John Garwell was awarded the DFC, with DFMs going to Dando, Kirke and Watson, though the unfortunate Bob Flux received no recognition. In effect, all those who survived the actual attack on the MAN factory were decorated, but those who did not survive or failed to reach the target, got nothing. Meanwhile, Hubert Crum and his crew were at large in the French countryside, endeavouring to make contact with the Resistence and to return home.

Back to Routine Operations and The Thousand Plan

While No 44 Squadron recovered from their heavy losses, the crews of No 420 Squadron continued to operate their war-weary Hampdens. Between 19 April and 3 May, the Waddington Hampden crews carried out eight attacks, which included three against Rostock and others against Bordeaux, Paris, Le Havre and Hamburg. In all, during this period, a total of 56 sorties were mounted without loss! On the night of the last attack in this period, No 44 Squadron returned to operations by despatching six Lancasters to Bordeaux. Among the crews taking part were the squadron stalwarts, Warrant Officers Wright and Stott. The Augsburg losses apart, one of the reasons for the lack of Waddington Lancasters taking part in Main Force operations, was that six crews had been detached (again) to Lossiemouth, in readiness for an attack on the battleship Tirpitz.

Following several postponements due to bad weather, the first attack took place on the night of Sunday 26 April. The Tirpitz was clearly identified and attacked, but subsequent photographic reconnaissance failed to reveal any damage to Tirpitz, the sister ship of the late unlamented Bismarck. Two nights later the attack was repeated, but once again the results were at best inconclusive. During the course of the two attacks, which had been carried out by 49 Halifaxes and 21 Lancasters, Bomber Command suffered the loss of eleven aircraft, one of which was a Halifax captained by the Commanding Officer of No 10 Squadron, W/Cdr Donald Bennett, who was later to become better known as Air Vice Marshal Bennett of Pathfinder Force fame.

Both Frankie Stott and 'Lucky' Wright reported as having placed their bombs either close to the Tirpitz or, possibly, other warships in the anchorage, though neither could claim any confirmed hits. Basically, the problem was that the Tirpitz defences, which included flak ships, shore-based guns, other warships and a smoke screen, had combined to create an effective barrier to a successful attack.

The month of May had begun, as had so many others for the Command, with a mixture of bombing attacks and minelaying. Sadly, on the night of 8/9 May, the crews of the two Waddington squadrons were again to experience heavy losses. A mixed force of 193 bombers carried out an attack on Warnemunde. The Station despatched fourteen aircraft, seven from each squadron. In all, nineteen aircraft were lost that night, which represented almost 10% of the attacking force. Among those lost was S/Ldr Campbell DFC and crew of No 420 Squadron, flying in PT-A (AT144). The sole survivor was S/Ldr Campbell, who became a PoW. Four of the seven aircraft of No 44 Squadron failed to return that night, which was a particularly heavy blow, coming so soon after Augsburg. What made matters worse was that among the four crews lost was that captained by W/Cdr Lynch-Blosse, who had only that day assumed command of the squadron. Also lost that night were the crews of Warrant Officers 'Pissy' Jones and Lamb, plus that of F/O McLagan; the latter's crew being the first all-Rhodesian crew to fly with No 44 (Rhodesia) Squadron. As a particularly sad footnote; John Nettleton's Augsburg bomb aimer, F/Lt Doug McClure DFC, was flying with the new squadron commander and perished with him. Subsequently, the squadron learned that McLagan's rear gunner, Sgt T D Moore alone had survived. Their aircraft had been hit over the target soon after releasing its bombs and crashed in one of the streets of nearby Rostock. Apparently, Moore came too the next morning, lying in the middle of a road, with a broken ankle and no recollection as to how he got there.

With the loss of nine experienced crews in three weeks, the operational capability of No 44 Squadron was severely reduced. Until the losses could be made good, there was no way that any crew could be rested. In other words, the same crews would have to fly on every attack. With this in mind, the Station Commander, Gp Capt Boothman, suggested to Bomber Command that the squadron be removed from its Order of Battle until replacement crews could be brought up to operational status. Command Headquarters had other ideas however, and directed that the squadron should be formed into two Flights; one operational and the other a training flight. Harsh though this may have seemed, Command did undertake to ensure that the operational flight would not be called upon to operate beyond its capacity (sic).

During the day of the attack on Warnemunde, S/Ldr Nettleton flew in from the Bomber Development Unit at Boscombe Down in Lancaster R5556, which had been fitted with an experimental mid-under gun turret. in the event, this project was not persevered with, which was to have unfortunate repercussions later in the air war. The following day, Marshal of the Royal Air Force, Viscount Trenchard again visited the Station and was introduced to the survivors of the Augsburg raid (less McClure). At around this time, another noteworthy visitor to the Station was the American film actor Gene Raymond, who came with other Hollywood luminaries. Raymond arrived in US Army uniform, together with several other American Army officers, one of whom was a Captain Schanniger. Most of the visitors, including Gene Raymond, were flown in a Lancaster of the Training Flight. According to 'those in the know', almost all the Army officers were destined to become 'Flak Position Officers'; though whatever that was, meant nothing to the RAF crews.

Yet another visitor was Bishop Neville Talbot MC DD, Bishop of Nottingham. The stated purpose of his visit was 'for an exchange of views'! But just what really was said or took place in the briefing room during this exchange, was not recorded!

The next major attack took place on the night of 19/20 May when the target was Mannheim. No 44 Squadron put up five Lancasters, while No 420 Squadron sent six Hampdens. This attack was subsequently assessed as having been not very effective, with twelve aircraft missing out of the 197 taking part. None of those missing were from Waddington. Although No 44 Squadron put up five Lancasters that night, only four actually left the aerodrome! Warrant Officer 'Lucky' Wright and crew, flying in Lancaster KM-R (L7581) had almost reached flying speed when the leading edge of the wing peeled back, destroying any semblance of lift on that side of the aircraft. The in-use runway that evening was the short 07/25 which ended at the A15 road.

As he struggled to retain control of his aircraft, Wright could see ahead of him, an Army convoy approaching a point on the road just off the end of the runway. Despite having insufficient speed, Wright hauled the control column back and managed to climb to about 50 feet, just clearing the terrified members of the convoy. Inevitably, the Lancaster then stalled and the starboard wing dropped, turning the bomber towards an aircraft dispersal to the east of the A15 road. Out of control, the aircraft crashed into two parked Hampdens of No 420 Squadron, Nos P2094 and X3149. These two machines were not on the flying programme that night and were sited side by side as their dispersal. Tragically, AC2 Commins, a wireless mechanic, was working on P2094 when the Lancaster crashed into it and received fatal injuries.

Having ploughed through the two Hampdens, Wright's aircraft continued on through a Nissen hut, which was unoccupied at the time (!) and finished up sliding sideways into a tree. As soon as their aircraft came to rest, the crew scrambled out and scattered; the unfortunate flight engineer requiring some assistance, as he had made violent contact with the swivelling inspection light sited over the control panel. The resulting damage to a sensitive part of his anatomy left him rather incapacitated. The crew were granted ten days leave, returning just in time to take part in the second 1,000-bomber attack of the war; the target for which was Essen.

A few nights after the Wright incident, No 420 Squadron redressed the balance when Hampden PT-P (AE399), flown by F/Sgt McDermid RCAF, swung on landing and collided with Lancaster R5842, which had only recently joined No 44 Squadron Training (Conversion) Flight. Two members of each crew were injured in the collision, luckily neither of them fatal.

Following the loss of W/Cdr Lynch-Blosse, W/Cdr K P Smales DFC had arrived on 10 May, to take command of the squadron. Ken Smales was no stranger to the squadron or to Waddington, having commanded 'B' Flight of No 44 Squadron between October 1940 and June 1941. On assuming command of the squadron, Ken Smales had to combine his duties of Commanding Officer with the need to convert on to the Manchester and the Lancaster. It was a measure of the man and his experience that he achieved operational status in just under three weeks; just in time to lead the squadron's effort in the first 1,000-bomber raid. This was Operation Millenium, the highly successful attack on Cologne.

On 13 May the Station personnel were delighted to learn of the immediate award of the DFM to two Sergeant Pilots of No 420 Squadron. On 4 May, during an attack on Stuttgart, Sgt W J Maitland RCAF, flying Hampden PT-S (P1314), had just crossed the Belgian coast near Ostend en-route to the target when his aircraft was bracketted by flak. One large calibre shell exploded very close to the bomber, injuring Maitland, setting the port engine on fire and peppering the aircraft with over 40 holes. Hit in the chest by shrapnel and with a badly damaged aircraft, Sgt Maitland would have been fully justified in ordering his crew to bail out. Instead, he turned back over the North Sea and made a safe landing at Martlesham Heath near Ipswich.

The other recipient of the DFM was F/Sgt Hiley RCAF, who was flying Hampden PT-X (P1187), also in the attack on Stuttgart. Having carried out a successful attack, Hiley and his crew were on the return flight, passing Luxembourg, when their Hampden was hit by flak. Some time later, they were attacked by a German Bf110 night fighter. During the attack, the lower gunner, Sgt Halward was killed and Hiley injured. The starboard engine was set alight and the aircraft suffered considerable additional damage. Despite this, the crew succeeded in shaking off the fighter while the injured Hiley got the fire under control. Despite the difficulties, Hiley eventually managed to carry out a successful crash landing at Great Bentley in Essex.

Another 'old boy' to return to Waddington around this time was the now S/Ldr D J Penman DSO DFC. Dave Penman had completed a tour of operations on No 44 Squadron, flying Hampdens, before converting to the Lancaster. Following his conversion training, he was posted to No 97 Squadron and took part in the Augsburg raid with that squadron. For his part in that attack he was awarded the DSO. He had returned to Waddington to join No 420 Squadron, having been posted to the Canadian squadron to assist them in their conversion to the Manchester, though subsequent events were to prove otherwise.

Another of the Augsburg survivors was also on the move. F/Sgt Frank Harrison, who had flown as John Nettleton's rear gunner, had decided to apply to remuster from Air Gunner to Air Bomber (Bomb Aimer). In his own words:

"Since air gunners were paid as Aircraft Hands General Duties (ACHGD), while the new trade of Air Bomber was paid the same rate as a pilot, Len Mutter (Nettleton's mid upper) and I decided to try for it. Our new CO, Ken Smales, approved my application and I joined a course which was run by a Rhodesian, F/O Vic Allen. On successfully completing the course, Vic Allen suggested that I join the crew captained by S/Ldr Burnett, the 'A' Flight Commander on No 44 Squadron. Burnett was a big, extrovert man, who had years of prewar RAF flying experience, some of it as an instructor. Having selected his personal aircraft and trained his crew to his satisfaction, he declared us 'ready for war'. It was in no small way due to his professionalism, that we got through our tour of operations unscathed". The late Frank Harrison went on to complete a further tour as a member of the Pathfinder Force; survived the war and eventually retired as a Flight Lieutenant.

In May 1942 the Air Ministry advised Headquarters RCAF in Europe, that two of their squadrons, Nos 408 and 420, were earmarked for conversion to the Manchester. Knowing only too well the problems that the RAF had experienced, and indeed were still experiencing with this aircraft, the Canadians declined to accept the Manchester, preferring to soldier on with the Hampden until something better was available (who could blame them?). As a result of this, Dave Penman was posted away from Waddington after only a brief stay. His new appointment was as OC No 28 OTU at RAF Wymeswold near Loughborough in Leicestershire.

When Air Marshal Harris had taken command of Bomber Command, its whole future was in the balance. Statistical analysis had shown that with few exceptions, the Command was not achieving meaningful results, and there were many who advocated dismantling the force and allocating its aircraft to Coastal Command and overseas theatres. Harris however was an almost fanatical believer in Bomber Command and its strategic role, and was determined to preserve it. Capitalising on the successful attack on Lubeck on 28/29 March, together with the subsequent success against Rostock one month later, he approached the Prime Minister and the Chief of the Air Staff, Sir Charles Portal, with a plan to attack selected German cities with a force of 1,000 bombers. Harris' persuasive arguments succeeded in convincing both Churchill and Portal, and the plan was put into effect. At the time, Bomber Command possessed little over four hundred front-line bombers and crews, so in order to gather together the necessary size force, the planners had to utilise the aircraft and crews of the various Operational training Units (OTUs).

By using staff/student crews and some student/student crews (!) from these OTUs, together with four from Flying Training Command, the staff at Bomber Command Headquarters managed to scrape together 1,047 bombers. this was achieved despite the late withdrawl of the promised 250 bombers from Coastal Command. This late change came about at the insistence of the Admiralty, who for their own reasons, did not wish the venture well. The raid itself was to be compressed into a 90 minute time frame, an unheard of concentration of aircraft; the force being led by experienced crews whose aircraft were equipped with the Gee navigation aid.

Of the 1,000+ aircraft taking part in this massive attack on Cologne during the night of 30/31 May, 153 came from No 5 Group. Of these, there were 73 Lancasters, 46 Manchesters and 34 Hampdens. Waddington despatched 11 Lancasters and 15 Hampdens, plus two Manchesters from No 44 Squadron's Training Flight. The war-weary Hampdens took off some 90 minutes ahead of the Lancasters in order to make good their timing over the target. The No 44 Squadron element was led by its new Commanding Officer, W/Cdr Smales, ably supported by the now S/Ldr 'Kipper' Herring DSO DFC, and F/O Henry Maudesley, both of whom flew the Manchesters of the Training Flight. As is a matter of historical record, the damage to Cologne and its unfortunate inhabitants was on an unprecedented scale. The force lost a total of 41 aircraft, only two of which were as a result of a mid-air collision, an unknown factor which had caused the planners at Command Headquarters some concern. All the Waddington aircraft returned to base, though one Hampden swung on landing and collided with a parked Lancaster (ibid).

One of the crews flying from Waddington that night was that of F/Sgt 'Happy' Taylor. He had flown eleven operations in Hampdens with No 144 Squadron, but when this unit was transferred to Coastal Command, he was posted to No 44 Squadron, following conversion to the Manchester and Lancaster at No 25 OTU at Finningley. As he recalled:

"On 28 May, everyone was confined to camp as there was to be a 'maximum effort', including the aircraft of the Training Flight, of which my crew and I were part. The groundcrews worked round the clock to prepare every aircraft for operations. There was great excitement because we all knew that something big was in the offing. One could feel the air of expectation everywhere. Then finally, on 30 May, operations were on! The briefing commenced in a hushed atmosphere, with the Station Commander, Gp Capt Boothman the first to speak. He told us that the target was Cologne and then went on to tell us the reason for all the secrecy and effort. Bomber Command was to send over one thousand aircraft in 90 minutes! We could hardly believe our ears, and all became very excited. At last, Jerry was going to be really hurt...

As we climbed into the evening sky we could see aircraft all around us, and this gave us a great feeling, difficult to describe. We reached our assigned height of

18,000 feet, just as we neared the Dutch coast. Surprisingly, we did not get the usual reception from the flak batteries at Texel and the adjoining islands. Then, as we crossed the coast, I saw a small glow in the distance and my second pilot, Sgt Richards, confirmed it. To me it looked just like a cigarette tip glowing in the dark. I called up my navigator, Sgt Edwards and confidently told him that I would not require his services to get to the target. He was not impressed by this and subjected me to a vociferous explanation of the need for accurate navigation. When I could get a word in, I suggested that he came out from behind his curtain and see for himself what I could see. On doing so, he agreed that it must be the target, adding that it was still over 150 miles away! As we approached Cologne, we could see two or three searchlights motionless in the sky and a huge pall of smoke which reached well above our altitude. Flying over the target area, it seemed to us as if the whole city was on fire, so we descended slowly in order to find a suitable place on which to drop our 4000lb 'Cookie' and the incendiaries. We eventually dropped our load near the centre of the city, close to the clearly visible river, having levelled off at 8000 feet. It was a sight that none of us would ever forget..."

'Happy' Taylor flew a full tour of operations with No 44 Squadron, much of it in Lancaster R5508, John Nettleton's original KM-B, in which he led the attack on Augsburg. Taylor and Henry Maudesley had collected it from Squires Gate and ferried it back to Waddington the day after Nettleton and crew landed there. In the light of what had happened to the other five aircraft, Taylor and Maudesley were surprised to find that the bomber had suffered hardly any damage at all. However, both were unhappy to find that later on, their groundcrew had painted a huge bomb on the nose, with the words 'Augsburg VC' surrounding it. The aircrew considered that this could cause them unecessary problems if they were forced down in enemy territory and insisted that the offending motiff be removed.

Determined to make the most of the undoubted success of Operation Millenium, Sir Arthur Harris ordered his staff to mount another 1,000-bomber attack while the force was still intact, and in which they could take advantage of the full moon. The second attack was scheduled to take place on the night after the attack on Cologne, but the weather proved to be unsuitable. The forecast for the following night was anything but ideal; but well aware that he could not keep his bombers standing by indefinitely, Harris chose to attack Essen on the night of 1/2 June. For various reasons, the Command could despatch only 956 aircraft, though doubtless the enemy were not aware of the shortfall! Waddington put up eleven Lancasters, one Manchester and thirteen Hampdens. The lone Manchester was again flown by Henry Maudesley. Once again, all Waddington aircraft returned safely, though one Lancaster and one Hampden had been forced to return early. The attack plan for Essen was similar to that employed against Cologne, except that the leading crews were to use more flares to mark the target for the main force. Unfortunately for the attackers, the weather proved to be worse than forecast, with haze and low cloud obscuring the city, which resulted in the bombing being very scattered.

With two massive attacks completed, Bomber Command reverted to its more usual size of attack of between one and two hundred aircraft, bombing whichever target offered the best weather conditions. During the next four months, the Command raided Essen four times, Bremen once and Emden four times, plus numerous other towns and cities. All these attacks were in addition to nightly minelaying sorties and various minor operations. An example of the considerable minelaying task taken on by the Command, was the despatching of 52 aircraft to lay mines off the coast near Lorient during the night of 23/24 June. Ten of these minelayers came from No 420 Squadron, all but one of which returned safely. Hampden PT-L (AD786), flown by the recently decorated F/Sgt Hiley DFM, crashed 20 minutes after take-off at nearby Boothby Pagnall. Fred Hiley survived the crash severly injured, but all three members of his crew perished. This particular loss brought the total losses from the Station during the four weeks following the Essen raid, to five; four from No 420 Squadron and one from No 44 Squadron.

Meanwhile, air operations apart, there was always something happening on the ground. One of the less edifying aspects concerned the by then large Rhodesian component of air and ground crews on No 44 Squadron. In their home country, these men had been brought up to accept the strict colour-bar as normal; blacks and whites just did not mix. So, when two West African groundcrew were allocated a billet occupied by Rhodesian groundcrew, they were physically ejected. The Station Commander immediately confined to camp the occupants of the billet in question. After a meeting, all the Rhodesians threatened to go on strike (mutiny in the armed forces) unless something was done! Following consultation with the senior Rhodesian officer on the Station, the two West Africans were posted to another station. Unfortunately, the problems did not end there; the Rhodesians threatened to boycott the local pub, the Horse and Jockey, if the landlord continued to serve West Indians who were serving in the RAF. Here again they had their way. However, there were those among the Rhodesians who could see that things were different in Britain and that they could not continue with their hard line. Once coloured aircrew began to appear, the problem became suppressed, if not entirely eliminated. The end to this local apartheid problem appears to have coincided with the arrival of a Rhodesian pilot, F/O W D 'Doug' Rail. He joined No 44 Squadron with a West Indian rear gunner, Sgt Gus Batty, in his crew. Some of the Rhodesians expressed their concern about this, but Rail insisted that Batty was an asset. As he (Rail) jokingly said, any German night fighter pilot coming up from behind would think that the rear turret was unoccupied, and suffer the consequences. Rail's determination to retain his gunner, plus the cheerful disposition of Batty himself, eventually won the Rhodesians over, to the extent that the aircrew christened Batty 'Midnight' or '2359'. Sadly, Rail and his crew were to die over Pilsen on 13 May 1943, while flying in KM-K (W4110).

Another less edifying activity on the ground was the thriving black market in petrol. In order to prevent the use of aviation fuel in cars, it was treated with a dye. Despite this, certain entrepeneurial spirits among the Station Instrument Section staff, had discovered that by passing the petrol through Silica Gell crystals, they could remove the dye, thereby preventing the Service Police from proving that a driver was using illicit fuel. Eventually, the police got wise to this practice and instituted a specific gravity test to identify aviation fuel. This in turn led some drivers to have a second fuel tank with a concealed selector switch; one tank for the legal 'pool' petrol and one for the illegal high octane aviation spirit.

Throughout the war, the Station, like all other military units, operated a seven day week. As some form of light relief, various social events and entertainments would be arranged from time to time. As LAC Green of the Instrument Section recalled:

"Station concerts were held in the Airmen's Mess after the NAAFI was hit by a bomb, and I particularly remember a Captain Scott and his eagle Mr Ramshaw (!). Scott would show films as well as performing with Mr Ramshaw, who would stand to attention on command. One of the Station airmen used to perform a drag act and could sing with a beautiful falsetto voice. Eventually, someone decided that he was just to good (!) and he was dropped. Rumour had it that some of the WAAFs became jealous and stirred things up..."

Among the non-flying officers on the Station was P/O H R Locke. Henry Locke was posted to Waddington as Adjutant of No 44 Squadron, just after Ken Smales assumed command. Henry was to remain at Waddington for the remainder of the war, moving from the squadron to the Station and, later, when the Base system was introduced, he became Adjutant to the Base Commander, Air Commodore Hesketh, who commanded No 53 Base (Waddington). Before his death in 1992, Henry gave a graphic account of the duties of a Squadron Adjutant in wartime:

"There was only one officer, the Adjutant, on a squadron who was not engaged on flying duties. All the others, such as the Officer Commanding and his Flight Commanders, were either on operations, asleep either post or prior to an operation, or on stand-down. This did not leave them much time for administration duties; this had perforce to be left to the Adjutant. For quite some time, aircrew were not permitted to sleep on the Station; instead they were billeted out in nearby private houses. During my time as Squadron Adjutant, I would be the one advised by Headquarters No 5 Group of the target over the scrambler telephone. I would then work out the fuel requirements and alert the groundcrew out at the dispersals. At some stage, the armourers would let me know what the bomb loads were to be. The Squadron Orderly Room (admin office) was manned 24 hours a day, and among its many duties was the issue of in-flight rations to the operational aircrew.

Administratively, we dealt with postings and promotions, plus the Squadron Commander's Orderly Room (disciplinary hearings). I had also to arrange for the bodies of any dead aircrew to be sent to their families, if so required by the next of kin. Each body had to have a rail ticket (sic) and travel in a separate compartment. In addition, we had to despatch a letter to the receiving undertaker, particularly when it would be unwise to open the coffin (!). In the event that an aircraft failed to return, we had to send off a stream of signals; some with regard to the crew; others concerned the aircraft. There was also the sacred 'G' Form, which had to be scrambled to No 5 Group Operations by 6.0pm each day. This form gave details of the number of pilots who were operational; ie, not on leave or non-effective - sick. The 'G' Forms were consolidated by Group HQ and sent on to Bomber Command, from where they were laid on the Prime Minister's desk at midnight. I remember on one occasion, the Squadron Commander (Smales) forbade me to include on the 'G' Form, any aircrew who might be sent on operations for a third successive night. He (Smales) was hauled out of bed in the middle of the night to explain his sudden loss of pilots! After that, he left the 'G' Form to me.

On 11 June, a six aircraft Flight from No 44 Squadron was detached to Nutts Corner in Northern Ireland, for anti-submarine duties with Coastal Command. The object was to narrow the gap in the Atalntic where U-boats could safely surface. Although the detachment did not last very long, some of the crews engaged in attacks on surfaced U-boats. The first of these anti-submarine patrols commenced the day following their arrival at Nutts Corner. Among the crews involved in the detachment were S/Ldr Weston, F/Lt Barlow, F/O Ball, P/Os Nicholson and Hackney, and Warrant Officers Wright and Dainty.

The first two days were uneventful, but on 14 June, a distress message was received from P/O Nicholson and crew, flying in KM-G (R5858). The message reported that they had lost power on both port engines and were ditching approximately 200 miles west of the Irish coast. In addition to the Lancaster's crew, there were two members of the resident No 220 Squadron on board, acting as advisors. No 220 Squadron of Coastal

Command were flying the American B17 Flying Fortress Mk I. In his message, Nicholson added that he could neither keep his aircraft straight, nor climb, and was commited to flying in circles.

Nothing more was heard from or about the crew, and the standard 'Missing in Action' procedure was put into effect. Some weeks later, W/Cdr Smales received a signal from the Gold Coast (now Ghana), saying that Nicholson and crew were there and that they would be sent on to Gibraltar. The signal added that the squadron was to arrange to collect the crew from 'The Rock'. In due course, two Lancasters were despatched to Gibraltar, one of them puncturing a tyre on some debris on the runway on landing and ground looped. The undercarriage collapsed and the aircraft burst into flames and burned out just beside the runway, much to the consternation of the crew of the second Lancaster, who had to land beside the blazing pyre. On his eventual return to the squadron, Nicholson explained that he finally decided to close down his remaining two engines before ditching his aircraft. After spending a night in their dinghy, the crew were picked up by a Royal Navy destroyer, its crew somewhat uncertain of their position while hunting for their convoy! Wireless silence and the convoy's route to the Gold Coast accounted for the time lapse before contact was made with the squadron.

Meanwhile, on 15 June, F/O Ball and crew sighted a U-boat on the surface only five miles from a convoy. They immediately dived to the attack and dropped six depth charges from a height of 50 feet, only fifteen seconds after the submarine had submerged. Unfortunately, they were very low on fuel and could not afford to remain on station to observe any results. They eventually landed back at Nutts Corner after a sortie lasting ten hours and 20 minutes. The same morning, F/Lt Barlow and crew had attacked another U-boat, which they had spotted at a range of three miles. At full throttle, Barlow dived to the attack and dropped a pattern of six depth charges from a height of 70 feet, just as the submarine submerged. The bomb aimer reported that he could see the U-boat about ten feet below the surface of the sea and that he saw the pattern of depth charges straddle the vessel.

A large patch of oil appeared on the surface of the sea and was being photographed when the obviously damaged submarine briefly broke the surface, before submerging almost immediately. Turning in at about 850 feet, Barlow dropped a 250lb anti-submarine bomb on to the swirl about 20 seconds after the U-boat's disappearance. With no discernable wreckage, Barlow and crew were credited with only a possible. Two days later, Barlow and crew were back in action when on reaching the reported position of a convoy, they found nothing. Barlow instituted a creeping line ahead search, and it was while so engaged that his gunners reported a Ju88 aircraft above them. Barlow turned towards the enemy aircraft and climbed up to engage, though just how and what he planned to do is not recorded. Possibly it was just as well that the Ju88 disappeared into cloud without apparently having seen that it was being pursued by a four-engined bomber! Not long after these incidents, the No 44 Squadron detachment was recalled to Waddington.

The reason for the recall was not long in becoming apparent. On the night of 25/26 June, the Command mounted the third '1,000-bomber' raid. The target on this occasion was Bremen, and a total of 1,123 aircraft took part in the attack. Waddington despatched eleven Lancasters, one Manchester and thirteen Hampdens. The lone Manchester KM-N (L7430), was flown by a Training Flight crew captained by P/O Farrington. This was to be the last time that a Waddington based Manchester was to fly on operations; doubtless coming as a relief to those crews who may have been tasked to fly the most unpopular bomber in the Command. Dense cloud over Bremen hindered accurate target identification, though on this occasion the Gee equipment worked well and the leading crews started many fires in the target area. On the other hand, moonlight reflecting off the layer cloud made conditions ideal for the Luftwaffe night fighters, resulting in the loss of 55 aircraft that night, which represented a loss rate of 5%; the highest suffered in a night attack to date. Away from operations; at the end of May, S/Ldr G G Avis had assumed command of 1506 BAT Flight, vice S/Ldr C W Bromley. Two weeks later, the award of the Air Force Cross (AFC) to S/Ldr Corwen Bromley was promulgated in the London Gazette.

Under its new dynamic commander, the pace of Bomber Command operations never slackened. Waddington aircraft were involved in numerous raids and mining sorties. In July, the Station's two squadrons took part in attacks on Bremen, Wilhelmshaven, Essen, Duisburg, Hamburg, Saarbrucken and Dusseldorf. During the course of these attacks the Station suffered the loss of one Lancaster and four Hampdens.

In early July, one of the new arrivals was Sgt Colin Watt. His recollections give an interesting insight into the early days of a 'sprog' pilot:

"*...after an interview with the CO, W/Cdr Smales, I was allocated to the Conversion Flight, which was 'C' Flight, the two operational Flights being 'A' and 'B'. Henry Maudesley, who was acting Flight Commander while John Nettleton was in the USA, explained that I would fly initially as second pilot before converting via the Manchester to the Lancaster. ...after a couple of days filling time with passenger trips and studying the many drills and systems, I joined the Station BAT Flight for Beam Approach training in their Oxfords and the Link Trainer. I returned to 'C' Flight on 26 July. That night the Station despatched 30 aircraft to Hamburg; thirteen Lancasters and seventeen Hampdens... ...on 29 July I was ON operations, flying as second pilot to S/Ldr Burnett, destination Saarbrucken... ...during our return* *trip we heard F/O Peter Ball radio base with the message that he was going to have to ditch. In the event he made it back to base, his problem being one of faulty gauges. Sadly, he and his crew were lost on 4 August during an attack on Essen".*

On the night of 31 July, the Command despatched a mixed force of 630 aircraft to attack Dusseldorf. Included in the force once again were aircraft from various conversion units, though this was in no way intended to be another 1,000-bomber raid. Waddington despatched sixteen Lancasters from No 44 Squadron and nine Hampdens from No 420 Squadron. The operation was a success, but casualties among the attackers were very heavy. Among the 29 bombers which failed to return was Lancaster KM-L (L7537), flown by F/Sgt N Tetley and crew of No 44 Squadron. This raid was to be the last undertaken by No 420 Squadron from Waddington. On 6 August, the Canadian squadron moved to Skipton-on-Swale in Yorkshire, and was transferred to No 4 Group. The original plan had been for the squadron to re-equip with the Manchester, and with this in mind, it had received a few of them the preceeding April. These were used by the squadron Conversion Flight for training purposes, but they were never flown on operations.

Following the refusal of Headquarters RCAF in Europe to order their crews to operate the Manchester, it became necessary to transfer the squadron to another Group. On moving to Yorkshire, No 420 Squadron re-equipped with the Wellington Mk III. Five months later, No 420 (Snowy Owl) Squadron became part of No 6 (RCAF) Group of Bomber Command. Later in the war the squadron flew Wellington Mk Xs, Halifax IIIs and finally Lancaster Xs, which it received in April 1945. The squadron was disbanded in Canada in September 1945. The Station personnel were sorry to see the 'Snowy Owls' depart, and entered wholeheartedly into the Canadians farewell party; one element of which was a red indian war dance around a real fire - in the middle of the Officers' Mess ante room! The repercussions and inevitable cost of replacing the carpet remain shrouded in mystery.

On Sunday afternoon, 2 August, the Luftwaffe intruders returned to Lincoln, dropping four bombs. Coldbath House was destroyed and one wing of the nurses home of the County Hospital was damaged.

With only No 44 Squadron remaining at Waddington, all effort was concentrated on its Lancaster operations. During the first week of August, the squadron took part in two attacks on Essen and in the fifth attack against Duisburg in three weeks. In all, the squadron despatched seventeen Lancasters in these operations, losing only one aircraft, that of F/O P A Ball DFM and crew, who were shot down on the first of the two attacks against Essen; theirs being the only Lancaster lost that night.

On 7 August, No IX Squadron arrived at Waddington from Honington, to convert from the Wellington to the Lancaster. The new arrivals were commanded by W/Cdr J M Southwell, and their arrival was remembered by one of the squadron's airmen, H W Pride of Nottingham:

"We arrived by train at Waddington railway station, each of us carrying a rifle because the LNER would not allow them to be carried in a trunk in the guard's van! Outside the railway station we were assembled and marched up the long steep hill to our new home. On reaching the main gate we were confronted by a huge banner, hung outside Station Headquarters and bearing the inscription 'SLOPPY SALUTING SIGNIFIES SLACKNESS'. Our immediate reaction was to wonder just what had we come to. After initially flying the dreaded Manchester, our aircrews started their Lancaster flying with No 44 Squadron's Training Flight."

One of No 44 Squadron's most experienced operators, 'Happy' Taylor was having his share of excitement. On 9 August, he took off for an attack on Osnabruck, but while still over the English Channel, they experienced engine failure, so returned to base and landed. In the debriefing room, his Co, W/Cdr Smales, asked Taylor where he had jettisoned his bombs. 'Happy' replied that he had not jettisoned them, but brought them back with him. On hearing this, Ken Smales and all the other executives in the room nearly had fits. It was pointed out to Taylor in the strongest possible terms, that he had obviously landed his aircraft well over weight, and had he crashed with a 4000lb 'Cookie' on board, he would have done considerable damage to the Station.

Also in August, there occurred an attack that was in itself not particularly noteworthy, but as a portent of things to come, it was most significant. On 17 August, twelve B17 Flying Fortresses of the United States Eighth Air Force carried out their first attack from England, the target being Rouen.

As if it was needed, on the night of 16 August, the Station personnel were given a reminder that aviation is inherrently dangerous, without the added risk of combat. That night, Lancaster KM-X (R5489), which had been named 'George' by his majesty King George VI, crashed on the approach to the Station. following an air test. The incident was recalled by the wireless operator, Sgt Frank Walshaw:

"We were making our landing approach to Waddington when the port outer engine caught fire. Ron Easom, our pilot, overshot and I heard him tell Jack our flight engineer, to feather the propeller and to operate the engine fire extinguisher. I immediately switched over from RT to WT to contact control and warn them of our problem. This action isolated me from the rest of the crew's intercom, but as I looked out of my small window, I could see the engine merrily blazing with the propeller still rotating at speed, while that of the adjacent engine,

which showed no sign of fire, was feathered and stationary! By this time our aircraft had lost flying speed and was heading for the ground. My immediate thought was 'This is curtains' and braced myself for the impact. The rest is etched indelibly in my mind; there was a rending of metal and the fuselage filled with dust and smoke as it split in two just in front of the mid upper gun turret. The radio transmitter broke away from its mounting and struck me in the chest. I scrambled out through the broken fuselage, followed closely by Ron Easom and our navigator. The wings were belching smoke and flames and bullets were exploding in all directions. Ron had been saved from serious injury by his seat harness, while our navigator, who had no seat harness at all, had survived solely by hanging on for dear life.

Our mid upper gun turret had been occupied by an LAC ground wireless operator who had come along for the ride. His flying helmet had been torn off and he had been cut badly about the face and ears when his head struck the rotating service joint. We extricated him via the break in the fuselage, by which time the whole front end was an inferno. Once clear of the wreck, it seemed as if the whole population of the village of Branston had materialised from nowhere and had come to help. Our aircraft had ended up on top of a pigsty and the squealing from the unfortunate pigs trapped underneath, added to the general confusion.Our rear gunner, Len Berrigan, had been trapped in his turret as the hydraulic lines had been fractured and his turret was locked fore and aft. The flames prevented us from entering the fuselage, so with the assistance of some villagers, we hauled on the gun barrels and manhandled the turret into the abeam position. After what seemed an age, we were able to open the turret doors and drag Len out to safety. He really was in a mess; his nose was broken and he had lost some front teeth when his head whipped forward into the gunsight. In addition, both his cheekbones were covered by large swellings.

Meanwhile, the crash wagon and the blood wagon (ambulance) had arrived and the medics were attending to our flight engineer. He had been catapulted into the instrument panel and then on down into what was left of the nose section, where our New Zealand bomb aimer, Dave Pullinger, had died on impact. Jack Fletcher was in a pitiful state and the sight of him made me retch. I too was not feeling too great; my chest felt as if it had been hit by a steam roller. Then a dear old lady from one of the nearby cottages appeared and offered us cups of tea. Len, together with the young airman and myself were taken to the Station Medical Centre, while Jack was rushed to Bracebridge Heath hospital where, mercifully, he died that night"

Ron Easom was soon back on operations, only to be lost over Hamburg on 9 November. Frank Walshaw also returned to operations, with another crew, with the minimum of delay; though not without understandable misgivings; that particular crash being his third! His first crash was in bad weather in a Hampden of No 14 OTU at Cottesmore on 23 December 1941. His second occurred at Waddington in June 1942, followed soon after by the crash of 'George'.

On 18 August, the London Gazette announced the award of the DFM to Sgt Albert John Newton of No 44 (Rhodesia) Squadron. The citation went on to state: 'This airman was the rear gunner of an aircraft (Lancaster) which carried out an attack on Essen in daylight (?). While flying near the Dutch coast, his aircraft was intercepted by two enemy fighters. The enemy made successive attacks from astern. During the third attack, Sgt Newton, who had vigorously defended his aircraft throughout, was wounded in the feet. Despite this, he continued to engage the enemy and, following an accurate burst from his guns, one of the fighters went into a steep dive and was not seen again. The remaining fighter closed in for another attack, but Sgt Newton, although in considerable pain, met it with resolute fire. The attacker broke away and terminated the engagement. By his courage and devotion to duty, this airman contributed materially to the safe return of his aircraft'.

By this stage of the war, some of the old hands, and indeed some of the not so old hands of No 44 Squadron, were begining to show signs of strain. As Charlie Churchill, Nettleton's wireless operator on the Augsburg operation recalled:

"By now I was begining to feel nervous, because it looked as if I might actually survive my tour. I felt as if I had been on ops for years, yet now, suddenly, I could imagine myself free from that feeling of perpetual doubt. At the start, I had been full of enthusiasm and held on to the thought that it was always the other chap who bought it. As the number of my trips mounted and friends failed to return, I was rapidly becoming one of the longest surviving members of the squadron. My awareness of this fact caused me to feel that I was living on borrowed time. By this time I was sporting an Irving Caterpillar Club badge and had survived the Augsburg raid, for which I had been awarded the DFM. Surely I would survive the few remaining trips of my tour?"

It was not to be! Churchill and the crew of P/O W H Day were posted as missing following an attack on Munich on 19/20 September. Their Lancaster, KM-Q (R5554), was shot down by a night fighter, only three members of the crew surviving to become PoWs. But Charlie Churchill's luck had not deserted him entirely; he was one of the three survivors. The trip to Munich was the final trip of his tour, following which he was to have been screened!

While No IX Squadron was going through its conversion to the Lancaster, the crews of No 44 Squadron operated on fifteen out of 31 nights. Included in their operations tally for that period were four nights minelaying, plus attacks on Duisburg, Osnabruck, Mainz, Kassel, Frankfurt, Nuremburg, Saarbrucken, Karlsruhe and Bremen. Of these attacks, those against Osnabruck and Karlsruhe were particularly accurate. That against Frankfurt on 24/25 August was the second attack to be led by the new Pathfinder Force, though it was not particularly accurate. The attack on Kassel by 306 aircraft on 27/28 August, was a disaster in that the attackers suffered a 10% loss rate!

With good weather and an increasing number of heavy bombers becoming available, Bomber Command stepped up its offensive against German targets. Aircraft from Waddington took part in thirteen operations during the month of September. In all, the Station launched 192 sorties; 57 of which were flown by No IX Squadron. The cost to the Station was the loss of eleven aircraft; seven from No 44 Squadron and four from No IX Squadron. On 10 September, four No IX Squadron Lancasters, led by their Commanding Officer, W/Cdr Southwell, took part in a 479 aircraft attack on Dusseldorf. This was a particularly accurate attack, with the Pathfinder Force (PFF) using modified 'Pink Pansy' target markers for the first time.

The attack on Essen on the night of 16/17 September, marked the end of their tour for 'Lucky' Wright and his crew. In all, they had completed 38 trips and could now look forward to being rested. However, on his return from'end of tour' leave, their Canadian rear gunner, Bud Gill, was informed that as the RCAF had not seen fit to arrange a posting for him, he was to resume operations. Understandably, he was singularly unimpressed with this, and after two very close calls, made his feelings known in no uncertain manner. Almost immediately, Bud was returned to Canada for staff duties at a Command headquarters. He had experienced a particularly close call during an attack on Essen. On the run-in to the target at 12,000 feet, a flak burst under the port wing flipped their Lancaster on to its back, at which point all four engines cut out. Somehow, Wright managed to get the bomber back on an even keel and by 6000 feet had managed to re-start two engines. By this time they were in the middle of a balloon barrage, but got away with it. Eventually, Wright got the other two engines started and they made a successful return to Waddington. Following this escapade, 'Lucky' Wright made an entry in the Sergeants' Mess 'Line Book' - 'There I was, upside down, nothing on the clock, four engines feathered and still climbing'.

Among the new arrivals at Waddington at this time were two aircrewmen who had not actually undergone any heavy bomber or Lancaster conversion courses. One of them was the late Sgt Walter Farraday, who flew five trips with the Wright crew. An ex-Corporal engine fitter, Farraday had volunteered to remuster as a Flight Engineer. He was still under training at Swinderby when a volunteer was called for to go to Waddington 'for a few days'. Walter Farraday volunteered and as a result flew as a totally untrained flight engineer in attacks on Bremen, Duisburg, Dusseldorf, Frankfurt and Karlsruhe. He ended the war as one of the few commissioned flight engineers, having eventually completed his training. His first 'qualified' tour was with No 61 Squadron, before he returned to No 44 Squadron in December 1943 for his second tour. During the time that Farraday flew with the Wright crew, the mid upper gunner was F/Sgt Wilfred Bickley, who was later to be awarded the Conspicuous Gallantry Medal (CGM), which is second only to the Victoria Cross for non-commissioned officers. At the time of the award in 1944, Bickley was serving on No 617 Squadron. The citation for his CGM referred to the fact that among his many achievements, he had flown over 70 operations over enemy territory between March 1940 and May 1944. Another noteworthy member of the Wright crew was the then P/O John Evans, the navigator. He subsequently went on to become S/Ldr J H Evans DFC and bar - quite an achievement for a navigator.

Walter Farraday was not the only member of No 44 Squadron to join without having enjoyed the advantages of a conversion course. P/O Eric Dudley arrived at the time that Bomber Command was desperately short of air gunners; hence his posting direct from the air gunner training unit to an operational squadron. He was one of the very few commissioned air gunners, and survived the war in Bomber Command, leaving the service as a Flight Lieutenant DFC.

Air Marshal Harris was becoming increasingly concerned at the mounting loss rate. As the Command's aircraft still lacked an accurate navigation aid that was useable over Germany, he considered that the results did not justify the losses. Accordingly, he tended to concentrate on coastal targets which could be more easily identified than those well inland. However, from time to time he did despatch his main force to major inland targets. One such target was Munich, which was attacked on 19 September, almost on the anniversary of the unsuccessful Nazi Putsch of 1923. This particular raid was well remembered by Charlie Churchill with good cause:

"...we set off for Lake Constance where we were to rendezvous with the other 67 aircraft taking part in this attack. It was a beautiful clear, moonlight night with the target area clearly defined. Nevertheless, in order to ensure a really accurate attack, our bomb aimer insisted that we descended to a height from where he could be sure of seeing the designated aiming point. Once we had dropped our load we turned for home, and what a glorious feeling that was; my last trip of this tour! Some time later, our flight engineer, Bill Downie, reported that the port inner engine was overheating. The engine was shut down, the propeller feathered and we continued our homeward journey on three engines. Since this meant that our maximum altitude was now very much lower, we naturally did not feel too happy. Despite our misgivings we reached France without further incident. At this stage we normally opened up to full power and increased

speed in a gentle descent, up to our maximum speed, but on this occasion, with our reduced power, this was not feasible. Then it happened! A loud explosion was followed rapidly by flames which quickly enveloped our aircraft. I later learned that we had been hit by cannon fire from a Ju88 night fighter.

Through the confusion came Bill Day's voice "Everybody Out". His voice was already becoming distorted as the fire ate away at the aircraft intercom wiring. In a matter of seconds, we were well and truly ablaze, especially the rear of the aircraft, which gave our rear and mid upper gunners little chance of survival; their parachutes having probably burned before they had any chance to reach for them. By the time I was able to get out from behind the radio, our Lancaster was completely out of control, plummeting towards the ground. Luckily, I was wearing my parachute when the attack took place, but as I moved into the aisle, I was suddenly catapulted down into the bomb aimer's compartment. There I found myself lying on top of Jock Glynn, our bomb aimer; then on top of me came George Wylie our naviagator. During my fall into the nose compartment my parachute had snagged on something and was partially open. Fortunately, I had the presence of mind to grab it with one hand to prevent it from spilling out in the aircraft.

As we hurtled down, the light from the flames illuminated everything with horrifying clarity. Somehow I became aware that George's weight had gone from my back. Turning and looking upwards, I could see the sole of his flying boot hooked in the emergency exit. The exit was normally in the floor of the nose, but now it was upright, just like a door. I managed to push myself up off Jock's body and, using my free hand, I unhooked George's flying boot and saw it fall away. This acted as a spur and I pushed myself erect and backed to the exit, pushing myself out with both feet. As soon as I felt that I was clear of the aircraft, I released my grip on the folds of my parachute, which opened immediately and I found myself seemingly floating gently through the black night. I was barely aware of the flash as our aircraft hit the ground and exploded.

I landed in a forest near, as I learned later, Valenciennes. My parachute had snagged in a small tree from which I was able to free myself. I cut off the parachute number and buried the rest. I next tied my identity discs together with a piece of rigging line and hung them round my neck. Sitting under a tree, I tried to recall what we had been taught about evading capture and making contact with the Maquis. I had my emergency kit and the crude button compass; thus equipped I set out to walk home!"

The pilot, P/O W H Day, a Rhodesian, perished with his flight engineer and the two gunners in the wreck of KM-Q (R5554).

On the non-operational side of the Station, the Beam Approach Training Flight received its first USAAF pilots, when four of them joined No 77 Course for training. It was also during September that an unscheduled flying machine landed at Waddington. The newly formed Airborne Forces element of the British Army consisted of parachute troops and glider-borne units, most of which in 1942, we based well away from Bomber County (Lincolnshire). Be that as it may, in September of that year an Airspeed Horsa glider landed at Waddington, though whether this was by accident or design is unknown.

The month of October was a successful month for the two Waddington Lancaster squadrons. Between them they despatched 155 aircraft for the loss of only three aircraft from No 44 Squadron. Sadly, among those lost was F/Sgt Leonard Mutter DFM, another of Nettleton's Augsburg crew. He was flying as bomb aimer with S/Ldr Stewart and crew in KM-G (W4188), taking part in an attack on Osnabruck on the night of 6/7 October.

To Le Creusot in Daylight

Among the targets attacked during the month of October were the Italian cities of Genoa and Milan. These attacks were planned to coincide with the opening of General Montgomery's Eighth Army offensive at El Alamein. The attack on Milan was a daylight operation and was considered to have been very successful, having been carried out by 88 Lancasters for the loss of four aircraft. However, the most notable raid in October was the low level daylight attack on the French Schneider works at Le Creusot near Chalon. In late July, the Air Staff had issued a list of additional targets in France, among which were the Gien Ordnance Depot; the Citroen works in Paris, and the Schneider Armament and Locomotive works at Le Creusot, near the Franco/Swiss border.

With these targets in mind, Bomber Command decided that selected Lancaster squadrons of No 5 Group would provide the crews for a low level daylight attack; this despite the recent losses on the Augsburg raid. It was felt that only by carrying out the attack in daylight, could the risk to French workers living in close proximity to the factory be minimised. Accordingly, those crews selected commenced low level formation flying training on 1 October. Initially, each of the nine squadrons practiced separately, leading eventually to three squadrons combining to form a Wing. Ultimately, the three Wings combined to create a Group. The attack by 86 aircraft was led by the very experienced W/Cdr Leonard Slee of No 49 Squadron, and was codenamed 'Operation Robinson'. This was something of a departure from the norm for codewords; the standard practice being that the actual codeword should have no apparent connection with the particular activity to which it referred.

Apart from minimising the risk to French civilans, the planners felt that one heavy, accurate attack would be less costly than several smaller, less accurate raids, which would serve only to make the Germans increase the local defences. The attack apart, the practices too had their moments. As one of the No 44 Squadron pilots, Colin Watt, recalled: "*On 7 October, our crew leave was scrubbed, so we felt that something big was on. The next day we were airborne taking part in a daylight formation training sortie, led by S/Ldr Burnett. It was exhausting work because during each of the practices, we spent three and a half hours on the deck. As we passed overhead, animals scattered in all directions, while on one occasion near Yatesbury, we almost cleaned up a Percival Proctor as it prepared to land... further exercises followed on 9 and 10 October, involving progressively larger formations, culminating in an evident dress rehearsal of some 80 plus Lancasters on 11 October. We flew to an RV at Upper Heyford and thence to Lands End and out to sea, returning via Aberystwyth to bomb a range...*"

As part of the practice, the formation was intercepted and attacked by fighters, at least two Spitfires of which crashed when they got caught in the bombers' slipstream at low level. Among the members of No 44 Squadron taking part in the Le Creusot attack was F/Sgt Frank Harrison DFM. As he later recalled:

"In early September, Nettleton's four NCO crew members were informed that their medals would be presented at Buckingham Palace in about one month's time. Within three weeks, I was the only one left! Despite having been spread through different crews, the others had all got the chop! The start of rehearsals for another daylight attack convinced me that I would not be keeping the appointment either. In the event, weather delayed the Le Creusot raid, so I was able to attend the investiture before taking part in the raid".[3]

The weather forecast for 17 October was favourable, though it was thought that it might deteriorate for the return. Accepting this, Command Headquarters set the operation in motion. Of the 95 Lancasters detailed for the operation, 86 actually took off for the rendezvous. All eighteen Waddington aircraft made a successful rendezvous at Upper Heyford and took part in the attack. The squadrons taking part in the operation were Nos IX, 44, 49, 50, 57, 61, 97, 106 and 207 Squadrons. There was no fighter escort; the formation relying on staying below enemy radar cover. From the RV at Upper Heyford the bombers flew at 1000 feet to Lands End, successfully negotiating low cloud over the West Country moors. Leaving Lands End, the force descended to well below 500 feet. Over the sea the clouds were very low and the force ran into rain, which made close formation keeping an absolute necessity. Ahead of the bombers by fifteen minutes, a small force of Coastal Command Whitleys had carried out a sweep to drive any lurking U-boats down, so that they would be in no position to record the bombers' passage and to broadcast a warning to the German defence system. Once clear of the rain, the formation opened out and flew southwestwards until they were well out into the Bay of Biscay, before turning East to the French coast.

As they neared the coast, the weather improved and the crews closed up and bunched into pairs or threes in order to provide some form of mutual protection in the event that they were intercepted. The formation crossed the coast on track, just off the southern tip of the Ile d'Yeu, some 50 miles south of St Nazaire, the scene of the successful but costly commando raid the previous March. By this time the bombers were flying at about 100 feet above ground and had still got over 300 miles to go before they reached their target. For a force whose training and experience had been optimised for high level night attacks, it was a remarkable achievement, particularly in view of the minimal amount of training that they had carried out. The navigators and bomb aimers were map reading all the way from the coast to the target area. They had been provided with strip maps which had the more prominent features highlighted on them. A considerable number of the air gunners took the opportunity to machine gun any German troops that appeared (!) to be in range. En route, the main hazard proved to be that of birds, with several Lancasters experiencing birdstrikes of one sort or another.

At a pre-determined point some 45 miles from the target, the bombers climbed and spread out into a fan-shaped formation, just as they had done during the group formation practices prior to bombing the training ranges. Having reached the required height band of between 4000 and 6000 feet, the aircraft again converged, forming a narrow but deep front for the actual bombing run. The first bombs were dropped at dusk (1806hr British Summer Time). The attackers were engaged by only one gun, a 37mm anti-aircraft gun which, after firing one short burst, ceased fire. Surprise was obviously complete, as at no time did enemy fighters put in an appearance. The bombing appeared to the crews to be accurate, though the target soon became obscured by dense black smoke. In all, the Lancasters dropped 120 tons of high explosive bombs, plus 40 tons of incendiaries.

Among those of the Waddington crews who reported seeing their results, S/Ldr Burnett reported seeing his load of five 1000lb bombs hit a long shed, while Sgt Morris and crew reported that they had dropped their load of 112 30lb incendiaries, which were observed to have burst on the target. F/O Silcock and crew reported that they had dropped their load of

---

[3] Of the four NCO members of John Nettleton's crew who were with him on the Augsburg raid:

- Sgt D N 'Buzzer' Huntley DFM (front gunner) was killed in action during an attack on Bremen on 13 September 1942.
- F/Sgt Charles Churchill DFM (W/Op) was shot down during an attack on Munich on 19 September 1942. He became a PoW.
- F/Sgt Leonard Mutter DFM (mid upper gunner) was killed in action during an attack on Osnabruck on 6 October 1942.
- F/Sgt Frank Harrison DFM (rear gunner) went on to survive the war, ending up as a commissioned (F/Lt) bomb aimer in the Pathfinder Force.

five 1000lb bombs in the target area, but were unable to determine which were theirs among so many others!

The intelligence specialists at Bomber Command had to wait for the results of a photographic reconnaissance sortie the next day before they could begin to assess the results of the attack. At the time of the raid, it was too dark to take daylight photographs and too light to use flash photography. Subsequent photographs showed that the steel rolling mills had been severely damaged; the forging and armour-plate bending shops had both been heavily damaged, and that varying degrees of damage had been caused to the locomotive works and machine shops. Against this, was the evidence that a considerable number of bombs had overshot the designated target area and had fallen on houses to the East of the factory complex. The final conclusion at Command was that though the attack had been successful, the accuracy of the bombing had been less than expected. In retrospect, this should have come as no great surprise, as those taking part had been trained for night area attacks and, in the main, that was where their experience and expertise lay. To then require them to undertake a complex daylight operation, with mimimal amount of specialised training was, to say the least, optimistic. That being said, it brought home to the German High Command that they could not afford to concentrate all their defences in the Ruhr and in the west coast towns and cities; they had to employ defence in depth, thereby diminishing the defences in any one area.

Bomber Command Reaches Out to Italy

Five days after the attack on Le Creusot, Lancasters from both Waddington squadrons took part in a night attack on Genoa. This was to be the first of six such attacks by Bomber Command in support of the Eighth Army's desert offensive. To again quote Frank Harrison:

"There hadn't been an Italian trip for some time and W/Cdr Smales wanted to go and see for himself. I was horrified to see my name on the Operation Order to fly as his bomb aimer. I don't think that any of us in his crew for that night had ever flown with each other before; a typical Smales crew! He had taken command of the squadron just after it had sustained very heavy casualties and, naturally, morale was very low indeed. Ken Smales pulled the squadron together by sheer example and leadership. Of small stature and with a reserved personality, he was the very antithesis of the Hollywood idea of a leader. His method was simple and effective, though dangerous. He flew only when an operation was known to be 'a stinker' and he never had a regular crew. This approach was considered by the 'old hands' to be a very special form of suicide. He was undoubtedly the bravest man I ever flew with. I have a particular memory of a big, tough and barbary Canadian F/Sgt, who had himself survived several close calls, saying in effect "If he can do it, so can I", though his phraseology was far more colourful.

We were the first of the No 44 Squadron element to take off, just after the last of No IX Squadron. We were still climbing for height over Waddington when an engine failed. My immediate thoughts were 'Great; now we will have to land, and its off to the village for me'. No such luck; Smales simply said 'This makes us like a Halifax', and off we went all the way to Genoa on three engines! Our crossing of the Alps had its moments, as so marginal was our height performance that I had to level my bomb sight in order to predict whether or not we would clear the next rock obstruction ahead! We literally scraped past some of the peaks during our ten hours and five minutes trip; my longest ever in more ways than one. W/Cdr Smales was awarded a well deserved DSO".

The attack on Genoa was carried out by 112 Lancasters of No 5 Group, the target being marked by the Pathfinders. Bombing was extremely accurate, with not one Lancaster being lost.

Two days after Genoa and only five after the Le Creusot attack, 88 Lancasters took off for another daylight attack. This time the target was Milan, and the two Waddington squadrons each despatched eleven aircraft, all of which returned safely. Among the crews from No 44 Squadron taking part was a young American volunteer, Sgt Robert Raymond. He was a recently arrived aircraft captain and was flying on this occasion as co-pilot with the experienced F/Sgt Elgar. Raymond had volunteered for service with the RAF in 1940 when he left the American Volunteer Ambulance Corps, with whom he had served in France up to the capitulation. Better known as 'Kansas', Raymond was to complete a full tour of operations and earn a DFC before transferring to the USAAF, who utilised his experience on instructional duties in the USA. His crew's aircraft was Lancaster KM-A (R5729) which they christened 'The Flying Jayhawk', which was badly damaged twice, before being shot down during an attack on Brunswick on the night of 14/15 January 1944.

Another crew taking part in the daylight attack on Milan, was that of an Australian pilot, F/Sgt Colin Watt. They were still on the ground at Waddington when Watt broke radio silence (strictly forbidden) to report a fault with one of his gun turrets. With the fault cured, but well aware that he would be in trouble for violating the strict rule of radio silence, Watt took off only eight minutes late. Their problems however, were not all behind them. As he recalled

"...our arrival at the RV at Lake Annecy was eight minutes early, so we circled to gain height prior to crossing the Alps. Geneva lay off to port and quite a few crews went over to take a look. We had just set heading towards Milan when, without warning or signs of malfunction, the starboard engine packed up on us. At our reduced speed of 130kts we gradually drifted back

through the bomber stream. At one stage, a No IX Squadron Lancaster came close to take a look at us. Up ahead we could see Lancasters wheeling in the sky like vultures as they descended over the target. Below us, through an intervening layer of broken startus at around 5000 feet, we could see roads and railways leading to the city of Milan. We bombed from 10,500 feet, which was disappointing, as I would liked to have gone in at low level and shot the place up. Had we done so however, we would never have gained sufficent height in time to get back over the barrier of the Alps. Our route home had us flying into the sun and we watched it set behind the Alps, a really beautiful sight. Then of course, it rapidly grew cold and I was still flying in shirtsleeves. As we passed Mont Blanc seven miles off to starboard, we had another magnificent view as the moon came up and illuminated the partly snow-covered mountains... ...Flying Control stacked us at 6000 feet for our recovery because of enemy intruder activity, but eventually, after flying for ten hours and five minutes, we were down; tired but happy to have made it.

The next morning the F/Sgt Discip informed me that an escort had been waiting to place me under close arrest for breaching radio silence before take-off. However, everyone thought that we had done a good job in carrying on with only three engines, so the whole business had been dropped when I landed. Some time later, S/Ldr 'Happy' Harmon, the Senior Air Traffic Control Officer, told me that as I had been just about to take off, the Station Commander ordered him to give me a 'red'. Harman had declined, explaining that it was too late and that in any case "You wouldn't have stopped would you?" This episode subsequently appeared in the national daily paper, the News Chronicle, and Colin Watt was awarded the DFM for his night's work.

Despite the onset of winter, the pace of operations did not slacken. A total of 157 bombers were despatched from the Station on nine operations during November, seven of which were either to Genoa or Turin. In addition, a detachment of No 50 Squadron came over from nearby Skellingthorpe and operated from Waddington for four nights, despatching a total of 20 Lancasters. The Station suffered only two losses to enemy action during the month of November, both from No 44 Squadron. Sgt O R Shepperson SAAF and crew, flying in KM-D (W4180), went down over Hamburg, while P/O S E R Young and crew were lost during an attack on Stuttgart in KM-C (W4304). Sadly, No IX Squadron lost two Lancasters in particularly tragic circumstances. On the night of 7/8 November, the Station despatched eleven Lancasters from each of the two resident squadrons, to take part in an accurate and concentrated attack on Genoa. On their return, the Station aircraft were stacked overhead the aerodrome for recovery. At 0210hr, Lancasters WS-R (R5916) and WS-L (W4265) collided above the aerodrome and crashed near the Lincoln to Sleaford road. All fourteen members of the the crews of F/O K A Mackenzie DFC RCAF and F/Sgt A J McDonald RCAF, perished.

On the 9th November, No 1661 Heavy Conversion Unit (HCU) formed at Waddington. The unit comprised the Conversion Flights of Nos IX and 44 Squadrons, which became 'A' and 'B' Flights respectively of the new unit. In addition, No 49 Squadron's Conversion Flight at RAF Scampton, became 'C' Flight, but remained at Scampton. No 1661 HCU was commanded initially by S/Ldr J D Nettleton VC, but on moving to RAF Winthorpe near Newark on 30 December, it came under the command of S/Ldr T C Murray DFC and bar. He in turn handed over command to W/Cdr Beauchamp DSO DFC.

Two days after the formation of No 1661 HCU, the Station was thrown into turmoil. As the recalcitrant Colin Watt recalled:

"On 11 November, administrative bedlam followed the news that 'Bomber' Harris was to visit the Station. The rapidly organised parade rehearsal was followed by a day of 'bulling up'. At 0900hr on a fogbound 12 November, frozen Station personnel stood on parade with aircrews in pairs behind their respective captains. One hour later, it was His Majesty King George VI who arrived, accompanied by the AOC No 5 Group, Air Vice Marshal Coryton and Churchill's Chief of Staff, General Ismay".

On 22 November, a mixed force of 222 aircraft bombed Stuttgart. Among the attackers were eleven Lancasters from No IX Squadron, nine from No 44 Squadron and seven from No 50 Squadron. Lancaster KM-C (W4304) of No 44 Squadron, flown by P/O S E R Young and crew, was one of the five Lancasters that failed to return that night. Among the other Lancaster crews taking part in this attack, was that of Colin Watt. His navigator, Frank Walshaw recalled:

"It was the practice on our squadron, for one crew to remain in the target area until bombing had ceased (!) in order to assess the success or otherwise of the raid, and on this particular occasion, it was our turn. It was a brilliant moonlit night, so to avoid the attentions of the enemy night fighters, we descended to very low level and stood off from the target. When the bombing ceased we made a low level run over the city, which by then was well alight. Below us I could clearly see people running in the streets and individual incendiaries burning where they had fallen on to rooftops. It was bright enough for me to be able to see houses in which the curtains were on fire, as were the room behind them. This was the first time that I had seen at close quarters the havoc wrought by the combined effects of bombs and incendiaries, and the scene brought home the horror and futility of war. I even experienced momentary guilt about harming fellow human beings. After leaving the target area, we remained at low level for the trip home. Somewhere near

Chaumont sur Somme we encountered a slow moving goods train and our two gunners clamoured for a chance to have a go. To their delight, Colin made two low passes, but there was no immediate evidence of their having inflicted any real damage, although I should not think that the train crew were too impressed by our escapade."

The month of December 1942 was the worst month of the year for overall Lancaster losses within the Command. A total of 28 were lost on operations, with eight others being lost as a result of accidents associated with operations. In addition, a further six were lost in training; making in all a total of 42 Lancasters written off. The month was particularly bad for the Station too. 196 sorties were despatched, for the loss of 13 aircraft (6.6%) Eleven of these were as a direct result of enemy action, and two as a result of a collision on climbing out soon after take-off. The Command was keeping up the pressure on the Italians and it appeared to be most effective. Intelligence reports indicated that the effect on civilian morale was enormous and out of all proportion to the damage caused. All aircraft attacking targets in Italy had, perforce, to carry a reduced bomb load in order to carry the extra fuel required for such a lengthy round trip. It was reported that 300,000 people fled Turin after the second attack and that the panic was as great, if not greater, following the daylight raid on Milan.

On the night of 17/18 December, Bomber Command called for a selection of small scale raids by 27 Lancasters on eight small towns in Germany. At the same time, a mixed force of sixteen Stirlings and six Wellingtons from No 3 Group, were targetted against the Opel works at Fallersleben. In addition, 50 other bombers laid mines from Denmark in the North, to the Bay of Biscay in the South. These small scale operations proved to be costly failures. Ten of the Lancasters were lost; seven of them from Waddington, while a further six Stirlings and two Wellingtons also failed to return. These losses represented a 17.3% loss rate; far more than the Command could afford. It appeared that there was much truth in the old adage - 'safety in numbers'. No 44 Squadron lost three aircraft and No IX Squadron lost two, as did No 50 Squadron, whose aircraft had flown from Waddington, being among those engaged in minelaying operations.

The next Main Force attack was against Duisburg, on the night of 20/21 December. It was on this operation that tragically, a No 44 Squadron Lancaster KM-P (W4259), flown by the experienced F/Sgt Elgar and crew, collided with a No IX Squadron Lancaster WS-B (W4182), flown by Sgt Hazell and crew. The collision occured during the climb-out, an ever-present hazard, and both aircraft crashed into Canwick Road at Bracebridge Heath, just south of Lincoln. Elgar's close friend 'Kansas' Raymond was hit hard by his death, and wrote at length on the accident to his fiancée in America. He mentioned in particular the fact that Elgar was only one week away from being commissioned. To Raymond, it was a double tragedy as his rear gunner, Sgt Harmston, was flying as a stand-in gunner in Elgar's crew; their own rear gunner being off sick. In death, Harmston joined both his brothers and three cousins, all of whom had been killed in air operations! In addition to the two aircraft lost in the collision, No IX Squadron lost a further aircraft WS-N (ED347), flown by Sgt J W Tyreman and crew, who were shot down by a night fighter over Holland.

Bomber Command Counts Its Losses

By the third anniversary of the outbreak of war, Bomber Command statistics made for grim reading. The Command had mounted a total of 86,800 sorties, in the course of which it had suffered the loss of 11,366 killed, 1655 wounded or seriously injured, and a further 2814 were prisoners of war. On top of this, 2534 aircrew had been killed or injured in non-operational flying incidents. In other words, almost 20,000 aircrew were not available for operations. At this time, all aircrew were required to fly at least 30 completed operational sorties in the course of their first tour of operations. On completion of their first tour, they could expect to be rested for a minimum of six months before becoming liable for a second tour of the same length as the first. Being 'rested' usually meant flying as an instructor at one of the many training units; quite often as hazardous as operations - some rest!

Those who managed to survive their second tour of operations would then be 'screened' and no longer liable for operational duties. Statistics show that of the 125,000 aircrew who flew with Bomber Command, 7,000 'volunteered' for a second tour, with several hundred going on to undertake a third tour! Sadly, many of these became examples of 'the pitcher that went to the well too often'. Of the 125,000 bomber aircrew, less than 75,000 (60%) survived the war. The final figures were to be: 55,000 dead, 20,000 wounded and 12,000 taken prisoner. As Air Vice Marshal Donald Bennett said: 'The contribution of an aircrew member of Bomber Command who completed an operational tour, or died in the process, measured in terms of danger or death, both in intensity and duration, was in my view far greater than that of any other fighting man, RAF, Army or Navy'.

Despite their heavy losses so close to Christmas, the Waddington crews, in common with the hundreds of others operating from the many airfields close to Lincoln, made the most of the available entertainment. The dances in the Assembly Rooms, better known as 'The Arse and Belly Rooms', were always popular, as were the numerous hostelries such as 'The Unity' in Broadgate; 'The Saracen's Head' near Newport Arch; 'The Lion and Snake' in the Bailgate, and of course, 'The Saracen's Head' (Snakepit) near the Stonebow.

The latter tended to be the preserve of the aircrew, though there was no formal arrangement. Possibly, the 'Snakepit' prices had something to do with it. The first 'Saracen's Head' on this site was built in 1496, but it was rebuilt several times on various occasions. Once one of the old coaching inns, it eventually became the largest hotel in the County, with more than 70 bedrooms, many of which had names, such as 'Tudor Room', 'Kitchener Room', 'Beatty Room' etc etc. As Daphne Kitchen, a lively young Lincoln lass at the time recalled:

"After The White Hart Hotel, which pre-war was really quite exclusive; indeed even during the war it retained a certain air of aloofness, the Saracen's Head was the best hotel for miles around. Pre-war, it too had been rather a classy joint, but with the advent of war, hordes of high-spirited young aircrew rapidly made it 'their own'. One entered through heavy double doors into a long wide entrance hall; on the left of which was a small room, which I seem to recall was, in the early days of the war at least, a bar reserved for Officers and their guests only. In any event, it was always packed to capacity.

At the end of the hallway was a beautiful wide, sweeping double staircase, leading up to the powder room and guest bedrooms. To the left of the staircase was a large dining room, presided over by an elderly, austere head waiter who appeared to view the somewhat impecunious new generation of diners with a slightly jaundiced eye. To the right of the staircase was a lounge which, although well patronized, was rather more subdued than the bar previously mentioned. The atmosphere of the whole place was somehow unique; high spirits, at times almost desperate gaiety, together with the close comradeship of the aircrew, combined to generate a magical 'something' that no other local hotel ever achieved".

Closer to home was the Horse and Jockey (Whore and Jockstrap) in Waddington village. Again, there seemed to be an unwritten understanding that this was the aircrew pub. It was managed by Albert Titmarsh and his wife; she being referred to among the aircrew as Anna Mae Wong, after an American film actress of the day. Apparently Mrs Titmarsh was considered somewhat oriental in appearance. Many were the rumours concerning the contents of the various dishes in the upstairs restaurant, but it did not seem to prevent the aircrews from using the establishment throughout the war. Rumour had it that on VE Night, the Australians 'suggested' to the landlord that he should declare drinks on the house, in recognition of nearly six years of aircrew drinking - otherwise there might have been a fire!

Another of the legends associated with Waddington concerned a chalked notice on the Operations Board one night. Against the name of an Australian pilot was the terse inscription 'Scrubbed-pilot shot himself'! Apparently the pilot in question was in the habit of carrying a loaded revolver in one of his flying boots. During a rather protracted wait for the green flare signal to start engines, he somehow contrived to accidentally fire the gun into his foot.

❖ ❖ ❖

6. Bomber Command Grows Stronger

By the end of 1942, No 5 Group possessed one non-operational and nine operational squadrons equipped with Lancasters. The start of the New Year coincided with the Lancaster's fuel problem being resolved, thereby enabling the Command to make better use of the new bomber's capabilities. It was the CinC's intention to proceed with the plans for the progressive destruction of German towns and cities. As a result of the meeting of the Allied leaders at Casablanca, the subsequent directive, among other things, detailed five main targets for attack. Such a broad directive suited Harris, leaving as it did, scope for him to select his targets. In the event, things were not to be so simple. The Admiralty and the Prime Minister had become increasingly concerned at the shipping losses from U-boat attack. Accordingly, much to Harris' irritation, he was directed to mount a series of attacks against selected U-boat bases on the French Atlantic coast. This despite the fact that intelligence reports and photographic reconnaissance had shown that the Kriegsmarine had provided its U-boats with (then) bomb-proof shelters which, as Harris pointed out, would result in the necessity to 'area bomb' the nearby French towns.

With an increasing number of four-engined heavy bombers taking their place in the Bomber Command Order of Battle, the CinC felt able to progress from the 'preliminary' phase of his campaign to the 'main' phase. In parallel with the improvement in aircraft came the long-awaited radio and radar navigation aids. However, coincident with the improvement in Bomber Command's equipment, were the improvements in the enemy's defence organisation and equipment. This had not gone unoticed in Bomber Command, and towards the end of 1942, the Command commenced a series of major efforts to disrupt the German defence system, and to provide passive defences for the aircraft of the main force.

Three radio countermeasures were introduced in quick succession. Shiver was the first, this being a jamming device optimised against night fighter radar. Its use was soon discontinued when it was discovered that its transmissions gave away the presence of the carrying aircraft. The next piece of equipment to come into service was named Tinsel. This consisted of a carbon microphone installed in the port inner engine nacelle. The operating procedure of Tinsel was for the bomber's Wireless Operator to search for the enemy's R/T between slected frequencies on the 3-6mc/s band. Once the R/T transmissions were picked up, the W/Op immediately back-tuned the transmitter to the receiver, put the transmitter selector switch to the R/T position and transmitted the engine noise over the enemy's night fighter R/T frequency. This system, with a few modification, remained an effective aid for the remainder of the war.

The third countermeasure carried by the main force bombers was codenamed Mandrel. This was optimised against the German long range Freya radar systems. As with Shiver, the problem with this equipment was that the operation of Mandrel gave the German defences early warning of the approach of aircraft operating the equipment. Despite this shortcoming, it remained in use, but more in the form of a screen, being carried by special aircraft, flying off the enemy coast, backed up by ground stations.

Nos IX and 44 Squadrons carried out all the early experimental work on radio and radar equipment within No 5 Group. The first airborne early warning equipment fitted to main force bombers was called Boozer. This was designed to give bomber crews early warning of their being illuminated by a night fighter radar. The first sets were installed in aircraft of No 44 Squadron in January 1943. However, as the squadron was in process of changing over from Lancaster Mk Is to Mk IIIs, it was decided to give No IX Squadron priority, as they had completed re-equiping with Mk IIIs. Accordingly, all the No IX Squadron Lancasters were fitted with Boozer, making it the only squadron in No 5 Group to retain Boozer. The system had been superceded by Monica, which had proved to be incompatible with Boozer. The eventual outcome was that the No 5 Group allocation of Boozer equipments was passed on to other Groups within the Command, while No 5 Group squadrons awaited the arrival of Monica.

The Monica Mk I covered an astern arc of 120 degrees in azimuth and from 45 degrees upwards to 90 degrees downwards. Its maximum range was 3000 feet and it gave warnings by means of 'pip' sounds over the bomber's intercomm, but not without some drawbacks. The problem with Monica Mk I was that it could be activated by another bomber in the stream closing in from astern. Eventually, improved marks of Monica came into use, employing visual indicators. These improved Monica Mk III sets were installed in aircraft that were not equipped with the new H2S radar. It later became apparent that the enemy night fighters could home in on the Monica transmissions, so all Monica sets were removed from Bomber Command aircraft.

At squadron level, the increasing availability and importance of radio aids, resulted in the establishment of a commissioned Wireless Operator as the Squadron Signals Leader. This appointment was usually filled by a Flight Lieutenant.

In early 1943, the introduction of the TR1196 radio, with its two frequencies for local flying control, enabled the radio specialists at Group Headquarters to implement their No 5 Group 'Quick Landing Scheme'. This system utilised the employment of two frequencies at different stages of an aircraft's approach to land. A similar, locally devised scheme was employed at Waddington using VHF R/T equipment, which proved to be even more successful than the Group version. As a result of this, Waddington became the centre for numerous experiments in the homing and landing of an aircraft stream.

For the personnel at Waddington, the New Year's operations began on the night of 3/4 January, when the target was Essen. The aiming point was marked by Pathfinder Mosquitos using 'Wanganui' sky-marker flares. This was a small scale raid carried out by only nineteen Lancasters, five coming from Waddington. Sadly, F/Lt Lonsdale and crew of No IX Squadron, flying in WS-B (W4840), failed to return. This attack on Essen was the first time that the Wanganui system of marking had been used in the sort of weather conditions it had been specifically designed to overcome; complete overcast. For the German defenders, it was yet another ominous portent of things to come. Indeed, it was at about this time that aircraft of Bomber Command dropped a particular 'Nickel'. It was entitled **'Le Courier de l'Air'**, being sub-titled **'Le Chef du Bomber Command au Peuple Allemand'.** (Though why a message to the German people should be written in French is anybody's guess). This leaflet contained the following message:

From C-in-C Bomber Command to the German People

Here is the text of a message from Air Marshal Harris, Commander-in-Chief Bomber Command. This message has been broadcast in the European service of the BBC, and has been distributed in Germany by pamphlets dropped by the RAF. It is the first time that a man who is directing air attacks against a country has sent a message to the country concerned.

I, Air Marshal Harris, Commander of the bombers which are attacking Germany, have taken the decision to send this message to the German people.

We in Great Britain have known all about air raids for long enough. For ten months your Luftwaffe bombed us. You began with day bombing. Then, when we made that impossible, you bombed us by night. You then had a powerful bomber force. Your aircrew fought well. They bombed London on 92 consecutive nights. They carried out very strong raids on Coventry, Plymouth, Liverpool and other British towns. They caused a great deal of damage. Forty-three thousand British men, women and children were killed.

You believed, and Goering promised you, that you would be sheltered from the bombs. In fact, throughout that period, we were able to send only a few aircraft to bomb you in turn. But now the roles are reversed. Now you send only a few aircraft to attack us, whereas we make heavy raids on Germany.

Why are we behaving in this way? It is not by way of reprisal - although we do not forget Warsaw, Belgrade, Rotterdam, London, Plymouth or Coventry, but we bomb you in order to make it impossible for you to continue the war. Such is our goal. Thus we shall pursue it relentlessly. City after city: Lubeck, Rostock, Cologne, Emden, Bremen, Wilhelmshaven, Hamburg - the list is growing, always to get longer. Allow the Nazis to drag you down with them if that is what you want; the choice is yours.

When the weather is fine, we bomb you by night. Already a thousand bombers are able to meet over a city like Cologne, and destroy a third of it in an hour of bombing. We know this because the photographs prove it. When the weather is overcast, we bomb your factories and your naval dockyards by day. In this way we have got as far as Danzig. We come by day and by night. No corner of the Reich is safe.

In Cologne, in the Ruhr or at Rostock, Lubeck or Emden, you think perhaps that our bombing is beginning to hurt. But this is not our opinion. In comparison with what will happen when our output of bomber aircraft reaches its maximum, and given that American production will first double and then redouble, all you have experienced up to now will seem to you to be very little indeed.

I am going to talk to you frankly. Is it our policy to bomb fixed military objectives or entire cities? It is obvious that we would prefer to bomb your factories, your naval dockyards and your railways, because in this way we would hit Hitler's war machine the hardest. But those who work in these factories live near them. Thus we hit your houses - as well as yourselves when we bomb. We regret the necessity of doing so. The workers at Humboldt-Deutz, the diesel engine manufacturers, for example - some of whom were killed on the night of 30 May last, must inevitable run the risks of war. In the same way as the men of the merchant ship crews, which the German submarines (equipped with Humboldt-Deutz engines) would torpedo. Were the aero-industry workers of Coventry not as much in the front-line as the aero-industry workers and their families in Rostock? But it was Hitler who decided thus.

It is true that your anti-aircraft defences inflict losses on our bombers. Your commanders seek to reassure you in telling you that our losses are so high that soon we shall no longer be able to continue to bomb you. Those among you who believe them will be bitterly disappointed.

I, the Commander of the British bombers, I am going to tell you honestly and truthfully what our losses are. They are less than 5% of the aircraft we send over Germany. So small a proportion of losses, far from weakening our fighting force, can have absolutely no effect on our enormous bomber fleet, deriving from the ever-growing production of our factories and those in the United States. America has scarcely joined the fray. The first American squadrons, the vanguard of a complete air armada, have arrived in England. Do you realise what will be coming to you when these in their turn begin to bomb Germany? Soon, we shall be back every day and every night, come rain or wind or snow, and the Americans will come with us. I have just spent eight months in America, I therefore know exactly what is going to happen. We are going to crush Germany, from one end to the other if you force us to do so. You cannot prevent us and you know it.

You have no chance of winning. You were not able to beat us in 1940, at the time we the British were alone and almost disarmed. Your commanders made a mistake in attacking Russia and America. (But your commanders are mad, everyone knows it, except Italy). How can you expect to win now that we are so strong; now that Russia and America are our Allies, and you are more and more exhausted yourselves? Remember that whatever the advance of your armies may be over the ground, they can never get to England. They were unable to get there when we were disarmed. Whatever their victories, there will always be the air battles with the Americans and with us. That is one battle you will never win. We are already winning it.

One last word: it is up to you to put an end to the war and to the bombing. You can overthrow the Nazis and make peace. It is not right to say that we anticipate a year of reprisals. That is the lie of German propaganda. But it is true that we shall take great care that no German government will again be able to start a total war. Is that not as necessary in your interests as in ours?

A T HARRIS

Commander in Chief

British Bomber Command

On the night of 8/9 January, another small scale raid, this by 38 Lancasters, attacked Duisburg led by three Pathfinder Force (PFF) Mosquitos. Each of the two Waddington squadrons despatched six aircraft. All six aircraft of No 44 Squadron returned safely, but Lancaster WS-Y (W4159) of No IX Squadron, flown by Sgt Foote and crew, failed to return. In addition, Lancaster WR-R (ED308), flown by Sgt Doolan and crew, was hit in the tail section by flak which killed the rear gunner, Sgt Robinson. The Flight Engineer and W/Op managed to drag the gunner from his badly damaged gun turret with great difficulty, but despite giving him first aid, he died of his injuries before they got back to base.

While the attack on Duisburg was taking place, six crews from No 44 Squadron, together with three from No IX Squadron, were engaged in minelaying off the North German and Danish coasts. Despite minelaying being considered much safer than bombing, two crews from No 44 Squadron failed to return.

The attacks on German towns and cities continued, Essen being a regular target. Then, on the night of 16/17 January, the target was Berlin. This was the first raid on the German capital since 8 November 1941. A total of 201 bombers took part, consisting of 190 Lancasters and 11 Halifaxes. According to the No IX Squadron War Diary, the announcement that Berlin was to be the target was received with delight by the squadron (sic). No 44 Squadron despatched fourteen aircraft and No IX Squadron sent eleven. The first of the No 44 Squadron Lancasters to take off was piloted by the Squadron Commander, W/Cdr Smales. He was closely followed by OC 'A' Flight, S/Ldr Nettleton VC. Similarly, the first of No IX Squadron's aircraft to go was flown by its Officer Commanding, W/Cdr Southwell. Flying as the navigator in W/Cdr Smales' 'scratch' crew, was F/Lt Des Sands DFC, who had been John Nettleton's navigator on the Augsburg raid.

Over the target, the crews were surprised at the weakness of the flak defences; concluding that as the city had not been bombed for over a year, most of its guns had been moved out to defend the Ruhr Valley targets. The raid itself was not particularly successful, despite having caught the German warning system off guard. On his approach to the target area, a heavy calibre flak shell hit W/Cdr Smales' aircraft, severely injuring his right arm. Despite his injury, he jettisoned his bombs and made a successful recovery to Waddington. With the W/Cdr in his aircraft was the Daily Mail air correspondent, Colin Betnall, who subsequently wrote a glowing tribute to Ken Smales' courage in getting his aircraft and crew (plus an air correspondent) safely back to base. The wound itself was not life threatening, but it developed into severe blood poisoning, resulting in Smales being taken off operations. Two weeks later the new Commanding Officer, newly promoted W/Cdr John Nettleton VC, assumed command of No 44 (Rhodesia) Squadron.

The following night, Bomber Command returned to Berlin, when a mixed force of 187 Lancasters and Halifaxes attacked the city, led by the PFF. As with the previous attack, this raid was not particularly successful and the attackers suffered severe losses to the enemy night fighters, with 22 bombers (11.8%) being shot down. Among those lost were four out of the eleven despatched by No IX Squadron, and one from No 44 Squadron.

Having lost seven crews in fourteen days while engaged in re-equipping with Mk III Lancasters, No IX Squadron did not operate again until the last raid of the month when, on the night of 30/31 January, eight of the squadron's aircraft joined ten from No 44 Squadron as part of a 148-strong force attacking Hamburg. This particular attack was the first to be carried out by aircraft of Bomber Command using H2S radar to identify the target. The codename given to the ground marking of targets by use of H2S radar was 'Parramatta'. Once again, it was not a particularly successful attack, and among the five Lancasters reported missing, were two from No IX Squadron. One of the two was that flown by F/Sgt F Nelson and crew, all of whom perished when their aircraft WS-N (ED481) crashed en-route to RAF Leeming, having been diverted from Waddington. The other IX Squadron aircraft which failed to return that night, was that flown by F/Sgt J F Thomas and crew. Their aircraft WS-O (ED477) was shot down over enemy territory.

The heavy losses suffered by No IX Squadron kept their Adjutant extremely busy. He was the sitting Member of Parliament, Bob Boothby, and his frequent absences from the squadron on House of Commons duties, resulted in an even heavier workload for the Squadron Signals Leader, F/Lt Skinner, who doubled up as Assistant Squadron Adjutant. Still on matters political, one week after the two January attacks on Berlin, the Combined Chiefs of Staff issued 'The Casablanca Directive'. It was this document that eventually led to what was to be called 'round the clock bombing', by the combined air fleets of the RAF and the USAAF. The main theme of the Directive was clear and concise: *'Your (Bomber Command and the USAAF) primary objective will be the progressive destruction and dislocation of the German military, industrial and economic system, and the undermining of the morale of the German people to a point where their capacity for armed resistance is fatally weakened'*. As Harris himself said in front of newsreel cameras: *'Having sown the wind, the enemy is about to reap the whirlwind'.*

Before aircraft from Waddington, or any other bomber airfield could take off on a raid, the many and varied departments on the Station would have worked long, hard hours in their particular specialist field. Among these departments was that of the Intelligence Section. At Waddington, one of the staff was a young WAAF, Doreen Byrne. She was to marry F/Sgt Terry Byrne, the W/Op on 'Lucky' Wright's crew, once they reached the end of their tour of operations. Both Wright and Byrne were on their second tour, each having completed one tour of operations on Hampdens. Some insight into the workings of the Intelligence Section can be gained from a letter she wrote to a friend some years after the war:

'The Operations Department was on the ground floor of Station Headquarters, near the Signals Section. We (Intelligence) were on the first floor, where we occupied three large rooms and two small ones. The Intelligence Officer had one of the small rooms, while the other was used by Sgt Skinner and three airmen. The Briefing Room was similar to any throughout the Command, containing a large blackboard, numerous tables for the crews, plus cabinets full of maps. The maps were the domain of the Station Navigation Officer and his two assistants, Cpl Ada Cox and LACW Doreen Nash. Next to the Briefing Room was the room where I spent most of my working life. This was used mainly by the crews when they came back from an operation and where they had tea and a smoke while waiting to be debriefed. During the day, this room was used for all kinds of office work, tea making etc etc. The room next door was the Intelligence Library, which possessed one of the largest desks I had ever seen. Also in this room was the secret 'scrambler' telephone, connected to Group Headquarters. All round the room were large settees and armchairs; this being where the crews came to be debriefed, sometimes three or four crews at a time. If it had been a big raid, there would be two debriefing officers.

My first task of the day as the Section Runner, was to ensure that the Squadron Leader's desk and office were in tip-top order. There was not much to do until Group came through on the telephone, which would initiate the hectic part of the day. Within fifteen minutes of the receipt of the message from Group, I would be called upon to take the familiar brown envelope and my little book to the operational squadrons' hangars, with always the same instruction - It was to be given to no one but the Squadron Commander. The crews would nearly always be sitting around the crew room, and would invariably greet me with "Here comes trouble" or "Where are we going"? They never believed me when I said that I did not know.

On returning to the Section, it was all one mad rush. The place would be like an ants' nest, with everyone dashing somewhere and phones ringing all over the place. Ada Cox would be up to her eyes in maps, getting them ready for the briefing, while Sgt Skinner would be well into the job and already at panic stations! He had a lot to do, which included typing the list of beacons for the night, before tasking me to run off copies for him with a horrible sticky roller. It was a difficult job, as it had to be done using rice paper which, because of the sensitivity of the material, had to be done behind closed doors. This of course, always led to a few mock raised eyebrows and earthy comments. Once the task was completed, the lists were placed into folders and locked in the safe until briefing time. Meanwhile, down in Operations, they were equally busy, and I used to think that my legs would drop off through repeatedly dashing up and down the stairs between the sections. it was amazing how it was all organised in such a short space of time; dedicated teamwork being the order of the day.

By the time a hurried lunch had been taken, it was almost time for the briefing. The crews would arrive and wait on the stairs until the Station Navigation Officer and other specialists arrived. A certain F/Sgt (her fi-

ancee) was always first to arrive, and we were glad of the chance to snatch a few moments together before the others arrived. Then it was always teasing and leg-pulling to cover up a lot of tense feelings. By this time, I would invariably be feeling sick inside, especially if it was going to be a bad target for the crews; not that there were any easy ones at this stage of the war, but some were definitely worse than others. Terry said, many years later, that he always watched my face, but not once did I show how anxious I was. It was a terrible feeling to want to say and express so much, but have to remain silent. After the briefing, it was quiet and the Section runner (me) could go to tea. After my tea I would come back with the others who were off duty, and we would sometimes watch the aircraft taking off. Then it would be over to the Officers' Mess to collect sandwiches etc for the Officers on night duty. Next I would go to the Sergeants' Mess to collect tea, milk and sugar etc for the crews on their return.

The next part of the job was by far the worst; the terrible waiting, listening to the big Air Ministry clock on the wall, ticking away, knowing just when they would be over the target! One of the girls from Operations, Doris Cheswell, would dash upstairs the minute Terry called in after crossing the coast. She always gave me the 'thumbs up' sign, which was such a relief. By this time, one of the girls would have the tea ready for the crews, and I would be standing ready to collect the foreign money pouches and their revolver bullets, as they had all to be booked in. I hated to bother the tired crews right away, though I must admit that some were rather naughty and just dumped them anywhere, which made it difficult to check. The crews would then go to the library where, sometimes, they would be kept waiting for quite a time, which must have been most frustrating for them after so long and dangerous a night.

About one hour before the aircraft were due back, the Station Commander, the Medical Officer, sometimes the Padre and W/Cdrs Smales and Southwell, plus the Station Navigation Officer, would join our officers, and I would make endless cups of tea, taking some down to Operations for the staff down there. No one would speak, it was just a very tense silence with Officers, WAAFs and everyone else not saying a word. In our section upstairs, it would be just the same; I do not think that I could find words to describe the tension. There were just people, walking up and down the room, tapping their feet, looking at the clock and then at one another..."

Among the debriefing officers involved in the interminable waiting, was Section Officer Laura Barnett-Gray, who arrived at Waddington in February 1943 and remained there until the end of the war.

During February, the Station despatched over two hundred aircraft against a variety of targets including Cologne, Hamburg, Turin, Milan, Lorient, Wilhelmshaven, Bremen and Nuremburg, as well as carrying out the inevitable mine-laying sorties. In terms of losses, this was a good month for the Station, losing only three aircraft from each squadron. By the middle of the month, the town and dockside of Lorient was almost completely destroyed, with its unfortunate population dispersed throughout France. Although the attackers' bombs could not penetrate the thick concrete roofs of the U-boat pens, they ensured that no infrastructure could exist in the immediate vicinity. In all, Bomber Command had flown 1,853 sorties in eight attacks in response to the Admiralty inspired Directive from the Air Ministry.

Two of the attacks during the month of February were particularly successful. For the attack on Wilhelmshaven on the night of 11/12 February, the Station despatched five Lancasters from each squadron as part of a 177 aircraft strong attack. Although the PFF found the target completely covered by cloud and were therefore forced to use their least reliable system of target marking, that of sky-marking by parachute flares (Wanganui) using H2S, the city suffered very heavy damage. Many crews reported seeing a huge explosion through the clouds, which was later confirmed as having been the Mariensiel naval ammunition depot exploding. The other really successful attack was that on Milan on the night of 14/15 February, when the Station despatched a total of fourteen aircraft as part of a 142-strong force of Lancasters. The bombing was accurate, carried out in good visibility, with crews reporting seeing the fires from over 100 miles away as they flew home. The Lancaster WS-Y, flown by F/Lt Verran and crew of No IX Squadron, orbitted the target during the raid while a cine film was taken of the attack. (Doubtless this was soon being seen on cinema newsreels throughout the country). For their part in this attack, both Waddington squadrons received letters of congratulation from the AOC.

Apart from their filming activities, the Verran crew had a particularly eventful time over Milan that night. They were on the final stages of their own bomb run, with their bomb aimer calling corrections to the pilot, when it happened! As was standard practice in Verran's crew, the W/Op, Sgt John Moutray, was standing on the step with his head in the astrodome, keeping an eye open for night fighters. For reasons which he could never explain, Moutray glanced vertically upwards, not something he had ever done before. To his horror, there, 30 or so feet above him, gaped the open bomb bay of another Lancaster! In the reflected glow from the taget fires and searchlights, the 4000lb 'Cookie' looked enormous. Realising that the bomber above them must be close to bomb release, Moutray shouted over the intercom "Break port hard, now!" Without waiting to question his W/Op, Verran stood the bomber on its wing tip and hauled it round in a tight turn. Thanks to a combination of luck, awareness, rapid reactions and professionalism, the Verran crew made it safely back to base.

New Zealand born Jim Verran had a remarkable series of lucky escapes. Two weeks after his near miss over Milan, Verran and his crew were returning from an attack on Berlin on the night of 1/2 March. As their Lancaster and its weary crew were on the downwind leg of the Waddington landing pattern, without warning, a Lancaster of No 57 Squadron from Scampton, collided with them head on! Verran was knocked unconscious and seriously injured, regaining consciousness in a ploughed field, surrounded by broken and burning pieces of Lancaster. He had apparently been catapulted out through the canopy roof. Three members of his crew perished, along with all those in the No 57 Squadron aircraft, which crashed near its base. Some five months later, on 27/28 August, S/Ldr Verran and crew were shot down over Denmark. Jim Verran was on his third (!) tour, this time as a member of the Pathfinders. A badly burned Verran and his bomb aimer were the only survivors.

Among the other crews flying from Waddington with No IX Squadron, was that of F/O G F 'Robbbie' Robertson. He and his crew flew their first twelve operations from Waddington before moving with their squadron to nearby Bardney. Robertson recalled two particular incidents which occurred during his time at Waddington:

"...*we were taking off towards Lincoln on the famous (!) grass runway which had a dip in the middle; you either bounced before or after the dip, depending upon the strength of the wind. As we reached a point about half way along the runway, the port inner engine blew up! It was too late to stop as we had just got airborne, so we just sat there and prayed, just managing to clear the towers of the cathedral by literally a few feet. Among the crew, nobody spoke for quite a time, the silence being broken eventually by Johnny Knell who, as we climbed towards the North Sea jettison area, said: "Skip, I really did not realise how much pigeon droppings there were on the cathedral tower"!*

Robertson's second Waddington incident concerned an attack on Berlin, and gives some idea of the strength of superstition among many crews; used as a mental shield against the unthinkable. As Robertson recalled: "...*take-off was postponed three times and eventually, when we were called to man our aircraft, we were in such a rush that I forgot my 'operational' cap. This had become part of a ritual every time we went on an operation. As Skipper, I would hand my cap to the navigator, who would pass it to the W/Op, who in turn, hung it on a special hook. When my crew realised that I had forgotten my cap, I very nearly had a mutiny on my hands, especially as there was the usual radio silence in force. We did eventually take off, but without the cap as the crew van had long since departed, and it was too late to go and fetch the wretched cap. Needless to say, we returned safely, but it was a long time before I was forgiven.*"

'Robbie' Robertson flew Lancaster WS-X (ED499) which was named by the crew 'Panic II'. Robertson ended his tour as a Squadron Leader, while the seven members of his crew could boast five DFCs and four DFMs between them. One of his post-flight Captain's Reports reads: "*Some silly ****** dropped a full load of incendiaries all over our aircraft when we were over the target...*"

One crew that was starting their first operational tour that February was that captained by F/Sgt Ken Brown RCAF. This crew made such an impressive start to their first tour that they were accepted by W/Cdr Guy Gibson for his 'X' Squadron at RAF Scampton. The Brown crew took part in the Dams raid, attacking the Sorpe Dam, making an accurate drop on their eleventh attempt after having dropped incendiaries to light their way in to their target. For his perseverence, Ken Brown was awarded the rare Conspicuous Gallantry Medal (CGM).

During February, No 1506 BAT Flight moved out of Waddington to Fulbeck near Sleaford. The WAAFs were particularly sorry to see them depart, as with them went their main source of 'joy rides'. At about this time, the award of the first DSO of the war to a member of No IX Squadron was announced; the recipient being S/Ldr D Clyde-Smith DFC. The citation recorded his determination to attack targets accurately, often from low level.

Among the recollections of the groundcrew at this time was that of H V Pride of Nottingham. He came to Waddington with No IX Squadron when they moved in from Honington. One particular occurence is firmly etched in his memory, as he recalled:

"*At the time that No IX Squadron operated from Waddington, there were no runways and the Lancasters would often take off three abreast from the wide expanse of grass. From time to time, whenever the wind was in a particular direction, the married quarters would be evacuated just in case an aircraft failed to get airborne. On one particular foggy morning, all the Station aircraft were grounded, so we groundcrew were playing cards in our home-made dispersal hut, by the side of the Sleaford Road (A15). We heard an aircraft fly over and expressed our sympathy for the crew, who were obviously trying to find an airfield clear of fog. The next we knew was our hut being tipped violently over, with a Lancaster's propellers chopping through the side wall!*"

With regard to the reference to the home-made dispersal hut; many of these were minor works of art. As Ken East recalled:

"*There were never more than three Lancasters in a hangar at any one time, for fear of air raids; ergo, our Lancasters were either in the air over unfriendly or friendly territory, or in a dispersal in, more often than not, bad weather. Because of the weather, groundcrews were driven to constructing crew shacks at the side of their particular aircraft's dispersal. These shacks were used as a shelter from the elements while awaiting instructions as to fuel load, bomb load etc, or while awaiting our aircraft's return. These shacks were a new and varied style of military architecture and were built with 'borrowed night materials', so called because the materials were 'borrowed' at night!"*

These unofficial structures would never pass a modern day fire inspection. With coal being scarce and rationed, many shacks possessed a crude but effective, if dangerous, heating system.. It consisted of a five gallon can cut in half and filled with sand. This would be sited inside the hut, while outside there would be a tank filled with waste oil and some 'scrounged' petrol (AVGAS). This fuel was fed to the stove in the hut by means of a rubber hose. The rate of flow was governed by various screw-clip devices - all in all highly dangerous! Indeed, from time to time these devices would 'blow back', resulting in injuries of varying seriousness to the occupants. Occasionally, the whole edifice would go up in flames, only to be replaced by a bigger and better specimen with the minimum of delay." (Similar devices were later to be found in the front line 'hoochies' of the Commonwealth Division in the Korean War, some ten years later!). On a different subject, I recall that just across the Sleaford Road from our shack, was a small pyramid-shaped dump of gas bombs. They were covered in camouflage netting and remained there for a long time. We never saw any form of guard or police cover, and were not aware of anyone taking care of them, though we supposed that someone looked after this particular form of frightfulness."

The month of March was to be another that was badly affected by the weather, with the second half of the month being particularly bad. However, it at least gave the aircrews some welcome relief from the strain of operations. Despite the weather, Bomber Command mounted eleven major attacks on a variety of German targets, in addition to carrying out numerous minelaying sorties. There were also three attacks on St Nazaire, the next U-boat base earmarked for destruction. Following these three attacks, the port was virtually destroyed and the unfortunate French civilian population had to be evacuated. In a report, Admiral Raeder stated that "St Nazaire and Lorient have been eliminated as main U-boat bases. No dog,, cat, or car is left in these towns; nothing remains but the pens in which the U-boats are repaired..."

According to Sir Arthur Harris, he considered the period from the Spring of 1943 until the Spring of 1944 to be his 'main offensive'. Throughout the winter, while maintaining his offensive, he concentrated on building up his force of heavy bombers and the development of new equipment and techniques. He now possessed 65 squadrons, of which 37 were operating four-engined heavy bombers. With the introduction of the blind bombing equipments such as Oboe and H2S, Harris now felt that the time was ripe for an all-out offensive against Germany, and that to get the results he required, the attacks would in the main be concentrated on the Ruhr. The Ruhr contained the highest concentration of German defence industry complexes and was well within the range of Oboe, probably the most accurate and reliable blind bombing aid available to the Command. Furthermore, all targets in this area could be attacked under cover of darkness, even during the shorter Summer nights. But, he was well aware that he could not concentrate solely on this area, as this would have inevitably led to the German High Command concentrating all their air defence forces in this area. Instead, while giving targets in the Ruhr the highest priority, the Command's aircraft continued to attack targets as far apart as Stettin on the Baltic, Turin in Italy and Pilsen in Czechoslovakia.

The first target attacked in March was Berlin or, to give it the name by which it was known to the bomber crews, 'The Big City'. The two Waddington squadrons despatched ten Lancasters apiece as part of a 302 strong force. This proved to be the heaviest raid on Berlin to date and by far the most destructive. The four-engine Lancasters and Halifaxes were now carrying heavier bomb loads, including the 8000lb high capacity blast bomb, more usually referred to as the 'Super Cookie'. Four nights later, on 5 March, Harris opened his 'Battle of the Ruhr' with a 442-strong force attacking Essen. Seventeen Lancasters from Waddington took part, all returning safely. The target was marked by Oboe equipped Mosquitos, which were backed up by PFF Lancasters, which dropped red markers and green target indicators (TIs). Hitherto, Essen had been protected by a layer of industrial haze which had prevented accurate target identification. But on this occasion, there was no requirement for the main force crews to be able to see the target; they were simply required to aim at either the red markers or the green TIs which had all been accurately placed over the Krupps armament works, located in the heart of Essen. All crews reported that the raid was well concentrated, some adding that they could still see the fires as they crossed the Dutch coast on their return journey. Subsequent reconnaissance photographs confirmed the crews' reports, showing 160 acres of destruction.

That attack on Essen was followed by another, one week later when sixteen Waddington Lancasters took part in an attack by 457 aircraft. As before, Oboe-equipped Mosquitos marked the Krupps works, which suffered 30 per cent more damage than in the earlier successful attack. Despite these gratifying successes in the Ruhr, Bomber Command had to acknowledge the fact that attacks farther afield, outside the range of Oboe, were in the main not particularly successful. During the month of March 1943, Waddington despatched a total of 243 Lancasters for the loss of six aircraft.

On 15 March, W/Cdr Southwell DFC handed over command of No IX Squadron to W/Cdr K B F Smith DSO, who commenced operating with his new command on the night of 27/28 March, when he led his squadron element of eleven aircraft in a 396 bomber attack on Berlin.

Among the crews taking part in a follow-up attack on 'The Big City' on the night of 29/30 March, was Flight Engineer, Mike Bachinski. He was flying as a member of 'Happy' Taylor's crew on their first trip as a crew. Taylor, by now P/O Taylor DFM, was back on No 44 Squadron for a second tour. Bachinski was a Canadian and, as he later recalled;

"Initially, I was on No 421 (Fighter) Squadron RCAF as a member of the groundcrew. Then the call came for volunteers from among the qualified groundcrew to train as Flight Engineers on the new heavy bombers being operated by the RAF. I volunteered and after various training courses, I crewed up with Sgt George McCready at No 1654 Heavy Conversion Unit (HCU) at Wigsley, where we undertook our conversion training. Firstly, we flew Manchesters and then moved to the Lancaster. Upon completing our course at Wigsley under the tutelage of ex-No 44 Squadron, 'Kipper' Herring, by now S/Ldr Herring, our pilots were asked to pick numbers out of a hat to decide which squadron they went to. When George picked No 44 Squadron, we all groaned. We had heard of this squadron and its reputation as having the greatest number of casualties in the Group, mainly because they had been one of the first squadrons to try out the new bomber on a daylight raid, with disasterous results.

Soon after our arrival at Waddington we were put through the preparation phase for operations, during which George McCready was assigned to Sgt Elgar's crew as a second dickie to gain the necessary experience. Even before he went up for a night flying test with this crew, George had a premonition that things were not going to work out and that he was not going to make it. He even went so far as to give us some of his personal belongings to hold in case his feelings proved to be accurate. We tried to cheer him up and reminded him that he would be flying with an experienced crew. That evening, I went into Lincoln to the cinema and while there I heard and felt a big 'bang'. My first thought was that enemy intruders were having a go at Waddington, but nobody in the cinema seemed concerned and there was no air raid siren, so I settled down to enjoy the film and forgot all about it. Upon my return to base, I noticed the gloomy looks on the faces of the rest of the crew, but before I could ask what was the trouble, they told me that George had died in a mid-air collision between a Lancaster of No IX Squadron and that of F/Sgt Elgar and crew.

We discussed our situation and decided that the rest of us would try to stay together as a crew, since we worked well together. We approached our Flight Commander and asked if we could get another pilot. He said that there were some Rhodesian pilots coming in for a second tour and that he might be able to set us up with one of them. The next day I was detailed as a 'spare bod' to replace a sick flight engineer from another crew. My crew did not like this idea, so I went to our Flight Commander again. He convinced me that the crew I would be flying with had already done nineteen trips and that it would be good experience for me. He added that it would also put me one up on the rest of my own crew. This last point appealed to me and I duly flew to Munich on 21 December 1942 with Sgt Shattock and his crew. Two weeks later, P/O Shattock and crew failed to return from another attack on Munich!

In due course our new pilot arrived; S/Ldr John Nettleton VC. After he had interviewed each of us, he accepted us as his crew. Our first operational trip as a crew with Nettleton was on 16 January, when we went to Berlin. In all, we flew five operations with John Nettleton, but he was then promoted to W/Cdr and became OC Operations, and as such had little use for a crew of his own. Our next pilot also came from southern Africa, and like Nettleton, had returned to No 44 Squadron for his second tour. As a crew we were delighted to have another experienced 'skipper'. P/O 'Happy' Taylor was outwardly an easy-going character, but his DFM was evidence that he knew what he was doing where operational flying was concerned. On every return from operations with 'Happy' we made a point of flying low(ish) over Lincoln cathedral to give thanks for our safe return and to also let the girls in the nearby cafe know that we were back!"

Despite the fact that April, with its shorter nights, made attacks on distant targets even more hazardous, Bomber Command took the opportunity of the slightly better weather to attack targets as far apart as La Spezia in Italy (twice), Stettin on the Baltic and Pilsen in Czechoslovakia. In addition, the Ruhr and other German targets were attacked, that on Kiel on the night of 4/5 April being the heaviest non-1,000 bomber raid mounted since the war began. A mixed force of 577 aircraft took part, 21 of them from Waddington, all of which returned safely to base. For No IX Squadron, the attack on Kiel without loss was to prove to be an exception. The month of April was to be a bad one for the squadron as, in all that month, they were to lose a total of nine aircraft on operations and one on a training flight, when one of its Lancasters crashed near Mildenhall airfield. Among their casualties that month was the recently arrived Squadron Commander, W/Cdr Smith, who was lost during an attack on Frankfurt on 10/11 April. His aircraft, WS-R (ED501) crashed near Mainz in Germany. All seven of the crew now lie in the Rheinberg War Cemetery.

P/O Eric Dudley, an air gunner flying with S/Ldr Whitehead DFC, a Flight Commander on No 44 Squadron, recorded in his scrap book, that during an attack on Berlin at around this time, they carried a Major S Bartlett of the United States Army Air Corps. Dudley added that the American must have been the first of his countrymen to bomb Berlin. As a footnote, he included the comment that the trip "...was a shaky do, with lots of flak and searchlights…" and that they had to return on 2.5 engines! On his safe return to London, Bartlett gave a press conference accompanied by his wife, the film actress Helen Drew. After the war, Bartlett was to co-write the aviation classic 'Twelve O'Clock High', which was made into a highly successful film. Bartlett himself went on to become a successful Hollywood film producer.

April was to be the last month that No IX Squadron was to operate from Waddington. The construction of numerous wartime satellite aerodromes, now more commonly referred to as 'airfields' (an American importation), had resulted in RAF Waddington being allocated two satellite airfields, namely Bardney and Skellingthorpe. RAF Skellingthorpe had in fact been an unofficial satellite of Waddington since it opened in October 1941. One month later it had become the home of No 50 Squadron. RAF Bardney was declared to be ready on 4 April 1943 and the advance party of No IX Squadron arrived there three days later. They were soon joined by their new squadron commander, W/Cdr P Burnett. The new Commanding Officer had been posted in from Headquarters No 5 Group at very short notice. On their departure from Waddington, No IX Squadron took with them their unofficial Battle Honours board. This board incorporated the squadron crest and a list of a targets attacked since its days as a Wellington squadron. Included on the board was the unofficial squadron motto, which had been coined by the then Commanding Officer, S/Ldr P C Pickard (hero of the propaganda film 'Target For Tonight' and later, for the low level attack by Mosquitos on Amiens Prison). The motto reads 'There's Always Bloody Something'. This board remains in the possession of the squadron to this day.

Following the first of the two attacks on La Spezia on 13/14 April, the returning aircraft of No IX Squadron landed at Bardney, most of the non operating aircrew and the groundcrew having moved across that morning. Their feelings on having exchanged the relative comfort of a pre-war station for the spartan conditions to be found on a wartime satellite airfield, can only be imagined. The squadron was given only 24 hours to become operational at Bardney, such was the pace of operations. On landing at Bardney at around 0630hr in the morning of 14 April, the crews were met by their groundcrews, who had seen them off from Waddington the night before. By dint of very hard work on the part of all concerned, the squadron produced the required five aircraft for the attack on Stuttgart on the night of 14/15 April.

Among all the comings and goings at Waddington in April, was the arrival of the new Station Commander, Gp Capt S C Elworthy DSO DFC AFC. 'Sam' Elworthy, a qualified barrister, had a distinguished war record flying Blenheim IVs as both Flight Commander and Squadron Commander of No 82 Squadron from August 1940 until May 1941. An outspoken man, on being posted to Headquarters No 2 Group, he took issue with his AOC on what he (Elworthy) saw as senseless losses. Following his subsequent posting to HQ Bomber Command, he played a part in the planning and execution of the first 1000 bomber raid. He would eventually retire from the RAF as Chief of the Defence Staff, and was to be the first RAF Officer to be elevated to the peerage since the end of the war.

Included among the Station Commander's personal staff was the Station Adjutant, F/Lt Henry Locke. 'Lockie' had arrived at Waddington as the Squadron Adjutant of No 44 Squadron, but had been moved to the Station post on the arrival of Gp Capt Lewis. He was to remain at Waddington until well after VE Day, eventually leaving to become a schoolmaster and deputy head of Rutlish Grammar School in Wimbledon. Among his latter-day pupils was the author, one who was to become a bishop, and the future Prime Minister, John Major. In January 1945, Henry Locke wrote the first draft of the recommendation by Air Commodore Hesketh, for the award of the Victoria Cross to F/Sgt George Thompson of No IX Squadron. In conversation with the author, Henry Locke said that he had hoped to remain in the RAF at the end of the war, but was considered too old to be offered anything other than a short term engagement - the RAF's loss, many schoolboys' gain.

It was at around this time that a second ground defence squadron of the RAF Regiment, No 2956 Squadron, was formed at Waddington.

Duisburg was fast becoming one of the most heavily bombed towns in Germany. It had been attacked towards the end of March and was to suffer three attacks in April and another in May. The attack on the night of 8/9 April is well remembered by the crew of F/O Pilgrim's aircraft KM-V (ED433). As Pilgrim recalled:

"*…that morning we returned from a fighter affiliation sortie to find that we were on 'Ops' that night. The forecast was for ten tenths cloud out and back and we were briefed to bomb on the PFF markers. As we approached the target, we were suddenly enveloped in a flash of blinding white light; a nearby aircraft with a full bomb load and considerable fuel had bought it in an instant, and seven young men had been vapourised. I immediately became aware that I no longer had control of our aircraft. The gyros had all toppled, leaving me with nothing but the basic pressure instruments. Nevertheless, it quickly became apparent that we were upside down, for I found myself hanging in the seat straps, while Jack Skilton, the Flt Eng, was in a ball in the roof! I began to pull back on the control column, planning to carry out a half loop, painfully aware as I did so that such a manoeuvre under power and with a full bomb load, ran the risk of overstressing the airframe to such an extent that our aircraft could either break up or, at best,* *mean our having to bail out. I called to Jack to close the throttles, totally overlooking the impossibility of such a task from his present position. Simultaneously, an anxious gunner shouted out for me to drop the bombs, to which I replied with some feeling "How can I, they are on the roof?" As we bottomed out of the half loop, Jack Skilton fell to the floor. He immediately reached for the throttles and reduced power, but by then, we were climbing rapidly towards completing the rest of the loop. I now called for the extra power demanded by our changed circumstances, but again this was none too easy for the engineer as he was on his way back to the roof! Fortunately, he managed to hang on to the throttles and I got the necessary power to complete the manoeuvre."*[4]

Understandably, at night with a limited instrument panel, our recovery to something approaching normal flight was preceeded by a few unsteady turns, dives and climbs. Eventually, we settled down and I took stock prior to deciding on our next course of action. Although these events had taken but a minute or two, to me it seemed like an eternity. Fortunately, I had been actively engaged throughout, but my crew had been forced into the position of helpless spectators, and to this day I am both surprised and relieved that they did not bail out at the first opportunity. We were obviously damaged, although I did not know to what extent. The options open to us were to turn immediately for home or to continue to the target. I chose the latter, as a solo transit home was a dubious proposition at the best of times; in a damaged aircraft that was unable to evade, it would have been suicide. In any case, my gunners were unable to fire their guns as the contents of the ammunition boxes and feed channels were distributed throughout the fuselage, as indeed were the contents of the Elsan! To make matters worse, the navigator's charts and instruments were nowhere to be found, so he was unable to calculate any new route home.

As a result of our experiences, our Lancaster flew somewhat uncertainly, especially with the bomb doors open, and at a much slower speed than normal. We had decided to continue with the operation, but our bombing run was extremely difficult, and the subsequent bombing probably not as accurate (sic) as we would have wished. Later, our arrival back at base could best be described as 'an arrival' rather than a landing." (Note. Lancaster KM-V, ED433 was withdrawn from service, pending repairs. It eventually returned to complete a few more operations before being lost over Kassel on 3 October 1943).

Another crew that had good reason to remember April 1943, was that of 'Happy' Taylor. As previously mentioned, Taylor had returned to his old squadron for a second tour, though he nearly did not make it. He might just as easily have gone to join the newly forming No 617 Squadron. As Taylor recalled:

"I was on the staff of No 1485 Bombing and Gunnery Flight at RAF Fulbeck when W/Cdr Gibson called in to recruit aircrew that had completed a tour of operations. He said that he wanted 'old hands' for a new squadron that he was forming; later to be allocated the number 617 Squadron. Being Rhodesian and knowing that there were very few of us left on my old squadron of that name, I told W/Cdr Gibson that if No 44 (Rhodesia) Squadron was unable to take me direct, without my having to go through an OTU, I would be prepared to join his squadron. To my surprise, he accepted this proviso without a murmur. Accordingly, I visited Waddington and had an interview with OC Operations, W/Cdr Nettleton VC, who informed me that there was a crew (his) without a pilot and that he would arrange for my transfer forthwith. So began my second tour with No 44 (Rhodesia) Squadron.

On the night of 20 April, our target was Stettin. As far as we were concerned, it was quite an easy target. The attack was to consist of approximately four hundred aircraft, with the bomber stream passing over the target inside 20 minutes. As usual, the poor old Stirlings took off from their bases first, followed by the Halifaxes and then the Lancasters. it was a moonlit night and the plan called for us to fly at low level across the North Sea and Denmark before climbing to our operational height over the Baltic. All went well, and as we flew across Denmark, the local people flashed 'V' for Victory with their lights. Following a successful bombing run, we set heading for Denmark on the return leg. Over Denmark I spotted a Halifax on our port side, weaving madly, though why he was doing so I couldn't imagine, as we were far too low for the defences to have a go at him. As I was not weaving, we were slowly overtaking him; so as we got closer, I kept my eyes on him for any unexpected manoeuvre. Suddenly, at the same instant that I heard a shout from my flight engineer, Mike Bachinski, I felt our aircraft shudder. Looking ahead, I saw the giant single tail fin of a Stirling right in front of me. I pulled hard on the control column, but failed to avoid striking the Stirling's tail. Our Lancaster rode up the Stirling's fin and we were extremely lucky that our engines were not flooded with foam as the Graviner switch indicators flickered. I called to the rear gunner to see if the Stirling went down. He reported that he had seen it pass underneath us, but that he had observed no signs of a crash. I called for an examination of our aircraft, and it transpired that we had an elongated tear in the port side of the nose and the bomb doors were badly buckled. The cockpit had filled with smoke or dust and the blast of air through the aircraft blew away the navigator's log and chart. We stuffed the hole in the nose with our Mae West lifejackets and flew home, albeit somewhat slower than the main stream. By coincidence, when we eventually arrived back at Waddington, the press were in attendance and made the most of our collision report. We

[4] All this went on in pitch dark in the middle of the bomber stream of some 392 aircraft while being engaged by flak!

subsequently read headlines in the morning press such as - 'Aircraft so thick en-route that two collided etc etc'. We later flew over to Newmarket airfield and met the crew of the Stirling and heard the saga of their return flight".

'Happy' Taylor and his crew had an eventful tour, not all of it as a result of enemy action. During the early stages of the arrival of the American Eighth Air Force bomber crews, some of their pilots came to Waddington to see for themselves how a front line bomber squadron operated. One of the American pilots volunteered to fly with the Taylor crew in an attack on a Ruhr target; an experience that left him quietly thoughtful! On another occasion, Taylor and crew carried the captain of a Royal Navy mine-laying submarine on a mine laying sortie to the entrance to the Kiel Canal. As Taylor later recalled: "*We dropped our six mines, and the 'naval bod' seemed suitably impressed*". After the post-flight debriefing, the submarine Captain invited 'Happy' to join him on a three week minelaying sortie into the Baltic; an offer which was gracefully declined with regrets!

Among other visitors to Waddington around this time was a party of Russian Air Force officers. They too had come to see how an RAF bomber station operated. To again quote 'Happy' Taylor:

"*...on one occasion after the briefing, a signal came in cancelling the attack because of a change in the weather. To the surprise and obvious displeasure of our Russian visitors, it was apparent that the crews were delighted with the cancellation and rushed off to their various messes or into town. As far as we were concerned, it meant that we would live another day and were determined to make the most of it. We felt that our performance did little to enhance Soviet/RAF relations, though they obviously did appreciate the fact that, despite our patriotic shortcomings, we did an efficient job of bombing the Germans in their homeland, something they (the Russians) were unable to achieve*".

Towards the end of the month, on the night of 29/30 April, Bomber Command despatched a total of 207 aircraft on minelaying sorties. This represented the largest single concentration of airborne minelayers to date, with a total of 593 mines laid off the North German coast. The force however, paid a heavy price, with 22 aircraft being lost (10.6%). The cause of such heavy losses on what was considered to be a relatively safe task, was low cloud over the German and Danish coasts. This forced the minelayers to fly low when determining their position before laying their mines. This requirement to fly low enabled the German coastal light flak units and those aboard flak ships, to engage the minelaying bombers. Five of the minelayers came from Waddington, one of which was flown by F/O Rail, who reported: "...starboard wing tip damaged by hitting the sea while taking evasive action from flak...".

An indication of the crews' attitude to minelaying can be gained from the recollections of F/O Pilgrim of No 44 Squadron:

"When I first joined the squadron, minelaying or Gardening sorties were mounted whenever the weather precluded Main Force bombing operations. Consequently, minelaying was not too popular as it interfered with 'nights off'. The mines had to be laid accurately; not only to be effective but also to safeguard operations by our own ships and submarines. A minelaying sortie required a night descent, often in murky conditions, down to low level in order to pick up a visual reference point. From this visual reference point, a time and distance run was made to the dropping point. With our primitive navigation aids at low level, mostly dead reckoning, even locating the visual reference point could involve the crew in a square search (in enemy territory!). This activity carried the associated risk of encountering a flak ship which had been strategically placed to engage such missions. The whole business could indeed be most hazardous. Towards the end of my tour (September 1943), our navigation aids had improved to the extent that mines could be accurately placed from heights of around 10,000 feet. This made a considerable difference and virtually relegated minelaying to 'Freshman' operations."

During the early days of May, all the talk at Waddington concerned the imminent closure of the Station and the move of No 44 Squadron to nearby RAF Dunholme Lodge. Bomber Command had long since commenced a programme of runway and dispersal building on all its operational airfields, as the increased size and weight of the four-engined heavy bombers made grass airfields no longer viable. The plan for Waddington involved the demolition of the existing World War I hangars on the south side of the airfield. Compulsory purchase orders had been served for the acquisition of land to both the north and the south of the existing complex, in order to facilitate the construction of three runways and a weapons storage facility (bomb dump). The main northeast/southwest runway was to be 2000 yards long, with the other two runways being 1500 yards in length, aligned along the axes 350/170 and 250/070. The old Mere Road (B1178), alongside which had been sited the old southern hangar complex,, had served as the southern boundary of the aerodrome since its inception. This road was to be permanently closed to the public for the duration (or longer if necessary). In addition to the extensions to the north and south, land to the east of the A15 road had been also taken over to provide an additional fifteen aircraft dispersals.

Despite the pending closure of the Station, operations continued throughout the month of May, though the weather resulted in the Station being able to operate on only seven nights. The Ruhr was still the centre of attention for Bomber Command, and six attacks were mounted against various towns and cities in this area. The one exception was the attack on Pilsen. This attack was possibly mounted to demonstrate to the German High Command that the attackers could be expected anywhere within the borders of its territory. During the course of the seven operations carried out during May, the Station mounted 98 sorties for the loss of five aircraft and crews. Most of the attacks evidenced the fact that with better aids and a more experienced PFF, the Main Force was capable of causing severe damage to virtually any target that it attacked. In particular, the last operation of the month; that against Wuppertal on the night of 29/30 May, caused what was probably the phenomenon known as a 'firestorm', albeit rather smaller than that which was to engulf Hamburg in the near future.

At about the same time that No 44 squadron was scheduled to move to Dunholme Lodge, plans were in hand to move Headquarters No 5 Group from its pre-war location at St Vincent's in Grantham, to Moreton Hall near Swinderby. The actual move eventually took place on 24 October 1943 when the Group Headquarters moved into RAF Swinderby itself. The reason for the sudden change was the requirement to find a suitable location for the Headquarters of the recently arrived Ninth Troop Carrier Command of the USAAC, who in due course took up residence at Moreton Hall.

On a humanitarian note, two Lancasters from Waddington were despatched to search for the crews of two American B17 Flying Fortresses, which had been reported as having ditched in the North Sea. Many hours later, the two Lancaster crews returned having found nothing. Fortunately, not all contacts with the Fortresses of the USAAC were as unfortunate. As one member of No 44 Squadron recalled:

"...during a daylight air test, an American Fortress appeared out to starboard and formated on us. After an exchange of waves, the American pilot feathered an engine and stared pointedly at us. When we followed suit, he promptly feathered a second engine. In reply, our pilot, Frank Phillips, feathered two more engines, maintaining position on the one remaining engine. At that our American friend called it quits, waved and restarted his engines. As he pulled away he gave a wing-waggle, leaving us quite elated, both with our piece of one-upmanship and with the performance of our Lancaster".

The Americans were not the only ones to be impressed with the Lancaster's performance. It had come as an unpleasant surprise to the German fighter pilots. By mid 1943, Bomber Command had been operating the Lancaster for almost eighteen months. In that time, the Command had built up a wealth of experience on the new bomber. From this experience, most of it gained in combat, evolved the Command's classic evasive manoeuvre for countering an attack by a night fighter. Known as the 'corkscrew', it combined the components of rapidly changing speed, altitude and direction, while at the same time, giving the bombers' gunners the best opportunity to engage the fighter, outgunned though they were. This remarkable evasive manoeuvre resulted in at least one very experienced and high scoring German night fighter pilot advising his novice pilots, to "...break off and leave it alone...go and look for a less capable crew..."

As far back as December 1942, Bomber Command proposed making changes to the Command structure; these changes being officially approved in March 1943, with the first coming into effect in June that year. From the beginning of the war, Headquarters Bomber Command had controlled the bomber offensive from its underground command post near High Wycombe in Buckinghamshire. The Headquarters' requirements regarding the target, number of aircraft, bomb loads, take off times, route and altitude, were all relayed to its stations and squadrons through their respective Group Headquarters. Each station was responsible for the provision of airfield facilities, maintenance, accommodation and other support services for its resident squadron(s), with each squadron functioning as a semi-autonomous unit, with its own servicing and administration elements. While the system worked well, it was very labour intensive, a commodity in increasingly short supply. To reduce the manpower requirements and to streamline the overall organisational structure, Bomber Command introduced the operational 'Bomber Base' system.

A 'Base' was to comprise a Base or Parent Station, with one or more satellite stations. In most instances, the Base Station would be one of the better equipped pre-war permanent airfields, from which the base would take its name. The smaller, less well equipped satellites were, in the main, the hastily constructed temporary airfields, scattered throughout Lincolnshire and East Yorkshire. The Base Station would house one or two bomber squadrons, as would the satellites. However, Station Headquarters on the main station would assume full responsibility for the aircraft maintenance and administration of all base and satellite squadrons. To facilitate this, a central maintenance facility was to be established on the main base to provide engineering support to all the operational squadrons. The consequent reduction in manpower establishments meant that squadron strengths were reduced to aircrew, plus a small cadre of ground staff to carry out daily servicing and any operational duties. With the main station taking over responsibility for the major servicing of all aircraft, it was provided with additional technical facilities and, in some cases, additional hangars.

In September 1943, Bomber Command issued a directive that the new 'Bases' were to be identified by a number, not the previously accepted geographical location. This number was to be a two figure combination; the first number of which would serve to identify the Group. The second number being peculiar to the

Base itself. Thus, RAF Waddington became known as No 53 Base; ie., Number Three Base of Number Five Group. No 53 Base came into being officially on 15 November 1943 and consisted of the Headquarters and Base Station of RAF Waddington, plus the two satellites or sub-stations of Bardney and Skellingthorpe. RAF Waddington continued to be comanded by a Group Captain (Gp Capt Elworthy), while No 53 Base as a whole came under the command of Air Commodore A Hesketh OBE DFC. When at full strength, No 53 Base would eventually operate five operational squadrons. RAF Waddington was to become the home of two Australian squadrons, Nos 463 and 467 Squadrons RAAF, while Bardney was the home of No IX Squadron and Skellingthorpe that of Nos 50 and 61 Squadrons. Between them, these squadrons were capable of putting 100 Lancasters in the air on operations when called for by HQ Bomber Command.

The new system worked well and achieved the aim of reducing the manpower requirement, but it did give rise to some administrative problems from time to time, as recalled by the Base Adjutant, F/Lt Henry Locke:

"...aircrew had a room in their repective Mess, but were required to sleep off camp at night. Non aircrew were readily granted permission, even encouraged, to live off base; in which case they had no room in their Mess or barrack block, but were still entitled to take meals in the Mess. The point to remember is that Bomber Command was essentially a night bomber force, so that when they returned from an operation, and after debriefing, they would sleep in their allocated billet. But, of course, many spent the night where they had spent the evening whenever not on operations - with their girl friends! This could sometimes lead to chaos whenever crews went missing. Their next-of-kin expected to receive their personal belongings; but if they (the belongings) were with the girl friend, we would be unable to find them as we did not keep a record of girl friends!"

After a series of parties, Waddington said a last goodbye to No 44 (Rhodesia) Squadron on 31 May 1943, when the aircraft and crews flew across to Dunholme Lodge. The groundcrew moved out by road, apart from the lucky few who managed to scrounge a flight in 'their aircraft'. The night before their departure, an impromptu, but nevertheless enormous party developed in the aircrew Sergeants' Mess. It started out as simply a farewell, but soon developed into a 'lets drink the bar dry' party. As Sgt Palmer recalled:

"...we just had to drink it... we had the assistance of the entire Officers' Mess, the groundcrew Sergeants' Mess, most of the WAAFs and a good many Corporals and Airmen as well. Some not very brilliant landings were made at Dunholme Lodge the next day and the R/T procedure was highly unorthodox to say the least, but all the aircraft got down in one piece."

The last two aircraft to take off from Waddington that day were flown by F/Lt Pilgrim and a Canadian F/Sgt Cliff Shnier. Acting in accordance with an obviously pre-arranged plan, the two Lancasters were seen to join up and turn towards the airfield. Side by side the two huge bombers flew across the airfield at virtually zero feet, heading straight for the Watch Tower, pulling up steeply at only the last moment, breaking to left and right. Two months later, newly commissioned P/O Shnier, then of No 97 Squadron PFF, was reported missing in an attack on Hamburg.

With the departure of the Station's aircraft, Waddington quickly presented a forlorn appearance. Vast heaps of earth appeared, trenches were dug and tons of concrete were laid as the contractors constructed three runways and numerous dispersals. It was at this time that the old World War I hangars beside Mere Road were finally demolished. During this major construction project, the decoy sites at Potter Hanworth, Branston Fen and Gautby were dismantled and abandoned.

During the five months that the airfield was non-operational, Bomber Command maintained its offensive. In June, Dusseldorf experienced its heaviest air raid when 783 bombers carried out an accurate attack. That same month, aircraft of the Command undertook the first 'shuttle' raid when, following an attack on Friedrichshaven, the force flew on south and landed at Blida in Algeria. After a one day break, most of the force flew back to their bases in England, attacking the Italian naval base at La Spezia on the way. In early July, the national press carried the report of the death of General Sikorski, the head of the Polish Government in Exile in London. He was killed when the Liberator he was flying in as a passenger, crashed on take-off from Gibraltar. The co-pilot of the Liberator, who also perished in the crash, was S/Ldr 'Kipper' Herring, who had earned the award of an immediate DSO when he brought a No 207 Squadron Manchester back from Berlin on one engine on 7 September 1941.

On 24 July, Bomber Command launched 'Operation Gomorrah' against Hamburg, when a force of 791 aircraft dropped 2284 tons of bombs in 50 minutes.

Window was used for the first time, causing insoluble problems for the German radar operators on the ground and those in the night fighters. During the next ten nights, Bomber Command attacked Hamburg on four of them. Aircraft of the Command flew a total of 3,091 sorties, dropping nearly 10,000 tons of bombs. Apart from the actual bomb damage, the unfortunate city was to experience a major firestorm, which was caused when numerous individual fires joined up, becoming one huge conflagration which drew air into it with storm force.

As a result of considerable intelligence activity, Bomber Command was ordered to mount an attack on the German 'V' weapon research establishment at Peenemunde on the Blatic coast on the night of 17/18

August. For the first time, a major attack was controlled by a 'Master Bomber', who kept up a controlling commentary throughout the attack. The planners had deliberately chosen a moonlit night in order to make it easier for the crews to find the target. It was accepted that this would also make the enemy night fighters' task easier, but the urgency of the situation overuled safety considerations. The attackers lost 40 out of the 596 aircraft taking part (6.7%), but the attack was a success and it put the German 'V' weapons programme back by at least six months. Another first that night was the use by the Luftwaffe night fighters of their new 'Schrage Musik' weapon. This was a twin upward-firing pair of 20mm cannon, installed in the rear cockpit of the Bf110s. These twin cannon were set to fire upwards and forwards at an angle of between 10 to 20 degrees from the vertical. For sighting, the pilot used a reflector gun sight mounted in the canopy roof above his head. This installation enabled the night fighters to attack the bombers from behind and below, in what was virtually the bombers' blind spot. As the guns were not loaded with tracer, the first that the unfortunate victim knew of an attack, was as the shells exploded in their aircraft. It has to be said that British intelligence was slow to accept that the Germans were employing a new type of weapon, even though such an installation had been employed by the RFC/RAF in the Sopwith Dolphin on the Western Front towards the end of World War I. It was not to be until early 1944 that close examination of some damaged bombers which had made it back home, convinced higher authority that the Luftwaffe had some sort of upwards firing weapon. In the main, it was the Australians and the Canadians who made use of the ventral gun position in their bombers to provide some sort of counter to the 'Schrage Musik' threat.

On the night of 3/4 September, Bomber Command carried out its third attack on Berlin in eleven nights. In all, a total of 1,665 sorties had been mounted against 'The Big City' in the course of these attacks, for the loss of 125 aircraft (7.5%). However, this was not part of an all-out assault on Berlin; that was to commence in November and continue through to the end of March 1944.

On 8 September it was announced that Italy had surrendered all its forces. The next day, Allied forces carried out a successful amphibious assault at Salerno, south of Naples. Five weeks later, the new Italian government declared war on Germany.

As part of the developing air war, the RAF night bombing offensive was enhanced by the formation of No 100 Group. This unit's role was to be that of radio countermeasures. Among its first operations in support of the Main Force, was Operation Corona. This involved broadcasting German language transmissions on the night fighter frequencies. In time, this activity was to be developed, culminating in the use of German-speaking operators being carried by selected squadrons. These 'ghost' controllers would carry out lengthy test transmissions, issue conflicting instructions, read heavy passages from various German philosophers and even play records of Hitler's speeches.

Work on Waddington's runways was completed in October and, on 11 November, advance elements of No 467 Squadron Royal Australian Air Force (RAAF), moved in from Bottesford near Nottingham. The crews of No 44 Squadron had been looking forward to returning to Waddington and were not particularly happy to hear that they were to remain in the quagmire that was RAF Dunholme Lodge. As one of the disgruntled aircrew recorded: *"The top brass knew what it was doing. If they had sent the Aussies to the Dunholme swamp, they would have given them more troubles than the Germans"*.

The arrival of the Australians at Waddington coincided with the start of what was to be called 'The Battle of Berlin'. Despite the losses, Bomber Command had continued to grow throughout 1943. Most of the obsolete twin-engined bombers had been replaced by the more powerful four-engined 'heavies', though a few Wellingtons had remained in front-line service until October 1943. This improvement in capability was coincident with the improvement in navigation aids and electronic defence systems, though unfortunately not in bomber defensive armament. The Command's crews were to soldier on with the outdated and outmoded 0.303" machine guns, due in the main to political intransigence, despite their Commander in Chief's efforts to get them the harder hitting 0.5" machine gun, as used by the Americans.

During 1943, Harris had conducted two major battles within the overall bombing campaign. The first was the 'Battle of the Ruhr', which ran from March to July; the second being the 'Battle of Hamburg' which, though of shorter duration than that of the Ruhr battle, was far more concentrated. By November 1943, Bomber Command possessed a total of 65 four-engined bomber squadrons, divided between six Groups. 33 of these squadrons were equipped with the Lancaster, 22 with the Halifax, nine with Stirlings and one in process of replacing its Stirlings with Lancasters. These were the aircraft and squadrons that would fight the the next 'Battle', the 'Battle of Berlin'. However, as the battle progressed, it became evident that the inferior performance of the Stirlings and Halifaxes was giving rise to an unacceptable loss rate. Consequently, the Lancaster squadrons were to bear the brunt of the battle and the losses.

The Battle of Berlin commenced on the night of 18/19 November. Despite horrendous losses, it was to continue until the night of 24/25 March 1944. By the end of the battle, Bomber Command had mounted 9,112 sorties against the German capital for the loss of 495 aircraft; a loss rate of 5.4%. In all, the Command's aircraft had dropped a total of 30,000 tons of bombs and incendiaries on and around the city.

In a minute to the Prime Minister, Harris wrote: "We can wreck Berlin from end to end if the Americans will come in on it. It will cost between 400-500 aircraft; it will cost Germany the war". In the event, the Commanders of the American Eighth Air Force (8th AF) declined to play a major part in the assault on Berlin. Their argument was that their crews were not trained to operate at night, and that their heavy losses on the Schweinfurt/Regensburg raids had demonstrated all too clearly that deep penetration raids into the heart of Germany were prohibitively expensive. This was to remain the position until the arrival of the Merlin-engined version of the North American P51 Mustang fighter, which could escort the bombers of the 8th AF all the way to Berlin and back.

Although the period between November 1943 and March 1944 came to be known within the Command as 'The Battle of Berlin', the heavy raids carried out by Bomber Command were not confined to 'The Big City' alone. Aircraft of the Command attacked the German capital on sixteen occasions during the course of the battle, but during the same period, they carried out nineteen other major attacks, plus numerous small scale raids. All this being in addition to the on-going minelaying programme.

The Australian Era Begins

The relative peace and quiet that had reigned at Waddington for about five months ended on 13 November 1943, when the Lancasters of No 467 Squadron RAAF arrived from Bottesford, under the command of W/Cdr J R Balmer OBE DFC. 'Josh' Balmer had already gained a reputation as an offensively-minded airman. In 1942, he was in command of No 100 Bomber Squadron RAAF, equipped with Bristol Beaufort torpedo bombers, based at Milne Bay. It was while under his command, that No 100 Squadron took part in the first defeat of the Japanese forces in New Guinea. Indicative of his attitude was the notice fixed above the door to his office - 'Abandon Hope All Ye That Enter Here'.

The Australian Lancasters and their crews had been preceeded by elements of their groundcrews. Among the earliest arrivals were two armourers who were tasked with carrying out modifications to incendiary cans. These two, LACs 'Slim' Applebee and Hodson, arrived at their new station perched atop a load of incendiary cans in the back of a three ton lorry. Slim Applebee recalled being frozen stiff on an extremely cold winter's day, but still feeling glad to have said goodbye to Bottesford. The Leicestershire aerodrome was a wartime airfield, with pre-fabrictaed T2 hangars, Maycrete administration buildings and Nissen huts for accommodation. To Slim and his 'mates', Waddington was untold luxury, with its central heating, large hangars, a NAAFI, and barrack blocks with the baths and showers inside. Gone were the days of a quick sprint from the Nissen hut to the ablutions block to wash and shave, mostly in cold water. The Waddington pre-war barrack rooms contained double-banked iron beds and could accommodate up to 40 airmen in each room which, while resulting in considerable overcrowding, was still considered by the new occupants, a vast improvement on uninsulated Nissen huts. As F/O Jack Wainwright (later to become S/Ldr DSO) put it: "*...at least from Waddington one could fight a gentlemen's war...*"

Just over one week after No 467 Squadron moved into Waddington, 'C' Flight, under the command of F/Lt H B Lock DFC, was hived off to form 'A' Flight of the new 463 Squadron RAAF, temporarily under the command of newly promoted S/Ldr H B Lock DFC. He and his crew had already flown 26 operations and very soon completed their tour. On 11 March, S/Ldr H B Lock DSO DFC and his crew left the Station to join No 97 Squadron PFF.

No 463 Squadron's first Commanding Officer was the recently promoted W/Cdr R Kingsford-Smith, who had originally been posted from Australia to join No 10 Squadron RAAF, flying Short Sunderlands in Coastal Command. However, in true Service fashion, the 'its all been changed' syndrome meant that instead, he would go to Bomber Command. 'Rollo' Kingsford-Smith was a nephew of the famous Australian aviator Sir Charles Kingsford-Smith.

Among the aircrews flying into Waddington from Bottesford, was that of P/O McClelland, flying in Lancaster PO-S (R5868). Much has been written about this particular Lancaster, which now resides in the RAF Museum at Hendon. Its operations tally of 137 made it one of the two top scoring Lancasters in Bomber Command. Though it became something of a Public Relations man's property, it was not always particularly well regarded by some of its crews. Warrant Officer Steve Bethell, the mid upper gunner in McClelland's crew, recalled the crew's feelings following their air testing PO-S on its maiden flight on No 467 Squadron on 14 September 1943. They assessed the aircraft as being 'clapped out'. Further reference to the squadron's Operations record Book (ORB) ellicits the following comments:

28 September '43. P/O Finch - "Recommend that after 78 Ops, this aircraft is unreliable for operations".

18n October '43 Anon - "This aircraft is only fit for a Conversion Unit".

Despite the above comments, PO-S (R5868) was to survive 59 further operations, during one of which it collided with another Lancaster over Berlin! It is now the pride and joy of the RAF Museum, having been lovingly restored by Mr Ted Willoughby who, as LAC Willoughby, flew into Waddington aboard 'his' aircraft on 13 November 1943.

One week after moving to Waddington, No 467 Squadron despatched 20 aircraft as part of a 440 strong force of Lancasters attacking Berlin on the night of 18/19 November; the Battle of Berlin had started! Waddington had actually produced 21 Lancasters for this attack, but during pre-flight preparations, Len Durham and crew of No 50 Squadron, found that their aircraft was unserviceable. As No 467 Squadron had more aircraft than crews at the time, Durham and crew were rushed from Skellingthorpe to Waddington to fly a spare aircraft. They were late taking off and had been told that if they could not make up for the time lost, they were to return and not fly as a straggler behind the Main Force. They never did catch up, but elected to press on regardless, completing an incident-free, successful trip.

Four nights later, the target was again Berlin, with No 467 Squadron providing sixteen out of the mixed force of 764 bombers. Unfortunately, one of the Waddington Lancasters did not leave the airfield. That flown by F/Sgt Schomberg and crew suffered engine failure at a critical stage in the take-off run, swung off the runway and crashed into a partially completed building. The crew suffered minor injuries, while bombs and incendiaries were scattered around the wreck; many of the latter burning. The nearby barrack blocks were evacuated while the Squadron Armament Officer, P/O Fishburn, defused the 4000lb Cookie, which was resting among the burning incendiaries. The next night, that of 23/24 November, it was back to Berlin, when Waddington despatched another sixteen Lancasters as part of the mixed force of 383 bombers. In less than one week, No 467 Squadron had despatched a total of 52 Lancasters without loss, whereas the Command as a whole had lost 55 aircraft. Writing of the 23/24 November attack in his diary, Hitler's henchman Joseph Goebbels wrote: *"I just cannot understand how the English are able to do so much damage to the Reich's capital during one raid. The picture that greeted my eye in the Wilhelmplatz was one of utter desolation, blazing fires everywhere..."*

Obviously the Station's luck could not last; finally running out on the night of 26/27 November. This was the occasion of the fourth attack on Berlin. A total of 443 Lancasters, together with seven Mosquitos, took part in the attack, which included fourteen Lancasters from No 467 Squadron and six from No 463 Squadron. The attacking force lost 28 Lancasters, one of them being that flown by F/Sgt Fowler and crew of No 463 Squadron. This was to be the first of the 78 aircraft that the squadron was to lose in the skies over Europe. Although No 467 Squadron did not lose any aircraft on this occasion, it was to suffer the loss of 110 Lancasters on operations during the war. Although No 467 Squadron did not lose any aircraft on the night of 26/27 November, it was a close run thing. F/O Jack Colpus and crew were flying in PO-S (R5868). The 'to be famous' 'S' Sugar was on its eightieth operation when it collided with another Lancaster over the target, just after completing the bombing run. For getting his aircraft back to base despite the damage, Jack Colpus was awarded a Green Endorsement by the Station Commander, Gp Capt Elworthy. In the remarks column of Colpus' log book, the Group Captain penned the following: 'Whilst on operations, his aircraft came into collision with another Lancaster over the target area and sustained severe damage to the port wing. F/O Colpus, by good pilotage, succeeded in bringing his aircraft back to base and made a safe landing without further damage.'

In a letter to the author, Jack Colpus gives a detailed account of the incident which, typically, does little to convey the trauma of such an event taking place at night over a burning enemy city, with flak, searchlights and enemy night fighters combining to make a real 'witches brew':

"Our bomb load was 1 x 4000lb Cookie, 56 x 30lb incendiaries and 105 x 4lb incendiaries. From take-off to landing was a flight time of 8 hours and fifteen minutes. We arrived over Berlin at about 20,000 feet. Contrary to the met forecast, there was no cloud cover. The whole of Berlin was a mass of waving searchlights, about 40 miles in diameter. We had completed our bombing run and had just selected 'bomb doors closed' when we were 'coned' by searchlights. They seemed to come from all directions at once. Evasive action corkscrew turns were made in an attempt to escape, but without success. Heavy flak bursts thumped in all round us, with flashes and puffs of smoke and cordite smell; the latter indicating just how close the flak burst had been. After a while, which seemed like an eternity to us, the flak stopped as if by magic. This meant only one thing - fighters were closing in! I decided on desperate measures and dived steeply down to the left, picking up speed to 300mph as we passed 10,000 feet before pulling up to starboard. At that instant, the searchlights lost us, although I was still dazzled with no night vision at all. We were climbing as quickly as possible in order to get out of the range of the light automatic flak and back into the bomber stream, when suddenly our aircraft lurched and dived to port.

I thought that we had lost power on one engine, but the rear gunner called out that we had hit another Lancaster. Full right rudder plus full rudder bias and full aileron trim was applied, but 'Sugar' still kept turning to the left. Obviously further action was necessary, so power on the port engines was increased and that on the starboard side was decreased until we were able to maintain a steady heading. All four engines were then switched to run off the port wing fuel tanks in an effort to eventually raise the port wing to a near level position. We jettisoned the empty Small Bomb Containers (SBC) to lighten the load. Our aircraft was now under some form of control, flying at the low speed of 140mph and gradually losing height. We decided to fly home direct to base, as at 140mph we would soon be out of the bomber stream, which was taking a dog-leg route back home. Full right rudder was required throughout the four hour trip back. My Flight Engineer, Sgt Smith, went down into the bomb aimer's compartment and assisted me by holding the rudder pedal with a strap round it, in order to take some of the load off my leg. On nearing the English coast, we were diverted to Linton-on-Ouse, as Waddington was covered in fog. At Linton, we were given priority landing behind an aircraft which was overshooting. At this time we were at about 500 feet; too high for a normal approach, but I decided to land anyway. As we touched down at approximately 120mph, about 20mph too high, due to the steeper angle of descent, the port wing stalled. If I had made a normal approach at the correct speed, the aircraft would have stalled on the approach and crashed. As it was, 'Sugar' ground-looped at the far end of Linton's runway, due to our high landing speed and my excessive braking.

Subsequent inspection of the damage revealed that about five feet of the wing tip was missing, while part of the remaining damaged area was bent down at right angles. It was this that had caused the turning problems. 'Sugar' was classified as Cat 'Q' and sent back to the manufacturers, not returning to the squadron until early February 1944.

As a post-script, the other Lancaster, from No 61 Squadron at Skellingthorpe, was also coned in searchlights and taking avoiding action when we collided. The skipper of the other Lancaster confirmed this when he landed at Waddington a few days later, especially to see me in order to discuss the circumstances of our 'meeting'."

Berlin was again the target on the night of 2/3 December, when a mixed force of 458 aircraft carried out an attack, and experienced the loss of 40 aircraft (8.7%). Luckily, there were no losses among the thirteen Lancasters despatched by No 467 Squadron or the six from No 463 Squadron. However, it was a near thing! F/O Dave Gibbs and crew, flying in Lancaster PO-L (DV277), collided on landing with another Station Lancaster which had stalled on the runway. Luckily there were no casualties among either crew. By coincidence, on another occasion some time later, Dave Gibbs and crew were taxying towards the upwind end of the duty runway, prior to crossing it to join up with other Lancasters taxying round the peri-track. Without warning, one of the Lancasters crashed on take-off right in front of his (Gibbs') aircraft. The crew of the Lancaster in question escaped from their aircraft just as their load of incendiaries detonated. But, trapped in their aircraft, Gibbs crew could only sit and wait for the crashed aircraft' s 'Cookie' to explode. Luckily, it did not, and Warrant Officer Fishburn of the Station Armament Section, dashed into the still burning wreck and defused the big bomb. He was subsequently awarded a 'Mention in Despatches'.

Among the crews operating over Berlin on the night of 2/3 December was one of No 467 Squadron's Flight Commanders, S/Ldr Bill Forbes. He was carrying Mr A W King, a reporter on the Sydney Morning Herald. Although Mr King's report was only briefly covered in the British press, it received much more attention in the Sydney Herald. Arthur King's words, though somewhat histrionic, do convey just what a Dantesque scene was displayed to the bomber crews over a heavily defended target:

"Superb in the savage beauty of its light, but terrifying as a spectacle of devastation by explosives and burning, was the scene in a part of Berlin as it appeared last night from a Lancaster of one of the Australian bomber squadrons in which I flew.

Hundreds of searchlights probed the skies and coned several bombers. Scarecrow flares [There were no such things, they were exploding bombers – author] soared up and burst into a cascade of light which turned night into day. Other flares broke into ominous red and green orbs and flak burst in angry blobs.

The skies over the target were indeed in turmoil, but the target area itself was in even greater turmoil as 4000lb bombs - 'Cookies', smashed amid the built-up area and thousands of incendiaries cascaded down and took hold among the blocks of buildings in fantastic alphabetical designs.

Symbolic of the purpose of the attacks, one of the early strings of incendiaries flared up in an almost perfect 'V' for Victory. Other strings formed 'i's, 't's and 'l's. Cookies exploded in seemingly slow mushroom-like glows. They burned a dull red for some time and then died in plumes of smoke.

The pilot of the crew with whom I flew was S/Ldr William A Forbes, 23... The Flight Engineer was P/O Frank Miller...The other crew members comprised two Scots, two Englishmen and a Canadian. They were doing their 27th operation together, and their Lancaster 'G' for George was on its eleventh. It had not been scarred, not even scratched on its previous ten sorties, which were represented on the fuselage, not by orthodox bomb replicas, but by foaming mugs of beer. 'Why that symbol' I had asked Sgt Laurie Parker, one of the groundcrew, as I waited to board the aircraft. Parker grinned and said 'Trips to the Land of Mugs - big mugs', he said laconically. The experienced crew brought 'George' efficiently and uneventfully past heavily defended areas on the way to the 'King of Targets'. Then the crux of the tense drama began.

Clouds protected us practically the whole way. Then, ten miles from the target, it became wispy. Visibility was perfect over the target itself. But, if the break in the clouds made the job easier for the bomb-aimers, it enabled the defenders to concentrate hundreds of searchlights and light and heavy flak against the raiders. The Germans used all their defensive devices, but we saw one raider perfectly coned in searchlights without fighters attacking it or flak directed at it.

'George' was among the first waves of bombers over the target, which had been defined with remarkable

clarity by the Pathfinder Force a few minutes earlier with Target Indicators of different colours. The bomb aimers' particular objectives stood out like beacons amid a confusion of colours. From the time we sighted them, about ten miles out, until we passed beyond them, was the most exciting ten minutes through which I have lived. The two central figures in that brief period were Forbes and the bomb aimer, P/O William Grime of Ealing, London; two 'Bills' who co-operatively directed and instructed each other over the intercom phones.

I stood behind the imperturbable Forbes and watched the fascinatingly fantastic (sic) scene over his shoulder. As soon as he sighted his Target Indicators, for which he was on the lookout, Forbes asked Grime whether he had seen them. Grime answered confidently in the affirmative and then gave the pilot a slight alteration of course, adding 'You can weave a bit Bill.' Forbes weaved to lessen the danger from flak, but it was only for seconds. Then Forbes settled down to hold his plane to the level, undeviating run so essential for accurate bombing. Flak poured upwards, though none burst close enough to 'George' (PO-G JB140) to threaten the crew's safety. But these were those few seconds which bomber crews dread and against which they must summon up all their courage, determination and imperturbability. A few seconds in which they never know whether the next flak-burst is going to extinguish their life, smash their limbs, cripple their plane, or whether they will slip past the German gunners.

This was the climax of the flight; almost four hours from base to target. Down below, four miles below, The flak, to the uninitiated reporter, seemed desperately dangerous, but according to 'George's' veteran crew of youngsters, it wasn't much. Whether heavy or light, it failed to disturb George's steady bombing run. Over the intercom, from the bomb aimer's compartment came Grime's calm voice; 'Bomb doors open', words that thrill even the most hardened crews. 'Okay' came from Forbes. Seconds passed; then from Grime came the even more magic words in his unruffled voice 'Cookie gone'. 'Okay', came from the equally unruffled Forbes. I counted slowly to myself...one, two, three four, five. Then Grime again spoke 'Incendiaries gone' 'Okay' came from Forbes. We had delivered, free of charge, to Hitler and company, a 4000lb building blaster and morale shaker, and many fire raisers. The early comers had already started fires and our waves stoked them thoroughly.

As they illuminated George, I - the spare part in the plane, had the best opportunity to watch those fires increase in numbers and from a band, seemingly to join in an immense conflagration. Amidst them glowed 'Cookies', angry explosions like boils on white flesh. Some billowed and grew in volume above the flames. Below George, another Lancaster nosed forward silhouetted sinisterly against the flaming background like a shark in an aquarium pool. It was not without cost that the inferno in Berlin's heart was lit. Three flak bursts seemed simultaneously to hit one Lancaster and it burst into flames. Another seemed to get into difficulties and later several parachutes could be seen floating down [straight into the inferno beneath them! – Author]. For many miles beyond Berlin's outskirts, the flames and their reflections in the sky could be seen. The later waves had done their work as efficiently as the early comers. All the bombing was completed in less than a quarter of an hour. Forbes crew compelled my admiration with their thoroughness, confidence and attention to their duties. Typical of George's crew's keeness and efficiency, was the work of the navigator, P/O James Robertson, a likeable young Scot from Elgin who, cooped up in a cramped compartment, pored over maps, made calculations and kept George on the planned course and brought the aircraft to the right place at the right time. Another Scot, Sgt Willie McLeod of Ardrishaig, tended the radio instruments with loving care and enlivened the intercom conversations with his broad accent.

One must not forget in telling this drama of the skies one other actor - 'G' George, who carried us without a hitch. Every crew which flies 'George' worships him. He bears a charmed life. His engines for seven hours last night did not miss a beat. The 5000 horses in them gave unstintingly of their power. His body protected us in a temperature of 70 degrees Farenheit. He gave us all the shelter and usefulness a good bomber should.

If emphasis is given to the drama's climax, both the earlier and later acts had fascinating features. From the time S/Ldr Forbes, having moved George along the runway, asked 'All set'? 'Okay, here we go' and without hesitation gathered speed and soon became smoothly airborne until George's wheels touched down, new and absorbing experiences jostled one another for this reporter. We set off with a sliver of the blood-red sun sitting prettily on top of a bank of slate-grey clouds. We soared up over lovely English fields, and as we gained height, George's occupants busied themselves in the settling process. Forbes completed odds and ends of instructions and checking necessary for success. Everything was shipshape in five minutes. George began a steady climb which was to take us into the high region in which the crew had been instructed to fly. There was little sensation of flying. George was as steady as the deck of an ocean liner in a smooth sea. The moon shone on a wierd and wonderful cloudland far below, like a crumpled snowfield. Now and again we saw other bombers, all, like George pursuing height. The oxygen was turned on after half an hour and we wore masks like characters in a Wellsian fantasy.

For six hours the crew was silently intent for long periods because Forbes, like all good skippers, disliked intercom chatter, which some film producers have romanticised. Miller confided presently that the temperature was minus 20 degrees centigrade. The flight proceeded without incident until we crossed the coast into enemy occupied territory, where the first flak feebly challenged us, doing service in breaking the monotony, which is one of the bomber crews' most insidious enemies. The crew kept an anxious and intent watch against collision with other bombers in the cloud masses through which we passed. Occasionally they reported sighting other kites we knew to be bombers from dozens of RAF stations linking up in the large attacking force; a real bombers procession to Berlin. Orange-red flak bursts studded the clouds from time to time along the route, but it remained for a strongly defended area to provide the most remarkable spectacle of the outward journey. A thick cloudbank interposed itself between George and the ground. Eighty or one hundred searchlights, ranged in rows with almost geometrical precision, probed through our protecting cover, but failed to penetrate it. The searchlights crests seemed to squat on top of the clouds like large diamonds on a black cushion in a jeweller's shop. This area sent up more flak. We picked up markers which our Pathfinders had laid for us and saw the first of the lanes of red fighter flares, which recently had become a feature of Germany's aircraft defences. Soon after passing this strongly defended area, our run into Berlin began.

On our homeward journey, flak gave us a nasty three or four minutes with several bursts sufficiently close beneath George to set it tossing resentfully. On the rest of the homeward trip it was sheer monotony (sic), in complete cloud, until the last half-hour, in which we descended into clearer levels. Then came the thrill of the aerodrome's welcoming lights, and after circling it several times to allow earlier arrivals to land, George touched down as smoothly as it had left, and I at least breathed a sigh of happy relief, despite the thrills of an experience I would never have missed. All the crews..."

Two other reporters were flying that night; one was Captain Nordhal Greig of the Daily Mail, a Norwegian related to the composer. The other was Mr Norman Stockton of the Sydney Sun. They were flying in a Lancaster of No 460 Squadron RAAF from RAF Binbrook and were lost with their aircraft.

The trip to Berlin carrying Mr King was Bill Forbes' last trip of his tour with No 467 Squadron. However, five months later he was to return to Waddington, this time as a Flight Commander on No 463 Squadron. He would arrive on 20 May 1944; assuming command of the squadron just over one month later, on 26 June, following the loss of the newly arrived squadron commander, W/Cdr Don Donaldson, who was flying on his first trip with his new squadron. The target on this occasion was the missile site at Prouville in France. Fortunately, Don Donaldson evaded capture and returned to England courtesy of the French Resistance.

Despite the loss of the two reporters with Bomber Command over Berlin, the well-known American broadcaster Mr Ed Murrow flew on an attack against Leipzig the following night. Murrow flew with a crew from Woodhall Spa, which together with eleven aircraft from Waddington, helped make up a mixed force of 527 bombers. The aircraft in which Ed Murrow flew returned safely, as did all the Waddington aircraft that took part. Unfortunately, Lancaster PO-G (JB140), piloted by F/O C I Reynolds crashed on take-off. The ever popular 'G' George suffered a double engine failure and swung off the runway. As the heavily laden bomber careered across the airfield, it swept through a group of groundcrew, severly injuring Sgt Hobbs. Crossing the taxiway, the aircraft struck and killed Sgt Laurie Parker, who was cycling back to the Sergeants' Mess, having just seen off his aircraft - 'G' George! When the Lancaster finally came to a violent stop, the rear gunner, Sgt Frizzell, was thrown from his turret. He died of his injuries the next day in Rauceby Hospital.

Bad weather prevented the Command from carrying out any major attacks for almost two weeks. During this period, Mosquitos of the Light Night Striking Force were operating in small numbers, carrying out attacks on a variety of targets. Then, on the night of 16/17 December, Bomber Command despatched a force of 483 Lancasters and Mosquitos to Berlin; 24 of the Lancasters came from Waddington, all of which returned safely. Cloud cover over the target necessitated sky-marking, but despite this, the attack was accurate. On their return, the bombers experienced very low cloud over England which resulted in 29 Lancasters either crashing or being abandoned by their crews. In all, 148 men died in the crashes or mishaps while parachuting. Although Waddington suffered no losses on this occasion, the Station had been extremely lucky earlier in the day. F/O Ross Stanford and crew were taking off on a night flying air test (NFT) when, just after lifting off the runway, they flew into a flock of lapwings that lifted up from the grass beside the runway. Many of the birds were killed by the propellers, but one came right through the windscreen and struck Stanford on the left earpiece of his flying helmet. A few inches to the right and the bomber must have crashed, with the inevitable consequences to all on board. As it was, the Stanford crew went to Berlin that night, in the spare aircraft!

Weather again restricted the operations of the Command, and it was three days before a mixed force of 650 aircraft was despatched to Frankfurt. Berlin was out of the question as a target that night due to weather over 'The Big City'. Waddington despatched 23 Lancasters to Frankfurt, all of which returned safely, though the crew of PO-M (ED532) had some interesting moments. They had air tested their aircraft the morning of the raid, their Lancaster having just had its 200 hour check. Notwithstanding a faultless air test, the aircraft's port outer engine developed problems on the way to the target, well before they had crossed the east coast of England. The skipper, S/Ldr Stuart Crouch, elected to continue at a reduced power setting on the affected engine. Despite their engine trouble, they reached the target on time and at the briefed height of 20,000 feet. While on the bombing run, with the bomb doors open, their aircraft was coned by six searchlights. The resulting glare blinded the pilot and the two air gunners, so with night fighters above them and flak bursting all round them, Crouch had only one option; he put the bomber into a steep dive. By the time they managed to break free of the searchlight beams, the crew estimated that their aircraft was doing over 400mph (TAS). Crouch levelled off at 10,000 feet and asked the navigator, Arnold Camps, for the course home. At this point, the bomb aimer, John Kennedy, reported that they had not dropped their bombs and requested that they go round again! Some members of the crew were not too impressed with the idea and made their views known; Crouch however had other ideas. Telling the disenters to pipe down, he climbed laboriously back up to 20,000 feet. This took quite a time as, while coned by the searchlights, one of the starboard engines had been damaged by flak and it too was not giving full power. Luckily for the crew their second bomb run was uneventful, though they saw a nearby Lancaster coned and receiving the full treatment.

With two engines on reduced power, they gradually fell behind the homeward bound main stream of bombers, but experienced no night fighter attacks. Then, while still some minutes from crossing the Dutch coast, the port inner engine developed power loss! Despite their increasing engine problems, Crouch and crew made a safe landing back at Waddington, some time after the other 22 crews.

The year ended with two attacks on Berlin; one on the night of 23/24 December, and the other, six nights later. On the first of these attacks, the Station despatched 20 aircraft, one of which, flown by P/O Heap and crew on their second operation, failed to return. On the last attack of 1943, Waddington despatched a total of 24 Lancasters to Berlin, losing that of P/O Tait and crew who, like P/O Heap, were on their second operation.

Aircrew leave was a rather unique system which, with heavy losses, could give rise to some crews; the lucky ones, doing quite well. The basic arrangement was that as a crew came back from leave, their names went to the bottom of the roster. Similarly, new crews went to the bottom of the roster on arrival. After each operation, any missing crew was removed from the leave roster and all those below them moved up. Consequently, the more crews posted as missing, the more frequent the survivors would go on leave. To quote one survivor: *"All you had to do to benefit from this system, was to stay alive"!*

F/O Reynolds and crew, who had crashed on take off on the night of the attack on Leipzig, were again in the wars. While still 200 miles from Berlin on the night of 29/30 December, they were hit by flak. They were again hit while on their bomb run, but on this occasion, their incendiaries were ignited, setting fire to the aircraft. Reynolds jettisoned the incendiaries and continued with the attack, his bomb aimer releasing their 4000lb Cookie on the Target Indicators (TIs). Then, with his aircraft still on fire, Reynolds extinguished the flames by a combination of a steep dive away from the target while his crew used all available fire extinguishers to fight the fire in the bomb bay. Their combined efforts proved successful and they returned to Waddington. Sadly, less than a week later, this hardy crew were to perish during an attack on Stettin.

While the aircrews were taking part in Harris' Battle of Berlin, the groundcrews were playing their part in meeting the many calls for a 'maximum effort'. As one of them recalled:

"...aircraft maintenance at that time was covered by a system known as repair and inspection (R & I). This included post-operation inspection and repairs. At Waddington, the two centre hangars (currently Nos 3 and 4) were used for the purpose, being marked 'RI' in large white letters. The hangar nearest to the guardroom (currently No 5) was used by Avro for Category B inspections. Owing to the number and pace of operations being undertaken by Waddington and its two satellites of Bardney and Skellingthorpe, it proved to be impossible for the squadrons to keep pace with the requirement for Major Inspections of the aircraft. These were scheduled at every 400 flying hours. As a result, a new servicing system was introduced, that of Base Major Servicing (BMS). Personnel required for the new system came from the existing squadron servicing staff. At Waddington, this new system necessitated the use of the two remaining hangars. Until the introduction of BMS, No 1 hangar had been used for 'Makers and Command' modifications work, while No 2 hangar was used for Major Inspections and repairs. ...it became Command policy for a tourex flight crew to be assigned to a Base for air testing duties. These crews were required to air test all aircraft after every Major Inspection... Furthermore, it was common prectice for the NCO i/c a maintenance gang to fly on the air test, a chance that most of them jumped at. The Flight Sergeant in charge of the BMS Section from its inception until VE Day was F/Sgt W Felstead. Apart from being an experienced engineer, he was an enthusiastic middle distance runner. Of the two Maintenance Gangs which formed part of the BMS, No 1 was led by Cpl Cull and No 2 by Cpl Rudman."

Among the Waddington groundcrew at this time was Sgt J E Pease, a compass adjuster. He had joined the RAFVR in 1941 as a trainee pilot, but a minor eye problem ended his hopes of aircrew duties. On remustering, he was told that if he still wished to fly, the duties of a compass adjuster would enable him to do so. Sergeant Pease in later life became better known as Lord Gainford.

Another member of the hard working groundcrew at Waddington was D W Moore, an engine fitter, who remembered quite clearly the engineering system at No 53 Base:

"Outside of the servicing carried out by personnel on the 'flights', such as between-flight inspections, daily inspections and refuelling etc, other maintenance of a more intensive nature was undertaken by what was known as the 463/467 Servicing Echelon in the hangars. Within the Echelon, our chain of command was separate from the squadrons, consisting in the main of engineering officers covering most specialisations. Our Senior Engineering Officer was S/Ldr McCabe RAF, who had been at Waddington for some time before the Australian squadrons moved in. The trade groups in the Echelon were divided into two groups of engine fitters, airframe fitters, electricians, armourers, instrument fitters, wireless specialists and safety equipment workers. Teams of these maintenance personnel would carry out inspections of every aircraft, in accordance with the established schedules every 50 flying hours (If the aircraft survived that long!). This was later increased to 75 hours. These were known as 1, 2, 3, and 4 Star Inspections, each increasing in the depth of servicing, according to the Star rating. The 4 Star Inspection would, in time, be followed by a Major Inspection, which was virtually a complete overhaul, with many components being replaced by new or rebuilt parts.

The Servicing Echelon was also responsible for acceptance checks on replacement aircraft for those lost on operations or in accidents. This included the painting of the appropriate squadron codes, together with the individual aircraft letter. Another important task was battle damage repair, which could include such tasks as propeller and/or engine changes, patching up flak damage and bullet holes and, sometimes more exciting, the removal of unexploded incendiaries which had been dropped on an aircraft from one flying above it in the target area. On one occasion, a maintenance crew working in a hangar, actually found an unexploded flak shell lodged inside a Lancaster! Minor airframe damage had to be repaired and, quite often, gun turrets replaced when damaged by enemy action. We were also required to service two Hurricane fighters and a Beaufighter which were based at Waddington (?). I believe that these were on the Station for airfield defence purposes.

Repairs of major battle damage to aircraft were carried out by the Avro team, who occupied one of the hangars. The Avro team were all civilians, and they would also undertake modifications to aircraft. On one occasion, I recall seeing a Lancaster of No 617 Squadron standing outside the Avro hangar. This aircaft had been modified to carry the 'Upkeep' dams bomb and was presumably waiting to be returned to standard fit, or changed again to enable it to carry one of the Dambusters' special weapons such a 'Tallboy' or 'Grandslam'.

The Servicing Echelon also provided personnel for the 'Duty Crew'. This was a continuous, seven day duty. The Duty Crew were on call throughout the seven days and were billeted on the ground floor of the control tower. Their main function was to guide aircraft from the end of the runway to the appropriate dispersal, before handing over to the aircraft's own groundcrew. The Duty Crew had also to deal with visiting aircraft and those diverted to the Station. On one occasion, we had to deal with about 30 to 40 USAAF Flying Fortresses and Liberators that had been diverted to Waddington on their return from an operation. The only place that we could find to park them was on the grass, in lines, on each side of the control tower.

Obviously, to have such a large number of diverted aircraft from the Americans was unusual and caused a lot of interest among all Station personel. Much to everyone's surprise, because of the American regulations, nobody was allowed near the aircraft until the Norden bombsights had been removed and secured. The American aircrews had orders to leave one crew member in their aircraft until armed guards arrived to escort the bombsights off the Station (what price Allied solidarity?). In due course a contingent of armed USAAF police arrived and were joined in the accompanying transport by the aircrews. As the embarrassed American aircrews left the Station, they had to endure a barrage of good natured RAF/RAAF banter.

The Servicing Echelons prided themselves in having all the aircraft assigned to operations repaired, inspected, air tested and returned to 'the flights' in good time for operations, particularly when a 'maximum effort' was called for by Command. This latter requirement was usually conveyed to all concerned by the firing of flares from the control tower as soon as the requirement was confirmed."

❖ ❖ ❖

7. An Anglo/Australian Station

The New Year opened for Bomber Command on the night of 1/2 January 1944 when 421 Lancasters attacked Berlin. The two Waddington squadrons despatched a total of 20 aircraft, losing one crew from each squadron. F/Sgt Lawson and crew of No 463 Squadron were on their second operation, their first having also been to Berlin in late December. The missing crew from No 467 Squadron, was that of F/O Patkin. They were on their eleventh operation and were shot down near Celle. There were no survivors from either crew. A cross check of German night fighter records indicates that the Patkin crew were probably shot down by one of the Luftwaffe's top scoring night fighter pilots, Major Heinrich Prinz zu Sayn-Wittgenstein of IV./NJG5. This pilot and his crew accounted for six Lancasters in 40 minutes that night between 0150hr and 0230hr. His Ju88C-6 carried the state-of-the-art SN2 radar and upward firing 'Schrage Musik'. However, the Prinz was not destined to survive Patkin by very long. On the night of 21/22 January, he was killed in action, probably by a vigilant Lancaster air gunner near Magdeburg. At the time of his death, his score stood at 83 victories.

Apart from its heavy defences, one reason why an attack on 'The Big City' never found favour with the crews of Bomber Command, was its distance. Any attack on Berlin meant a round trip of about eight hours, at least seven of which would be over enemy territory. The distance in a straight line from Waddington to Berlin was approximately 600 miles, but the attackers never flew a direct route. In attempts to mislead the enemy fighter controllers, the Main Force would be routed to their target via a series of feints or dog-legs. This resulted in a time to Berlin of between three and four hours. As Arnold Camps, one of the Australian navigators recalled, when discussing the attack on Berlin on the night of 26/27 November 1943, the crews experienced a westerly wind of over 100mph, which meant that they reached their target in a little under two hours. However, the return trip took over six hours! Heavy losses among the Halifax and Stirling squadrons during the early phase of the Battle of Berlin, resulted in their being withdrawn, leaving the Lancaster squadrons to battle on alone.

For the Lancaster crews, it was back to Berlin again on the night of 2/3 January, when a force of 383 aircraft attacked the German capital, of which sixteen came from Waddington. The attackers lost 27 Lancasters (7%) that night, one of them from Waddington. F/Sgt Weatherill and crew of No 463 Squadron failed to return; there again being no survivors.

Bad weather precluded any attacks on Berlin for the next two weeks, but Stettin and Brunswick were attacked by 348 and 496 aircraft respectively. The attack on Stettin was particularly accurate, though No 467 Squadron lost the crews of F/O Reynolds and P/O Connolly; there being only one survivor out of the fourteen crew members. Sgt King, the flight engineer on the Reynolds crew survived to become a PoW. The attack on Brunswick ten days later, was not considered a success. On the other hand, the German night fighters were very successful. They got into the bomber stream soon after it crossed the Dutch/German border and claimed most of the 38 aircraft shot down that night (7.6%). Eleven of the bombers lost that night were from the PFF, but all the Waddington aircraft returned safely.

It was back to Berlin on the night of 20/21 January, when 26 Lancasters from Waddington formed part of a 769 strong force. This was thought to be a particularly successful attack, with massive damage being inflicted on railways, factories and power stations, though German records for this night are blank. Once again losses were high with 35 bombers being lost (4.6%) though none of them were from Waddington. The next night the target was Magdeburg, followed by three more attacks on Berlin before the end of the month. To support the attack on Magdeburg, a small force of 22 Lancasters, including some from Waddington, joined forces with 12 Mosquitos in a diversionary attack on Berlin. Its purpose was to draw enemy night fighters away from the Main Force attacking Magdeburg, but unfortunately it failed to achieve its aim. The Berlin aiming point for the diversionary force was the airfield at Tempelhoff, and as P/O Doug Harvey's crew ran in to bomb, their mid upper gunner reported six enemy night fighters flying in line astern, passing a few hundred feet below. Luckily the fighters failed to spot Harvey's aircraft and they returned safely. One Waddington aircraft failed to return from the Magdeburg attack. P/O J Mitchell and crew, flying in PO-K (ED803) were on their fourth operation when they were shot down. As was so often the case, there were no survivors.

The attack on Berlin on the night of 20/21 January had been the heaviest assault on 'The Big City' to date.

The increased hitting power of Bomber Command was now becoming all too evident to the hard-pressed German defenders. Each attack on Berlin in the second half of January was carried out by over five hundred aircraft. Such was the quality of the crews and the planning, that the bomber stream had become particularly condensed, with over 20 aircraft per minute passing over the designated target.

The Station lost three crews in the attack on Berlin on the night of 27/28 January. No 467 Squadron lost F/O O'Brian and crew flying in PO-T (ED539) on their fourth operation, and P/O Grugeon and crew flying in PO-C (ME575) on their seventh operation, five of which had been to Berlin. No 463 Squadron lost F/O Leslie and crew flying in JO-N (ME563), who were also on their seventh operation. This particular attack by a force of 515 aircraft, 26 of them from Waddington, cost the attackers the loss of 33 Lancasters (6.4%). S/Ldr Bill Brill, OC B Flight of No 463 Squadron got back to base safely, but not before he had experienced a narrow escape. He and his crew were flying in JO-R (DV274) when their aircraft was hit and severely damaged by falling incendiaries, dropped from an aircraft above them. Brill gave the order to stand by to abandon the aircraft, but having regained control, he cancelled it and flew what the crew subsequently described as 'a nightmare return trip'.

The next night, Berlin was again the target; this time for a force of 677 bombers, 32 of them from Waddington. This attack was subsequently recorded by the German authorities as having been the heaviest attack on the city during this period of sustained assault. Two of the Station's aircraft failed to return. No 467 Squadron lost F/Lt Ian Durstan and crew, flying in PO-T (ED867) on their 25th operation. Once again, none of the crew survived.* No 463 Squadron lost F/Lt Cooper and crew, an experienced team on their fourth successive attack on Berlin. They were flying in JO-S (HK537) when they were shot down; none of the crew surviving.

Despite the bad weather, January had been an active month at Waddington, along with the rest of the Command. The Station had despatched a total of 215 aircraft to a variety of targets, including six attacks on Berlin. In all, the two Australian squadrons lost fifteen crews in this, the first month of 1944. The last raid of the month was to be particularly costly to the Station. On the night of 30/31 January, the target was Berlin and No 467 Squadron put up ten aircraft, suffering the loss of P/O A D Riley and crew who were flying in PO-C (DV378). Tragically, No 463 Squadron lost three crews out of fourteen that same night, all of whom were experienced operators. These crews had the misfortune to arrive on the squadron just before 'The Battle of Berlin' commenced and all three had participated in several attacks on the German capital. Among the crews lost was that of F/O Messenger who, together with his crew, had flown sixteen operations with No 467 Squadron before being moved to their sister squadron. Among the sixteen operations were three to Berlin. Messenger and crew were on their sixth operation with their new squadron (five of them to Berlin) when they were shot down. The wireless operator was Sgt Wooldridge, who was older than the average for aircrew, and had been married for eleven years. He and his wife very much wanted to start a family, but he died not knowing that his wife was expecting their first child. His daughter was born eight months after he was killed in action. The losses that night (6.2%) however were not entirely one-sided. One of the No 463 Squadron air gunners saw a JU88 outlined against the sky markers and on opening fire scored numerous hits before it broke away. In addition, Sgt Colin Campbell, the mid upper gunner in F/Lt Bruce Simpson's crew was credited with 'a probably destroyed' Bf110.

The last attack of the month against Berlin was, as has been shown, particularly costly for the two Waddington squadrons. Apart from the loss of F/O Messenger and crew in JO-G (ED772), No 463 Squadron lost P/O Dunn and crew in JO-A (ED949) and P/O Hanson and crew in JO-O (JA873). Dunn and crew were an experienced team and had flown six trips to Berlin out of their last seven operations. Similarly, Hanson and crew had flown five trips in succession to Berlin before being shot down. Of the 21 members of the three crews from No 463 Squadron, nineteen were killed and two became PoWs. The loss of P/O Riley and crew of No 467 Squadron was a particularly heavy blow, as they were a very experienced crew flying on their sixteenth operation. Only the bomb aimer survived to become a PoW; all in all, only three survivors out of the 28 crew members.

Apart from having to face the prevailing adverse winds on the return trip, the English weather could add further problems and hazards to the weary crews, sometimes returning in damaged aircraft and with injured crew members. On one occasion, F/Lt Jack Colpus and crew returned to find the whole of Lincolnshire covered in thick fog. Determined to land at their own base, they eventually located Waddington and received permission to land. Colpus' call of 'funnels' was acknowledged and he received 'a green' from the runway caravan. As he rounded out, Colpus realised that the runway lights he was looking at were goose-neck flares which were no longer used at Waddington. They landed on a grass runway with a thump and headed off blind into the fog with the brakes hard on! Colpus was more than a little concerned as, apart

* The Durston crew's aircraft was located in what was East Germany in August 2001 by a group of German amateur historians. The missing six bodies were found in the wreck and accorded a full militarily funeral in the Berlin War Cemetery on 15 July 2003. It transpires that the Durston crew experienced a technical fault to their rear gun turret, which delayed their take-off Despite this, they elected to press on alone, some two hours behind the main bomber stream.

from realising that he was not on a Waddington runway, he did not know where he was or the length of the grass runway. Eventually the Lancaster came to a stop and a relieved Colpus called to the Waddington tower to report; "Pancaked and clear of the runway". To which the puzzled voice of the WAAF R/T operator came through: "Hello N Nan; where are you"? Colpus' reply of "You tell me and we will both know" was the cause of considerable hilarity among a very relieved crew. They had in fact landed at the nearby night fighter airfield of Coleby Grange.

Jack Colpus has other less exciting memories of his time on No 463 Squadron at Waddington. As he recalled:

"There was a family atmosphere at Waddington. This was evident at the take-off point, where a large group of men and women would gather of their own accord. They would stand beside the runway caravan in all sorts of weather, just to wave the crews away, for many of whom, it was to be their last farewell. It was also very heartening, after returning from an operation, no matter at what time in the early hours, to be greeted with a 'Glad you made it', and to have a mug of hot tea placed in your hand, particularly from someone who you knew was not on duty. The Officer in charge of the WAAFs, the Mess Steward and two sisters, Nellie and Kathleen Coupland, always seemed to be there. The Met Office was another place where you were made to feel welcome. The Met Officer, Barry, and his staff of Mary Turner, Eleanor Rolfe, Norah Dann and Dorothy Jepson, would always come up with a cup of tea for a visitor. I remember also, sharing an Australian fruit cake from home with our groundcrew over a cup of NAAFI tea, while we nattered together before the morning night flying test (NFT)."

Life on a bomber squadron was one of numerous paradoxes, not the least of which was the fact that one element, the aircrew, had one of the most dangerous roles in any of the three services. On the other hand, the groundcrews, to all intents and purposes had what appeared to the unknowing, one of the safest. However, as in most things, all was not as it may have appeared. To obtain some idea of the life of a member of Bomber Command groundcrews, the recollections of one of them, Bill Yates, gives a comprehensive picture:

"Each aircraft had its own aircrew and groundcrew. The latter would normally consist of an NCO, two or three fitters and a rigger. Our working day began at 0800hr with daily inspections and repairs to any damage that had been reported by the night flying groundcrew team. Next, the aircraft would be refuelled to the minimum load of 1450 gallons. Some time later, the aircrew would arrive at the dispersal to check their equipment and have a quick chat with their groundcrew, before possibly carrying out a NFT. With the aircrew's checks completed, the bomb train would arrive and the armourers would commence bombing up. Sometimes the 4000lb 'Cookie' would have been delivered the previous night, soon after the aircraft had taken off on an operation. It would be left on its trolley beside the dispersal, albeit without any arming devices fitted. In the early days, all bombs had to be winched up into the bomb bay by hand; not an easy task for an armourer, kneeling on the floor inside the fuselage, using the manually operated winch. With bombing up complete, the fuel bowser would arrive and top up the fuel to the load required for that night's operation. Most groundcrew would hazard a guess at the possible target, based on the bomb and fuel loads, but they would not really want to know, just in case they mentioned it when they should not have done so. With refuelling complete, all was ready and the team could go to the mess hall for a meal. However, it did not always go as smoothly as that. If there were problems, the team would have to carry on until they were solved. We could then, and only then, sign the Form 700 and be told the start-up time; usually about one hour before take-off.

Ideally, there would be three men in a start-up team, though two could do the job at a pinch. In any case, the whole team would normally turn out, unless they had something special to do. The start-up team would either hang about the dispersal or wait in their homemade dispersal hut until they heard the aircrew arrive in the bus or three ton truck. This was always the difficult part; everyone trying to act normally, all hiding their true feelings. Eventually, the aircrew would board the aircraft, some having first performed some good luck ritual. The pilot would start the engines and carry out a mag drop check on each of them and then shut all four engines down. The crew would then leave their aircraft and join us for a chat and a smoke. There would normally be about half an hour before take-off; time to tell a few more jokes, throw a cricket ball or kick a football about. In other words, anything to take all our minds off what the aircrew would soon be flying into. It was obvious to us that the strain on the aircrew, trying to act normally during the day while being fully aware of what awaited them, was terrific. For us, the groundcrew, the worst part was having our crew fail to return. We would start off hoping that they had landed somewhere else, before going over to another aircraft to lend a hand; anything to take our minds off the possibilities.

Inevitably, it would be time to start engines. The crew would climb in and in due course, all four engines would be running. A last thumbs up and a wave, and the big bomber would taxy out to join the long line of Lancasters forming up on the perimeter track. To see and hear something like 24 Lancasters, one behind the other, each with all four engines running, was an awsome sight and sound. The air would vibrate; even the ground seeming to shake. Our part completed, we would make our way to the runway caravan to join the group that always gathered there. It would be a mixed bag; aircrew not flying that night, WAAFs and Station HQ personnel, all waiting to wave off each of the bombers as it commenced its take-off run. They would go with a roar, one after the other, with the sky above seemingly full of Lancasters circling and climbing, before heading off towards the coast. With their noise fading away, there would be little for us to do but await their return. At least one of us would be on night flying duty; the tasks being to marshal the aircraft into its dispersal on its return, fit the control locks and place covers on the tyres and gun turrets. To sit high up on the nose of a Lancaster while struggling with a turret cover, trying to fit it over the nose turret, while at the same time battling against the eternal Lincolnshire wind, had hazards all of its own.

The night flying duty crews on nearby dispersals would sort out some sort of rota so that everyone could get away to the mess hall for supper or go to the NAAFI. This unofficial rota would ensure that there would always be someone on hand to deal with any boomerangs - an aircraft that returned early with a problem. Out on the dispersal, we had two WAAF drivers, one on the tractor and one driving the three tonner, but they were stood down once all the aircraft had returned. Night flying duty usually came round every other night, but we could normally get our heads down for a few hours in the dispersal hut. As soon as it was nearing the time of the expected return of the aircraft, everyone would be listening out for them. Eventually, the telephone would ring and it would be the control tower telling us that one of our Flight was about to land. With a 'Maximum Effort', we would have despatched twelve Lancasters from our Flight and as such, there would be six of us on duty, three to each of the two networks of adjoining dispersals. If we were lucky, the first one down would be on our side of the network. We would take the WAAF tractor driver with us to the aircraft and tow the bomber backwards into its dispersal without delay. However, if the other side of the network got to use the tractor first, it would require some juggling to get the aircraft sorted out and in the correct dispersal, facing the right way.

Back at the dispersal, the duty man would wait until his Lancaster turned off the peri-track into the dispersal track. He would be standing in the middle of the track, holding a torch in each hand. As the big bomber passed the neck of the dispersal pan, the pilot would be signalled to stop and cut the engines. Then, before the crew had made their way to the door of their aircraft, the tractor would close on the rear of the aircraft and hook up to the tail wheel assembly. Meanwhile, the duty man would have made his way to the door of the bomber where he would wait for the crew to open it and pass out the ladder. Once the ladder was hooked on to the sill, the crew would climb down. They would be weary and glad to be back; to have survived another night and with one less operation to do. There would be time for just a few questions such as 'Everyone OK; good trip, kite OK' before the aircrew climbed aboard the waiting three ton truck and went off to debriefing and the post-flight meal. In the meantime, the duty crew awaited the arrival of the next aircraft, when they would go through the whole procedure again, repeating it until the last aircraft was down, or they were told that all those that were coming back had done so! Once all the aircraft had been put to bed, it would be back to the Flight Office before heading for the billet and bed. A night duty crew were allowed to stay in their billet until after lunch the next day, but in many cases they would report for work as usual and not knock off until their aircraft was declared serviceable and ready for operations. There were seldom any spare bods to fill in, apart from those whose aircraft had failed to return and who were waiting for a replacement aircraft and a new crew.

So much for a 'normal' day, which could be quite pleasant in the summer, but barely tolerable in the winter. On a sunny summer's day members of the groundcrew would strip down to just a pair of shorts, but in the winter they would don their Flight Deck Suits which, it was rumoured, had been obtained from the Navy. A particularly good day would be when the sun shone, the aircraft had not flown the night before and there were no operations scheduled for that night. This rare occurrence would leave the groundcrew with little to do. On these occasions, the aircrew would often come over to the dispersal and join us without the pre-operation tension spoiling the atmosphere. On the other hand, a particularly bad day would be when the weather was awful, the groundcrew struggling to carry out their alloted tasks in the cumbersome Flight Deck Suits, and the squadron had suffered heavy losses.

All dispersals eventually possessed their own home-made dispersal hut. Ours was the work of our Australian Corporal, Lance Compton. He acquired (!) bits and pieces from all over the Station and elsewhere, and before long we were the proud owners of a hut built of wood and corrugated iron, complete with windows, a stove, a work bench and numerous seats which were fastened to the walls.

For recreation, we spent most evenings in the NAAFI singing round the piano, or in the camp cinema which was on the first floor of the mess hall. There were also dedicated schools playing cards, Monopoly or 'Uckers'. Although we were not paid very much, we would go to one of the many public houses in the local area or in Lincoln. The Horse and Jockey pub in Waddington village was always popular, especially the upstairs restaurant. There you could drink for an extra hour if you were eating. I felt sure that the 'H & J' was in league with the local poachers, as the menu was invariably rabbit, hare, pigeon or some other sundry country fare. If a meal was beyond the pocket, we could always go to the dance in the villager hall, which was well supported by the RAF, WAAF and the locals. Then, on the way back to the hole in the hedge entry to the camp, we could stop off at Peatman's the village bakers, and buy whatever was on offer at the back door. Sometimes, particularly when our aircrew were celebrating something special, we would join them in the 'H & J' and then move on with them to the aircrew Sergeants' Mess. This was particu-

larly popular when there was a mess dance in progress. To get away with this, the NCOs in the crew would lend each one of us their spare jacket".[5]

The month of January 1944 ended with a heavy fall of snow. At one stage it posed such a problem for the snow clearing parties, which included all Station personnel including the aircrew, that the Station's aircraft were towed out of their dispersals and lined up along the edge of the runway. To ensure that the snow did not prevent operations, the clearing work went on by day and by night. During the hours of darkness, the working parties, equipped with nothing more sophisticated than shovels, worked by the light of searchlights. This period of bad weather lasted for about ten days and virtually prevented any heavy raids taking place until mid February. After this two-week break, the Main Force commenced operating again on 15 February with an 891 aircraft attack on Berlin. This was the heaviest non-1,000-bomber attack to date and by far the heaviest on Berlin. A total of 2,645 tons of bombs were dropped, causing extensive damage, including the large industrial complex in the Siemenstadt district. Fortunately for many Berliners, they had been evacuated from the city, and as a result the civilian casualties were far less than they would otherwise have been. The attackers lost 43 aircraft (4.8%), but all the Waddington aircraft returned safely.

A week before the massive attack on Berlin, the Bishop of Chichester, Dr George Bell, speaking in the House of Lords, questioned the morality of the RAF policy of area bombing. He went on to say that while he did not forget what the Germans had done to Warsaw or Coventry, his concern was whether the government understood what area bombing was destroying. Apart from the obvious material destruction, the Bishop was concerned with the implications for future relationships among the people of Europe. It was apparent that, with few exceptions, the Bishop's concerns were not shared by the British people nor by those of the occupied countries.

Coming close behind the Bishop's expressed concerns, some other bodies, for whatever reasons, expressed doubts as to the efficacy of Bomber Command's attacks.Post war analysis showed that under Albert Speer, the brilliant Nazi armaments minister, weapons production in Germany rose steadily. Tank production increased from 760 a month at the begining of 1943 to 1229 in December that year. Similarly, the production of aircraft rose from 15,288 in 1942 to 25,094 in 1943. While these figures are not disputed, the question has to be asked: "What would these figures have been had they been allowed to expand without let or hinderance"? It should be remembered also that the attacks by Bomber Command caused a massive diversion of resources to the air defence of the Reich, thereby depriving the German army in Russia, Italy and in the West of vital air support. Similarly, the one million and more men engaged on home defence, plus thousands of guns and aircraft and associated facilities, meant that they were unavailable for front-line duties. The cold hard fact was (and still is) that from 1939 to 1944, Bomber Command, and later the American Eighth Air Force, was the only Allied weapon capable of bringing the war home to the German people. Most, if not all the counter proposals regarding the diversion of the resources allocated to Bomber Command to other spheres, were inherrently concerned with defensive measures; not a war winning philosophy.

In early February, F/O A J Saunders and crew were posted to No 83 Squadron of the PFF. This crew flew their first operational trip with No 467 Squadron on the night of 23/24 November 1943 when they went to Berlin; not an easy start for a 'sprog' crew! Two days later, they were posted across the road to No 463 Squadron. On their new squadron they flew six sorties; four to Berlin and one each to Frankfurt and Brunswick, before volunteering for Pathfinder Force duties.

Four nights after the Berlin attack, the Command despatched 823 aircraft to attack Leipzig on 19/20 February. This could be considered the opening attack of what the American Eighth Air Force termed 'The Big Week', a major assault on German fighter production. Leipzig was the location of four Messerschmitt factories, plus a ball bearing factory. On this occasion, the target was cloud covered and had to be bombed using sky markers (Wanganui), never the most accurate form of attack. The German fighter controlling authority correctly predicted the target and the bomber stream was subjected to continuous attack both to and from the target. The attackers lost 78 aircraft (9.5%), one of which was P/O Fayle and crew of No 463 Squadron, flying in JO-C (DV338). This was their ninth trip, seven of which had been to Berlin. From a coldly analytical Station point of view, the loss of one aircraft out of the 35 despatched, was a far better result than most other stations in the Command could report. The Halifax squadrons in particular suffered grievous losses (almost 15%), and as a result, the Halifax Mks II and V were permanently withdrawn from attacks on Germany.

One of the crews taking part in the attack on Leipzig was that captained by S/Ldr Henry Crouch, OC 'A' Flight of No 467 Squadron. His navigator, F/Lt Arnold Camps, recalled that they were on their last operation

[5] With the end of the war in Europe, 'Bomber' Harris wrote to the Chief of the Air Staff, Air Chief Marshal Sir Charles Portal, requesting that a Bomber Command medal be struck for those who served in the Command on the ground. He expressed his concerns that under the plans as he knew them, his groundcrews, having served in the British Isles, would be entitled to only the Defence Medal. In his letter to Portal, Harris stated: "...it is apparent to me that few people appreciate the terrible miseries and discomfort, and the tremendous hours of work under which the ground personnel of Bomber Command on the airfields have laboured for nearly six years..." As is a matter of record, Harris was unsuccessful in his endeavours to obtain due recognition for his groundcrews; another victory for the chairborne warriors!

(25th) and that it became one to remember. Before the Lancasters at Waddington could move, the runway had to be cleared of snow. The crews eventually got airborne just before midnight in the middle of a full scale blizzard, making the take-off run particularly dangerous as the pilots could barely see the runway ahead of them. While climbing up to their assigned height, Camps found that the meteorological forecast winds were hopelessly wrong. As a result, the Crouch crew had to dog-leg on the route across the North Sea in order to lose enough time to arrive at the first turning point at anything like the planned time. While carrying out the dog-leg, the Crouch crew had several near misses with other aircraft in the bomber stream. They later noted that some other crews were not so lucky. These had elected to lose time by orbiting the first turning point, and Camps logged several mid-air collisions in the area as the orbiting aircraft fell foul of the incoming bomber stream. In the meantime, the Luftwaffe controller had despatched some of his night fighters to the area of the first turning point, evidenced by considerable signs of air to air combat. Having turned on to the second leg of their route, the Crouch crew noted that while they were corkscrewing, two Lancasters flying on either side of them, were flying straight and level. Both were shot down almost within seconds of each other. Continuing to corkscrew, Crouch and crew were left alone by the night fighters for some time. Inevitably, it became their turn, but with the two gunners calling out evasive turns, combined with the corkscrew, they made it to the target and back home, albeit having been attacked several times.

The day after the Leipzig raid, the Americans commenced their 'Big Week'. On that day, the Eighth Air Force despatched 1,028 bombers, accompanied by 800 fighters, plus 16 RAF fighter squadrons. The targets were the industrial complexes in Leipzig, Rostock, Oschersleben and Tutow. This massive assault, the first of the 'Big Week' series of attacks, was part of the Eighth Air Force's effort to meet the requirements of the 'Pointblank' directive, which called for the defeat of the German fighter force, both in the air and on the ground, together with the associated industrial production complexes.

For the crews of Bomber Command, the target on the night following the Leipzig raid, was Stuttgart, which was attacked by a force of 598 aircraft, 29 of which were from Waddington. Once again the Station was lucky and experienced no losses. Four nights later on 24/25 February, the target was Schweinfurt, when the Command despatched 734 aircraft in a follow-up attack to that carried out by 266 American B17 Flying Fortresses the previous day. On this occasion, Bomber Command elected to try a different tactic. The attacking force was split into two waves, two hours apart. The first wave of 392 aircraft took the brunt of the defences, losing 22 aircraft (5.6%), while the second wave of 342 aircraft lost just over half that number (3.2%). The attack itself was not accurate, being one that Harris had opposed on the grounds that the target was distant, difficult to locate and was one of what he termed 'panacea targets', the destruction of which, according to the 'experts', would cripple the enemy at a stroke (sic), but which in reality never did so. On this occasion, No 467 Squadron remained lucky with no losses, but sadly, No 463 Squadron was not so fortunate, losing the crews of F/Lts Martin and Mortimer.

The navigator of the Mortimer crew, F/Lt Bill Baggie, flying in JO-M (LL740), recalled that this trip was to be the crew's thirtieth and last of their tour. Their route to Schweinfurt included, for them, a diversionary dummy attack on Stuttgart. As Baggie recalled:

"A dummy run on Stuttgart to draw the night fighters away from the real target area was a good idea if you got away with it. To my knowledge, seven aircraft were shot down turning north from Stuttgart. It was a perfect (sic) starlit night with unlimited visibility. Our seven Lancasters were flying almost wing tip to wing tip when we were attacked, and one by one we were all shot down. We were the fifth to fall and all our evasive tactics were to no avail. I was told later at my interogation by the Germans, that only seven crew members in total survived, six of them from our crew. What a magnificent tribute to our pilot, F/Lt Mortimer, that although he sacrificed his life, six members of his crew bailed out... During our three months on No 463 Squadron at Waddington, we had lost ten crews and I was horrified to learn from my captors that we were the first from our squadron to be interrogated.

At my first interrogation at the night fighter base near Stuttgart, I met the German pilot who claimed to have shot us down. In fact he claimed credit for all seven Lancasters. Apparently, he was 27 years of age, a graduate from Oxford University and spoke English with a beautiful Oxford accent. Under different circumstances, I had the odd feeling that he would have been an extremely likeable bloke."

Bill Baggie and the other surviving members of the crew later reported that their bomb aimer, F/O Young, was shot by the Germans (!) after interrogation. The circumstances surrounding this are uncertain, and it would certainly have been a rare occurence as the crew were in the hands of the Luftwaffe, not the SS or the Gestapo.

No 463 Squadron's other loss that night, that of F/Lt C J Martin, also affected their sister squadron, No 467 Squadron. Martin was flying on his eighteenth operation, with a No 467 Squadron crew in LM444 when they were shot down. The only survivor was the navigator, F/O D B White, who became a PoW.

The last attack of February was another 'Big Week' attack and was against Augsburg on the night of the $25/26^{th}$. A force of 594 bombers, including 23 from Waddington, attacked this ancient town, achieving an outstandingly successful result. This was another split-wave attack and the losses were comparatively light, though two crews from Waddington failed to return, those of P/O Stuchbury of No 467 Squadron and P/O McKnight of No 463 Squadron. None of the fourteen crew members survived.

The month of March commenced with the the first real attempt to put into effect the requirements of the 'Combined Bombing Directive'. This had originated in the Casablanca Directive of January 1943, which called for much closer integration of the efforts by both the British and American bombing offensive. At the time, neither were in a position to actively pursue the requirements of the Directive, which called for '...the progressive destruction and dislocation of the German military, industrial and economic system, and the undermining of the German people to a point where their capacity for armed resistance is fatally weakened...' In the event, both forces had pursued their own policies, for a variety of reasons. However, from this point on, France was to feature more often on the target programme, interspersed with attacks on the German aircraft industry. Aircraft of Bomber Command carried out numerous raids in March, four of which were large scale attacks, three of which consisted of over 800 aircraft. Among the targets attacked by aircraft from Waddington that month included Stuttgart and Frankfurt twice each; Marignane and Aulnoye in France, plus Essen, Nuremburg and Berlin. While the Waddington aircraft took part in these nine attacks, numerous other operations were carried out by other units of the Command. The attack on Berlin was to prove to be the last major attack on the 'Big City'. This was not a particularly successful attack and was to become known in the Command as 'The Night of the Strong Winds'. A strong northerly wind which had not been forecast, blew the bomber stream well to the south of its intended route, both going to and returning from Berlin. The result was that many aircraft flew unwittingly over heavily defended areas and suffered the consequences. In all that night, the Command lost 72 aircraft (8.9%), though there were no losses among the 33 Waddington aircraft taking part. Of minor interest on the national political front, the National Coalition government managed to defeat a call for pay increases for servicemen by only 23 votes. This compared unfavourably with the usual 580 majority. As a result, it was announced that "...the War Cabinet would undertake a review of service pay..." (sic).

In terms of losses, Waddington had a relatively good month in March, the last operation being that against Nuremburg on the night of 30/31 March. This attack has been well documented and can be classed only as a disaster for the Command. A force of 795 bombers, including 35 from Waddington, carried out the attack under a moonlit sky, with little or none of the promised cloud cover en route. Instead, the crews were faced with a cloud covered target and an unforecast very strong wind. The Luftwaffe controller ignored all diversionary activity and concentrated his fighters astride the route to Nuremburg. In all, 82 bombers were shot down on the way to the target and in the target area. A further thirteen were lost on the return, by which time, most of the enemy night fighters had been forced to land having run low on fuel or ammunition, or both. In all, a total of 95 bombers were lost over enemy territory (11.9%), with an additional fourteen aircraft crashing in England or off the coast. This represented a total loss of 109 aircraft (13.6%), or to put it another way, almost 763 crew members. These heavy losses, combined with 78 on the Leipzig attack, plus another 73 in the attack on Berlin only six nights previous to the attack on Nuremburg, ended the 'Battle of Berlin'. However, in a perverse way, it proved to be a turning point in the air war, with the combined bomber forces gaining the ascendancy over the Luftwaffe.

In mid March, No 463 Squadron said farewell to OC 'A' Flight, S/Ldr H B Lock DSO DFC. He and his crew had flown a total of 26 operations with No 467 Squadron before he was posted to No 463 Squadron on its formation. At the end of his tour at Waddington, he formed a new crew of volunteers and left to join No 97 Squadron of the Pathfinder Force. It was quite a crew that he took with him, which was in fact, his old No 467 Squadron crew, and it made impressive reading:

S/Ldr Lock DSO DFC Pilot

F/O Hooton DFC Flt Eng

S/Ldr Makepiece DFC Nav

F/O Nedwich DFC B/Aimer

F/O Boultbee DFC W/Op

F/O Lacey DFC Mid Upper Gunner

F/O Bridgeman DFC Rear Gunner

Some critics of Bomber Command take a perverse delight in linking the two costly attacks, those on Berlin and Nuremburg, while totally ignoring the raid on Essen which occured between them, which was extremely successful, with a loss rate of only 1.3%. Based on the losses for their two linked attacks, the critics claim that Harris' 'Battle of Berlin' was a costly defeat. It has to be admitted that defeat it was, as Harris had not succeeded in wrecking Berlin from end to end, thereby bringing the war to an early end. However, as whether or not it was a total defeat is open to question. Bomber Command mounted 8,700 sorties in 16 major attacks on Berlin between November 1943 and March 1944. Of these, approximately 500 aircraft (5.8%) failed to return. Harris' own parameter of a maximum acceptable loss rate was 5%, which unarguably was exceeded, but other raids were usually well below this rate. So in terms of loss rate, the figures were acceptable, though no doubt those taking part would not have agreed. These statistics were known to Bomber Command, but by the end of March Harris was under orders to concentrate on the 'Transportation Plan'; the attacks in support of the coming invasion of Europe. In summary, the Battle of Berlin certainly did not achieve the Cin C's stated aim. However, being the Nazi capital, it had to be defended, and as such thousands of troops, guns and aircraft were employed against the attacks by Bomber Command. These assets were therefore denied to the German forces facing the Russians, the Allies in Italy and those preparing to defend ' 'Fortress Europa' in the west. The bomber offensive became what it was inevitably destined to become, a war of attrition, with victory going to whoever was still on their feet at the end of the contest. In this regard, the gallant crews of Bomber Command won!

Aircraft from Waddington took part in nine attacks during the month of March, mounting a total of 275 sorties for the loss of five aircraft. The first losses occured on the night of 15/16 March when P/O J Roberts and his experienced crew, with 28 operations to their credit, failed to return while flying in ME573 of No 463 Squadron. The squadron lost a second crew that night when the Lancaster JO-E (ED606), flown by F/Sgt W A Graham, collided with a Lancaster of No 625 Squadron from Kelstern while preparing to land. The Graham crew were on their first operation when the collision occured over nearby Branston; there were no survivors from either crew.

Two nights later the target was Frankfurt, when 40 aircraft from Waddington formed part of an 846-strong force. This attack caused widespread heavy damage, leaving 55,000 people homeless. The aircraft flown by P/O J W Gardner and crew, JO-S (EE191), was shot down and all seven crew members killed. The Gardner crew had joined No 463 Squadron in December 1943 and began their tour with seven successive operations against Berlin! The attack on Frankfurt was their twelfth operation, by which time they had proved to be an extremely efficient crew, noted for the accuracy of their bombing. Their aircraft EE191 was flying on its 115th operation, though probably because of its failure to return, it is not listed anywhere among those Lancasters achieving over 100 operations.

A follow-up attack on Frankfurt took place four nights later when Waddington despatched 35 aircraft as part of an 816 strong force. The damage done to the unfortunate city was even more severe than that of the preceeding attack, with another 120,000 people being made homeless. This particular night attack was followed 36 hours later by a daylight raid by 162 B17s of the USAAF. On this occasion, the Americans elected to attack Frankfurt as a secondary target when they found their primary target of Schweinfurt covered by cloud. Eventually, the Americans overcame the problem of cloud covered targets by use of what became known as the 'Scouting Force'. Tour expired bomber pilots, flying in P51 Mustangs, flew ahead of the American main force and would radio back weather conditions en-route and in the target area.

An entry in the Frankfurt City Diary, in referring to these raids, includes the following entry:

"The three raids of 18, 22 and 24 March were carried out by a combined plan of the British and American air forces and their combined effect was to deal the worst and most fateful destruction to Frankfurt, a blow which simply ended the existence of Frankfurt, built up since the middle ages". (Stadtarchiv Frankfurt am Main, Chroniken 85/140, Vol 6, page 988).

A few hours after the American daylight attack on Frankfurt, Bomber Command launched the last Main Force attack on Berlin, when 811 bombers carried out a costly attack, losing 8.9% of the force. Luckily for the crews from Waddington, all 33 Lancasters returned safely. Among the facilities in Berlin that were badly hit that night was the depot of the Waffen SS Liebstandarte Adolf Hitler Division. This too was the day that 76 RAF prisoners of war took part in 'The Great Escape' from Stalag Luft III, with fatal consequences for most of them.

The remainder of the month was almost loss free at Waddington, until the fateful attack on Nuremburg, when No 467 Squadron lost two aircraft. The missing crews were those of F/O Llewelyn in PO-D (DV24) and F/Lt Simpson in PO-O (LM376). Llewelyn and four members of his crew were killed, the other two becoming PoWs. On the other hand, the Simpson crew were lucky. Five of them evaded capture, with Simpson and three others returning to England. Post war investigation revealed that their aircraft had been shot down by the 25 year old Luftwaffe night fighter ace Oberleutnant Martin Drewes who, having set the Lancaster's wing ablaze using his upward firing 'Schrage Muzik', followed it down, declining to fire again. As a result all members of the Simpson crew succeeded in bailing out, Their aircraft crashed at Creppe, 4km south of Spa in Belgium. Oberleutnant, later Major Drewes, went on to fly 235 missions, being credited with the destruction of 50 'viermots (four engine bombers), 43 of them at night flying in his Bf110. He survived the war and eventually settled in Brazil.

Much has been written about the disastrous attack on Nuremburg on the night of 30/31 March., though from the Waddington point of view, it was not a bad night, though the returning crews were under no illusion as to the scale of the losses. One of those who recorded their thoughts was the then OC 'B' Flight of No 467 Squadron, S/Ldr Arthur Doubleday DFC. On his return to Waddington he was asked by the AOC, Air Vice Marshal Sir Ralph Cochrane, how things had gone. The AOC was visiting Waddington at the time and was already aware from radio intercepts that Luftwaffe night fighter activity had been very high and effective. Doubleday's reply to his AOC was brief, to the point and typically Australian: *"I believe the Jerries scored a century before lunch today".*

Arthur Doubleday, who was to end the war as W/Cdr Doubleday DSO DFC MiD, was on his second tour of operations, having completed his first with No 460 Squadron at Binbrook, as indeed had most of his crew. He was to become one of the stalwarts of the Waddington squadrons and was remembered with affection by the the then Station Commander, Group Captain, later Marshal of the Royal Air Force (MRAF) Lord Elworthy, who said that he considered Arthur Doubleday and Bill Brill, magnificent leaders. Even more indicative of the quality of Arthur Doubleday was the recollection of his then AOC, Air Chief Marshal Sir Ralph Cochrane. Writing his tribute in the book written after the war by Nobby Blundell entitled 'They Flew From Waddington', Cochrane recorded: "...*On another occasion a nearby squadron* (No 61 Squadron at Skellingthorpe) *was in trouble and needed a firm hand to sort things out, so S/Ldr Doubleday found himself a Wing Commander in command, and quickly restored morale...*"

Another distinguished leader who flew with No 467 Squadron while OC Operations at Waddington, was W/Cdr J B Tait. He had already achieved an impressive record of operations and was subsequently to volunteer to take command of No 617 Squadron. He ended the war as Gp Capt Tait, DSO and three bars, DFC.

Air Marshal Elworthy made specific reference to Bill Brill when recalling his days in command at Waddington. Bill Brill was OC 467 Squadron from 12 May 1944 to 12 October 1944, ending the war with a DSO and a DFC and bar. He completed his first tour of operations with No 460 Squadron, being a contemporary and close friend of Arthur Doubleday. On returning from the debacle of Nuremburg, Doubleday was more than a little concerned at the non appearance of his mate Bill Brill. Much to his relief, Brill got back late, landing in very poor weather. Apparently he had flown into the debris of an exploding Lancaster just short of the target, and a belt of ammunition had penetrated one of his engines (!), causing a consequent loss of power for the return trip. On another occasion, the Brill crew returned to Waddington with their aircraft riddled with bullet holes and with both air gunners completely out of ammunition. This same experienced crew were caught out during a pre-operation air test (NFT) in the local area. Without warning, one of the Merlin engines caught fire and resisted the best effects of the Graviner fire extinguisher to put it out. Luckily, Bill Brill managed to dive the fire out, which was just as well, as none of the crew had bothered to take their parachutes with them!

From April 1944, Bomber Command came under the overall direction of the Supreme Allied Commander, General Eisenhower, and was ordered to concentrate its main effort on all forms of transportation in France. This was planned as part of the prelude to the forthcoming invasion. The knowledge that they were to get some respite from the incessant attacks on German targets must have come as some relief to the crews of the Command. Night after night, these young men had pitted themselves and their aircraft against the most sophisticated air defence system in the World. That they persisted in their task, despite horrendous losses from time to time, is a testament to their courage and devotion to duty (or was it devotion to each other and the squadron?) During the period 18 November to 31 March, Bomber Command mounted 29,459 sorties and lost a total of 1230 aircraft (4.2%) including those that crashed in England on their return. Though some of the crews of aircraft that crashed in England survived, the loss of 1117 aircraft over enemy territory represented the loss of 7819 aircrew or, in other words something approaching 60 plus squadrons! Of these losses, most were credited to the bomber's main enemy, the night fighters.

April was to be another good month for the two Waddington squadrons. In all, a total of 306 aircraft were despatched for the loss of one from No 467 Squadron and two from No 463 Squadron. During the month, the Command carried out 32 Main Force attacks, with Waddington aircraft taking part in ten of them. Among the targets in France that were attacked were Toulouse, Tours, Juvissy, La Chapelle, plus two on St Medard-en-Jalles. Coincident with these operations were several against various German targets, including Brunswick, Dusseldorf, Karlsruhe, Munich and Schweinfurt. During the month, all service leave was stopped and the exciting word 'invasion' was on everyone's lips.

The attacks against targets in France were all part of the list of objectives detailed in the tripartite Casablanca Directive of January 1943. This directive detailed the target priority in the following terms: 'Your primary objective will be the progressive destruction and dislocation of the German military, industrial and economic systems, and the undermining of the morale of the German people to a point where their capacity for armed resistance is fatally weakened. Within that general concept your primary objective will, for the present, be in the following priority:

a. German submarine yards.

b. The German Aircraft Industry.

c. Transportation.

d. Oil Plants.

e. Other targets of the enemy war industry.

However, in the light of heavy American bomber losses, General Eaker, the Commander of the Eighth Air Force, asked for changes in the priority list. Accordingly, in view of the gradual ascendancy of Allied naval forces over the German U-boats in the Battle of the Atlantic, the Chiefs of Staff accepted the case for changes. On 10 June 1943, they issued the Point Blank

Directive, which gave first priority to attacks on the German aircraft industry. That apart, the wording of the original Casablanca Directive remained unchanged. Then, in January 1944, Air Chief Marshall Sir Trafford Leigh-Mallory and his staff drew up a detailed Air Plan for Operation Overlord, the invasion of Normandy. Their plan was to become known as the 'Transportation Plan', but it was immediately opposed by Harris and the American General Spaatz, the Commander of the United States Strategic Air Force in Europe. But the two air commanders were overuled by their political masters and, on 15 April 1944, they were ordered to put the 'Transportation Plan' into effect.

At Waddington, the Station had bad a fond farewell to Gp Capt Elworthy on 31 March and waited to see what the new man would be like. The 'new man' was Gp Capt David Bonham-Carter, who was to make a strong impression on all personnel of the Station. At the time, No 463 Squadron was still commanded by W/Cdr Rollo Kingsford-Smith, while No 467 Squadron was led by W/Cdr Sam Balmer. A study of W/Cdr Kingsford-Smith's log book for this period reveals some interesting facts. On the night of 18/18 April, he carried the Squadron Adjutant, F/Lt Bill Hodge, in an attack on the Juvissy railway yards! Then, on the night of 22/23 April when the target was Brunswick, among his crew was an eighth member, F/Lt Moorhead, who was listed as 'mid-under gunner (0.5 Browning)! This was something that the Canadians of No 6 Group had been advocating (and employed unofficially) for some time. Lastly, on the penultimate attack of the month, the Wing Commander carried a Major Greenhowe, whose role was listed as that of 'anti-aircraft assessor'! Doubtless most Bomber Command crews would have considered this to be a completely unnecessary duty; they were more than aware of the quality and quantity of the German flak defences.

The No 463 Squadron Adjutant, F/Lt Bill Hodge, whose assigned role was solely that of unit administration, obviously developed a taste for operations, as he would occasionally fly as a mid-under gunner whenever his primary duties allowed.

Between the attacks on Juvissy and Brunswick, the Command carried out two other heavy attacks in addition to numerous minor operations. On 20/21 April, a force of 247 Lancasters attacked the railway yards at La Chapelle, just north of Paris. This was an extremely accurate and concentrated attack on an important rail centre. The other operation was against Cologne, which was attacked by a 357 strong force. This too was a concentrated and effective attack, causing considerable damage and many casualties.

The 38 Waddington crews taking part in the attack on La Chapelle, were joined by W/Cdr Tait, who flew a No 463 Squadron aircraft (LM548) with a No 467 Squadron crew. Sadly, F/O Feeney and crew of No 467 Squadron were shot down on this their sixth operation; not one crew member survived. The next night it was the attack on Brunswick, in which 36 out of the 238 Lancasters taking part, came from Waddington. This was the first occasion in which the No 5 Group low level marking method was used over a heavily defended German target. This was not considered to have been a particularly accurate attack, and cost the Station the loss of P/O Schomberg and crew of No 463 Squadron flying in JO-L (LL892). They were flying on their eleventh operation, four of which had been to Berlin. None of the crew survived, but after the Allied armies pushed into northern Holland, the wreck of their aircraft was located near Nieuwolda, to the East of Groningen.

Among those who remembered April 1944 was Jim Marshall's Flight Engineer, Sgt Basil Oxtaby, who recalled:

" On a trip to France, we took the new Station Commander, Gp Capt Bonham-Carter, as our second pilot. We were briefed not to log him, as he did not have permission to go on operations. Our skipper, Jim Marshall declined the Group Captain's request to 'go over and look at those pretty lights'. What he was looking at was light flak tracer, which he had never seen before. We had and we wanted nothing to do with it!"

The Marshall crew completed a full tour of 32 operations before being screened. Their navigator, F/Lt Arnold Easton DFC was one of a select few to have his route winds broadcast back to Group HQ, who averaged out the figures received from the selected navigators. These averaged winds would then be rebroadcast as a mean wind to all Main Force crews. The aim of this being to reduce the number of aircraft straying off course and into heavily defended areas. It was during this period that a Station Lancaster returned to base with the rear gunner fast asleep in his turret, with his fingers still curled round the triggers of his four Browning machine guns. As the tail-wheel dropped on to the runway, a burst of tracer streaked across the airfield, some of it passing through the control tower. Fortunately, there were no casualties, but some embarrassing questions had to be answered.

On the night of 24/25 April, 244 Lancasters carried out what was described by the German post-raid report, as the most destructive raid on the city of Munich to date. 33 of the attackers came from Waddington, including the Marshall crew, who were flying on their 31st and penultimate operation. This crew had good cause to remember this particular attack, as their bomb aimer called for two dummy runs over the target before being satisfied that he could properly identify the aiming point. The crew's comments on and after the third run in to bomb are not on record!

In early April, W/Cdr Tait had assumed command of the Film Unit based at Waddington and he was again operating with a hybrid crew from No 463 Squadron during the attack on Brunswick. Though he was not a member of either squadron, the Aussies had great respect for Tait, particularly because of his willingness to fly on operations when he need not have done so. This was even more laudable as it necessitated his flying with a motley collection of odds and sods; a practice not recommended for a long and happy life. On one occasion, while climbing to his assigned height, with the auto-pilot engaged (not something practiced by most pilots), Tait was passing the time reading a map, though some sources say that it was a novel, not a map. Suddenly, there was a panic call from the bomb aimer saying that an electrical fire had broken out in his compartment. Without putting his map (or novel) down, Tait snapped "Well put the bloody thing out then". The crew then continued on their way to the target. Of such things are legends made.

On the night of 26/27 April, Bomber Command was out in force over Germany yet again. This time the target was Schweinfurt, when a force of 206 Lancasters from No 5 Group carried out an attack which was subsequently assessed as having been a failure. The attackers met with unexpectedly strong headwinds, which delayed the marker aircraft, and the subsequent marking was inaccurate. Despite a coincident attack on Essen, the Luftwaffe night fighters were present in considerable strength and exacted a heavy toll. In all, 21 Lancasters were lost (9.3%), though all 27 aircraft from the Station made it back to base; but only just!

Flying in Lancaster LL881, F/O Dudley Ward and crew of No 463 Squadron had just completed their bombing run when they had to shut down their starboard outer engine. Some time later, as they passed Orleans, the port outer failed. Carefully nursing his aircraft homeward, Ward's problems became acute when a third engine failed! Ordering his crew to take up ditching positions, he attempted to re-start one of the two other engines. Luckily, with a 100-mile sea crossing ahead of them, he was successful and eventually landed at Tangmere. Sadly, Dudley ward and his crew were all killed in action five operations and two weeks later, during an attack on Lille.

Among the non-operational elements at Waddington at this time was a little known detachment known as the Base Test Crew. Their job was to carry out any required air tests of No 53 Base Lancasters, plus quite a number for other No 5 Group bases. The captain of the crew was Australian F/O Douglas Toovey DFC and bar. All members of his crew had completed their first tour of operations with No 50 Squadron at RAF Skellingthorpe, one of the Waddington satellite stations. During the course of their first tour, the Toovey crew undertook eight attacks on Berlin. They arrived at Waddington in January 1944 and by August of that year, all members of the crew had been commissioned. Sgt, later F/O Bill Kelbrick, was the mid upper gunner, and he recalled:

"...we would collect an aircraft direct from the factory at Woodford and fly it to Waddington. Once Base Major Servicing, under the leadership of W/Cdr Brown and S/Ldr Hobbs ('Green') had completed the necessary modifications, we took it up and tested it in every department: guns, electrics, navigation equipment, radio and bombing etc etc. For testing the bombing systems, we would carry out academic bombing runs on targets in the Wash bombing ranges, using practice bombs. We would also test the aircraft's ability to fly first on three engines, then on two. On one occasion, we tried it out on one engine; something that we never repeated! All in all, we must have tested over two hundred aircraft, some of them having been flown into Waddington by the pilots of the Air Transport Auxiliary (ATA) I recall that on one occasion we were more than a little surprised to see a female ferry pilot climb out of a Lancaster that she had just flown into Waddington on her own, with no co-pilot or flight engineer. When we tested an aircraft, we would deliver it direct to the station or squadron to which it had been allocated. On hand-over, the Lancasters were fully operational and in many instances, would fly on operations that same night. During our time as the Base Test Crew, we took part in aircraft carrier trials (sic). The airfield that we used for this purpose had an aircraft carrier deck painted on its runway. The main object as far as we were concerned was to test and evaluate some new form of approach and landing system.

Among the Station personnel I can recall were:

- *W/Cdr Engineering – W/Cdr Day; later W/Cdr Brown*
- *W/Cdr Operations – W/Cdr Tait; later W/Cdr McFarlane*
- *OC RAF Regimen –t W/Cdr Shepherd-Nunn (a concert pianist)*
- *Base Adjutant – F/Lt H R Locke (a schoolmaster)*
- *W/Cdr Administration – W/Cdr Sherlock (an ex regular F/Sgt)*
- *Senior Air Traffic Controller – S/Ldr Knox*
- *AVRO Liaison Manager – Mr 'Snowy' Langton*

For the crews of the two Waddington squadrons, the month of May opened with nine consecutive attacks on targets in France and Belgium. The rest of the month included one attack each on Brunswick, Duisburg and Eindhoven, plus three more against French targets. The first attack of the month was that on Toulouse, where the designated aiming points were an aircraft assembly plant and an explosives factory.

The Station despatched 20 Lancasters, all of which returned safely, as did all the 139 aircraft taking part. Sadly, this was not to be the case on the next operation. There had been some concern in high places that the Command's Main Force crews would not be accurate enough to hit the small targets of the type nominated for pre-invasion destruction. Furthermore, there was even more concern regarding the distinct possibility of many French and Belgian civilians being killed when the Main Force took on these targets. In the event, Bomber Command was to prove that its crews could, and did, bomb extremely accurately, though on some occasions the target selection could have been better.

Mailly-le-Camp

On 3 May, the Command selected for destruction the old French army camp on the outskirts of the village of Mailly, known as Mailly-le-Camp. The camp was near Rheims in northern France and was used by the Germans for the training and reinforcement of front-line Panzer regiments. It was a large complex, containing barracks, workshops, adminsitrative buildings, together with an extensive tank training area. Allied intelligence staffs considered that such a unit, only 80 miles East of Paris and within relatively easy reach of the invasion area, would pose a distinct threat; ergo, it had to be eliminated despite its close proximity to the village of Mailly, and the concomitant risk to French civilians. The meteorologists had forecast a cloudless night over northern France and this, together with a three-quarter moon, made conditions ideal. In view of the relatively small size of the target, Command decided to send aircraft from only two Groups; Nos 1 and 5, both of which were equipped with Lancasters.

The plan of attack had two critical components. Firstly, because of the risk of killing many French civilians, it was imperative that both the placing of target markers and the subsequent bombing had to be extremely accurate. Secondly, in order to catch as many troops as possible in unprotected buildings, the attack had to develop quickly, before these troops could get into shelters. This second element also included an assessment that an accurate attack completed quickly, should give the Main Force crews time to get away before the intervention of German night fighter units based further to the East. Despite the dichotomy between the two components, speed and accuracy, a plan was eventualy pieced together and set in train. The plan called for the attack to commence at midnight on 3 May. There were to be three aiming points; one at each end of the barracks complex and one on the workshops. The target area would be illuminated by PFF crews from Nos 83 and 97 Squadrons, enabling W/Cdr Leonard Cheshire to lead in his four Mosquitos of No 617 Squadron. Their role was to accurately mark the first of the designated targets. Then, with one end of the barracks marked, approximately 180 Lancasters of No 5 Group, including 22 from Waddington, would bomb the markers laid at low level by the Mosquitos. Ten minutes later, the marker aircraft would mark the other end of the camp complex, which would then be attacked by the second wave of approximately 170 Lancasters; these from No 1 Group. During these two attacks, a separate No 1 Group marker force would mark the workshops complex which, in turn, would be bombed by a force of 30 Lancasters, again from No 1 Group. All the attacking aircraft were to carry a mixed load of 4,000lb 'Cookies' and 500lb medium capacity bombs.

W/Cdr Cheshire had been designated the Marker Leader, with W/Cdr Deane of No 83 Squadron acting as the Master Bomber. Deane would be backed up by S/Ldr R N M Sparks, also from No 83 Squadron. The attack schedule called for the 346 Lancaster attack to last for a little under 30 minutes. The Waddington component joined up with other Lincolnshire based squadrons and set heading for Reading, one of the Command's regular turning points. From Reading their route took the attackers to Beachey Head and on to the French coast, just north of Dieppe, which they crossed at 12,000 feet. Having cleared the enemy's coastal defences, the force of Lancasters commenced a descent at speed, in order to reach their assigned holding areas, fifteen miles north of the target.

The Luftwaffe air defence system picked up the raiders and initiated some interceptions, none of which were successful. Indeed, the Lancaster air gunners claimed three enemy night fighters shot down during this early phase. In the meantime, the illuminators had done their work well and Cheshire had no trouble in placing his target markers in the area of the first aiming point. However, he was not satisfied that they were close enough to the target, so he called up another Mosquito to put down new markers. This was done accurately by F/Lt David Shannon of No 617 Squadron. Satisfied, Cheshire called up the Master Bomber and told him to call in the first wave. W/Cdr Deane did as directed, but it was at this point that things started to go horribly wrong. Deane's transmission to the Main Force, who were orbiting a yellow Target Indicator, could not be heard. The transmissions from his TR1196 VHF set were being drowned out by a more powerful American Forces Broadcast news programme. Realising that the Main Force had not received his call to come in and bomb, Deane ordered his wireless operator to re-transmit the same message using WT morse code from his TR1154/1155. This too proved to be ineffective. It was subsequently discovered that the set in Deane's aircraft was 30kcs off frequency. Despite the frequency discrepancy, a few of the orbiting bomber crews heard a disjointed order to bomb, through the louder American radio station, and commenced the attack. A few other crews followed their example despite not having heard the order themselves. Tragically, the majority of the bomber crews remained steadfastly orbiting the marker as ordered. Those crews that did bomb in this early stage, placed their loads accurately on the red Spot Fires.

Seeing what was happening and noting that the exploding bombs were begining to obscure the red Spot Fires, Cheshire called up the Master Bomber (Deane) and requested that he call in the second wave. His action had a degree of urgency as he (Cheshire) could see the begining of an air battle between the orbiting bombers and the night fighters of the Luftwaffe. Again, W/Cdr Deane attempted to call in the still orbiting bombers, who were by now under heavy attack from night fighters. As previously, the Main Force could not hear the message. Realising this, Cheshire attempted to call them in himself. When this too failed, he ordered the attack to be abandoned and for the force to return to their bases; this too went unheard! By this time, a thoroughly frustrated Cheshire was getting desperate. In a final attempt to get the Main Force in to attack, he called in all his remaining marker crews to mark selected parts of the target area. All the red Spot Fires were accurately placed at low level, the marker aircraft (Mosquitos and Lancasters) carrying out their tasks underneath the falling bombs of those Main Force crews which had decided to attack regardless, having seen the earlier markers go down.

Back at the yellow Target Indicator, over 300 Lancasters were still orbiting, despite being under constant air attack. The Luftwaffe night fighter crews could hardly miss the bright marker, and must have been astonished at the behaviour of their enemy. At this point, some of the crews' patience and nerve gave out and there were numerous pointed and derogatory remarks transmitted to the Master Bomber and Marker Leaders by the still orbiting Lancaster crews. Suddenly, over the air came the first loud and clear instruction. The Deputy Master Bomber, S/Ldr Sparkes, had also been unable to hear the Master Bomber's transmissions, but on seeing some bombs exploding in the target area, he ordered the crews to stop bombing and await instructions! Sparkes was now faced with a virtually insoluble problem; he could hear the Master Bomber transmitting, but could not determine what he was saying. Should he overule the Master Bomber's unknown instructions and take control himself. Eventually, having seen many bombers exploding in mid-air, or going down in flames, Sparkes managed to make contact with the Main Force and took control of the attack.

Having finally received the long-awaited order to bomb, the orbiting Lancaster crews peeled off and, with scant regard for an ordered approach, literally swamped the target area with a mixture of 4000lb 'Cookies' and 500lb medium capacity bombs. At a bombing height of 5000 feet, the bombers were rocked by the blast of their own bombs, not something they experienced when bombing from their usual height of around 18000 feet. For many, it was a frightening experience. The night fighters too were still busy, continuing their attacks during the bomb run and on the withdrawl from the target. Among those shot down in the later stages of the attack was S/Ldr Sparkes and crew, all of whom survived. Post attack photographic reconnaissance pictures revealed that the 1,500 tons of bombs dropped had destroyed over 100 buildings, almost 50 workshops, plus various other buildings and facilities. In addition, over 200 Panzer troops, most of whom were experienced NCOs, were killed plus many more wounded. Of the over 200 vehicles destroyed, almost 40 were tanks. On the debit side, Bomber Command lost 42 Lancasters shot down and a further two that, although they had returned to their bases, were so badly damaged that they were classified as 'write-offs'. Coming as it did so soon after the heavy losses on the Nuremburg attack, it was hard for the crews to take, but take it they did and were back in the air three nights later. The two Waddington squadrons lost one crew each during the attack. No 463 Squadron lost F/O Fryer and crew, who were all killed in action flying JO-G (LM458). No 467 Squadron lost P/O Dickson and crew, flying in PO-G (JB134). Five of the crew were killed in action, but the bomb aimer and the wireless operator parachuted to safety. Subsequent enquiries determined that no French civilians were killed by bombing, though some died under crashing bombers.

The Bombers' War Continues

An interesting insight into the fatalistic attitude of many crews of Bomber Command can be gained from two entries in the diary of F/O Ernie Biddiscombe, the navigator in the Lillecrap crew of No 467 Squadron. In the first, he recorded a brief conversation between a replacement crew member and one of the regulars in another crew. The replacement was flying on his first operation:

Replacement: - *"Look, there are the track markers going down"*.

Old Hand: - *"Yeah, Jerry fighters doing it for us"!* (The supposed 'markers' were burning bombers).

The second entry refers to an attack on German Navy ships in a well defended harbour:

An anonymous flight engineer, on seeing the heavy flak and tracer coming up from the ships and shore batteries, called out: *"Christ, do we really have to go in there"?*

Two other such examples occured over Mailly-le-Camp. A voice was heard over the R/T during the protracted orbit, to ask *"Why can't we bomb...?"* To which someone responded *"Oh dry your eyes..."*

Later in the attack on the still orbiting bombers, a voice was heard to call *"Christ. I am on fire..."* To which an Australian voice replied *"If yer going to die, do it like a man - quietly"!*

Two days after Mailly-le-Camp, 23 Lancasters took off from Waddington as part of a 68 aircraft attack on an ammunition dump at Sable-sur-Sarthe in France. Crews reported a continuous chain of explosions, culminating in one enormous, spectacular explosion. The Master Bomber for this attack was S/Ldr Harry Lock, who until early March had been OC 'A' Flight of No 463 Squadron. The following night, a lone Lancaster took off from Waddington; PO-Q (ED953), flown by W/Cdr Tait and crew, tasked with photographing a 53-strong Lancaster attack on the airfield at Tours. Among the crew were two members of the RAF Film Unit, P/O Herbert and Warrant Officer McNaughton. W/Cdr Tait had assumed command of the Film Unit only three weeks before its first operation.

The next night, Waddington despatched 22 Lancasters as part of a 58-strong force to attack the airfield at Lanveoc-Poulmic near Brest. As with the attack on Sable-sur-Sarthe, an ex-Waddington pilot was flying with the PFF. F/O Allan Whitford DFC had moved from Waddington in December 1943 and, following PFF training, joined No 83 Squadron, whose crews were part of the PFF element supporting the attack. On this operation, the No 5 Group force was led by S/Ldr Brill, OC 'B' Flight of No 463 Squadron. Flying in Lancaster JO-P (DV229), Bill Brill along with other Waddington crews, obtained a perfect aiming point photograph despite, in Brill's case, being badly damaged by flak on the bombing run. His aircraft lost most of one tail fin and the power from two engines, but made it back to base. A few days later, Bill Brill was promoted to Wing Commander and assumed command of No 467 Squadron. The night following the attack on Lanveoc-Poulmic, another solo Lancaster took off from Waddington. As with the sortie on 7 May, the purpose was to again carry two members of the RAF Film Unit. On this occasion, the two cameramen were P/O Morris and, as previously, Warrant Officer McNaughton. Their task was to film the attack on the Gnome-Rhone and other factories near Gennevilliers. This was to be F/Lt Bill Marshall and crew's last trip of what had been an exceedingly eventful tour. However, the Marshall crew were not overly impressed with having to fly their last trip with photographers instead of bombs! Having attacked Berlin six times and other 'hard' targets, they felt that it was something of an anti-climax. As one of the crew said: *"Bomber crews felt that bombs were rather important in view of the risks involved..."* This smale scale attack by 56 Lancasters and eight Mosquitos was relatively expensive, with five Lancasters failing to return; a loss rate of 8.9%.

Although the crews of Bomber Command were only too well aware that there were no 'easy' targets, no matter how short the distance to the target, the night of 10/11 May possible have served as a reminder to the staff at Command Headquarters. Waddington despatched a total of 31 aircraft as part of a 506 strong mixed force attacking the railway yards at Courtrai, Dieppe, Ghent, Lens and Lille. The Waddington component took part in the successful attack on Lille, but at great cost. No 467 Squadron lost the crews of S/Ldr Don Smith DFC, F/O Felstead and F/O Hislop, while No 463 Squadron Lost the crews of S/Ldr Powell, F/Lt Scott and F/O Ward. Of the 42 crew members involved in these losses, 40 were killed, one became a PoW and one evaded capture. The successful evader was S/Ldr Don Smith who, on his return to Waddington in September 1944, reported that his aircraft had been hit by flak just after bomb release. He eventually managed to make contact with the Resistence, who brought about his safe return. This was a minor raid of relatively short duration, but it cost the two Australian squadrons their heaviest losses in a single night.

Sugar's Century

The large military complex at Bourg-Leopold in Belgium was the target for a 190-strong force on the night of 11/12 May. 25 Lancasters left Waddington, one of which was the now famous PO-S (R5868), flying on its 100th operation. The Master Bomber called off the attack half way through because the target was totally obscured by dust and smoke, making it dangerous for the civilians living nearby. The fact that this was 'Sugar's' 100th was made much of by the Command Public Relations people. Although the attack on BourgLeopold was one of the veteran bomber's shorter operations, it proved to be far from routine. Due to a major error in the forecast winds, many of the bombers arrived late in the target area. 'Sugar' was being flown on this occasion by P/O Tom Schofield and crew, who were on their fifth operation. In his post-flight report, Schofield reported:

"The weather conditions were clear but hazy when we arrived in the target area at 0018hr. We were unable to see any red Spot Fires, so decided to carry out a time and distance run from a 'Green' at the southwest sector. While on the bomb run we received a 'Stop Bombing' message at 0026hr. Nine minutes later the Master Bomber ordered 'Return to Base'. As we were leaving the target, we were picked up by two Ju88 night fighters, which commenced a series of coordinated attacks. These attacks lasted for nine and a half minutes, but due to excellent coordination between the two gunners and the wireless operator on the Monica set, we forestalled the ten or so attacks, despite being handicapped by a full bomb load (1 x 4000lb and 16 x 500lb bombs)."

At the commencement of the attacks, PO-S was flying at 16000ft. By the time the Ju88s gave up, the Lancaster was down to 6000ft. Once over the North Sea they jettisoned their bombs and set heading for Waddington. In view of the rather unique occasion (very few Lancasters got anywhere near 100 operations; about 25 in all), as many ground personnel as could, waited for 'Sugar's' return. Eventually, to considerable relief, Tom Schofield and crew landed at 0122hr and taxied the century maker into its dispersal. The next day the PR people set up the 'official' welcome. Tom Schofield and crew stood on a trestle platform, high up by the nose of the bomber, while the rest of the Station personnel, including the Station Commander and the Base Commander, Air Commodore Hesketh, gathered around beneath them. The crew drank a toast to their aircraft while the assembled company raised their hands in salute and gave three cheers. Some of the official photographs of the occasion show a Hurricane on the ground behind the Lancaster. Despite numerous enquiries, there remains something of a mystery about the presence of an obsolete fighter on an operational bomber base. One ex-Waddington stalwart, Dennis Moore, managed to shed some light on the matter: "*...as far as I can remember, they (Hurricanes) arrived at Waddington in early 1944 and were still there in July. In addition to the Hurricanes, there were a few Beaufighters, though I never really found out for certain just what they did...*"

The euphoria over the safe return of 'Sugar' was tempered by the loss of W/Cdr Sam Balmer and crew of No 467 Squadron. The Wing Commander and all seven members of his crew perished during the attack on Bourg-Leopold. Among his crew that night was S/Ldr Roy Nordon-Hare, more popularly known as 'Jugo', who was flying as 'mid under' gunner on the last trip of his first tour. W/Cdr John Raeburn Balmer DFC OBE had been posted to command No 467 Squadron on 19 August 1943, following the loss of W/Cdr Gomm. The trip to Bourg-Leopold was to be Balmer's last trip of his second tour, he having been short toured on his promotion to Group Captain!

Another crew that had problems on the Bourg-Leopold operation was that captained by F/O John Waugh, flying in PO-W (DV277). Like the crew of 'Sugar', they were unable to bomb before the raid was cancelled, and they too found themselves singled out by a night fighter. Although they managed to drive the fighter off, their aircraft was badly damaged, and to add to their problems, they were unable to jettison their bombs. Their aircraft became progressively harder to control, so once they were in the Waddington area, John Waugh gave the order to bail out, which they did over the village of Coleby. With five of his crew down safely by parachute, Waugh and his Flt Eng, Sgt Fred Peacock, landed the damaged Lancaster at Waddington without further incident.

A few days after the public relations exercise concerning 'Sugar', the members of the press were again at Waddington, this time to cover the visit of the Prime Minister of Australia, Mr John Curtin. A great believer in aviation, he is on record as having said: "*...the strength of Australian defence must lie in aviation. If we cannot afford, as we cannot, a floating navy equal to that of a World power, it is yet within our means to sustain an aerial fleet equal to any that can be brought against us...*"

The Main Force crews of Bomber Command had a week free of major operations after the attacks of 11/12 May, not recommencing their assault until the night of 19/20 May. That night the Command divided its attention between eight targets, six of them being railway yards and two, coastal gun positions. The 28 Waddington crews taking part that night formed part of a 113 strong force attacking Tours. This attack required extreme accuracy because of the proximity of the target to the residential district of Tours. The raid itself was a great success, but fog on return resulted in all the Waddington aircraft diverting to Silverstone and Wigsley. It was the day that Mr Curtin was visiting, and he waited in vain for the crews' return. Prior to the operation, the PR people had photographed the Prime Minister talking to F/O Bill Mackay and crew. The Mackay crew had not been too happy about this as it was considered bad luck to be photographed before taking off on an operation. In the course of the attack, Mackay had to dummy run on his first run in, and then collided with another Lancaster during his second attempt! Luckily the damage was not too serious and a successful third attempt was completed. On their return, the Mackay crew vowed never to be photographed again before take-off, regardless of any pressure.

The month of May ended with three extremely accurate attacks, the first of which was against the railway junction at Nantes, on the night of 27/28 May. The 31 Lancasters from Waddington formed part of the 100-strong attacking force. In the event, the first 50 crews bombed so accurately that the Master Bomber ordered the remaining crews to retain their bombs and to return home. The penultimate attack of the month took place the following night, when Waddington despatched 21 of the 181 Lancasters carrying out an attack on German coastal gun batteries at St Martin de Varrevilles. These guns covered the approaches to the Cherbourg peninsular. The last operation of May was against the railway junction at Saumur, when over a quarter (27) of the 82 strong force came from Waddington. The raid took place on the night of 31 May and was a complete success. The Waddington component had taken off in the middle of a violent thunderstorm and, as the aircraft climbed to height, they experienced the phenomenon known as St Elmo's Fire; quite frightening if you are not expecting it, or have never experienced it before. All in all that night, the Command mounted 820 sorties for the loss of eleven aircraft (1.3%). The attack was followed up one week later when No 617 Squadron wrecked the Saumur tunnel with the first use of the 12,000lb 'Tallboy'.

The month of May had proved to be a busy and costly month for the Station. Between them, the two squadrons had mounted 354 sorties to 15 targets, for the loss of 12 crews. Of these, 80 were killed in action, one became a PoW and three evaded capture. During the month, the Station's aircraft took part in eleven attacks on French and Belgian targets, one in Holland and two in Germany; the 'Transportation Plan' was well under way!

Despite the sadness occasioned by the loss of friends, something that the crews of Bomber Command had come to accept, life went on and the young aircrew made the most of their free time. On the occasions when the blackboard in thew foyer of the aircrew Sergeants' Mess carried the chalked notice 'NO WAR TONIGHT', the crews would frequently arrange a get-together in either a local village pub or one of the many in Lincoln. Sergeants Les Bird (air gunner) and Eric Green (W/Op) at the ripe old age of 19 and 20 respectively, preffered to go for a drink in one of the Waddington village pubs followed, at closing time, by a visit to Peatman's bakery where they would sit in the back room, eat jam tarts and just chat with the bakery workers. Les Bird had flown as under gunner with W/Cdr Balmer on the operation immediately prior to that on which he (Balmer) and his crew failed to return. The under gun in a Lancaster was a rarity, introduced it was said, by the Canadian crews of No 6 Group as a counter to the upward firing guns of the Luftwaffe night fighters. In practice it was a 0.5" calibre Browning heavy machine gun. The RAF had very little 0.5" ammunition, despite the CinC's attempts to get the gun turrets of his four engine bombers upgunned. This dearth of 0.5" ammunition resulted in various methods, fair and foul, being used by those squadrons employing under guns, to obtain what they needed. At Waddington for example, any diverted American bomber that was left unguarded by its crew, would be extremely unlikely to leave the Station with any 0.5" ammunition still on board! Les Bird recalled that the under gun fired through the floor of the Lancaster and that he was strapped into a bucket seat looking down towards the rear, through a hole in the floor.

For those who elected not to indulge in a pub crawl or a visit to the cinema, there was always the various informal Mess activities. As F/O Dave Gibbs DFC recalled:

"Picture a long ante room in the Officers' Mess, with a large fireplace at one end. Deep in their armchairs nearest to the fire, various Wing Commanders and Squadron Leaders of the administrative or engineering staffs are engrossed in the 'The Times'. Down at the other end of the room the boys are busy talking shop. Suddenly, there is consternation among 'The Times' readers as the fireplace bursts into a red inferno. Some joker has managed to get the contents of a red Verey cartridge, wrapped in newspaper, into the flames and made himself scarce. Such an event occurred one evening as W/Cdr Kingsford-Smith was warming himself in front of the fire. On this occasion, the perpetrator had not bothered to remove the contents from the cartridge case, but had wrapped two complete cartridges in paper and dropped them into the fire. In due course they detonated and sections of red and green pyrotechnics flew through the unfortunate Wing Commander's legs, luckily causing no injury, other than to injured pride."

Another pastime, with the beer flowing freely, would be games of 'Saddle My Nag' or 'High-Cock-Alorum'. Those taking part might range in rank from Pilot Officer to Wing Commander (sometimes Group Captains and Air Commodores would join in), and in the main were confined to the aircrew officers. An acceptable alternative to these somewhat dangerous games would be the piling up of the ante room furniture in the middle of the floor, in the form of a rather unstable pyramid. With the structure complete, the participants would take it in turn to ascend the less than steady edifice and implant a soot-encrusted imprint of their hands, feet, or another part of their anatomy on the ceiling.

Dave Gibbs and crew completed a full tour of operations, which included eight attacks on Berlin. Their narrowest escape among several, was on their return from Berlin on the night of 2/3 December 1943. Having been cleared to land, seconds after touching down they collided with another Lancaster, which had stalled on the runway. Luckily, nobody in either aircraft was seriously injured. The Gibbs crew ended their tour at the end of April 1944 and were posted to various training establishments. Some months after leaving Waddington, Gibbs was instructing at No 27 OTU when, in company with F/Lt Arthur Bowman (ex No 463 Squadron) he was tasked with taking two Wellingtons, loaded with trainee air gunners, for an air firing exercise in the Wash weapons range. Their old Station of RAF Waddington being close to their intended route, they decided to to take a low level look at their beloved Waddington. To avoid being identified, they elected to pass directly over the top of the air traffic control tower. Accordingly, they gave the Station 'a buzz'. Unfortunately for them, the Station Commander, Gp Capt Bonham-Carter, the Base Commander and various visiting Air Marshals, were on their way to the tower to witness a demonstration of the first Lancaster to be fitted with reverse pitch propellers. The Station Commander had no difficulty in identifying the code letters on the two Wellingtons and duly had the two miscreants paraded in front of him. Gibbs and Bowman accepted their dressing down, but reckoned that their old Station Commander might at least have complemented them on their tight formation!

Despite their CinC's reservations, the crews of Bomber Command quickly proved themselves capable of carrying out accurate attacks on relatively small, sensitive targets in occupied Europe. Since the Combined Chiefs of Staff agreed to place Bomber Command and the USAAF 8th Air Force under the control of General Eisenhower, Bomber Command had undertaken some 8,000 sorties and dropped 41,000 tons of bombs on the 37 railway targets allocated to them under the Transportation Plan. By D-Day, over half the targets attacked had been so badly damaged that no follow-up attacks were considered necessary. Allied intelligence services had calculated that a German infantry division of 15,000 men, would require approximately almost 70 trains to support it. Similarly, a Panzer division would need approximately 80 such trains.

The month of June 1944 opened for the crews at Waddington with an attack on the important German signals station at Ferme-d'Urville. 26 out of the total of 96 Lancasters taking part, came from Waddington, and the target was completely destroyed, with all the attacking aircraft returning safely. The early days of the month were to be particularly hectic for all at Waddington and every other Bomber Command base. An ex-armourer, LAC Wyatt, recalled that in the run up to D-Day, they had to be ready for quick turn-rounds and/or load changes. They had also to paint daylight identification markings on the tail fins of the Lancasters; some of which were changed almost daily. Similarly, as ex-engine fitter Reg Kemp recalled:

"We had to paint three white stripes on our aircraft, as carried by all Allied aircraft taking part. Of course, as the blackout regulations were still in force, this painting was frequently carried out by torchlight. The results, the following mornings were plain to see - not a straight line in sight! However, it was good enough for the aircraft to be able to take part, and we eventually tidied up the artwork some time later."

D-Day and Normandy

On the night of 5/6 June, a mixed force of 1,012 bombers attacked a variety of coastal gun batteries. The 28 Lancasters from Waddington formed part of the force assigned to attack St Pierre-du-Mont as their part in Operation Flashlamp, the neutralising of all German coastal gun batteries in the invasion area. In the event, virtually all the bombing was based on Oboe marking as all but two of the targets were covered by cloud. In all, 5,000 tons of bombs were dropped; so far, the greatest tonnage dropped in one night by the Command.

One of the Waddington aircraft, PO-V (LL846), flown by F/Lt Lawrence Hawes and crew, carried two members of the RAF Film Unit: F/O B T Lendrum and P/O Morris. To enable the film people to obtain worthwhile footage, Hawes brought his Lancaster down to 3000ft in order to get below the cloud base, while the bombers up above dropped their loads blind! So tight was the timing, that the advance units of the invading forces were ashore in Normandy before the last of the bombers had landed at their home bases. Three aircraft were lost during these attacks, but all the Waddington aircraft returned home safely.

The next morning, D-Day, the Station despatched 36 aircraft as part of a mixed force of 1,065 aircraft attacking various railway and road targets along the German lines of communication. All the targets were in or near French towns and the bomber crews did their utmost, often at great risk to themselves, to avoid causing any French civilian casualties. Sadly, some were inevitable in view of the weight of bombs being delivered. This particular attack was to be W/Cdr Kingsford-Smith's 27th operation. Among the other Waddington crews taking part was a composite crew captained by F/O Bill Mackay of No 467 Squadron. He had just returned to the Station from tour-expiry leave but managed to talk his way on to the operation, despite the fact that the only available regular member of his crew was F/Lt Harry Bentley, his mid upper gunner. Harry Bentley too, had returned from leave just in time to take part in the memorable events of the day. The rest of the crew got back too late, and were disappointed to have missed it. That Bill Mackay and Harry Bentley should volunteer to take part in an operation while they were 'screened' is all the more surprising, when among their 32 operations, the name of Berlin features nine times! The Mackay crew on this auspicious occasion were as follows:

PO-H (ED532)
F/O Bill Mackay DFC RAAF (Pilot)*
Sgt V L Johnson RAF (Flt Eng)
F/Lt P E McCarthy DFC DFM RAAF (Nav)
Sgt R O Norfolk RAF (BA)
P/O T H Ronaldson RAF (W/Op)
F/Lt H C J Bentley DFC RAAF (MU/G)
Sgt G T Tipping RAF (R/G)

Two nights later, the targets were various railway complexes behind the German lines. A total force of 483 bombers took part, 29 of them from Waddington. Rennes was considered by the crews to be something of a 'softy'; not far inland and probably not heavily defended, but for F/O Noel Sanders and crew it would turn out to be a night to remember. This was their 13th operation and they were flying in their favourite aircraft, JO-V (ED611), better known as 'Uncle Joe'. 'V' Victor had already flown 50 operations when it was passed on to the Sanders crew in May 1944. It was eventually to be 'Struck Off Charge' (SOC) on 20 June 1947 with over 100 operations to its credit.

On this particular evening, the Lancaster carried a bomb load of 4 x 1,000lb and 9 x 500lb bombs, together with a fuel load of 1,600 gallons. They were seen off by the usual crowd of well wishers, which on this occasion included the Base Commander, the Station Commander and some high ranking visitors. All seemed to be going well until about half-way down the runway when, with the airspeed indicator showing 95mph, there was a loud bang under the starboard wing, followed by the aircraft swinging to starboard. Realising that he had a burst tyre and that it was too late to pull up, Sanders rammed the throttles through the gate and dragged the heavily laden bomber off the ground. Meanwhile, the spectators, to a man (or woman) seeing what seemed certain to be certain disaster, threw themselves to the ground, rank notwithstanding!

---

* Later shot down in an attack on Gelsenkirchen on 21 July 1944.

The personnel in Air Traffic Control likewise had a few terrifying moments as the huge Lancaster barely missed the tower as it lurched across the airfield. With a terse call of "Tyre on the runway", Sanders and crew set off for their target! Once over the target, the bomb aimer, F/O Eric Rosenfeld had great difficulty in picking up the aiming point. He called for several dummy runs before being confident of hitting the target and not the nearby French houses. The consequent delay left them virtually isolated in the target area and, inevitably, the radar-predicted flak scored a hit. The explosion on the port side tore a gaping hole in the fuselage, right beside the navigator's station, tearing away one leg of his battledress trousers and part of one sleeve; all this without touching him. It was definitely F/Sgt Max Greacen's lucky day. Subsequent inspection of the aircraft revealed a total of 43 holes in 'Uncle Joe'. On nearing Waddington on their return, the crew were warned that the Station was fogged in and that they were to divert to the FIDO equipped crash strip at Carnaby near Bridlington. Despite the damage and the lack of a tyre on the starboard side, Sanders made a successful landing, though the thought of veering off the runway and into the fuel-filled FIDO pipes must have been rather disconcerting. Following a week of repair work on their aircraft, Noel Sanders and crew were reunited with 'Uncle Joe' and went on to complete a full tour of 33 operations by the end of August 1944.

Less fortunate than the Sanders crew that night was the crew of F/O H A Parkinson, flying in PO-A (LM440). The attack on Rennes was their eighth operation, during which they were badly damaged by flak. They too were ordered to divert because of the fog and, while attempting to land an almost uncontrolable aircraft at Catfoss near Beverley, they struck a tree on their approach and crashed. The only member of the crew to survive was the W/Op, F/Sgt Mossenson.

During the days which led up to D-Day, both squadrons had been kept busy, mostly flying daylight operations. To reduce the weight of the aircraft, the ground crews were tasked with removing the exhaust flame dampers (shrouds) from the engines. The returning aircraft, with their blue exhaust flames sometimes visible in the dull light, were often watched by numerous spectators, who had previously had little opportunity to see the Station's bombers return; normally in the early hours of the morning. On one particular occasion at this period, a returning Lancaster was seen to have lost one tail fin. Word spread quickly and a sizeable crowd gathered to watch the landing. It transpired that the aircraft had been struck by a bomb falling from another aircraft flying higher. As the Lancaster approached the runway, the watchers could see that not only was there a fin missing, but that there were incendiary bombs sticking up out of the wings and fuselage! There was a spontaneous cheer and burst of applause as the damaged bomber made a perfect landing.

On the night of 10/11 June the target was, once again, the railways feeding the German front line. In all, a force of 423 bombers were assigned to attack four major rail centres. The 30 Lancasters from Waddington were allocated the Orleans rail complex. This was quite an expensive attack, with fifteen Lancasters and three Halifaxes being lost. Among those missing, was one from No 463 Squadron. Flown by P/O Fletcher and crew on their seventh operation, Lancaster JO-P (DV229) had 'Admiral Shite Hawk' emblazoned on the port side of the nose. In addition, this aircraft, which was flying on its 59th operation, carried Winston Churchill's words painted on the side of the nose - 'We Shall Return Them Tenfold'.

At the debriefing following the attack on Orleans, several crews complained that they had been fired upon by naval vessels as they crossed the Channel. As the Kreigsmarine was conspicuous by its absence, the vessels in question could have only been Allied warships. Furthermore, some crews reported hearing Fletcher calling up Southampton naval base while being fired upon. Whatever the facts, approximately 20 minutes after leaving the target area, Fletcher's port inner engine burst into flames, followed soon after by his port outer. He turned his aircraft towards the Allied bridgehead in order to get over friendly territory as soon as possible, but soon realised that they were not going to make it. Fletcher ordered his crew to bail out, which all six did successfully. Fletcher however had left it too late to escape himself, holding the aircraft straight and level as his crew abandoned their bomber. That he, along with many others in similar situations, received no gallantry award for their sacrifice is just one of many injustices. Of his crew, four became PoWs, while two managed to evade capture and were eventually handed over to advancing troops by the French. The day after the loss of the Fletcher crew, a newly joined crew on No 467 Squadron crashed, having been on the squadron for three days. They were on their first squadron training sortie, flying in PO-D (LM552), when they disappeared without trace over the Irish Sea.

The railway yard at Poitiers was the target for aircraft of No 5 Group on the night of 12/13 June. In all, a mixed force of 671 aircraft attacked a variety of communications targets, though the attack on Poitiers was singled out by Bomber Command as being the most accurate of the night. All 32 aircraft despatched from Waddington returned safely. The day after the attack on Poitiers, the Army reported that major German army units were forming up in the Aunay-sur-Odon and Evrecy areas. Accordingly, two operations were prepared and executed that night. At Aunay, 223 Lancasters of No 5 Group carried out a precision attack which completely destroyed the combat capability of the enemy units, without loss. This operation was W/Cdr Kingsford-Smith's thirtieth and last operation, and he carried with him, two film unit personnel to record the attack.

W/Cdr D R Donaldson assumed command of No 463 Squadron on 18 June, taking over from W/Cdr Rollo Kingsford-Smith DSO DFC. Meanwhile, aircraft of Bomber Command were being diverted from their task of supporting the ground forces to counter a new and most dangerous threat. The German 'V' weapons sites had been accorded a lower priority than those forming part of the 'Transport Plan', or the support of the invasion forces, as far back as February 1944 when the so-called 'Crossbow' targets were listed as second principal targets. All this changed on 13 June when the first of the V1 flying bombs began falling on London and south-east England. On 16 June, 73 of the new weapons fell on Greater London. There was considerable concern at high level about the effect that these attacks, ineffective in themselves, were having on public morale. Accordingly, Bomber Command was diverted to join with the Tactical Air Force in destroying the storage depots and launching targets; not an easy task as they were well concealed and made of reinforced concrete. This new task resulted in numerous additional French targets appearing on the Command's target list. On the night of 19/20 June, a special force of Lancasters and Mosquitos was targetted against the German flying bomb store at Watten near St Omer in France. Aircraft of No 617 Squadron dropped the special 'Tallboy' bombs, but visibility in the target area was so poor that the follow-up attack by 29 Waddington Lancasters, was cancelled.

It was back to Germany on the night of 21/22 June for 34 Waddington crews. Their target was was the synthetic oil plant at Wesserling near Gelsenkirchen. This was a bad night for the bomber crews, losing 37 of their number out of a force of 133 aircraft (27.8%). Three of the crews that failed to return were from Waddington. No 463 squadron lost the highly experienced F/Lt E A L Smith and crew who were flying in JO-S (DV280) on their 23rd operation. Flying with them as co-pilot on his first operation was F/O Bill Gossip. Left without a pilot, Bill Gossip's crew flew with the newly arrived CO, W/Cdr Donaldson, in place of his own crew who he had sent on leave while he settled in. Two days after losing their skipper, they were shot down while flying with the Squadron Commander on his first operation as Commanding Officer. All managed to abandon their aircraft, three ending up as PoWs, while the remaining four evaded capture and eventually returned home. No 467 Squadron lost two crews on the Wesserling attack. F/O Edgar Dearnley DFC and all members of his crew were killed in action while flying in PO-M (ED532) on what was their 33rd operation! Lost too was F/Lt Brine and crew, flying in LL971. The sole survivor of the Brine crew was F/Sgt Bernard Sutton, the bomb aimer. Shot down by a night fighter, their Lancaster crashed three miles from the German/Dutch border. As Bernard Sutton stated in his report:

"We were shot down by a night fighter at about 0135hr, just as we were approaching the Dutch border. Our starboard wing caught fire (Schrage Muzik?)...our pilot ordered 'Put on parachutes'. I had just clipped my parachute pack on the right side only of my harness when our aircraft seemed to blow up. I found myself falling. so I pulled the 'D'-ring, eventually landing in a swamp..."

F/Sgt Sutton successfully evaded capture, courtesy of numerous brave Dutch and Belgian men and women.

On 22 June, the Duke of Gloucester visited the Station. He viewed various aircraft and spoke to a number of crews. He paid particular attention to JO-N (LM130), the mount of P/O Hattam. This aircraft had been badly damaged by flak during an operation the previous night; the bomb aimer, Sgt Hamblin, being severely wounded and subsequently awarded the DFM. The Duke congratulated Hattam and crew on their safe return, but declined politely an offer to have his name added to the coming night's Battle Order.

Following a highly successful attack on the railway yards at Limoges, Bomber Command despatched a force of 739 aircraft to attack a variety of previously attacked flying bomb sites. The 34 Lancasters from Waddington were among those tasked with attacking the site at Prouville, which they bombed at low level. It was a clear, moonlight night and the Command suffered the loss of 22 aircraft, all of them Lancasters. It was another particularly bad night for the two Waddington squadrons; this being the night that No 463 Squadron was to lose its new Commanding Officer and crew. In all, the squadron lost three crews including W/Cdr Donaldson. Also lost were F/Lt J M Tillbrook and P/O J F Martin together with their crews, only one of whom survived to be taken prisoner. F/Lt Tillbrook and crew were on their twelfth operation and all seven were killed in action. P/O Martin's crew were also on their twelfth operation, eight of them having been flown in a period of only seventeen days. They were shot down near Abbeville, the bomb aimer, F/Sgt Malcolm, being the sole survivor of the crew, ending up as a PoW.

In his subsequent debrief, Don Donaldson reported that his aircraft JO-C (LM597) was hit by flak under the port inner engine which immediately caught fire. The rudder controls and electrics had also been damaged and he was unable to control the swing of the aircraft. He gave the order to bail out; in due course doing so himself. As he was descending by parachute, he saw some members of his crew being engaged by searchlights and light flak! During his assisted evasion, he passed through Amiens, noticing that the bomb damage from the attack on 12/13 June was severe and that the population "...seemed very upset..."! He decided against identifying himself there and moved on to the nearby village of Douai. Don Donaldson arrived back in England on 1 September 1944.

Of the two missing crews from No 467 Squadron, F/Lt Arthur Berryman perished in his aircraft, but all six members of his crew survived; five as PoWs and one, the navigator,F/O Jack Down, evaded capture and returned to England on 5 September. Sadly, there were no survivors from the crew of F/Lt Roland Cowan DFC, flying in PO-L (ND729). This crew were on their 33rd operation, which was intended to be the last of their tour! Though not on the list of crews lost that night, the crew of F/O Sam Johns might so easily have been so. During the attack on Prouville, they in turn were attacked by a night fighter, their aircraft, PO-V (LL846) being badly damaged and set on fire. The rear gunner, F/Sgt Jack Fallon, was blown out of his turret without his parachute, while the fire in the fuselage forced the mid upper gunner to bail out. Gallant efforts on the part of the rest of the crew succeeded in extinguishing the fire and they made a successful return to base. One month later, Johns and his old crew plus two new members, were to be hit by flak on the way back from an attack on Stuttgart and were eventually forced to ditch in the North Sea, just after crossing the enemy coast. After three days at sea in their dinghy, they were picked up by a German vessel and became PoWs. Sam Johns and crew were on their 29th operation; so near the end of their tour. The attack on Prouville lasted approximately only one hour, but in that time the Station suffered the loss of 37 crew members; 22 killed, ten made PoW and five left evading capture.

At Bomber Command Headquarters, it had been decided that the attacks on the French and Belgian targets did not merit being credited as a full operation. This resulted in the crews being required to fly more operations than the number elsewhere. Obviously, the crews themselves strongly disagreed with this assessment, but had litle choice in the matter. Eventually, the Command staff were forced by events to recognise the grim truth that there were no 'soft targets'. If nothing else, Prouville must have gone some way to proving the point. As the No 463/467 Squadrons historian, Nobby Blundell, put it *"Five aircraft and 37 men lost from a Station effort of 34 aircraft; this in an operation that took only three hours and 20 minutes from take off to landing. Some soft target!"*

The month ended with an attack on the rail yards at Vitry, followed by one on the flying bomb site at Beauvoir. Records show that JO-S (DV280) of No 463 Squadron was lost, flown by F/O Rowe and crew, but the post-war Squadron historian records that they evaded capture and were again on the Battle Order two nights later! However, their aircraft, DV280 is recorded as being lost in an attack on 21 June and again on 26 June. What is not in dispute is the fact the Rowe crew were all killed in action on their 28h operation on 30 August in an attack on Konigsberg. It just goes to show that wartime records were only as accurate as the recorder (whoever) made them. No 467 Squadron lost F/O Geoge Edwards and crew on the Beauvoir attack, which was their second operation and the squadron's first full daylight operation. Four managed to bail out to become PoWs, but Edwards was killed in action along with the flight engineer and the wireless operator. The statistics for the Station for the month of June 1944 read as follows: 431 sorties flown to 14 enemy targets; 13 crews lost with 54 killed in action; 24 becoming PoWs and 15 evading capture. On the credit side, eight of the crews completed their tours of duty, and F/Sgt Keith Hamblin of No 463 Squadron, was awarded the DFM. Hamblin was the bomb aimer in Ray Hattam's crew, and during the attack on Gelsenkirchen on 21/22 June, he was severely wounded. In the words of the official citation: "...when nearing the target area, the aircraft was struck by shrapnel. F/Sgt Hamblin was badly wounded in the leg, but despite this he remained at his post and continued to direct his captain through a successful bomb run. Not until the aircraft was well clear of the target area did he inform his captain of his injury. First aid was administered and he afterwards insisted in fulfilling his duties until the English coast was sighted..."

Following the loss of W/Cdr Donaldson, S/Ldr W A Forbes, OC 'B' Flight was appointed to command the squadron. This was a particularly popular appointment, and the genial young man with the commanding manner, led his squadron from the front., improving on its already acknowledged high standard of efficiency. F/O Bill Forbes commenced his first tour of operations on 14 June 1943 on posting to No 467 Squadron, then at RAF Bottesford. One week later he led nine of the squadron's Lancasters in a 700-aircraft attack on Krefeld. Bill Forbes completed 27 operations on his first tour, being declared tourex on 12 January 1944. After a brief spell in the Command training system, he returned to Waddington on 20 May 1944 as S/Ldr Forbes DFC. On assuming command of No 463 Squadron, he was particularly fortunate in having two very forceful Flight Commanders. S/Ldr Des Sullivan DFC commanded 'A' Flight, while command of 'B' Flight passed to S/Ldr Bill Radford. Both were very experienced operators, flying on their second tour.

On the non-operational side of Station life at this time, it too had its highs and lows. From time to time, Army glider pilots from the 1st Airborne Division, who were located nearby, would pay courtesy visits. They were only too happy to accept the offer of a trip in a Lancaster that was being checked out by the Base Test Crew. One such test crew had the reputation of proving that each Lancaster assigned to them for testing, could fly on one engine, and it was quite common to see one or two glider pilots looking very relieved to be safely back on the ground after a trip with the crew in question.

By this stage of the war, the need for light relief in the form of entertainment had been recognised and established. In addition to the occasional Entertainments National Service Association (ENSA)* show, there were visits by the RAF Symphony Orchestra, most members of which had been professional musicians before the war. Their concerts at Waddington were held in the NAAFI and were always well attended. On one memorable occasion, the conductor was the well-known Basil Cameron. On this particular visit, it was a warm summer evening, and at dusk the orchestra were playing a Mendelssohn symphony. Then, in the distance came the sound of the first Merlin engine coughing into life; operations were on! The noise of the engines steadily grew in volume, followed soon after by the familiar droning sound of heavily laden Lancasters taxying round the perimeter. Finally came the throbbing sound of Lancasters on their take-off run, all of which, to the listeners, seemed to keep time to the tempo of the music. To many of those present, it was a moving and significant contrast.

In the Officers' Mess, one of the most popular records was 'Coming in on a Wing and a Prayer'. Another was 'For All You Know', sung by the popular group The Inkspots. Apparently this record would be played repeatedly after the briefing and until the crews left for their aircraft. One afternoon, an officer who was always complaining how inappropriate the song was, took it off the turntable and smashed it. Ironically, he failed to return from his next operation.

In the Sergeants' Mess, Les Bird, the rear gunner in Dave Gibbs crew recalled:

"If the blackboard in the foyer carried the chalked notice **WAR TONIGHT**, *we would all go about our various specialist duties. The air gunners and W/Ops would most likely go out to the dispersal area to check the guns, turrets and radio equipment. The pilots, navigators and bomb aimers would go to their various sections to get the detailed 'gen' (information) relevant to their specialisation. Then when it came time for briefing, we would all go to the briefing room for the main briefing. This would be where we would find out just where we were going and the route we would be taking. Various other pertinent items of information were given to us, such as new flak concentrations, latest enemy tactics and information on any operations in support of our efforts. With the briefing over, we would then return to our quarters for whatever last minute things we had to do. We had to leave behind all personal or squadron identification. Most of us carried passport-type photographs sewn behind the maker's lable in our battle dress blouse. When the time came, we would go to the Mess for a pre-flight meal before making our way via the locker room, to the waiting transport. The vehicles would drop us off at our aircraft, where we would have a brief chat with our groundcrew before boarding the aircraft. I always took an empty beer bottle with me to drop over the target; a pint size for most targets, but a quart bottle for 'The Big City'. It always gave us a great feeling to see the group of people who gathered at the end of the runway to wave us off..."*

Another recollection is that of Sgt Richard Goodburn, which serves to show just how close members of a bomber crew came to be: "...I misread my leave pass on one occasion and was still at home when I received a frantic call from my skipper (Ray Hattam) asking why I was not back on base. After some very lucky hitch-hiking, I just managed to get back to Waddington as my crew were getting into the waggon taking them out to the aircraft. Nobody had reported my absence, my crew being quite willing to go on an operation without their errant rear gunner! We were well on the way to the target before I found out where we were going."

In the 56 days following D-Day, Bomber Command flew a total of 33,746 sorties. Waddington's squadrons flew in 425 of them against 19 targets. In all, 15 Waddington crews were lost with 83 men listed as killed in action, 17 as PoWs and six successfully evaded capture. Of the Station's 19 targets, 16 were in France and Belgium, the rest in Germany. There were four attacks on flying bomb sites, eight against railway complexes, two in direct support of the Army and four against strategic targets, one of which was an oil facility. With 15 crews lost, July, along with the preceding January, was the worst month for losses by the two Waddington squadrons.

The first attack of the month of July was on the night of 4/5 July when 31 aircraft from the Station took part in a 246 aircraft attack on the flying bomb site at St Leu d'Esserent. This was an extremely accurate attack, mostly employing 1,000lb bombs, but two crews from No 463 Squadron, F/Lts Buckham and Hattam, were tasked with dropping 20lb fragmentation bombs on gun sites surrounding the target. No 463 Squadron suffered the loss of the crews of F/Lt Webb and P/O Carter. The former was on his 24th operation, while P/O Carter and crew were on their first. Lost with the Webb crew was the 'A' Flight gunnery leader, F/O M J McLeod, who was flying as mid-under gunner. There were no survivors from either crew. In total, the Command lost thirteen (5.3%) Lancasters on this attack, all to night fighters. During the course of five years of night attacks by Bomber Command, the 'nachtjag' of the Luftwaffe had developed their night fighting techniques into a deadly form of aerial warfare.

The Station aircraft did not operate for the next two nights, which came as a welcome break for the aircrews and a chance for the hard working groundcrews to catch up on outstanding tasks. During this brief break, the Station took delivery of a replacement Lancaster; this one coming from No 1662 HCU at nearby Blyton. During the course of an acceptance air test, and with three groundcrew on board, the aircraft suffered a

* Unofficially said to stand for 'Every Night Something Awful'.

malfunction of the undercarriage, but was landed successfully, much to everyone's relief.

On the night of 7/8 July, the Station despatched 28 aircraft as part of a 221 strong force, making a repeat attack on the flying bomb site at St Leu d'Esserent. The 'V1' dump was located in a group of tunnels that had formerly been used for the cultivation of mushrooms. Once again, enemy night fighters intercepted the raiders and 29 (13%) Lancasters and two Mosquitos were lost. No 467 Squadron lost two crews; those of F/O Ryan, all of whom perished, and F/Lt Reynolds, two of whom survived and successfully evaded capture. Lost with the Reynolds crew was P/O Driscoll, who was flying as second pilot on his first operational flight. Following this second attack on St Leu d'Esserent, all crews taking part received the following message from the AOC No 5 Group, AVM Sir Ralph Cochrane:

'All members of aircrew taking part in Friday night's attack on St Leu d'Esserent have reason to feel proud of their achievement. Day photographs show a concentration of bombs on and around the aiming point which would have been considered excellent had there been no opposition. In the circumstances, the accuracy achieved is a magnificent tribute to captains and crews. It is now known that the enemy ignored all other attacks that night in order to concentrate his whole strength in defence of this one target. He brought to bear some 100 twin and 30 single-engined fighters, many being concentrated over the target. Losses would have been far heavier had it not been for the excellent discipline and strict adherence to the Flight Plan, especially the timing of the attack and the dispersal after leaving the target. The plotted positions of aircraft 20 minutes after bombing shows an even spread over a front of 60 miles, and in height between 5000 and 20,000ft. As a result, interceptions quickly diminished after leaving the target. Although the cost of the operation was high, it achieved its purpose and has received from the Press the recognition which you so fully earned. I believe it to be the best achievement yet put up by No 5 Group, and an indication to the Germans that even under conditions most favourable to them, they are still unable to stop attacks on the targets they value most highly. Well done.'

The railway yards of Vaires outside Paris was the Command's target on 12 July, when a force of 159 bombers were tasked with its destruction. Although the Station aircraft were not actively involved in this attack, F/Lt Fred Merrill DFC and crew took a Film Unit aircraft JO-L (LM587) to cover the operation. The target was obscured by cloud, so the Master Bomber ordered the attack to be abandoned as it was too close to French houses for blind bombing. Merrill and crew had already completed a 30 operation tour on No 463 Squadron, but had volunteered to stay on and fly the Film Unit aircraft. They completed a further fifteen operations before being rested. Throughout their first tour, Merrill and crew flew almost all their operations in the same aircraft JO-O (LL790), named 'Ogling Olwyn From Oodnadatta' after Merrill's home town. 'Olwyn' was eventually lost over Konigsberg in August.

On the night of 12/13 July, Bomber Command commenced what was to develop into series of three attacks on the Revigny railway complex. These attacks included railway targets at Culmont-Chalendry, Tours, Villeneuve St Georges, Aulnoye and Revigny itself. The first two attacks, those on 12/13 and 14/15 July were only partially successful, with some of the attacks having been aborted. In the course of these two attacks, Bomber Command lost 12 out of 378 Lancasters on the first raid, and seven out of the 242 on the second. Four days later, after two operations against after two operations against different targets, the Command despatched 253 Lancasters back to Aulnoye and Revigny. This time the attack was successful, but at the cost of 26 Lancasters (10%) shot down by night fighters. In total, the Command lost 45 Lancasters in efforts to destroy these important transport targets.

Waddington experienced mixed fortunes during the course of the attacks on the Revigny rail complex. The Station despatched 24 aircraft on the first operation, that against Culmont-Chalendry, and a further fifteen on the second attack when the target was Villeneuve St Georges. There were no losses among the Station aircraft on either of these operations. However, on the third attack, when sixteen of the Station's aircraft were targetted against Revigny itself,, No 467 Squadron lost the crews of F/Os Dave Beharrie and Tom Davis, while No 463 Squadron lost the crews of F/Os Gifford and Worthington. This represented a 25% loss rate for the Station on one operation. Of the 28 crew members involved, eighteen were killed, four became PoWs and six evaded capture. Dave Beharrie was actually commissioned on the day that he was shot down. Prior to joining the RAAF, he had served as an Able Seaman in the Royal Australian Navy.

On being attacked by a night fighter, their Lancaster PO-C (PB234) exploded, throwing four of the crew clear, all of whom parachuted to safety. F/Sgt John Brown, the bomb aimer, Sgt Bill Johnson, the flight engineer, and F/Sgt Fred White, a stand-in rear gunner, all landed safely and were spirited away by the French Resistance. F/Sgt Eric Brownhall, the navigator, broke his collar bone and suffered other cuts and bruises in addition to losing both his flying boots in his descent, which was a common occurrence with the big, floppy suede flying boots. Eric Brownhall was handed over to the Germans for medical treatment, and it was while in a nearby hospital that he was visited by a Luftwaffe pilot who claimed to have shot down his Lancaster. On passing over a gift of chocolate, he added "Of course, we knew you would be coming"!

As a sequel to the sad events that July night, two of Eric Brownhall's fellow crew members, John Brown and Bill Johnson, visited the site of their wartime crash in 1981. The French people with whom Bill Johnson had remained in contact, made a great fuss of them, and a local farmer made himself known to them before handing them Eric Brownhall's flying boots. Since the visit, the three have got together and remain in contact.

Between the second and third attack on the Revigny rail complex, the Station despatched seventeen aircraft as part of a 222-strong force of Lancasters attacking the marshalling yards at Nevers on the night of 15/16 July. F/Lt William Murphy DFC and crew of No 467 Squadron, failed to return, all being subsequently reported as killed in action. Three nights later, the target was the French town of Caen, when the Station provided 31 aircraft as part of the 942 strong force carrying out the operation. The No 5 Group component was led by the new Commanding Officer of No 463 Squadron, W/Cdr Bill Forbes. He carried with him S/Ldr Green, a Group Tactical Officer (?) as observer. The raid was in support of Operation Goodwood, an armoured attack on the German defences around the town of Caen. The unfortunate recipients of the 6800 tons of bombs dropped were those French residents remaining, plus the troops of the 21st Panzer Division and the 16th Luftwaffe Field Division. This attack was considered to be the most successful attack in direct support of the Allied ground forces to date. The Station suffered no losses in this attack, but only just! The aircraft flown by F/O G R Campbell and crew was in the middle of the bomb run when, watched by a horrified flight engineer, Sgt Dave Burr, and mid upper gunner F/O Jack Hamilton, another Lancaster just above them, released its load of 1000lb bombs. The first bomb of the stick passed between the two starboard engines, the second went clean through the wing, the next two passed just behind the trailing edge of the tailplane, with the rest falling astern. Despite the damage, the Campbell crew completed their attack and returned to Waddington.

It was at about this time that the government began a second evacuation of some non-essential citizens from London, in view of the increasing spate of V1 attacks. By 18 July, nearly half a million mothers and children had been evacuated. Although the defences were improving, some 200,000 houses had been destroyed or damaged. But of more immediate relevance to the aircrews of Bomber Command was the landing at Woodbridge in Suffolk of a German Ju88 night fighter. The crew had got themselves hopelessly lost and landed at Woodbridge by mistake, thereby presenting the Allied intelligence staff with a complete, intact, state of the art, Luftwaffe night fighter. British scientific intelligence specialists, under the direction of their head, Professor R V Jones, were soon studying its equipment in detail. What they found came as a nasty shock. On board the fighter were three different radar sets. The FuG220 was found to be impervious to 'window', while the FuG227 or 'Flensburg' radar enabled the fighter to home in from a range of 50 miles, to within 1000 yards of an aircraft fitted with the 'Monica' tail warning radar as carried in Bomber Command aircraft. Equally alarming was the discovery that the FuG 'Naxos', enabled them to home in from 40 miles on to the H2S transmissions of attacking bombers. As a result of the scientists findings, Headquarters Bomber Command ordered the complete removal of 'Monica' from its aircraft. Similarly, orders were issued for crews to reduce H2S transmissions to a minimum.

Despite the heavy losses on the Revigny raids, the Command was out again the next day attacking flying bomb sites. The seventeen aircraft from Waddington were targetted against a site at Thiverny; all returning safely. The next night the Station despatched 30 aircraft as part of the 302 strong force attacking the railway junction at Courtrai. The Bomber Command report on this raid states that the target was 'devastated', though not without cost. Out of a total of 702 heavy bombers operating that night, the Command lost 37 aircraft (5.3%), two of them from Waddington. Both the missing crews were from No 467 Squadron. F/O D Jeffrey and crew had flown six operations in their 21 days on the squadron, and all were killed in action that night. F/O Barlow and crew had flown two operations in their eleven days on the squadron, and again, there were no survivors.

Having concentrated on targets in France since D-Day, the attack on Kiel during the night of 23/24 July, caught the German defences by surprise. The target was the port of Kiel, with the U-boat docks being given special emphasis. It took only 24 minutes for the 629 bombers to carry out a very accurate attack. The losses were relatively light, with only four aircraft lost, none of which were from Waddington. The following night the target was a double blow, taking in Stuttgart and Donges. The Station despatched seventeen aircraft as part of the 614 strong force which carried out an accurate attack on Stuttgart. A second wave of sixteen aircraft left Waddington to join in a 104 aircraft assault on the oil centre at Donges. All the Station's aircraft returned safely, but again, only just!

F/O Sweeney and crew, flying in JO-P (LM223) on their fifth operation, were hit by heavy flak which shot off their tail wheel and one elevator. In addition, the remaining elevator was so badly damaged as to be virtually useless, while the rear gunner suffered minor shrapnel wounds. Sweeney got his aircraft back to base, making a rather spectacular landing. He was to perform a somewhat similar feat two months later when he returned with a completely unserviceable undercarriage and with a 2000lb bomb 'hung up' in the bomb bay.

The following day the target was the airfield and signal centre at St Cyr in France. 94 Lancasters and six Mosquitos, all from No 5 Group, carried out an accurate attack for the loss of one Lancaster. The missing aircraft was from No 463 Squadron and was being flown by F/O Don Grundy and crew, who were flying their sixth operation in their ten days on the squadron. Their aircraft JO-Y (LM589) was hit by heavy flak while on the bomb run, which started a fire in the starboard outer engine and one inside the fuselage. Five members of the crew bailed out successfully once they had releasd their bombs, but the aircraft crashed before the pilot and the wireless operator could make their escape. All five survivors became PoWs, though two of them were detained in hospital in France and were freed when the area was overun by Allied forces about one month later. The surviving crew members were convinced that Don Grundy had remained at the controls to give their young W/Op a chance to escape. They felt most strongly that this should have been recognised by an award, but those in authority decided otherwise. JO-Y fell to earth very close to the site of an earlier air crash which had occurred some fourteen years before, when the ill-fated R101 airship crashed in the same area.

The remainder of the month of July was taken up with attacks on the rail yards at Givors, a return to Stuttgart, the rail yards at Joigny-la-Roche and Rilly-la-Montagne (another split force attack), and a close support attack in the Villers Bocage - Caumont area; this in support of an American ground assault. All the French targets were attacked without loss, but that on Stuttgart cost the Station three aircraft. The loss of F/O S Johns and crew has already been covered; the other two crews being those of F/O Fotheringham of No 467 Squadron and F/O Wilkinson of No 463 Squadron. None of the fourteen members of the latter two crews survived. F/O Fotheringham and crew, flying in PO-T (ME856) became the 87th aircraft shot down by the Luftwaffe's top-scoring night fighter pilot, Major Schnaufer.

The month of August was to be a particularly busy month for the two Waddington squadrons. Between them they flew a total of 568 sorties against 19 targets for the loss of nine aircraft. Of the missing 63 men, 55 were killed in action, six became PoWs and two evaded capture. On the other hand, five crews completed their tour of operations, two of which were posted (volunteered?) to the Pathfinder Force.

The first five attacks carried out in August by aircraft from Waddington were all against flying bomb sites. In all, during the course of the five operations, the Station despatched 135 aircraft for the loss of two crews. During the attack on the flying bomb site at Bois-de-Cassan on 2 August, the Lancaster (ME853) flown by F/O A R Bradley and crew on the second operation, was struck by bombs dropped from an aircraft above them. One wing was sheared off and in falling out of control, the doomed bomber collided with PO-E (ND346), flown by F/O A H Dyer and crew. All fourteen members of No 467 Squadron perished. The crew of F/O Bradley had been on the squadron for just three days.

The following day the Station despatched 30 aircraft to Trossy-St-Maxim on another successful attack on a flying bomb storage site. All the Station's aircraft returned, though that of F/O Bill Ryan and crew of No 467 Squadron (PD218) made a belly landing at Wittering. The cause, was their being hit during their bomb run by falling bombs, one of which smashed through the port wing, taking the main undercarriage with it. A second bomb struck the trailing edge of the starboard wing just behind the inboard engine. The incidence of crews experiencing or observing hits by bombs falling from above in daylight, raises the question as to how many losses at night were due to the same cause?

During the second week of August the two Waddington squadrons took part in five operations, four of them against railway yards or oil depots. However, that on the 7th August was in support of the Army Operation Totalize I. This was a combined assault by British, Canadian and Polish armour and infantry, in an attempt to close a trap on the German forces at Falaise. As one of the supported tank men recorded: "...the Secqueville woods blazed under the weight of RAF bombs, not one of which fell in the massed columns of tanks only 1000 yards away..."

The first attack of the month against a German target took place on 12/13 August when Bomber Command despatched a mixed force of 297 aircraft to attack the Opel motor factor at Russelsheim. This was not an accurate attack and of the 34 aircraft despatched from Waddington, one failed to return. F/O Mellowship and crew of No 467 Squadron, flying in PD230 were all killed in action. This crew had flown thirteen operations in less than one month, foregoing leave after their first five, as was usual practice. During this attack on Russelsheim, a minor, but rather unique event took place when F/O Baggott and crew had to borrow a navigator from No IX Squadron at Bardney. P/O W S A Richardson was a West Indian and was loaned to No 467 Squadron for one trip. Richardson went on to complete his first tour and was half-way through his second tour when the war ended.

Another split wave attack took place on 14 August when the Station despatched twelve aircraft in an attack on Brest harbour. The aim of the attack was to sink the numerous large ships in the harbour, thereby denying the enemy the opportunity to use them as block ships. This attack resulted in the sinking of the French battleship Clemenceau and the cruiser Gueydon. In addition, two medium-size tankers were left ablaze and sinking. The second wave of 21 aircraft from Waddington formed part of a 411-strong force attacking German armoured forces trapped in the Quensay area. This attack was to be a mix of great success and tragic error. The German Panzer regiment in the area had taken nearly two months to reach the Quensay area as a result of Bomber Command wrecking the Saumur railway line and tunnel, but it was now ready to take its Mark VI (Tiger) heavy tanks into action against the inferior Allied Sherman and Churchill tanks. It was the main German force blocking the Allied breakout from Normandy, but the Allied ground tactics had succeeded in manoeuvring the Panzers into an area where air power could be brought against it. The attack by Bomber Command destroyed the Panzer regiment, allowing the Canadian armour, infantry and artillery units to overun the German positions with little or no opposition. They immediately sent a message of congratulations and thanks to the RAF. The surviving German troops taken prisoner were found to be suffering from what would now be called 'Post Traumatic Shock'. Tragically for the troops of the 12th Canadian Field Regiment, Royal Artillery, who were located in a quarry, they were using yellow flares for identification purposes, while the PFF were using yellow Target Indicators. This unfortunate coincidence resulted in 70 of the attacking bombers unloading on what they thought were yellow TIs, which were in fact the Canadians' yellow flares. The surviving Canadians were found to be in the same state of shock as the German Panzer troops. As far as is known, this is the only recorded instance of Allied heavy bombers hitting friendly forces during the battle for Normandy.

Holland had not featured on the Bomber Command target schedule for some time, but on 15 August a force of 1,004 bombers attacked nine airfields in Holland and Belgium, as a prelude to a renewing of the night offensive against Germany. The 32 aircraft from Waddington, led by S/Ldr D J Sullivan, were targetted against the Dutch airfield of Gilze Rijen. The airfield was utterly wrecked, with all the Station aircraft returning to base, but not without cost. Once again, there was an instance of falling bombs striking another aircraft. Lancaster JO-R (LL844), known as 'Ginger Meggs', was being flown by S/Ldr Langlois and crew when it was hit by a bomb from above. The rear gun turret was sheared off carrying the unfortunate gunner, F/O Hamilton, with it.

It was back to the business of night attacks on German targets on the night of 16/17 August when a force of 461 Lancasters attacked the port and industrial area of Stettin. Waddington despatched 33 aircraft, all of which returned safely; indeed, the whole force lost only five aircraft. One minor drama was acted out over the target when the Master Bomber, W/Cdr Porter of No 97 Squadron, was hit while controlling the bombing. He was heard to call: "*Wev'e been hit; this is it; going in now; goodbye...*" then nothing! Two daylight attacks on French targets followed; one on a supply depot, the other an oil storage tank complex. After that it was back to Germany. On the night of 25/26 August the target was Darmstadt, when 190 Lancasters carried out what was deemed to be an unsuccessful attack. All 37 Waddington aircraft returned safely. The following night a force of 174 Lancasters carried out an attack on the distant supply port of Konigsberg. All 29 Waddington aircraft returned safely, though they were diverted to Wigtown near Luce Bay in Scotland. On hearing this, the Station Commander, Gp Capt Bonham-Carter, flew a Lancaster with 22 Station personnel on board up to Wigtown to welcome his crews back from what had been the longest distance raid of the war so far.

Three nights later it was back to Konigsberg for 39 Waddington aircraft as part of a 189 strong force of Lancasters. The target was at the extreme limit of the range of a Lancaster (925 miles) and each aircraft was restricted to no more than 2.5 tons of bombs. Despite the limited bomb loads, severe damage was caused around four separate aiming points. The presence of low cloud in the target area resulted in the Master Bomber putting the Main Force into a 20 mile orbit until it cleared; this by aircraft already at the extremity of their range! Despite all the problems, Command intelligence staffs estimated that over 40% of all houses and 20% of all industrial units had been destroyed. One week after the attack, the following message was received by all No 5 Group stations from the Commander in Chief (Harris): 'Congratulations to all concerned in the devastating attack on Konigsberg. In spite of severe weather difficulties, the entire city has been virtually destroyed at that immense range by a comparatively small force'. The operations had indeed been successful, but fifteen of the Lancasters (7.9%) were missing. Waddington suffered the loss of four aircraft, two from each squadron. No 463 Squadron lost F/Lt T G J Parker and crew together with that of F/O M J Roe, whose crew were on their 29th operation. There were no survivors from either crew. Meanwhile, No 467 Squadron lost the crews of F/Os J A Richards and D J Sandell. Five of the Richards crew survived to become PoWs, but there were no survivors from the Sandell crew. In addition, the Station lost Lancaster LM237, flown by F/Lt Tattershall and crew who were attached to No 467 Squadron from No 83 Squadron of the Pathfinder Force. This was the crews seventh operation from Waddington and only the navigator, F/O Sutcliffe RCAF survived to become a PoW.

Following the attacks on Stettin and Konigsberg, all Swedish shipping was withdrawn from the Baltic. Of interest is the entry in the log book of one of the participants in these attacks. F/Lt Robert Faulks, the navigator in F/O Stewart's crew, recorded on the line in his log book giving details of the attack, the cryptic comment: 'I hope we never get that trip again'! One can but hope that the Soviets appreciated the effort.

The crew of 22 year old F/O David Hughes, flying in PO-G (LM239) on their seventeenth operation, had good cause to remember their first trip to Konigsberg on the night of 26/27 August. As their bomb aimer, F/Sgt Harry Johnstone recalled:

"*...we had been briefed on two previous occasions for the attack on Koningsberg, but on both occasions the raid had been called off, either due to weather or because* *of a possible security leak. ...our bomb load consisted of a 4000lb 'Cookie', several 1000lb bombs, fitted with various time delay fuzes, and numerous cases of incendiaries. ...our all-up weight was in the region of 66000lb and with this weight we used the full length of the runway before lifting off. At the main briefing, the intelligence officer had referred to the fact that our routes to and from the target took us over Sweden. He went on to add that although they were neutral, the Swedes were sympathetic to the Allied cause. Should we encounter any anti-aircraft fire, we would not have to worry as it would be fired only to keep us high, and in no way would it be aimed at us. Later, as we flew over Sweden and were being engaged by very accurate flak, I found myself doubting the intelligence officer's veracity! That apart, after about six hours of relatively uneventful flying, we found ourselves approaching the target area. The navigator handed over to me for the bomb run. We had been briefed that if mid-air collisions were to be avoided over the target, each individual aircraft had to keep as near as possible to the course, height and speed assigned to us. As we approached the aiming point, searchlights began sweeping the sky around us and flak was bursting directly ahead of us. It always looked impenetrable, due to its concentration, but it never was. On the bomb run I gave the final course correction in order to bring the red TIs under the cross of my bomb sight. It was then that it happened!*

Our aircraft was picked up by the much feared blue/white master searchlight. Within seconds numerous other searchlights coned us. Being illuminated like this left us feeling as naked as a new-born baby. Dave, our pilot, instinctively pushed his control column forward in order to gain as much speed as possible and to break free of the beams. At the HCU, our instructors had emphasised that once 'coned', our life expectancy could be measured in seconds rather than minutes if we did not get out of the beams instantly. .. I had earlier noticed that when we were flying at our assigned altitude of 18000 feet, we were just below a layer of cloud, but our pilot's instinctive reaction to dive for speed was simply taking us further into clear air, so I called out for him to climb, not dive, and to get above the cloud, though what good this would do against radar controlled guns is highly questionable. However, Dave acknowledged my call and told our flight engineer to put on five degrees of flap to assist us in our climb. What happened next probably inadvertantly saved our lives. Somehow or other, in all the stress and confusion, our flight engineer pushed the flap selector lever down and watched the indicator to show that we had the required five degrees. But, he forgot to return the selector lever to neutral, so the flaps continued to move down until they reached the fully down position. We were soon in cloud, which at least diffused the brilliant light from the searchlights and gave us some feeling of security. Suddenly, our aircraft gave a sickening shudder and the nose dropped; we had stalled! Pandemonium reigned, with every loose item of equipment hitting the roof. In the nose, I experienced the sensation of weightlessness as I floated up off my prone position and found myself pressed hard against the base of the nose gun turret. I was later told by our flight engineer that he found himself spread-eagled face upwards against the perspex roof of the cockpit canopy.

Just as I was gathering my wits about me, I heard our pilot call to the flight engineer that he had put full flap on. By this time our aircraft was hurtling towards the ground in an almost vertical dive at over 300mph; this with a full bomb load on board. On hearing the pilot's call, the Flt Eng forced himself off the canopy and grabbed hold of the flap selector lever, holding it until the indicator showed zero flap; he then centered it. We were now faced with the risky task of returning our aircraft to a straight and level attitude without the wing roots collapsing under the strain of the pull out. This was virtually impossible with a full load of bombs on board. It flashed across my mind that our only chance was to get rid of the bombs without delay. I called to the skipper to open the bomb doors so that I could release the bombs as soon as it was safe to do so. Dave agreed and, while using all his strength to haul the control column back, managed to open the bomb doors. As soon as I saw that we were coming up to something resembling straight and level, I pressed the bomb release button and away went our bombs, though not towards the TIs!

Eventually, our pilot got the aircraft under control and back to straight and level, though we had lost over 3000 feet of height. Our rather unconventional and rapid descent had taken us well below the radar predicted box barrage intended for us and we turned for home. Our return trip was uneventful, despite the presence of enemy night fighters. I saw two of our aircraft shot down on the way back. Any time a bomber hit the ground, it would appear as a brilliant expanding explosion, followed by orange liquid fire spreading out over the ground; seven young lives had just been snuffed out! At our subsequent debriefing at Wigtown, we decided to omit any reference to our unique method of flak avoidance".

The Hughes crew went back to Konigsberg three nights later, without incident, going on to complete a full tour of 32 operations. Following the second attack on Konigsberg, the Hughes crew, together with several others, were roused from their beds after only a few hours sleep, in order to carry out a cross-country training exercise against a captured Luftwaffe Ju88 night fighter.

The last operation of the Command in August was against nine suspected V2 storage sites. The 31 aircraft from Waddington attacked the site at Rollencourt in France. All the Station aircraft returned safely, but another No 83 Squadron crew on attachment, this time to No 463 Squadron, were lost on a training sortie. F/O Beddoe and crew all perished when their Lancaster (PD259) crashed near Kingussie.

With the Allied ground forces well established on the Continent, German targets became more frequent as the CinC Bomber Command resumed his preferred option of destroying the enemy's capacity to wage war. In September, Station aircraft flew 382 sorties against 14 targets for the loss of 12 crews. Of the 84 crew members involved, 48 were killed in action, 27 became PoWs and nine evaded capture. Notwithstanding the C-in-C's enthusiasm for attacking German targets, the first three operations in September were against enemy defences in and around Brest and Le Havre. Neither the Station nor the Command suffered any losses in these three attacks.

By early September, Duncan Sandys, then a junior minister, could tell the British public that the attacks by German V1 flying bombs were virtually over; this new menace having been defeated. In the two and a half months since they began to fall on London, 2300 had got through to the capital, killing 5475 people, injuring 16000 others and destroying 25000 houses. Unfortunately, on the very day that Sandys made his announcement, the first of the V2 rockets fell on Chiswick!

During the briefing for the night attack on Darmstadt on 11/12 September, the Station Commander read out the following messages which had been received at Headquarters No 5 Group:

From: Lt. General Crerar. 1st Canadian Army.

'Heavy bombers did absolutely first class job on Le Havre defences and contributed greatly to fine attack carried out today by British formations of Canadian Army'

From: GOC 1st British Corps.

'All ranks unanimous in their praise of absolute accuracy of bombing and timing on every occasion. On 10 September all targets were covered just as we wanted. Prisoners testify to its efficiency. On behalf of all ranks 1st British Corps wish to thank you for your wholehearted co-operation. Would much appreciate if all crews taking part could be informed of admiration, appreciation and gratitude of us all'.

Following this verbal pat on the back, the Station despatched a total of 34 aircraft as part of a 226-strong force of Lancasters, which carried out an extremely accurate attack on Darmstadt. This attack combined with the weather conditions to create the dreaded 'firestorm' phenomenon. To Bomber Command, this was an outstanding success, indicative of the Command's improved techniques and performance. To the unfortunate German people, it was another example of 'terror bombing'; a case of 'reaping the whirlwind', with a vengeance. During the attack on Darmstadt the Lancaster flown by F/O Gordon Stewart and crew of No 467 Squadron was intercepted by a Ju88 night fighter. On its second attack, a cannon shell from the fighter hit the mid upper gun turret, putting one of the guns out of action and injuring the air gunner, F/Sgt David Morland. To add to the crew's problems, two guns in the rear turret became irretrievably jammed. The Ju88 carried out three further attacks which Dave Morland helped to counter by firing his one remaining gun while calling out evasive moves to his pilot. Eventually the night fighter was forced to break off the attack with smoke and flames pouring from one engine. For his courage and professionalism, F/Sgt Morland was subsequently awarded the DFM. There was a total of twelve Lancasters shot down that night over Darmstadt, one of which was that flown by F/O J W Taylor and crew of No 463 Squadron. Their aircraft, JO-F (LM242) failed to return and there remains some confusion regarding the fate of the crew, who were flying on their fourth operation.

The day of the attack on Darmstadt saw F/Lt Bruce Buckham and crew ferry their Lancaster JO-L (LM587) to nearby Woodhall Spa in readiness for Operation Paravane, the Nos IX and 617 Squadrons' attack on the German battleship Tirpitz. Some time before this however, towards the end of August, S/Ldr Eric McCabe, the Senior Engineering Officer of No 53 Base (Waddington), had been sworn to secrecy before being briefed by the Base Commander, Air Cdr Hesketh. McCabe was told that a special operation was being planned and that he was to select a small servicing party of 23 men. At the time, No 617 Squadron was commanded by W/Cdr Tait who, when he left Waddington, took over command of 'The Dambusters' from W/Cdr Leonard Cheshire. It is of interest to note that the AOC No 5 Group, AVM Sir Ralph Cochrane, had Leonard Cheshire screened after his 100th operation, whereas 'Willie' Tait already had over one hundred operations to his credit before he assumed command of the prestigious unit.

Bruce Buckham and crew had been selected to fly the camera aircraft, complete with three camermen and two war correspondents. The full compliment of JO-L was as follows:

F/Lt B A Buckham (Pilot)
F/Lt J A Loftus (Cameraman)
F/O R W Broad (Nav)
P/O Kimberley (Cameraman)
F/O J L Manning (B/A)
Mr Guy Byam (BBC Correspondent)
F/O E J Holden (W/Op)
Mr W E West (Assoc Press)
P/O W Sinclair (FE)
F/O D W Proctor (RG)
F/Lt E H Giersh (MUG)[6]

[6] Eric Giersh also filmed the attack from the mid upper gun turret, though his usual station was that of rear gunner.

The saga of the first, unsuccessful attack on the Tirpitz by Nos IX and 617 Squadrons is well known, but the part played by the Waddington based Film Unit is not so well documented. As Bruce Buckham recalled: "...so on 15 September the force of Lancasters took off (from their Russian base of Yagodnik) and headed towards Alten Fjord at fairly low level It was a good two hours flight across Lapland and, as we approached the fjord, a quick climb to the assigned bombing height was carried out. The force levelled off at a height of between 13000 and 18000 feet. We had been told that the 12000lb 'Tallboy' bomb reached terminal velocity from a dropping height of 13000 feet. 21 of the Lancasters carried Tallboys, while a further six carried the 500lb 'Johnny Walker' oscillating mine. As we climbed up to our dropping height, fifteen miles from our target, we could see that the enemy had received early warning of our approach and literally hundreds of smoke canisters on board the ship, on the shore and in the water, were doing a thorough job... ...the others flew back to Yagodnik airfield near Archangel, but we returned direct to base; a fifteen and a half hour flight, which I believe was the longest recorded for a bomber..."

Bruce Buckham and crew were not solely there to film the attack. Their aircraft carried twelve 500lb Johnny Walker oscillating mines in addition to the two correspondents, plus the two cameramen and their equipment. This attempted attack on the Tirpitz in Kaa Fjord was the only occasion that the Johnny Walker mines were used operationally.

While Bruce Buckham and crew were on detachment with Operation Paravane, the crews of the two Waddington squadrons continued to take part in Main Force operations. On the night of 12/13 September, the Station despatched 34 aircraft on a 204-strong Lancaster attack on Stuttgart. The attack was successful, but it cost the Station the loss of two crews, both from No 467 Squadron. F/Lt D D Brown and crew were on their 24th operation, flying in PO-P (LM226) and were all killed in action with the exception of the rear gunner, F/Sgt Rennick, who became a PoW. The other crew that failed to return was that of F/O A L Bright, flying in LL789. This crew were on their second operation, having been on the squadron for ten days. The only members of the crew to survive were Bright himself and his rear gunner, F/O Manchester, both of whom became PoWs.

On 17 September, 112 Lancasters, together with 20 Mosquitos, attacked German flak positions in the Flushing area in support of the opening phase of Operation Market Garden, the airborne assault on Holland. Meanwhile, a further 762 bombers attacked German positions around Boulogne, in preparation for an attack by Allied ground forces. The Main Force dropped a total of 3,000 tons of bombs, which resulted in the early surrender of the defending German troops. Two aircraft were lost in this attack; one Lancaster and one Halifax. The missing Lancaster was that flown by F/O E J Tanner and crew (LM675) of No 463 Squadron. Remarkably, all seven members of the crew survived and managed to reach Allied lines. In his subsequent report, Tanner stated:

"...as we ran in to bomb we were hit by heavy flak. This blew a hole in our port wing, approximately eleven feet by six feet, and damaged the port aileron. The No 3 fuel tank was blown out of the wing and exploded behind us (!) By this time the aircraft was out of control, so I ordered the crew to bail out. The rear fuselage door was jammed, so all crew members apart from the rear gunner, bailed out from the front hatch..."

Although Tanner managed to regain some control of his aircraft by the time it was down to 4000 feet, he was unable to prevent it from spinning the moment he let go of the controls in order to abandon it himself. So, with the port engines at full power and the starboard engines throttled back, he made a reasonable (sic) controlled landing in a field full of anti-invasion posts. By the time his aircraft came to a stop, a fire in the starboard wing was out of control, so Tanner left the wreck in haste! This operation had been the crew's 25th and by the time they returned from leave they had been declared tourex and were posted into the Command training machine.

Bremerhaven was the target for 206 Lancasters on the night of 18/19 September, of which 36 were from Waddington. This attack caused the fearsome 'firestorm' phenomenon which gutted the centre of the town and the port area.. All the Station's aircraft returned safely, and such was the success of this operation that Bremerhaven never again featured on the Command's target list.

A force of 227 Lancasters attacked the twin towns of Monchengladbach and Rheydt on the night of 19/20 September. Waddington despatched 36 aircraft, of which one failed to return. F/O Alec Findlay and crew of No 467 Squadron, flying in PB299, force landed their badly damaged Lancaster near Vouziers, north of Chalons. Findlay and possibly one other member of the crew evaded capture, three became PoWs and two (possibly three) were killed. On his return to Waddington, Alec Findlay formed a new crew and continued operating until the end of April 1945. It was said of him in jest, that he spent more time on the ground attending courts of inquiry than flying, as he crash landed twice more before the end of the war. Also lost on this operation was W/Cdr Guy Gibson VC DSO* DFC* who was flying 'just one more trip'. He was acting as the Master Bomber, flying in a Mosquito with S/Ldr Jim Warwick DFC, the RAF Coningsby station navigation officer. Bob Faulks, the navigator on F/O Gordon Stewart's crew, recorded in his diary that the crews were not impressed by that night's performance by the PFF, as they (the Main Force) were kept orbiting for 20 minutes, awaiting the order to bomb.

The next day the Main Force attacked German positions around Calais. There were 646 bombers taking part in this attack, but Waddington was tasked with the provision of one crew only. Bruce Buckham and crew, flying in JO-L (LM587) again, were tasked with filming the attack. As on the Tirpitz operation, F/Lt Loftus was the senior camera operator, this time assissted by F/O Buckland.

The Main Force was out in strength again on the night of 23/24 September, when three major raids were mounted. A force of 549 aircraft attacked Neuss near Dusseldorf, while a force of 113 bombers attacked the Munster/Handorf night fighter airfields. Meanwhile, a further 136 Lancasters of No 5 Group attacked the Dortmund-Ems canal. This wretched canal had been the subject of numerous attacks by aircraft of Bomber Command from the earliest days of the war. Waddington despatched 36 aircraft for the attack on the canal at Ladbergen. A total of fourteen Lancasters were lost (10%) in the attack on the canal, three of them from Waddington. No 467 Squadron lost F/O C A Brown and crew, who were flying on their first operation. The sole survivor was the rear gunner, Sgt Turnbull, who survived to become a PoW. The crew had been on the squadron for only five days! The other two missing crews were from No 463 Squadron. These two losses were particularly tragic. P/O Staples and crew all died in JO-P (LM223) when they collided with Lancaster JO-Y (LM309) in the target area. JO-Y was being flown by F/O Lindquist and crew on their second operation; Lindquist and two of his crew survived to become PoWs but the other four perished. P/O Staples and crew were flying on their first operation, but their aircraft, JO-P had quite a record. It had been badly damaged by enemy action five times, but each time, its groundcrew, led by 'Nobby' Blundell, managed to repair it, but in 'Nobby's' words: " *It had so many patches that it looked like a spotted dog*".

Less than twelve hours after the attack on the canal, a force of 188 aircraft, fifteen of them from Waddington, carried out an attack on various German positions around Calais. The target was covered by cloud, so the Master Bomber brought some of the Main Force down below the cloud base to bomb visually when it became apparent that the Oboe-dropped markers were not achieving the required accuracy. Some crews came down as low as 2000 feet, suffering the attentions of very accurate light flak for their troubles. This light flak claimed eight aircraft, one of which came from Waddington. Lancaster JO-O (DV171) of No 463 Squadron, was being flown by F/O R A Jones and crew on their eighth operation. Jones and two of his crew perished, but the other four survived to become PoWs.

The night after the gallant remnants of the British First Airborne Division withdrew across the Rhine near Arnhem, Bomber Command was out on an attack on Karlsruhe. A force of 266 Lancasters carried out a concentrated attack, leaving a large area of the city devastated. 31 of the attackers came from Waddington, two of which failed to return. F/O K V Millar and crew were flying in PO-G (LM239) on their 33rd operation when they were shot down. Six members of the crew survived; the mid upper gunner having been killed in the action. Their loss was keenly felt as they were a very experienced crew, right at the end of a very successful tour. Lost with them was the No 467 Squadron Gunnery Leader, F/Lt Cleary, who was flying as rear gunner on the thirteenth operation of his second tour. The other crew lost that night was that of F/Lt A B Tottenham. They were flying Lancaster JO-L (LM587) and were tasked with filming the attack. As there were no survivors, it has to be assumed that two unknown camera operators of the Command Film Unit were lost with them. These camera aircraft were fitted with camera mountings in the front gun turret, the fuselage door and in a ventral position. F/Lt Tottenham commenced his operational tour with No 467 Squadron, with whom he flew eleven operations, seven of them in PO-S, 'Sugar' (R5868) before being transferred to No 463 Squadron and picking up a new crew. He was considered to be something of a camera specialist and was flying on his 36th operation when he was shot down.

The medium sized city of Kaiserslauten was attacked by the Command once only. On the night of 27/28 September, Waddington despatched 31 aircraft as part of a 217 strong force targetted against the unfortunate city and its inhabitants. Just over 900 tons of bombs were dropped, causing widespread destruction, with 36% of the city's built-up area being destroyed. The one Lancaster lost on this operation, was that flown by F/O R J Miller and crew of No 463 Squadron. This crew, flying in JO-T (PB263) were on their first operation and none of them survived. There could so easily have been an additional loss that night. F/O M F Sweeney and crew, flying in JO-R (LL844) or 'Ginger Meggs' to give it its unofficial name, were badly shot up and lost all hydraulics. This resulted in a wheels up landing at Waddington on the grass beside the runway. The crew elected to remain with their aircraft rather than bail out, despite the knowledge that they had a 2000lb bomb hung-up in their bomb bay! Sweeney was awarded the DFC for this action, which was not the first time that he and his crew had been in the wars. Only one month earlier, Sweeney's aircraft JO-P (LM233) had been hit by heavy flak, losing an elevator and the tail wheel. Despite this, Sweeney made an excellent if somewhat noisy landing. This was one of the aircraft that was lost in the mid-air collision over the Dortmund-Ems canal with the Staples crew. On the other hand, 'Ginger Meggs' went on to complete a total of 86 operations.

The attack on Kaiserslauten was the last for the Station in September. Among the crews flying on operations during the month, had been the Station Commander, Gp Capt Bonham-Carter. Bomber

Command was not over keen on Station Commanders flying on operations, but those of the calibre of David Bonham-Carter continued to do so, though not without a degree of difficulty. The Station Commander flew five operations with No 467 Squadron, three of them with crews on their first operation! He actually led the attack on Gilze-Rijen airfield in August with a No 463 Squadron crew, and was again flying with No 463 Squadron in September in the attack on Rheydt. On that occasion he flew as second pilot to F/O C J Lynch and crew, who were on their fourth operation. One of the problems that the Station Commander had to overcome in order to fly on operations, was recalled by John Brown, the bomb aimer on Dave Beharrie's crew, who were shot down over Revigny on 18/19 July 1944:

"Gp Capt Bonham-Carter was rather deaf and had to use a rather cumbersome, battery-operated hearing aid; hence his nickname of 'TR9' among the air and ground crews. He invariably wanted to fly in PO-S (R5868), but 'Sugar's' groundcrew were particular who they let fly her. Having flown over one hundred operations, they preferred that their aircraft was flown by a full-time operational crew, rather than any 'now and againers'. Accordingly, they organised a very efficient bush telegraph system, whereby they were kept informed of the Station Commander's operational flying urges. As soon as they received a warning that he was talking about flying in 'Sugar', it would be towed into the hangar and two engines whipped out; 'Sugar' was 'non-available'.

Despite the onset of autumn, there was no let-up in the pace of operations. During the month of October, the Station despatched 321 aircraft on operational sorties against a total of 12 targets. In terms of losses, it was to be a slightly better month than any of the five preceeding months. In all, the Station lost six crews in October; of the 42 aircrew involved, 21 were killed in action, 12 became PoWs, while nine evaded capture.

On 5 October, the day that Germany reduced the call-up age to sixteen, Bomber Command despatched a force of 227 Lancasters in a daylight attack on Wilhelmshaven. Waddington put up 33 aircraft, all but one of which returned safely. The attack was not particularly successful as the Main Force had to bomb through complete cloud cover using H2S radar. The missing Waddington aircraft was the only loss suffered by the attackers in that operation. The aircraft, PO-R (DV373), flown by F/O M J Feddersen and crew, was ditched in the North Sea, having been forced to turn back short of the target . On their return to the Station two days later, the crew told their story. Approximately two hours after take-off and while flying at 1500 feet, the port engine failed. With an almost full load of fuel, plus the bomb load, the Lancaster dropped down to 1000 feet before Feddersen was able to stabilise it. He feathered the propeller and endeavoured to keep up with the formation. However, it quickly became apparent that this was not going to be possible, and in a very short space of time they were two miles behind the formation, with the gap ever widening. Deciding that pressing on was not a realistic option, Feddersen turned back. During the turn, the flight engineer reported that the fuel warning lights for the port outer engine were illuminated and that power was rapidly falling off. This engine too then failed completely, by which time the Lancaster was down to 800 feet and losing height all the time, despite full power on the two starboard engines. Feddersen realised that ditching was imminent and ordered his crew to take up ditching positions.

Ditching a Lancaster was always a risky undertaking, but with a full bomb load, which could not be jettisoned because of their low altitude, it must have seemed tantamount to suicide. As the bomber sank towards the sea, the wireless operator, F/Sgt Houston, fired off two red Verey signals and transmitted a continuous SOS. The ditching was copy-book, along the swell and at just the right attitude. Despite this, the aircraft sank in under two minutes. The multi-seat dinghy was released from its stowage in the wing and inflated, whereupon most of the crew managed to board it without getting too wet. Unknown to Feddersen and crew, their ditching had been witnessed by an American B24 Liberator, flying at 20,000 feet. Eventually, after an uncomfortable night and most of the following day in their dinghy, a Warwick aircraft of the Air Sea Rescue Service (ASR) dropped an airborne lifeboat nearby.

Once aboard, Feddersen and crew made full use of the boat and its equipment. The Warwick remained on station over the lifeboat until 10pm that night. The next morning, two days after their ditching, a second Warwick appeared overhead, followed by Mustangs and Fortresses of the American ASR. Feddersen and crew were finally picked up by two ASR motor launches at 5pm that day. On the way back to Great Yarmouth, the launches diverted to pick up the crew of an American B17 Flying Fortress that ditched almost in front of them. Sadly, after an all too brief 'survivors leave', the entire crew perished one month later on 11 November, while taking part in an attack on Harburg. It was the crew's fourth operation and their first after their ditching.

A luckier crew on the night of the attack on Wilhelmshaven was that of F/Lt McRae of No 463 Squadron. They were attacked five times by a Bf109 'Wilde Sau' (Wild Boar) fighter and a Do217 night fighter, over a period of about twelve minutes. Fortunately for the crew, McRae was an above average pilot who had amassed 1000 hours in Flying Training Command before commencing operations with Bomber Command. His tight corkscrewing, aided by the gunners' calls, completed negated every attack by the fighters. Tiring of their lack of success, the two fighters broke off and went looking for easier prey.

The town of Bremen had been attacked by Bomber Command on 31 separate occasions before the Main Force returned for the last time on the night of 6/7 October. The 35 Waddington aircraft formed part of the 246-strong force which carried out an outstandingly successful attack. A total of 1,021 tons of bombs were dropped, 868 of which were incendiaries. It was a clear night with a three-quarters moon and the bomb aimers could not have had better conditions. The damage achieved was such that the Command's bombing analysts reported that a return to the town at a later date would be unecessary. One of the five Lancasters which failed to return belonged to No 463 Squadron. F/O Tointon and crew were flying on their ninth operation when they were shot down by a night fighter. Tointon and two members of his crew were killed in action; three became PoWs, but the flight engineer, Sgt John McLellan, evaded successfully, despite several close calls.

The day after the attack on Bremen, the Command carried out simultaneous attacks on Kleve, Emmerich and Walcheren. A total of 121 Lancasters were targetted against the sea wall near Flushing on the southern shore of Walcheren. The 23 Waddington aircraft took part in the attack against the sea wall and all returned to base - just! F/O Gordon Stewart and crew, flying in PO-Q (NF910), were in the wars again. On their initial bomb run they were hit by flak which left the Lancaster with 25 holes in the fuselage and wings. On landing back at base, fuel was still leaking from ruptured fuel tanks. For their actions during this operation, two members of the crew were decorated. F/O Stewart was awarded the DFC, while his bomb aimer, F/Sgt Robert Calov, received the DFM. In the words of the joint citation: 'As pilot and bomb aimer respectively, this officer and airman were detailed to attack the Nolle Dyke in daylight in October 1944. In the first run-in to the target, their aircraft was hit by a heavy shell and sustained damage. The windscreen of the bomb aimer's compartment was smashed (!) F/Sgt Calov was struck in the eye by flying particles of glass. His injury was most painful and he became temporarily blind in the affected eye. Despite this, he successfully attacked the target at the fourth attempt...' These awards, added to that to F/Sgt Morland a month earlier, meant that there were three decorated members in the Stewart crew.

Four days after breaching the sea wall at Flushing, a force of 115 Lancasters attacked German gun positions on the north bank of the river Scheldt near Flushing. Waddington despatched 36 aircraft, all of which returned safely.

On 13 October, the CinC Bomber Command received a directive from the Deputy Chief of the Air Staff, Air Marshall Sir Norman Bottomley, which gave details of Operation Hurricane I and II. In brief, the common objective was to demonstrate to the enemy the overwhelming superiority of the Allies, and the futility of continued resistance. Hurricane I provided for the concentration of effort in time and space against objectives in the Ruhr. Hurricane II provided for the maximum concentration of Allied air attacks against precise targets, anywhere else in Germany. By maximum concentration, the Combined Operational Planning Committee envisaged the employment of Bomber Command and the USAAF Eighth Air Force for Hurricane I, and of Bomber Command and the VIIth and VXth Air Forces of the USAAF for Hurricane II.

The first attack of Hurricane I took place on 14 October, when the target was Duisburg. The Main Force had undertaken no operations for two days, and as such the Command could put up a total of 1,013 aircraft, comprising 519 Lancasters, 474 Halifaxes and 20 Mosquitos. This massive force was escorted to and from the target by a total of 473 fighter aircraft of the RAF. At the same time, the American Eighth Air Force despatched 1,051 B17 and B24 bombers to Cologne, escorted by 749 fighters of the USAAF. In all, approximately 3,500 aircraft were airborne on the first operation of Hurricane I. Only one aircraft from Waddington took part in the assault on Duisburg. F/Lt Buckham and crew of No 463 Squadron, flying in JO-Y (PD239), and carrying F/Lt Loftus and F/O Buckland as camera crew, were tasked with filming this, the heaviest daylight raid of the war by Bomber Command.

Operation Hurricane I continued that night when Bomber Command despatched 1,005 aircraft to carry out a second attack on Duisburg. In all, almost 9,000 tons of bombs hade been dropped on the unfortunate town in approximately 36 hours. Meanwhile, an additional force of 233 Lancasters attacked Brunswick. In spite of numerous earlier attacks, Brunswick seemed to bear a charmed life, but this time it was to suffer its worst attack of the war, with the old part of the city centre being completely destroyed. The city was divided into six identifiable areas for the attack, each area having two bomber squadrons assigned to it. The 39 aircraft from Waddington joined those from Skellingthorpe in attacking the most northerly area. The targets were marked by aircraft of No 5 Group, using their own methods which finally achieved the results they had been striving for. The various spoof diversions and night fighter support were also extremely successful, resulting the loss of only one Lancaster. All the Waddington aircraft returned safely to base. The attack on Brunswick rendered 80,000 people homeless, many of whom were subsequently fed from the kitchens carried on a special train, the 'Hilfzug Bayern', which came from distant Bavaria.

Apart from despatching eleven aircraft as part of a 47-strong force attacking the sea wall at Westkapelle on 17 October, the Waddington squadrons were not called upon until the night of 19/20 October. On this occasion, Bomber Command carried out two attacks, one against Stuttgart and the other against Nuremburg. The

40 Lancasters from Waddington formed part of the 263-strong force targetted against the scene of many Nazi rallies, Nuremburg. The raid was only partly successful and certainly not the knock-out blow that Command had hoped for. There were no losses among the Waddington aircraft. Earlier that day, W/Cdr Brill had handed over command of No 467 Squadron to W/Cdr Keith Douglas DFC AFC. The squadron's new commanding officer had flown his first tour of operations with No 103 Squadron at Elsham Wolds. He commenced his second tour with No 460 Squadron at Binbrook, and had completed a grand total of 60 operations when he was given command of No 467 Squadron.

There followed a three day respite for the crews at Waddington before being tasked for a 'maximum effort' against the German gun batteries at Flushing. This was to be another bad day for Waddington, with three out of the 41 aircraft despatched failing to return. No 467 Squadron lost F/O Ted Rowell and crew, flying in PO-P (NF989). They were seen by other aircraft to be on their way home over the North Sea but appeared to be in trouble. Sadly, they joined many other gallant crews of both sides who found their final resting place beneath the sombre, cold waters of the North Sea. No 463 Squadron lost the crews of F/Os Cyril Borsht and John Dack. Cy Borsht and crew were flying in JO-L (NF977) when they were hit by flak on the bomb run. The first hit struck the starboard wing, while further hits tore into the fuselage killing the flight engineer, Sgt Leigh. Fires broke out in the navigator's compartment, with others further back in the fuselage and in the bomb bay. Left with no alternative, Borsht gave the order to bail out.

The five other crew members plus Borsht all landed safely, some more so than others. F/Sgt 'Snowy' O'Connell landed in four feet of water, which now covered parts of the island of Walcheren. Apart from a few sundry small shrapnell wounds, O'Connell felt fit enough to evade capture, which he succeeded in doing. He eventually joined up with four Italians who had escaped from a forced labour gang and all five decided to lie up on the island until it was captured by the British army, which they felt could not be long delayed. O'Connell was content to survive on a diet of tinned peas (!) which had been left behind by the evacuating Germans; not so his fellow escapers. The Italians decided that their co-residents were expendable and accordingly three Dutch cats appeared on the menu! According to Brian O'Connell, the killing, skinning and eating of these unfortunate creatures was the most unnerving episode of the whole business. He was eventually repatriated in early November. Of the other members of the crew, Cy Borsht and two others became PoWs, while the bomb aimer, F/Sgt Laing, and the rear gunner, F/Sgt Cooper, both succeeded in remaining free.

The third crew which failed to return, that of John Dack, were flying on their 32nd operation when they were shot down by flak. In the crew transport on their way out to their waiting Lancaster, this experienced crew ruminated on the wisdom of sending black painted night bombers on a 4000 feet daylight attack against a well defended target. While they were waiting to board JO-P (PB260), they were visited by their Flight Commander, S/Ldr Des Sullivan, who informed them that their target had been changed and that they were now to bomb four artillery gun positions in the town of Flushing. He added as an aside, the news that Bomber Command had just reduced the tour length from 33 to 30 operations, so that even if they did not go, they had completed their first tour. The crew politely suggested that perhaps they could be excused this operation in view of the fact that they were already two operations over the requirement. Des Sullivan said that it was only a short trip, and as they were all ready to go, they might just as well go and be done with it.

On reaching the target area they found the cloud base to be just below 4000 feet, so they descended to get below it. No sooner had they cleared the cloud when the mid upper gunner called that he could see light flak coming up all around them. Almost immediately, their Lancaster was hit and caught fire, filling the fuselage with dense, choking, yellow-brown smoke. It did not require John Dack to give the order to bail out, the necessity to do so was patently obvious. Dack was the last to leave the aircraft, dropping through the nose hatch with his parachute clipped to only one side of the harness. Despite his unbalanced descent, he survived the fall, landing in the Scheldt river. Dazed and suffering from shock, it was some time before he realised that the reason he was having difficulty staying afloat, was that he had forgotten to inflate his life jacket. At some stage he passed out, regaining consciousness in a farm house being treated by a German army medical orderly. The following day he was re-united with the other two survivors of his crew, the bomb aimer, Warrant Officer Jim McWilliam and his flight engineer, Sgt Lofty Lee. A German army captain who questioned John Dack told him that they had picked him up by boat, but that the rest of the crew had been shot (sic). What he actually meant by this is something of a mystery; possible getting confused in the translation, but the sad fact remains that four of the crew were killed. Of the fourteen members of the two crews, five were killed in action, six became PoWs and three evaded capture.

Five days later, 35 Waddington Lancasters took part in an unsuccessful attack on the German U-boat pens at Bergen in Norway. Three of the Station aircraft were damaged by flak over the target area, but all three returned to base. Sadly, the aircraft flown by F/O A T Ley and crew, flying in ND332 on their third operation with No 463 Squadron, failed to return. Only the rear gunner, Sgt MacIntyre, surviving to become a PoW.

Two other Station crews were flying that night, both of No 467 Squadron and both flying on their first operation. Both crews had good cause to remember the occasion. F/O Walter Boxsall and crew, flying in PO-U (LM746), were carrying out the standard radius of action timing procedure when they collided with F/O Lillecrap's aircraft, PO-W (NN714). Both Lancasters suffered severe damage to their starboard wings. After some initial problems, Frank Lillecrap regained control of his aircraft, cancelling the 'prepare to abandon' order and flew to the Wash weapons range where they jettisoned their bombs. Following a low speed handling check at 11000 feet, and two overshoots, Lillecrap made a successful landing at Waddington. On inspection, it was found that his Lancaster had lost three feet of starboard wing and that the outer engine in that wing had seized at the moment of impact. In the other aircraft, 'Kitch' Boxsell bailed out four members of his crew before making a good landing at the crash strip at Carnaby near Bridlington.

On their return to Waddington, the rest of the Station aircraft were diverted to nearby Fiskerton where they landed with the rather frightening aid of FIDO (Fog Investigation Dispersal Operation or Fog Intensive Dispersal Of - whichever version you prefer). Some crews subsequently described their landing between the two rows of blazing petrol pipes as being the most frightening part of the whole operation.

Led by W/Cdr Tait, 36 Lancasters of Nos IX and 617 Squadrons took off from Lossiemouth on 28 October to attack the Tirpitz, which was at anchor off Tromso in Norway. With them went F/Lt Buckham and crew in one of the Film Unit aircraft JO-Y (PD329). As on previous occasions, the camera crew was F/Lt Loftus and F/Sgt Buckland. All the aircraft took off in heavy rain at the start of their six hour flight to the target. On reaching Tromso, the attackers found the mighty battleship obscured by low cloud and were forced to bomb 'blind'. On being debriefed following their return to Lossiemouth, those crews that had actually bombed made no claims, but unknown to them, the ship had been badly damaged by one or two near misses, which had blown in part of the warship's hull plates, letting in over 800 tons of water. These same near misses also caused severe distortion of at least one of the propeller shafts.

During the attack, Buckham had descended to about 8000 feet and witnessed the first bombs exploding about 100 yards from the ship, and saw two others explode on contact with the anti-torpedo nets surrounding the Tirpitz. The film crew's last glimpse of the ship was of her afloat with all secondary weapons in action. On his return to Waddington after a flight of 14 hours and 20 minutes, Bruce Buckham had to carry out a landing on one wheel. At some stage in the return flight over the North Sea, the crew felt and heard a tremendous crash, but it was not until the first light of day that they could see that the starboard main wheel was hanging down, the engine nacelle panels flapping loose and that there was a gaping hole in the wing. It transpired on later investigation, that a shell had passed through the undercarriage bay, carried on through the Numbers 1 and 2 fuel tanks and out through the wing, without exploding. Luckily, the self-sealing system of the fuel tanks had worked as advertised!

The last trip of the month of October for the Waddington crews took place in daylight on 30 October. Once again the target was enemy gun positions on Walcheren. Of the 102 aircraft taking part, 26 were from Waddington, all of which returned safely to base, though some later than others. The Lillecrap crew was once again in the wars, on this their second operation. The crew had been allocated PO-T, but somehow or other, a bomb fell from the bomb bay as the crew were carrying out their pre-flight checks! This resulted in a mad scramble to the spare aircraft and the consequent rush to get off on time. They made it, but just after taking off, their aircraft ploughed through a flock of birds, one of which came through the bomb aimer's blister, covering the unfortunate Bruce Lindsay in a cocktail of blood, feathers and guano! Another bird's corpse could clearly be seen jammed in the radiator cowling of the port inner engine.

Despite all this, they managed to catch up with the outbound formation, just in time to witness a No 467 Squadron Lancaster have its starboard tailplane chopped off by the propeller of another aircraft. The Waddington aircraft was last seen spiralling down over the sea, jettisoning its bomb load. The Lillecrap crew were delighted to hear on their return that the aircraft in question, landed safely. The two crews actually involved in this mini drama were those of F/O Gordon Stewart DFC in PO-X (LM686), and F/O E W Thomas in PO-Q (NF910). Subsequently, the Squadron Commander awarded the Stewart crew an operation for getting their aircraft back in one piece. On the other hand, he refused to credit the Thomas crew with an operation, despite the fact that they pressed on to the target, because 'he did not consider that their bombing was accurate enough'!

Despite the autumn weather and the onset of winter, there was still no let-up in the pace of operations. By this time, Waddington was becoming seriously overcrowded. Each barrack block or billet was required to house twice the number of personnel for which it had been designed. To overcome the problem of lack of space, higher authority introduced the double, or two-tier bunk system. This in itself was not a major problem, but as Victor Sweetman, one of the groundcrew recalled:

"...as there was always chaps in bed, having been on night flying duties, the blackout curtains never came down. The atmosphere at times could be pretty grim, what with all the problems of too many people crowded into too small a space for too long a period..."

A more light hearted aspect of the flying was that of the unofficial one-upmanship between Lancaster crews and those of the American Flying Fortresses. Lyle Pattison, the navigator in Merv Bache's crew, recalled being engaged in a training flight over central England when Bache spotted a Fortress and closed in on it until flying in formation. The American pilot took this as a challenge and feathered one engine, whereupon Bache followed suit. The American then feathered a second engine; again copied by Bache. Moments later, it became apparent that the Fortress was struggling, so Bache proceeded to cavort around the sky, performing two-engine manoeuvres all round the Fortress. Tapping his forehead, the Fortress pilot opened up his two feathered engines and peeled off. Some weeks later, a similar competition occured, this time involving the Lillecrap crew.

November 1944 saw the Australian squadrons at Waddington commencing their second year in residence. The month was to be a hard one for the Station as, in the course of 275 operational sorties, it would have to bear the loss of nine crews in attacks on nine targets. Of the 63 aircrew involved in these losses, 32 would be killed in action, 20 become PoWs and eleven would successfully evade capture. In addition, the Station would suffer the loss of two crews from No IX Squadron who were flying with No 463 Squadron for experience.

The month commenced with the Station despatching 36 aircraft as part of a force of 226 Lancasters to bomb the Meerbeck oil installation at Homberg. All the Waddington aircraft returned safely to base. The next night, 2/3 November, the Command despatched 992 aircraft on the last attack of the war on Dusseldorf. Thirty of the attackers came from Waddington, two of which failed to return. No 463 Squadron lost F/O Smith and crew, flying in JO-C (PD338) on their third operation. Smith and five members of his crew became PoWs, but their wireless operator was killed in action. No 467 Squadron lost F/O Leslie Langridge and crew who were flying in PO-B (DV396) on their ninth operation. Langridge and his rear gunner were killed, but the other five members of the crew bailed out safely over Allied lines. PO-B was shot down by the combined efforts of a night fighter equipped with 'Schrage Muzik' upward firing cannon, and a free flying 'Wilde Sau' (Wild Boar) FW190.

With the port outer engine on fire and one tailplane shot away, the Lancaster fell away into a spin, but not before the mid upper gunner, Sgt Derek Allen, managed to get in some telling hits on the night fighter. Langridge gave the order to bail out, but their stand-in rear gunner was trapped in his turret. Although knowing that they were at a dangerously low height and falling rapidly, Derek Allen went to his aid with a crash axe, chopping away the turret doors. Having freed the rear gunner, Allen grabbed his parachute and started to make his way to the forward escape hatch. Luckily for him, the violence of the spin broke the damaged fuselage apart just where he was busy trying to clip on his parachute, while avoiding being thrown around the fuselage by the 'g' forces. He survived the descent but was knocked unconscious when he crashed into some trees, which saved his life. When he came round suspended from a tree,, he decided to put as much distance as he could between himself and the blazing ruins of his aircraft. As he moved off, he heard a lot of shouting, which he eventually recognised as being English.

With considerable relief, he surrendered to some American soldiers, where he was reunited with the four other surviving members of the crew. F/O Langridge's body was found inside the burned out wreck of his aircraft; that of the rear gunner being found some distance away having apparently bailed out too low for his parachute to function. After three weeks survivor's leave, Derek Allen was allocated to another crew and completed his tour of operations. However, on 14 January 1945, in recognition of his gallantry that night, he was recommended for the award of the rare Conspicuous Gallantry Medal (CGM).

One of the other Waddington crews taking part in the heavy attack on Dusseldorf was that captained by Frank Lillecrap, known on the squadron by his nickname of 'Sweet Violets'. His rear gunner, 'Paddy' Jones, recalled daring only to glance at the inferno below that was the city of Dusseldorf, in case he spoiled his night vision. Over the intercomm he heard the voice of their flight engineer saying "Skipper, what's that up ahead?" This was followed by Lillecrap's terse "The target". Back came the response "Christ, have we got to go in there?" The mid upper gunner in the Lillecrap crew was Sgt Frank Clements who, at 30 years old, was the daddy of the crew. Clements was an ex-Metropolitan Police Officer who had volunteered for aircrew duties. He and Paddy Jones were to be commissioned on the same day; a rare thing indeed for two gunners on the same crew. At the end of his operational tour, Frank Clements was seconded to the RAF Provost Branch.

Two days after the attack on Dusseldorf, the Command despatched 174 Lancasters to bomb the newly repaired Dortmund-Ems Canal. 24 of the force came from Waddington, with all but one of them returning safely. No 463 Squadron lost F/O Reilly and crew, flying in JO-X (NE133). This crew had experienced a particularly hard tour, having been hit by flak on several occasions, and their loss on their sixteenth operation was keenly felt on the squadron. There were no survivors. However, it was a different story for the crew of F/Lt Stanley George of No 467 Squadron, who were flying on their 26th operation, this time in PO-L (JB286). They were attacked simultaneously by two fighters, their aircraft being badly damaged, and the bomb aimer, Warrant Officer David Beattie being seriously wounded in the head. Excellent cooperation between the two gunners and the pilot succeeded in beating off the attacks and the crew pressed on to the target.

On the return journey, they were again attacked by fighters, but as before, succeeded in driving them off. Stanley George elected to land at the first airfield in order to get medical help for his bomb aimer, who was by then in great pain. Immediately after landing at the emergency crash strip at Woodbridge in Suffolk, Beattie was rushed to hospital. Sadly, though he survived, his injuries were particularly severe, resulting in the loss of sight in both eyes. This particular operation was well remembered by the crew navigator, F/Sgt Ed Ward (later F/O Ward), who recollected:

"...the fighters attacked from below and directly ahead of our aircraft; the night fighter flying on a reciprocal course. The first indication of the attack was the stream of tracer... ...apparently our bomb aimer, lying in the nose, must have been hit by one of the first of the high explosive bullets fired by the fighter, as he gave no advance warning of the attack; something he would normally have done on seeing any attack coming in towards the front of our aircraft. Stan George immediately put our Lancaster into the standard Bomber Command corkscrew manoeuvre. Performed correctly, this manoeuvre prevented an attacking fighter pilot from getting his sights steady on the bomber, involving as it did, changes in height, speed and direction. It also had the advantage of maintaining an average course and airspeed as required by the navigator.

'Up Down Up Down'

'Stbd Stbd Port Port'

Weaving a fully loaded bomber could be quite dangerous and difficult for the pilot, as each change of height and direction was quite violent. Navigation was almost impossible as all portable instruments and equipment would float around the cabin (negative 'g') and would have to be found and retrieved at the end of the action. Luckily, after a period of weaving, we obviously lost the enemy fighter and resumed normal straight and level flying at our assigned height. Not long after this we could see that we were getting close to the target, where we could see the coloured markers put down by the PFF. Once we had settled down after completing several corkscrews during the fighter attack, Stan called up each crew member in turn to confirm that they were alright and to report any damage. As to the damage, we had lost the exhaust flame shroud on the port inner engine, resulting in the exhaust flame extending to about twelve feet behind the wing. This airborne beacon could only serve to attract the attentions of any prowling night fighter, not to mention the flak crews. In addition, the port fin and rudder and the aileron were all damaged, causing the aircraft to fly badly until Stan managed to correct it by juggling with the trim tabs. Two crew members had failed to respond when Stan had asked us to check in. Neither Cliff the mid upper gunner nor Dave the bomb aimer had responded, so Stan asked me to check up on Dave, while Pat, our wireless operator, checked up on Cliff. Pat reported that Cliff's only problem was that his intercomm plug had become disconnected. I on the other hand, had a much more serious report to make.

On ducking under the instrument panel and moving down into the bomb aimer's compartment, I could see him slumped over his bombsight. I called Pat down to help, and between us we managed to extricate Dave from the nose and get him over the main spar and down the fuselage to the folding bed near the mid upper gun turret. Our problem was not made any easier by the fact that Dave recovered partial consciousness and began to struggle in order to get back to his bombsight. Eventually, we managed to get him on to the bed and administered morphine to our badly injured friend. We found that a bullet had entered his head below the left eye and exited above the right eye, leaving both eyes out of their sockets, lying on his cheeks. In the poor light, we could not tell if he had any further injuries and reported as much to Stan, adding that we did not think that Dave would survive the trip home.

Meanwhile, Stan had told Ted Stokes, our flight engineer, to get down into the bomb aimer's position and do the best he could. Ted talked Stan through a second bomb run and dropped our load of fourteen 1000lb bombs on the PFF flares. Post raid analysis of our release point photograph showed that we hit the canal. As if what we had experienced was not enough, on our way home we were attacked again by a night fighter. Once again, Stan lost our opponent by using the violent corkscrew evasive manoeuvre, though not before we had suffered additional damage. From the time of the first attack, on our way to the target, until the second attack as we were leaving, was only about fifteen to 20 minutes, though to us it seemed more like five hours. All this time, I had given no thought to the navigation, and it was not until Stan called for our position and a heading for home that I got back to work. Estimating our bearing and distance from the burning target, I gave an approximate heading for base, which I hoped would keep us in the returning bomber stream and marginally safer from further attack by night fighters, despite the glowing banner streaming back from our shroudless engine.

Once on course for home, we carried out a more thorough check for damage to our aircraft. One engine was obviously damaged and overheating, so it was shut down and the propeller feathered. Our radio had been hit and was completely out of action, leaving us both deaf and mute. We could see that the wings had been hit and that there were holes of various sizes in both of them. Suddenly our rear gunner called out that a night fighter was closing in from astern and almost immediately opened fire. Stan put our Lancaster into another tight corkscrew and this, combined with Jim Cox's fire caused the enemy pilot to either lose us or break off his attack and look for an easier target. Later, just after crossing the Dutch coast, we lost a second engine, leaving us with the prospect of a two-engined crossing of the North Sea - not a happy thought! As it was, we could not maintain height, so this, combined with the need to get medical treatment for Dave without delay, necessitated a diversion to the crash strip at Woodbridge.

It was standard procedure in Bomber Command on returning from an operation, to cross the English coast at a predetermined position, at a planned height and time, as detailed in the pre-flight briefing. This was 'supposed' to ensure that our anti-aircraft defences did not fire upon returning bombers. However, we of course were nowhere near our assigned coast-in point, were well behind time, and much lower than the briefed altitude. In fact, by this time we were down to around 2000 feet. As we could not let anyone know of our predicament, we could only await the inevitable. Our problems were compounded by the fact that the coastal area was cloud covered, rendering our aircraft almost invisible to those on the ground, though not so the glow from the exhaust flames from our damaged port inner engine. Taking us to be an incoming V1 flying bomb, the anti-aircraft gunners opened fire at relatively close range. Their fire was accurate as evidenced by numerous shrapnel hits and lots more holes appearing. Our wireless operator was frantically firing off the colours of the day from his Verey Pistol, but these took time to drift down through the clouds. Luckily for us, the ground gunners eventually spotted them and ceased fire. After what seemed an age, Stan put our battered Lancaster down on the runway at Woodbridge in a 45 mph crosswind. We were met by an ambulance at the end of the runway and Dave Beattie was quickly but gently passed through the fuselage door and was whisked away to hospital. He remained on the critical list for several months, but eventually pulled through, though he never regained his sight. Despite this, he made a successful career for himself in post-war Australia."

Subsequent inspection of 'L' Love reveailed that the aircraft had been holed in over 70 places and that Stan George had put the bomber down with only two pints of hydraulic fluid remaining in the undercarriage system. As for the crew, they went on to complete their remaining four operations and were posted away. In due course, they were awarded the following decorations:

F/Lt George (P) DFC

F/Sgt Ward (N) DFM (Later commissioned)

F/Sgt Beattie (B /A) DFM

Sgt Stokes (FE) DFM

F/Sgt White (W/Op) Mentioned in Despatches

[One would think that the rear gunner at least should have got something!]

On the night of 6/7 November, it was another canal attack. This time it was the junction of the Mitteland Canal with that of the Dortmund-Ems Canal near Gravenhorst. The marker Mosquito pilot dropped his marker flares so accurately, that they fell in the canal and were extinguished. Only 31 of the 235 Lancasters taking part dropped their bombs before the Master Bomber gave the order 'Frogmarch' - abandon the attack. In all, ten Lancasters were lost, three of them from Waddington. The Station had despatched a total of 35 aircraft; the three missing aircraft all coming from No 463 Squadron. All fourteen crew members of the aircraft flown by F/O J Austin (NG191) and F/O P J Bowell (JO-O PD311) were killed in action. F/O C J Lynch and crew, flying in JO-P (NF900), survived to become PoWs. By coincidence, some of the Lynch crew were to be among the PoWs repatriated in aircraft of their old squadron, as part of Operation Exodus, the flying home of British PoWs in May 1945.

As if the loss of three crews from one squadron was not enough, the returning crews were warned that Lincolnshire was fog-bound and that they were to divert to Seething in Norfolk. This airfield was the home of the B24 Liberators of the 448th Bomb Group USAAF. Among the diverted aircraft was OC A Flight of No 463 Squadron, S/Ldr Des Sullivan. He and his crew were flying in JO-S (NG256) which had been damaged by flak in the target area. On the final stages of Sullivan's approach into Seething in appalling visibility, his aircraft fell in the undershoot and was written off. Despite having a full bomb load of fourteen 1000lb bombs on board, there were no injuries among the crew, which on this occasion included an Army Major named Greenhough. He had gone along in the capacity of 'Flak Observer', but his comments regarding the flak do not appear to be on record!

All the crews that were diverted to Seething were most impressed by the treatment they received while guests of the Americans. They took the opportunity to eat well and to look inside the Liberators. All were particularly impressed with the ten 0.5" calibre machine guns, expressing the wish that they had the same hitting power. In their turn, the American crews were amazed at the sight of fourteen 1000lb bombs in one aircraft; their Liberators being capable of carrying only an 8,000lb bombload.

Bomber Command operated at a reduced level for the next few days, possibly due to bad weather. Whatever the reason, the Waddington crews were not called upon until the night of 11/12 November, when the target was the Rhenania-Ossag oil refinery near Harburg. The American heavy bombers had attacked this target several times in daylight, but it was apparent that it was either still, or was back, in operation. The Station provided 33 out of the 237 Lancasters taking part in this operation. On this occasion, it was No 467 Squadron that suffered losses, with two crews failing to return. As previously mentioned, F/O Feddersen and crew, flying in PO-W (NN714) were undertaking their first operation since ditching in the North Sea one month earlier. This time there was to be no rescue; none of the seven man crew survived. The other missing crew was that of F/O T F Eyre, flying in PO-Q (NF917) on their eighteenth operation. Six of the crew were killed in action; the only survivor being the rear gunner, F/Sgt T A Nilen, who became a PoW.

Among the lucky crews who got back to base that night was that of F/Lt Bill Kynoch, flying in PO-M (LM233). During the attack on the canal, their aircraft was hit by flak which started a fire in the fuselage. While the crew were fighting the fire, their aircraft was attacked by a night fighter and their rear gunner was wounded. With a badly damaged aircraft and an injured crew member, Bill Kynoch put his aircraft down at the first airfield he saw, which in this instance was the crash strip at RAF Manston in Kent. The rear gunner quickly recovered from his wounds and was back in his turret three weeks later. Sadly, during his first operation on his return, which was an attack on Heilbron, Sgt Steele was killed in the course of a lengthy combat with a night fighter. On this occasion the crew were flying in PO-D (LM100).

The Death of the Tirpitz

The day before the Main Force had attacked the oil refinery at Harburg, on 10 November, Numbers IX and 617 Squadrons were ordered to return to Lossiemouth in preparation for yet another attack on the Tirpitz. Once again Bruce Buckham and crew, plus the cameramen F/Lt Loftus and F/O Rogers, left Waddington in JO-Y to join up with the bombing force. Take off from Lossiemouth was scheduled for 0300hr on 12 November, but by this time the Scottish airfield was under a thick blanket of snow. Fortunately, by early afternoon the sky had cleared and things looked promising, so the crews were taken out to their aircraft. On arriving at JO-Y, the Buckham crew found it to be covered in frozen snow. The bomb aimer and flight engineer set to work with brushes and glycol and eventually managed to clean up their aircraft. Then, to add to their problems, it started to snow again, quickly assuming blizzard proportions. As Bruce Buckham taxied out, he noted several Lancasters had bogged down, so he was particularly careful as he weaved his way round them. By this time, the snow was well up the sides of their Lancaster's main wheels. Eventually, somewhat later than intended, the photographic aircraft got airborne and set off after the nineteen Lancasters that had made it into the air.

In accordance with the plan, the attackers crossed the North Sea and on passing over the Norwegian coast, flew to the mountainous border between Norway and Sweden. They then turned north, keeping the mountains between themselves and the German radar units. As Bruce Buckham recalled:

"*...November 13th had dawned perfectly clear and still in the target area. It was a magnificent sight as we climbed to our planned height; there was Haakoy Island, a large snow-covered mound in the middle of Tromso Fjord. There, anchored in the tranquil waters, pointing towards us, was the huge shape of the Tirpitz. We still had about fifteen miles to go, but already, vast explosions were occurring in the middle of, and all around our loose gaggle of aircraft. Tirpitz was firing her 15" main armament at us using short delay fuzes. As we got closer we came under fire from the ship's secondary armament, together with fire from shore batteries and two flak ships; things were getting hot! We went in to film at 6800 feet just as Willie Tait and the others lined up to carry out their individual bombing runs.*

We were soon made aware that our height was very unhealthy, so I descended to 2000 feet. By this time the bombers were right overhead us and in the final stages of their run in. As they dropped, the 12000lb MC 'Tallboy' bombs looked to us like high divers as they fell in a curve towards their target. The first two bombs were very near misses, quickly followed by two or three direct hits. Suddenly, there was a tremendous explosion on board the battleship and she appeared to heave right out of the water. Carried away by the excitement and the suddeness of it all, we had unknowingly descended to 200 feet. Our cameras had been running all the time, recording the assault on this mighty battlewagon. Once the actual bombing ended, we flew over the Tirpitz, around it and all about it. But still she sat there, under a huge mushroom cloud of smoke, which plumed several thousand feet up in the air. We could see numerous fires and explosions on board and a huge gaping hole was visible on the port side, where a whole section of the hull had been blown out.

After we had been flying close to Tirpitz for the best part of half an hour, I decided to call it a day and set heading for the mouth of the fjord. Then, suddenly, our rear gunner, who was operating a camera, called out that he thought that Tirpitz was rolling over. I turned back to port to have a look and sure enough, she was listing over at an angle of 70 to 80 degrees. This time we flew in at 50 feet and watched with bated breath as she heeled over to port ever so slowly, majestically even, in a way almost gracefully. I made one more pass up at 5000 feet and then set off for Waddington, where we landed after a flight time of 14 hours and 19 minutes."

On landing at Waddington, the crew were debriefed in the presence of their AOC, Air Vice Marshal Sir Ralph Cochrane. On being asked how it went, Bruce Buckham replied: "Well we will not have to go back after this one; Tirpitz is finished." In addition to all the messages of congratulations, Bruce Buckham was awarded an immediate DSO, with DFCs going toF/Lt Giersch (RG), F/O Proctor (MUG), P/Os Holden (W/Op) and Manning (BA), with F/O Broad the navigator receiving a bar to his DFC. Why the flight engineer, P/O Sinclair was omitted, is something of a mystery; one of the many concerning the award of decorations. At Waddington, all personnel were invited to a showing of the film of the attack, which was screened in the Airmen's dining hall. Sometime later, the same film was given World-wide release.

Back to Business as Usual

After the excitement following the sinking of the Tirpitz, it was back to business as usual. On 16 November, Bomber Command despatched a mixed force of 1,188 bombers, escorted by nine squadrons of Spitfires and Mustangs, to attack three towns behind German lines. The towns were Duren, Heinsburg and Julich, and the attacks were in support of an assault by the American First and Ninth Armies. This was to be an extremely bloody battle, which came to be known as 'The Battle of the Hurtgen Forest', in which the Americans suffered horrendous casualties. The ground battle continued until February, with the unfortunate troops taking part in it calling it either 'The Green Hell' or 'The Death Factory'. By the the time the battle was over, the two American armies had suffered 30,000 casualties. This apart, the preliminary attack by Bomber Command took place in ideal conditions and all three towns were virtually destroyed. 30 aircraft from Waddington led by the Station Commander, G/Cpt Bonham-Carter all returned safely. As the last of the Command's aircraft left the smoking ruins of the three towns, 1,239 bombers of the American Eighth Air Force attacked what was left.

The Station had a five day break before despatching 30 aircraft as part of a 1,315 aircraft attack on six targets, which were attacked simultaneously. These targets were a mixture of oil production centres and communication facilities. The aircraft from Waddington were among those targetted against the Dortmund-Ems Canal near Ladbergen. Despite having to descend to 4,000 feet to get below cloud, there were no losses among the 123 Lancasters assigned to this particular target. Once again, the recently repaired breach was blown out and the water drained out of that section of the canal.

During the five day break prior to the attack on the canal at Ladbergen, a minor event occurred on the Station which, if anything at all, must have typified the 'life must go on' spirit. While the groundcrews were carrying out the routine Daily Inspections (DI) on their instruments of death, a cry went up on one of the dispersals "I don't believe this"! For there, in all its glory was the local hunt, at full gallop heading straight across the airfield. The spectators later estimated that there must have been 20 to 30 riders and countless hounds, though there was no sign of the fox!

Apart from an abortive attack on the U-boat pens at Trondheim on the night of 22/23 November, the Station was not tasked again until the night of 26/27 November, when the target was the home of Naziism - Munich. This was to be the Station's last operation in November and all 36 crews returned safely, though one crew did so via a crash landing in France! The attack on Munich had an inauspicious begining as far as Waddington was concerned. The weather was the worst in which any large force of the Command's bombers had ever taken off. The cloud base was down to below 600 feet and visibility was less than the length of the runway in use. Similarly, many crews reported severe icing in the area of the target. The crew that failed to make it back home, was that of F/O Alec Findlay, flying in PO-Q (PD398). Findlay had previously force landed in France in September, while taking part in the attack on Rheydt. On that occasion, he and one other member of the crew evaded capture and returned to Waddington, where Alec Findlay collected another crew and recommenced operations. During the operation against Munich, the crew navigator became ill and eventually passed out through lack of oxygen. An inexperienced crew, flying in 10/10 cloud without a navigator, they soon became hopelessly lost. By the time they managed to determine their position, they were down to only 80 gallons of fuel. Despite trying the 'Darkie' and 'Referee' emergency service, to which they received no response, they were left with no alternative but to force land. Selecting an open space where he could see US Army vehicles, Findlay carried out a successful wheels up landing near Brieulles. Their aircraft was a write-off, but all the crew members emerged from it uninjured. They were flown back to England in an American Air Force Dakota. Alec Findlay was living up to his reputation as spending more time attending Courts of Inquiry than flying on operations.

As the aircrews at Waddington and all other stations in Bomber Command entered the last month of 1944, it was obvious to all but the most incurable optimist that the war would not be 'over by Christmas'. On the contrary, there remained several more bloody months to come before their services would no longer be required.

For the Station's aircrews, operations commenced in December on the night of the fourth; the day after the Home Guard (Dad's Army) held their disbandment parade in front of King George VI in Hyde Park. The target for the 41 Waddington aircraft was the rail complex in the city of Heilbron. This was the first and only time that Bomber Comand attacked this target and it was virtually destroyed in a matter of minutes. The 282 Lancasters and ten Mosquitos dropped 1,254 tons of bombs and incendiaries, causing the dreaded 'firestorm' phenomenon, destroying 82% of the city, with heavy loss of life. A total of 12 Lancasters were lost in the attack, two of them from Waddington. No 467 Squadron lost F/O J B Plumridge and crew, flying in PO-N (PB470) on their first operation; the only survivor being the bomb aimer, F/Sgt Penman, who became a PoW. No 463 Squadron lost the crew of F/O J K Waring, who were also flying in their first operation. Their aircraft, JO-Q (PB792) was also flying its first operation, and the tragic circumstances of the loss of this aircraft must be almost unique.

The sole survivor from the Waring crew was the rear gunner, F/Sgt Cheesman, who subsequently reported that they had carried out a successful attack and were on their way home. He recalled that at some point on the return journey, the navigator warned the pilot that they were below the safety height for that area, to which the captain replied that he wanted to get down clear of the cloud. Soon after that exchange their aircraft hit a hillside, hurling Cheesman backwards out of his turret. He ended up unconscious inside the fuselage under the mid upper turret. When he eventually regained consciousness, he called to the other crew members but, receiving no reply in the darkness, he decided to remain in the fuselage until daylight. At dawn, Cheesman could see that it was snowing heavily. Finding one of his flying boots which had been torn off his foot in the crash, he experienced great difficulty in pulling it on because of a broken right arm and left hand. Crawling out of the wreck, he found that the Lancaster had broken in two, just aft of the wings. The hillside was covered in young trees about 20 to 30 feet high. Having already ascertained that the mid upper gunner was dead in his turret, Cheesman searched for signs of the rest of his crew. He found their bodies scattered around the wreck, about 20 yards away. Having satisfied himself that all were dead, he set off heading southwesterly, towards the Allied lines. He was eventually picked up by members of the French Forces of the Interior (FFI), who in time handed him over to the American Army.

The Station lost one other crew member that night. F/Lt Bill Kynoch and crew, flying in PO-D (LM100), had an extended combat with a persistent night fighter. In the course of the battle, their rear gunner, Sgt R W Steele, was killed. It was his first mission after returning to operations, having been injured on the night of 11/12 November. His aircraft was so badly damaged that Bill Kynoch put it down on the emergency crash strip at Manston in Kent.

Two nights later, the target was the town and rail complex of Giessen. This was another of the Command's triple target attacks. While the Main Force attacked Osnabruck and Leuna, the 38 aircraft from Waddington formed part of the 255 strong force attacking Giessen. It was an accurate attack, with one of the eight missing Lancasters coming from No 463 Squadron. F/O R R Young and crew, flying in JO-K (PB290), were shot down on their fourth operation; there were no survivors. The Waddington element of the attack on Giessen was led by W/Cdr Bill Forbes, OC No 463 Squadron. Flying with him on this trip as the mid-under gunner was F/Lt Winston, who normally flew as mid upper gunner in the crew of F/Lt John Padgham.

Between the 8th and 11th December, the Command mounted three separate attacks against the same target, employing a total of 693 Lancasters. The target was the Urft dam; the purpose of the attacks being to breach the dam so that the Germans could not do so when Allied troops reached a position which would make them vulnerable to flood water. On the first attack, cloud cover affected the bombing and no results were observed. The second attack was recalled due to bad weather in the target area. Although the dam was actually hit on the third attack, no breach was achieved. In all, Waddington despatched 97 aircraft on these attacks, all of which returned safely.

The day after the commencement of the German offensive 'Wacht am Rhein' in the Ardennes (The Battle of the Bulge), Bomber Command mounted another three target operation. A mixed force of 523 bombers attacked Duisberg, while another force of 317 Lancasters attacked Ulm. This attack on Ulm was to be the first and only attack by the Command on the cathedral city. Meanwhile, a force of 280 Lancasters carried out an extremely accurate attack on Munich. In all that night, the Command lost eight Halifaxes and four Lancasters; just over 1% of the total force. Of the four Lancasters, which were all lost in the attack on Munich, two were from Waddington. No 463 Squadron lost the crew of F/O K E H Bennett, flying in JO-D (LL847) on their sixth operation. In the crew, flying as second pilot on his first operation, was F/O J H Ogilvie. The only member of the crew to survive was the navigator, F/Sgt Easton, who became a PoW.

The Ogilvie crew were subsequently posted to No IX Squadron at Bardney, where they were assigned a new Captain. No 467 Squadron lost F/O Terry Evans and crew flying in PO-F (PD215) on their fourteenth operation. In modern parlance, it has to be sadi that 'it just wasn't their day'. Soon after take-off the rear gunner reported that the hydraulic drive to his turret was not functioning properly. By the time they crossed the French coast it had failed completely, leaving the rear turret operating only manually. Next, their starboard outer engine instruments showed that the oil temperature was excessively high; soon after this initial indication, the engine began to run rough.

The flight engineer, using a combination of boost and revolutions, managed to keep things within the accepted limits until the required climb to 16000 feet to clear the Alps. Despite their problems, they pressed on and in time turned on to the attack heading. As they did so, the mid upper gunner reported another Lancaster flying parallel to them some 600 yards away on the port beam. Just as the crew spotted the green TIs going down, Terry Evans sighted another aircraft coming up under the port wing. Left with no alternative, he hauled back on the control column and applied full power. Immediately, the rough engine cut out completely and the starboard wing dropped.

At that instant the other aircraft crashed into the lower part of the starboard fin and rudder, before slicing twelve feet off the wing, which included the aileron and part of the flap. Unaccountably, at this very instant, the starboard outer picked up, causing the Lancaster to flick into a spin. There in the dark near Munich, PO-F performed a complete flat orbit, right in the middle of the Main Force bomber stream! Eventually, Evans managed to regain control by applying full port aileron and rudder. The strain of doing this was enormous and he was assisted in his efforts by the flight engineer and the bomb aimer, who took it in turns to share the load. When approximately 20 miles from Munich the 4000lb 'Cookie' was jettisoned. This was achieved by chopping through the cabin floor to get at the bomb release mechanism, as neither the electrical nor mechanical release systems were functioning. Evans elected to retain the incendiaries to prevent the possibility of route marking and drawing night fighters into the bomber stream. In any case, he reasoned that the Small Bomb Container (SBC) release mechanism would not have worked.

As Evans and crew limped home across Europe, it proved virtually impossible to maintain height, but they eventually achieved some degree of stabilisation at arounf 4000 feet, with a stalling speed of 150mph. To add to their problems, the No 1 fuel tank developed a leak, necessitating the running of all four engines from this tank in order to make maximum use of the available fuel. Shortly before midnight, with oil pressure having fallen to almost zero, the starboard outer burst into flames and, to add to their problems, could not be feathered. Despite operating the Graviner engine fire extinguishers, the fire continued to burn furiously. Within a matter of what seemed like seconds, the Lancaster became almost uncontrollable, eventually falling away into a descending turn to starboard. At this point, Evans gave the order to bail out; their height at this time being around 3,000 feet.

The bomb aimer tried to jettison the escape hatch, but it was jammed. In desperation, he jumped on it and disappeared through the aperture, quickly followed by the rest of the crew apart from the rear gunner who left via his turret. By the time Terry Evans came to leave the stricken aircraft, it was down to 1500 feet. He left his seat and dived head first out of the front hatch, but was caught by one leg. As he dangled under the aircraft, desperately kicking and pulling to free himself, he saw the starboard engine, still on fire, fall away from its mountings. Realising that he was gettting perilously close to the ground, Evans pulled the ripcord of his parachute and hoped! It worked; though his parachute was damaged in the process, resulting in his making a heavy landing.

Their Lancaster crashed near Chalon sur Marne, behind the Allied lines. In due course the crew returned to Waddington and resumed operations in February 1945. They went on to complete a further ten operations before the war's end. The flight engineer, F/Sgt Bob Brownjohn, was awarded the DFM for his efforts that night. (Note: The author flew with him some 30 years later, in the Lancaster of the RAF Memorial Flight).

The night after the attack on Munich, 34 Lancasters from Waddington formed part of a 236-strong force attacking the port of Gdynia in the Baltic. The Waddington crews, among others, had been briefed that their aiming point was the pocket battleship Lutzow, formerly the Deutschland. The port area was severely damaged and the elderly battleship Schleswig-Holstein was hit, eventually burning itself out in the harbour. Eight other ships anchored in the port also were sunk. All the Station aircraft returned safely.

After two nights off, Station aircraft were again on the Order of Battle on the night of 21/22 December. This time, the target was the huge synthetic oil refinery at Politz near Stettin. 207 Lancasters were assigned to this target, 34 of them from Waddington. Following the operation, which caused severe damage to the complex, Air Chief Marshal Portal, the Chief of the Air Staff, expressed the view to the CinC Bomber Command, that he should have used a larger force, to which Harris disagreed and said as much! A total of eight Lancasters were lost in the operation; three over Europe and five in crashes in England.

When the force returned to their bases, they found most of them shrouded in fog, causing most of them to be diverted to Scotland. Unfortunately, many of them did not have sufficient fuel remaining to make it to Scotland and had to make a stab at getting in at their home base. Two of the Waddington crews found themselves in exactly that situation. F/O R H Halstead and crew flying in JO-M (PB688), had suffered some battle damage to their aircraft and their radio was not working. Unknown to Halstead and crew, one of the returning aircraft had managed to land in the fog, but after that Air Traffic Control ordered the remainder to divert. Having not received the diversion order, Halstead continued his approach, crashing just short of the airfield. The sole survivor was the mid upper gunner F/Sgt Nation, who suffered severe injuries.

Another Waddington aircraft that returned so low on fuel that a diversion to Scotland was not a viable option, was that flown by Bill Kynoch and crew. Flying in PO-M (NG366) they actually got down on to the runway, but ran off on to the grass in the fog, damaging their aircraft, but fortunately, they all escaped injury.

The attack on Politz was 'S' Sugar's 117th operation, and the aircraft was flown on this occasion by F/O Gordon Stewart and crew. Between them, this crew boasted one DFC and two DFMs. However, this could so easily have been Sugar's last trip. At one stage the crew thought that they would have to bail out, owing to fuel shortage. Luckily, they made it - just! The McRae crew, flying in JO-W (PD203), were even luckier. As they taxied round the perimeter at Waddington en route to their dispersal after the operation, all four engines cut out through lack of fuel. They had to remain with their aircraft as it was towed into its dispersal, before they could report for debriefing and the welcome cup of rum-laced tea.

The crews that had diverted to Lossiemouth following the attack on Politz had to remain there over Christmas, not managing to return to Waddington until Boxing Day. Christmas festivities or not, Bomber Command continued to operate, though Waddington was not called upon until the 27th of the month, when the target was Rheydt. The 27 Station Lancasters joined up with 173 others in an attack on the railway yards, all returning safely to base.

While over 300 aircraft attacked targets at Monchen Gladbach and Bonn on 28/29 December, the Station despatched ten aircraft as part of a 67-strong force of Lancasters attacking a large naval unit in Oslo Fjord. No hits were claimed and no aircraft were lost.

The last attack of 1944 for the crews of the two Waddington squadrons was against Houffalize. This was a supply bottleneck for the German Army, and the attack by 154 Lancasters was in support of the American Divisions' on-going counter-attack in the Battle of the Bulge. The Station despatched 24 aircraft, all of which returned safely.

So ended 1944, the fifth year of the war.

❖❖❖

8. The Last Year of the War

The first month of 1945 was to be relatively quiet; due in the main to bad weather affecting operations. On the home front, the government had recently released some statistics concerning the country's war effort. The figures showed that the output per head of population was greater than that of any other other nation. The output of war weapons in the preceeding five years included 102,600 aircraft, 25,000 tanks, 722 warships and 4.5 million tons of merchant ships. Other figures showed that one civilian had been killed for every three servicemen and that one in three houses had been destroyed or damaged. As if to underscore the fact that all were in the struggle, whether in uniform or not, various members of the Rolls Royce workforce would visit the Station to see for themselves, air operations being mounted. On one occasion, two of the visitors were particularly 'bolshie' and seemed determined to be unimpressed by anything they saw. Despite this, their hosting crew did their best for them right up to leaving in the crew transport to go out to their aircraft. This particular operation was a daylight attack on a target in France, so the crews taking part were back at base well before the visitors left. Sadly, the hosting crew in question were among the missing; a fact that caused a complete and moving change of attitude in the two workers in question.

The first operation of the New Year for the crews of RAF Waddington was a daylight attack on the Dortmund-Ems Canal at Ladbergen (again). This took place in the morning of new Year's Day. 25 Station aircraft joined forces with 77 others in breaching and draining the canal. On their way to the target, as they crossed the Channel, some of the crews spotted the snake-like vapour trail of a V2 rocket over Holland. For his leadership of this attack and his leadership of No 463 Squadron on his second tour, the 25 year old W/Cdr Bill Forbes was awarded the DSO to add to his DFC.

Another DSO was awarded as a result of the New Year's Day attack. The award went to F/Lt 'Merv' Bache who, together with his crew, was flying in PO-H (PA169). The attack height was low at only 4500 feet and, as the crews approached the target, they could see what one of them described as *'a cubic mile of flak'*, which lay between the bombers and their target. Almost immediately, Bache's aircraft was hit in the port wing and the bomb bay. Detecting no apparent affect on the handling of the Lancaster, Bache pressed on and completed his attack. Almost immediately after the bomb aimer called "bombs gone", the aircraft was hit again, this time in No 1 fuel tank. The same hit tore away the side of the port inner engine, which emitted considerable flames and smoke. The propeller was feathered and the Graviner switch operated, which successfully extinguished the flames. The W/Op fired off four red Verey cartridges, but the fighter escorts apparently failed to see them. Not long after this, the port outer engine was hit, but although it ceased to function, it did not catch fire. By this time PO-H was approximately 20 miles from the Rhine.

The only way in which Bache could maintain control, having lost both engines on the port side, was by applying full starboard aileron and rudder, together with applying full power from the two starboard engines. To relieve the load on his pilot's legs, the bomb aimer managed to fasten a gun loading cable between the rudder pedal and a convenient projection. Despite all his own problems, Bache noted a Lancaster hit by flak, well on fire and going down in a spiral dive to port (more on this later). Merv Bache had ordered his crew to put on parachutes and be ready to make a rapid exit if necessary, when the port inner caught fire. Meanwhile, they struggled along with their aircraft in a permanent 40 degree bank to starboard, yawing and gradually losing height, while falling further and further behind the Main Force. With all his problems, Bache still retained his sense of humour. In his post raid report he commented that as they approached the Rhine, they were passed by a Lancaster flying on three engines, "making a magnificent turn of speed"! At about the time that they were overtaken, the crew became aware of a group of Hawker Tempests, which they (the crew) hoped would observe their predicament and act as escorts. Unfortunately, the fighter pilots did not to see the battered Lancaster limping along.

Between them and relative safety, the Bache crew could see a Lancaster being engaged by considerable flak. It was obvious to them that, crippled as they were, they would have to fly through it, with no hope of taking evasive action. In an effort to gain sufficient power to maintain height and reach Allied lines, Bache restarted the burnt port inner engine. It ran for a few minutes before cutting out completely. Just after this, the battered Lancaster was in turn engaged by the flak they had seen in front of them. Unable to take evasive action, Bache's problems were further compounded by the need to throttle back his starboard outer engine in order to counter a swing to port. By this time, they were down to 5000 feet as they crossed the Rhine. PO-H finally crossed the Maas. They were now down to around 3500 feet and, while still struggling through the last of the flak barrage, they were struck by shrapnel in the front gun turret, the bombing panel, front fuselage floor and roof, the starboard wing and the DR master compass in the rear of the fuselage by the entrance door.

Confident that they had finally reached the safety of the Allied lines, Bache gave the order to bail out. Inevitably, as soon as he released his grip on the control column, the aircraft started to roll over. Well aware that time was running out, Bache succeeded in forcing his way out of the nose escape hatch. He pulled the ripcord as soon as he was clear of the aircraft and almost immediately crashed into the top of a pine tree, which broke off, causing him to fall heavily to the ground. All seven members of the crew landed safely, though most suffered minor injuries of one sort or another. It was for this performance that Merv Bache was awarded an immediate DSO. All members of the crew but one recovered quickly from their injuries, and after their survivors' leave were back on operations by late February. They went on to complete a further nine operations before the war's end.

The burning Lancaster noted by Bache was a No IX Squadron aircraft WS-U (PD377), flown by F/O Harry Denton and crew. Their squadron was based at Bardney, one of the Waddington (No 53 Base) satelllites. For his gallantry in rescuing fellow crew members from an on-board fire, the W/Op, F/Sgt George Thompson, was awarded a posthumous Victoria Cross. The citation for the award was drafted for the Base Commander by the Adjutant of No 53 Base, F/Lt Henry Locke, the ex No 44 Squadron Adjutant who had been on the Station since the Hampden days.

Less than 12 hours after despatching 15 aircraft to attack the Dortmund-Ems Canal, the Station launched a further ten Lancasters as part of a 152-strong force attacking another canal. This time it was the turn of the Mitteland Canal at Gravenhorst to receive the attentions of Bomber Command. All the attackers returned safely having destroyed approximately half a mile of canal banking. These attacks on the canals took place despite the fact that Waddington, in common with much of eastern England, was covered in deep snow. The subsequent landings on icy runways following their return were fraught with danger and the cause of various accidents.

With its high casualty rate, the crews of Bomber Command became used to having to deal with the loss of friends in action, but the Station was particularly hard hit by the loss of F/O N V Allamby and crew who, while flying a training sortie in PO-C (NF908), crashed four miles north of Leek in Staffordshire on 3 January. The crew arrived on No 467 Squadron on 1 December and had carried out five operations; their last being the attack on Gravenhorst, two nights prior to their fatal crash. To the Station personnel, it seemed such a tragic and unfair way to go.

The next operation set in train by Bomber Command has been, and in some quarters still is, the subject of considerable controversy. The target was the small town of Royan, situated at the mouth of the River Gironde, north of Bordeaux. Here, the German garrison was conducting a stubborn and costly defensive action, thereby denying the Allies the use of the port of Bordeaux. Tragically for the citizens of Royan, this was a very political scenario and they were to suffer the consequences. The task of capturing Royan had been assigned to the 12000 men of General Koenig's French Forces of the Interior (FFI), commanded by Free French officers appointed by General de Gaulle. Indeed it was at de Gaulle's insistence that the FFI were alloted the task. The FFI, being at best light infantry, lacked artillery or armour, and as a result, made little progress in subduing the defences. A humane German garrison commander gave the residents of Royan the opportunity to leave the town, but most elected to remain in order to care for their property and belongings. It is estimated that there were approximately 2,000 civilians in Royan at the time of the attack by Bomber Command.

The root cause of the tragedy which followed was the result of a combination of incompetence and inefficiency. Some weeks before the raid, on 10 December, a meeting took place between French officers and an American officer from a tactical air force unit in France. The problem of Royan was discussed and the American suggested that in view of the lack of artillery, the defences could be 'softened up' by bombing. The French officers apparently agreed, emphasising that the only civilians remaining in the town were collaborators. This of course was totally incorrect. The request for bombing support was passed on to Supreme Headquarters Allied Expeditionary Force (SHAEF), who in turn passed the task to RAF Bomber Command. As one of the crews involved in the attack recalled; the brief to the crews taking part included the phrase "To destroy a town strongly defended by the enemy and occupied by German troops only". It was later claimed that SHAEF ordered a last-minute cancellation because of growing doubts concerning the presence of French civilians in the town. This order, if actually issued, was not received by Bomber Command in time and the preparations continued.

A force of 347 Lancasters, 24 of them from Waddington, dropped a total of 1,576 tons of bombs, including 285 'blockbusters'. Subsequent French reports stated that nearly 90% of Royan was destroyed. The estimated number of deaths among the civilian population varied between 500 and 800; the German dead numbering less than fifty. Following this devastating attack, a local truce was arranged between the

German defenders and the besieging FFI. This truce lasted for ten days while the search for survivors continued. The German garrison held out until mid April!

There followed numerous recriminations, among which was that directed at Bomber Command. Subsequent investigation cleared the Command of any blame. However, this was not before Harris received a blunt request for information from the Chief of the Air Staff (CAS). In his memo, Portal wrote: "...you will have seen in today's German communique the statement that some 1,000 French civilians were killed during your recent attack on Royan, and that German losses in dead were thirteen. Other evidence confirms this statement. Since we are almost certain to be asked why this place was attacked, I should be grateful if you would inform me fully of the dates and particulars of any dealings you may have had with SHAEF on the subject. I am making similar enquiries unofficially of SHAEF, particularly about the intelligence to support a statement, which I saw in one of your liaison messages; to the effect that only Germans were in the town..."

In his equally blunt but respectful reply, Harris laid the blame squarely on SHAEF. His letter dated 11 January 1945 makes interesting reading:

"Your letter of 9 January, on the subject of the attack on Royan. I have already written officially to the Air Ministry protesting against the misinformation, with regard to the civilian inhabitants, on which this attack was based. No doubt the DCAS will show you this letter. This attack was ordered by SHAEF. It was undertaken in accordance with those orders and the priority rating on an occasion when nothing else could be done anywhere else. I understand (although this is subject to confirmation) that SHAEF were asked to make the attack by the French authorities, and that it was the French authorities who assured them that there were no French civilians in the town.

General Bedell Smith at SHAEF is, I am told, personally instituting enquiry into both the initiation of the attack by SHAEF, and the matter of the civilian inhabitants. I have instructed Oxland to give me full details as soon as they are available. I would add that for obvious reasons, I have particularly warned SHAEF that all Army support targets which they send me on their priority list to be carried out under specific order, are accepted without question by me, unless they contravene some overiding prior instruction, or custom, and that we must also, for as obvious reasons, rely entirely on them for the clearing of the target; eg during the German advance (The Battle of the Bulge) they might have sent me an order to bomb a French town, which from the information in my possession, appeared to be in American hands. But in view of the circumstances in which such orders are received, provided I am convinced that they come from the correct authority, I cannot question them. I have not always the material information at the time.

This matter arose when they put on Limburg Marshalling Yards as an urgent priority Army support target, which we attacked without question. In the process we hit an American prisoner of war camp and, I believe, caused considerable casualties. On examination of the photographs, it (the camp) was discovered to be only six hundred yards from the Marshalling Yard they (SHAEF) had laid us on to.

I am sure you will agree that we cannot have divided authorities in the matter of ordering and clearing ad hoc Army targets, and that those who have the right to order attacks must be solely responsible for clearing the target from every point of view. Nevertheless, this is the third occasion on which the Army has misinformed or misled us, viz: le Havre, Royan and Limburg..." [7]

The recriminations were to rumble on long after the war's end. Following enquiries made by the American General Walter Bedell Smith, Eisenhower's Chief of Staff, the American air force officer who passed on the original proposal to SHAEF to attack Royan, was removed from his post. However, it was among the French where the real divisions came to light. The accusations and counter-accusations persisted. So bitter did these exchanges become, that one French General committed suicide. Even General de Gaulle became involved when, in his book 'Memoires de Guerre', he blamed the Americans in a totally inaccurate recollection. Notwithstanding all this, the basic facts are that nearly 1,000 French civilians died, while the Germans held out for over three more months before finally surrendering on 18 April 1945.

As far as the crews of Bomber Command were concerned, Royan was just another target, bombed in support of the ground forces. The furore that erupted did not concern them, indeed they were totally unaware of it. Of more immediate concern to them was the fact that they had to help with clearing the runways of snow before they could take off on the operation against Royan, from which two Waddington crews failed to return. No 463 Squadron lost F/O Milne and crew, flying in JO-R (PB695) on their third operation. Their aircraft crashed in the town of Royan and there were no survivors. The other missing aircraft was PO-V (LM677) of No 467 Squadron, which was flown by F/O R B Eggins and crew on their sixth operation. On their way back from the target, their aircraft collided with a Lancaster (ME300) of No 189 Squadron, based at Fulbeck. Aware that he was losing control, Eggins gave the order to bail out. Five of the crew did so immediately, but the rear gunner had difficulty rotating his turret before he could leave the aircraft. The consequent delay in waiting for his rear gunner to bail

[7] Air Vice Marshal R D Oxland (Station Commander of RAF Waddington, December 1926 to March 1927) was at the time of this matter, SASO Bomber Command. Soon after the Royan incident, he left to take up an appointment of Senior Bomber Command representative at SHAEF. (A political attempt to shut the door after etc etc...?)

out resulted in Eggins leaving the Lancaster somewhat late. Luckily, all seven members of then crew made safe(ish) landings and were back on operations one month later. Sadly, one month after their return to flying duties, they failed to return from their twelfth operation, with only the bomb aimer, F/Sgt Grady, surviving to become a PoW.

On the night of 5/6 January, while the Main Force attacked Hannover, 18 Waddington Lancasters joined with 113 others in another attack on the town of Houffalize, a German supply bottleneck. This was an extremely accurate attack for the loss of two Lancasters, neither of which were from Waddington.

Two nights after supporting the American ground forces fighting near Houffalize, Bomber Command was again over Munich. A force of 645 Lancasters carried out a successful attack, for the loss of 11 aircraft (1.7%). One of those lost was the aircraft flown by F/O W A McNamee and crew of No 467 Squadron. They were flying in PO-L (JB286) on their sixth operation, as part of the 27 strong Waddington component. In common with nearly all other crews, they experienced severe icing throughout the long trip. Running out of fuel, McNamee gave the order to bail out as soon as they estimated that they were over England. Tragically, their 'fix' was inaccurate and they bailed out over the North Sea! Despite a long search of their known area, nothing was found, but their aircraft eventually crashed at Eye near Peterborough.

After a week of **'NO WAR'**, the Station squadrons were back on operations on the night of 13/14 January, when the target was the oil installation at Politz near Stettin. This had been planned as an H2S radar bombing attack, but as the weather in the target area was found to be clear, the No 5 Group marker crews employed their tried and tested low level marking technique. The accuracy of the subsequent attack reduced the installation to a shambles. All 31 Waddington aircraft returned safely to base.

The next night the Station despatched 28 aircraft as part of a 573-strong force of Lancasters attacking the synthetic oil plant at Mersberg-Leuna. At his post-war interrogation, Albert Speer, Hitler's Minister for Armaments, stated that in his opinion this was one of the most damaging raids on the German synthetic oil industry. Two of the Waddington crews failed to return, but both eventually made it back - on foot! F/O F J Howells and crew, flying in JO-G (LL865), were hit by heavy flak, which put the hydraulics out of action, effectively immobilising the gun turrets. They continued with their bombing run and were hit again, which set the port inner engine alight. Howells feathered the propeller and operated the engine fire extinguisher, which doused the fire. They were then attacked by a FW190 fighter, but the mid upper gunner managed eventually to drive it off. As they turned for home, their aircraft was again hit by flak, this time puncturing the starboard wing fuel tanks. Knowing that he had insufficient fuel to make it back, Howells set course for Juvincourt in France, where he made a successful landing after having blown the undercarriage down using the emergency air system. The crew returned to Waddington and were back on the battle order in early February. Sadly, after completing six further operations, they were shot down on their nineteenth, with only the bomb aimer and the rear gunner surviving to become PoWs.

The other Waddington crew missing after the attack on the Mersberg-Leuna complex was that of F/O R A Leonard. Flying in JO-U (NG193), their aircraft was so badly damaged that they too had to divert to Juvincourt, where they made a successful emergency landing. This crew had completed 21 operations by this time and on their return, were screened from further operations.

48 hours after attacking Mersberg-Leuna, the Command was carrying out another major multi-target operation. Magdeburg was subjected to an area attack by a mixed force of 371 aircraft, while at the same time, the Zeitz synthetic oil installation was attacked by 328 Lancasters and the Benzol plant at Wanne-Eickel was attacked by 138 Lancasters. Meanwhile, the huge synthetic oil installation at Brux in western Czechoslovakia was destroyed by a force of a further 231 Lancasters. 28 Waddington aircraft took part in the attack on Brux and all returned safely.

The last operation of January as far as Waddington was concerned was Gelsenkirchen, when Bruce Buckham flew his last operation of his second tour. Flying in his favourite JO-Y (PD329), he and his crew filmed the attack by a mixed force of 152 aircraft. Following this operation, F/Lt Bruce Buckham DSO DFC returned to Australia. In all, he had flown 49 operations, having undertaken two tours without a break.

Despite the bad weather which seriously affected operations throughout the month of January, the Station had not had an easy time. It had mounted 181 sorties against nine targets, for the loss of six crews. Of these 42 men, 14 were killed in action and 28 successfully evaded, or managed to reach Allied lines before bailing out or crash landing. In addition, another Station Lancaster was severely damaged when it crashed during an air test.

On a lighter note, the Australians insisted on celebrating ANZAC Day on 26 January. The British element of the crews did not require too much encouragement to join in the festivities. As the two squadrons were on stand-down, there was no reason not to celebrate in style. Sgt Stan Bridgeman, the flight engineer on the Farrow crew, entered into the spirit of the evening with considerable enthusiasm. Late in the evening he made a somewhat unsteady journey to his room in the Aircrew Sergeants' Mess. Feeling in need of some fresh air, he opened the window and stuck his head out into the cold night air. While taking in the refreshing Lincolnshire air, he had a rather garbled conversation with the crew wireless operator, Jack

Wiltshire, who was just above him. Eventually, his fellow room-mates decided that enough was enough and dragged Stan Bridgeman from the window and put him to bed. It was some time later, when the effects of celebrating ANZAC Day too enthusiastically had worn off, that it dawned on him that as his room was on the top floor of the Mess, Jack Wiltshire must have been sitting on the roof during their conversation! It would seem also that one of the local horses took part in the ANZAC Day activities, as it was found the next morning in the Mess snooker room.

February was to be another hard month for the two Waddington squadrons. In all, the Station would mount 304 sorties against 12 targets, for the loss of 11 crews. Of the 91 aircrew involved, 47 were killed in action, 35 became PoWs and nine evaded capture. By this time, many crews were flying with an eighth crew member, apart from carrying a tyro captain from time to time. This eighth crew member was a mid under gunner, manning the single 0.5" machine gun firing through the floor. Among those killed in action were both Squadron Commanders; W/Cdr Keith Douglas of No 467 Squadron and W/Cdr Bill Forbes of No 463 Squadron. In addition to the standard bombing sorties, two film unit sorties were flown.

The month commenced with the Command carrying out another simultaneous three-target assault on the night of 1/2 February. Over 300 aircraft attached both Ludwigshaven and Mainz, while a further 271 Lancasters attacked the railway complex at Siegen. Waddington despatched 40 aircraft to Siegen, but the attack suffered the effects of very high winds in the target area and was not considered to have been successful. Two of the three Lancasters lost over Siegen were Waddington aircraft. No 463 Squadron lost F/O Frank Smith and crew flying in JO-K (NG275). This was an experienced crew, flying on their 23rd operation. All members of the crew, with the exception of the navigator, survived to become PoWs. No 467 Squadron lost F/Lt Keith Livingstone and crew, flying in PO-G (NG197). This was another experienced crew, who were flying on their 22nd operation. The navigator of the Livingstone crew was S/Ldr Des Sands DSO DFC, an Australian serving in the RAF. Des Sands was John Nettleton's navigator on the ill-fated low level daylight attack on Augsburg on 17 August 1942. At the time he was posted missing, Des Sands was OC A Flight. All members of the crew, including F/O Eagle, a new pilot on his first operation, flying as second pilot to gain experience, managed to bail out while Keith Livingstone held their aircraft steady. Livingstone left it too late to escape himself and perished in the crash. All those who had bailed out became PoWs.

The hazards of operations were not confined to flights over enemy territory. Prior to taking part in an attack on Karlsruhe on 2/3 February, Jack Wiltshire and Stan Bridgeman, respectively the wireless operator and flight engineer, went out early to their aircraft JO-N (LM130), better known as 'Nick the Nazi Neutralizer'. Jack wanted to carry out a full check of his radio equipment, while Stan planned to run up all four engines. By the time Stan Bridgeman had stowed his gear and carried out the pre-start checks, Jack Wiltshire had completed all his radio checks, so he asked his flight engineer friend if it was OK to switch the Ground/Flight switch to Flight. Stan agreed to this and the wirless operator accordingly moved the switch across from Ground to Flight. The operation of the switch was immediately followed by a loud 'clang'. A surprised flight engineer called out to his W/Op: "*What the ---- was that?*" Before Wiltshire could answer, one of the groundcrew shouted to them through the rear gun turret clear vision panel to get out as the 4000lb 'Cookie' had fallen on to the hardstanding. Stan Bridgeman ever after claimed to hold the World speed record for the journey from the cockpit of a Lancaster to the rear door; not an easy journey by any means. Jumping from the door, he sprinted across the pan and dived behind the earth mound surrounding the dispersal; all of some 50 feet from a 4000lb bomb!

After several nerve-wracking minutes, during which time nothing happened, the groundcrew started to reappear. Following their example, Bridgeman and Wiltshire climbed the mound and walked over to survey the weapon, which was lying under the open bomb bay of their Lancaster. The arrival of their CO, W/Cdr Forbes and S/Ldr Sullivan, their Flight Commander, was the signal for a burst of frenetic activity as the bomb was re-hoisted into the bomb bay. The net result of this incident was that the Farrow crew were well behind the Main Force when they eventually arrived over Karlsruhe. Here they were the sole recipients of the attention of the resident flak batteries! The postscript to this saga belongs to Stan Bridgeman, who commented that "*Not many Cookies were dropped in two countries on the same night*".

While the Farrow crew were sorting out the problem of their rogue Cookie, the 34 other Waddington aircraft formed part of the 250-strong force of Lancasters on their way to Karlsruhe. This was to be the last major attack on the city by Bomber Command and was considered to have been a 'complete failure' due to cloud over the target area. The attackers lost 14 aircraft on this operation (5.6%), whereas the total lost over the other two targets attacked that night was seven out of 818 aircraft taking part (0.8%). Three of the aircraft lost over Karlsruhe were from Waddington. No 463 Squadron lost F/O E K Oliver and crew flying in JO-B (ME298). This was their second operation and only the flight engineer and navigator survived to become PoWs. No 467 Squadron lost two crews and very nearly a third. F/Lt N S C Colley was an RAF pilot, and he and his crew were shot down flying in PO-J (PB306) on their 21st operation. None of the crew survived.

F/O A N G Robinson and crew were flying on their twelfth operation in PO-D (LM100) when they too were shot down. Only the bomb aimer, F/Sgt Jarrett survived to become a PoW. In his post-repatriation report, Jarrett stated that while they were over France the starboard inner engine caused problems, so their captain decided to shut it down and to feather the propeller. The flight engineer activated the feathering button for that engine, but on doing so, he called to the pilot that all four engine propellers were feathering! Despite instant action to reverse the process, it proved to be ineffective, resulting in a total loss of power. Robinson gave the order to abandon the aircraft, but only the bomb aimer and the rear gunner got out in time. F/Sgt Jarrett hit the ground some 20 seconds after his parachute opened. The rear gunner was not so lucky; he hit the ground before his parachute was fully deployed. The remaining five members of the crew perished in the subsequent crash.

A luckier crew that night was that of F/O Keith Swain, flying in PO-T (PD231). During the attack on Karlsruhe, they had to fight off a very determined attack by an enemy night fighter. Their Lancaster suffered severe damage and the port inner engine caught fire. Their initial attempts to extinguish the fire proved unsuccessful, so Swain gave the order to bail out. The two gunners and the wireless operator bailed out just before the fire was brought under control. Seeing this, Swain cancelled the bail out order and decided initially to try to reach Allied territory. Having crossed the front line, Swain decided to press on and recover to Waddington, which he did, arriving somewhat late. The remaining four crew members went on to complete a tough 35 operations tour, all against heavily defended targets.

Five nights later it was back to the wretched Dortmund-Ems Canal at Ladbergen. That night, the Command mounted 1,205 sorties against three targets; the towns of Goch, Kleve and the canal. At the canal, a force of 177 Lancasters dropped delayed action bombs, but the attack was considered to have been inaccurate and the canal was not breached. Of the 24 aircraft despatched by Waddington, one failed to return. The Commanding Officer of No 467 Squadron, W/Cdr Keith Douglas DFC AFC and his crew were shot down some time after having left the target area. Flying in PO-U (NG455), with F/O L W Baines RCAF as second bomb aimer (?), W/Cdr Douglas and two members of the crew were killed in the action; four others became PoWs, while the W/Op, P/O Strickland made contact with some Dutch civilians who hid him until a British Army reconnaissance patrol moved into the area. None of the surviving crew members could say whether it was flak or a night fighter that shot them down. All they could recall was a mighty crash and their pilot calling for them to bail out. Strickland returned to Waddington on 1 April 1945.

W/Cdr Douglas had completed his first tour of operations while serving on No 103 Squadron at Elsham Wolds. He commenced his second tour with No 460 Squadron and had completed six operations when he was promoted and posted to command No 467 Squadron. He and his crew were on their thirteenth operation of their second tour when they were shot down.

On the credit side that night, was the action by F/O Chris Peart and crew, flying JO-T (NN721). Having completed their bombing run they were homeward bound when they were attacked by several Ju 88 night fighters. In the ensuing combat, the combined actions of the two gunners and their calls for corkscrews held the enemy at bay. However, one of the fighter pilots appeared determined to destroy the bomber, and closed in on the rear of the Lancaster until at virtually point blank range. Just as he fired his first burst, the two Lancaster air gunners concentrated their fire upon him, scoring numerous strikes. Almost immediately, the Ju88 burst into flames and fell away as fire engulfed both wings. The fighter was seen by both gunners to hit the ground and explode.

The following night the target was again the synthetic oil plant at Politz. The Command had launched a total of 1,020 sorties against three targets that night; Krefield, Wanne-Eickel and Politz. The 31 aircraft from Waddington formed part of the 475-strong Lancaster force which wrecked the Politz plant so thoroughly that it produced no further oil during the remainder of the war. All the Station's aircraft returned, though F/O Wicks and crew, flying in JO-U (RF141), made it only as far as the Emergency Landing Strip (ELS) at Carnaby near Bridlington. Following the usual debrief, the Wicks crew were credited with damaging a Ju88 night fighter before releasing their bombs and with destroying another just after clearing the target. Two enemy Ju88 night fighters had attacked JO-U before the crew had commenced their bombing run. The attack set ablaze No 1 port inner fuel tank; the hydraulic system was damaged and the mid upper gunner's intercom lead was severed. Despite the fire and threat of explosion in the port wing, they managed to shake-off the fighter and commenced their bombing run! As soon as they had dropped their bombs, Wicks shut down the port inner engine and feathered the propeller, but the fuel tank fire only increased in intensity.

They were then attacked again by another fighter. It could hardly miss seeing them, with a blazing fire in the wing. Wicks put the Lancaster into the corkscrew evasive manoeuvre, which in addition damped down the fire, but did not extinguish it. During the course of the corkscrew, the rear gunner, Sgt Cottroll, shot the fighter down, the crew witnessing it crash and explode. With the fire in the wing showing no sign of abating, Wicks ordered the crew to stand by to abandon the aircraft. Then, in one last attempt to extinguish the fire, he put the Lancaster into a steep dive, which eventually blew the fire out. They then set course for home on three engines, with bomb doors open without hydraulics to close them, ten degrees of flap, artificial horizon out of action and with no intercom to either gunner. The navigator worked out a short cut over Denmark and they made a successful landing at Carnaby; all this in an aircraft that was barely capable of staying in the air. For his performance that night, Milton Wicks was awarded the DFC. The crew went on to complete a tour of 26 operations.

Ernie Biddiscombe, Frank Lillecrap's navigator, when recording his impressions in his comprehensive diary, commented on this Politz raid: *'Kites going down right and left of us as we neared the target. Looks as if the enemy has anticipated us. The fiery trails of the falling Lancs is a grim sight indeed. Two were seen to explode in mid air; no doubt hit with their bombs on board'* (Fourteen young men instantly vapourised). In all, the Command lost twelve Lancasters over Politz that night.

Much has already been written about the attack on Dresden on the night of 13/14 February 1945. Some of the material could best be described as ill-conceived if not inaccurate. From the point of view of many, if not most of the bomber crews briefed to attack Dresden, it was just another target among dozens; just another German town. Very few of the young men of Bomber Command were students of medieval Germany, and none had the benefit of hindsight, a characteristic so essential to revisionist historians. One of the more common reactions among those crews at the Dresden briefings was "What a bloody long way to go!"

Dresden, together with Berlin, Chemnitz and Leipzig were all part of Operation Thunderclap. This plan was concerned with the proposal to carry out a series of particularly heavy area raids on German cities, with a view to creating administrative and commercial collapse. In addition, these particular towns, situated just behind the German front lines on the Eastern Front, had become vital supply and communication centres. There was also the intention to prevent the German High Command transferring reinforcements from the Western Front to that in the East.

Operation Thunderclap was put into effect by an Air Ministry directive to the CinC Bomber Command. It is a matter of record that Prime Minister Churchill and the War Cabinet played a direct part in the final planning phase of Thunderclap. Later, when the scale of the devastation visited upon Dresden became known, in true political fashion, the members of the War Cabinet distanced themselves from the whole business. This left all the odium to fall on Harris and his crews. Whatever criticisms may be fairly levelled at the CinC Bomber Command; for all his faults he was in the final analysis the servant of his political masters, and it is there that the blame, if blame there be, should lie. Harris coined the term 'unctious rectitude' when commenting on possible criticisms of the reference to 'drunks' and 'parties' in Gibson's book Enemy Coast Ahead. Such a term could well be applied to those who endeavour to lay the blame for Dresden at Harris' door. Some of those who villify Harris seem to have conveniently overlooked the fact that for nearly six years, this country had been engaged in a war to the death. A war that we could not afford to lose, for our own sake and for that of much of Europe. It is truly in the nature of the beast, that in war, horror begets horror.

Bomber Command despatched 796 Lancasters to Dresden, 36 of them from Waddington. A total of nine Lancasters were lost, representing a loss rate of 0.01%. Of the six aircraft lost over Germany, one came from Waddington. F/O Fernley-Stott and crew, flying on their 22nd operation in JO-E (NG234) failed to return. Their aircraft was seen by the Lillecrap crew to suffer a direct hit by flak and to explode in mid air; there were no survivors.

Chemnitz was the target the night after the attack on Dresden. This was another Thunderclap attack, but it was not a success. Meanwhile, a force of 224 Lancasters carried out a moderately successful attack on an oil refinery at Rositz, a small town near Leipzig. Waddington despatched 32 aircraft, all but one of which returned safely. The missing aircraft JO-T (NN721), was flown by F/Lt Padgham and crew on their eighteenth operation. Their aircraft was hit by flak twice in quick succession; two of the crew being killed. The remaining members of the crew parachuted to safety, but all were captured and became PoWs. On this occasion, the departure of the Station's aircraft was recorded by an Air Ministry film team, though what has become of the film is unknown. On their return from Rositz, all crews reported severe icing problems en-route to the target.

The attack on the Bohlen synthetic oil plant on the night of 19/20 February, was not considered to have been successful. 35 of the 254 aircraft taking part, came from Waddington, all of which returned safely, with the exception of the unfortunate F/O Alec Findlay. He and his crew, flying in PO-Y (PD362), were back in strife again. On this occasion, all their navigation equipment ceased to function, but despite this they pressed on to the target. On their return, while attempting to land at Friston in Sussex in very poor visibility, their Lancaster was badly damaged, though the crew emerged unscathed. Once again, Alec Findlay found himself attending a Court of Inquiry!

During the attack on Bohlen, many Main Force crews heard the following exchange over their radios:

"Bomber Controller to Marker Leader; take over Johnny, take over."

"Roger pal; good luck."

This brief exchange marked the death of the crew of the Master Bomber, W/Cdr E A Benjamin DFC* The loss of the Master Bomber early in the attack probably accounts for the lack of success that night.

On landing back at Waddington that morning, Lancaster PO-Y (PB754), flown by Frank Lillecrap and crew, suffered a jammed throttle on the starboard inner engine. At full throttle, this caused the bomber to swing violently to port. Seeing that he was heading straight for another Lancaster, Lillecrap managed to swing his aircraft out of line, scattering numerous groundcrewmen as it swerved towards them. Luckily for all concerned, he managed to bring his aircraft to a stop without damage.

24 hours after the abortive attack on Bohlen, Bomber Command carried out a four-target assault, one of which was the Mitteland Canal at Gravenhorst. Twenty of the 154 Lancasters attacking the canal came from Waddington; all of which returned safely. The attack itself was virtually a non-event as the target area was completely covered by cloud, causing the Master Bomber to call the attack off and order the bombers home. By this stage of the war, the Mitteland Canal had been attacked almost as often as the Dortmund-Ems Canal and was referred to as 'the milk run'. However, in view of what was to occur when the crews returned the next night, the term 'milk run' could be considered somewhat inappropriate. A standing black joke among the aircrews was to the effect that, the aircraft of No 5 Group bombed the Mitteland Canal so often that the German flak gunners just left their guns aimed and ready for the next attack. With good weather forecast for the next night, the Command despatched 165 Lancasters back to the Mitteland Canal at Gravenhorst. This attack was coincident with attacks on Duisburg and Worms. It was a clear night and the canal was breached, but at a high cost to Waddington.

In all, the Command lost nine Lancasters attacking the canal that night, three of them from Waddington. Possibly the hardest loss for the Station to accept was that of No 463 Squadron's commander, W/Cdr Bill Forbes. He and his crew were flying in JO-A (PB804) when they were shot down by a night fighter on their way back from the target. Bill Forbes and his mid upper gunner, Warrant Officer Norman were killed in the attack, while the remaining members of the crew, which included F/Lt John Loftus, a camera operator, all bailed out and were taken prisoner. Among those lost with the Squadron Commander was the Bombing Leader, F/Lt Grime DFC; the Navigation Leader, F/O Costello; the Assistant Signals Leader, P/O McLeod and the Flight Engineer Leader, F/Lt Dean.

Wing Commander W A Forbes DSO DFC completed his first tour of operations with No 467 Squadron between June and December 1943. Among his 26 operations were four trips to Berlin at the height of the Battle of Berlin. After a rest (sic) he returned to operations, this time as the Commanding Officer of No 463 Squadron. He was on his 46th and last scheduled operation when he was killed; at the age of 25. The wording of the citation for the award of his DSO, says it all: 'Acting W/Cdr W A Forbes DFC RAAF, No 463 Squadron RAAF. This officer has completed a large number of operational missions as the captain of an aircraft. In January 1945 he led a force of aircraft to attack the Dortmund-Ems Canal in daylight. The results were spectacular and the canal was drained and put completely out of action. Throughout his two tours of operational duty, this officer has consistently displayed outstanding leadership and determination. As a Flight and Squadron Commander, he set an exceptionally fine example, which has been reflected in the efficiency and fine fighting spirit of his unit.'

The second Waddington crew lost that night was that of F/O L R Pedersen, flying in JO-P (LM548). Pedersen had taken over F/O Eagle's crew following his (Eagle's) loss flying as second pilot with F/Lt Livingstone of No 467 Squadron, during the attack on Siegen on 1/2 February. Having carried out a successful bombing run, the crew were on their way home, about 45 minutes from the target, when they were hit under the mid upper gun turret and in the port wing by a burst of fire from a 'Schrage Muzik' equipped night fighter. Only the bomb aimer and the flight engineer managed to parachute to safety before the Lancaster exploded in mid air. It crashed near the town of Weert in Holland, there being no other survivors. In his post return report, the bomb aimer, Warrant Officer Dixon, reported seeing 'scarecrow' shells bursting below them at the time they were hit. He also stated that the only other crew member to escape, Sgt Freeman, joined him in an Army Casualty Clearing Station in Holland, but that he was still there as he had been severely injured. Warrant Officer Dixon had been passed on to the Army by Dutch civilians at considerable risk to themselves.

This reference to 'scarecrow' shells was the term used by bomber crews to describe what they believed to be a special type of anti-aircraft shell, used by the German defenders to lower the morale of the bomber crews as, when they exploded, they gave the appearance of a bomber exploding in mid air. Post war interrogation of German weapons specialists elicited the fact that they (the Germans) possessed no such weapon. What the crews saw all too often was a real bomber exploding in mid air!

The third No 463 Squadron crew to fail to return that night was that of F/O Graham Farrow. This crew, flying in JO-Z (NG329), were on their sixteenth operation. Having completed their attack, they too were on their way home and were approaching Venrai in Holland when they were attacked by a night fighter. This was another 'Schrage Muzik' equipped night fighter, a Bf110. With an uncontrollable fire in the starboard wing, Graham Farrow gave the order to bail out. All seven members of the crew made it to safety, though the flight engineer, F/Sgt Stan 'Lofty' Bridgeman was wounded in both legs by fragments from cannon shells. The luckiest member of the crew was the pilot, Graham Farrow. By the time he came to jump from the burning bomber, it was on its back and falling into a steep dive. Somehow or other, Farrow managed to push himself free of the machine and parachuted to safety.

A post war (40+ years) discussion with the late Stan Bridgeman and the mid upper gunner, Frank Bone, revealed some points of interest. They were in the last wave of Lancasters to attack and were on their way home. In the minutes leading up to the attack upon their aircraft, they counted seven aircraft going down under night fighter attacks. Suddenly, without any sign of their assailant, they were hit in the starboard inner engine and fuel tanks. Both men recalled seeing the tracer streaks of the cannon shells as they flashed past the wireless operator, Jack Wiltshire and destroyed the accumulator and the navigator's table! That the shells missed the wireless operator and the navigator, F/O Peter Harris, must be considered little short of miraculous. The shells came up through the floor at an angle of approximately 60 degrees. With a wrecked accumulator, it proved impossible to feather the propeller of the damaged engine, though it would have had little effect on the eventual outcome.

With the exception of Lofty Bridgeman, who remained in hospital for some time, the crew were back on operations two weeks later, their target being Essen! As a result of considerable research by Stan Bridgeman[8] it has been established that the Farrow crew and possibly those of W/Cdr Forbes and F/O Pedersen, were shot down by the German night fighter ace, Major Heinz Wolfgang Schnaufer and his crew of IV/NJG1. This unique crew, all holders of the Knight's Cross (Ritterkreutz) were credited with shooting down seven Lancasters during the attack on the Mitteland Canal. Their submitted locations, and the timings of 2044, 2048, 2051, 2055, 2058, 2100 and 2103hr were all confirmed by Luftwaffe intelligence. In one letter from a bulky file of correspondence with Stan Bridgeman, Schnauffer's radar operator, Fritz Rumpelhardt, stated that they also carried out an eighth attack, but that after firing a few rounds, their cannons ceased firing (probably out of ammunition). They registered hits on this eighth bomber, but broke off without observing any result. This last attack occured at 2110hr, one minute before the recorded time that the crew of JO-Z bailed out. So, the chances are that Graham Farrow and crew were Schnauffer's eighth victim in the space of 26 minutes! Schnauffer and crew ended the war with a total of 121 victory tallies marked on the tail fin of their Bf110 (Werk No 720260). One of the fins is in the Imperial War Museum in London; the other is in the Australian War Museum in Canberra.

[8] The author contacted Stan Bridgeman in the course of researching material for the Waddington history. During one of numerous telephone conversations, Stan laughingly mentioned that while his fellow crew members were enjoying their post operation breakfast, he had to make do with Army hospital gruel! On his subsequent visit to Waddington with the late Frank Bone, Stan ordered steak pie for lunch. Instead, he was served a full fried breakfast! The RAF may have been late in serving him his post operation breakfast (40 years late), but the debt was duly settled (and eaten).

W/Cdr Forbes' place was taken by W/Cdr Keith Kemp DFC. He had arrived on No 463 Squadron on 17 January and was due to assume command, following Bill Forbes' final operation. As previously mentioned, Forbes was killed in action on what was scheduled to be the last operation of his second tour. Keith Kemp was no stranger to operations; his first having been as the Commanding Officer of No 2 Squadron RAAF. This squadron was equipped with Lockheed Hudsons, flying out of Darwin in northern Australia. He was awarded an immediate DFC for his leadership of an attack on Dobo in the Aru Kep archipeligo, off the coast of New Guinea on 3 March 1943. He was later credited with shooting down a Japanese aircraft with the two 0.303" fixed machine guns in the nose of his Hudson; no mean feat. Kemp subsequently commanded the re-formed No 13 Squadron RAAF at Cooktown, North Queensland, which was by then, flying the American built Vega Ventura bomber.

On 22 February, Bomber Command despatched 167 Lancasters in an accurate attack on oil refineries atGelsenkirchen and Osterfeld. The attack was filmed by F/Lt Allen Perry DFC and crew, flying in JO-L (PD337). This crew had only recently completed their first tour; but instead of going to training units or whatever, they volunteered to press straight on for a second tour as a photographic crew. The next night, 367 Lancasters carried out a devastating area bombing attack on Pforsheim; the attack again being filmed by Perry and crew in JO-L. The attackers dropped 1825 tons of bombs in 22 minutes, resulting in a death toll of 17000, with 83% of the town destroyed in the subsequent fire storm. German raid assessment records lists this as the third most effective attack of the war, after Hamburg and Dresden.

The last operation of the month of February was a daylight attack on the Dortmund-Ems Canal on the 24th of the month. The 166 Lancasters, including 29 from Waddington, found the target covered by low cloud and mist, resulting in the attack being cancelled. All those taking part returned safely to their bases, though the attack was not without loss. A No 61 Squadron Lancaster (RF137) blew up after returning to Skellingthorpe, necessitating the diversion of all the satellite's aircraft to Waddington. One of the crew members taking part in this operation, recorded his pleasure at seeing numerous Mustang fighters 'cutting capers around the bomber formation, obviously spoiling for a fight which never materialised'.

On a lighter note, it was the custom on the two Waddington squadrons, among many in Bomber Command, to paint various designs on the nose of the aircraft. An example of this 'art work' was that of PO-E (ME432), known at Waddington as 'Easy Two'. This No 467 Squadron Lancaster carried the unofficial crew heraldic shield, which was painted by one of the aircraft's groundcrew, Sgt Frank Skillington. The actual device in no way conformed to the rules of heraldry, but consisted of a shield divided into four (party per cross), surmounted by a pair of crossed (saltire) crutches. According to the crew, the crossed crutches were indicative of the number of times that the Bache crew (it was their aircraft) limped home. They (the crutches) could also be said to refer to the actual crutches used by their wireless operator, F/Sgt Dreger, following his injury after bailing out on New Year's Day 1945. In the top left hand quadrant of the shield was a tankard of ale - the symbolism obvious! Next to that, in the top right hand quadrant, was a lighted candle, meant to depict night operations and other nocturnal activities! The bottom left hand quadrant contained a chamberpot,; the meaning being self-evident when taken in conjunction with the motto 'Semper in Excreta' which referred to the fact that this crew were repeatedly shot up by flak throughout their tour. The bottom right hand quadrant was blacked out, symbolising the crew's opinion of the frequency of times they were kept in the dark as to what they were doing.

Despite the successes of the Allied ground forces, there was no easing of the demands made upon the Command's crews during the month of March. Between them, the two Waddington squadrons would mount 371 sorties against 17 targets, for the loss of four crews from each squadron. Of these 56 men, 44 were killed in action; five became PoWs, while seven evaded capture.

By the 2nd of March, the city of Cologne was virtually in the front line. Accordingly, Bomber Command mounted a two-wave daylight attack by a total of 858 bombers. The Pathfinders marked the target in clear weather and the resulting bombing was both accurate and concentrated. Four days later the city was captured by troops of the American First Army, who found that about three quarters of the city had been destroyed by the combined effects of bombing and shellfire. Remarkably, the Gothic cathedral remained virtually undamaged. Waddington's participation in the Command's last attack on Cologne was limited to the provision of a photographic aircraft. No 463 Squadron despatched JO-L (PD337), flown by F/Lt Graham Skelton DFC and crew, plus F/O Rogers and Sgt Pearce as camera operators. The Skelton crew had completed their first tour with No 467 Squadron at the end of October 1944 and, following two weeks leave, were posted 'across the road' to No 463 Squadron as the Film Unit crew; a duty for which they had volunteered! After flying nine operations as the camera crew, the Skelton crew were screened and flew no further operations.

It was back to the Dortmund-Ems Canal at Ladbergen again on the night of 3/4 March. A force of 212 Lancasters, 30 of them from Waddington, breached the aqueduct in two places, putting the canal out of action for the remainder of the war. Sadly, this success was not achieved without cost. Of the seven Lancasters lost that night, four were from Waddington. No 463 Squadron lost F/O Howells and crew, flying on their nineteenth operation in JO-D (NG469). They were shot down; only the bomb aimer and the rear gunner surviving to become PoWs. The other three Station crews lost that night were from No 467 Squadron. Flying on their third operation, F/O R T Ward and crew were shot down in ME453, none of the crew surviving. This crew, less F/O Ward, had flown one trip in February to Gravenhorst with Gp Capt Bonham-Carter, at the very start of their operational tour. A more experienced crew was that of F/O R B Eggins, who were flying in PO-V (LM677). As previously mentioned, this crew had survived a mid-air collision over France two months previous. This time they were not to be so lucky; only the bomb aimer surviving to become a PoW. The third No 467 Squadron crew lost that night was that of the Squadron Commander, W/Cdr Eric Langlois DFC. This crew had been posted from No 463 Squadron when Langlois was appointed to command the squadron following the loss of W/Cdr Douglas. At the time he was shot down, W/Cdr Langlois had been in command of the squadron for less than one month. He and his crew were flying on their 17th operation of their second tour, aboard Lancaster PO-W (PB806). There were only two survivors, the bomb aimer and the mid upper gunner.

The Station was fortunate not to lose a fifth crew that night. F/O Wicks and crew, flying in JO-O (NG439) suffered an engine failure on take-off. After several terrifying minutes of '*interesting*' flying, Wicks managed to put the fully loaded bomber back on the runway without further mishap.

As if the loss of four crews over enemy territory in one night was not enough, the Luftwaffe chose this night to put into effect Operation Gisela. It is believed that this was the brainchild of the leading German night fighter ace, Major Schnauffer. He had found that once the returning bomber stream crossed the front line, they ceased jamming and dropping 'window'. He put forward the proposal that a force of night fighters should shadow the departing bombers until they reached the North Sea, when they should then be attacked. The Commander of the Third Air Division, Major General Grabmann, became very enthusiastic about the proposal, extending it to include attacking the bombers as they were preparing to land back at their bases. British intelligence learned of the plan (Ultra?) and wasted no time in ensuring that the Germans knew that the plan was known to the Allies. Notwithstanding this weakness, after some delay, Operation Gisela was given the go-ahead. The Luftwaffe units employed were all equipped with the Ju88G-6, and it involved something between 100 and 200 aircraft. In all, these intruders accounted for 22 Bomber Command aircraft, though not without loss to themselves.

One of those who recalled the effect on Waddington of Operation Gisela, was Jim Craig, the navigator on the recently arrived crew of F/O Beer. The crew had been on the Station just over one week and had yet to fly on operations. Craig was in the Aircrew Seregeants' Mess when over the Tannoy broadcast system came "Air Raid Warning Red". Such an occurence was new to most of the crews, who, instead of making for the shelters, made their way out to the Flight Line *"To watch the fun"*. While awaiting 'the fun', the assembled crews heard over the Tannoy, which must have been tied into the Air Traffic Control frequency, a No 467 Squadron aircraft call up for permission to land. The communications went as follows:

"Hello Slangword (Waddington's callsign), this is Lustral N Nan Over (No 467 Squadron's callsign)" [Mozart was No 463's callsign]. Immediately, over the broadcast system came the ATC reply, which to say the least was non-standard: "Shut your ------ mouth". Such a departure from the norm shocked even the hardened Aussie aircrew.

Despite the airfield being in total darkness, the pilot in question carried out a successful landing. Meanwhile, a No 463 Squadron crew that had landed a few minutes earlier, were met at their aircraft by a WAAF driver in a crew bus. LACW Crane was the driver and, as she made her way round the perimeter track, one of the enemy intruders straffed her bus. Luckily, nobody in the vehicle was hit, but one of the bullets had penetrated the driver's door and passed between her legs and the front of her seat, before hitting the handbrake, which was in the middle of the floor near the gear lever. The intruder remained in the area for some time, dropping anti-personnel 'butterfly' bombs and machine gunning anything that caught his attention. In the event, the only real damage was a hit on the pyrotechnic store, which caught fire. The store held the Station and Base stock of pyrotechnics and the many target markers and indicators such as Chandeliers and others. It was later to be claimed (sic) that it was possible to read the newspaper in the streets of Lincoln from the glow from Waddington. However, the main worry at the time was that the fire might spread to the main bomb dump, with disastrous consequences. It was mainly due to the efforts of one of the armament officers, a New Zealander, F/O Hector, that the fire was brought under control quickly and the danger averted. On a happier note, just about every air defence weapon on the Station was fired that night, many of them by enthusiastic amateurs. The intruder was not hit; luckily, neither was anything else of any consequence.

Subsequent research has revealled that the intruder that night was flown by Hauptmann Heinz Rokker, a 64 victory night fighter ace of NJG2, operating out of Twente in occupied Holland. For some time after the attack, Station personnel were continually reminded of the dangers of approaching the anti-personnel 'butterfly' bombs. Despite this, one sergeant picked one up intending to keep it as a souvenir and suffered the inevitable fatal consequences.

The Trials of Gus Belford and Crew

Two nights later, Bomber Command despatched 760 aircraft in an attack on Chemnitz, with an additional 248 Lancasters attacking the synthetic oil plant at Bohlen. The Station provided 30 aircraft for the Bohlen operation, all but one of which returned safely. The missing aircraft was JO-G (NG401), flown by F/O Gus Belford and crew. They were in the middle of their second (!) bomb run when their aircraft was hit by heavy flak. Their first run had been aborted due to a combination of heavy flak and the loss from sight of the Wanganui sky marker. As Belford banked steeply to starboard to recommence the bombing run, his Lancaster was bracketed by five bursts of flak. One of the shells was a direct hit on the starboard wing between the rear wing spar and the No 3 outer fuel tank. Shrapnel from the other four shells caused considerable damage to the VHF transmitter, the TR 11 radio and the Loran navigation equipment. However, it was the direct hit that sealed their fate. The No 3 fuel tank, outboard of the starboard outer engine, was blown through the top of the wing and trailed in the slipstream behind the starboard outer No 4 engine. The same hit had also demolished the inner three hinges of the starboard aileron, and blasted it (the aileron) upwards. The slipstream forced the bent section to the rear, resulting in full port aileron deflection. Despite strenuous efforts, it remained in this position throughout the remainder of the flight. Among the other damage, was that to the fuselage, which had been torn open beside the mid upper turret, together with dozens holes of varying sizes along the full length of the starboard side of the fuselage.

In addition to the flak damage to the aircraft, four members of the crew suffered injuries of varying degrees. The mid upper gunner, F/Sgt Shipperd, was wounded in the temple, neck and in his right side, and rendered unconscious. The rear gunner, F/Sgt Jobson, was wounded in the throat and left eye, being rendered temporarily blind. Gus Belford and his navigator, F/O Wheeler, both suffered minor injuries. The remaining members of the crew, including F/O Beer, flying as co-pilot on his first operation, all escaped injury.

The effect of the deflection of the aileron was to cause the aircraft to roll into a vertical starboard bank and drop into a spiral descent. Belford gave the order to prepare to abandon the aircraft, but failed to receive any acknowledgement from the crew stations at the rear of the bomber. Realising that something was seriously wrong, Belford sent the wireless operator back to give assistance if required, and to report back over the intercom. Meanwhile, F/Sgt Polkinghorn, the bomb aimer, jettisoned the bombs, which enabled Belford to regain a measure of control of his aircraft, eventually managing to stabilise the Lancaster in level flight using ten of the twelve divisions of port rudder trim. For the remainder of the flight, the aircraft flew with approximately six degrees of yaw to starboard. On receiving the report from the wireless operator concerning the injuries to his crew members, Belford realised that his two gunners required treatment without delay. Cancelling the order to prepare to bail out, he asked his injured navigator for a course to the nearest Allied airfield. Despite the fact that nearly all his navigation equipment was unserviceable, Wheeler gave him a perfect course for Juvincourt near Reims.

They flew on, in cloud, without radio contact and with only the Gee set providing navigation information. Eventually, with only 20 minutes fuel remaining, F/O Wheeler set up a simulated beam approach using the Gee information. They broke cloud at 700 feet, with the runway dead ahead, about two miles distant. With no aileron control, Belford had earlier decided on a wheels up landing,, influenced by the fact that he could not be certain that they would be in a position to make the runway whenever they broke cloud. The watchers in the tower at Juvincourt realised that the approaching Lancaster was in trouble, and gave a series of flashing green signals, indicating that he had priority. With limited (sic) control, and a strong cross-wind, the bomber drifted off the line of the runway, so Belford elected to put down in the dark, using the perimeter track lighting to judge his height. Just as he was about to cut the engines, the Juvincourt control tower loomed up dead ahead. There was no way that the bomber would stop before crashing into the tower, so Belford applied full power and, while still yawing to starboard, managed to clear the top of the tower, but removed its radio and radar aerials as they passed over its terrified occupants.

Remaining below cloud and keeping in sight of the runway, Belford decided to try to minimise the damage to his already battered aircraft, by lowering the undercarriage, though he left this until at about 200 feet above the ground - "*Just in case!*" Unknown to him, the port mainwheel had not come down, the resulting drag causing the Lancaster to yaw further away from the line of the runway. He called to the flight engineer to raise the undercarriage, but the hydraulic fluid had leaked away in the lowering phase, accordingly, nothing happened. With his aircraft nearing the ground, Belford tried once again to lower the undercarriage, this time using the emergency air bottle; this too was unsuccessful. So, with considerable yaw to starboard and rapidly running out of height and airspeed, Gus Belford had no choice but to put the aircraft down regardless. Those watching were of the opinion that the one wheel landing was well executed, spoiled only by being ripped off as it sank into a shell crater. The battered Lancaster finally came to rest 300 yards down the runway and some 30 yards off to one side, facing back the way it had come.

With the exception of the two hospitalised air gunners, the crew were flown back to Waddington and were back on operations in less than three weeks. The attack on Bohlen had been their 23rd operation, and by VE Day they had completed a further six. For his performance that night, F/O A C Belford was awarded an immediate DSO. Despite this hair-raising introduction to operational flying, F/O Beer went on to complete seven operations as captain of his own crew before the end of the war in Europe.

The Whirlwind Continues

With the loss of W/Cdr Langlois, command of No 467 Squadron passed to W/Cdr Ian Hay DFC. The new CO was an experienced operator, having flown two operational tours with Nos 2 and 15 Squadrons RAAF before coming to Europe. His original posting had been to No 463 Squadron, but with the loss of W/Cdr Langlois he was moved 'across the road'. He was to remain in command of the squadron until its disbandment at Metheringham in October 1945. On a personal note; Ian Hay's wife served for some time at Waddington as an LACW. They met at Waddington and were married before his return to Australia. Another wedding occasioned at Waddington was that between Warrant Officer Thompson, the flight engineer on Reg Ellis' crew of No 463 Squadron, and Warrant Officer Welsh WAAF, the youngest Warrant Officer in the WAAF and the first in Bomber Command.

The Station's aircraft operated on the two nights immediately following the attack on Bohlen. On the first night, 26 aircraft were despatched as part of a 191 strong force, attacking the small port of Sassnitz on the island of Rugen, north of Stettin. The harbour was crowded with warships and merchantmen engaged in moving troops to Norway, and in evacuating high ranking Nazi officials from the Eastern Front areas that were at threat from the advance of the Red Army. The following night, 27 Station aircraft formed part of a 234-strong force of Lancasters attacking the oil refinery at Harburg. This was to be a bad night for Bomber Command, with fourteen Lancasters (6%) failing to return, though on this occasion none of those lost were from Waddington.

Thousands of miles from Waddington at this time, across the other side of the World, a force of 300 American B29 Superfortresses carried out a firebomb attack on Tokyo. Approximately sixteen square miles of closely packed industrial and domestic areas in the city were destroyed. Estimates of the number of people killed in this attack vary from between 83,000 to 130,000. This devastating attack, in many ways as destructive as the later atomic bomb attacks, received little media attention at the time, and ever since has been overshadowed by the atomic bomb attacks on Hiroshima and Nagasaki.

On 11 March, the Command mounted its heaviest attack of the war. A total of 1,079 bombers dropped a total of 4,661 tons of bombs on Essen, which was 32 tons more than that dropped on Cologne in the first of the Command's 1,000-bomber raids in May 1942. Although Essen was cloud covered, a feature which for so long had been its best defence, this time it did not save the city. The Pathfinders dropped Oboe directed sky markers (Wanganui) and an accurate and devastating attack ensued. After over five years of trying, aircraft of Bomber Command finally destroyed the 2,000-acre Krupp's armament works. All 26 Waddington aircraft returned safely, though sadly, the Station did lose a crew that day. Newly arrived P/O Orchard and crew, flying in JO-N (LM130), were taking part in a fighter affiliation training exercise when they collided with a Hurricane (PZ740) of No 1690 Bomber Defence Training Flight (BDTF). Both aircraft crashed in fields near Metheringham; there were no survivors.

The Lancaster in which P/O Orchard and crew were flying, JO-N, was better known as 'Nick the Nazi Neutralizer'. It had just undergone a Major service, a very rare occurence for any squadron Lancaster! It had originally come to Waddington from the Armstrong Whitworth factory at Coventry in May 1944. Allocated to No 463 squadron, it went on to complete 83 operations prior to its 'Major'. Its operations tally was depicted by 'devil's forks' as opposed to the more normal bomb tallies. The forks related to the nose art, which was that of 'Old Nick' himself. Lancaster LM130 had served only on No 463 Squadron and was well and truly a Waddington Lancaster.

The day after the heavy attack on Essen, Bomber Command despatched an even greater number of bombers against a single target. A mixed force of 1,108 aircraft attacked Dortmund in daylight. This was the greatest number of bombers ever sent to attack a single target and remained so up to the end of the war. In addition to the huge bomber force, a mass of RAF fighters provided escort. All in all, there were over 2,000 British aircraft taking part in the attack. 31 of the bombers came from Waddington, whose bomb loads formed part of the total of 4,851 tons dropped on the unfortunate Dortmund. This too was a record that was to stand for the remainder of the war in Europe. Two bombers were lost, but neither came from Waddington. Post war assessment of this attack concluded that it put Dortmund out of the war. Air Marshal Harris' words were coming true with a vengeance - The Nazis had indeed sown the wind, and were now well and truly reaping the whirlwind.

Two nights later, on the night of 14/15 March, 35 Waddington aircraft formed part of a 244-strong force attacking the Wintershall synthetic oil installation at Lutzkendorf. While this attack was taking place, a further 568 aircraft attacked a variety of other targets. The attack on Lutzkendorf was costly, with 18 Lancasters (7.4%) failing to return. Again, Waddington was lucky, with all its aircraft making it back home safely. It was during these operations, that the Command flew its last Stirling (LJ516) sortie.

On 15 March, No 463 Squadron despatched F/Lt Perry and crew in JO-L (PD337) to film an attack on the Benzol plants at Bottrop and Castrop-Rauxel. Both attacks were successful, with all the Lancasters returning, though No 4 Group lost a Halifax. This particular operation proved to be one that the Perry crew and the two camermen would long remember. All went well and according to plan until the take-off run when, as their aircraft reached 95-100mph and fast approaching the end of the runway, the port outer engine emitted a large cloud of white smoke, the engine revolutions dropped and the heavily laden bomber yawed violently to port. With a fully loaded Lancaster, weighing something in the region of 68,000lbs, Allen Perry had no time for finesse. He just held all the engines at full power and dragged his aircraft off the ground. Once safely airborne, they set course for the Wash emergency jettison area and dropped their bombs 'safe', two of which exploded on contact with the sea! This brought their overall weight down to some 58000lb and a safe landing on three engines was made back at base.

Allen Perry and crew were airborne again the next night, in a different aircraft. Flying in Lancaster JO-Y (PD329), they were to film the attack on Wurzburg. Waddington despatched 32 aircraft as part of a 225-strong force attacking Wurzburg. At the same time, a mixed force of 317 Lancasters and Mosquitos attacked Nuremburg for the last time. The Wurzburg force dropped 1127 tons of bombs within seventeen minutes with great accuracy, destroying 90% of the city. Of the six Lancasters lost in this operation, one came from Waddington. F/O Thomas and crew were an experienced crew on their twentieth operation, flying in PO-T (PD231) when they were shot down. The sole survivor was the rear gunner, Sgt B A Davies. It was the Thomas crew that had an operation discounted when they collided with another squadron aircraft during the attack on Flushing on 30 October. In all, Bomber Command lost 30 Lancasters (4.2%) in the two attacks that night.

Two days later, the Command despatched small forces of Lancasters to attack the viaduct at Arnsberg and the bridge at Vlotho near Minden. Only one Station aircraft took part in these attacks. No 463 Squadron despatched one aircraft, flown by F/Lt Perry and crew. Flying in JO-Y (PD329) again, they were tasked with filming the attack on the Arnsberg viaduct. They joined up with 37 Lancasters of Nos IX and 617 Squadrons, who were tasked with the destruction of the two railway targets. The aircraft of No 617 Squadron dropped six 22000lb 'Grand Slam' bombs which resulted in the collapse of the viaduct. Perry and his camera operators, P/O Buckland and Sgt Pease, filmed the huge bombs as they fell away from the dropping aircraft, and managed to follow the flight of the bombs all the way down to impact (This film is in the RAF Museum archives). The attack on the bridge at Vlotho was unsuccessful. On this occasion, all the aircraft taking part returned safely.

In his report on the Arnsberg attack, Perry reported: "We saw a Grand Slam hit the western span and the whole span disintegrated, with the roofs of nearby houses being blown off. On our second pass, only the crater was visible. We arrived over the target in company with a No 617 Squadron aircraft, YZ-C (PG996), which was 300 feet off on our immediate starboard. Front turret No 1 camera filmed the Grand Slam leaving YZ-C and followed it down. The mid under cameraman filmed the bomb hitting the viaduct's western span. The crew felt our aircraft vibrate when the bomb exploded - we were at 13000 feet at the time! Fighter escort was excellent." The No 617 Squadron aircraft filmed by Perry and crew was that flown by F/O Phillip Martin and crew.

Two weeks after the unsatisfactory attack on the synthetic oil plant at Bohlen, 224 Lancasters went back to finish the job. This was an extremely accurate attack and the plant was put out of action, and remained so up to the day that it was overun by American troops several weeks later. Though successful, it was a costly attack, the raiders losing nine of their number, including one of the 33 despatched from Waddington. The overall loss rate that night was 4%. The missing Waddington crew was that of F/O R S Bennett, flying in JO-C (PB845). This crew were on their fourth operation and there were no survivors.

On 22 March, the Command mounted attacks on five separate targets. 227 Lancasters attacked Hildesheim; 124 Halifaxes and Lancasters attacked Dorsten; 100 Lancasters attacked Bocholt; 130 Halifaxes and Lancasters attacked Dulmen, while 102 Lancasters attacked the rail bridges at Bremen (82 aircraft) and Nienburg (20 aircraft). 35 Waddington aircraft participated in the attack on Bremen. In addition, F/Lt Perry and crew joined in to film the attack. Perry later reported that the bridge was still intact when it disappeared from view under the protective smoke screen. This attack was carried out without loss.

For the Allies and the Germans, the Rhine was not simply a vital military objective, being the last 'ditch' before the open North German Plain. It was also an important psychological barrier, and had always symbolised German strength and unity. In the north, Montgomerie's 21st Army Group was faced with having to cross the Rhine at its widest. That the Germans would strenuously defend it, had never been in doubt. The focal point for the 21st Army Group was the town of Wesel, primarily because of its road network, that opened the way to the plain. In brief, the 51st Highland Division was to make the initial crossing, while the 1st Commando Brigade would assault Wesel immediately after a heavy bombing attack by Bomber Command. This was to be followed by a daylight drop by troops of the 6th Airborne Division. In preparation for the assault, the Commandos crossed the Rhine on the night of 23/24 March and moved into position about 1500 yards west of Wesel.

To carry out the precision attack on Wesel, Bomber Command gave the task to 195 Lancasters of No 5 Group, plus 23 Mosquitos from the Pathfinder Force. Of the Lancaster force, 32 were from Waddington, and the force dropped a total of 1000 tons of bombs in nine minutes, from the relatively low height of 9000 feet. All the attackers returned safely. This massive, concentrated attack, left the German defenders either dead or too dazed to fight effectively. The assault troops of the 51st Highland Division were crossing the Rhine before the last of the bombers had left the target area. The fortified town of Wesel was in British hands before midnight. In his subsequent message of thanks to the Command, Field Marshal Montgomerie wrote:

'My grateful appreciation for the quite magnificent cooperation you have given us in the Battle of the Rhine. The bombing of Wesel last night was a masterpiece and was a decisive factor in making possible an entry into that town before midnight'.

A follow-up message came to Waddington from HQ No 5 Group:

'Aircraft of Nos 463 and 467 Squadrons last night took part in an attack on the town of Wesel. The outstanding success of the raid can be judged by the message from the Army Commander. The Commandos send their hearty thanks to Bomber Command for their brilliant attack on the fortress town of Wesel last night. Only one stick of bombs missed the aiming point and no damage resulted from it. Wesel was taken this morning with only 36 casualties'.

Little over twelve hours after the attack on Wesel, the Command despatched three forces, each of approximately 175 aircraft, to attack separate targets. This represented a total daylight effort of 537 sorties, for the eventual loss of four aircraft. Waddington' part was limited to the provision of a Film Unit aircraft by No 463 Squadron. Once again flown by Allen Perry and crew, JO-Y filmed the attack on Sterkrade railway yards. This rail complex was packed with supply and troop trains in support of the German forces opposing the British breakout from the Wesel area. The rail yards were completely destroyed without loss. On this, the Perry crew's last operation, the camera crew was P/O Ancell and Sgt Corder.

Back at Waddington, No 463 Squadron experienced a minor incident when JO-O (NG439) crashed on the Scopwick/Nocton road, just south of the airfield as a result of engine failure. Fortunately, there were no serious injuries.

The last attack of March for the Waddington crews was against Farge. This was an oil storage depot and U-boat shelter. No 617 Squadron provided the 20 Lancasters targetted against the U-boat pens, while 115 others took on the oil storage depot. The newly constructed U-boat pens were protected by a 23 foot thick concrete roof, but this proved to be no defence against the two 'Grand Slam' bombs which penetrated it. The subsequent explosions collapsed the roof, rendering the shelter unuseable. The results of the attack on the oil installation were unknown as all the attackers dropped delayed action bombs. The decision to use delayed action fusing was to ensure that the target did not become obscurred by smoke and dust, which would have resulted in an incomplete attack. All 34 Station aircraft returned safely to base.

The official report on the Farge attack stated that no aircraft were lost, but this is at odds with the log entry made by Ernie Biddiscombe, the navigator of the Lillecrap crew. In it he recorded that while flying in PO-Y (PB754), the crew witnessed an Me262 jet fighter attack on the bomber formation. The crew's two gunners, Frank Clement and John (Paddy) Jones, both opened fire at the fast approaching fighter without any apparent effect. Luckily for the Lillecrap crew, the shells from the fighter's four 30mm cannon hit a Lancaster some way ahead of them. They witnessed it break in two and fall in flames; no parachutes being observed.

Biddiscombe reported that they were later told that two similar attacks had taken place further back in the bomber stream, which accounted for two more Lancasters.

The month of March 1945 had been something of a record breaking month for Bomber Command, in which it had dropped a total of 68000 tons of bombs and incendiaries.

It was at about this time that there were various rumours circulating the Station concerning certain unofficial activities. One concerned a particular RAF policeman who, took a perverse delight in giving the NCO aircrew a hard time. Apparently, so the rumour went, one evening he was jumped upon, bound and gagged and had a bag pulled over his head. The unfortunate policeman was then carried to the perpetrators' aircraft and pushed into the fuselage, being hidden by the rest bed. Here he remained throughout a night trip to a German target. On returning to Waddington, he was smuggled away from the aircraft and left to free himself while his kidnappers left discreetly. The word was that he was a much sadder and wiser man thereafter. Apocryphal maybe; but it might just be true! Another rumour concerned the Base Adjutant, F/Lt Henry Locke. Henry had been at Waddington since the Hampden days, but had been denied the chance to remuster as aircrew because of his age. However, it was fairly common knowledge that he flew on several operations 'just to see for himself'. Less likely, is the rumour concerning a WAAF who was reportedly smuggled aboard a Lancaster one night and taken on an operation, from which the aircraft in question did not return.

The weather was appalling towards the end of March, causing several operations to be cancelled. This bad weather continued into the first week of April. Though obviously not known to the crews of the two Waddington squadrons, April was to be the last month of their war. During the month, the Station was to mount 227 sorties against nine targets, in the course of which, four crews would be lost, all from No 463 Squadron. Mercifully, of the 28 aircrew involved, all but six would survive. 15 evaded capture, while the remaining seven would be interned briefly in Sweden.

The Station's first target of the month, on 4 April, was the underground secret weapons establishment at Nordhausen, east of Halle. 38 of the 243 Lancasters taking part came from Waddington, all of which returned safely. Tragically, what was believed to be a military barracks, was in reality the accommodation for concentration camp workers and forced labourers. This attack had been planned originally to take place at midnight, but other factors delayed it until 0915hr in the morning. The formation was escorted by a mixed force of Spitfires and Mustangs. The Lillecrap crew witnessed the loss of the only Lancaster on this operation. It was hit from above by a falling bomb and exploded in mid air, with only one parachute seen to emerge from the debris.

Two days after the attack on Nordhausen, 20 aircraft from Waddington joined forces with 34 others to attack a group of enemy supply ships which had beaten the Allied naval blockade of western Holland. The target was Ijmuiden, but the attack had to be called off due to bad weather and the concomitant danger of killing Dutch civilians.

The next night the target was the oil refinery at Molbis near Leipzig. 175 Lancasters took part, fifteen of them from Waddington. This was an accurate attack and the plant ceased production. All the Lancasters, plus the eleven Mosquitos taking part returned safely. The following night, on 8/9 April, Bomber Command despatched 231 Lancasters in an attack on the oil refinery at Lutzkendorf. The target, which had been attacked unsuccessfully the previous night, was marked by Mosquitos of No 5 Group and was rendered 'inoperative' for the rest of the war. In all, six Lancasters were lost on this operation, two of them from the 21 despatched from Waddington.

F/O Baulderstone and crew, flying in JO-V (NX584), were on their seventh operation. As they ran in towards the target they were hit by heavy flak on the starboard side. Their aircraft immediately rolled to port, but Baulderstone managed to regain control, while at the same time ordering his crew to put on parachutes. By this time the red TIs had gone down and the bomb aimer cooly commenced his run up commentary. The bomb load having been released on to the TIs, Baulderstone turned away from the target and set heading on the return route. Almost immediately, the flight engineer called up reporting a fire in the starboard wing, and requested that both engines be shut down and the propellers feathered. Baulderstone declined to do so, instead he ordered his crew to prepare to abandon the aircraft as quickly as possible. He next asked the navigator how far it was to the Allied lines, to which F/Sgt Hill replied that it was approximately 30 miles. Realising that they would never make it, Baulderstone gave the order to abandon the aircraft. Just what went wrong will never be known, because the only survivor was the rear gunner, Sgt Don Broadhead, who reported seeing the aircraft hit the ground while he was still in his parachute descent. Don Broadhead evaded successfully and just over two days later, linked up with American troops, who passed him back to their rear areas and eventually to London.

The other Waddington crew shot down that night also fell victim to heavy flak. F/O Ferris and crew, flying in JO-M (ME478), were on their fifth operation when they were hit in both wing roots, which resulted in the loss of both inner engines. Pressing on with his two remaining engines, Ferris intended to make an emergency landing at Juvincourt, but unfortunately the starboard outer engine failed also, leaving them with no alternative but to bail out. The crew abandoned their aircraft at 3200 feet, all landing without injury. They all managed to evade capture and eventually made contact with Allied troops. They arrived back at Waddington in time to take part in the attack on Tonsberg on 25/26 April, which was to be their sixth and last operation.

The last major attack by Bomber Command on Hamburg, had taken place on the night of 8/9 April, when a force of 440 aircraft attacked the shipyards. At the time of the Hamburg attack, Waddington aircraft were attacking Lutzkendorf. The following day a small force of 40 Lancasters attacked the oil storage depot at Hamburg, while seventeen 'Special' Lancasters of No 617 Squadron attacked the U-boat pens with Grand Slam and Tallboy bombs. Both attacks were successful and all 21 Waddington aircraft returned safely to base. The Station component on this attack was led by W/Cdr Kemp, OC No 463 Squadron. During the course of this operation, the bombers were attacked by Me262 jet fighters, which dived through the protective screen of Spitfires and Mustangs to get at the bombers.

Although all the Station aircraft returned from the attack on Hamburg, that flown by F/Lt McGregor and crew, flying on their first ever operation, in JO-R (SW269), was hit by shrapnel from a five-shell burst of predicted heavy flak. Apart from the loss of the starboard inner engine, no other serious damage resulted. Then, some fifteen minutes later, while on the homeward course, they were attacked by an Me262. The Luftwaffe pilot pressed home his attack until almost colliding with the Lancaster. The two air gunners returned fire (6 x 0.303" machine guns versus 4 x 30mm cannon!) The Lancaster was hit in the starboard wing and fuselage and on the mid upper gun turret. However, the return fire from the two gunners was seen to hit the starboard wing root of the jet fighter, which dived away and was not seen again. The McGregor crew saw other Lancasters under attack by the jets, two of which were observed going down in flames. No parachutes were seen to come from either bomber. With one engine out of action and coolant leaking from another, McGregor made a successful landing at the emergency landing strip at Woodbridge in Suffolk. One week later, the crew were back on operations.

After the Hamburg raid, it was a week before the Station was put on the alert for another operation; possibly, the Command was running out of worthwhile targets. On this occasion, the target was the railway yards at Pilsen in Czechoslovakia. 29 Lancasters took off fromWaddington to join up with the other 193 taking part in this operation. The attack was accurate, with only one aircraft being lost. Unfortunately for the Station, the missing aircraft was JO-L (ND733), flown by F/O Hagley and crew on their first operation. They were on the outbound route and still climbing, in the vicinity of Wurzburg, when they were atttacked by an unidentified fighter. Their Lancaster was hit in the starboard inner engine, the starboard wing, the flight engineer's panel and the starboard side of the cockpit. Other damage included the loss of oil supply to the starboard outer engine, the rupturing of No 1 fuel tank and the loss of hydraulic supply and some electrical services. In addition, both the navigator's and the wireless operator's stations were damaged. In no time at all, the interior of the fuselage was awash with hydraulic fluid, followed by the starboard inner engine bursting into flames. Hagley wasted no time in closing the throttle and feathering the propeller, before operating the Graviner fire extinguisher bottles.

With the fighter continuing its attack, Hagley threw his aircraft into a successful corkscrew, which eventually resulted in their assailant either breaking off the attack or simply losing them. On resuming straight and level flight, Hagley conducted a damage survey which, apart from the previously listed damage, showed that the starboard outer engine was rapidly losing oil. With no hope of making it to the target, Hagley called for a course for the jettison area in the English Channel. However, it soon became apparent that they were unable to maintain height with their full load of 1 x 4000lb Cookie, plus thirteen 500lb bombs still on board. They duly jettisoned all the 500lb bombs 'safe' near Hanau. With the resulting lightening of the load, Hagley managed to climb the bomber up to 4800 feet. They then altered course to the diversion airfield at Juvincourt in France. Lacking any serviceable navigation equipment, the only aid available to them were the stars. Using the astro sextant, their navigator, F/Sgt Bruhn, brought them to within sight of Juvincourt, which appeared some miles off to port at about 5am. At the moment they sighted the lights of Juvincourt, the starboard outer engine seized, causing considerable vibration. Hagley ordered his crew to put on parachutes and to stand by to abandon the aircraft. The rudder was then lashed with rope to assist the pilot in maintaining some semblance of control. By this time, JO-L was steadily losing height, though the intention was still to make a landing. The Cookie was jettisoned 'safe' over open country near Juvincourt. Then, without warning, the starboard outer engine burst into flames. Lacking the required electrical services, they were unable to feather the propeller, resulting in the imminent danger of an explosion, as the windmilling action of the propeller was forcing fuel into the engine nacelle. With his options exhausted, Hagley gave the order to jump, by which time the Lancaster was down to 1700 feet, four miles north of Juvincourt. All seven members of the crew left the aircraft without difficulty and watched as, enveloped in flames, it crashed in open country. The crew arrived back at Waddington on 19 April and were sent on survivors' leave. By the time they returned, the war in Europe was at an end.

It was back to Czechoslovakia two nights later on 18/19 April, when the target was the railway complex at Komotau (now known as Chomutov). Waddington provided 35 of the 114 Lancasters taking part in the operation. The attack was a complete success and all aircraft returned safely.

The Station had a five day break before being tasked again. This time, the target was the railway yard and port areas of Flensburg on the German/Danish border. In the event, the raid had to be abandoned by the Master Bomber as the target was covered by cloud and there was a very real risk of killing many Danish civilians. All aircraft returned safely, including the 20 despatched from Waddington.

Though it was not known to be so at the time, the last attack of the war by the two Waddington squadrons took place on the night of 25/26 April. The targets were the oil refinery and U-boat fuelling depot at Tonsberg in southern Norway. 28 of the 107 Lancasters took off from Waddington, with all but one returning safely to base. The experienced F/O Arthur Cox and crew were flying in JO-Z (RA542) on their 22nd operation, and were a rarity at Waddington, being an all RAF crew. On this occasion, their crew navigator was unable to fly, so the the acting Squadron Commander, S/Ldr Des Sullivan arranged for his own navigator, F/O Jack Wainwright, to fly with the Cox crew. In fact, Des Sullivan and crew had been screened, but Jack Wainwright was a couple of operations short of a full tour and wished to put this matter to rights. This, despite it being his second tour!

On crossing the North Sea on their way to the target, the Cox crew were pleasantly surprised to find that the cloud cover broke up more or less where the meteorological staff had predicted it would. This, together with Jack Wainwright's skill as a navigator, resulted in an accurate landfall. Without warning, soon after crossing the coast, they were hit by a prolonged burst of cannon and machine gun fire from a Ju88 night fighter equipped with 'Schrage Muzik'. The worst of the damage was concentrated in the nose of their aircraft, with the metal frame and perspex bombing blister being torn apart and much of the bomb aimer's equipment destroyed. F/Sgt Bob Smurthwaite, the bomb aimer, who had been lying in the prone position in the nose, was blown back into the fuselage, ending up seriously wounded behind the navigator's seat. The flight engineer, Sgt George Simpson, was wounded also, suffering serious injuries to his left shoulder and hand. In addition to the damage to the nose section of the aircraft, some of Cox's flight instruments were put out of action, as was much of the navigation equipment. To add to their problems, all the navigator's maps and charts were sucked out through the shattered nose.

Just as Arthur Cox shouted the order over the intercom to "prepare to abandon", he heard the rattle of his gunners machine guns. The rear gunner, Sgt 'Jock' Hogg had spotted the Ju88 coming in again and was engaging it. Unfortunately, the mid upper gunner, Sgt Fred Logan, was unable to rotate his damaged turret and as such, was able only to engage on one one side of the bomber. Cox heard him muttering a 'prayer' that the enemy pilot would attack from his effective side, which he obligingly did. Neither gunner claimed to have shot the fighter down, but they did report that they felt that it would have had difficulty in flying with all the extra metal that they had added to it. In fact, the two gunners' return fire had been more effective than they realised, as the Ju88G-6 crashed at Iveland, some 60km west of Arendal, killing the crew of three. This was the only interception recorded by the Luftwaffe controllers that night.

Immediately following the attack, the bomber had fallen off into a steep dive, but eventually Cox and the injured Simpson, working together, managed to bring it under control. With a shattered nose, there was an icy blast coursing through the aircraft causing, among other things, the packets of 'window' to unfurl and decorate the inside of the Lancaster like a wierd Christmas tree. Cox repeated his "prepare to abandon" order, but his crew expressed little desire to jump out into the icy cold and dark. It was this, combined with Jack Wainwright's report on the injuries to their bomb aimer, that convinced Cox that Bob Smurthwaite would stand little chance of survival if they baled out. Cox despatched George Simpson down into the nose compartment to assess the extent of the damage. This in itself was no mean feat as, unknown to his pilot, Simpson was bleeding heavily from his injuries and had little use of his left arm and hand. In the dark of the shattered nose and in a howling, icy gale, Simpson almost fell out of a gaping hole in the floor. Despite this, he managed to work the jettison bar and released fourteen out of their sixteen bombs. On returning to the cockpit, he mentioned nothing of his danger or injuries, simply commenting: "Can't bomb; sights u/s; engines OK". Meanwhile, Jack Wainwright was busy giving first aid to the bomb aimer; the efficacy of his aid later prompting a Swedish surgeon to testify that it was only Wainwright's prompt first aid and care that had saved his comrade's life. Having administered morphine and bandaged the wounds, Wainwright asked his captain for permission to open Smurthwaite's parachute and wrap it round him as protection against the sub zero blast entering through the shattered nose. It was this that finally decided Cox that he had no alternative but to try and make it to Sweden.

Despite his injuries, George Simpson continued to assist his pilot in controlling the aircraft. He used himself as a shield to protect Cox from the slipstream; in so doing, he added frost-bite to his already badly injured hands. His first aid duties over, Jack Wainwright endeavoured to give his pilot directions to Sweden from memory. His memory must have been sound as they eventually identified the lights of Gothenburg. Some two hours after the attack on their aircraft, Cox landed on the grass airfield of Jonkoping by the lights of several cars! Their landing was quite spectacular, with a 100 foot high bounce. The unfortunate Cox's hands were so frozen that he could not hold control column; instead, he was flying by holding it with his arms, hugging it to him at roundout. Once down, the Lancaster performed a massive groundloop, nearly finishing up in a lake. When it eventually came to a stop, Cox passed out and collapsed over the control column, leaving Simpson to cut the throttles and switch off the engines and fuel system

Arthur Cox's recollections of their arrival in Sweden are typical of the Bomber Command aircrews' capacity for understatement. He recalled the comments made by his crew: *"Typical Cox effort; a hell of a bounce, followed by a barely controlled crash, ending in a screaming ground loop to avoid going into a lake"*. What he omitted to mention was the fact that he was painfully wounded and was frozen to the controls of his aircraft by blood. The Swedish medical team had to exercise considerable care in removing his hands from the control column before they could despatch him to hospital. Six weeks later, following their return from internment in Sweden, George Simpson was recommended for (and received) the Conspicuous Gallantry Medal (CGM), second only to the Victoria Cross. Arthur Cox and Jack Wainwright both received the DSO. The award of these three prestigious decorations to one crew must be something of a record. Their Lancaster, JO-Z (RA542) was the last of over 3,300 Lancasters lost during the war. After the end of the war in Europe, the remains of JO-Z were classified by the Air Ministry as Beyond Economical Repair and were sold to the Swedish Air Force for spares.

The Whirlwind Is Over

The Tonsberg operation was Waddington's last offensive operation of the war, but the two squadrons still had several trips to make over Europe. For a variety of reasons, higher authority decided that returning PoWs should be ferried home by the Allied force of transport aircraft, together with some of the heavy bombers. This evacuation of ex-PoWs, known as Operation Exodus, commenced on 3 April, a month before the war's end. For Waddington, Exodus began on 27 April when several Station Lancasters flew to Brussels, where each one was loaded up with 24 ex-PoWs and flown to Dunsfold. Although it cannot have been a very comfortable trip, none of their passengers complained, despite having to make the journey sitting on the floor of the fuselage. For the many prisoners released by the American Army in southern Germany, it was decided to use the airfield at Juvincourt (coded A68), situated midway between Reims and Laon in northern France. Juvincourt had been a major Luftwaffe airfield, with three concrete runways; later taken over by a combined USAAF and RAF team. The USAAF used it as a fighter airfield during the day, while the RAF used it as the Bomber Command Advanced Emergency Airfield (BCAEA). This airfield was ideal as it also possessed a High frequency Direction Finding (HFDF) unit, which had provided navigation assistance to aircraft in distress. From then on, Operation Exodus really got under way.

During the first week of May, Juvincourt became a major pick-up point for PoWs. To ensure a rapid and efficient turnround, several servicing parties were despatched to the French airfield to look after the Lancasters. The operation continued until 25 May, by which time virtually all the PoWs from Germany had been flown home; a total of 74,195 men in the 3,586 sorties flown by aircraft of Bomber Command. On their arrival at Juvincourt, the Lancasters would be marshalled in echelon along the length of one side of an out-of-use runway. As soon as all the bombers were in position, a convoy of huge American-made Army trucks would arrive, each stopping opposite a Lancaster on the other side of the runway. When their assigned aircraft was ready, 24 men would jump from their lorry and hurry across to their Lancaster. The two Waddington squadrons ferried back over 1,000 PoWs, many of them ex-Bomber Command men. A fitting end to what had been a long and bloody campaign.

One last task remained for the crews of the Command. As a reward for their efforts and privations, many ground crew personnel were given the chance to see for themselves what their Command had been doing to the enemy. Known to the groundcrews as 'Cook's Tours', they were flown on round trips over targets that had been just names to them. Several aircrews who carried airmen on these trips commented that what began as a high-spirited joy ride, gradually subsided into a stunned silence as their passengers could see the scale of retribution inflicted on the enemy. As one airman commented on climbing out of a Lancaster "How on earth did they carry on for so long?"

Tuesday 8 May 1945, **VE Day**! The official announcement of the end of the war as far as the Station was concerned, was made by the Station Commander, Gp Capt Nelson, who had taken over from Gp Capt Bonham-Carter in April. Once it had become apparent that the war in Europe was virtually over, advance arrangements had been put in hand to hold a grand VE Day dance in No 4 hangar. The assigned hangar was cleared of aircraft and equipment and a sizeable workforce got down to the task of removing years of accumulated oil and grease from the floor. Many gallons of 100 octane aviation fuel were used and eventually the floor was rendered spotless. This was then covered in French Chalk, 'borrowed' from the Dinghy Section. At the time, there was a national shortage of beer, but fortunately someone on the Station had an uncle who owned a brewery. Accordingly, several aircraft were despatched to RAF Middleton St George, the nearest airfield to 'uncle', to collect the necessary lubrication. Meanwhile, bunting had been conjoured up, and this, together with 'Window' folded into streamers, turned the hangar into a rather large and unique, ballroom.

In the centre of the hangar, the Station boxing ring had been erected and it was from here that the Station Dance Band played. With a largely male population on the Station, an open invitation had been made to the good people of Lincoln (particularly the young women). Hundreds of them streamed up Cross O Cliff and Canwick Hills on foot to the Station. As a safety precaution, all the Station transport vehicles had been moved to the far end of the runway, well away from any over-enthusiastic revellers. The seal was set on a wonderful occasion by the return of Gp Capt Bonham-Carter who, it was rumoured, had flown across from Canada just to be with them.

A Special Order of the Day

On 10 May 1945, the Bomber Command Routine Orders contained a 'Special Order of the Day' from the CinC, Air Chief Marshal Sir Arthur Harris. The following is an exact copy of a Waddington Station Routine Order:

Men and women of Bomber Command. More than five and a half years ago, within hours of the declaration of war, Bomber Command first assailed the German enemy. You were then but a handful. Inadequate in everything but the skill and determination of the crews for that sombre occasion and for the unknown years of uncertain battle which lay beyond horizons black indeed.

You, the aircrews of Bomber Command, sent your first tons of bombs away on the morrow of the outbreak of war. A million tons of bombs and mines have followed from Bomber Command alone. From Declaration of War to Cease Fire, continuity of battle without precedent and without relent.

In the Battle of France your everyday endeavour bore down upon the overwhelming and triumphant enemy. After Dunkirk your country stood alone - in arms but largely unarmed, between the Nazi tyranny and domination of the World.

The Battle of Britain, in which you took great part, raised the last barrier, strained but holding in the path of the all-conquering Wehrmacht, and the bomb smoke of the Channel ports choked back down German throats and the very word 'Invasion'; not again to find expression within these narrow seas until the bomb-disrupted defences of the Normandy beachheads fell to our combined assault.

In the long years between, much was to pass.

Then it was that you, and for long alone, carried the war ever deeper and ever more furiously into the heart of the Third Reich. There the whole might of the German enemy in undivided strength, and - scarcely less a foe - the very elements, arrayed against you. You overcame them both.

Through those desperate years, undismayed by any odds, undeterred by any casualties, night succeeding night, you fought. The Phalanx of the United Nations.

You fought alone, as the one force then assailing German soil, you fought alone as individuals - isolated in your crew stations by the darkness and murk, and from all other aircraft in company. Not for you the hot emulation of high endeavour in the glare and panoply of martial array. Each crew, each one in each crew, fought alone through black nights, rent only, mile after continuing mile, by the fiercest barrages ever raised and the instant sally of the searchlights. In each dark minute of those long miles lurked menace. Fog, ice, snow and tempest found you undeterred. In that lonliness in action lay the final test, the ultimate stretch of human staunchness and determination.

Your losses mounted through those years. Years in which your chance of survival through one spell of operational duty, was negligible. Through two periods, mathematically nil. Nevertheless survivors pressed forward as volunteers to pit their desperately acquired skills in even a third period of operations, on special tasks.

In those five years and eight months of continuous battle over enemy soil your casualties over long periods were grievous. As the count is cleared, those of Bomber Command who gave their lives to bring near to impotence an enemy who had surged swift in triumph through a Continent, and to enable the United Nations to deploy in full array, will be found not less than the total dead of our National Invasion Armies now in Germany. In the whole history of our National Forces never had so small a band of men been called to support so long such odds. You indeed bore the brunt.

To you who survive I would say this. Content yourselves and take credit with those who perished, that now the Cease Fire has sounded, countless homes within our Empire will welcome back a father, husband or a son whose life, but for your endeavours and sacrifices, would assuredly have been expended during long further years of agony to achieve a victory already ours. No Allied nation is clear of this debt to you.

I cannot here expound your full achievements. Your attacks on the industrial centres of northern Italy did much toward the collapse of the Italian and German armies in North Africa and to further the invasion of the Italian mainland. Of the German enemy, two to three million fit men, potentially vast armies, were continuously held throughout the war in direct and indirect defence against your assaults. A great part of her industrial war effort went towards fending your attacks. You struck a critical proportion of the weapons of war from enemy hands on every front.

You immobilised armies, leaving them short of supplies, reinforcements, resources and reserves; the easier prey to our advancing forces. You eased and abetted the passage of our troops over major obstacles. You blasted the enemy from long prepared defences where he essayed to hold. On the Normandy beaches; at the height of the battle of Caen; in the Falaise Gap. To the strongpoints of the enemy held Channel ports, St Vith, Houffalize and the passage of the Rhine. In battle after battle you sped our armies to success at minimum cost to our troops. The Commanders of our land forces, and indeed those of the enemy have called your attacks decisive.

You enormously disrupted every enemy means of communication, the very life-blood of his military and economic machine. Railways, canals and every form of transport fell, first to decay and then to chaos under your assaults. You so shattered the enemy's oil plants as to deprive him of all but the final trickle of fuel. His aircraft became earthbound, his road transport ceased to roll, armoured fighting vehicles lay helpless outside the battle, or fell immobilised into our hands. His strategic and tactical plans failed through inability to move.

From his war industries, supplies of ore, coal, steel, fine metals, aircraft, guns, ammunition, tanks, vehicles and every ancilliary equipment, dwindled under your attacks. At the very crisis of the invasion of Normandy, you virtually annihilated the German naval forces then in the Channel; a hundred craft and more fell victim to these attacks. You sank or damaged a large but yet untotalled number of enemy submarines in his ports, and by mine laying in his waters. You interfered widely and repeatedly with his submarine training programme. With extraordinary accuracy, regardless of opposition, you hit and burst through every carapace which he could devise to protect his submarines in harbour. By your attacks on inland industries and coastal shipyards, you caused hundreds of his submarines to be stillborn.

Your mine-laying throughout the enemy's sea lanes, your bombing of his inland waters and his ports, confounded his sea traffic and burst his canals. From Norway, throughout the Baltic; from Jutland to the Gironde; on the coast of Italy and North Africa, you laid and relaid minefields. The wreckage of the enemy's naval and merchant fleets litters and encumbers his sea lanes and dockyards. A thousand known ships and many more as yet unknown, fell casualty to your mines.

You hunted and harried his major warships from hide to hide. You put out of action, gutted or sank most of them.

By your attacks on experimental stations, factories, communications and firing sites, you long postponed and much reduced the V weapond attacks. You averted an enormous further toll of death and destruction from your Country.

With it all, you never ceased to rot the very heart out of the enemy's war resources and resistance.

His capital and nearly one hundred of his cities and towns, including nearly all of leading war industrial importance, lie in utter ruin, together with the greater part of the war industry which they supported. Thus you brought to nought the enemy's original advantage of an industrial might intrinsically greater than ours and supported by the labour of captive millions, now set free.

For the first time in more than a century, you have brought home to the habitual aggressor of Europe, the full and acrid flavour of war, so long the perquisite of his victims. All this and much more you have achieved during these five and a half years of continuing battle, despite all opposition from an enemy disposing of many geographical and strategic advantage with which to exploit an initial superiority in numbers.

Men from every part of the Empire and most of the Allied nations fought in your ranks. Indeed a band of brothers.

In the third year of war, the Eighth Bomber Command and the Fifteenth Bomber Command of the USAAF from their Mediterranean bases, ranged themselves at our side, zealous in extending every mutual aid, vieing in every assault upon our common foe. Especially, they played the leading part in sweeping the enemy fighter defences from our path and, finally, out of the skies.

Nevertheless, nothing that the crews accomplished - and it was very much, and decisive - could have been achieved without the devoted service of every man and woman in the Command. Those who tended the aircraft, mostly in the open, through six bitter winters; endless intricacies in a prolonged misery of wet and cold. They rightly earned the implicit trust of the crews. They set extraordinary records of aircraft serviceability.

Those who manned the Stations, operational headquarters, supply lines and communications. The pilots of the photoraphic reconnaissance units, without whose lonely ventures far and wide over enemy territory, we should have been largely powerless to plan or to strike.

The operational crew training programme of the Command, which through these years of ceaseless work by day and night, never failed, in the face of difficulty and unpredicted calls to replace all casualties and to keep our constantly expanding first line up to strength in crews trained to the highest pitch of efficiency; simultaneously producing near 20.000 additional trained aircrew for the raising and reinforcement of some 50 extra squadrons, formed in the Command and despatched for service in other Commands at home and overseas.

The men and women of the Meteoroligical Branch who attained prodigious exactitudes in a fickle art and stood brave on assertion where science is inexact. Time and again they have saved us from worse than the enemy could have ever achieved. Their record is outstanding.

The Operational Research Sections, whose meticulous investigation of every detail of every attack, provided data for the continuous confounding of the enemy and the consistent reduction of our own casualties.

The scientists, especially those of the Telecommunications Research Establishment, who placed in undending succession in our hands the technical means to resolve our problems and to confuse the every parry of the enemy. Without their skill and their labours, beyond doubt we could not have prevailed.

The Works Services, who engineered for Bomber Command alone, two thousand miles of runways, track and road, with all that goes with them. The Works Staff, designers and workers who equipped and re-equipped us for battle. Their efforts, their honest workmanship, kept in our hands indeed a shining sword.

To you all, I would say how proud I am to have served in Bomber Command for four and a half years and to have been your Commander-in-Chief through more than three years of your saga.

Your task in the German war is now completed. Famously have you fought. Well have you deserved of your Country and her Allies.

Signed A T Harris
Air Chief Marshal
Commander-in-Chief
Bomber Command

It is a matter of record that despite their Commander-in-Chief's final paragraph, political expediency took precedent and the men and women of Bomber Command were never to receive their just and due recognition and reward. They were even denied a campaign medal of their own, despite the fact that their campaign was only marginally shorter than that of the Royal Navy's Battle of the Atlantic. The reason given being that, as with many other servicemen and women, the groundcrews of Bomber Command had never left the country; surely as specious an answer as any.

The war in Europe over, all eyes turned to the almost forgotten war in Asia. The British Pacific Fleet had been operating alongside the massive American fleet since the summer of 1944. When in August 1945 it was combined with the East Indies Fleet they became the greatest Commonwealth fleets ever. However, at Waddington in May 1945, rumours abounded; the most popular being that both Australian squadrons would form part of Bomber Command's force destined for the Pacific War. The unit was collectively known as 'Tiger Force' and was scheduled to be based on an island close to Okinawa, which itself had finally fallen to the Americans on 21 June 1944. The island of Okinawa was already an operating base for the giant American B29 Superfortresses, a quantum improvement on the bombers of RAF Bomber Command or those of the USAAF Eighth and Fifteenth Air Forces.

In the event, only No 467 Squadron was earmarked for Tiger Force; apparently, No 463 Squadron would not be required. As part of the build up of the Force, the assigned crews commenced a programme of long distance navigation exercises, many of them lasting over twelve hours. On 15 June, No 467 Squadron moved to nearby RAF Metheringham, lately the home of No 106 Squadron. Their task was to work up as part of the Main Force component of Tiger Force. In due course, they were scheduled to re-equip with Lancasters fitted with special long range, 400-gallon fuel tanks. Two weeks later, No 463 Squadron moved to the No 53 Base satellite of Skellingthorpe. The squadron carried out some desultory training flights, albeit without a great deal of enthusiasm until, on 25 September, it was disbanded. With both of its resident wartime squadrons relocated, Waddington became the home of Nos IX and 617 Squadrons. The latter arriving on 17 June, followed on 6 July by No IX Squadron. These two squadrons, among the best in No 5 Group, had been earmarked for operations against the Japanese using the 12000lb Tallboy and the 22000lb Grand Slam bombs. At about the same time, a batch of Mk VII (Special) Lancasters were delivered to Waddington. These particular Lancasters were fitted with enlarged bomb bays and uprated Merlin engines.

Following the dropping of the atomic bombs on Hiroshima and Nagasaki, the war in the Far East came to an end on 15 August 1945. A few weeks later, Tiger Force was disbanded, never having really got off the ground as a cohesive force. Five days after its sister squadron had ceased to exist, No 467 Squadron was itself disbanded on 30 September 1945.

So ended the Second World War for Waddington and other units of Bomber Command.

The C-in-C had been promoted to Marshal of the Royal Air Force and retired to South Africa, having declined the offer of a peerage by the new Prime Minister, Clement Attlee. His efforts to obtain a specific campaign medal for all members of the Command failed, much to his disgust, leaving his groundcrews to qualify for only the Defence Medal. As he was to write in his book 'Bomber Offensive', "...every clerk, butcher or baker in the rear of the armies overseas had a campaign medal..." It would seem that the 8,000 deaths among the groundcrews, together with additional thousands of serious injuries and illness, counted for nought with the paladins of Whitehall.

In closing the story of the war effort of those at RAF Waddington, a brief reminder of the overall cost would not be out of place. Bomber Command lost a total of 55,500 aircrew killed. Of this number, 8195 were killed in accidents and crashes. In addition, 9838 became prisoners of war, many of them wounded. Furthermore, there were another 8403 aircrew that suffered injuries in operations or in accidents of one sort or another. This makes a total of 73,741; this out of a total strength of 125,000 aircrew. In other words, there was a 59% chance that a member of aircrew would not survive unscathed. A high price indeed, and one worthy of better than to have been described as 'useless' by W H Auden, an Oxford Professor of Poetry, who had spent the entire war in the safety of the United States, before being invited to become a member of the United States Strategic Bombing Survey Team - *Semper Eadem*!

❖❖❖

1 RAF Waddington 5 April 1918 (Aircraft are RE8s, BE2cs and DH 6 and 9s). *L G Stuart-Leslie*

2 Waddington hangars under construction (Aircraft is an Avro 504A). *R W Elliott thro'* G Stewart-Leslie

3 The ante room of the Officers' Mess April 1917 *V J Clow*

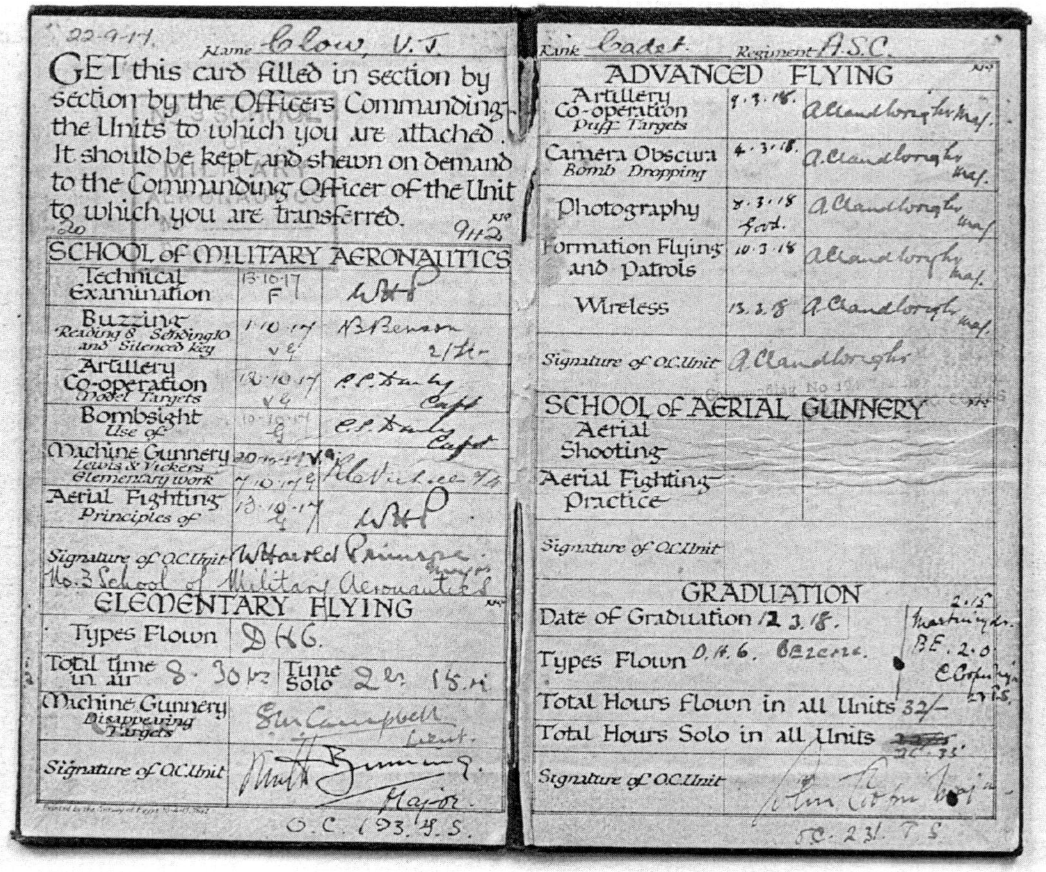

22-9-17. Name Clow, V.J.

GET this card filled in section by section by the Officers Commanding the Units to which you are attached. It should be kept and shewn on demand to the Commanding Officer of the Unit to which you are transferred.

No 9142

SCHOOL of MILITARY AERONAUTICS		
Technical Examination	13-10-17 F	WHP
Buzzing Reading & Sending 10 and Silenced key	1-10-17 V G	H Benson 2/Lt
Artillery Co-operation Model Targets	12-10-17 V G	C.C. Darley Capt
Bombsight Use of	10-10-17 G	C.C. Darley Capt
Machine Gunnery Lewis & Vickers Elementary work	20-10-17 V G / 7-10-17 G	R.C. Wilcox 2/Lt
Aerial Fighting Principles of	13-10-17 G	WHP

Signature of O.C. Unit: W Harold Primrose Major, No. 3 School of Military Aeronautics

ELEMENTARY FLYING	
Types Flown	D.H.6.
Total time in air	8. 30 hrs; Time Solo 2 hrs 15 m
Machine Gunnery Disappearing Targets	G.W. Campbell Lieut.

Signature of O.C. Unit: Major, O.C. 193 T.S.

Rank Cadet Regiment A.S.C.

ADVANCED FLYING		
Artillery Co-operation Puff Targets	9.3.18.	A Claudborough for Maj.
Camera Obscura Bomb Dropping	4.3.18.	A Claudborough Maj.
Photography	8.3.18 Good.	A Claudborough Maj.
Formation Flying and Patrols	10.3.18	A Claudborough Maj.
Wireless	13.3.18	A Claudborough Maj.

Signature of O.C. Unit: A Claudborough

SCHOOL of AERIAL GUNNERY	
Aerial Shooting	
Aerial Fighting Practice	

Signature of O.C. Unit:

GRADUATION

Date of Graduation 12.3.18.

Types Flown D.H.6. Elezene. BE.2.C

Total Hours Flown in all Units 32/-

Total Hours Solo in all Units

Signature of O.C. Unit: Major, OC 231 T.S.

4 A Waddington student's training record *V J Clow*

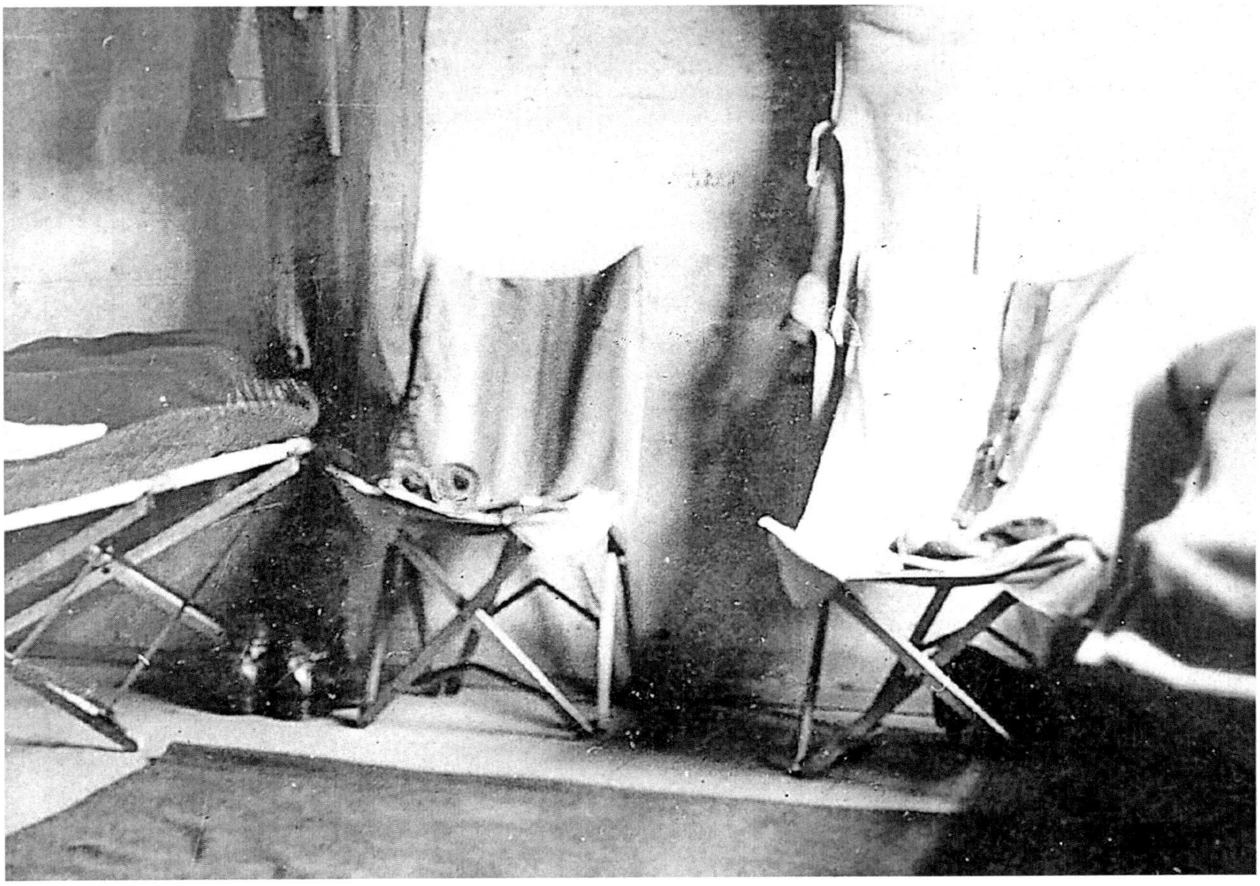

5 Student accommodation at Waddington *V J Clow*

6 A DH6 at Waddington R W Elliott thro' G Stewart-Leslie

7 Staff of No 27 Wing at Waddington *Whitby*

8 Headquarters Staff of No 27 Wing at Waddington *Whitby*

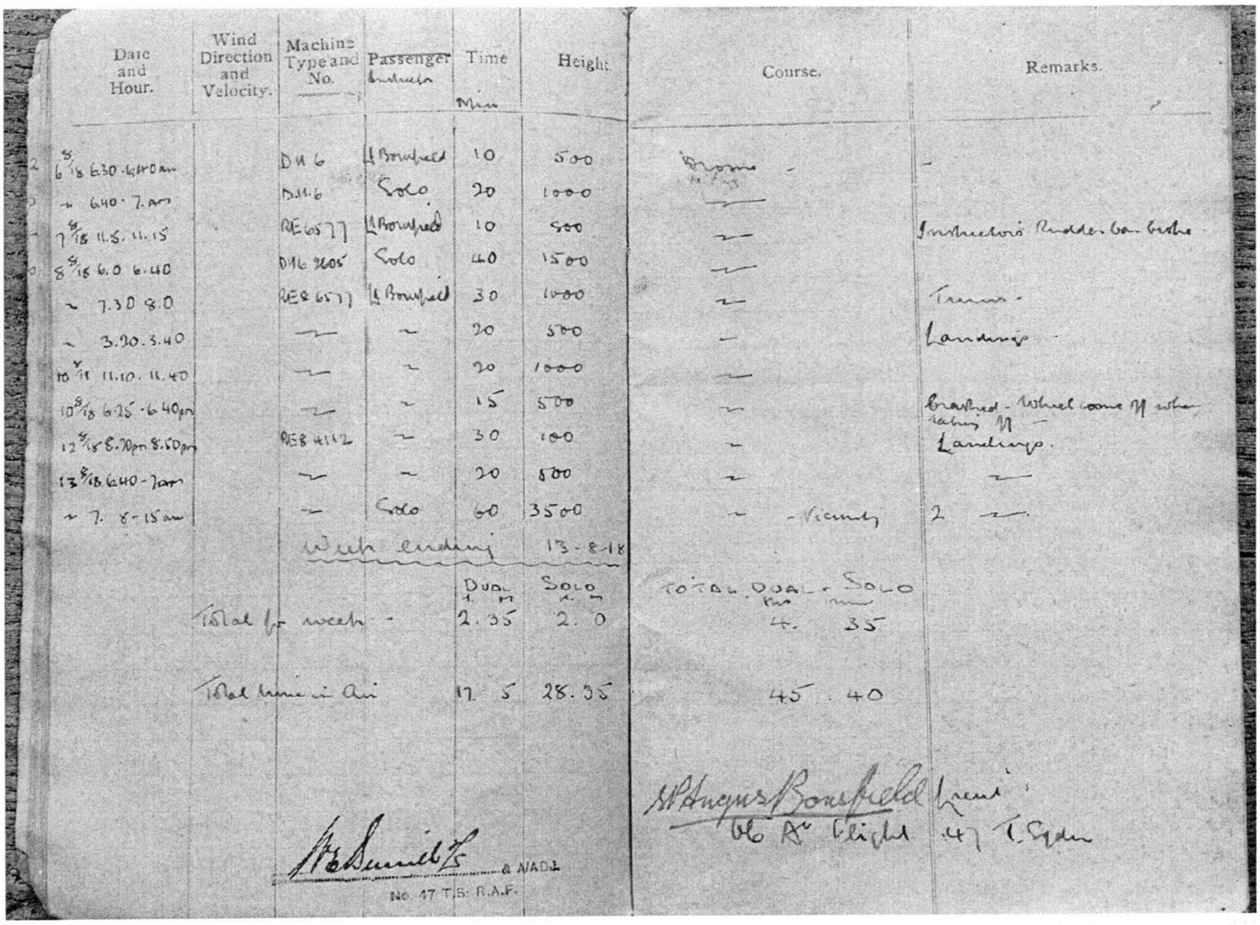

Date and Hour.	Wind Direction and Velocity.	Machine Type and No.	Passenger Instructor	Time Mins	Height.	Course.	Remarks.
6/8/18 6.30-6.40am		DH6	Lt Bousfield	10	500	Drome	-
" 6.40-7.am		D.H.6	Solo	20	1000	"	
7/8/18 11.5-11.15		RE6577	Lt Bousfield	10	500	"	Instructor's Rudder bar broke
8/8/18 6.0-6.40		DH6 2605	Solo	40	1500	"	
" 7.30-8.0		RE8 6577	Lt Bousfield	30	1000	"	Turns
" 3.20-3.40		"	"	20	500	"	Landings
10/8/18 11.10-11.40		"	"	20	1000	"	
10/8/18 6.25-6.40pm		"	"	15	500	"	Crashed - wheel came off when taking off
12/8/18 8.30pm-8.50pm		RE8 4112	"	30	100	"	Landings
13/8/18 6.40-7am		"	"	20	800	"	"
" 7.8-15am		"	Solo	60	3500	" - Vicinity	2 "

Week ending 13-8-18

	Dual h m	Solo h m	Total Dual + Solo hr m
Total for week	2.35	2.0	4.35
Total time in Air	17.5	28.35	45.40

H Angus Bousfield Lieut.
i/c 'A' Flight 47 T. Sqdn

[illegible signature] & A/AD1
No. 47 T.S. R.A.F.

9 A page from the Log Book of 2/Lt V J Clow *V J Clow*

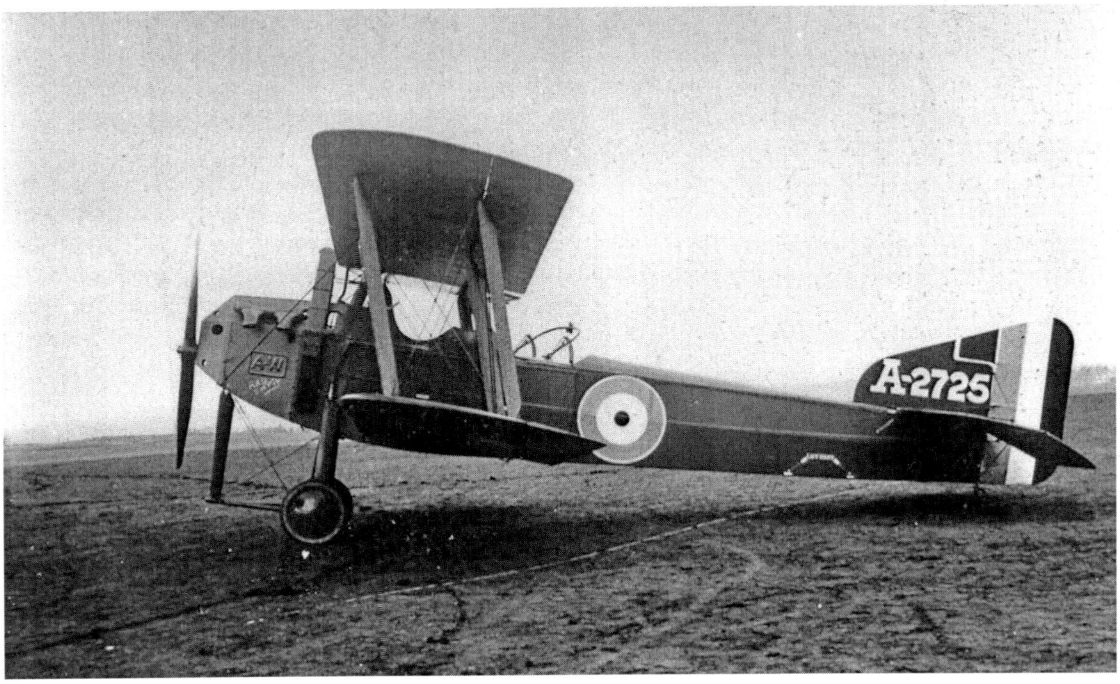

10 An FK 8 'Big Ack' at Waddington *C G Stevens*

11 Warrant Officer H J Hiatt a Waddington Instructor The aircraft is a Graham White XV *Waddington Collection*

12 A crashed Maurice Farman 'Shorthorn' on the roof of a Waddington hangar - April 1917 *R W Elliott thro' G Stewart-Leslie*

13 A Waddington RE8 looking much the worse for wear *C G Stevens*

14 A fatal crash at Waddington. Note the burned body ! *Author's collection*

15 A Waddington Avro 504A on its nose. *Author's collection*

16 An FK3 'Little Ack' (A1479) near Waddington *G Stewart-Leslie*

17 The Waddington buildings seemed to attract the students' aircraft. *Waddington collection*

18 A Waddington DH6 embedded in the roof of the WRAF hut! *V J Clow*

19 One of the Waddington instructors Captain 'Charlie' ! Note the unique flying boots *Whitby*

20 A random collection of Waddington students *G Stewart-Leslie*

21 Cadet C G Stevens and his FE2b; Waddington 1917 *C G Stevens*

22 2/Lt Reggie Pohlmann; Waddington October 1917 *W Owen*

23 Lt Smith in flying kit at Waddington *Whitby*

24 One of the Americans who trained at Waddington *Whitby*

25 A selection of Russian student pilots at Waddington *Whitby*

26 A Fairy Fawn of No 503 'B' Squadron; Waddington 1928 *D. Allison*

27 The early volunteer pilots of No 503 Squadron *D. Allison*

28 Fairey Fawn (J7980) during an Air exercise, August 1928 *D. Allison*

29 Ground staff of No 503 Squadron *D. Allison*

30 A Fairey Fawn of No 503 Squadron *D. Allison*

31 Starting up a Fawn (Napier Lion engine) *D. Allison*

32 No 503 'County of Lincoln' Squadron *D. Allison*

33 Among the first to join - T H Worth; D G Allison; N D Wardrop; R Maw *D. Allison*

34 The old Officer' Mess at Waddington; it was replaced by Newell House. *D. Allison*

35 Refuelling a 503 Squadron Fawn in 1928. The casual figure leaning on the wing is 'Speedo' Barrow, 'ts pilot. *D. Allison*

36 Some of the ground staff of No 503 Squadron - (L-R) Sgt Burton/Sgt Major Rippon/ ? /Kinsley/Waller, with Cpl Bunn in the cockpit. August 1928 *Peter Green Collection*

37 One of the Waddington hangars, with a Fawn inside and a AW Atlas of No 26 Squadron outside. Waddington 1929. *Peter Green Collection*

38 An Avro 504N (Lynx Avro) of 503 Squadron *D. Allison*

39 A Handley-Page Hyderabad of No 503 Squadron. Note the badge on the nose. *R C Browne*

40 Two 503 Squadron Hyderabads in 1930 *D. Allison*

41 The Blankney Hunt meeting on Waddington aerodrome around 1930. *C. Cole (LLA)*

42 503 Squadron Hyderabads *D. Allison*

43 The hangars of No 503 Squadron at Waddington *D. Allison*

44 Ungainly to say the least; a 503 Squadron Hyderabad *Peter Green Collection*

45 Progress ! A HP Hinaidi of No 503 Squadron *D. Allison*

46 A line up of 503 Squadron Hinaidis in 1930 *D. Allison*

47 "I do not believe it". Re-rigging a crashed 503 Squadron Hinaidi. The man with his back to the proceedings is the Commanding Officer,Wg Cdr Twisleton-Wykham Ffiennes. *D. Allison*

48 A 503 Squadron Westland Wallace II in 1936 *Peter Green Collection*

49 Three Wallace IIs of No 503 Squadron *Waddington Village Historical Society*

50 A Wallace II of No 503 Squadron with three of its ground crew. *Peter Green Collection*

51 A Blenheim Mk I of No 44 Squadron, not long before the outbreak of war. Note the 50 Squadron Hampden in the background. *C Waterfall*

52 Some pre-war Waddington pilots: (L-R) Good/Bennett/Lloyd Bagley/ ? / Pollard *P C S Bagley*

53 A Hawker Hart I of No 503 Squadron over Lincoln. Note the cathedral *Waddington Village Historical Society*

54 A Hawker Hind of No 50 Squadron at Waddington *P Knight*

55 A 50 Squadron Hind outside one of the new Waddington hangars *Waddington Collection*

56 No 50 Squadron Hinds in full flight *Waddington Collection*

57 A Hawker Hind of No 44 Squadron in 1936 *Mr Rudd*

58 Plt Off Jack Peel of No 503 Squadron *Peel family collection*

59 The fatal crash of No 503 Squadron Hart (K3025) in which Plt Off Forte and LAC East were killed; 6 February 1937. *H. Willers*

60 The funeral in Lincoln of LAC East *Mr Rudd*

61 No 50 Squadron Hinds in formation *Waddington Collection*

62 A No 44 Squadron Hampden (L4399) at Waddington in July 1939. Note the pre-war code letters for 44 Squadron - JW. The figure in the foreground is Sgt Percy Nixon - KIA while minelaying on 19/20 July 1940. *C. Waterfall*

63 Two No 50 squadron Hampdens on standby during the Munich Crisis. Note: QX-D (L4078) *J Taylor*

64 RAF Waddington just before the outbreak of war. Note that one WW I hangar is still in use by the side of Ermine Street (now called High Dyke). Also, note that the old hangar complex is still there; it was removed when the concrete runways were installed *C G Jefford*

65 Hampdens of No 44 Squadron at Waddington in July 1939. The aircraft behind them could be an Anson or an Oxford. The Hampden on the left is L4171; that on the right is L4087 *C. Waterfall*

66 A battle damaged Hampden of No 44 Squadron (AD982). The result of a night fighter attack 2/3 September 1941. Note the damage below the rear turret and along the fuselage *J Taylor*

67 A group of air gunners of No 44 Squadron posing beside one of their aircraft. (L-R): 'Bill' (Keith) Street DFM RNZAF (KIA 1942), Jim Taylor **(sole survivor – PoW), 'Ginger' Bell** (KIA 1940) Jerry Preston (KIA 1941) Pete McLaren RNZAF (KIA 1941) *J Taylor*

68 Hampden X2997 of No 44 Squadron hit the roof of one of the WW I hangars during a 'blind approach' training sortie. This shows the damage inside the hangar. *C Waterfall*

69 Hampden VN-Z (AE 184) of No 50 Squadron *No 50 Sqn Collection*

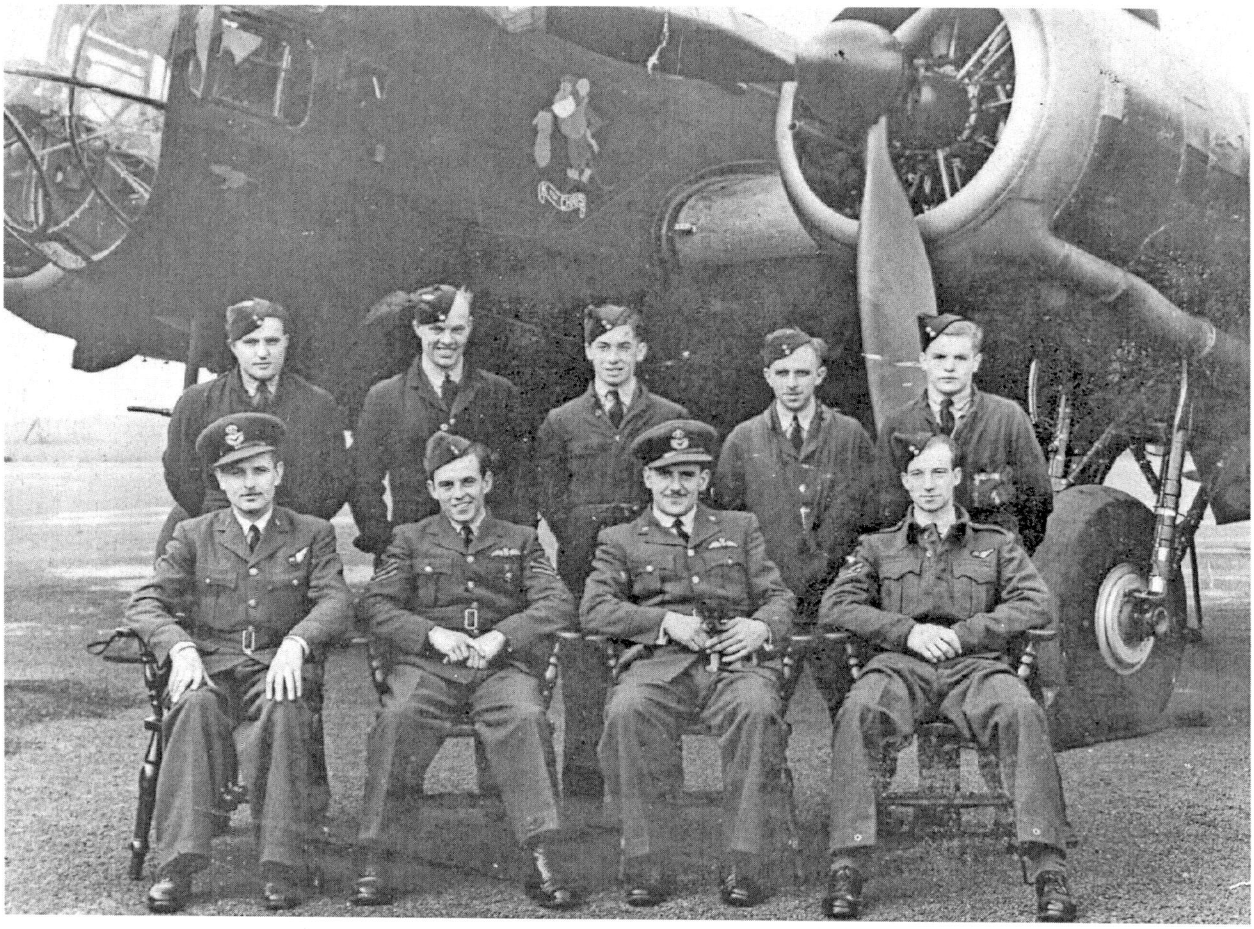

70 Fg Off Ford and crew in front of their No 50 Squadron Hampden 'K' for Chris ! Their groundcrew are standing in the back row. *No 50 Sqn Collection*

71 A Hampden of No 50 Squadron. Note the twin Vickers 'K' guns in the rear upper turret *H Moyle*

72 The Duke of Kent is greeted by the Station Commander on the occasion of his visit to RAF Waddington *Waddington Collection*

73 A Waddington crew leave their aircraft after a sortie. Note the variation in flying clothing. *E. McCabe*

74 The remains of the village church in Waddington village after having been struck by a landmine. *M. Dragon*

75 A close up view of No 44 Squadron Hampden KM-Z. Note the exhaust flame dampers and the fixed nose mounted machine gun. *J Taylor*

76 A thoughtful group in Flying Control at Waddington (L-R): Flt Lt Hobson FCO / Sqn Ldr Burton-Gyles OC No 44 Sqn / Wg Cdr Lewis Acting Stn Cdr / Sqn Ldr Laborne Senior FCO *Mrs P Brimson*

77 Sgt Jim Taylor of No 44 Squadron in his W Op/AG's upper gun position in a squadron Hampden. Note the twin Vickers 'K' guns and the deflector. *J Taylor*

78 Manchester EM-S (L7515) of No 207 Squadron at Waddington. Delivered in October 1941 *N Hyde*

79 A No 207 Squadron Manchester EM-H (L7288) *R Glynn-Owen*

80 Manchester EM-D (L7284) of No 207 Squadron over Lincolnshire *P Brimson*

81 On 23 November 1941, Manchester EM-F (L7300) crashed in Fiskerton Lake near Lincoln after a double engine failure. *R.Kirby*

82 Practicing for Augsburg. John Nettleton's original KM-B Lancaster L7578. He actually flew R5508, coded KM-B, when L7578 went to No 97 Squadron. Note the shadows of the formation on the ground *J. Garwell*

84 Four good friends! (L-R): Plt Off Dave 'Toffee' Appleton *(KIA), Fg Off Peter Ball DFM* (KIA), Flt Lt 'Gunner' Halls DFC (Missing June 1942), Fg Off John 'Daisy' Garwell DFM DFC (PoW April 1942) *J H Evans*

85 Sqn Ldr John Nettleton VC and his bride, Section Officer Betty Havelock on the occasion of their wedding on 1 July 1942 *J H Evans*

86 Warrant Officer 'Frankie' Stott DFM and crew. The aircraft is Nettleton's Augsburg Lancaster (L-R): Sgt Miller (W Op/AG) F/Sgt Glynn (F Eng) WO Stott Unknown 2nd pilot under training F/Sgt Willan (Nav) F/Sgt Allison (W Op) F/Sgt Braines (AG) *Bud Gill*

87 Am Aiming Point Certificate awarded by HQ No 5 Group and signed by the AOC AVM Ralph Cochrane *E Dudley*

88 The bomb damaged Airmens' Mess and NAAFI at Waddington *N Ray*

89 Another view of the damaged Mess Hall and NAAFI *N Ray*

90 A burned out Waddington Lancaster in a field near the aerodrome *E McCabe*

91 American visitors to Waddington. Second from the left is Gene Raymond the Hollywood film star *D Laird*

92 A No IX Squadron crew after an attack on Hamburg as part of Operation Gomorrah in July 1943 *C Waterfall*

93 Lancaster PC-Q (NF910) of No 467 Sqn; Winter 1943 *H R Cull*

94 Internal flak damage *E McCabe*

95 The Operations Room at Waddington in 1944 *W Hodge*

96 Winter at Waddington, early 1944. The 'X' marks the point where one of the Lancasters went off the taxyway and got bogged down, blocking the rest of the taxying aircraft. It was freed and hauled back on to the taxyway in short order. *D L Gibbs*

97 Fg Off T N Schofield (far left) and the crew of 'S' Sugar (R5868) after what was reputed to have been her 100th operation in May 1944. The crew on this attack were (not in order): Fg Off T N Schofield (P), Sgt R H G Burgess RAF (FE), Fg Off I Hamilton RAF (N), F/Sgt F E Hughes (B), F/Sgt R T Hillas (WOp), Sgt J D Wells RAF (MUG), and F/Sgt K E Stewart (RG) *W Hodge*

98 Lancaster PO-S (R5868) after her 100th Operation. (L-R): Sgt Harry South (Aussie) Cpl Andy Cowton RAF Unknown Nick Hodson RAF Alf Mansell RAF Derek Mason RAF Unknown Air Cdr Hesketh (No 53 Base Commander). Chalking on the bomb is LAC Ted Willoughby RAF. *A. Tongue*

99 PO-S after a servicing, showing 96 operations completed. *C. Offe*

100 Lancaster JO-U (ED61 1) of No 463 Squadron. The smeary patch to the left of Stalin originally showed stars for raids completed prior to coming to Waddington. They have been painted out and added to those flown by No 463 Squadron *Sharman*

101 Lancaster JO-N (LM130) 'Nick the Nazi Neutralizer'. This was one of the few Lancasters to qualify for a MAJOR inspection. She flew 86 operations. *S Bridgeman*

102 JO-R (LL844) 'Ginger Megs'; another 86 operations survivor. This was taken after a wheels up landing on 28 September 1944 after an attack on Stuttgart. She still had all her bombs on board when she ended up behind the Station rifle range. *D. Hill C. Allen*

103 Part of a daylight formation attack. The rearmost aircraft is PO-S (R5868) 'S' Sugar *L. Pattison*

104 Fg Off John Dack (rear row, centre) and crew; taken before they were shot down on the last operation of their tour. *D. Hill*

105 Fg Off John Dack in the cockpit of JO-P (PB260). The raid tally shows 31 ops. He was shot down on his 32nd operation, which was to have been his and his crew's last one *D. Hill*

106 Celebrations at Waddington on VE Day *R. Milne*

07 Preparing JO-V (RF270) for Operation Exodus, the repatriation of PoWs. The Waddington squadrons averaged 500 PoWs a day *W. Hodge*

108 Operation Exodus. A bunch of PoWs, waiting to board their transport home. *S. Bridgeman*

ROYAL AIR FORCE STATION

WADDINGTON

FOR FAITH AND FREEDOM